D0065844

America Disarmed

America Disarmed

Inside the U.N. and Obama's Scheme to Destroy the
Second Amendment

Wayne LaPierre

Published by WND Books, Washington DC. For information regarding special sales or
licensing, please contact the publisher: WND Books

ISBN 978-1-936488-43-8

Printed in the United States of America

Contents

This book would never have seen its way into print if not for the expertise and kind assistance of two of my longtime colleagues. Sincere thanks go to David B. Kopel, research director at the Independence Institute, and to noted constitutional law expert Stephen P. Halbrook. In sections of this work, you will see their exhaustive research and insights unfold, since their findings are so powerful as to demand inclusion along with my own firsthand observations. Both men serve every day as freedom fighters on the front lines in the battle to defend the Second Amendment, and I am proud to call them friends.

Foreword

In 2009, the United States joined 152 other countries in endorsing the United Nations Small Arms Treaty, a resolution designed to disarm America and others across the globe.

Specifically, the resolution establishes an international conference to be held in 2012, where leaders from various countries—many of which have deplorable human rights records—will craft an international scheme to severely restrict our right to own a firearm.

As Professor Larry Bell detailed in a popular column for *Forbes* magazine in early 2011, this global agreement will surely pave the way for gun bans, mandatory gun registration, and eventually, the confiscation of civilian-owned firearms. President Obama, Hillary Clinton, and the U.N. all claim that the only purpose of the treaty is to fight terrorism and international crime syndicates. Americans should not be fooled.

According to Professor Bell, should the U.S. Senate ratify the treaty it will almost certainly force America to:

- Enact firearms licensing requirements, creating additional bureaucratic red tape for legal firearms ownership;
- Confiscate and destroy all "unauthorized" civilian firearms;
- Ban the trade, sale, and private ownership of all semiautomatic firearms; and
- Create an international gun registry.

Bell also notes that the treaty will override our national sovereignty and, in the process, give license to the federal government to assert preemptive powers over state regulatory powers guaranteed by the Tenth Amendment.

You can see why gun control activists in the United States have been lobbying for this treaty for a long time.

Former U.N. ambassador John Bolton, the preeminent expert on the inner workings of the global body, recently told me there is no doubt that the U.N.'s real agenda here is domestic firearms control:

> "After the treaty is approved and it comes into force, you will find out that it has this implication or that implication and it requires the Congress to adopt some measure that restricts ownership of firearms," Bolton warns. "The [Obama] administration knows it cannot obtain this kind of legislation purely in a domestic context…They will use an international agreement as an excuse to get domestically what they couldn't otherwise."

The NRA has been warning America's gun owners about this ticking time bomb for nearly two decades and has committed serious resources to fighting the U.N. and President Obama's global gun ban schemes.

Hillary Clinton has not been shy about her determination to push for Senate ratification of the U.N.'s gun ban treaty. And you can bet that if Obama wins a second term, he'll move full speed ahead to implement the U.N. treaty's mandates. Popular or not, it won't matter, because Obama won't need to appeal to voters for reelection.

Ironically, the U.N.'s gun ban treaty will make citizens of the United States and other countries more vulnerable to terror, not less.

Historic and current events show us that rogue governments, not private citizens, pose the greatest threat to innocent civilians across the globe. This horrible truth is visible every day in Africa. The mass murders that tyrants carry out are made possible by the confiscation of privately owned firearms—and firearm confiscation is made possible by the licensing and registration of gun owners, firearms, and ammunition.

According to political scientist, noted author, and international conflict expert Rudy Rummel, the fifteen worst regimes during the twentieth century killed 151 million of their own citizens. That comes to 1.5 million victims per year. For many unfortunate people around the world, government poses a much a larger threat than the guy next door.

Of course, President Obama and Secretary Clinton have never bothered themselves with the facts surrounding firearms ownership. They have spent their entire careers demonizing American gun owners and doing everything in their power to make gun ownership more expensive, more difficult, and, in many cases, illegal.

Now they want to unleash the entire U.N. gun-ban axis on our right to keep and bear arms.

NRA's chief executive officer and executive vice president Wayne LaPierre does an excellent job blowing the lid off this backdoor scheme to use the United Nations to force mandatory gun registration and confiscation on America.

The pages herein will show you exactly what Obama means when he says he is working for gun control "under the radar." And it's my hope that after reading this you will help NRA sound the alarm on this treacherous abdication of U.S. sovereignty.

Chris W. Cox, Executive Director
National Rifle Association Institute for Legislative Action

Introduction

The U.N. Gun Ban Treaty

It was 1996, in the dark days of the Clinton administration, when I first began to sound the alarm to the unsuspecting gun owners of our nation. The gun-ban lobby, having been forced to a standstill in Congress, was looking for new avenues on which to attack our Second Amendment rights. At the same time, the vast apparatus of the United Nations and its associated nongovernmental organizations was fresh off a global campaign to ban land mines and looking for a new rallying cry. It was 1997 when a U.N. panel of "government experts on small arms" delivered a formal recommendation for a global conference to be held in the near future. The goal? A global treaty to restrict "small arms and light weapons."

The U.N. had plunged headlong into the gun-ban business.

Upping the ante in 1999, the U.N. issued another demand for a small-arms conference to be held in 2001. They were making a high-stakes bet on the outcome of the 2000 presidential election. They were counting on Al Gore to not only take the Oval Office, but also to encourage the creation of the global gun-ban manifesto as the next step of the relentless Clinton-Gore drive to destroy our Second Amendment rights. So, the conference was slated for July 2001, to make sure the newly elected Gore would have enough time to install the antigun lobby's operatives into key positions with authority over America's negotiating positions. Self-appointed social engineers all over the world were silently cheering for the Gore campaign, and the major funders of the global gun-ban movement poured their resources into shadowy political operations intended to ensure a Gore victory.

The plan was simple, and the bets were laid. But the silk-stocking set forgot to account for a single, major political force that would come to play a pivotal role in the presidential election—the National Rifle Association, and more important, its base of grassroots supporters.

NRA president Charlton Heston and I went on the road for weeks leading up the presidential election. In every city we visited, our message was simple: our gun rights could not survive another four years of Clinton-Gore assaults. We took our message to the heartland and to the battleground states. Just before the elections, we held our last rallies in Tennessee and Arkansas—to make sure that the voters who had first elected Clinton and Gore would know exactly how far their favored sons had strayed from their home states' political values. At every venue, capacity crowds jammed shoulder to shoulder to hear our message and to join our battle cry in unison—to "Vote Freedom First" and elect George W. Bush to the U.S. presidency.

The outcome is now well charted in history. During the agonizing weeks spent on the Florida recounts, analysts were musing over results that indicated vast departures from past voting history. Against all odds and predictions, George W. Bush carried Arkansas, Tennessee, and three other states that Bill Clinton himself credited the NRA with helping President Bush win.[1] Once the Supreme Court put an end to the partisanship in Florida, the victor was declared.

We were all exhausted for weeks. It had taken every penny we could muster to pay for the advertising, direct mail, phone banks, and political rallies. It had taken every ounce of personal energy to keep up the breakneck pace of weeks of political rallies, some of them held in three different cities per day. And it had taken every last vote we could summon from the nation's sportsmen and -women to Vote Freedom First, defeat Al Gore, and protect our rights from another four years of withering assault in the nation's capital.

But the U.N. was another story entirely.

It was too late for the U.N. puppet masters to beat a strategic retreat. The plan for the gun-ban conference and treaty continued right on pace.

The global gun-ban forces planned to avenge their defeated champion, Al Gore. They knew that the Bush administration would not let them run roughshod over the constitutionally guaranteed freedoms of American citizens, so they were going to turn the event into a media circus.

And then they made another bet. The demands issuing from the conference would include another conference in 2006, for another bite of the apple after the 2004 presidential elections. And here we were about to witness the U.N.'s second concerted effort to strip the Second Amendment from our Constitution. This time, however, we didn't have to worry about the drafting of a wide-ranging treaty to demand that our rights be sacrificed on the altar of global political correctness.

Because this time, the treaty was already in place. It had been for five years.

In July 2001, the conference stage was set, and I traveled to New York City just to observe the spectacle. The official title of the meeting was "United Nations Conference on the Illicit Trade in Small Arms and Light Weapons in All Its Aspects"—not the first or last time the U.N. crowd would demonstrate its passion for long, ambiguous phrases to describe the proceedings.

You see, there really are no definitions at the U.N. Specific meanings for terms of discussion would force the diplomats to abandon their rambling rhetoric. Diplomacy as practiced at the U.N. includes intentional vagueness, apparently intended to spare the diplomats from being forced to make concrete decisions over agreed-upon terms. Often, there are no definitions, and no votes. The only progress made by the body as a whole would come in the celebrated process of "consensus." Consensus, to my observation, meant wearing down your opponents with media ambushes and other confrontations designed purely to reduce resistance.

But it was immediately clear to me what the terms "small arms and light weapons" meant to the U.N. delegates. As I climbed the steps to the U.N. building on that morning, I came across the most prominent statue on the plaza. It shows a revolver with its barrel twisted into a knot. And when I stepped in the doors, I saw another special piece of "artwork" commissioned specifically for the conference. It consisted of more than seven thousand rifles, pistols, and shotguns, crushed into the shape of a cube. From overhead a single light shone, "epitomizing hope for change in the future." Other themed artworks designed to inspire the conference included murals titled *Guns 'R Us* and the *Mural of Pain*, the latter showing photos and drawings of "victims of gun violence."

There were no pictures of mortars, shoulder-fired rockets, heavy crew-served machine guns, or anything else you and I might consider to be "small arms and light weapons." There was no criticism of rogue military forces or genocidal governments. The conference and its artwork focused only on the "scourge of small arms" and the "flood of weaponry," with all fingers pointed to the United States and our "lax gun laws" as their source.

No, the target of the conference was revolvers, pistols, shotguns, and rifles. Your guns. And your rights.

The day before the conference opened, the spectacle was fully under way. And what a show! Remember, the staff and diplomats at the U.N. are outnumbered manyfold by the representatives of nongovernmental organizations, or NGOs. Thousands of these groups are accredited at the U.N. and make a full-time living from pressing their demands before the body. The largest and most influential NGOs serve as puppeteers for delegates who support their extremist agendas. With supreme arrogance, the NGOs refer to themselves and their pet delegates at the U.N. as "civil society."

Media grandstanding is part and parcel of their program. Even before the conference was officially under way, supporters took to the streets with giant protest puppets, most depicting the newly elected President Bush in a less-than-flattering light. The U.N. itself made its plaza available for a daylong series of speeches, exhibits, displays, posters, and video-loop "documentaries." The crowning touch was a page from the U.S. antigun lobby playbook, the so-called Silent March, where thousands of shoes were arranged on a red carpet. There were candles and incense, singing, and much holding of hands.

It had all the hallmarks of protest marches in the nation's capital, complete with hundreds of NGO activists, except here the protesters were also the professionals. The next day, they would move into the U.N. building in force, and play a major role in the outcome of the negotiations.

Let's talk about what happens during a U.N. conference. Most folks probably envision the typical TV shot of a U.N. chamber, with delegates plugged into headphones offering translation to their native tongue. This scene did play out during the conference, but it is only the smallest part of the proceedings.

The bulk of the theater takes place outside the U.N. building, with staged events and media productions built around themes assigned to different days of discussion. The first day of the gun-ban conference was called "Small Arms Destruction Day," complete with a U.N.-issued handbook "to aid those in charge of such destruction." Countries around the world were encouraged to destroy "confiscated, collected, seized, or surplus" firearms and to invite the local media for maximum exposure.

Other themes to play out during the conference included "Children's Day" and "Women's Day," as well as Africa, Asia, and Latin America Days. And the U.N. helpfully published a daily *Disarmament Times* newspaper to help keep activists up to speed on the day's events. A total of 119 NGOs attended the conference, dispatching 380 representatives. Some of those NGOs were umbrella groups, such as the International Action Network on Small Arms (IANSA), which in turn includes hundreds of other NGOs. That made for plenty of street theater during the conference.

Back in the U.N. headquarters building, the discussions proceeded at several levels. The only visible evidence of the conference came in the form of regular speeches offered by delegates of participating countries. These vague, rambling lectures touched on various issues within the negotiations, occasionally offering a nation's perspective but still couched in blurred, equivocal rhetoric that seemed essentially meaningless. The U.N. also allowed the NGOs to make their own presentations to the delegates, a process that reminded me of the frequent sight on Capitol Hill of a lone Congressman speaking to an empty chamber.

The real action went on in dozens of conference rooms deep in the bowels of the building. That's where hundreds of staff-level negotiators from the major participating nations hammered out specific language to propose to their country's delegates upstairs. The United States had representatives present from its headquarters U.N. staff, the Department of State, the Department of Defense, and dozens of smaller agencies. But it's impossible to know what's going on in these discussions, as they are closed to the public and to NGOs as well. In fact, the entire two final days of the conference were conducted in closed session, when the major nations finally began to negotiate in earnest over the final document.

It struck me as more than mildly ironic that the U.N., an institution purportedly striving for democracy and representative government all over the globe, would conduct its business behind an unyielding facade of official silence. Where was the outrage? My professional lifetime has been devoted to affecting the policy decisions of elected lawmakers. In the fifty state legislatures and U.S. Congress, not even our fiercest enemies ever tried to deprive us of the opportunity to witness debate and affect the outcome of votes. Here, there would be no voting. There would be no opportunity to witness the real debate over the provisions of the treaty. And there was certainly no way to lobby the delegates for or against anything in particular, if by chance you could find out what was really under discussion behind closed doors.

The process needed a central focus, a starting point from which to draw our battle lines. And that's when Undersecretary of State John Bolton showed up.

Undersecretary Bolton was then fairly new to the job. Appointed by President George W. Bush, Bolton had a reputation as a hard-liner in foreign policy, one that was well deserved. Bolton was once asked, under questioning from a Congressman, to explain his approach to negotiating foreign policy with other nations. The Congressman suggested to Bolton that perhaps a carrot-and-stick approach would be more fruitful. Bolton cut him off, saying curtly, "I don't do carrots."

But he brought his stick to the U.N., appearing before the delegates on July 9, 2001. He began his address with the typical flourishes of the U.N. idiom, addressing the audience as "Excellencies and distinguished colleagues . . ." But the niceties stopped there, and Bolton went directly to the heart of the matter, first attempting to force some definitions into the process.

"Small arms and light weapons, in our understanding, are the strictly military arms—automatic rifles, machine guns, shoulder-fired missile and rocket systems, light mortars," he said. "We separate these military arms from firearms such as hunting rifles and pistols, which are commonly owned and used by citizens in many countries."

Bolton went on: "As U.S. Attorney General John Ashcroft has said, 'just as the First and Fourth Amendments secure individual rights of speech and security respectively, the Second Amendment protects an individual right to keep and bear arms.' We therefore do not begin with the presumption that all small arms and light weapons are the same, or that they are problematic."

Bolton then outlined the United States' opposition to many of the treaty's proposed elements, saying, "We do not support measures that would constrain legal trade and legal manufacturing of small arms and light weapons . . . We do not support the promotion of international advocacy activity by international or non-governmental organizations, particularly when those political or policy views advocated are not consistent with the views of all member states . . . We do not support measures that prohibit the civilian possession of small arms, [and] the United States will not join consensus on a final document that contains measures contrary to our Constitutional right to bear arms."

He closed by calling the opposition's bet on a 2006 conference, saying, "The United States also will not support a mandatory Review Conference, which serves only to institutionalize and bureaucratize this process . . . Neither will we commit to begin negotiations and reach agreement on any legally binding instruments, the feasibility and necessity of which may be in question and in need of review over time."[2]

Timid applause greeted the end of his remarks, but many of the delegates were silently fuming. Bolton had just slammed the door on U.S. participation in the holy grail of the conference—a legally binding global treaty, designed and intended to restrict the rights of American citizens. But again, the U.N. would not be so easily defeated. The forces behind the gun-ban treaty retreated overnight to recalculate their strategy. By the next morning, their tactic was clear: proceed under the framework established by Bolton's comments, continue negotiations over treaty language considered "politically binding" but not legally binding, and wear down the United States until it surrendered.

Bolton returned to D.C. but left behind his enormous team of negotiators from the various U.S. agencies. The United States also appointed three "public" members of the official delegation, all of whom understood the political implications of the proposed treaty: Congressman Bob Barr of Georgia, former Congressman Chip Pashayan of California, and former U.S. ambassador to Switzerland Faith Whittlesey.

Still, the next ten days played out as David and Goliath, with the United States alone in the position of fighting off the biased media, antigun delegations from countries such as Japan and Canada, and the relentless fervor of the hundreds of antigun NGOs represented at the conference.

Other nations that opposed elements of the treaty were content to sit back and let the United States take the heat, knowing from Bolton's speech that the U.S. position was firm, and that they wouldn't have to get their own hands dirty. The central talking point of the global gun-ban elite was to claim that the United States had isolated itself against a global consensus to restrict firearms in a U.N. treaty. On Main Street, USA, this is a claim to glory. But in the hallways of the U.N. building, isolation was considered a major offense against the very concept of the U.N. itself.

Chip Pashayan later told NewsMax.com, "It was magnificent to see the U.S. stand up against these forces and not buckle under to what was international political pressure, which was very formidable notwithstanding the fact that the U.S. is the big boy on the block."[3]

Second Amendment scholar David Kopel, who monitored the discussions, later wrote in *National Review*:

> The U.S. delegation consistently rejected efforts at "compromise," which would have kept some antigun language in the treaty but made it softer and more ambiguous. An American delegation that was terrified of being "isolated" would have accepted the ambiguous language—on the theory that the Americans could later apply a pro-rights interpretation to the ambiguities. The Bush delegation was wiser: It recognized that, at the U.N., a conference final document is just the starting point. From there, U.N. bureaucrats will "monitor" how a country "complies" with such documents, and the bureaucrats resolving the ambiguities will favor their own radical agendas.[4]

The antigun delegates were befuddled. In the past, they had successfully worked together to wear down the United States in negotiating the specifics of other treaties. The U.S. negotiators were conditioned to moving their positions incrementally in the process, and checking back frequently with their bosses in Washington to see what they could live with. In his NewsMax interview, Pashayan noted, "The people from the State Department would have been more inclined to compromise to produce an agreement, that's their business. But they were prepared to follow the directions coming from above to stick with the 'redlines' and not go along with watered-down language."[5]

Going completely against the consensus process, Bolton's speech had drawn a line in the sand. The United States team had no intention of allowing that line to be crossed, despite the relentless and growing pressure.

The standoff would last beyond the scheduled closing of the conference, forcing negotiators to go into an all-night bargaining session on the final night.

Delegates were huddled in Conference Room 4 of the U.N. General Assembly building. It was Friday, July 20—slated as the final day of the conference. Tense negotiations had gone on late into the night on Thursday. The major bones of contention had boiled down to two of the "redlines" established in Bolton's speech.

The U.S. team refused to budge on language to prohibit small arms exports to "non-state actors," an artful term coined by the diplomatic set to describe anyone who was not an official government recognized by the U.N. The American team rightly refused this language outright, noting that it would prohibit support for freedom fighters, people resisting tyrannical governments (such as our colonial minutemen at Lexington and Concord) or even longtime allies like Taiwan that are not formally recognized by the U.N. as a state.

The other redline was drawn over language to "seriously consider legal restrictions on unrestricted trade in and ownership of small arms and light weapons." In the alarmingly vague U.N. vernacular, this language amounted to a direct attack on the civilian ownership of firearms of any kind.

Some African delegations were insisting on the "non-state actor" language, due in no small part to their desire to solidify and consolidate power behind their current dictatorial governments, and strip opposition forces of the means to challenge their power.

Antigun delegates moved to preserve some shred of the language prohibiting civilian ownership. Conference president Camillo Reyes of Colombia attempted to mediate, proposing a compromise in which the language would be moved to the preamble of the document, where it would be perceived as having less force. At every impasse, Reyes complained about the Americans' stubborn refusal to entertain compromise, and ordered the conference to finish debate over some other, unresolved language irrelevant to the core negotiations.

It was by then Saturday morning, about 4 a.m., and the core dispute could be avoided no longer. Canadian negotiators introduced another watered-down version of the "non-state actor" language, which would say only that a nation "has to bear special responsibility when it would send arms to non-state actors." Canada dangled a package deal; if the U.S. would accept this vague statement, it would agree to deletion of the language on civilian ownership. Negotiators fell into silence as they realized that Canada had decided to push the United States to the edge of the envelope.

We said no.

Reyes again criticized the United States and ordered a break. Pashayan told NewsMax that some exhausted members of the negotiating team wanted to accept the Canadian compromise, although it, too, could hamper a future U.S. president in foreign policy. Drawing on more than a decade's experience as a Congressman, Pashayan counseled a steady hand, suggesting that the U.S. simply refuse the deal and see what happened next.

Pashayan's counsel was correct. When the conference reconvened, the African nations dropped their demands. Following their lead, the developed nations opposing the U.S. position said they would follow the Africans' lead. As the sun rose over Manhattan, the final document was readied for consideration while the negotiators got a few hours' sleep.

The document was consolidated into a single draft and headed with the title "Programme of Action." It would be considered "politically binding," meaning that it lacked legal authority but nonetheless represented the consensus of participating nations. It did not violate any of the Americans' stated redlines, at least not technically, and it allowed the opposition to salvage some "face" for the time and effort spent on negotiations. In sum, it was the perfect political deal—no one was particularly happy with it, it meant essentially nothing in terms of binding law, but it nonetheless allowed everyone involved to say they had "done something" about the problem, whether real or imagined.

U.S. negotiators were not pleased, however, that the final draft still contained a call for a follow-up conference in 2006. But it was too late for more discussions. Reyes quickly brought the final document up for consideration, and pronounced it passed by consensus. The delegates then proceeded to deliver a lengthy series of speeches congratulating Reyes for garnering approval, but expressing disappointment that the Americans had prevailed in negotiations.

Pashayan summed up the experience for NewsMax: "This is not the end. This is the beginning skirmish of a war . . . All of this has to be understood as part of a process leading ultimately to a treaty that will give an international body power over our domestic laws. That is why we must make sure that there is nothing, express or implied, that would give even the appearance of infringing on our Bill of Rights, which includes the Second Amendment."[6]

Not surprisingly, the Programme of Action has had no effect on containing or preventing global conflict. So the next natural step is to accuse nations of noncompliance, demand far more restrictive language, and insist that the next conference produce a document that is legally binding. Translation: All fingers pointed at America, and all of their demands once again focused on your gun collection.

If no changes are made in the Programme of Action, what impact could the existing document have on our rights?

The answer is: plenty. The language is vague and sweeping, and it doesn't take much imagination to see how the gun-ban crowd could insist on the most extreme reading of its elements. Here's a rundown of the major existing provisions agreed to by consensus in 2001, quoted directly from the document.[7]

> To put in place, where they do not exist, adequate laws, regulations and administrative procedures to exercise effective control over the production of SALW (small arms and light weapons) within their areas of jurisdiction, and over the export, import, transit or retransfer of such weapons.

Read it again, and remember: there is no definition of "small arms and light weapons." Not to mention "adequate laws," "effective control," and "transit or retransfer." Who decides what is adequate? Who defines "effective control"? I do know the meanings of *transit* and *retransfer*, and these terms encompass merely traveling with firearms, or giving or selling firearms to friends, family, or at a gun show.

> Ensure that comprehensive and accurate records are kept for as long as possible on the manufacture, holding and transfer of SALW.

"Comprehensive and accurate records, kept as long as possible." The United States already does that for the manufacturing of firearms, but "holding and transfer" means possession and purchase. Taken in sum, this provision is code for a massive, international gun registration database, a deep pond for unlimited fishing expeditions by U.N. bureaucrats and investigators.

> Develop adequate national legislation or administrative procedures regulating the activities of those who engage in SALW brokering.

What is a gun dealer if not a broker between the manufacturer and customer? And here again, what exactly is "adequate"? As the U.S. team realized during negotiations, the answers to these questions will come not from a dictionary or neutral party, but from U.N. bureaucrats who are already on record opposing our constitutional freedoms.

> Ensure confiscated, seized or collected SALW are destroyed.

Any Americans who aren't worried about firearms being confiscated have their heads in the sand. In 2005 we saw authorities going house to house in New Orleans after the Hurricane Katrina disaster, pounding on doors and illegally confiscating firearms. The National Rifle Association stopped them in court, and the judge ordered the confiscated guns returned, but if the U.N. has its way, there would be nothing to return but scraps of metal and heaps of ashes.

> Develop and implement, where possible, effective disarmament, demobilization, and reintegration programmes.

So after we are disarmed, the U.N. wants us demobilized and reintegrated. I can hear it now: "Step right this way for your reprogramming, sir. Once we confiscate your guns, we can demobilize your aggressive instincts and reintegrate you into civil society."

No thanks.

> Encourage regional negotiations with the aim of concluding relevant legally binding instruments aimed at preventing, combating and eradicating the illicit trade, and where they do exist to ratify and fully implement them.

The antigun forces are encouraging countries to use other multinational groups, such as the Organization of American States, the European Union, and various African regional groups, to negotiate stricter treaties, make them binding, and push them through to ratification. It's intended to open up other fronts of attack, and it has been successful, as you will learn.

> Encourage the strengthening of moratoria or similar initiatives in affected regions or subregions on the transfer and manufacture of SALW.

This one is simple. "Moratoria" is the plural of *moratorium*, a fancy word for "ban."

Finally, the real whopper:

Promote a dialogue and a culture of peace by encouraging education and public awareness programmes on the problems of the illicit trade in SALW.

Let's connect the dots here. "SALW" means our guns. "Illicit trade," to many U.N. delegates, means any civilian trade whatsoever. So the "culture of peace" means no guns in civilian hands—a monopoly of force held by the state.

We don't need a dialogue about that concept; our Founding Fathers had a vigorous dialogue when they crafted the Bill of Rights to the U.S. Constitution. They expressly rejected a monopoly of force held by the state, and for good reason. But if the U.N. has its way, our cherished constitutional freedoms will be obliterated to reach the naive fantasy of a "culture of peace."

I can hear some readers now: "Oh, Wayne's just overreacting. That's not what these people really want." It is. And you don't have to take my word for it.

In 2004, I traveled to London to publicly debate Rebecca Peters, head of the International Action Network on Small Arms (IANSA). She was the chief of an umbrella group of NGOs, hundreds of them, who are all working together toward a global gun ban. Debating before an audience at King's College, I was amazed at how openly Ms. Peters was willing to admit the long-term goals of their movement.[8]

Peters quoted U.N. head Kofi Annan as saying, "The easy availability of small arms has contributed to violence and political insecurity, and have [sic] imperiled human security in every way." She told the audience that "guns are involved in human rights abuses . . . guns obstruct peacekeeping activities . . . guns hinder development, investment, and tourism."

That's a long indictment! But she was just getting started.

"Guns don't respect borders," she continued, citing the same argument of our national gun-ban groups when they complain about "lax" gun laws in our rural states causing crime in major cities. "There is a patchwork of laws globally," she said, echoing another canard of our domestic debate. And she grabbed one last arrow from the rhetorical quiver of the U.S. gun-ban lobby, claiming that increased crime rates in Great Britain were due not to their gun bans, but to the "loophole" of failing to ban airguns and replicas. And then she told the group that the Programme of Action represented only "moderate measures" to "reform" gun laws globally. She stated that the U.N.'s efforts to pass a gun-ban treaty represented "civil society saying, 'Stop!'" to the United States.

It became clear that in Peters's view, our guns were equivalent to military ordnance and weapons of mass destruction. "Treaties are how we deal with nuclear, chemical, and biological weapons," she said. "Only guns are exempt." She vented her wrath on the United States, saying, "The U.S. should recognize it's not exempt from the world, contributes disproportionately to world problems, and should cooperate."

An audience member pointed out that the U.S. Constitution prevented her vision of "cooperation" with the gun-ban treaty, but she persisted, complaining that the U.S. position represented the attitude that American citizens are "more equal than others."

Peters detailed the starting point of the "moderate reforms" she wanted the U.N. to ram down the throat of America's law-abiding citizens: owner licensing, registration, certain categories of guns should not be available, and limits on the number of guns civilians can own. Her goal, she claimed, was to "keep guns out of the hands of people who are irresponsible." When asked who that might be, she shrugged, saying that "good people sometimes do bad things" and that lawful self-defense "only happens in the movies."

I told the audience that if Peters and the U.N. couldn't tell the bad people from the good, we were all going to be in a lot of trouble. The audience pressed Peters for more detail on what type of firearms Americans should be allowed to own.

Peters responded, "I think American citizens shouldn't be exempt from the rules that apply to the rest of the world . . . Americans should have only guns suitable for purposes they can prove."

An audience member told Peters that his target-shooting guns had been confiscated, and asked if this disturbed her in any way. She responded, "Countries change; laws change; why are firearms exempt? The definition of sporting activity is always under pressure. Target shooting is not a legitimate sport! If you miss your sport, take up another!"

Now the audience was riled, and Peters was flustered when she delivered her closing remarks, saying: "Guns cause enormous suffering in the world at large. So much for guns and freedom. The U.S. is the country with the largest proportion of its population in prison . . . We should be talking about prevention. People have a right to live free from fear. Wayne has been watching too many movies. Common sense dictates that guns do not make people or societies safer."

The audience had grown skeptical, and I tried to put her words in a larger perspective. I told the crowd that we saw the IANSA mission for what it was: the reemergence of the same old socialist fantasies of the twentieth century—fantasies that prey on citizens who fall for the false promise of social engineering. I described the global gun-ban forces as elitists who think they know better than we do how to live our lives, spend our money, educate our children, and protect our homes. They are people who believe that if they could just be in charge, they could make our lives perfect. Their basic premise now is that if you will surrender your right to own a firearm to the whims of a new global bureaucracy, you will be safe. But I counseled the audience to study the history of nations where the social engineers have had their way, and suggested they should think twice about the bargain.

Americans simply won't fall for it, I explained. We are the freest nation in the world, and the false promise of the social engineers is precisely the bargain rejected by our forefathers.

I explained why Peters's vision was so frightening to Americans. Her vision is sweeping international police powers, offensive to every notion of our Bill of Rights. I told the audience to look at her own words, papers, and testimony, and they would find endless demands for recordkeeping, oversight, inspections, supervision, tracking, tracing, surveillance, marking, verification, paper trails, and databases.

And I pointed out that—no matter what Peters's lofty words and noble rhetoric were—nowhere in her documents would you find any provision by which oppressed people would be liberated or freed from dictatorship. Nowhere in her work is there a thought about respecting the rights to self-defense, privacy, property, due process, or political freedom of any kind.

I closed by asking the audience to join the fight for freedom—because these competing visions will now clash again on the debate floors of the U.N. in New York City.

The U.N. conference is not the only battlefield; it's just the largest. The global gun-ban forces have spent the years since the first conference opening new fronts for the clash of competing visions, and each one poses a unique threat to our freedoms. Each is also intended to add to the growing global clamor for the U.S. to surrender its principled stand on the private ownership of firearms.

Right now, the U.N. is negotiating an Arms Trade Treaty (ATT), aiming to have it ready for signature before the November 2012 presidential election in the United States. The push for the ATT received a significant boost at an October 3, 2005, meeting in Luxembourg where foreign ministers of the European Union "backed demands for a new international treaty on the arms trade to outlaw small arms," according to an article in *Defense News*.[9] Proposed by Great Britain's foreign secretary Jack Straw, the statement was greeted gleefully by global gun-ban groups. Simon Grey, the arms control campaign manager at the NGO Oxfam, "hailed the decision as a 'massive step toward stricter' controls on firearms."

That same month, a hemisphere away, in our own nation's capital, the Organization of American States (OAS) held a two-day meeting "aimed at developing steps to prevent and combat illicit arms trafficking in the Western Hemisphere," according to a press release from our very own Department of State.[10] The assistant secretary-general of the OAS called the arms trade a "transnational scourge," and said its effect on society "ranks among the most disastrous criminal activities against humankind." The meeting was led by a delegate from Colombia and held in accordance with the OAS "Inter-American Convention against the Illicit Manufacturing and Trafficking in Firearms, Ammunition, Explosives, and Other Related Materials." In the press release, the Colombian delegate called the convention "'groundbreaking and unique' as it is the first binding legal agreement on this issue."

Wait a minute. Isn't this the same "legally binding" concept we're fighting at the U.N.? And why did you never hear about the Senate approving this treaty?

Because it never has. The OAS treaty was first proposed in 1998, during the Clinton years. Since then, the career State Department bureaucrats, and President Obama, have pushed for Senate ratification of the proposed OAS treaty, but the Foreign Relations Committee has never taken it up.

The bureaucrats are surely proud of their work. In the press release, they stated that "the entry into force in 1998 of the Inter-American convention against illicit arms trafficking made the OAS a leader in multilateral efforts to address the problem of illicit weapons trafficking."[11] How did the "entry into force" happen without Senate ratification? The press release states, "The United States is a signatory to the convention and supports efforts to 'aggressively' implement its provisions."

So now we have treaties that are supposedly applicable to the U.S. without Senate ratification, merely because the president signed them.

So much for checks and balances.

The clash of competing visions is not limited to the United States versus the global gun-ban groups. In the midst are career bureaucrats, both here and abroad, whose jobs depend on negotiating agreements, not making principled stands. They are pushing forward on multiple fronts, out of the public eye, and seemingly without supervision.

This is their business, and we are newcomers to the process, vastly outnumbered by their legions. They are operating in venues that didn't even exist a few years ago. They are supported by the global media and reinforced by the work of paid NGO staffers who are dedicated solely to moving a global gun ban forward. We are vastly underfunded compared to the billions of dollars received by NGOs in "international aid and development" grants used to promote gun prohibition, some of which originate in our very own tax coffers. There are times when I wonder whether it's even possible to beat them at their own game.

But then I am reminded that this debate is not about process, policy, or global politics. At its core, this debate is about people, and the value we place on freedom.

Another development in October 2005 reminded me of freedom's enduring appeal. Social engineers in Brazil placed a binding gun-ban referendum on the national ballot for the October 23 elections. With majority support, the ballot question would completely outlaw the sale of firearms and ammunition to private citizens. Rebecca Peters awaited the results of the vote on the edge of her seat, telling the *Nation*, "If it passes, the referendum will show other countries that the gun lobby can be beaten. If that happens, we believe campaigns will arise in other countries, in Latin American and elsewhere, for a moratorium, or for serious restrictions, on the proliferation of guns."[12] There's their favorite word for "ban" again, "moratorium." And now she's talking about "serious" restrictions, not just the "moderate" ones she outlined in our debate. No wonder she was so excited at the prospect of a national vote in Brazil to ban guns.

On the day of the vote, voters stood in long lines to cast their ballots—voting is mandatory in Brazil, with failure punishable by a fine. Political observers predicted the ban would pass by a landslide. At the end of the day, however, the referendum was rejected by a vote of nearly 65 percent. Freedom's enduring appeal had triumphed again.

But not for long.

Despite all the pundits who said the referendum would set a global precedent, Brazil's gun-ban groups vowed to try again. The vaunted "will of the people" only seems to count when the people agree with the gun-ban agenda. "This closes the issue now, but maybe the next generation will be able to have this discussion again," said a local leader of the gun-ban campaign. "I hope the whole world will be able to deal with this again."[13]

The whole world will certainly deal with it again, and freedom will face its fiercest challenge yet, from the concerted forces of the global gun-ban corps who have spent the years since 2001 gearing up for more attempts to destroy the freedoms that are as American as apple pie.

The chapters that follow will confirm the stakes of this epic battle. And they will illustrate how critical it is for every freedom-loving American to join this battle and work together to ensure that freedom prevails again.

The U.N., which recently celebrated its sixty-fifth anniversary, was founded with the highest hopes to promote peace among the world's nations and human rights for the world's peoples. Yet when it comes to both its peacekeeping and human-rights missions, the U.N. has proven itself utterly bankrupt. For example, the U.N.'s so-called Human Rights Council includes some of the worst human rights violators in the world, such as Cuba, Libya, and Saudi Arabia.

Add to this the almost daily reports in the media of U.N. corruption, including what can only be described as a "culture of rape" among U.N. "peacekeepers" around the world. Decent men and women, not only in America but worldwide, must vigorously oppose U.N. attempts to disarm civilian populations—especially those in dire need of the tools for self-defense.

Not long after the United Nations was founded, Sir Winston Churchill offered the following about the new world body: "We must make sure that its work is fruitful, that it is a reality and not a sham, that it is a true temple of peace in which the shields of many nations can some day be hung up, and not merely a cockpit in a Tower of Babel."[14]

When this great leader said "we," he was really speaking of you and me. What would he say today?

Chapter 1

Global Repression: The International Gun Control Movement

S tymied by the outcome of elections in the United States—solidifying pro–Second Amendment majorities in the U.S. House and Senate—the gun-prohibition lobby turned to the courts, filing meritless suits against gun manufacturers with the hope of imposing prohibition through industry bankruptcy. As the lawsuit strategy fell apart, gun-prohibition groups sought victory through international law. Under their new strategy, the further the locus of decision making moved from democratic, American control, the better the chances for success in achieving universal disarmament through an international, U.N.-backed treaty.

Rebecca Peters

Until July 2010, billionaire George Soros's protégé Rebecca Peters ran the International Action Network on Small Arms (IANSA), which coordinates the gun prohibition efforts of groups around the world, including the Brady Campaign in America. (As of September 2010, the IANSA website has not revealed a new "Director," and there is no indication from IANSA that its future efforts will not continue in Peters's extremist path.) IANSA claims more than eight hundred accomplice groups worldwide and is funded with countless millions from governments, international foundations, and billionaires such as Soros. In spreading its dangerous doctrine of civil disarmament, IANSA receives the patronage of the same governments that push gun prohibition at the U.N. In effect, IANSA is the cutting-edge public relations arm of the U.N.'s gun prohibition campaign.

When I debated Peters at King's College in London on October 12, 2004, she was very forthright in saying that the gun prohibition movement was aimed squarely at Americans: "Americans are people like everyone else on Earth. They should abide by the same rules as everyone else."[1]

Peters would deny firearms, the proven means of self-defense to resist tyrants and genocide, to good citizens worldwide: "It's not going to be up to each individual person to be like a hero in a movie defending against this threat to freedom."[2]

At the debate, I reminded the audience of NRA's public awareness campaign, which asked: "Would you shoot a rapist before he slit your throat?" She responded by denying even rape victims the right to defend themselves against violent attack: "Women need to be protected by police forces, by judiciaries, by criminal justice systems. People who have guns for self-defense are not safer than people who don't . . . having a gun in that situation escalates the problem."[3]

When Peters claimed that all she wanted was "moderate" gun control, I repeated her mantra, in which she advocates banning every hunting rifle and works toward eliminating firearms of any kind:

> Your definition of "moderate" is the most extreme definition imaginable. From your own words, here you are in a CNN interview in October 2003. You want to ban every rifle that can shoot over 100 meters. That's basically a football field for people back in the U.S. That's every hunting rifle in the United States. The founding document of IANSA, your very own organization says, and I quote, "Reduce the availability of weapons to civilians in all societies." Duck hunters . . . in Australia. Taking away their pump shotguns. Here's your ad, and I can give you all these NGOs you

work with. Pamphlet after pamphlet after pamphlet, I can stack them to the ceiling, where you call for no [right] to individual armament. So let's be honest. You want to take guns away from all people, a global bureaucracy to do it. We're not going to let it happen.[4]

The moderator asked her, "So is that true?" She answered honestly: "We want to see a drastic reduction in gun ownership across the world. Yes. We want to see much lower proliferation of guns among the civilian population, and also among governments . . . Yeah, we want to reduce the number of guns in circulation around the world."[5]

Her "moderate" gun-ban plan includes more than just banning every hunting rifle. She and IANSA want to ban every semiautomatic shotgun, every semiautomatic rifle, and every single handgun:

Moderator: Do you believe, as you said in the past, that semiautomatic rifles and shotguns have no legitimate role in civilian hands?

Rebecca Peters: Yes, I do. Semiautomatic weapons are designed to kill large numbers of people. They were designed for military use. Many people have bought them for other purposes, for example, for hunting because they've been available. But there's no justification for semiautomatic weapons to be owned by members of the civilian population. Yes, I believe that semiautomatic rifles and shotguns have no legitimate role in civilian hands. And not only that; handguns have no legitimate role in civilian hands.[6]

Her long-term objective is a worldwide gun ban, which would be enforced against the U.S. In her generosity, she would allow selected Americans to prove that they need a single-shot rifle—with a range of fewer than 100 meters—for hunting:

I think American citizens should not be exempt from the rules that apply to the rest of the world. At the moment there are no rules applying to the rest of the world. That's what we're working for. American citizens should have guns that are suitable for the legitimate purposes that they can prove. I think that eventually Americans will realize that their obsession with arming themselves in fear, in a paranoid belief that they're going to be able to stave off the ills of the world through owning guns, through turning every house into an arsenal, eventually Americans will go away from that. I think Americans who hunt—and who prove that they can hunt—should have single-shot rifles suitable for hunting whatever they're hunting. I mean American citizens should be like any other citizens of the world.[7]

Peters extolled a decree she would impose on the U.S., already in effect in Australia and Great Britain: prohibition of defensive gun ownership. In those countries, she proclaims, "You were not allowed to have guns for self-defense. If you had a gun for self-defense, you were breaking the law."[8]

Peters shares that worldview with Neil Arya, who formerly headed Physicians for Global Survival in Canada. He told the U.N. in 2001 that physicians do not care whether firearms are involved in incidents where the shooter was a gangster, a soldier, or a law-abiding gun owner. In this perverse view, no distinction exists between an armed criminal murdering a robbery victim, an innocent victim saving her life by shooting the violent felon, a Nazi soldier shooting a Jew, or an American soldier shooting a Nazi soldier.[9] Yet it's a view espoused by the U.N., which is run by dictatorships that practice genocide, rape, kidnapping, and slavery around the world. And this is the bankrupt organization that Peters believes should impose its "culture" on the U.S. During our debate, when the question was posed, "Why do you place such unquestioning trust in governments and the United Nations, when you clearly do not trust individuals for the best way to protect themselves and their families?" she replied:

It's called civilization. Individuals come together. They form societies. They form governments. That's part of the contract that we make. It's a long time gone now since Thomas Hobbes described society as being characterised by a continual fear and danger of violent death and the life of man is solitary, poor, nasty, brutish and short. I have confidence that people coming together into countries are going to operate better than a whole lot of individuals making up their own rules, taking the law into their own hands.[10]

In other words, the dictatorial governments of Iran, North Korea, Cuba, Syria, and China should be empowered to mandate whether peaceful citizens may defend themselves against violence. Exercising the God-given right to protect oneself would no longer exist.

To fully understand the danger the global enemies of freedom pose to our Second Amendment, Americans must understand the ever-shifting vocabulary and bizarre legal theories masking the endgame of the international gun-ban movement.

For the true, sinister meaning of benign-sounding phrases such as "gun control," or "gun law reform," or "sensible firearms regulation," or "violence prevention"—the phony, deceptive vocabulary of the international gun-ban crowd—look no further than the mind of Rebecca Peters and her allies. Their ideology—wherever it is applied—is deadly to freedom.

With IANSA and Peters, there are no words or phrases that mean what average world citizens might naturally construe. They live in the murky sea of newspeak of their own invention—IANSA-speak, if you will.

Their doctrine is based on a concept of collective punishment or a kind of neo-Marxist redistribution—where guilt is transferred from evildoers, criminals, or mass killers, to be assigned to the innocent masses—law-abiding gun owners. In applying this twisted view on a global scale, their goal is to implement total civil disarmament through the U.N., either by an overriding binding treaty or piecemeal, one country at a time, outlawing and confiscating whole classes of firearms.

To understand what Peters has been pushing for on the world scale—what is intended for firearms owners in every nation—those working to protect freedom must study her past to define her words and actions today. The nightmare for peaceable gun owners in Australia is a glimpse into the future for those who are not vigilant and strong.As the proclaimed architect of the 1996–97 long-gun confiscation in Australia,[11] Peters saw law-abiding firearms owners forfeit more than seven hundred thousand rifles and shotguns for destruction under the guise of what she and the government called a "buyback."[12] The confiscation scheme, which Peters said "is the world's biggest,"[13] is the seminal example of gun control. And gun control shouldn't be about punishing criminals. "There is in America," she sniffed, "a very entrenched idea that the purpose of gun laws is to punish bad guys."[14]

Australia, Peters has often said, is the standard for the rest of what she calls "civil society"—meaning, a society without gun ownership. She always refers to the seven hundred thousand confiscated and destroyed rifles and shotguns banned in Australia as "inherently dangerous" "weapons of war," as "battlefield weapons," or as "military style-weapons," and the media always obliges by adopting her IANSA-speak.[15]

But the semiauto and pump shotguns and the self-loading rifles she marks as being "inherently dangerous" were almost all ordinary sporting arms. The official government forfeiture list included all semiauto .22s, including the Ruger 10/22, Winchester Model 1905, and Remington Nylon 66. As for shotguns and center-fire rifles, the list included the Winchester Model 12, Remington 870, Mossberg 500, Browning Auto-5, Remingtons 1100 and 11-87, Remingtons 740 and 7400, and the Winchester Model 100.[16] Think of any semiauto sporting long gun and any pump shotgun; whatever the make, those firearms became contraband under Peters's "weapons of war" big lie.

The collected words of Rebecca Peters and IANSA resemble a

Shakespearean aside; they say one thing to the other actors on the stage, then something else past the back of their hands to be heard by their agreeable global partners. For example, at our King's College debate, Peters mocked the use of the term "gun confiscation." She claimed that "the gun lobby has very much overstated . . . confiscation, which seems to be the preoccupation of the gun lobby. There has [*sic*] not been mass confiscation programs."[17] Apparently, in IANSA-speak, the Australian government's seizure of seven hundred thousand sporting long guns from law-abiding citizens was not "mass confiscation."

Nailing Peters and IANSA down as to their real worldview is simple. Don't believe what they may have said to sound moderate—perhaps before an American audience—but bank on what they have said when they're pushed into a corner.

Again in the King's College debate—broadcast to a worldwide audience—Peters characterized her international plan for global gun control through the U.N. as "very, very moderate."[18] Then she defined "moderate" by describing what any American gun owner would recognize as extremist and oppressive.

> We're not talking about banning all guns . . . but "moderate gun control" means people who own guns should have a license. Guns should be registered. It means ensuring that certain categories of guns are not available to private citizens . . . for example, high-powered, rapid-fire ones like the ones we banned in Australia. And there should be a limit on the number of guns civilians can own.[19]

The public outcry that Peters and her fellow gun haters orchestrated and the media hysteria that they manipulated to create Australia's long-gun ban came as a result of a mass killing in the Tasmanian resort town of Port Arthur on April 28, 1996. A lone gunman—a violent sociopath who had repeatedly been brought to the attention of police and mental health authorities to no avail—killed thirty-five people using two semiautomatic rifles, which he had stolen from a licensed collector, after murdering the man and his wife.[20] Port Arthur came weeks after a mass murder of children in Dunblane, Scotland, by a depraved pedophile wielding a handgun. Britain reacted with a ban on all registered handguns; Australia went after all semiauto rifles and shotguns and all pump shotguns in private hands.

Punishing gun owners in those two formerly free nations made no sense—except when IANSA's extremist theories were applied. Peters spelled them out very clearly in Australia, where her concepts for gun control remained out of sight and her goals unachieved until Port Arthur. Then she was everywhere, managing the media, spoon-feeding Australia's prime minister and gun-ban legislative politicians in the states and territories, and pressing them to embrace her model legislation.

One of her international sisters in the global gun-ban movement, Adèle Kirsten, a founding member and later director of Gun Free South Africa, wrote a lengthy paper comparing various ban efforts around the world. She shed light on the Australian experience:

> The Australian campaign was not just the result of public outrage to the Port Arthur massacre. A group of social activists had been working on the issue for several years prior to the events . . . They were surprised when the national media outlets said: "we need uniform gun laws, we need registration of all guns, and we need to ban all semiautomatics."[21]

She quoted Peters here, saying, "We thought we were still trying to establish this as the norm, but in fact what happened is that it had become so established that these newspapers and TV thought this was their opinion." Kirsten said it this way: a "defining moment doesn't just happen—it is constructed by social actors."[22] In other words, the media were willing gun-ban allies.

Peters's notions of gun control were like a long-dormant pathogen incubating. Her ideas—accepted blithely by the media and government as an answer to dealing with a crazed mass murderer—never had anything to do with Port Arthur, or with real crime. They had—and always will have—one central intent: disarming innocent people. For Peters, the Australian gun ban is the global model. She says it over and over. The absolute key element is registration and licensing—which she calls "moderate" and "common sense."

As a reward for her gun-ban success in Australia, Peters received a grant from George Soros's Justice Foundation to "research gun violence and gun control laws internationally, so that countries considering the reform of their gun laws can be informed by the experience elsewhere." Under that arrangement, she became a fellow at the Center for Gun Policy and Research at the Johns Hopkins Bloomberg School of Public Health.[23]

From there, Peters was elevated by her sugar daddy to Programme Director for the Funders' Collaborative for Gun Violence Prevention at Soros's Open Society Institute in New York. With Soros's funds, Peters bankrolled the most notorious destructive lawsuits to destroy the U.S. firearms industry, and she became the ultimate global carpetbagger—demanding a handgun ban in a nation where she no longer lived, demanding registration and licensing of a nation where she was a guest, and then making demands as a self-styled citizen of the world on all free nations.

In a paper designed to give credence to her new demand for a handgun ban in Australia, Peters and Roland Browne, her former cochair at Australia's National Coalition for Gun Control, laid out a manifesto—the basis for everything she now does on the world stage. The road map is titled "Australia's New Gun Control Philosophy: Public Health Is Paramount."[24]

In that seminal November 2000 declaration, Peters expanded her theory that if guns were taken from society, all the ills associated with firearms misuse would be curtailed. It is what has always guided IASNA. Of Port Arthur, she said, "Those killings also propelled Australia to the forefront of the global movement for rational gun laws. The regulatory scheme created by our Police Ministers in 1996 exemplified the new approach to gun policy: treating gun violence as a public health issue, rather than simply as a crime."[25] She suggests that without private firearms ownership by all ordinary citizens, victims of other violence would be better off:

> Likewise a gun law based on the public health approach seeks to reduce the likelihood of threats, assaults and suicide attempts, but especially to improve the victims' chances of survival if those events do occur. An assault with a machete is preferable to one with a gun, because fewer people are likely to be injured and they are more likely to survive their injuries.[26]

Possibly she should try to peddle that curious notion in Rwanda. As part of her transferral of guilt to innocent gun owners, she offers what has become a common theme in her global gun-ban aspirations:

> Regulation based on the public health approach recognises that most illegal guns are simply legal guns that have been stolen or sold secondhand. Since the supply source for the illegal market is legal owners, imposing greater accountability on legal owners will cut down the flow to the illegal market.[27]

And "greater accountability on legal owners" means that they must forfeit their legal property to prevent it from falling into illegal use. Peters, moreover, ridicules what she says is the downside of the gratuitous punishment she would inflict upon innocent gun owners—loss of their property, loss of their rights, and loss of their dignity as human beings by the unjust transfer of public guilt:

> From a narrow political perspective, the public health model comes at an electoral price. It involves an obvious encroachment

on (perceived by some) rights, being the "right" to own or possess a firearm. The supposed encroachment on this perceived right is heightened in the minds of some gun owners, because, they would say, they have "done nothing wrong."[28]

Those few words sum up the insanity and the injustice of the IANSA-Soros-Peters worldview, where honest, decent, and above all, innocent people are punished on a massive scale under the twisted gun-ban dogma. Indeed, in IANSA-Soros-Peters world, the very act of owning guns, of exercising a right, is doing something wrong.

Although IANSA/Soros have clearly sketched out the long-term goal of a worldwide gun ban, the international gun-prohibition movement is willing to proceed one step at a time. Recognizing the practical difficulty in disarming every civilian in the world at once, a 2002 U.N. book offers a model national law to require licensing and registration of all gun owners, with no gun owner allowed to possess more than a single handgun, or five guns of any type. Periodic "competency testing" would be required for all gun owners.[29]

Before the 2001 U.N. antigun conference, IANSA and its allies released a public letter equating guns with terrorists, calling them "a new source of terror: the glut of small arms and 'civilian' weapons that are seeping from many industrialized nations, through channels both legal and illegal, to virtually all four corners of the globe." Note that the very idea of civilians owning firearms was highlighted by scare quotes.

Of course if a gun-hating government, like the one in South Africa, wants to make gun ownership impossible, it merely has to impose a licensing and testing requirement, and then make it nearly impossible to take the test, and to ensure that the licensing system imposes such extreme delays as to make it impossible to acquire a license to own or sell firearms.[30]

International Gun-Control Groups

The number and extent of international gun-control groups is mind-boggling, and, unlike our homegrown radicals, they do not usually maintain a high public profile. They don't have to; they are not particularly interested in affecting the opinions of voters, members of Congress, or state legislators. The people they are trying to influence are the decision makers in the international arena who are generally somewhat removed from domestic political pressures: officials in foreign ministries.

These international gun-banners work quietly and behind the scenes. Most American gun owners have neither heard of them nor have any idea of the resources at their disposal. It is this vast government and foundation money that has enabled these groups to grow at a frightening rate and influence policy all over the world. Let's examine this international web.

International Action Network on Small Arms (IANSA)

The group was started in 1998 and grew out of the relationship between academics/consultants and the U.N. Department for Disarmament Affairs. In 1998, IANSA was an association of thirty-three NGOs from 10 countries, but by 2010 it had more than eight hundred member associations from 120 countries. It is the leading antigun NGO and coordinates the attendance and participation of its member associations at the various U.N. workshops and conferences. IANSA has a permanent staff and maintains a headquarters in London.

Funding IANSA are the governments of the United Kingdom, the Netherlands, Belgium, Sweden, and Norway.[31] It also receives funding from a broad collection of left-wing foundations, including the Ford Foundation, the Rockefeller Foundation, the Compton Foundation, the Ploughshares Fund, John D. and Catherine T. MacArthur Foundation, and the Samuel Rubin Foundation.[32]

The namesake of the Samuel Rubin Foundation, not coincidentally, was a member of the Communist Party USA. Rubin's daughter, Cora Weiss, now runs the foundation, which is headquartered on United Nations Plaza in New York City. The Foundation funds a variety of far-left and antigun groups,[33] and Cora Weiss is famous for her December 1969 trip to North Vietnam, after which she claimed that American POWs were comfortable in their "immaculate" facilities, and that two released POWs who challenged her claims were "war criminals."[34]

One of IANSA's members is Barbara Frey, a University of Minnesota law professor who is the U.N.'s special rapporteur on "the Prevention of Human Rights Violations Committed with Small Arms and Light Weapons." Notice that her very title precludes any consideration of the use of firearms to prevent human rights violations, including genocide.

IANSA's website carries features on U.S. domestic gun-control issues in which readers are urged to take action in support of restricting Second Amendment rights—such as by fighting against the sunset of the so-called "assault weapons" ban or by opposing the passage of the "Protection of Lawful Commerce in Arms Act," which rightfully shielded firearms manufacturers from lawsuits designed to bankrupt the industry. The involvement of such an NGO, financed by foreign government money, in U.S. domestic political issues is totally improper and unacceptable.

In addition to its member organizations, IANSA has spawned regional affiliates all over the world, including the Southern Africa Action Network on Small Arms (SAANSA), the Nigeria Action Network on Small Arms (NANSA), the Congolese Action Network on Small Arms (RECAAL), the Argentina Network for Disarmament (Red Argentina para el Desarme), the Japan Action Network on Small Arms (JANSA), the Cameroon Action Network on Small Arms (CANSA), the Liberian Action Network on Small Arms (LANSA), the Togo national network, La Coalition de la Société Civile Togolaise de Lutte Contre la Prolifération des Arms Légères et pour La Paix (Coalition of Togolese Society for Combat against Light Arms and for Peace), and the Serbian national network, Mreza za Mirovnu Politiku (Network for Peace Politics).

The most visible IANSA spin-off is Control Arms. That group was created in October 2003 by IANSA, Amnesty International, and Oxfam, for the purpose of lobbying for a U.N. Arms Trade Treaty—and of course lobbying to make the treaty as repressive as possible against innocent gun owners.

The Small Arms Survey

The Small Arms Survey (SAS) is unique and dangerous.[35] Basically a research institute specializing in gun control issues, it is housed at the Graduate Institute for International Studies in Geneva, Switzerland. The SAS authors a yearly Small Arms Survey, published by the Oxford University Press. It also prepares numerous reports looked upon by many governments as objective sources of information on small arms, and does substantial consulting work for the U.N.

The SAS is a large organization with full-time employees and consultants. It is funded by grants from the governments of Australia, Belgium, Canada, Finland, Denmark, France, the Netherlands, New Zealand, Norway, Sweden, Switzerland, and the UK. Given its resources, credibility, and relationship to the U.N., the SAS is a formidable foe.

Centre for Humanitarian Dialogue

Also operating out of Geneva is the Centre for Humanitarian Dialogue, or CHD.[36] It has forty-eight full-time staff, although not all are devoted to small arms issues. According to its website, "Donors in 2010 include Norway, Sweden, the United Kingdom, Switzerland, Denmark, Ireland, Australia, the MacArthur Foundation, the Netherlands, Belgium, Open Society Institute, Liechtenstein, the European Union and the City of Geneva."[37]

The CHD has made opposition to civilian possession of firearms its own particular cause. For example, to assist the Brazilian gun ban referendum, from March 16 to 18, 2005, CHD hosted a major workshop in Rio de Janeiro, Brazil, entitled "Regulating Civilian Ownership of Weapons."[38] Though there was a request to include representatives of the hundreds of millions of legal firearm owners in the meeting, it was specifically rejected. The conclusions of the workshop were the usual gun control panaceas: bans, registration, and the like.[39]

Other International Antigun Groups: Who and What Gun Owners Face

While IANSA works with American gun-ban groups, most of the active international antigun NGOs are not from the U.S. and, with the exception of Amnesty International and Oxfam, are not well-known in this country. The network of global antigun activists includes:

- Amnesty International.
- BASIC (British American Security Information Council): Its main focus is on nuclear issues, but it has become active on the "small arms issue."
- Bonn International Center for Conversion: a German disarmament think tank.
- GRIP (Groupe de recherche et d'information sur la paix et la sécurité), Brussels: One of the most active international antigun NGOs, it has produced numerous reports on firearms marking, tracing, and brokering.
- ISS (Institute for Security Studies): a South African think tank.
- Oxfam: Originally the "Oxford Committee for Famine Relief," this British NGO has turned into a lobby for all sorts of extreme left causes.

- Ploughshares: a major Canadian "peace" NGO, extremely active in the small arms issue from the very start.
- Saferworld: major U.K. anti-defense organization.
- SIPRI (Stockholm International Peace Research Institute), Sweden: also active in the small arms issue for more than ten years.

These individuals are among the leaders of the international gun-ban movement:

- Philip Alpers, New Zealand: former television producer, now a "gun control" researcher who edits *Gun Policy News*
- Ilhan Berkol, Belgium: GRIP
- Loretta Bondi, U.S.: currently a speechwriter for the UN Office of the High Commissioner for Human Rights
- Cate Buchanan, Switzerland: Centre for Humanitarian Dialogue
- Wendy Cukier, Canada: Ryerson University, and president of the Coalition for Gun Control
- Owen Greene, UK: Bradford University
- Adèle Kirsten, South Africa: Gun Free South Africa
- Edward Laurence, U.S.: Monterey Institute of International Studies: formerly an adviser or consultant for the United Nations Office of Disarmament Affairs, Human Rights Watch, and the Small Arms Survey; and cofounder of IANSA.
- Lora Lumpe, Norway: Norwegian Initiative on Small Arms Transfers

Overall there are dozens of full-time paid NGO activists working on the gun-ban issue, with budgets of millions. Remember this is an effort aimed at a small, select group of international decision makers, and not at fifty legislatures and the U.S. Congress. Given the size of the target audience, this international gun-ban effort represents a large, well-financed movement.

Here is a partial list of materials international gun control groups distributed to delegates at the 2005 Biennial Meeting of the States on Small

Arms that occurred at U.N. Headquarters July 11–15. In contrast to the 2001 and 2006 U.N. conferences, the 2005 event was a relatively unimportant interim meeting. Yet the gun prohibition groups showed up with a vast array of slick, very professionally-produced propaganda materials to distribute to the delegates. These items were given out by the hundreds.

- 4 different books
- 13 individual book-size reports
- 4 DVDs or software packages on CDs
- 20 different posters
- 6 different T-shirts
- 40 assorted brochures
- 30 separate position papers
- 5 different bumper stickers
- 3 miscellaneous items (folding guides on small arms, etc.)

Regional International Organizations

As the U.N. pushes for international gun control, there are also numerous regional efforts. Here is just a very brief overview.

- European Union:[40] The E.U. has been extremely active in the small arms field, issuing proposals to the U.N. and developing its own comprehensive policy.

- Organization for Security and Cooperation in Europe (OSCE):[41] Most Americans have never heard of the OSCE, a European regional group founded to address security issues. Regardless, it has been very active in the small arms issue, especially the destruction of firearms possessed by civilians in Eastern Europe.

- Economic Community of Western African States (ECOWAS): This African regional organization adopted a moratorium on the import and manufacture of small arms in 1998.[42]
- Nairobi Small Arms Protocol:[43] Similar to ECOWAS, these African countries in the Kenya regional adopted their own antigun protocol in 2003.
- South African Development Community:[44] SADC is a regional group and has adopted its own firearms protocol.
- Organization of American States: The OAS adopted a gun control convention known as "CIFTA" (for its Spanish acronym) in 1997, and the Treaty entered into force in 1998.[45] President Clinton signed, but the U.S. Senate has not ratified this treaty.

Firearms Owners Respond

The National Rifle Association has been defending gun owner rights on the international stage since the mid-1990s and has reached out to hunting and sport shooting groups all over the world to establish a common front against the threat.[46]

In 1997, NRA and several other groups formed the World Forum on the Future of Sport Shooting Activities—the WFSA.[47] The WFSA now has dozens of different groups, including associations from Australia, Austria, Canada, Denmark, Finland, France, Germany, Italy, Japan, Malta, Spain, South Africa, Switzerland, and the UK. In 1999, the WFSA became an official U.N. Non-Governmental Organization (NGO).

International gun control has been institutionalized at the U.N. It is entrenched not only in the Office for Disarmament Affairs, but also in the Development Programme, the Human Rights Council, the General Assembly First Committee, and elsewhere. It is on the U.N.'s permanent agenda. It is not going to go away. If there is one thing the U.N. does well, it is stubbornly staying with a cause year after year. American gun owners have to be at the ready year after year, and we must unify every hunter, sport shooter, and firearms owner in the world if we are to succeed in quashing the fashionable hysteria peddled by gun banners.

It may be tempting to dismiss the threat. Who really takes the United Nations seriously? As international analyst Stefan Halper observed, "After more than a half century, the verdict on the United Nations is in. The data on reform or lack thereof are available for all to see—and they are not a pretty picture. There is abundant evidence that waste, fraud, and abuse are rampant throughout the U.N. system."[48]

Yet the enemies of the right to bear arms are both determined and patient. As is often the case in politics, a small number of activists, with ample funding and sympathetic media coverage, can create the illusion of a consensus—in this case, one for a global gun ban. They see the U.S. Constitution as but a small barrier to their global ambitions. International activists have undertaken a more insidious strategy as well, working to change not only the public perception that individual Americans have a right to own a firearm, but the legal understanding that the Constitution guarantees the right to gun ownership.

The U.N. and its many conferences seem far removed from most Americans. But its actions have real consequences, and it is intent on eliminating the right of self-defense for every man and woman on earth. In this way the gun-banners will destroy freedom, for the freedom of self-defense underlies all other liberties.

The governments pushing for a global gun ban recognize this. After all, the vast majority of the regimes pushing the arms treaty don't allow their citizens the individual freedoms guaranteed to Americans under the Bill of Rights. It's not just that other governments aren't concerned about liberty, believing that it's not very important. Most actively oppose individual rights. These governments desire to expand their own authority, and gun owner rights stand in the way.

Anyone can look around the world and see how most governments use excessive power. Some honest gun-control activists acknowledge that citizens often purchase firearms because their governments do not protect them.[49] One report even admitted "some make the argument that where democratic institutions are weak, curtailing civilian possession may simply be a means of strengthening the control of authoritarian regimes."[50]

What the advocates of a global gun ban so often ignore is that virtually all firearm atrocities and massacres around the world aren't committed by individual criminals. Instead, the vast majority of wanton killings around the globe are committed by governments—the members of the U.N. themselves. The same governments that now want to extinguish the right to self-defense in America and every other nation so that only governments will have guns.

Most discussions at the United Nations are deservedly obscure, but the debate over guns really matters. It's about firearm ownership. But not only gun ownership—it's also a fight for individual liberty and national sovereignty. It's a battle for America's soul.

Chapter 2

The U.N.'s Disarmament Agenda: Looking Back, Looking Forward

One would think that the end of the Cold War would have little to do with the U.N. global gun-ban movement, but its impact was enormous. The most compelling, dramatic issue of the Cold War involved the possibility of nuclear conflict between the United States and the Soviet Union, spawning what could be called the "disarmament establishment."

The disarmament establishment comprises U.N. disarmament agencies, disarmament bureaucrats, agencies in the various foreign ministries, foreign policy think tanks, academics, and nongovernmental organizations (NGOs)—a formidable institution in the truest sense of the word. And like all institutions, it has institutional survival at the top of its agenda, no matter its public rhetoric.

Notwithstanding the fact that President Ronald Reagan's steadfastness did more to end the Cold War than any arms treaty, disarmament per se continues as an article of faith in the U.N.'s mind-set. That is, arms are bad because they cause wars, and arms cause violence in and of themselves. Once the Cold War ended, the disarmament establishment literally needed a mission, and it wasn't much of a leap for the disarmament crowd to see small arms as its next target. They needed the work, and willingly focused on small arms prohibition in a world beset with terrorism, nuclear proliferation, and government-sponsored genocide.

Sowing the Seeds

While both U.N. and U.S. policy-making are political processes, the U.N. disarmament movement has its roots in and depends in large measure on academic conferences, where contacts are made and strategies formulated.

The creation of the modern global gun prohibition lobby occurred February 24–25, 1994, at a conference titled "International Trade in Light Weapons," held in Cambridge, Massachussetts, and organized by the American Academy of Arts and Sciences. The list of thirty-nine participants reads like a Who's Who of the international gun control movement. Participants from the U.S. government were present, as was Jody Williams, the American who would later win the 1997 Nobel Peace Prize for her work to ban land mines.

The academics gathered in Cambridge that winter mapped out a gun-ban strategy that is still being pursued more than sixteen years later:

> As can be seen in the long debate on gun control in the United States, nothing happens as long as the "recipients" [gun owners!] can make the argument that possession of such weapons is defensive in nature and adds to stability. [We] would submit that the legislation outlawing semiautomatic weapons in the United States only passed when a majority of the public concluded that it was the guns themselves that were a major factor in killings taking place in their cities and neighborhoods. In regard to international transfers of light weapons, this may be difficult to achieve even at the national level, although many states have well-established norms against the possession and trade in these kinds of weapons. But, as noted above, the surfeit [oversupply] of such weapons in the wake of the end of the Cold War makes the problem at a minimum regional or international in nature.
>
> The campaign initiated by human rights and development NGOs to ban antipersonnel land mines serves as an excellent

example of what can be done to establish such a norm. In this age of the Internet and CNN, much more could be done to change world opinion regarding the negative consequences of the light weapons trade.[1]

These academics were, and are, the intellectual foot soldiers of the international gun-ban movement. What we have accomplished intellectually in the domestic gun control debate, with scholars such as David Kopel, Don Kates, Steve Halbrook, and others of national repute, has yet to penetrate the international arena where in the past sixteen years the other side has put out dozens of books arguing its case for global disarmament.[2]

The Land Mine Treaty

In 1997 a watershed event in the history of international relations occurred: the adoption of the international treaty banning land mines, known as the Ottawa Treaty. Significantly, NGOs were its driving force. The effort was unique: NGOs were involved in the actual negotiations of the treaty, and the work was done outside of the U.N. system itself, with Britain's Princess Diana the iconic symbol for the movement.

The adoption of the land mine treaty inspired and empowered the NGO movement. NGOs had been the prime sponsors of the treaty and had, in effect, arranged an alliance with like-minded governments, which made the treaty possible. The second effect was to motivate governments to get ahead of the process and not let NGOs take too much of a leadership role. Another effect was to dangle the ultimate reward in international relations, the Nobel Peace Prize, before the eyes of U.N. gun-ban advocates. A Nobel Prize means a place in history, celebrity status, credibility on just about any issue you want to discuss, a lifetime of lucrative honorariums and social events—and cash.

The thinking, after the successful land mine treaty, was intoxicatingly simple: ban small arms and win the Nobel Peace Prize again.

The litany of heinous murders in Montreal, Dunblane, Port Arthur, and Columbine allowed unscrupulous politicians to ban and confiscate firearms in Canada, the UK, and Australia. The Montreal crime occurred in 1989, Dunblane and Port Arthur occurred in 1996, and Columbine in 1999. While the U.S. successfully resisted the gun-ban hysteria, these tragic events energized gun-ban movements throughout the world. Antigunners such as Wendy Cukier of Canada, Rebecca Peters of Australia, and Adèle Kirsten of South Africa formed the leadership cadre of the international gun-ban movement. The U.N., although ostensibly concerned with international matters, also found it convenient to cite these tragedies as justification for its own gun-ban agenda.[3]

Disarmament and arms control have long been priorities at the U.N. The Conventional Arms Register came into operation in 1992, and various academics seek to expand it to small arms. Today, several U.N. delegations, including France, have taken up the cause of putting firearms in the Conventional Arms Register. Some countries already voluntarily supply this information to the U.N. registry. For example, Bulgaria reported that in 2008 it exported 1,004 revolvers and self-loading pistols to the United States.[4]

The global gun control issue was raised to prominence by then U.N. secretary-general Boutros Boutros-Ghali in a supplement to an Agenda for Peace in January 1995.[5] Boutros-Ghali used a new term, "microdisarmament," a concept which was being pushed by the grand dame of the U.N. Department for Disarmament Affairs, Swadesh Rana, a high-caste Indian woman and long-term U.N official whose job was to lecture the world on how to behave properly.[6]

"Microdisarmament" means disarming one country at a time, rather than expecting to disarm the whole world all at once. It is a modern version of the principle that the Soviet Union's dictatorship adopted in 1924, of "socialism in one country." After Lenin died, the Soviet tyrants faced the reality that they were not going to take over the whole world as quickly as they had once hoped, so they set about imposing their totalitarian vision in the one country they did control. Like Soviet Communism, microdisarmament aims for a radical transformation in a short period of time, but is content to impose that transformation country by country, as opportunities present themselves. The long-term goal, however, remains to cover the globe with a totalitarian system: Communism (favored by the Soviets), or elimination of gun ownership and the right of self-defense (favored by the U.N.). So in 1995, two parallel U.N. attacks on firearms owners began.

One came out of the U.N. Department for Disarmament Affairs at its New York headquarters, while the other emerged from the U.N. Office on Drugs and Crime located in Vienna, Austria.[7]

The U.N. Department for Disarmament Affairs began a series of studies that led to the U.N. Conference on Small Arms in 2001. The 2001 Conference generated the Programme of Action against small arms that continues to this day to be the focal point of much of the international gun-ban effort.

The U.N. Office on Drugs and Crime began its own formal study of firearms, which would lead to the U.N. Firearms Protocol in 2001. Gun control via the Protocol continues today.

Over time, many more U.N. agencies and departments would join the global gun ban campaign. The campaign is founded on extensive, well-financed efforts involving hundreds of U.N. personnel, national government officials, NGO members, and academics. Walk into one of the many conferences on small arms conducted at U.N. headquarters in New York, and you would be awestruck by the size of the conference, the numbers of people involved, and the extensiveness of the program: five hundred–plus diplomats, U.N. officials, and NGO gun banners all gathered to do one thing—take guns away from every law-abiding citizen in the world. Then you realize how serious the threat is.

Politics in the "Global Village"

On October 18, 1992, a sixteen-year-old Japanese exchange student, Yoshihiro Hattori, misread an address on the way to a Halloween party and tried to enter a homeowner's garage in Baton Rouge, Louisiana. The owner tragically mistook Hattori for a burglar and shot him. Hattori died, and though the homeowner was charged, he was eventually found not guilty. This incident, however, laid the foundations for Japanese efforts at international gun control. The tragedy received major attention in the Japanese media, and Hattori's parents gathered 1.7 million signatures on a gun-control petition, which was presented to President Bill Clinton.[8]

The Clinton administration was sympathetic to the gun prohibitionists, and in a speech in 1996, the U.S. ambassador to Japan, Walter Mondale, adopted the following theme:

> Our ability to lead in Asia will be largely colored by what we do at home . . . Many look at violence in America, especially the wanton availability of guns and argue that our emphasis on the individual really means personal license at the expense of social stability.
>
> The importance of this issue has been brought home to me by the number of Japanese citizens who have been killed in America since I have been Ambassador. I have met loving parents who sent young and innocent students to the United States only to have them lose their lives . . . Failure to deal with violence in America, failure to restrict the use of guns as weapons of wanton bloodshed, is no longer just a domestic issue. It is costing us terribly as world leaders.[9]

Clearly, Walter Mondale was willing to sacrifice American gun owners' Second Amendment rights for Japanese goodwill. And this would prove to be just the opening salvo.

Since the mid-1990s, Japan, which profits from its significant sporting firearms export industry (it claims that it doesn't produce small arms, because only military firearms are small arms), has seen to it that gun control stays atop of the U.N. disarmament agenda.

On December 12, 1995, the U.N. General Assembly passed the first of many resolutions on small arms (A/RES/50/70 B).[10] It called for a panel of government experts that was appointed in April 1996, chaired by Ambassador Mitsuro Donowaki of Japan.[11] The effort was staffed by the previously mentioned Swadesh Rana, and the U.N. hired as its consultant Dr. Edward J. Lawrence from the Monterey Institute for International Studies in Monterey, California. Lawrence had been doing consulting work for the U.N. Department for Disarmament Affairs since 1992. More important, he was also one of the academics who met in Cambridge in 1994,[12] typifying the incestuous relationship between the disarmament lobby and the U.N. The U.N. is a source of funding for the academics, and the U.N. receives the benefits of the spadework of these advocates. Tracing money in the arcane U.N. system is a difficult task, but it was common knowledge that Japan was paying for a substantial part of all of these efforts.[13]

In 1997, the panel of experts issued its report.[14] An early draft was inadvertently circulated, and it contained recommendations for strong limits on civilian possession of small arms. After protests from America, these recommendations were toned down, but the report still contained twenty-four recommendations, not the least of which was that the U.N. hold an international conference on small arms. The report defined what was included in the category of "small arms," with five definitions that cumulatively covered virtually every firearm possible.[15]

In response to the 1997 report, the U.N. General Assembly passed a resolution that called for the appointment of a group of government experts to continue the work on small arms prohibition.[16] The group was appointed in April 1999, and was again chaired by Ambassador Donowaki and staffed by Swadesh Rana. The consultant this time was another disarmament advocate, Dr. Owen Greene, from the University of Bradford in the UK.

The group submitted its report in August 1999.[17] The U.N. General Assembly has already resolved to convene an international conference on firearms,[18] and the experts recommended that the conference address "the illicit arms trade in all its aspects."[19] The last four words in that phrase were to cause the most trouble for the eventual conference. The advocates of international gun control resemble the old Tammany Hall politician: "I seen my opportunities and I took them!"[20] Their opportunity was to use all of the factors we have discussed to hijack the existing mechanisms and institutions for disarmament between states and use them for good old-fashioned "gun control."

Since America opposes illicit trafficking in small arms—just as on the domestic front we remain opposed to the criminal misuse of firearms—we tried to steer U.N. efforts toward illicit trafficking. International gun-control advocates, however, were determined to expand the focus, thus the addition of the key words "in all its aspects."

The theme throughout all of these international conferences remained constant: to control illicit small arms, the number of legal arms owned must be reduced. This is why the phrase "in all its aspects" was the opening gun banners sought.Three formal preparatory committee meetings and innumerable workshops were held prior to the 2001 Conference. This process produced a draft Programme of Action (PoA) that the conference was supposed to adopt. This was not to be a treaty, but a commitment on behalf of the agreeing states to continue the U.N. small arms program for at least a five-year period.

The draft PoA[21] considered by the 2001 Conference was highly objectionable, written using "U.N. language"[22] and filled with references to humanitarian and development issues. There were no references to the rights of firearms owners, hunting, or sport shooting. The tone was exceedingly anti-firearm and internationalist. Many of the issues were totally inappropriate for the U.N. even to be considering. Here are just a few of the provisions found objectionable by the firearms community:

- Article II Paragraph 2—a reduction in the number of small arms; that is, destroying firearms
- II/4—Increased control
- II/7 and II/10—recordkeeping over transfers, which amounted to massive gun registration requirements
- II/13—A prohibition of transfer of arms to "non-state actors," meaning the U.S. could never arm any freedom fighters, no matter how oppressive the regime
- II/16—"Stockpile" control; again, gun registration
- II/17—Destruction of all surplus arms, which would have the effect of making the U.S. Civilian Marksmanship Program illegal, because that program uses surplus arms from the U.S. Department of Defense
- II/19—Arms destruction to be public, thus institutionalizing anti-firearms propaganda events and publicity
- II/20—A ban on civilian possession of military weapons
- II/23—"Public awareness" programs—more propaganda
- II/24—regional moratoria on manufacturing, export, and so on
- II/35—an international instrument of tracing, involving firearms marking or an international registration scheme
- II/38—working with "Civil Society"—in other words, institu-tionalization of the role of gun prohibition NGOs
- II/39—the promotion of a "Culture of Peace," a euphemism for antigun propaganda
- III/6—more state legislation
- III/8—which would allow the U.N. to get permanently involved in "stockpile management"
- III/18—funding of advocacy programs
- IV/1/a—a review conference in the year 2006
- IV/1/c—a treaty on "tracing"
- IV/1/d—a treaty on restricting manufacturing

These provisions were being strongly advocated by Japan, Canada, numerous African countries, and most of South America. The U.S., on the other hand, was strongly opposed to most of these proposals. America let it be known that there were certain "red line" items, which, if adopted, would cause the U.S. to reject the conference outcome completely. These included:

- Any limitation on civilian possession
- Any restrictions on manufacture
- Any attempt to ban transfers to "non-state actors"
- Any attempt to commit the U.S. to negotiate legally binding treaties on "marking," "tracing," or "brokering"

The stage was set when the conference opened July 9, 2001. Nearly all of the U.N. member states were represented by 500 delegates, and 177 NGOs were also approved to attend. Twelve of the 177 NGOs were from the firearms community.[23] Ambassador Camillo Reyes, of Colombia, was selected as president of the conference. Again, these conferences are huge events that include not only regular "plenary sessions" where states, NGOs, and others speak, but innumerable side shows, literature tables, demonstrations, video presentations, press conferences, and other events. A mobile home–sized sculpture of crushed guns adorned the main U.N. lobby, while the infamous sculpture of a revolver with a knotted barrel stood outside.

On July 16, 2001, the NGOs made their presentations. Thirty antigun NGOs and all twelve pro-freedom groups spoke, among them the National Rifle Association (NRA). Although significantly outnumbered, the firearms community NGOs were given an hour to speak, one-third of the three-hour plenary session for NGO presentations.[24] The difference between the two groups was striking. In short, respectful presentations, gun owners' representatives emphasized civil rights, the heritage of hunting and sport shooting, and the necessity to find real solutions to the issue of violence worldwide. The antigun groups' presentations were an emotional litany of recycled clichés—guns are bad, guns cause violence, and so forth.

Theoretically, decisions are made at most international conferences by consensus. This essentially means that everybody has to agree. It is not that a vote, such as in Congress or the legislatures, cannot be held, but this is usually avoided at all costs. Further, some countries are more equal than other countries. Countries are pressured into agreements at a conference, and diplomats are programmed to compromise and not fight.

To the chagrin of the international gun banners, this was not to be the case at the 2001 conference. On the opening day, Undersecretary of State for Disarmament Affairs John R. Bolton categorically and unequivocally stated the U.S. positions. In the strongest possible terms, Bolton laid down America's position. Here are excerpts from his remarks:

> Excellencies and distinguished colleagues, it is my honor and privilege to present United States views at this United Nations Conference on the Illicit Trade in Small Arms and Light Weapons in All Its Aspects.
>
> The abstract goals and objectives of this Conference are laudable. Attacking the global illicit trade in small arms and light weapons (SA/LW) is an important initiative which the international community should, indeed must, address because of its wide ranging effects.
>
> The illicit trade in SA/LW can be used to exacerbate conflict, threaten civilian populations in regions of conflict, endanger the work of peacekeeping forces and humanitarian aid workers, and greatly complicate the hard work of economically and politically rebuilding war-torn societies. Alleviating these problems is in all of our interest.
>
> Small arms and light weapons, in our understanding, are the strictly military arms—automatic rifles, machine guns, shoulder-fired missile and rocket systems, light mortars—that are contributing to continued violence and suffering in regions

of conflict around the world. We *separate these military arms from firearms such as hunting rifles and pistols, which are commonly owned and used by citizens in many countries. As U.S. Attorney General John Ashcroft has said, "just as the First and Fourth Amendments secure individual rights of speech and security respectively, the Second Amendment protects an individual right to keep and bear arms." The United States believes that the responsible use of firearms is a legitimate aspect of national life.* Like many countries, the United States has a cultural tradition of hunting and sport shooting. We, therefore, do not begin with the presumption that all small arms and light weapons are the same or that they are all problematic. It is the illicit trade in military small arms and light weapons that we are gathered here to address and that should properly concern us.

Believing that it is in our interest to stem the illicit trade in military arms, the United States has avidly promoted and supported such international activities as the Wassenaar Arrangement and the U.N. Register of Conventional Arms. Bilaterally, we offer our financial and technical assistance all over the world to mitigate the illicit trade in SA/LW. We have worked with countries to develop national legislation to regulate exports and imports of arms, and to better enforce their laws. We have provided training, technical assistance, and funds to improve border security and curb arms smuggling in many areas of the world where this problem is rampant. And in the past year, we have instituted a program to assist countries in conflict-prone regions to secure or destroy excess and illicit stocks of small arms and light weapons.

[W]e strongly support measures in the draft Programme of Action calling for effective export and import controls, restraint in trade to regions of conflict, observance and enforcement of UNSC embargoes, strict regulation of arms brokers, transparency in exports, and improving security of arms stockpiles and destruction of excess. These measures, taken together, form the core of a regime that, if accepted by all countries, would greatly mitigate the problems we all have gathered here to address.

There are, however, aspects of the draft Programme of Action that we cannot support. Some activities inscribed in the Program are beyond the scope of what is appropriate for international action and should remain issues for national lawmakers in member states. Other proposals divert our attention from practical, effective measures to attack the problem of the illicit trade in SA/LW where it is most needed. This diffusion of focus is, indeed, the Program's chief defect, mixing together as it does legitimate areas for international cooperation and action and areas that are properly left to decisions made through the exercise of popular sovereignty by participating governments:

We do not support measures that would constrain legal trade and legal manufacturing of small arms and light weapons. The vast majority of arms transfers in the world are routine and not problematic. Each member state of the United Nations has the right to manufacture and export arms for purposes of national defense. Diversions of the legal arms trade that become "illicit" are best dealt with through effective export controls. To label all manufacturing and trade as "part of the problem" is inaccurate and counterproductive.

Accordingly, we would ask that language in Section II, paragraph 4 be changed to establish the principle of legitimacy of the legal trade, manufacturing and possession of small arms and light weapons, and acknowledge countries that already have in place adequate laws, regulations and procedures over the manufacture, stockpiling, transfer and possession of small arms and light weapons.

We do not support the promotion of international advocacy activity by international or non-governmental organizations, particularly when those political or policy views advocated are not consistent with the views of all member states. What individual governments do in this regard is for them to decide, but we do not regard the international governmental support of particular political viewpoints to be consistent with democratic principles. Accordingly, the provisions of the draft Program that contemplate such activity should be modified or eliminated.

We do not support measures that prohibit civilian possession of small arms. This is outside the mandate for this Conference set forth in UNGA Resolution 54/54V. We agree with the recommendation of the 1999 U.N. Panel of Governmental Experts that laws and procedures governing the possession of small arms by civilians are properly left to individual member states. *The United States will not join consensus on a final document that contains measures abrogating the Constitutional right to bear arms.* We request that Section II, paragraph 20, which refers to restrictions on the civilian possession of arms, to be eliminated from the Program of Action, and that other provisions which purport to require national regulation of the lawful possession of firearms such as Section II, paragraphs 7 and 10 be modified to confine their reach to illicit international activities.

We do not support measures limiting trade in SA/LW solely to governments. This proposal, we believe, is both conceptually and practically flawed. It is so broad that in the absence of a clear definition of small arms and light weapons, it could be construed as outlawing legitimate international trade in all firearms. Violent non-state groups at whom this proposal is presumably aimed are unlikely to obtain arms through authorized channels. Many of them continue to receive arms despite being subject to legally binding

UNSC embargoes. Perhaps most important, this proposal would preclude assistance to an oppressed non-state group defending itself from a genocidal government. Distinctions between governments and non-governments are irrelevant in determining responsible and irresponsible end users of arms.

The United States also will not support a mandatory Review Conference, as outlined in Section IV, which serves only to institutionalize and bureaucratize this process. We would prefer that meetings to review progress on the implementation of the Program of Action be decided by member states as needed, responding not to an arbitrary timetable, but specific problems faced in addressing the illicit trade in small arms and light weapons. Neither will we, at this time, commit to begin negotiations and reach agreement on any legally binding instruments, the feasibility and necessity of which may be in question and in need of review over time.

Through its national practices, laws, and assistance programs, through its diplomatic engagement in all regions of the world, the United States has demonstrated its commitment to countering the illicit trade in small arms and light weapons. During the next two weeks, we will work cooperatively with all member states to develop a final document which is legitimate, practical, effective, and which can be accepted by all nations. As we work toward this goal over the next two weeks, we must keep in mind those suffering in the regions of the world where help is most desperately needed and for whom the success of this Conference is most crucial.[25]

Almost two weeks later, when the conference closed in the early morning hours of June 21, 2001, the U.S. had prevailed on every point but one—a review conference in 2006. The Americans had taken one of the toughest pro-freedom stances ever at an international conference. On the final night, pressured by the Europeans, the Japanese, the Canadians, and the Africans, the U.S. steadfastly refused to budge on key issues. The other side blinked. The U.S.'s four red lines had not been crossed!

Gun control advocates at the conference were incensed, and antigun NGOs predictably blamed NRA. Typical was Aaron Karp, writing in the *Brown Journal of World Affairs*:

> As activists mobilized in recent years to support efforts to control the spread of small arms, they triggered a response from gun advocates. In a twist of Newtonian physics that should surprise no one, the reaction was opposite and overpowering.
>
> The immediate catalyst was the U.N. Conference which compelled the gun advocates—led by the National Rifle Association—to take the defensive. *The contradictory result of the U.N. Conference was leading the NRA to become internationally active for the first time.* Even if America's final position at the event had been assembled under President Al Gore, the immense clout of one of the country's most effective single-issue lobbies would still have been felt. As it was under the George W. Bush administration, the impact was just plain huge. *At the Conference itself, the NRA emerged as a greater force than all the 180 other NGOs there combined,* dominating the American delegation to a degree few had previously imagined possible.[26]

John Bolton, of course, would go on to become U.S. ambassador to the U.N. and one of the strongest defenders of American interests to serve in that role in years. Antigunners never seem to realize that some public officials support the Second Amendment not because of the power of NRA but because they truly, sincerely, and personally support that inalienable right. And, much to the dismay of the international crowd, there are public officials in other countries who support the concept behind the Second Amendment: the basic human right to defend oneself from tyranny and other criminal violence.

Despite Bolton's success in 2001, U.N. efforts to ban firearms continue, with numerous small arms projects funded by the U.N. national governments and by foundations. Each country is supposed to have a "national point of contact" on small arms and to file reports with the U.N. on its activities. Sweden alone reports that it has spent $50 million on small arms projects. The process internationally has no end in sight.

Opening Shots: The United Nations Firearms Protocol

The U.N. office on Drugs and Crime in Vienna launched its efforts at the Ninth U.N. Congress on the Prevention of Crime and the Treatment of Offenders in Cairo, Egypt, April 29 to May 8, 1995. There, Japan introduced its first resolution for international gun control.[27] The Japanese developed the basic theme and concept of international gun control that remains today: international gun control means domestic gun control in all of the U.N. member states. The background paper supporting the resolution recommended universal registration, bans of civilian possession of military weapons, and a whole series of other onerous measures.[28]

The Japanese media picked up the drumbeat: "Strict gun control is a major contributing factor to the safe society we are proud of [and] Japan must become a leader in gun control in international society."[29]

This was the first international diplomatic event where NRA had a presence. An NRA member attending the Congress on another matter, offered to monitor the Japanese effort. We gratefully accepted his offer, and NRA's very presence had an effect on the meeting. The Cairo meeting set in motion a series of actions. An international study of firearms regulation in the various U.N. jurisdictions was authorized.[30] The study was supervised by Canadian James Hayes and paid for by Japan, Canada, and Australia.[31]

A series of four regional workshops on firearms regulations was scheduled: Ljubljana, Slovenia, September 22–26, 1997; Arusha, Tanzania, November 3–7, 1997; São Paulo, Brazil, December 8–12, 1997; and New

Delhi, India, January 27–31, 1998. The workshops would reach absurd recommendations: paying taxes before being allowed to own a firearm; a limit of one firearm per person; a medical exam; upper and lower age limits; smoothbore firearms only; and no collecting of firearms except by museums. Both NRA and antigun groups were present at these workshops, but there was a systematic exclusion of these NGOs from many of the meetings on the grounds that sensitive "law enforcement matters" were being discussed.

In 1998, a General Assembly resolution was adopted accepting the international firearms study and starting the process of drafting an "international instrument to combat the illicit manufacturing of and trafficking in firearms, their parts and component and ammunition." The actual form of this instrument was that of an attachment, or "protocol," to the international "convention" against transnational organized crime that was being drafted at the same time. A "convention" is the modern term of art for a broad treaty signed by more than two states.

The United Nations Firearms Protocol: An Exercise in Hypocrisy

The effort to draft what became known as the "firearms protocol" proceeded until March 2, 2001, when it was adopted as one of the four protocols attached to the United Nations Convention against Transnational Organized Crime. The firearms protocol was modeled on a draft of the Organization of American States Firearms Protocol.

The U.N. firearms protocol does not contain any of the more radical proposals mentioned earlier, but it serves as an excuse for states that sign it to pass more and more harassing firearms legislation. The most objectionable aspects of the firearms protocol are what it does not do.

Throughout the drafting of the protocol, and the parallel effort on the disarmament side, there did emerge a very limited consensus on a few things that might actually impact illegal trafficking of firearms. One of these was that all firearms should be marked with a unique serial number.

This of course is long-standing U.S. law. It was on this point that real hypocrisy of U.N. gun-ban efforts emerged.

Although there is a requirement, under the protocol, that all firearms be marked with the name of the manufacturer and a unique serial number, there are two exceptions to this rule. One exception is galling, and the other is a scandal.

The basic marking requirement reads:

Article 8—Marking of firearms

At the time of manufacture of each firearm, either require unique marking providing the name of the manufacturer, the country or place of manufacture and the serial number.[32]

The first exception is found in Article 4 of the Protocol:

Article 4—Scope of application

2. This Protocol shall not apply to state-to-state transfers or to state transfers in cases where the application of the Protocol would prejudice the right of a State Party to take action in the interest of national security consistent with the Charter of the United Nations.[33]

In other words, a state can transfer arms that do not have serial numbers to another state. In addition, if a state decides that "in the interest of national security"[34] it wants to manufacture and transfer small arms without serial number, it can. This is astounding considering that these types of transfers are the root of many of the problems with small arms—such as one tyrant selling unserialized guns to another tyrant so that the victims and the international community will never know where the guns came from.

These are precisely the kinds of guns that should not be exempt from a marking requirement.

So why did the U.N. exempt tyrant-to-tyrant firearms sales? The answer is simple: it is a lot easier to regulate legal firearms owners than it is to control rogue states dumping arms across borders. It is the same hypocrisy we find with domestic gun control efforts, writ large: it is easier to take guns away from law-abiding citizens than to take them away from criminals. If this example of U.N. hypocrisy were not bad enough, the second exception to the marking requirement is an outrage.

The United Nations Firearms Protocol: The Chinese Outrage

Like the beasts in George Orwell's *Animal Farm*, all nations in the U.N. are equal, but some are more equal than others. The U.S. may be the only superpower in the world, but China is the emerging "number two," and everybody at the U.N. knows it. While players at the U.N. love to criticize the U.S., they willingly kowtow to China.[35] This is what happened with the U.N. Firearms Protocol. Earlier I quoted the first part of the protocol marking requirement. Here is the rest:

Article 8—Marking of firearms

At the time of manufacture of each firearm, either require unique marking providing the name of the manufacturer, the country or place of manufacture and the serial number, *or maintain any alternate unique user-friendly marking with simple geometric symbols in combination with numeric and or alphanumeric code, permitting the ready identification by all States of the country of manufacture.*[36]

As our academic friends say, let's "deconstruct" this. There are two marking requirements found in the article. You can mark firearms with the name of the manufacturer, country/place of manufacture, and a serial number, or you can meet the alternative requirement. And what does this alternative require? Well, first, it says "or maintain"—meaning countries have to be doing this already. What country is using "simple geometric symbols"? That would be China. This discloses "the country of manufacture," but it does not provide a unique serial number. The bottom line is that there is a special exception in the marking requirement for China, which only places sufficient information on the firearm to allow one to tell that it is from China. This makes a mockery of the whole protocol. Every country in the world that agrees to the protocol must place unique serial numbers on the firearms it manufactures—except China.

How did this happen? The drafting of the protocol in Vienna went until late into the evening of March 2, 2001. At about 10 p.m., the translators were far beyond their usual overtime, and the hundreds of officials attending the meeting were faced with the possibility that there would be no agreement because time was running out. That's when the Chinese made their bid to insert special language into the marking article. The head of the U.S. delegation met privately with the Chinese in a closed session without her advisers who usually dealt with firearms matters. Elizabeth Verville was a human rights specialist from the U.S. Department of State and was not all that familiar with firearms issues. Verville, like so many State Department regulars, could not face the idea of leaving Vienna without an agreement. She may not have even understood what the language meant. Regardless, she agreed to the Chinese exemption.

The new language was read on the floor, and there were immediate objections from those who understood the Chinese proposal. Attorneys attached to the U.S. delegation and experts from the E.U. explained to their delegations the effect of the language. Both the U.S. and the E.U. then tried to amend the Chinese language to include a requirement for an individual serial number. The proposals were rejected.[37]

The Chinese exception is not only in the firearms protocol but also in the PoA, as well as other U.N. instruments. So all the pious talk about "marking and tracing" as a tool to save lives in the Third World amounts to a bunch of hokum. Legitimate manufacturers in the U.S. and Europe now face additional paperwork and regulatory burdens in their sales to law-abiding exporters. Meanwhile, the Chinese government is explicitly allowed to feather its nest by continuing the corrupt sale of unmarked guns to evildoers.

Shocking though this special treatment of a totalitarian state may be, it is hardly surprising. As we shall see beyond all doubt, cozy deals and political corruption are a way of life at the U.N.

Chapter 3

CIFTA, the U.N. Antigun Conferences, and the Arms Trade Treaty

The opponents of the Second Amendment have been working on three international treaties to stifle our rights.

The first treaty comes from the Bill Clinton years, and is the product of the Organization of American States (OAS). At the very least, it would require that most American gun owners be licensed the same way firearms manufacturers currently are. And the treaty has the potential to do much more harm.

The second treaty is a binding legal document to be created to implement the United Nation's "Programme of Action" for global gun control. Thanks to the heroic John Bolton, United States ambassador to the United Nations, the pro-freedom side was able to stop the creation of a binding international instrument at the U.N.'s major antigun conferences in 2001 and 2006. But the U.N. came back with another conference in 2010, and this time, the U.S. delegation—chosen by Hillary Clinton—was on the side of the gun-banners. There, the U.S. delegation supported using some of the worst parts of the OAS treaty as guidelines for the Programme of Action. These could be adopted at the next conference on the Programme of Action, scheduled for 2012, while Obama and Clinton will still be in charge.

The third item is the Arms Trade Treaty (ATT). Its stated purpose is to prevent arms transfer to human rights violators. That's a great idea, except that the ATT will do nothing to make arms embargoes more effective against actual violators of human rights, such as the tyrannical governments who control much of the U.N.

The ATT will, however, lead to arms embargoes against democracies, with Israel and the United States being the top targets. Israel because the international gun control movement is very much a part of the U.N.'s hate-Israel movement. And the United States because U.S. gun ownership laws are themselves violations of human rights, according to the United Nations. Why? It's because U.S. laws allow crime victims to shoot rapists, arsonists, and carjackers. The final version of the ATT is expected to be produced in 2011 or 2012, providing President Obama with an opportunity to sign the treaty.

CIFTA

The Organization of American States (OAS) is made up of nations of the Western Hemisphere. It was founded in 1948 to encourage regional cooperation.

Back in 1997, President Bill Clinton took another step to advance the global gun control agenda when he signed a new OAS gun control treaty. Obviously, with the Clinton administration in charge of the treaty negotiations, there was no one looking out for the rights of American gun owners.

Clinton apparently recognized that the chances of Senate ratification were slender, so although the treaty was submitted to the Senate in 1998, he did not push for ratification, lest the treaty be rejected.

President George W. Bush also did not send the treaty to the Senate, but he did not take the step of withdrawing U.S. signature from the treaty, as he did with the International Criminal Court treaty.

"CIFTA" is a Spanish acronym for *Convención Interamericana contra la Fabricación y el Tráfico Ilícitos de Armas de Fuego, Municiones, Explosivos y Otros Materiales Relacionados.*[1] In English: Inter-American Convention against the Fabrication and Illicit Traffic of Firearms, Munitions, Explosives, and Other Related Materials.[2]

A few weeks after taking office, President Obama announced that he would send CIFTA to the Senate for ratification.[3] According to the Obama

White House, CIFTA is a harmless expression of international goodwill. The White House also said that the National Rifle Association had helped to negotiate the treaty. The claim about the NRA is absolutely false, and the claim that CIFTA cannot harm American gun owners is quite dubious.

To begin with, CIFTA requires the abolition of law enforcement sales of firearms that have been confiscated from criminals.[4] The sales help the police raise revenue for law enforcement purposes, at no cost to the taxpayers. Of course all sales take place through federally licensed firearms dealers, and so all customers must be cleared by the National Instant Check System.[5]

The CIFTA ban makes no sense, except from a gun prohibition viewpoint. If the police confiscate a gun from a bad guy and put the bad guy in prison, the gun itself is not "bad." In the hands of the law-abiding person (such as someone who passes the National Instant Check System), the gun can be used to thwart or deter criminals. Banning the police sales is logical only if guns are viewed as intrinsically evil, so that any step to reduce the total gun supply is considered positive.

CIFTA would also require that all persons who reload ammunition get an ammunition manufacturing license. According to CIFTA, "illicit manufacturing" means any "manufacture or assembly of firearms, ammunition, explosives, and other related materials" without "a license from a competent governmental authority of the State Party where the manufacture or assembly takes place."[6]

Currently under both federal and state law, there is no license needed to reload ammunition for personal use. But Article IV would require licensing, and also mandate that unlicensed reloading be a crime: "State Parties that have not yet done so shall adopt the necessary legislative or other measures to establish as criminal offenses under their domestic law the illicit manufacturing of and trafficking in firearms, ammunition, explosives, and other related materials."[7]

Right now, if you do need a manufacturing license (for example, if you sell the reloaded ammunition), then you have to pay the Bureau of

Alcohol, Tobacco, Firearms and Explosives (BATFE) $150 every year for the license. The BATFE can raise the license fee whenever it chooses, without having to ask Congress for permission.

As a licensed manufacturer, your manufacturing facility (that is, your home) is subject to one unannounced inspection by BATFE annually.[8] CIFTA would require that every reloader be subjected to the same rules, even a man whose total annual production is a dozen rounds for his hunting rifle.

To make matters much worse, almost all other gun owners would also be defined as "manufacturers," and thus required to pay $150 for their "manufacturing" license, with their homes subject to unannounced inspections by BATFE.

Under current law, firearms manufacturing does require a license, and "manufacturing" is defined as making the receiver. A person who makes a firearm for his own personal use does not need a license, since he does not "engage in the business" of manufacture.[9]

However, CIFTA defines manufacturing much more broadly—so broadly that it includes activities such as putting on a scope or a sling, or replacing a worn-out barrel. And anybody who manufactures firearms accessories—such as slings or replacement grips—would also need a manufacturing license. Why? Because licenses, says CIFTA, are necessary to manufacture "other related materials"—defined as "any component, part, or replacement part of a firearm, or an accessory which can be attached to a firearm."[10] Among the things that can be "attached to a firearm" are any and every type of spare part, as well as magazines, bipods, recoil pads, slings, laser sights, scopes, scope rings, and so on. Similarly, licenses would be required to make replacement or aftermarket springs, screws, nuts, or other internal parts for firearms.

But it gets worse. It is not just the actual manufacturers of these items who would need a license. So would the *users* of the devices. CIFTA says that "illicit manufacturing" is "the manufacture *or assembly* of firearms, ammunition, explosives, *and other related materials*" without a license.[11]

If you buy some scope rings and put them on your rifle, or if you screw some aftermarket grips onto your handgun, you are obviously doing some "assembly." And under CIFTA, you can't do assembly unless you have a manufacturing license.

Similarly, the kind of gun repair that many gun owners do at home would also need a manufacturing license. When you replace a worn-out screw or barrel, add a new recoil pad, or take out an old spring and put in a new one, you are engaged in assembly.

Currently, the federal firearms laws do not apply to guns made before 1898 or to modern replicas of those guns (as long as there is no commercially available ammunition for the replicas).[12] In contrast, CIFTA has no exemption for antiques.

This means that if you assemble a flintlock Kentucky Rifle from a kit, then you would be a criminal, unless you have first obtained a federal firearms manufacturing license.

When you clean your gun, you disassemble it—such as by removing the slide from your Colt 1911, or detaching the barrel from the fore-end of your shotgun. Well then, when you put the clean gun back together, you are "assembling" it, aren't you? So people who clean their guns would also need a federal firearms manufacturing license.

By the way, once you have licensing, registration almost surely comes with it. Today, if you are a federally licensed manufacturer of firearms or ammunition, you have to keep detailed records of everything you make, and those records can be inspected by BATFE. If the manufacturing license requirement were expanded to include reloaders and gun owners, it would not be much of a stretch for BATFE to make reloaders keep records of the ammunition they manufacture, or to make gun owners keep records of the guns they "manufacture" (that is, the guns to which they add accessories, or that they disassemble for cleaning and then reassemble).[13]

Quite obviously CIFTA was not (despite what the Obama White House claims) negotiated with NRA input. If the NRA had been a participant, we certainly would have told the treaty drafters how insanely overbroad their definition of "manufacturing" is.

But we weren't at the negotiating table, and CIFTA now is what it is. CIFTA would mean that almost every gun owner in America would need to get a federal firearms manufacturing license.

The BATFE could not possibly handle the enormous flood of license applications it would be required to process. (And remember, the manufacturing license is only for one year, so people with existing licenses would have to renew them every year, if they thought that in the coming year they might want to clean their guns, or change a barrel, or so on.)

Indeed, BATFE could not even handle the huge number of applications that would be required from actual "manufacturers" of firearms accessories, such as the companies that sell screws to gun companies, or that make wooden stocks for flintlock rifle kits.

It's not BATFE's fault that it would be overwhelmed. BATFE is set up and staffed at personnel levels appropriate for licensing companies who make firearms and ammunition. BATFE's Federal Firearms Licensing Center would probably have to be a thousand or ten thousand times larger in order to handle all the extra licensing that CIFTA would mandate.

BATFE would face almost irresistible pressure to raise the licensing fee, in order to generate the revenue necessary to pay for such a gigantic expansion of its licensing staff.

CIFTA is quite clear that the comprehensive licensing system is necessary, along with criminal penalties for people who do not get the licenses: "States Parties that have not yet done so shall adopt the necessary legislative or other measures to establish as criminal offenses under their domestic law the illicit manufacturing of and trafficking in firearms, ammunition, explosives, and other related materials . . . the criminal offenses established pursuant to the foregoing paragraph shall include participation in, association or conspiracy to commit, attempts to commit, and aiding, abetting, facilitating, and counseling the commission of said offenses."[14]

So if you help your buddy put a scope on his rifle and give him a little advice along the way, and your buddy doesn't have a manufacturing license, you, too, must be criminally punished, for "aiding, abetting, facilitating, and counseling the commission of said offenses."

Now antigun CIFTA advocates in the Senate will point to the CIFTA Preamble, which says: "This Convention does not commit States Parties to enact legislation or regulations pertaining to firearms ownership, possession, or trade of a wholly domestic character."

Reassured? You shouldn't be. The preamble says that governments do not have to adopt new laws about "ownership, possession, or trade." Conspicuously absent from this list is *manufacturing*. CIFTA repeatedly says governments *must* adopt laws to require manufacturing licenses. Nothing in the Preamble gives governments the option not to license manufacturing.[15]

Now, the Obama administration might point to some other nations that have ratified CIFTA but have not required manufacturing licenses for changing a rifle scope, or putting new grips on a handgun. This is true, but the other nations already require a government license simply to own a gun. The other point is that many nations ratify international treaties, and then ignore their legal obligations under the treaties.

The United States, however, tends to be much more scrupulous about obeying the treaties that it signs.[16] As the last few years have shown, whenever some people think that the U.S. government is not obeying an international treaty, the noncompliance becomes a huge issue in the United States.

And besides, if we don't intend to do what CIFTA says, then why ratify it? If we don't think that treating every gun owner and reloader like a manufacturer is a good idea, and if we don't want to outlaw law enforcement sales of firearms, then there's no point in ratifying CIFTA. If the only purpose of CIFTA ratification (according to Obama's claims) is to make a gesture of solidarity with other OAS nations, it would be better for the Senate to pass an official resolution declaring our solidarity with other OAS nations.

When the Senate ratifies a treaty, it becomes the law of the land. It overrides every inconsistent state law, including state constitutions. To say that we should change the law of the land by adopting such an extreme and badly written treaty is crazy.

Or, perhaps, crazy like a fox. CIFTA looks like an awfully good way to move the United States into federal licensing for all gun owners.

Now, suppose that CIFTA were ratified by the Senate. Could the BATFE or other federal entities go ahead and start writing the regulations to ban police sale of firearms, and to require manufacturing licenses for all gun owners and reloaders?

Under traditional rules of international law, the answer would be no. Normally, treaties are not considered to be "self-executing." So, for example, when the Senate ratified the International Convention on Torture, the ratification did not, in itself, create a new federal criminal law against torture. The Senate and House, in order to fulfill the U.S. obligation under the Torture Convention, had to pass a separate federal statute that outlawed torture.

On the other hand, if the treaty expressly declares itself to be self-executing, then it immediately becomes a part of domestic law, without any further action by Congress.

CIFTA does not say that it is self-executing, so under the standard rules of legal interpretation, it would not be self-executing.

Unfortunately, we no longer live under the standard rules of international law. The most authoritative voice in interpreting the meaning of treaties is the legal adviser to the U.S. State Department. For the position of legal adviser, Secretary of State Clinton has picked Harold Hongju Koh. As I explain in chapter 20, Koh favors a ban on the *legal* trade in firearms, and he has vowed to make gun control one of his personal top priorities at the State Department.

Koh disagrees with what he calls the doctrine of "so-called self-executing treaties." He says that the Supreme Court cases that distinguish between self-executing and non-self-executing treaties are wrong.[17]

According to Koh, the Senate "should ratify treaties with a presumption that they are self-executing." So when the Senate considers CIFTA, the Senators ought to consider the very serious possibility that Koh is going to declare CIFTA to be self-executing, even if he promises during the ratification debate that he will not.

Koh has long been thinking about how to use CIFTA to push gun control in the United States. In his infamous Fordham speech "A World Drowning in Guns," he said that CIFTA must be supplemented by "supply-side control measures in the United States." One such control he especially liked was the "particularly intriguing idea" of "promoting 'smart' or perishable ammunition." That means, in his words, "bullets that would degrade and become unusable over time."[18]

So how about CIFTA as a basis for BATFE to outlaw the manufacture and sale of all primers that don't wear out within a couple of years?

Sometimes when ratifying a treaty, a country will add a "reservation." This is a statement that the country does not intend to obey a particular part of the treaty, or that it interprets a section of a treaty as inapplicable to some activity in the country. The U.S. Senate often adds reservations to treaties.

Perhaps in order to get CIFTA ratified, the Senate managers might agree to the addition of a reservation stating that CIFTA is not self-executing. But Koh thinks that reservations may have no legal effect. Writing about a Senate reservation to a different treaty, Koh said, "Many scholars question persuasively whether the United States declaration has either domestic or international legal effect."[19]

Once CIFTA was ratified, the gun ban movement in the U.S. would use it incessantly, and effectively, to promote their agenda. They could say, "Congress needs to pass a major new gun control statute in order to live up to our obligations under international law."

There are lots of people who don't care much about the gun issue, one way or another, but who do care that the U.S. obeys the treaties we have ratified. Again, if the Senate does not want to enact major new gun control laws, then it should not ratify a treaty that requires the enactment of major new gun control laws.

Let's imagine that the Senate ratified CIFTA, but Congress did not pass any law based on CIFTA, and that there were some magical way to keep Koh from declaring CIFTA to be self-executing. (Such a declaration would unleash BATFE to write the licensing and registration regulations discussed above). Even then, we would not be safe from CIFTA.

According to Koh, whenever the Senate ratifies a treaty, courts should allow private plaintiffs to bring lawsuits based on the treaty.[20] In other words, CIFTA would override the 2005 Protection of Lawful Commerce in Arms Act, which has barred junk lawsuits against gun makers and gun stores. (Usually, when two laws conflict, courts give the priority to the law that was enacted later, which would be CIFTA.)

Koh has already advised "human rights advocates" (a group which, in his thinking, includes antigun advocates) to bring lawsuits "not just in domestic courts, but simultaneously before foreign and international arenas."[21]

One possible venue for a CIFTA case against American gun companies (or against the United States government, for not enacting the licensing laws required by CIFTA) would be a complaint to the OAS Inter-American Commission on Human Rights, or a lawsuit in the OAS Inter-American Court of Human Rights.[22]

Another forum could be the World Court, which is part of the United Nations. The World Court (formal name "International Court of Justice") is only for government versus government cases; so Mexico or Brazil could sue the United States for its failure to enact the gun controls required by CIFTA. For the suit to move forward, the United States would have to consent to World Court jurisdiction, but it is not hard to imagine the Obama-Clinton administration consenting to the jurisdiction—and working behind the scenes to encourage strongly antigun governments such as Brazil or Mexico to sue.

Significantly, at the April 27, 2010, "Richard J. Daley Global Cities Forum," held in Chicago, Chicago mayor Richard "Daley convinced more than a dozen of his counterparts from around the world to approve a resolution urging 'redress against the gun industry through the courts of the world' in The Hague."

At a news conference, Daley explained, "This is coming from international mayors. They're saying, 'We're tired of your guns, America . . . We don't want those anymore because guns kill and injure people.'"

Among the supporters of the Daley resolution was Mexico City mayor Marcelo Ebrard Casauban, who said that "85 percent" of Mexican drug cartel guns come from the United States. Philadelphia mayor Michael Nutter also endorsed a World Court case.[23]

It would be dangerous to consider Daley's lawsuit plan to be an empty threat. In 1998, Chicago mayor Daley and New Orleans mayor Marc Morial filed the vanguard of what would become three dozen municipal lawsuits against the firearms industry. The lawsuits were not successful in court, but they did come very close to convincing firearms manufacturers to capitulate. The suits were finally ended by the Protection of Lawful Commerce in Arms Act, signed into law in 2005. In international courts, our Second Amendment would be of no legal significance.

Suppose the licensing laws required by CIFTA were enacted, and pro-rights plaintiffs brought a Second Amendment lawsuit against the new CIFTA licensing laws?[24] A lawsuit might point to *Heller's* language that says that regulation of the "commercial sale" of firearms is constitutionally permissible. So, by implication, requiring a license just to tinker with a gun you already own, or to reload your own ammunition for personal, noncommercial use, might be a violation of the Second Amendment. The lawsuit might also point to the well-established principle that a treaty cannot negate any part of the Bill of Rights.[25]

The Obama team is ready for that one too. First of all, Attorney General Holder and his staff would point out that CIFTA and its licensing requirements do not outlaw handguns, or any other type of gun. Neither do they prevent people from using guns for self-defense. Accordingly, Obama and Holder would argue that there is no violation of the Second Amendment right as protected by *Heller.*

Besides, as Koh could elaborate, courts should "construe domestic statutes consistently with international law," and "should employ international human rights norms to guide interpretation of domestic constitutional norms."[26] Koh wants our Constitution to be "co-ordinated" (that is, watered down) so that it meshes with international law.

President Obama may need only one more Supreme Court appointment, joining the four current antigun "transnationalist" justices (Ginsburg, Kagan, Breyer, and Sotomayor), to create a Supreme Court majority that will do exactly that.

There's more to the CIFTA threat. The OAS has drafted guidelines for how nations should implement CIFTA.[27] These guidelines go even farther in turning CIFTA into a tool for the destruction of lawful firearms use and ownership. If Koh's theory of self-executing treaties were to prevail, then Senate ratification of CIFTA could give BATFE the authority to impose by regulation all of the OAS guidelines.

The OAS urges that "unauthorized" acquisition of firearms or ammunition (e.g., buying a gun or a box of ammunition from a friend) be criminalized, because, supposedly, buying a gun or ammunition without prior government permission means that you are "trafficking" in weapons. Likewise, OAS proposes making it illegal for you to give ten rounds of ammunition to a friend at a shooting range, unless that transaction has been approved in advance by the government.

If you're suspected of having "illicit" firearms or ammunition (e.g., ammunition you reloaded at home), then a court "shall issue, at any time, without prior notification or hearing, a freezing or seizure order." So your property gets confiscated, by a judge who never gave you notice or the opportunity to present your side of the story.

The recommended prison term is from one to ten years.

Then there are the controls on "arms brokers." This does not just cover people who arrange for the sale of three thousand rifles to foreign governments. Rather, according to the system adopted by the OAS, an "arms broker" is anyone who "for a fee, commission or other consideration, acts on behalf of others to negotiate or arrange contracts, purchases, sales or other means of transfer of firearms, their parts or components or ammunition." In other words, someone like a hunting guide who arranges for the local gun store to have suitable ammunition on hand for the guide's clients.

Everyone who is an "arms broker" must have a license from the national government. The broker must file annual reports with the government, specifying exactly what arms and ammunition he brokered, and to whom. For example: "Oct. 10, 2011, arranged for Fred's Hunting Supply store to have a Remington 700 Mountain Rifle LSS, in .270 Win caliber, with a 22-inch barrel, on hand for Edward Smith to purchase, along with 50 rounds of ammunition: Winchester 270, 130 Grain Supreme Ballistic Silvertip. Smith's home address is 123 Main Street, New Sharon, Iowa."

The hunting guide's office records would be subject to government inspection, without need for any court order.

Then there's marking. "Wherever possible and appropriate States should consider requiring appropriate markings on other structural components (such as barrels and slides) manufactured or imported for use as replacement parts for firearms." This would raise the cost of a firearm by at least several hundred dollars, since manufacturers would have to ensure that the barrel and slide with a particular serial number were only assembled onto a receiver with the same serial number. If a serialized slide were rejected for quality control reasons, the barrel and receiver with the matching serial number would be worthless.

What about already-manufactured guns that don't have all these marks? According to the OAS's model laws for CIFTA, governments are required to outlaw these guns, creating the following criminal offense: "Except as authorized by the State, any person who deals in, transfers or possesses firearms that do not contain the corresponding markings required under Article 3." If there's any thought of grandfathering the possession of the current gun stock, the OAS guidelines statute makes no mention of it.

Governments are required to maintain a database of the gun's serial number, along with "the name and location of the owner and legal user of a firearm and each subsequent owner and legal user thereof, when possible." In other words, universal gun registration.

It's not just the gun owners and their guns that would be registered. So would every gun user. The registry must include "the name and location of the owner and legal user of a firearm and each subsequent owner and legal user thereof, when possible."

International Criminal Court

Gun owners sometimes ask me if the International Criminal Court could be a threat to gun rights. My answer is, there is a risk, but it's less immediate than many others that we face.

The International Criminal Court (ICC) went into operation in 2002 as a United Nations criminal court. It can prosecute people for genocide, crimes against humanity, and war crimes. In a few years, it will have the authority to prosecute for the ill-defined crime of "aggression."

Defendants before the International Criminal Court are deprived of many of the due process protections of the U.S. Constitution. There is no jury trial and no right to speedy trial. The prosecution has a right to appeal acquittals, and during the appeal the defendant remains incarcerated. Judges and prosecutors are drawn from a variety of nations, including dictatorships with no respect for due process. A person sentenced by the ICC may be sent to a prison anywhere in the world. Nongovernment organizations may suggest that a prosecutor bring charges against a particular defendant.

The ICC was created by the 1998 Rome treaty; during the ICC negotiations, President Clinton worked hard to include checks and balances in the Court's operation, so that it would be used for proper purposes (e.g., against warlords), but would not be politicized. Unfortunately, as President Clinton's chief negotiator, David J. Scheffer, recounted, a "small group of countries, meeting behind closed doors in the final days of the Rome conference, produced a seriously flawed take-it-or-leave-it text, one that provides a recipe for politicization of the court and risks deterring responsible international action to promote peace and security."[28]

Accordingly, President Clinton refused to sign the treaty setting up the court. Finally, he did sign, on December 31, 2000, but he said that he had no intention of sending the ICC treaty to the Senate for ratification. He was simply signing so that the U.S. could participate in negotiations to fix the ICC.[29]

No fixes were made, however, and in 2002, President Bush "unsigned" the treaty.[30]

Unfortunately, the Obama administration has a different view of the ICC. Secretary of State Hillary Clinton said, "This is a great regret that we are not a signatory. I think we could have worked out some of the challenges that are raised concerning our membership. But that has not yet come to pass."[31]

Presidents Bush and Clinton were both concerned about the risk of political prosecutions aimed at United States soldiers or their civilian superiors. They were right; the ICC has already begun collecting information that might lead to criminal prosecution of U.S. and NATO forces in Afghanistan.[32]

Another risk is for Americans engaged in the firearms business. The groups lobbying for the Arms Trade Treaty have called for International Criminal Court prosecutions for people who knowingly sell guns that will be used to perpetrate the crimes covered by the ICC statute. They likewise want ICC prosecutions for any government officials who allowed the arms transfers, under the theory that the government officials failed to exercise "due diligence."[33]

Now, if these principles were actually applied based on the ordinary meanings of the words in the ICC statute, I would be delighted. It would be great to see the Chinese army's gun manufacturers, and their corrupt Chinese government overseers, hauled before the International Criminal Court and put on trial for their role in aiding and abetting genocide by selling arms to Sudan's dictatorship.

I would enjoy watching an ICC prosecution of the despicable South African government officials who helped the Chinese "Ship of Shame" deliver weapons to Zimbabwe's genocidal tyrant Robert Mugabe.

If the ICC made any move in the direction of guns, the most likely initial targets would be the less politically powerful bad guys, such as Eastern Europeans (rather than Chinese) smuggling arms to African warlords. The precedents established in the smuggling cases could help lay the foundation for future prosecutions of the legitimate arms trade, since IANSA is always trying to conflate arms smugglers with the legitimate arms trade.

It is important to remember that in the Bizarro world of the United Nations, Israel is supposedly the worst human rights violator in the world, and the United States is the fifth worst. (Details later in this chapter.)

I think it's just a matter of time before the ICC starts persecuting Israelis, and Americans may not be far behind.

Of course Americans and Israelis don't commit the crimes over which the ICC has jurisdiction.[34] However, as Brett Schaefer and Steven Groves of the Heritage Foundation warn, the ICC can impose novel definitions or interpretations of these crimes.[35]

For example, if the U.N.'s forthcoming Arms Trade Treaty outlaws the transfer of arms to "non-state actors" (such as rebel groups fighting against a genocidal tyrant), then the International Criminal Court could decide that anyone who helped supply arms to the freedom fighters could be prosecuted for alleged misdeeds of the freedom fighters.[36]

Already, the United Nations has said that American gun laws that allow armed self-defense against rapists, robbers, arsonists, and carjackers are a violation of human rights. (See chapter 13.) Supposedly, if the rapist or the carjacker is not trying to kill you, then you are violating his human rights if you shoot him in self-defense.

The International Criminal Court could take the next step and declare that any arms sales to Americans are a "crime against humanity" because the sellers know of the near certainty that many of the guns will be used for human rights violations—that is, for shooting criminals.

Would the ICC have personal jurisdiction over an American whom the ICC wanted to prosecute for supposed "crimes against humanity" such as manufacturing guns for sale to Americans, or selling guns to freedom fighters?

There are three ways the ICC can get jurisdiction. First, a potential defendant's government can consent.[37] In other words, if the Obama administration says, "Go ahead and prosecute him," the ICC can arrest you and haul you off to Europe for trial.

The second basis for jurisdiction is if the conduct occurs in the territory of a country that has ratified the ICC treaty.[38] For example, if American gun manufacturers attend an international trade fair in Germany (a nation that has ratified the ICC), then the ICC would have jurisdiction over them for acts in Germany.

The third method is if the person is a national of a country that has ratified the ICC treaty.[39] The United States has not ratified the ICC; neither, so far, has President Obama urged ratification.

However, State Department legal adviser Harold Koh has devised a plan to start putting the United States under the ICC's thumb. He has instructed ICC advocates to "provoke interactions between the United States government and the ICC." For example, the U.S. might provide evidence in a case before the ICC. Then, the instance of U.S. cooperation with the ICC "could be used to undermine" President Bush's "unsigning" of the ICC Treaty. The small acts of cooperation would be declared to "constitute a de facto repudiation" of the "act of unsignature."[40]

Maybe it's just a coincidence, but that is exactly what the Obama administration has been doing. Obama's representatives have been providing U.S. assistance and support to some current ICC prosecutions (against defendants who are unquestionably bad men), and have been praising the ICC in the process.

That cooperation in itself does not bring U.S. citizens under ICC jurisdiction. But as Harold Koh might say, "It's a good first step."

The U.N. Antigun Conferences

In April 2006, my book *The Global War on Your Guns: Inside the U.N. Plan to Destroy the Bill of Rights* sounded an urgent warning about the U.N.'s antigun summit that was beginning just a few weeks later. This was the summit that the gun ban groups had been working toward for the last five years, ever since they were rebuffed in 2001.[41]

Their global propaganda machine had grown much bigger and more powerful, and the media were more compliant than ever about turning their press releases into "news" articles. At smaller conferences under the auspices of various U.N. agencies, they had used the 2001 Programme of Action to push gun prohibition in every country they could, and to build the foundation for their final triumph in 2006.

IANSA had acquired plenty of allies in the U.N. delegations. Some national delegations for the 2006 Conference had already decided to include IANSA members as delegates who would guide their decision making.

They even set up the Brazilian gun confiscation referendum for late 2005, intending to use it to prove that the people of the world wanted to get rid of guns. They got actor Michael Douglas to make commercials touting the conference.[42] Douglas, who is the official "U.N. peace messenger," has been a longtime gun control activist,[43] and he played the heroic, gun-banning U.S. president in the 1995 film *The American President*—whose D.C. opening was held as a fund-raiser for the legal arm of the Brady Campaign.[44]

But their plans began to unravel. The Brazilian people overwhelming voted against gun confiscation. Then, in May, June, and July of 2006, the U.N. heard from the American people. The National Rifle Association had urged Americans to send postcards and letters to the U.N., telling the U.N. to stop its schemes to undermine the Second Amendment.

The Conference was scheduled for June 26 to July 7, and when the NRA let the American people know that U.N. gun-banning was going to take place on the Fourth of July, there was quite a protest. The U.N. backed down and decided that the Conference would take a holiday on the Fourth.[45]

Sack after sack after sack of mail poured in to the U.N.—a hundred thousand letters and postcards. Secretary-General Kofi Annan said that the United Nations had no intention of interfering with gun possession in America, although the record of what the U.N. had been doing under his tenure showed that his statement was a flat-out lie.

I think the intensity of the American public's response was partly in reaction to Hurricane Katrina. The American people saw what happened in New Orleans, where guns were confiscated, and the good people were left defenseless. New Orleans proved beyond any doubt that Rebecca Peters and George Soros and the United Nations and the Brady Center are wrong when they say honest citizens don't need firearms.

Yet if the U.N. ever gets its way, we will all be just like those poor souls down in New Orleans whose guns were confiscated by force. They were left with no 9-1-1, no police, no protection, and no way to protect themselves. That's the United Nations' dream for America.

The U.N. claimed that it was not even reading your postcards and letters, and was just dumping them in the trash. But the message got through, and not just at the United Nations. American officials paid attention. Especially at the White House. Your actions helped the White House stand firm behind America's U.N. ambassador John Bolton. The U.S. delegation also included former United States Congressman Bob Barr, a Second Amendment stalwart.

The conference areas were filled with delegates and gun ban lobbies bashing the United States for its firearms freedom.

On the day the conference opened, Secretary-General Kofi Annan held a public event to welcome Rebecca Peters and receive an antigun petition that IANSA had collected. The secretary-general reaffirmed that the United Nations supported IANSA's campaign.[46]

At the conference, Bolton was like Horatio at the Bridge. He said that the United States was ready—in fact eager—to join in an international agreement to stop illicit arms trafficking. He pointed out that the United States already had the strongest controls in the world on arms exports.

But he insisted that the U.S. was not going to sign anything that would infringe the Second Amendment. Neither would we sign anything that would make it illegal for the United States to supply arms to people who were fighting for freedom against *genocidaires* or other tyrants.

He also insisted that the 2006 conference was going to be the last one. Once there was a real agreement on *illicit* trafficking, then there should not be future conferences at which the prohibitionists could keep coming back for more attacks on legitimate gun owners.

As is the norm at the United Nations, everything of substance at the conference took place behind closed doors, away from the view of the public and the press.

The gun prohibitionists adopted a strategy of taking what they could get in 2006, while preserving their opportunity to get more later. The Bolton-Barr team refused to relent on the idea of future conferences.

Finally, on the afternoon of the last day of the conference, the U.N. drafters presented the delegations with a take-it-or-leave-it final document. The document was a big improvement from the draft that had been presented at the opening of the conference, and it got rid of many of the provisions to which Bolton and Barr had objected. But the final document said that there would be two or more future antigun conferences. Ambassador Bolton said no.

The conference ended, with no agreement, no consensus document. The gun prohibitionists went home, bitterly complaining to the media that the United States had thwarted the conference, and that nothing had been accomplished. Actually, something quite important *had* been accomplished. John Bolton, Bob Barr, and NRA members had saved the Second Amendment.

It didn't take long for the prohibitionists to regroup. The 2001 Programme of Action was still in existence. It is not legally binding, but it has been, and continues to be, a great pretext for governments that wanted to infringe or eliminate gun rights.

The prohibition lobbies convinced the U.N. to convene another big antigun conference, which took place June 14–18, 2010. This time, the U.S. delegation did not include people like John Bolton and Bob Barr. Instead, it was composed of people eager to further the Obama-Clinton agenda.

And perhaps since the Mexican government has taken the lead in attacking American gun rights and saying that American gun owners cause international problems, the chairman of the 2010 U.N. Conference was Ambassador Pablo Macedo of Mexico. It does not seem to be a coincidence that the U.N. picked a chairman from the nation that is currently the most active advocate for restricting American gun rights.

At the U.N. meeting, Federico Perazza of Uruguay presented a working paper setting out a model for global gun controls that should be adopted by every nation. Included in that working paper was an endorsement of the recommendations that the Organization of American States has made for how nations should implement CIFTA. According to the United Nations Department of Public Information, "Stephen R. Costner (United States) said his delegation agreed with and supported 'virtually everything' in the working paper presented by Mr. Perazza. He noted a few comments for further consideration, but stressed that the paper was well thought out."[47]

Costner properly reminded the U.N. that the Senate has not ratified CIFTA. However, at the 2012 Review Conference, the U.N. could adopt a revised Programme of Action, with U.S. delegation support, based on Perazza's recommendations. And again with U.S. support, the U.N. could make the revised Programme of Action legally binding, as has been urged by U.N. secretary-general Ban Ki-moon, and by the Mexican diplomat who chaired the 2010 meeting.

The result would be that the United States would have accepted a legally binding international law obligation to impose the U.N. gun control restrictions. If Congress refused to enact the model restrictions, the United States would be globally criticized for failing to live up to its international law obligations.

Arms Trade Treaty

On October 31, 2008, the U.N. General Assembly did something really frightening. At the behest of IANSA and the rest of the Soros lobby, the GA ordered that drafting begin on an Arms Trade Treaty (ATT); that is, a "legally binding treaty" for "establishing common international standards for the import, export and transfer of conventional arms."[48] The drafters are supposed to have the treaty ready in 2011, although it is possible that the date might slip to 2012. In either case, the Treaty would be ready in time for President Obama to sign.

The leading international spokesman for the ATT is Costa Rican president Oscar Arias.[49] His Arias Foundation is funded by George Soros, and President Arias has been pushing Costa Rica to adopt an extremely repressive gun law, copied from the South African law that IANSA holds up as a global model.

The ATT is a sham. If its advocates really wanted strong, effective laws on international arms sales, they could just copy the United States arms export control laws, which are the toughest in the world.

The advocates of the ATT say that its purpose is to impose international arms embargoes on human rights violators. This is a great idea, except for a few problems:

- For actual violators of human rights—such as the (gun-banning) tyrannies in Iran or Burma, or the warlords in the Democratic Republic of the Congo—the ATT will do nothing to make embargoes any stronger.
- Hypocritical governments like China and South Africa will probably sign the ATT, and then go right on supplying arms to dictators and *genocidaires*, since these governments are already breaking existing laws on the supplying of arms.
- The ATT will probably create a "right" of governments to have weapons. As a result, it would be an international law violation if

a pro-freedom government (e.g., the United States) outlawed arms exports to a dictatorship (e.g., China, Syria, Venezuela, Vietnam) if the dictatorship had not been placed under an official U.N. embargo.

• When the ATT advocates talk about embargoing arms sales to "human rights violators," they are explicitly advocating an embargo on Israel, and implicitly advocating an embargo on the United States, since these two democracies are among the very worst human rights violators in the world, according to the U.N.

The ATT Will Not Work on Real Violators of Human Rights

In international law as it currently exists, there is nothing more powerful than an order from the United Nations Security Council. Unlike the U.N. General Assembly, which has no power to impose legal obligations on nations, the Security Council can order all member states to take particular actions.[50] No other entity in the world has the power to issue such universal orders.

Under present international law, the U.N. Security Council can impose a mandatory arms embargo.[51] Nothing that could be created by an ATT could be more legally potent than a Security Council resolution. Accordingly, the ATT will add nothing to the legal strength of an embargo.

Now the ATT advocates are hoping that the final version of the treaty would create a committee that could impose legally binding embargoes without the need for the approval of the Security Council.[52] If the advocates get their way, there would very likely be *more* embargoes, but these embargoes would not have any more legal force.

Creating embargoes without the need for Security Council approval would prevent any of the five permanent members of the Security Council (U.S., Russia, China, United Kingdom, France) from being able to exercise a veto.

For example, the United States would almost certainly veto any attempt to impose an arms embargo on Israel. The people of the United States and Israel are close friends because of their shared belief in freedom and human rights.

Similarly, the government of China has prevented a Security Council embargo of Robert Mugabe's tyranny in Zimbabwe. The dictators of China and Zimbabwe are close friends because of their shared practices of kleptocracy and mass murder.

Whether an embargo is imposed by the Security Council or by a new ATT bureaucracy, it is only as effective as the willingness of states to comply. Which means that failure is guaranteed.

For example, the Security Council has imposed an arms embargo against the warlords in the eastern Democratic Republic of the Congo. The embargo is legally binding on every member state of the United Nations. Yet these warlords are still being supplied with firearms by Albania, Burundi, China, Rwanda, South Africa, Sudan, Uganda, and Zimbabwe—as well as by the army of the DR Congo itself, and by U.N. Peacekeepers![53]

At the United Nations, you can't find a nation that is more self-congratulatory and self-righteous about its restrictive gun laws than South Africa. They got the model law that Soros and IANSA want to impose worldwide.

It's a terrible law, and, as I detail in chapter 7, an important reason why South Africa is the rape capital of the world. Yet there is a good provision in South Africa's Arms Control Act; the South African government must "avoid transfers of conventional arms to governments that systematically violate or suppress human rights."

In the spring of 2008, shortly after Robert Mugabe's dictatorship in Zimbabwe had stolen another election and murdered many pro-democracy citizens in Zimbabwe, a Chinese ship laden with arms showed up in South Africa. It was carrying firearms, mortars, and RPGs (rocket-propelled grenades) from Poly Technologies (a Chinese arms manufacturer controlled by the Chinese army); the arms were to be delivered to landlocked Zimbabwe.[54]

The South African Transport and Allied Workers Union did the right thing and refused to unload the ship, which became known as "the ship of shame." Human rights activists obtained an injunction against the ship. Yet the South African government—controlled by the same anti-West, pro-communist African National Congress party that had imposed the South African gun control act—approved the transfer of weapons to Mugabe.[55]

While human rights activists were heading toward the docks to serve the court injunction on the Chinese ship, it sailed away and turned off its transponder.[56] At sea, it was refueled by the South African navy.[57] Then it sailed off and found a port run by a dictatorship that was friendly with the Zimbabwe and China dictatorships (probably Angola, Tanzania, or Congo-Brazzaville), where the guns were unloaded and then airlifted to Zimbabwe.[58]

IANSA claims that an ATT would have "created stronger obligations on the exporter and transiting states."[59] But so what? The South African government won't even obey the laws it writes itself. There's no reason to think that the government will obey an Arms Trade Treaty.

Likewise, China violates the U.N. Security Council embargo on warlords in the Democratic Republic of the Congo—even though China (apparently for public relations purposes) did not veto the embargo in the Security Council.

The "Right" of Dictatorships to Buy Arms

While no one knows for sure what will be in the final version of the Arms Trade Treaty, the General Assembly's instructions to the ATT drafters affirms "the right of all States to manufacture, import, export, transfer, and retain conventional arms."[60] This would be a disaster.

Take Iran, for example. There is no United Nations conventional arms embargo against Iran. Yet some governments, including the United States, wisely prohibit their citizens from selling arms to the Iranian government—because Iran exports arms to terrorist organizations (such as Hezbollah) and supplies them to the Islamist terrorists in Iraq, and because the Iranian government imposes a vicious tyranny on the people of Iran. Yet with an Arms Trade Treaty, the Iranian mullahs could say that since there is no U.N. arms embargo, they have a "right" to acquire weapons, and that the U.S. arms embargo against Iran is a violation of international law.

In my view, people—unlike dictatorships—really do have a right to arms. The constitutions of four nations (United States, Mexico, Haiti, and Guatemala) specifically recognize this right, and the constitutions of many more recognize a right of personal self-defense, or of security in the home, or to resist tyranny—all of which imply a right to possess the necessary tools to defend one's life or home or nation (in the case of tyranny).[61]

Yet the General Assembly's drafting instructions made no mention of the importance of constitutional rights, or of respect for the internal affairs of member states. This was not an accidental omission; the Group of Governmental Experts that was advising the U.N. had recommended pro-constitution language, and the U.N. chose to reject it.[62]

Instead, the General Assembly said that governments that ratify the Arms Trade Treaty would have to apply the "highest possible standards" to prevent arms from being used in any "criminal activity."[63] The GA did not say "strong standards"; they said "the highest possible standards." Anytime you have a gun control law, you can always imagine a higher standard. If there's a registration law, then a higher standard would be to require that registration be renewed every year. If there's a one-week waiting period, a higher standard would be two months. If there's a licensing law based on a fingerprint-based background check, a higher standard would be to also add police interviews with at least ten people who know the license applicant. And on and on. Every gun law—even extremely repressive laws like those in the United Kingdom—can be made even more repressive. The "highest possible standard" is another way of saying "gun prohibition, or something very close to it."

An Arms Embargo on Israel

Even though dictatorships (and some democracies, such as South Africa) often ignore existing laws about arms transfers, and can be expected to ignore the Arms Trade Treaty whenever it suits them, some nations are more scrupulous. Many European nations do obey arms embargos imposed by the U.N. Security Council. The European Union also imposes its own arms embargos, beyond what the Security Council does. For example, the EU has embargoed arms sales to Zimbabwe, and most EU states appear to be complying with the embargo.

In fact, even if the ATT compliance committee did not have its own power to create embargoes, some European nations might use the ATT to create a national embargo. An official in some ministry of foreign affairs might say, "Look, our nation has signed the Arms Trade Treaty, which says we are not supposed to allow firearms to be exported to countries that violate human rights. Country X is a big violator of human rights. So since the Ministry of Foreign Affairs has the power to control arms exports, I hereby forbid any company in my nation to export arms to Country X."

A plausible scenario. And if it led to a cut-off in exports to tyrannies such as Syria, Iran, Vietnam, China, Venezuela, or Cuba, that would be fine. (Not that any of the dictatorships would have trouble acquiring substitute arms from other dictatorships, especially China.)

However, the countries I just listed are not likely to be the targets of arms embargoes implemented in the name of the Arms Trade Treaty. Israel is going to be one of the first victims, followed by the United States.

This is not a big secret. The Soros lobbies have publicly identified Israel as the top target. Rebecca Peters herself has said that an Arms Trade Treaty would outlaw arms sales to Israel. She claims that "the most obvious case" of arms being supplied in violation of international law "is the continuing US supply of arms to Israel."[64]

IANSA, along with Amnesty International and Oxfam (both of which used to be constructive organizations, but which are now run by the far Left), have jointly created an additional lobby, called Control Arms. That group, too, says that Israel is such an egregious violator of human rights that arms sales must be prohibited. To make sure Israel can't make its own arms, they also want a ban on selling Israel any of the materials (e.g., titanium) that can be used to manufacture arms.[65]

In an essay in the *New York Review of Books*, Soros urged an end to America's special friendship with Israel, and said that Americans who supported pro-Israel lobbies had far too much influence on American policy.[66] Israeli professor Gur Ofer, who unsuccessfully tried to convince Soros to set up a program to help Soviet Jews who had emigrated to Israel, said, "There's a non-Zionist or anti-Zionist element in his thinking. He believes that Jews should act within the societies where they live."[67] Zionism is, of course, the great movement that led to the reestablishment of Israel as a Jewish homeland; among its central beliefs were that Jews should reestablish their connection with the physical world, and should learn how to use arms to protect themselves.

Unfortunately, putting Israel on the fast track to destruction makes sense in the perverse logic of the United Nations. According to the United Nations, Israel is the world's worst violator of human rights. The "Eye on the UN" project at Touro Law School, on Long Island, has compiled a list of how often countries are subject to human rights condemnation by the United Nations. Since 2003, when "Eye on the UN" first began compiling the statistics, the most-condemned country has always been Israel. In fact, it is condemned more than twice as often as any other country.[68]

Now, let's say that the Arms Trade Treaty leads to embargoes on the five worst human rights violators. That would be the very least to be expected.

According to the U.N., Israel is far and away the worst. Who's next? Based on 2003–09 condemnations by the U.N., the second-, third-, and fourth-worst countries are Sudan, Democratic Republic of the Congo, and Burma.[69]

Who's the fifth-worst country? Well, according to the United Nations, it's an awfully bad one. From 2003 to June 2009, the U.N. condemned it 211 times for human rights violations. That's more than Cuba, Venezuela, and Libya *combined*.

That awful country is the United States of America.

The Inter Press News Service, in a story describing the ATT in terms favored by Control Arms (in fact, basing the entire story on what Control Arms said), explained that "the Arms Trade Treaty would set up a risk assessment system to determine the legality of an arms transfer on a case-by-case basis, based on the likelihood the weapons would be used to harm civilians or in some way other than national defense or law enforcement."[70]

Well, when arms are exported to the United States, there is a pretty huge risk that they will be used "in some way other than national defense or law enforcement." Tens of millions of Americans use guns for target shooting, hunting, collecting, or self-defense.

Moreover, when guns are used for self-defense in the United States, they are "used to harm civilians," according to the United Nations. As I detail in chapter 13, the United Nations Human Rights Council has already declared that when the government allows a crime victim to shoot a rapist, arsonist, burglar, or carjacker, the government is guilty of violating the criminal's human rights.

In addition, according to the U.N. Council, a country's failure to impose sufficiently stringent gun control is in itself a violation of human rights. And their definition of sufficiently stringent is so extreme that even the laws of Chicago, New York City, and Washington, D.C. (pre-*Heller!*), are considered violations of human rights, because they are not strict enough.

Would the U.N.'s Arms Trade Treaty commission actually impose an embargo on the United States? Well, law professor Kenneth Anderson was at the initial meetings in the 1990s, where the U.N. campaign against firearms began. He recounted that, although the supposed purpose had been to cut off arms to warlords, the objective quickly changed into an attack on American gun ownership:

I was director of the Human Rights Watch Arms Division, with a mandate to address the transfer of weapons into conflicts where they would be used in the violation of the laws of war, and small arms were the main concern. I was astonished at how quickly the entire question morphed from concern about the flood of weapons into African civil wars into how to use international law to do an end run around supposedly permissive gun ownership regimes in the US . . .

I dropped any personal support for the movement when it became clear, a long time ago, that it is about controlling domestic weapons equally in the US (or, today, even more so) as in Somalia or Congo.[71]

The U.N. might be much likelier to impose an embargo if United States delegates privately spread the word that President Obama and Secretary of State Clinton would not mind an embargo one bit. In fact, they would welcome it.

So it would not matter if Obama and Clinton could not convince two-thirds of the Senate to ratify an Arms Trade Treaty. The rest of the world does not need U.S. Senate approval in order to stop selling firearms to the United States.

Maybe you're thinking that you might miss being able to buy some of the fine guns manufactured in Italy or Germany or Belgium. And you probably don't know that a lot of American-label guns are actually manufactured in Japan.

But Control Arms is one step ahead. The embargo is not just for finished guns, but also for materials that can be used to manufacture them. (Imports of these materials could be allowed, as long as strict controls ensured that they were not diverted into firearms manufacture.)

Today, firearms are not made from pure steel, but from steel alloys. Among the more common alloy elements for firearms are boron, chromium, copper, manganese, molybdenum, nickel, phosphorous, silicon, sulphur, and vanadium.[72] Aluminum, titanium, scandium, and cobalt are also used in firearms manufacture.

The United States is self-sufficient, or close to it, in boron, molybdenum, phosphorous, scandium, and sulphur. We are completely or almost completely dependent on imports for manganese, nickel, and vanadium. Forty percent of our copper is imported.[73] The U.S. also imports a very large share of its needs for aluminum, chromium, cobalt, phosphorous, silicon, and titanium.[74]

Thus, a global embargo on metals used for firearms manufacture imports would make the production of some modern firearms impossible, and would require major production redesigns for most of the rest, with drastically increased prices.

It seems quite a stretch to start with a treaty that is supposed to be about banning arms sales to human rights violators, and ending up with a crackdown on U.S. imports of manganese and nickel. Yet as Professor Anderson observed firsthand, that is precisely what the international gun control movement has been all about, nearly from its inception. When the advocates of CIFTA, the U.N. Programme of Action, and the ATT talk about illegal guns, they are taking a roundabout way of saying that they will make your guns illegal.

Nobody knows for sure what the final ATT will contain, but based on what transpired in July 2010 at the Arms Trade Treaty Preparatory Committee meeting, there is a serious risk that the Treaty will mandate microstamping—a requirement that will add about two hundred dollars to the cost of a gun.

Microstamping is a patented process, and the patent holder has been lobbying governments to require the use of his product. With microstamping, the tip of the firing pin is laser engraved with the firearm's serial number. According to the sales pitch, when the firing pin hits the case, the case is stamped with the gun's serial number. So when the case is recovered from a crime scene, it can be linked to the owner of the gun. Of course, making this work would require that all guns be registered.

However, three separate studies have unanimously agreed that microstamping doesn't work.[75]

First of all, the patented device does not reliably stamp an identifiable number on the case. Second, a criminal can easily defeat the device by filing the firing pin head. Third, criminals could pick up empty casings from public firing ranges and dump them at crime scenes, thereby implicating innocent gun owners.

While failing to reduce crime, the two-hundred-dollar-per-gun cost of mandatory microstamping would succeed in making guns unaffordable, especially for poorer people. The Sporting Arms and Ammunition Manufacturers' Institute (SAAMI) explains that gun makers would have to spend millions of dollars in retooling their manufacturing and assembly processes.

By long-standing U.S. law, the serial number must be engraved on the gun's receiver. In assembly, that receiver would have to be mated with a firing pin containing the same unique number, even though the number on the firing pin is invisible to the naked eye. If a firing pin were rejected for quality control reasons, then the receiver (with the matching serial number) would be worthless.

The antigun lobbies are also pushing for the Arms Trade Treaty to require registration of every gun, and restrictions on arms sales, particularly on transfers between private individuals.

Ambassador John Bolton warns that Obama's established record of failure at the United Nations poses a particular danger of him trying a major initiative: "Where Obama may try something new is to emphasize his support for an 'Arms Trade Treaty,' currently in the initial stages of negotiation, that could dramatically restrict the private ownership of firearms worldwide, despite the clear constitutional protections of our Second Amendment."[76]

On the other hand, it is possible that the ATT might decide to leave domestic firearms ownership alone, and just focus on international sales. No one will know for sure until the last hour of the last day of Treaty drafting. The more active and politically engaged American gun owners and the NRA are, the better the odds that the ATT drafters will decide that a frontal assault on the Second Amendment is too much trouble.

Chapter 4

Demonizing Lawful Gun Owners

This is not the end. This is the opening skirmish of a war," announced retired representative Charles Pashayan (R-CA, 1979–91), a U.S. delegate to the July 2001 U.N. Small Arms Conference. Pashayan warned that issues of restricting private ownership of firearms and of banning gun sales to individuals not authorized by a government (e.g., freedom fighters) would return, even though they were defeated at the conference. As he explained, "All of this has to be understood as part of a process leading ultimately to a treaty that will give an international body power over our domestic laws."

U.S. senator Dianne Feinstein (D-CA) agreed: "[T]he Conference is the first step, not the last, in the international community's efforts to control the spread of small arms and light weapons."

As July 2001 approached, Americans sent the U.N. e-mails, protesting the upcoming small arms conference. The U.N. adopted a twofold scheme to deal with them. First, it turned many of the e-mails over to its security office, apparently under the theory that those citizens holding strong opinions on Second Amendment rights must be dangerous—even though not one of the letters made a threat.[1]

Second, it cranked out a press release claiming that the conference posed no threat to law-abiding gun owners.[2] The last claim was a patent falsehood, although many in the American media took the U.N.'s public relations at its word, and failed to observe the massive evidence that restricting domestic gun ownership was clearly the intended purpose of the conference.

The U.N. Conference on Small Arms was held in a room where a large poster proclaimed: SMALL ARMS KILL WOMEN & CHILDREN. The two-week conference was the result of General Assembly Resolution 54/54, adopted December 15, 1999. According to the U.N., the conference "was convened to address the increasing threat to human security from the spread of small arms and light weapons and their illegal trade." Note that illegal trade was only part of the threat; the spread of small arms (and that includes every firearm in your gun cabinet) was considered a threat in itself.

At the conference, speaker after speaker made it clear that "excessive" quantities of guns (i.e., any guns in civilian hands) was a problem in itself, separate from the issue of illegal trade. Rey Pagtakhan, the Canadian secretary of state, condemned the "excessive and destabilizing accumulation and uncontrolled spread of small arms."

Ireland's U.N. delegate declared, "States must stop [the] exporting of small arms and light weapons to all except other governments. All states must suppress private ownership of small arms and light weapons."

Yemen's Abdalla Saleh Al-Ashtal explained, "The goal is to prevent any further increase in the traffic in small arms. It is a problem which relates not only to the illicit trade, but to all issues connected with the legal trade." He touted the situation in Yemen, where "individuals voluntarily surrender their weapons. The media is used to convince people to hand over their weapons."

Burchell Whiteman, Jamaica's minister of education, youth, and culture, called guns and drugs "a double-barreled force of evil and mayhem." Since the imposition of Jamaican gun prohibition in the 1970s, the Jamaican government has used gun and drug prohibition as justifications for eliminating many privacy and due-process elements of the common-law legal tradition.[3] "The time has come," Jamaica's minister continued, "for the international community, particularly states which manufacture arms, to consider the implementation of measures that would limit the production of such weapons to levels that meet the needs for defence and national security." In other words, a ban on gun possession by citizens should spread worldwide.

Proposed language required signatory governments to "seriously consider" banning civilian ownership of small arms "designed for military purposes"—a proposal that would outlaw the M1 carbine, M1 Garand (designed for World War II), many antique firearms (designed for the Civil War), and scores of bolt-action rifles (designed for World War I). Since almost all guns are ultimately derivative of military designs (Col. Colt started making money by selling his revolvers to the U.S. Army), the language would have been a wedge for near-total gun prohibition. The U.N.'s January 9, 2001, Draft Programme of Action mandated that "[w]here appropriate, moratoria on the production, export and import of small arms and light weapons will be developed and implemented on a regional and subregional basis."[4]

The opening of the conference was marked by the unveiling of *The Art of Peacemaking*, a five-ton sculpture created by Canadians Sandra Bromley and Wallis Kendal, with a subsidy from the Canadian War Museum. The sculpture consists of seven thousand firearms welded together into a giant cube, designed to remind viewers of a tomb or a prison.[5] This sculpture perfectly symbolized the U.N. philosophy on guns: violence comes not from the human heart, but from "bad" objects, and the duty of the U.N. is to destroy those objects. The American media blazed with fury that the National Rifle Association was impeding U.N. efforts to control rocket launchers. But the U.N. definition of small arms plainly did include ordinary firearms, and encompassed revolvers, self-loading pistols, rifles in general, semiauto rifles in particular, and fully automatic firearms. The light weapons category included heavy machine guns, mortars, hand grenades, grenade launchers, portable antiaircraft or antitank guns, and portable missile launchers.

Notably, the *Art of Peacemaking* sculpture was not about grenades or rocket launchers; it celebrated the destruction of firearms. Likewise, the U.N. plaza does not feature a sculpture of a rocket launcher tied in knot; it features a revolver with a barrel tied in a knot. And the U.N.'s annual Destruction Day festival (detailed later in this chapter) celebrates the ritual destruction of firearms.

The U.N.'s draft protocol for the conference called for "tighter control over their [firearms and ammunition] legal transfer," for "strengthening current laws and regulation . . . concerning their use and civilian possession," and for "enhancing accountability, transparency and the exchange of information at the national, regional and global levels." This latter goal (a euphemism for universal gun registration in U.N.-run databases) was to be achieved by "systematic tracking of firearms and, where possible, their parts and components and ammunition from manufacturer to purchaser." Government-owned firearms were to be explicitly exempted from these controls.[6]

The European Institute (a D.C. think tank that focuses on trans-Atlantic relations) called for "obligatory liability insurance" for gun owners, plus an "ammunition tax" and "firearm recycling deposit"—whose proposed benefits including making guns less affordable. Further, ammunition calibers "5.56 (.223), 7.62 (.308), and 9mm would be reserved for the military and police." So, the thinking went, "In a period of less than 10 years compulsory changes of the calibers of weapons in private possession could be implemented." An ammunition ban "should be acceptable to all nations because it does not directly interfere with national regulations of private ownership of guns."[7]

Likewise pushing for severe domestic restrictions was the so-called Eminent Persons Group, consisting of twenty-three antigun politicians[8] including U.S. senator Dianne Feinstein and Robert McNamara. McNamara followed his failed tenure as U.S. defense secretary during the Vietnam War with an even more destructive tenure as president of the World Bank, through which he shoveled aid and loans to third-world kleptocracies that used the money to oppress their subject peoples. The indigenous victims of the World Bank/kleptocracy alliance are the very people whom the Eminent Persons Group would disarm.

Formally, the conference was intended to adopt a nonbinding protocol, but gun prohibitionists insisted that even a nonbinding document must lead to a mandatory review of national responses.

In short, the U.N.'s protestations that the conference had nothing to do with American gun possession were true only in a hypertechnical sense; the goal was to create long-term international pressure for severe restrictions on Americans' Second Amendment rights, even though the conference itself would not directly impose those restrictions.

The United States was denounced by the Toronto *Globe & Mail* on July 12, 2001, when the newspaper asserted that "the purpose of the U.N. initiative is not to take hunting rifles away from American good old boys. It is to stop the international trafficking of machine guns, rocket launchers and other lethal weapons."

But actually, the U.N. definition of small arms specifically included: "revolvers and self-loading pistols, rifles and carbines, sub-machine-guns, assault rifles, light machine-guns."[9] This definition was created in a report whose page 1 heading was "General and Complete Disarmament: Small Arms."

Simply because shotguns were not specifically named did not mean that they were excluded from the definition. Certainly the international gun prohibition movement never claimed that shotguns were not among its targets.

The U.N. Conference conveniently ignored data from the Small Arms Survey 2001, published by the Graduate Institute of International Studies in Geneva,[10] which reported that almost all small arms killing of civilians is perpetrated by organized crime, pirates/bandits, and rebel groups. Collectively, these groups possess about 900,000 guns—only two-tenths of 1 percent of all the small arms in the world. Fifty-six percent of the world's 551 million small arms are held by private citizens, 41 percent by armies, and 3 percent by police forces.

In other words, in the world as in the U.S., more than 99 percent of firearms are possessed by decent citizens or issued to military and law enforcement agencies. Firearms misuse is perpetrated almost exclusively by criminals who own a fraction of a percent of all the guns.

If the real objective were to reduce misuse, then nations would follow the lead of the U.S., which has extremely strict laws on the export of small arms, including firearms. All firearms made or sold in the U.S. must have registration marks, allowing for tracing. The American export controls are far more rigorous than the controls of the hypocritical nations such as the UK and Sweden, which impose near prohibition on their own people, while often turning a blind eye toward exports to terrorists and gangsters. And as in the

U.S., the misuse of two-tenths of 1 percent is a pretext for prohibitionists to outlaw every lawfully possessed firearm.

One of the newest factoids from the U.N.'s antigun propaganda machine is the claim that 740,000 people per year are killed as a result of armed violence. That figure comes from the "Geneva Declaration on Armed Violence and Development," which is the product of various global antigun groups working with U.N. support. Significantly, the creators of the Geneva Declaration refuse to let any outsiders see the mathematical calculations they used.[11]

Global Gun Registration:
The Explicit First Step to Confiscation

At the 2001 Small Arms Conference, one of the buzzwords of gun-prohibition advocates was the need for "transparency" in small arms. This was shorthand for saying that there should be no privacy regarding gun ownership, and government authorities should have a list of every gun owner and every gun in the country. Registration has been used over the years to facilitate gun confiscation in Canada, the United Kingdom, Australia, Jamaica, California, New York City, Nazi-occupied Europe, Soviet-occupied Europe, the Philippines, Bermuda, and many other places. Registration is a critical step to total gun prohibition. U.N. disarmament staff have explicitly stated the advantage of registration as a preparatory step toward confiscation.[12]

A U.N. press release touted mandatory gun registration for every (nongovernment) firearm anywhere in the world, but said that a U.N.-controlled registry was "premature"—not that a U.N. registry was a bad idea, just premature, in light of current political realities.[13]

The Canadian government, having sunk more than $2 billion into its domestic gun registry, and having used gun registration for gun confiscation, pushed hard for international registration mandates. Apparently the Canadian government's failed registration scheme would look less foolish if other governments followed suit.

At the 2010 U.N. conference on the Programme of Action, Canadian professor Gary Mauser explained that the ambitious plan for universal, hyper-detailed gun registration was simply not feasible: "Few countries in the world are capable of instituting complex regulatory schemes, such as owner licensing and firearms registration. Canada and South Africa both have strikingly failed to set up a workable national system."

For speaking truth to power, Professor Mauser was disrespectfully jeered during his speech by the delegates, and by the antigun lobbies who were present.

"Transparency for thee, but not for me" could be the U.N. motto. While trying to abolish privacy for gun owners, the U.N. barred the press from the debate and deliberation on the official Programme of Action. Americans would be appalled if Congress threw the press out of the Capitol while debating a gun law, but that is precisely what the U.N. did.

To the extent that gun "transparency" can actually help track down how criminals and terrorists obtain firearms, the world's responsible firearms manufacturers already provide it.

Since the Gun Control Act of 1968, all guns manufactured in or imported into the U.S. must have serial numbers and markings indicating the identity of the manufacturer and place of manufacture. In conjunction with the U.N. Conference, the world's firearms manufacturers, working through their World Forum on the Future of Sport Shooting Activities, signed an agreement with the Eminent Persons Group to provide similar markings on all their firearms. Such identification has never been objectionable to the manufacturers. At a previous international conference, the only reason that a binding agreement on markings was not achieved was that China objected. Later, the "Protocol against the Illicit Manufacturing of and Trafficking in Firearms" specifically exempted China—even though the hugely corrupt Chinese military is an enormous source of arms for warlords, criminal gangs, and despots throughout the Third World.

The U.S. has not signed the Protocol, but the Canadian government has. Canada's then ruling Liberal Party tried to use the Protocol as a pretext to require that all firearms imported into Canada undergo a special marking and stamping process that would add about two hundred dollars to the cost of each gun. The Protocol does require marking, but not the extreme process pushed by the Canadian government. Although the Liberal government finally backed down, and was later replaced by the much more pro-rights Conservative Party, the attempted abuse of the law in Canada shows how any international gun control treaty, if ratified by the U.S., could easily be twisted by an antigun U.S. administration to impose severe restrictions on law-abiding gun sales and ownership.

At the 2001 U.N. Small Arms Conference, the U.S. again supported firearms identification—provided that the language clearly did not open the door for registration of gun owners. That's good enough for legitimate investigations—but not good enough for the prohibition groups that planned to use the trade in illicit arms as a pretext for destroying the privacy of every (nongovernment) gun owner in the world.

Another component of the U.N.'s gun prohibition program is ammunition control, supported by falsehoods from the gun prohibition lobbies. For example, a 2005 report titled "Biting the Bullet" claims that ammunition is terribly dangerous, because it spontaneously explodes.[14] Rules against "stockpiling" ammunition (that is, owning a few hundred rounds) and against home reloading are clearly in the works.

U.N.-Sponsored Gun-Burning Festivals, Demonization of Gun Owners, and the World Health Organization

The U.N. is fiercely determined to eradicate "the gun culture." The beginning of the conference on July 9, 2001, was commemorated with the celebration of the U.N.'s Small Arms and Light Weapons Destruction Day. Around the world, governments made huge piles of firearms—not those owned by the government, but rather, those formerly belonging to citizens. Of course, guns meant for destruction could be crushed—but mere crushing would not excite the special symbolism of destruction by burning.

July 9 was not the first time bonfires were lit to destroy resistance to the power of the government. Nazi "Germany's Josef Goebbels ordered all Jewish books to be burned in public on May 10, 1933. University towns were centers of Jewish Books Destruction Day."[15] As the *Völkischer Beobachter* (*Populist Observer*) reported on May 12, 1933, "The German student body of the Berlin universities assembled yesterday for a torchlight procession on Hegel Platz. They formed up, accompanied by a truckload of 25,000 books and writings harmful to the people. The procession ended at Opera Platz, where as a symbolic act, these un-German writings were set aflame on a pile of logs."

The burning of Jewish and un-German books was followed within a few years by the burning of Jews and other supposedly un-German people. Jewish Books Destruction Day helped change popular consciousness so as to pave the way for genocide. Likewise paving the way for genocide was the systematic disarmament of Jews and all other opposition elements, in Nazi Germany itself and in conquered territories.

How long until a U.N.-declared official day of hate is celebrated with governments actually killing people?

That day has already come. The U.N.'s Office on Drugs and Crime has declared that every June 26 shall be celebrated as the U.N. International Day against Drug Abuse and Illicit Drug Trafficking. June 26 is the anniversary of the signing of the declaration at the 1987 International Conference on Drug Abuse and Illicit Trafficking. The declaration is the basis for the U.N.'s 1988 Convention against the Illicit Traffic in Narcotic Drugs and Psychoactive Substances. This treaty commits its signatories, including the U.S., to maintaining a policy of domestic prohibition.

The long-term objective of many at the Small Arms Conference was to replicate the success of their predecessors at the Drugs and Psychoactive

Substances Conference—creating an international regime of prohibition, enforced not only by individual governments, but by transnational power—a power explicitly designed to destroy the freedom of individual governments to change their prohibition laws in the future.

China celebrates U.N. drug hate day by executing drug criminals. Although the Chinese Communist government asserts that all the executed are "drug traffickers," Amnesty International has shown otherwise. In one case, a young woman was returning to her home province from her honeymoon in January 1996. An acquaintance offered to pay her to carry a package for him, as is common in China. On the train, she became suspicious, and attempted to open the package, but could not. A ticket checker noticed her agitation and notified the police. The Guangxi High People's Court sentenced her to death on June 26, 1996, in honor of the U.N. antidrug day.[16]

At a 2001 press conference, U.N. deputy spokesman Manoel de Almeida e Silva was asked about China's execution festival. While acknowledging that "as far as I am aware the convention does not provide for the application of the death penalty," the U.N. spokesman would not criticize the Chinese executions.

According to Harry Wu's Laogai Research Foundation, Chinese doctors are required to promptly harvest organs whenever a group of antidrug executions is scheduled. Kidneys, other organs, and even skin are sold for as much as fifteen thousand dollars.[17]

What does the future hold as "Small Arms and Light Weapons Destruction Day" on July 9 works its way onto the U.N. holiday calendar? Will the mass burning of firearms help set the stage for mass executions of gun owners? Will the U.N. sponsor events around the world designed to reinforce fears about small arms, and to forestall dissent about small arms prohibition? Regardless of whether one likes or dislikes the U.N. antidrug program, it provides the tested blueprint for a long-term U.N. program against guns.

Already, the public relations effort to equate guns and drugs has begun. The U.N. Development Programme announced that drugs are the largest illicit business in the world, and arms trafficking is second. At the Small Arms Conference, Durga P. Bhattarai of Nepal expressed the commonly held view that (nongovernment) guns were as pernicious as drugs, as he asserted that guns turn children into "addicted killers."

The European Institute for Crime Prevention and Control, which is affiliated with the U.N., was more explicit:

> Bringing the diffusion of firearms under control is not merely a legal act, it requires to overcome the latent gun culture whose "virus" is more firmly established in some societies than in others. Unfortunately the propagation of the gun culture is presently well entrenched in the global electronic media. Some non-governmental organisations like the US-based National Rifle Association strategically sponsor the gun culture.[18]

Kofi Annan has equated small arms to nuclear or chemical weapons—thus demonizing them and implying that they should never be in civilian hands.[19] He said that small arms are "'weapons of mass destruction' in terms of the carnage they cause."[20]

Annan further claimed that firearms "exacerbate conflict, spark refugee flows, undermine the rule of law, and spawn a culture of violence and impunity. In short, small arms are a threat to peace and development, to democracy and human rights."[21] It would be more accurate to say that U.N. Secretary-general Kofi Annan (and his successor Ban Ki-moon) and the corrupt U.N. exacerbate conflict, spark refugee flows, undermine the rule of law, spawn a culture of violence and impunity, and are a threat to peace and development, to democracy and human rights.

Back in the U.S., Second Amendment activists declared July 9 to be National Firearms Purchase Day, urging citizens to buy firearms or ammunition.[22]

The litany of disinformation produced by the U.N. and its various organs is staggering. For example, the U.N. and its gun prohibition allies claim that civilian possession of defensive arms impedes economic development. To the contrary, arms possession by law-abiding citizens helps promote the rule of law, and hence promotes economic development. The major cause of economic underdevelopment is corrupt government, a problem that the U.N. abets. Also harming economic development in the Third World are the malaria and AIDS epidemics, both of which are worsened by the U.N.'s war against DDT, and by its funneling of anti-AIDS money to governments that steal much of the aid.[23]

World Health Organization

Back in the 1990s, the federal Centers for Disease Control used your tax money to produce a barrage of junk science claiming that gun ownership by law-abiding citizens was a "public health" crisis. Finally, Congress, at NRA's urging, ordered the CDC to stop its unscientific propaganda.

Now, the task of producing antigun junk science in the name of public health has been taken over by the World Health Organization (WHO), which is part of the U.N.

Like the CDC, the WHO justifies its advocacy for antigun laws on the grounds that "violence" is supposedly a public health issue, and that the discipline of public health, with expertise in preventing infectious disease, can use that expertise to reduce violence. The WHO produces an enormous amount of antigun research. The organization also uses its periodic World Conference on Injury Prevention and Safety Promotion to network global gun ban advocates, and helps them develop joint strategies.[24]

Douglas Weil formerly served as research director at the Center to Control Handgun Violence, which was the research arm of Handgun Control, Inc. The groups later changed their names to "Brady Center" and "Brady Campaign." Weil left the Brady bunch to become a consultant to the World Health Organization.

As I will explain in chapter 15, the WHO is currently cooking up a tax on international firearm sales.

Not that the WHO spends all its time promoting gun control. The WHO has a broad political agenda, much of which is harmful to public health. For example, for years the WHO refused to admit a delegation from Taiwan, or even to allow Taiwanese journalists to cover WHO meetings. This was done to appease China, whose dictatorship demands that everyone pretend that Taiwan is part of China, even though Taiwan is now independent of China, and has been independent for almost all of Taiwan's history.

The WHO's kowtowing to Chinese imperial aggression endangered everyone's health. Because Taiwan was excluded from the WHO, Taiwanese health officials were denied information about the bird flu outbreaks in China. Likewise, the WHO shut itself off from information about bird flu in Taiwan.

Put another way, the WHO faced a choice between, on the one hand, increasing the risks of a deadly global flu epidemic, which could have killed millions, and, on the other hand, annoying the Chinese dictatorship. The WHO chose to endanger the entire world, just to appease the Chinese tyrants.

There are actually some places where the WHO's medical expertise could help reduce gun violence. For example, in Southern Sudan, the Murle people have a serious, unexplained problem with infertility. So the Murle have been kidnapping children from other tribes to raise as their own. This naturally results in a tremendous amount of intertribal violence. If the Murle infertility problem were solved, there would be less violence. However, the WHO has refused to address the issue. They have also refused to respond to questions from Dr. Paul Gallant and Dr. Joanne Eisen, of the Independence Institute, regarding why the WHO has decided not to help the Murle.[25]

The WHO spends huge amounts of money on fancy conferences about malaria. But in the real world, people are dying of malaria because the WHO will not pay for effective medications (artemisinin-based combination treatments), and instead buys medications (chloroquine and sulfadoxine/pyrimethamine) that fail up to 80 percent of the time. The WHO's medical malpractice kills thousands of people every year.[26]

Stopping Resistance To Tyranny

At the 2001 U.N. Small Arms Conference, Iran took the lead in promoting a ban on arms supplied to "non-state actors." The "non-state actors" clause would require manufacturers "to supply small arms and light weapons only to governments, or to entities duly authorized by government." The clause would make it illegal, for example, to supply arms to the Kurds or religious minorities in Iran, in case Iranian persecution or genocide drove them to forcible resistance. The clause would have made it illegal for the U.S. to supply arms to the oppressed Kurds and Shia of Iraq before the Saddam Hussein regime was toppled.

Had the "non-state actors" provision been in effect in 1776, the transfer of firearms to the American Patriots would have been prohibited. Had the clause been in effect during World War II, the transfer of Liberator pistols to the French Resistance, and to many other resistance groups, would have been illegal.

At the U.N. conference, the U.S. delegation stood firm against the "non-state actors" clause, rejecting compromise efforts to revise the language, or to insert it into the preamble of the Programme of Action. Although Canada pushed hard, the U.S. would not relent. U.S. Undersecretary of State John Bolton pointed out that the proposal "would preclude assistance to an oppressed non-state group defending itself from a genocidal government."

U.N. deputy secretary-general Louise Frechette (of Canada) explained that in some parts of the world, an AK-47 could be obtained for fifteen dollars or a bag of grain. Small-arms "proliferation erodes the authority of legitimate but weak governments," she complained.

U.S. delegate Faith Whittlesey replied that the U.N. "non-state actors" provision "freezes the last coup. It favors established governments, while taking away rights from individuals. It does not recognize any value higher than peace, such as liberty."[27]

According to the U.N., any government with a U.N. delegation is a "legitimate" government. This U.N.standard conflicts with the Declaration of Independence standard that the only legitimate governments are those "deriving their just powers from the consent of the governed."

A press release from Silent March (a group of antigun protesters) complained that the U.S. had "rejected a call for states to stop arming guerrillas in other countries." The press release came after Undersecretary Bolton had explained that the U.S. objected to the provision because it "would preclude assistance to an oppressed non-state group defending itself from a genocidal government."[28]

Silent March promoted itself as a humanitarian group concerned about gun death, but this concern apparently vanished when the victims are being murdered by governments. This is the morally upside-down world of the U.N. culture, in which victims who resist genocide, and governments that help the victims resist, are condemned as immoral.

Joining with Silent March and Iran to criticize the U.S. position was Gaspar Santos Rufino, vice-minister for defense of Angola:

> African leaders, in analyzing the causes of the proliferation and illicit trafficking of small arms, suggest that Member States and the suppliers should be more transparent in their conduct and go beyond national interests. This means, so far as possible, to impose limits on the legal production of certain basic goods, to exercise rigorous control of their circulation, and even to destroy surplus production of goods.
>
> It should be possible to do this with small arms and light weapons, as they are not basic goods and will not be missed by our people.[29]

Rufino, of course, is the defense minister of a communist dictatorship that was installed by the Cuban army's small arms and light weapons in 1975–76, and which has never permitted fair and free elections.

Rufino complained: "In Angola, men with guns in their hands have opposed the legitimate Government for many years. It should be clear that it is imperative to destroy surplus arms, regulate their production in the legislation of manufacturing countries, and sell them to legally constituted and authorized entities."[30]

The "men with guns in their hands" are the men of UNITA, one of the groups that (along with Rufino's communist organization) fought against the Portuguese colonial regime until Portugal surrendered in 1975. Rufino's side would have lost the civil war that followed but for Fidel Castro's modern-day Hessians.

What makes Rufino's dictatorship—created by Cuban "men with guns in their hands"—legitimate? As Rufino shows, beneath the veneer of humanitarian rhetoric, the objective of small arms prohibition is to ensure that dictatorships enjoy a monopoly of force.

The push for banning gun ownership by "non-state actors" is based on the faulty premise that "the government" is equivalent to "the state." To the contrary, as the Declaration of Independence teaches, it is a self-evident truth that governments are created by the people of a state, in order to protect the human rights of the people.[31] As sovereigns, the people have the authority to change the government when they determine that the government is no longer fulfilling its function of protecting the people's rights. The people are the only true and legitimate rulers of a state, and the government is merely their instrument and servant. To the extent that a government is not founded on the consent of the governed, it is illegitimate. As a U.S. federal district court put it, "the people, not the government, possess the sovereignty."[33]

The notion that gun possession by "non-state actors" is always illegitimate is directly contrary to the Second Amendment, which guarantees that the people retain the ultimate sovereignty. The conflict between the U.N.'s gun ban and the American Second Amendment reveals the essence of the modern U.N. vision: government is the master, and people are the servants.

Once we acknowledge that people may legitimately possess small arms in order to resist dictatorships, especially genocidal ones, then another favorite term of the prohibition lobby, "transparency," is easier to understand. Applied to individuals, transparency is a euphemism for the abolition of privacy. Applied to gun ownership, transparency means that governments keep track of everyone who owns a gun, and precisely what guns they own. In other words, transparency should be more properly defined as "government registration of private activities." No freedom-loving people would want to register the books they own or read, or their personal medical or health records. The same is true of firearms. Transparency has repeatedly been used by governments to facilitate confiscation of some or all guns—in democracies such as Bermuda, Canada, and England, and in dictatorships such as Nazi Germany, the Soviet Union, and the states conquered by them.

There is no legitimate reason for the government to monopolize firearms, newspapers, religious institutions, home ownership, or any other form of property that helps preserve a free state. Government is responsible to the people, not to itself. Thomas Jefferson, James Madison, and their fellow Patriots all understood this fundamental truth of political legitimacy. Indeed, America's Declaration of Independence and Bill of Rights are their legacy in enshrining our unique freedoms.

Chapter 5

Choking Off the Second Amendment in the United States

D id the work of the National Rifle Association members in the 2000 election matter? If Al Gore had won that election—and he would have won if the NRA had not put George W. Bush over the top in West Virginia, Missouri, Florida, Arkansas, and Tennessee—then the 2001 U.N. antigun conference would have had an entirely different result.

Rather than drawing a line in the sand against a binding international treaty, the U.S. delegation would have enthusiastically supported an extremely repressive treaty.

The Clinton-Gore administration was well aware—as a Kerry administration would also have been—of how effectively the U.N. can be used to impose extreme gun laws in the U.S. During the Clinton-Gore administration, when the draft protocol for the 2001 convention was being prepared in December 2000, it was the Colombian and Mexican delegations, not the American delegation, that offered optional language recognizing that some countries have legitimate traditions of sporting and other gun use.

Now, you may wonder what harm could signing a bad treaty do? After all, the U.S. Constitution requires that treaties be ratified by a two-thirds vote of the U.S. Senate.

There are many ways in which extreme U.N. gun laws could be enforced in the U.S., even without ratification of a repressive treaty by the U.S. Senate.

First of all, the president could call the document an "agreement" rather than a "treaty." Then, instead of needing two-thirds of the Senate, the document simply needs a majority in the U.S. House and Senate for approval. This tactic is precisely how President Bill Clinton convinced Congress to ratify the North American Free Trade Agreement (NAFTA), which never could have won two-thirds' support in the Senate.

As a practical matter, if a president's party controls both houses of Congress, it is nearly impossible to stop him from building a majority for anything he wants—if the president is willing to commit every resource he has to getting the bill passed. That is how the Clinton gun ban was approved in 1994—by a Democratic president applying extreme pressure (both threats and promises) to normally pro-gun Democratic legislators.

A back-door approach to extreme gun control would be an international treaty that, on its face, looks innocuous. The treaty might simply contain language about preventing arms transfers to criminals, and perhaps some requirements that countries enact strict controls on commercial firearms exports. (U.S. export controls are already the strictest in the world.) Then, a president might convince a majority of both houses—or two-thirds of the Senate—to make the document into law, since it appears to be harmless to U.S. rights.

The U.N. has a very long history of convincing nations to sign on to treaties with moderate, sensible language, and then—after ratification—twisting that language to impose extremist results.

Consider, for example, the U.N. Convention on the Elimination of All Forms of Discrimination against Women (CEDAW). If you read the CEDAW, and you believe that a woman ought to be able to work in any job for which she is qualified, you would probably find little to criticize in the language. Not surprisingly, many nations ratified the CEDAW, believing that they were simply affirming principles of nondiscrimination that they already believed in. The U.S., however, was more cautious, and did not ratify it.

As typical for U.N. conventions, CEDAW carried an attractive name, yet it has been perverted into a program for restricting freedom and eliminating choice for women and families. Patrick Fagan's excellent backgrounder for the Heritage Foundation details how U.N. bureaucrats in nations that have submitted to CEDAW are working to restrict religious freedom, eliminate parental choice about sex education classes, discourage the celebration of Mother's Day, deconstruct the two-parent family, and most of all, make it legally, culturally, and economically burdensome for women to choose to stay home with their children.[1]

With truth-in-labeling, the CEDAW would be called "the Convention for the Gradual Replacement of Mothers by Government." The bureaucrats who implement it are profoundly antichoice on family issues, especially the choice of mothers to take care of their children personally.

Similarly, the U.N. Convention on the Rights of the Child is being reinterpreted by U.N. bureaucrats in ways never agreed to by the governments that signed the convention. According to the U.N.'s Committee on the Rights of the Child, the convention means that all children, no matter how young, have—with no need for parental consent, or even in opposition to parental wishes—an unlimited right to reproductive and sexual services, and to freedom of association.

Obviously, none of the 191 ratifying nations meant to accept such a radical destruction of parental rights. But, as one U.N. watchdog has noted, "in light of such Committee actions, U.N. delegates fear it is impossible for countries to know what they are endorsing when they ratify international treaties. What is more, essential power may no longer rest with those who write treaties, but with those who get to interpret them."[2]

Thus, *any* U.N. firearms treaty that becomes law in the U.S. could become a platform for the imposition of extremist gun control, with U.N. bureaucrats, not U.S. voters, making the decisions.

Even worse, U.N. gun prohibition can be imposed in the U.S. without *any* form of approval from Congress. Let's suppose an antigun president—

say, Barack Obama or Hillary Clinton—signs a U.N. antigun treaty, but the treaty has not yet been ratified by Congress.

Now consider the Vienna Convention on Treaties. The Vienna Convention has not been ratified by the U.S., but the U.S. State Department has decided that the U.S. should almost always abide by its terms. The Vienna Convention provides the rules for how nations are supposed to obey international treaties. One of the rules of the Vienna Convention is that once a nation has signed (not ratified, just signed) a treaty, the nation may not undermine the treaty.

So, relying on the signed but unratified treaty, President Hillary Clinton could start issuing executive orders to impose various gun laws because, she could claim, without the executive orders, the U.S. would be illegally undermining the treaty.

Would American courts enforce the Second Amendment to defend our rights against international gun control—either in the form of a treaty, or in the form of executive orders based on an unratified treaty?

Not necessarily. It's true that a treaty, even if ratified by the U.S. Senate, cannot directly repeal constitutional rights.[3] Many judges, however, would interpret the Second Amendment so narrowly that the right to arms would always give way to the requirements of any "gun-control" treaty. Such judges believe in what they call a "living Constitution"—but what they really mean is a "dead constitution." They reject a Constitution whose text and intent are the law of the land, favoring instead a constitution that has no enduring meaning, but can be changed on the whim of a judge, based on the judge's determination of social policy.

Even worse, the very existence of international gun-control treaties, *even treaties that are never signed or ratified by the U.S.*, provides judges with a pretext for choking off Second Amendment rights.

The fact that many nations have nearly obliterated gun owners' rights and the right to self-defense is already an important reason, according to some judges, for interpreting the Second Amendment into protecting nothing at all.

The existence of international gun-control treaties reinforces their argument that the Second Amendment can be shriveled out of existence.

Supreme Court Justice Stephen Breyer told ABC's George Stephanopoulos that we must rise to "the challenge" of making sure the U.S. Constitution "fits into the governing documents of other nations."[4] In the case of *Knight v. Florida*, Justice Breyer wrote that it was "useful" to consider the death penalty jurisprudence in India, Jamaica, and Zimbabwe.[5] The notion that the U.S. Supreme Court should be guided by courts from the genocidal dictatorship of Robert Mugabe in Zimbabwe is outrageous. And while Jamaica and India have every right to enact their own laws, so does the U.S. The American people will no longer be sovereign if courts start interpreting the U.S. Constitution based on the laws of other nations.

In *Grutter v. Bollinger* and *Gratz v. Bollinger*, in which the Supreme Court was asked to interpret the Fourteenth Amendment to the U.S. Constitution and the federal Civil Rights Act of 1964, Justices Ruth Bader Ginsburg, David Souter, and Stephen Breyer cited the Convention on the Elimination of All Forms of Discrimination against Women.[6] And Justice Ginsburg, in a speech to the American Constitutional Society (a group of left-wing legal activists and academics), celebrated the Supreme Court's abandonment of the "Lone Ranger mentality" and their being "more open to comparative and international law perspectives."[7]

In the death penalty case *Atkins v. Virginia*, Justice John Paul Stevens wrote the opinion for the majority of the Court, citing an amicus brief from the European Union. He quoted the E.U.'s statement that "within the world community, the imposition of the death penalty for crimes committed by mentally retarded offenders is overwhelmingly disapproved."[8]

So according to Justice Stevens—and a majority of the Court— the European Union's disapproval is a good enough reason for the Supreme Court to change the meaning of our Constitution. The danger to the Second Amendment is quite obvious, since the EU also strongly disapproves of the American right to arms and the American right to self-defense.

An even greater peril is that the international gun prohibition movement needs neither a treaty nor the cooperation of even one branch of our government in order to destroy the Second Amendment.

Formal legal documents—such as treaties, conventions, agreements, and declarations—are one source of international law. But international law is also based on "norms" or "customary law." In recent decades, activist lawyers have become extremely adept at fabricating norms and customary law out of thin air. Courts do not always go along with these nonsense-on-stilts arguments, but some could.

So even without a treaty, gun prohibitionists can argue in U.S. courts that international norms compel the court to interpret the Second Amendment, and the states' individual constitutional rights to arms, restrictively.

Ominously, a supposed international norm against civilian gun ownership—especially gun ownership for defense against criminals or a tyrannical government—could also be raised in a foreign court. In "The Second Amendment and Global Gun Control," attorney Joseph Bruce Alonso describes how U.S. gun manufacturers could be sued in foreign courts.[9]

In a foreign court, the Second Amendment would provide no defense. Nor would any of the due process protections of the U.S. Constitution be applicable. American statutes such as the Protection of Lawful Commerce in Arms Act would be irrelevant.

The prospect of destroying our Second Amendment through foreign lawsuits is already being developed. In the fall of 2005, the national government of Canada urged Canada's provincial governments to sue American gun companies in Canadian courts. (So far, none of the provinces have acted, but they could change their minds at any time, based on political calculation.)

As I detailed in chapter 3, Chicago's despotic Richard Daley and a dozen of his global mayor allies are working on plans to sue firearms manufacturers in the World Court.

Importantly, if one day U.S. gun rights and self-defense rights are themselves considered human rights violations, then the American firearms industry could be especially vulnerable to suits in foreign or international courts.

The first steps have already begun. University of Minnesota law professor Barbara Frey is the U.N. special rapporteur on the relationship between guns and human rights. In her role, she works as a gun prohibition activist. For example, in early 2005, she participated in a strategy session in Brazil in which various nongovernment organizations plotted how to pass a total gun prohibition referendum in that nation in October. The conference was sponsored by the far-Left government of Brazil and by Viva Rio, the group that pushed the handgun ban.

In her official capacity as the U.N.'s special rapporteur, Frey declared that it is a human rights violation for a government not to impose some of the gun-control laws she favors. These controls include licensing for all gun owners, "safe storage" (that is, "lock-up-your-gun" laws that prevent guns from being used in an emergency against an intruder), and reducing the number of firearms.[10]

The next year, in 2006, Frey produced a lengthy report setting forth the view that American-style gun laws are human rights violations because they are insufficiently restrictive, and because America allows too much self-defense. As I will explain in chapter 13, that report was officially adopted by the United Nations.

Frey, IANSA, and the rest of the U.N. gun-ban bureaucracy are also working on creating a claim that international law already forbids supplying arms to a serious abuser of human rights.[11] The theory could, perhaps, lead to the supplier being sued in a foreign court, or even criminally prosecuted in the International Criminal Court (discussed in chapter 3).

Of course, it would be a good idea if the theory would be deployed against governments that actually are gross abusers of human rights—such as Sudan, Zimbabwe, or North Korea. But remember, according to the U.N., the worst human rights abuser in the world is Israel, and among the next worst is the U.S. In chapter 3, I discussed how antigun activists want to use the U.N.'s Arms Trade Treaty, which is currently being drafted, to impose an arms and arms component embargo on Israel—and that the U.S. might be one of the next targets.

In the Orwellian world of the U.N., America's first freedom amounts to a human rights violation. The total gun prohibition that the U.N. has imposed on citizens of other nations, leaving them helpless against criminals, is precisely what the U.N. wants to impose on the U.S. After all, as Rebecca Peters puts it, the United States has no right to be different from other countries.

The U.N. is the most lethal threat ever to our Second Amendment rights. Even though we avoided the worst possible results at the summer 2006 U.N. antigun conference in New York City, the U.N. and the international gun prohibition movement will continue their war against the Second Amendment. The danger to human rights in the U.S. and around the world grows deadlier every year. Already many thousands of people around the globe have been victims of genocide because of the "success" of the U.N.'s war on gun ownership. To close our eyes and pretend "it can't happen here" would literally be a fatal error.

Chapter 6

Congress and the Second Amendment: Views of the Popular Branch

It is no wonder that the gun prohibition lobbies so love the United Nations, because the U.N. is so insulated from democratic control. In contrast, when the American people have the opportunity to act through their state legislatures and through Congress, they tend to respect and protect the fundamental human right of self-defense, and the related right to possess and carry arms for self-defense.

For example, on four occasions in American history, Congress has enacted legislation that declared its unequivocal understanding of the meaning of the Second Amendment to the U.S. Constitution. The Second Amendment states: "A well regulated Militia, being necessary to the security of a free State, the right of the people to keep and bear Arms, shall not be infringed." The U.S. Congress adopted that wording and proposed it to the States in 1789 as part of the Bill of Rights, which the states ratified in 1791.

Throughout U.S. history, the American people have always understood that the Second Amendment means what it says: it is the people who have the right to keep and bear arms, and government may not infringe that right. The existence of this right would promote a well-regulated militia composed of the armed populace, which is essential to the security of not just any state, but a *free* state.

That plain meaning of the Second Amendment is reflected in Congressional action taken within vastly different historical contexts. Since Congress is elected (and hence held in check) by the people, Congress has never given any support for the notion of the gun prohibition lobbies that the Second Amendment fails to protect any right of the people, and instead ensures a nonsensical "collective right" of states to maintain militias. To the contrary, in the Constitution's vocabulary, states have powers, not rights, and the division of federal–state powers regarding the militia is dealt with elsewhere in the Constitution, in Article I, section 8.

On four occasions—in 1866, 1941, 1986, and 2005—Congress enacted statutes to reaffirm this guarantee of personal freedom and to adopt specific safeguards to enforce it.

The first two were enacted at times of great historical crisis. The 1866 declaration was enacted to protect the rights of freed slaves to keep and bear arms following a tumultuous civil war and at the outset of the subsequent, chaotic Reconstruction period. The 1941 enactment was intended to reassure Americans that preparations for war would not include repressive or tyrannical policies against firearms owners, and it was passed shortly before the Japanese sneak attack on Pearl Harbor, which forced the United States into World War II.

The two more recent enactments sought to reverse outrageous excesses involving America's legal system. In 1986, Congress reacted to overzealous enforcement policies under the federal firearms law by passing reform legislation. And in 2005, as a result of the misuse of the state and federal judicial systems aiming to destroy America's firearms industry, Congress stepped in to end this threat to the Second Amendment.

The history of these four enactments of Congress makes absolutely clear that keeping and bearing arms is an individual right that may not be infringed by the government, whether federal or state. The first part of that history, involving the civil rights of the newly freed ex-slaves, was at the heart of the Supreme Court's 2010 decision in *McDonald v. Chicago*, when the Supreme Court agreed with the NRA's argument to the Court that the Fourteenth Amendment makes the Second Amendment enforceable against all state and local governments.

The Freedmen's Bureau Act of 1866:
The Constitutional Right to Bear Arms

Like the rest of the Bill of Rights, the Second Amendment was viewed by the antebellum Supreme Court as guaranteeing individual rights against action by the federal government, but not against the states. At the end of the War between the States, slavery was abolished; however, Southern states continued to treat black freedmen as if they were still slaves, in part by prohibiting them from possessing firearms and sending militiamen to search freedmen cabins for arms. Sometimes the searches were carried out by terrorist organizations such as the Ku Klux Klan or the Knights of the White Camelia, with tacit approval from local "law enforcement."

In an effort to protect the Second Amendment rights of Southern blacks, Congress passed the Freedmen's Bureau Act in 1866, which declared protection for the "full and equal benefit of all laws and proceedings concerning personal liberty, personal security, and . . . estate . . . including the constitutional right to bear arms"[1] Congress also enacted the Civil Rights Act and proposed the Fourteenth Amendment to the states for ratification as an amendment to the Constitution.

The Fourteenth Amendment declares that all persons born or naturalized in the U.S. are citizens. It also prohibits the states from abridging "the privileges and immunities of citizens," and declares that no state shall "deprive any person of life, liberty or property without due process of law," or deny to any person "the equal protection of the laws."

The Freedmen's Bureau Act is key to understanding how Congress interpreted the Second Amendment some seventy-five years after it became part of the Constitution in 1791. The Act also demonstrates that the right to keep and bear arms was a fundamental right that the general clauses of the Fourteenth Amendment were intended to protect from violation by the states. Indeed, the same two-thirds of Congress that proposed the Fourteenth Amendment to the U.S. Constitution in 1866 also enacted the Freedmen's Bureau Act.[2]

This legislative history begins on January 5, 1866, when Senator Lyman Trumbull of Illinois introduced S. 60, the Freedmen's Bureau Bill, and S. 61, the Civil Rights Bill.[3] (Trumbull, the chairman of the Judiciary Committee, had previously coauthored the Thirteenth Amendment, which outlawed slavery.) To exemplify the need for civil rights legislation, black citizens of South Carolina had assembled in a convention and adopted a petition to be submitted to Congress. It stated in part:

> We ask that, inasmuch as the Constitution of the United States explicitly declares that the right to keep and bear arms shall not be infringed—and the Constitution is the Supreme law of the land—that the late efforts of the Legislature of this State to pass an act to deprive us of arms be forbidden, as a plain violation of the Constitution.[4]

The petition became the centerpiece of a speech on the Senate floor by the great antislavery senator Charles Sumner of Massachusetts, urging protection of the freedmen, saying:

> They also ask that government in that State shall be founded on the consent of the governed, and insist that can be done only where equal suffrage is allowed . . . They ask also that they should have the constitutional protection in keeping arms, in holding public assemblies, and in complete liberty of speech and of the press.[5]

On January 30, Representative Thomas Eliot of Massachusetts, chairman of the Select Committee on Freedmen, reported the Freedmen's Bureau Bill to the House of Representatives.[6] Eliot quoted from an ordinance of Opelousas, Louisiana, which contained the same deprivations of rights as under slavery, including the following:

No freedman who is not in the military service shall be allowed to carry firearms, or any kind of weapons, within the limits of the town of Opelousas without the special permission of his employer, in writing, and approved by the mayor or president of the board of police. Anyone thus offending shall forfeit his weapons, and shall be imprisoned and made to work five days on the public streets, or pay a fine of five dollars in lieu of said work.[7]

The Freedmen's Bureau Bill was initially broadly worded; so to ensure that there would be no mistaking its intent, Rep. Nathaniel P. Banks of Massachusetts called for it to be amended explicitly to provide for everyone "the civil rights belonging to white persons, including the constitutional right to bear arms."[8]

Freedmen's Bureau committee chairman Eliot did just that on February 5 by offering a substitute for S. 60.[9] Among the clarifications was the following:

The next amendment is in the seventh section, in the eleventh line, after the word "estate," by inserting the words "including the constitutional right to bear arms," so that it will read, "to have full and equal benefit of all laws and proceedings for the security of person and estate, including the constitutional right to bear arms."[10]

In a speech urging adoption, Eliot quoted from a report to General O. O. Howard, commissioner of the Freedmen's Bureau, which described the following conditions in Kentucky: "The civil law prohibits the colored man from bearing arms; returned soldiers are, by the civil officers, dispossessed of their arms and fined for violation of the law."[11] Commissioner Howard observed, "Thus, the right of the people to keep and bear arms as provided in the Constitution is *infringed*."[12]

The Freedmen's Bureau Bill, including the amendment characterizing "the constitutional right to bear arms" as a "civil right,"[13] passed the House by a landslide vote of 136 to 33.[14]

Senator Trumbull, as instructed by the Committee on the Judiciary, recommended that the Senate concur in the House amendments.[15] Trumbull explained:

> There is also a slight amendment in the seventh section, thirteenth line. That is the section which declares that negroes and mulattoes shall have the same civil rights as white persons, and have the same security of person and estate. The House have inserted these words, "including the constitutional right of bearing arms." I think that does not alter the meaning.[16]

Trumbull, the author of the Freedmen's Bureau and Civil Rights bills, made it absolutely clear that general language about civil rights and personal security was intended to include the right to bear arms, regardless of whether that right was explicitly mentioned.

The Senate concurred in S. 60 as amended without a recorded vote.[17] The House then approved some unrelated Senate amendments.[18] With that, Congress had passed the Freedmen's Bureau Bill.

As passed, the Freedmen's Bureau Bill provided that, in areas where ordinary judicial proceedings were interrupted by the rebellion, the president should extend military protection to individuals whose rights were violated. The text specified in part:

> Wherein, in consequence of any State or local law, ordinance, police or other regulation, custom, or prejudice, any of the civil rights or immunities belonging to white persons, including the right to make and enforce contracts, to sue, be parties, and give evidence, to inherit, purchase, lease, sell, hold and convey real and personal property, and to have full and equal benefit of all laws

and proceedings for the security of person and estate, including the constitutional right of bearing arms, are refused or denied to negroes, mulattoes, freedmen, refugees, or any other persons, on account of race, color, or any previous condition of slavery or involuntary servitude.[19]

Meanwhile, discussion on the need to guarantee the right to keep and bear arms continued. Representative William Lawrence quoted General D. E. Sickles's General Order No. 1 for the Department of South Carolina as follows:

I. To the end that civil rights and immunities may be enjoyed . . . the following regulations are established for the government of all concerned in this department . . .

XVI. The constitutional rights of all loyal and well disposed inhabitants to bear arms, will not be infringed.

Those who had fought for the South in the Civil War were allowed the same right after taking the Amnesty oath or the Oath of Allegiance.[20]

This "most remarkable order," which was published in the headlines of the *Loyal Georgian*,[21] a prominent black newspaper, was thought to have been "issued with the knowledge and approbation of the President if not by his direction."[22] "A Colored Citizen" asked, "Have colored persons a right to own and carry fire arms?" The editor of the *Loyal Georgian* responded:

Almost every day we are asked questions similar to the above. We answer *certainly* you have the *same* right to own and carry arms that other citizens have. You are not only free but citizens of the United States and as such entitled to the same privileges granted to other citizens by the Constitution.

The editor then quoted the following from a Freedmen's Bureau Circular:

Article II, of the amendments to the Constitution of the United States, gives the people the right to bear arms, and states that this right shall not be infringed. Any person, white or black, may be disarmed if convicted of making an improper or dangerous use of weapons, but no military or civil officer has the right or authority to disarm any class of people, thereby placing them at the mercy of others. All men, without distinction of color, have the right to keep and bear arms to defend their homes, families or themselves.[23]

President Andrew Johnson vetoed the Freedmen's Bureau Bill, although his objections had nothing to do with the reference to "the constitutional right to bear arms."[24] Lyman Trumbull criticized the veto, since the bill protected constitutional rights.[25] He quoted from a letter written by Colonel Thomas in Vicksburg, Mississippi, which stated that "nearly all the dissatisfaction that now exists among the freedmen is caused by the abusive conduct of this [State] militia," which typically would "hang some freedman or search negro houses for arms."[26]

The Senate attempted to override the veto, but mustered two votes less than the necessary two-thirds,[27] leaving no point in the House for conducting an override vote. This was the beginning of strained relations between Congress and the president, which would snowball into an unsuccessful attempt to impeach Johnson. Charged with eleven articles of impeachment, he was acquitted in the Senate by a single vote.

On March 7, Representative Elliot introduced a revised version of the Freedmen's Bureau Bill.[28] As before, it included "the constitutional right to bear arms" in the rights of personal security and personal liberty.[29]

Debate on the Civil Rights Bill was now in full swing. Representative John A. Bingham of Ohio quoted its provisions, including its guarantee of "full and equal benefit of all laws and proceedings for the security of person and property,"[30] and explained that "the seventh and eighth sections of the Freedmen's Bureau bill enumerate the same rights and all the rights and privileges that are enumerated in the first section of this [the Civil Rights] bill."[31] Bingham then quoted the seventh section of the first Freedmen's Bureau Bill, that provided that all individuals would "have full and equal benefit of all laws and proceedings for the security of person and estate, including the constitutional right of bearing arms"[32]

The Civil Rights Bill passed both the Senate and the House,[33] but on March 27 President Johnson vetoed it.[34] In the override debate in the Senate, Lyman Trumbull referred to the "inherent, fundamental rights which belong to free citizens or free men in all countries, such as the rights enumerated in this bill."[35] He quoted a prominent legal treatise as follows: "The absolute rights of individuals may be resolved into the right of personal security, the right of personal liberty, and the right to acquire and enjoy property."[36] The Civil Rights Bill was intended to protect these rights, which the Freedmen's Bureau Bill stated as including the right to bear arms.

The Senate successfully overrode the president's veto.[37] The *New York Evening Post* identified "the mischiefs for which the Civil Rights bill seeks to provide a remedy" as including "attempts to prevent their [blacks] holding public assemblies . . . [and] keeping fire-arms."[38]

By April 9, the House had also overridden President Andrew Johnson's veto, and the Civil Rights Act of 1866 became law.[39] As enacted, § 1 provided that

> . . . citizens, of every race and color, without regard to any previous condition of slavery or involuntary servitude . . . shall have the same right, in every State and Territory in the United States, to make and enforce contracts, to sue, be parties, and give evidence, to inherit, purchase, lease, sell, hold, and convey real and personal property, and to *full and equal benefit of all laws and proceedings for the security of person and property, as is enjoyed by white citizens.*[40]

That remains the law today.[41]

Now that action on the Civil Rights Act was complete, Representative Eliot, on behalf of the Select Committee on Freedmen's Affairs, reported H.R. 613, the second Freedmen's Bureau Bill.[42] As before, the new bill recognized "the constitutional right to bear arms."[43]

Meanwhile, the proposed Fourteenth Amendment to the Constitution passed the House.[44] On May 23, Jacob Howard of Michigan introduced it in the Senate.[45] Senator Howard referred to "the personal rights guaranteed and secured by the first eight amendments of the Constitution; such as freedom of speech and of the press . . . the right to keep and bear arms."[46] Howard explained: "The great object of the first section of this amendment is, therefore, to restrain the power of the States and compel them at all times to respect these great fundamental guarantees."[47] No one in the Senate disputed that statement. What became the Fourteenth Amendment was clearly intended to protect the right to keep and bear arms from violation by the states.

The Freedmen's Bureau Bill was also debated in the House on May 23.[48] Representative Eliot observed that § 8, which explicitly recognized the right to bear arms, "simply embodies the provisions of the civil rights bill, and gives to the President authority, through the Secretary of War, to extend military protection to secure those rights until the civil courts are in operation."[49]

Eliot recited a Freedmen's Bureau report by General Clinton B. Fisk, who reported about black Union soldiers returning to their homes in Kentucky after the war ended:

> Their arms are taken from them by the civil authorities and confiscated for the benefit of the Commonwealth . . . Thus the right of the people to keep and bear arms as provided in the Constitution is infringed, and the Government for whose protection and preservation these soldiers have fought is denounced as meddlesome and despotic when through its agents it undertakes to protect its citizens in a constitutional right.[50]

The freedmen, Fisk continued, "are defenseless, for the civil-law officers disarm the colored man and hand him over to armed marauders."[51] On May 29, the House passed H.R. 613, the Freedmen's Bureau Bill, by a vote of 96 to 32.[52] The House then took up the proposed Fourteenth Amendment.[53]

After further debate, the Fourteenth Amendment passed the Senate by a vote of 33 to 11,[54] a 75 percent margin, comfortably more than the required two-thirds to amend the Constitution. On June 13, the House passed the proposed Amendment by 120 to 32,[55] which was 79 percent of the votes, once more well beyond the necessary two-thirds.

A bill was also pending that mandated that the former Confederate states ratify the Fourteenth Amendment as a condition for reentry into the Union. As explained by Representative George W. Julian, the constitutional amendment was needed to prevent states from nullifying the Civil Rights Act:

> Although the civil rights bill is now the law . . . [it] is pronounced void by the jurists and courts of the South. Florida makes it a misdemeanor for colored men to carry weapons without a license to do so from a probate judge, and the punishment of the offense is whipping and the pillory. South Carolina has the same enactments; and a black man convicted of an offense who fails immediately to pay his fine is whipped . . . Cunning legislative devices are being invented in most of the States to restore slavery in fact.[56]

In other words, while the Civil Rights Act and the Freedmen's Bureau Bill were intended to guarantee the right to keep and bear arms and other rights, the Fourteenth Amendment was needed to leave no question as to the constitutionality of such enactments or of further possible enactments to protect civil rights.

On June 26, the Senate took up the Freedmen's Bureau Bill. Section 8, which included reference to "the constitutional right to bear arms," was renumbered as § 14.[57] The House rejected a motion by Senator Thomas

Hendricks of Indiana to strike out the section on the basis that "the same matters are found in the civil rights bill substantially that are found in this section."[58] (Hendricks was a leading Senate foe of civil rights, and had even opposed the Thirteenth Amendment.)

The two bills protected the same rights, responded Senator Trumbull, but the Civil Rights Act applied in areas where the courts were operable, and the Freedmen's Bureau Bill would apply where the civil authority had not been restored.[59] The bill then passed without a roll-call vote.[60]

After being sent to a conference committee, the bill was reported, and the Senate concurred.[61] A motion in the House to table the bill lost by a vote of 25 to 102.[62] The report was then adopted without another roll call vote.

President Johnson then vetoed the second Freedmen's Bureau Bill,[63] but the House overrode the veto by 104 to 33, or 76 percent,[64] and the Senate did so by 33 to 12, or 73 percent.[65]

As finally passed into law on July 16, 1866, the Freedmen's Bureau Act extended the Bureau's existence for two more years.[66] The full text of § 14 of the Act declared:

> that in every State or district where the ordinary course of judicial proceedings has been interrupted by the rebellion, and until the same shall be fully restored, and in every State or district whose constitutional relations to the government have been practically discontinued by the rebellion, and until such State shall have been restored in such relations, and shall be duly represented in the Congress of the United States, the right to make and enforce contracts, to sue, be parties, and give evidence, to inherit, purchase, lease, sell, hold, and convey real and personal property, and to have *full and equal benefit of all laws and proceedings concerning personal liberty, personal security,* and the acquisition, enjoyment, and disposition of estate, real and personal, *including*

the constitutional right to bear arms, shall be secured to and enjoyed by all the citizens of such State or district without respect to race or color or previous condition of slavery. And whenever in either of said States or districts the ordinary course of judicial proceedings has been interrupted by the rebellion, and until the same shall be fully restored, and until such State shall have been restored in its constitutional relations to the government, and shall be duly represented in the Congress of the United States, the President shall, through the commissioner and the officers of the bureau, and under such rules and regulations as the President, through the Secretary of War, shall prescribe, extend military protection and have military jurisdiction over all cases and questions concerning the *free enjoyment of such immunities and rights*, and no penalty or punishment for any violation of law shall be imposed or permitted because of race or color, or previous condition of slavery, other or greater than the penalty or punishment to which white persons may be liable by law for the like offense. But the jurisdiction conferred by this section upon the officers of the bureau shall not exist in any State where the ordinary course of judicial proceedings has not been interrupted by the rebellion, and shall cease in every State when the courts of the State and the United States are not disturbed in the peaceable course of justice, and after such State shall be fully restored in its constitutional relations to the government, and shall be duly represented in the Congress of the United States.[67]

In short, the "full and equal benefit of all laws and proceedings concerning personal liberty, personal security, and . . . estate" included "the constitutional right to bear arms," and those rights were to "be secured to and enjoyed by all the citizens," who were entitled to "the free enjoyment of such immunities and rights." It is noteworthy that the same more than two-thirds of Congress that enacted this language of the Freedmen's Bureau Act also enacted similar, albeit more general, language in the Civil Rights Act, which remains on the books today.

Even more significantly, more than two-thirds of Congress adopted the Fourteenth Amendment to the Constitution and submitted it to the states for ratification. First and foremost among the Bill of Rights guarantees that the Fourteenth Amendment was intended to protect from state infringement was the Second Amendment right to keep and bear arms. Not even the First Amendment right to free speech was singled out for such special emphasis as was the Second Amendment.

Members of the Reconstruction Congress clearly read the Second Amendment to guarantee a fundamental right of "the people," i.e., individuals. It would be another century before the spread of the "collective right" view of the Second Amendment, under which the Amendment protects nothing more than some undefinable power of States to maintain militias or a nonsensical right to bear arms in a militia, which is inconsistent with any military force. Indeed, Congress in 1866 recognized "the constitutional right to bear arms" by all persons, even newly freed slaves, and further saw the need to protect this and other rights from the state militias.

This first Congressional action took place in a great historical epoch just after our bloody Civil War, and at the beginning of a civil rights revolution. The next occasion in which Congress gave homage to the Second Amendment in a statutory declaration was in one of the darkest epochs in human history for civil rights abroad. It came just before America's entry into World War II.

The Property Requisition Act of 1941:

No Impairment of the Right of Any Individual
to Keep and Bear Arms

Just shy of two months before Japan's infamous attack on Pearl Harbor, Congress enacted the Property Requisition Act of 1941. It authorized the president to requisition certain types of property seen as necessary for national defense in the event that the United States was dragged into the war in Europe and Asia. The Act declared that it must not be construed "to authorize the requisitioning or require the registration of any firearms possessed by any individual for his personal protection or sport," or "to impair or infringe in any manner the right of any individual to keep and bear arms."[68]

Before examining the deliberations in Congress that led to this enactment, some background as to why Second Amendment rights were a matter of concern is in order. This was the Age of Totalitarianism, featuring Nazi Germany, Fascist Italy, Imperial Japan, and Communist Russia. Mass murder and genocide characterized these regimes, under which depriving firearms from would-be victims was essential. The Nazi experience illustrates that point.

Americans reading the *New York Times* or other newspapers in November 1938 were horrified at the headlines reporting what became known as the Night of Broken Glass: "Nazis Smash, Loot and Burn Jewish Shops and Temples Until Goebbels Calls Halt."[69] Homes were attacked and thousands of Jewish men arrested. Essential to the success of this pogrom was the prohibition on possessing arms:

> One of the first legal measures issued was an order by Heinrich Himmler, commander of all German police, forbidding Jews to possess any weapons whatever and imposing a penalty of 20 years confinement in a concentration camp upon every Jew found in possession of a weapon hereafter.[70]

The following year, after Hitler launched World War II by attacking

Poland, Americans would read about a U.S. citizen originally from Poland being executed by the Nazis for "having concealed a considerable quantity of arms and ammunition in violation of German regulations."[71] And fast-forwarding yet another year, with the collapse of France, the headlines read: "German Army Decrees Death for Those Retaining Arms and Radio Senders."[72] The *Times* observed:

> The best way to sum up the disciplinary laws imposed upon France by the German conqueror is to say that the Nazi decrees reduce the French people to as low a condition as that occupied by the German people. Military orders now forbid the French to do things which the German people have not been allowed to do since Hitler came to power. To own radio senders or to listen to foreign broadcasts, to organize public meetings and distribute pamphlets, to disseminate anti-German news in any form, to retain possession of firearms—all these things are prohibited for the subjugated people of France, as they have been verboten these half dozen years to the people of Germany.[73]

Given these events, Americans were in no mood to accept inroads on their own Second Amendment rights. Domestic prohibitionists had turned from violent crime to subversion as the excuse for watering down the right to bear arms. Not unexpectedly, they found little support. The *Times* reported:

> In the face of pleas for compulsory registration of firearms as a defense measure against fifth columnists, the National Conference of Commissioners on Uniform State Laws voted today, by a large majority, to exclude from its proposed Uniform Pistol Act a clause compelling householders to register their weapons . . . The suggested law retains the traditional right of the American citizen to keep arms as a matter of protection.[74]

Nonetheless, firearm registration was advocated by U.S. attorney general Robert H. Jackson, who recommended to Congress laws making wiretapping easier, indeterminate criminal sentencing, and "a law for national registration of firearms now exempt from such listing."[75] That would have meant that ordinary rifles, pistols, and shotguns would have been required to be registered, as were machine guns under the National Firearms Act of 1934. That proposal, made in early 1941, set off alarm bells among firearm owners and their allies in Congress.

Indeed, Jackson had argued two years earlier in the U.S. Supreme Court that the Second Amendment right is "only one which exists where the arms are borne in the militia or some other military organization provided for by law and intended for the protection of the state."[76] In deciding *United States v. Miller* (1939), the Supreme Court disregarded that argument, ruling instead that the Second Amendment protects possession of a firearm that "is any part of the ordinary military equipment or that its use could contribute to the common defense."[77] *Miller* focused on the nature of the arm, not on whether the possessor was a militia member.

In mid-1941, citing intelligence from a "source close to one of the groups which has been agitating for registration of all firearms," C. B. Lister, secretary-treasurer of the National Rifle Association, warned Representative Edwin Arthur Hall of New York that "an attempt might be made to incorporate such Federal registration of firearms in the pending tax bill."[78]

Soon after, in a hearing before the House Committee on Military Affairs, Representative Paul Kilday, a Democrat from Texas, attempted to ask questions of Under Secretary of War Robert P. Patterson, concerning a bill to allow the president to requisition property from civilians: "The reason I ask that is somebody made the boast they were going to get the other [firearms] legislation under this bill!" However, the committee then went into executive session, and the record does not reflect what happened next.[79]

As originally proposed in the Senate, the bill in question—S.1579— gave the president wide powers to authorize the requisition of machinery and other property of value for the national defense on payment of just compensation. The House Committee on Military Affairs added the following qualifications to the bill:

> That nothing herein contained shall be construed to authorize the requisition or require the registration of any firearms possessed by any individual for his personal protection or sport (and the possession of which is not prohibited nor the registration thereof required); nor shall this Act in any manner impair or infringe the right of any individual to keep and bear arms.[80]

The Committee Report included this explanation about the reason for adding this provision:

> It is not contemplated or even inferred that the President, or any executive board, agency, or officer, would trespass upon the right of the people in this respect. There appears to be no occasion for the requisition of firearms owned and maintained by the people for sport and recreation, nor is there any desire or intention on the part of the Congress or the President to impair or infringe the right of the people under section 2 [sic] of the Constitution of the United States, which reads, in part as follows: "the right of the people to keep and bear arms shall not be infringed." However, in view of the fact that certain totalitarian and dictatorial nations are now engaged in the willful and wholesale destruction of personal rights and liberties, our committee deem it appropriate for the Congress to expressly state that the proposed legislation shall not be construed to impair or infringe the constitutional right of the people to bear arms. In so doing, it will be manifest that, although the Congress deems it expedient to grant certain extraordinary powers to the Executive in furtherance of the common defense during critical times, there is no disposition on the part of this

Government to depart from the concepts and principles of personal rights and liberties expressed in our Constitution.[81]

While the declaration about the right to keep and bear arms was welcome, supporters of the Second Amendment were not so sure that no one contemplated future infringements. When the bill hit the House floor on August 5, Congressman Hall described what was happening abroad and anticipated violations here as follows:

> Before the advent of Hitler or Stalin, who took power from the German and Russian people, measures were thrust upon the free legislatures of those countries to deprive the people of the possession and use of firearms, so that they could not resist the encroachments of such diabolical and vitriolic state police organizations as the Gestapo, the Ogpu, and the Cheka. Just as sure as I am standing here today, you are going to see this measure followed by legislation, sponsored by the proponents of such encroachment upon the rights of the people, which will eventually deprive the people of their constitutional liberty which provides for the possession of firearms for the protection of their homes.
>
> I submit to you that it is a serious departure from constitutional government when we consider legislation of this type. I predict that within 6 months of this time there will be presented to this House a measure which will go a long way toward taking away forever the individual rights and liberties of citizens of this Nation by depriving the individual of the private ownership of firearms and the right to use weapons in the protection of his home, and thereby his country.[82]

Representative Walter G. Andrews of New York responded that the bill was strongly advocated by Under Secretary of War Patterson.[83]

The Senate then considered the House amendment. Senator Tom Connally of Texas described it as "safeguarding the right of individuals to possess arms."[84] Senator Albert B. Chandler of Kentucky argued that "we have no reason to take the personal property of individuals which is kept solely for protection of their homes."[85] Delegates to a conference committee were appointed.[86]

The conference committee deleted the ban on registration, but kept the declaration against infringing the right to bear arms.[87] In support of that version, Representative A.J. May, a Kentucky Democrat and conference manager, recalled the remarks in executive session of the under secretary of war in the Military Affairs Committee:

> Judge Patterson before the committee stated in answer to a question that the War Department had been considering regulations with respect to the requisitioning of personal property, that it had not yet occurred to them . . . that they might be called upon to register arms. If they were called upon to register arms, I do not think they would go out and say to every farmer in this country, to every workingman in this country, to every citizen, businessman, or whatever profession or calling he may have, that he must register the weapons he might have in his home, but to guard against that we undertook to give these brethren here concerned about their guns the proper kind of protection, and we did it in the language of the Constitution, or as nearly as we could, and I quote from the report: "Nothing contained in this act shall be construed to impair or infringe in any manner the right of any individual to keep and bear arms."[88]

Congressman May added his understanding of the Second Amendment as follows: "the right to keep means that a man can keep a gun in his house and can carry it with him if he wants to; he can take it where he wants to . . . and the right to bear arms means that he can go hunting . . . and that nobody has any right, so long as he bears the arms openly and unconcealed, to interfere with him."[89]

Commenting on registration, Representative Dewey Short of Missouri explained, "The method employed by the Communists in every country that has been overthrown has been to disarm the populace, take away their firearms with which to defend themselves, in order to overthrow the Government."[90] Representative Paul Kilday of Texas put it in historical perspective:

> For a period of perhaps 15 years there has been an element in this country seeking to require the registration of all firearms. That bill has been offered in almost every Congress during that period of time. It has never been reported out of the Committee on the Judiciary, and we now have another one of those subterfuges of getting under the name of national defense something that they have not been able to get over a period of years.
>
> I call attention to section 4 of this act, which provides that the President shall have the power to administer the provisions of the act, through any officer or agency that he may determine and to require such information as he may deem necessary in carrying out the provisions of the act. That gives the power to require the registration of every firearm in the United States because knowledge of the location and the owner would be the first information necessary for requisition.[91]

Merely enacting the words of the Second Amendment in the bill, Kilday noted, would provide no real protection:

> We are in the ridiculous position of being asked to vote for an amendment which copies the language of the Constitution into an

act of Congress . . . At the proper time I propose to offer a motion to recommit the conference report to the conference committee, to the end that they may pass on this and incorporate my amendment which provided that the bill shall not be construed to give the Government the power to requisition a firearm possessed by an individual, nor to require the registration of it. That must be put in here in order to make the bill constitutional. Judge Patterson testified. His one example was that they might need shotguns, and he felt that if they need shotguns they should have the right to take them from anybody.[92]

Kilday was referring to the remarks in executive session by Under Secretary of War Patterson in the Military Affairs Committee. Kilday further recalled, "Judge Patterson said they had already made their plans to require registration . . . Remember that registration of firearms is only the first step. It will be followed by other infringements of the right to keep and bear arms until finally the right is gone."[93]

Noting that the Russian Communist experience taught the wisdom of Second Amendment protection for "our right to bear arms as private citizens," Representative Lyle H. Boren, an Oklahoma Democrat, averred, "The gun I own in my home is essential to maintaining the defense of my home against the aggression of lawlessness."[94] He added about the American way of life:

I propose to defend it against the soldiers of a Hitler and against a government bureaucrat. All the invasions threatened against American democracy are not from without. I feel that the defense of democracy is on my doorstep and your doorstep as well as on the world's battlefields . . . I rebel against the destruction of freedom in America under the guise of emergency.[95]

Representative John William Wright Patman, a Texas Democrat, noted the constitutional safeguard provided by the framers against abuse of power by the president, who controlled both the army and the state militias when federalized. The answer was:

> The people have a right to bear arms. The people have a right to keep arms; therefore, if we should have some Executive who attempted to set himself up as dictator or king, the people can organize themselves together and, with the arms and ammunition they have, they can properly protect themselves . . .
>
> If we permit the people here in Washington to compel the people all over the Nation to turn in their arms, their ammunition, then the Chief Executive, whoever he is, gets control of the Army and the militia, how will the people be able to protect themselves?[96]

Patman characterized as "meaningless" the bill's language, repeating the Second Amendment guarantee. "The Constitution guarantees to the people those rights which they have asserted in this bill."[97]

"The Constitution guarantees to every citizen the right to keep and bears arms," asserted Representative John J. Sparkman, an Alabama Democrat. But he conceded that Under Secretary Patterson had stated that, if "it is necessary to take our shotguns, we ought to have the power to do it." Indeed, Sparkman even said, "If in order to defend this country it is necessary to come into my home and take my shotgun, my pistol, my rifle, or anything else I have . . . I say you are welcome to do it."[98] What distinguished this from totalitarianism was left unclear.

That argument fell on deaf ears, and the motion to recommit the bill to committee then passed by 154 to 24.[99] The resulting new conference report restored the ban on firearm registration.[100]

As passed and signed by President Franklin Roosevelt, the Property Requisition Act authorized the president to requisition broad categories of property with military uses from the private sector on payment of fair compensation, subject to the following:

Nothing contained in this Act shall be construed

(1) to authorize the requisitioning or require the registration of any firearms possessed by any individual for his personal protection or sport (and the possession of which is not prohibited or the registration of which is not required by existing law), [or]

(2) to impair or infringe in any manner the right of any individual to keep and bear arms.[101]

This law bore witness to the value that any war would be fought to preserve the Bill of Rights and other liberties, not to destroy them. And it was fitting that the Second Amendment would be declared to be of special importance as war clouds loomed, for Americans who were accustomed to keeping and bearing arms would make superior riflemen. In fact, the National Rifle Association played an instrumental role in training civilians in marksmanship throughout the war.

In less than two months after passage of the Act, the Japanese attack on Pearl Harbor would drag the United States into World War II. It was then a fight to the death to preserve freedom, and it would be victorious.

The Firearms Owners' Protection Act of 1986: The Rights of Citizens to Keep and Bear Arms

The world had changed considerably by the time Congress enacted the Gun Control Act of 1968. A new generation of zealots pushed the envelope against constitutional rights in favor of unprecedented powers being grabbed by the federal government. The Gun Control Act intruded into traditional areas of state regulation and created numerous victimless crimes, such as making it a felony to transfer a firearm to a person in another state, to sell an unspecified number of guns without a license, or to commit other harmless acts without any intent to violate the law.

By this time, prohibitionists denied that the Second Amendment protected any individual right whatsoever. U.S. attorney general Ramsey Clark led the charge for a bill to require the registration of all firearms and to imprison those who failed to comply.[102] After Michigan Congressman John Dingell, a Democrat, recalled how the Nazis used registration records to confiscate firearms, the Johnson administration produced a report reaching the preposterous conclusion that "there is no significant relationship between gun laws and the rise of dictators."[103] NRA officials testifying before the committee recalled the language of the Property Requisition Act, but the prohibitionists were in denial.

The prohibitionists' registration bill was defeated. Moreover, as passed, the Gun Control Act included a preamble that eschewed any intent to burden law-abiding citizens, although it included no explicit reference to the Second Amendment. In the ensuing years, however, experience substantiated the predictions of the act's opponents that the law would be used to ensnare innocent citizens. The enforcement policies of the Bureau of Alcohol, Tobacco, and Firearms (BATF) led to numerous abuses that would be well documented in Congressional hearings beginning in the late 1970s.

Increasing awareness in Congress of the need for reform led to the enactment of the Firearms Owners' Protection Act of 1986 (FOPA). FOPA represents the third time Congress made clear by statute that the Second Amendment enshrines an individual right. Actually, FOPA declared that the existing Gun Control Act and its enforcement by BATF needed correction in light of several constitutional rights as follows:

The Congress finds that

(1) the rights of citizens

(A) to keep and bear arms under the second amendment to the United States Constitution;

(B) to security against illegal and unreasonable searches and seizures under the fourth amendment;

(C) against uncompensated taking of property, double jeopardy, and assurance of due process of law under the fifth amendment; and

(D) against unconstitutional exercise of authority under the ninth and tenth amendments; require additional legislation to correct existing firearms statutes and enforcement policies; and

(2) additional legislation is required to reaffirm the intent of the Congress, as expressed in section 101 of the Gun Control Act of 1968, that "it is not the purpose of this title to place any undue or unnecessary Federal restrictions or burdens on law-abiding citizens with respect to the acquisition, possession, or use of firearms appropriate to the purpose of hunting, trap shooting, target shooting, personal protection, or any other lawful activity, and that this title is not intended to discourage or eliminate the private ownership or use of firearms by law-abiding citizens for lawful purposes.[104]

The finding in FOPA that the Second Amendment guarantees the rights of citizens to keep and bear arms was supported by a comprehensive report by the Senate's Subcommittee on the Constitution, which stated:

The conclusion is thus inescapable that the history, concept, and wording of the second amendment to the Constitution of the United States, as well as its interpretation by every major commentator and court in the first half-century after its ratification, indicates that what is protected is an individual right of a private citizen to own and carry firearms in a peaceful manner.[105]

In FOPA's substantive reforms, Congress implemented its recognition that the Second Amendment guarantees individual rights by deregulating substantially the purchase, sale, and possession of firearms, and by requiring proof of a "willful" or "knowing" violation for conviction under the law.

FOPA further enforced Second Amendment rights and reflected Congress's traditional rejection of registration in the following provision:

No such rule or regulation prescribed after the date of the enactment of the Firearms Owners' Protection Act may require that records required to be maintained under this chapter or any portion of the contents of such records, be recorded at or transferred to a facility owned, managed, or controlled by the United States or any State or any political subdivision thereof, nor that any system of registration of firearms, firearms owners, or firearms transactions or dispositions be established.[106]

Another important FOPA reform was the provision preempting state laws that prohibit travelers from transporting firearms throughout the United States.[107] This reflected Congress's recognition that the Second Amendment protects the individual right to keep and bear arms, which was made applicable to the states through the Fourteenth Amendment. Idaho senator Steve Symms introduced this provision with the explanation, "The intent of this amendment . . . is to protect the Second Amendment rights of law-abiding citizens wishing to transport firearms through States which otherwise prohibit the possession of such weapons."[108] In the House, Rep. Tommy Robinson of Arkansas stated that "our citizens have a constitutional right to bear arms . . . and to travel interstate with those weapons."[109]

FOPA, which was signed into law by President Ronald Reagan, represents a high-water mark for protection of Second Amendment rights by the U.S. Congress. When the Clinton administration pursued anti–Second Amendment policies, the American electorate cleaned house beginning in 1994, making further passage of prohibitionist legislation in Congress difficult. At the state level, the passage of "Right-to-Carry" laws ushered in further defeats for the prohibitionists, who then turned to the courts. They launched abusive lawsuits against the firearms industry, hoping to blackmail it through the threat of bankruptcy, and to destroy the Second Amendment by coercing manufacturers into submitting to extensive restrictions on the sales, marketing, and design of firearms.

The Protection of Lawful Commerce in Arms Act of 2005: To Preserve a Citizen's Access to Firearms

The prohibitionist attempt to bypass the legislative process and ban guns through litigation led Congress to enact the Protection of Lawful Commerce in Arms Act ("PLCAA") in 2005.[110] This Act represents the fourth occasion in the history of the U.S. Congress in which that body interpreted the Second Amendment to protect individual rights.

PLCAA is self-described as: "an Act to prohibit civil liability actions from being brought or continued against manufacturers, distributors, dealers, or importers of firearms or ammunition for damages, injunctive or other relief resulting from the misuse of their products by others." The bill was in response to more than thirty lawsuits brought by municipalities against the firearms industry aimed at ruining the industry and shutting down firearms commerce. The legislation was supported by the National Rifle Association, the Department of Defense, the National Association of Manufacturers, the

U.S. Chamber of Commerce, United Mine Workers of America, and other business and union organizations.

PLCAA begins with findings that go directly to the heart of the matter:

Congress finds the following:

(1) The Second Amendment to the United States Constitution provides that the right of the people to keep and bear arms shall not be infringed.

(2) The Second Amendment to the United States Constitution protects the rights of individuals, including those who are not members of a militia or engaged in military service or training, to keep and bear arms.[111]

The Act recognizes that having arms is a constitutional right, and thus it makes no sense to sanction lawsuits against federally licensed manufacturers merely for making this constitutionally protected product. Moreover, Congress asserted its constitutional power to protect Second Amendment rights.

Lawsuits were filed against the firearms industry for damages and other relief for the harm caused by criminals and other third parties who misuse firearms.[112] However, the manufacture, importation, possession, sale, and use of firearms and ammunition are heavily regulated by federal, state, and local laws.[113]

The Supreme Court of Illinois recognized this plain fact in 2004, ruling in *Chicago v. Beretta* (2004):

It seems that plaintiffs seek injunctive relief from this court because relief has not been forthcoming from the General Assembly. We are reluctant to interfere in the lawmaking process in the manner suggested by plaintiffs, especially when the product at issue is already so heavily regulated by both the state and federal governments. We, therefore, conclude that there are strong public policy reasons to defer to the legislature in the matter of regulating the manufacture, distribution, and sale of firearms.

Indeed, the federal Gun Control Act was originally passed under the Interstate Commerce Clause, adding further justification for this act. As the findings stated, businesses "are engaged in interstate and foreign commerce through the lawful design, manufacture, marketing, distribution, importation, or sale to the public of firearms or ammunition that has been shipped or transported in interstate or foreign commerce," and they should not be liable for the harm caused by unlawful misuse of firearms that function as designed and intended.[114]

Such imposition of liability on an industry abuses the legal system, erodes public confidence in the law, "threatens the diminution of a basic constitutional right and civil liberty," destabilizes other industries in the free enterprise system of the United States, and "constitutes an unreasonable burden on interstate and foreign commerce of the United States."[115]

Such liability actions, commenced by various state politicians, urban officials, and gun-ban groups, were unprecedented and not a bona fide expansion of the common law. The sustaining of these actions by a "maverick" judge or jury would expand liability in a manner never contemplated by Constitution's framers or by the federal or state legislatures. Congress's enforcement power under the Fourteenth Amendment was made clear in the further finding: "Such an expansion of liability would constitute a deprivation of the rights, privileges, and immunities guaranteed to a citizen of the United States under the Fourteenth Amendment to the United States Constitution."[116] Those rights include the right to keep and bear arms and the right to due process of law.

The liability actions at issue "attempt to use the judicial branch to circumvent the legislative branch of government to regulate interstate and foreign commerce through judgments and judicial decrees," undermining the separation of powers, federalism, state sovereignty, and comity between the sister states.[117]

PLCAA also included purposes clauses that further defined its constitutional bases. The immediate purpose was to prohibit causes of action against the firearms industry for harm caused by criminals and others who unlawfully misuse firearms.[118]

The values of the Second Amendment were reflected in the goal "to preserve a citizen's access to a supply of firearms and ammunition for all lawful purposes, including hunting, self-defense, collecting, and competitive or recreational shooting," and "to guarantee a citizen's rights, privileges, and immunities, as applied to the States, under the Fourteenth Amendment to the United States Constitution, pursuant to section 5 of that Amendment."[119] Section 5 is the Enforcement Clause, which allows Congress to enforce rights against state or local government violation.

Besides preventing such lawsuits from imposing "unreasonable burdens on interstate and foreign commerce,"[120] the law also protects the First Amendment rights of members of the firearms industry, including their trade associations, "to speak freely, to assemble peaceably, and to petition the Government for a redress of their grievances."[121]

PLCAA's substantive provision stated: "A qualified civil liability action may not be brought in any Federal or State court." Any such pending action "shall be dismissed immediately."[122] The rest of the law defined the nature of the prohibited civil action in contrast with the types of traditional actions, which would remain unaffected.

Debate on the bill focused on the substantive liability issues and proposed amendments. The propositions contained in the findings and purposes that the Second and Fourteenth Amendments guarantee an individual right to keep and bear arms went virtually uncontested.

Senator John Thune of South Dakota set the tone when he averred, "This bill is about law abiding gun owners, it is about law abiding gun dealers, it is about law abiding gun manufacturers who are having that Second Amendment right infringed upon by those who are trying to destroy an industry."[123] And Senator Larry Craig of Idaho—the bill's chief sponsor—maintained, "The Constitution also, I believe, imposes upon Congress the duty to protect the liberties enshrined in the Bill of Rights which includes the Second Amendment. If the firearms manufacturers are driven out of business, that Second Amendment will be nothing more than an illusion."[124]

Opponents of firearm ownership previously denied that the Second Amendment protected any individual rights, but in this debate hypocritically attempted to wrap themselves in the Amendment. New York Senator Chuck Schumer, a consistent antigun advocate, uttered these words: "The right to guns is a good thing. I support the Second Amendment." He then contradicted those words by vehemently urging defeat of the bill.[125]

The bill would pass the Senate with sixty-five yeas and thirty-one nays, a very comfortable margin.[126] This victory never would have been achieved without majority leader Bill Frist of Tennessee and his tireless efforts to ensure that the bill received a fair hearing and that it was not "poisoned" with antigun amendments. Sen. Max Baucus of Montana helped Senator Craig marshal this reform effort through the Senate, aided by strong support from Senate majority whip Mitch McConnell of Kentucky and Senate Republican Conference chairman Rick Santorum of Pennsylvania. A filibuster-proof sixty votes were needed to ensure PLCAA's passage; of course, this would have been impossible without support from senators from both parties, and that certainly included minority leader Harry Reid of Nevada.

In House debate, representative Lamar Smith of Texas declared, "to allow frivolous lawsuits to constrain the right of Americans to lawfully use guns is both irresponsible and unconstitutional."[127] Noting the need to stop "this abuse of the legal process," representative Sam Graves of Missouri explained: "This bill will protect the firearms industry from lawsuits based on the criminal or unlawful third party misuse of their products. This law is necessary to prevent a few state courts from undermining our Second Amendment rights guaranteed by the Constitution."[128]

Representative Joe Schwarz of Michigan said it in a nutshell:

The Second Amendment was not written as a mere exercise in constitutional thought. It had a practical purpose: first, to ensure that citizens would have the tools to protect their families and their homes and, second, to ensure that an armed militia could be called up to defend the country in emergencies.[129]

The PLCAA—with Cliff Stearns of Florida and Rick Boucher of Virginia its chief House sponsors—passed the House overwhelmingly with 283 yeas and 144 nays[130] and was promptly signed into law by president George W. Bush. The anti—Second Amendment litigators, who earlier filed the abusive lawsuits the act was designed to eliminate, filed motions claiming that the PLCAA was unconstitutional.

In 2008 and 2010, large bipartisan majorities of both houses of Congress joined in amicus curiae briefs to the United States Supreme Court, in *District of Columbia v. Heller*, and *McDonald v. Chicago*. The briefs explained to the Court the history of congressional protection of the individual Second Amendment right to keep and bear arms for all lawful purposes.

Future history will determine if Congress will deem it necessary once again to protect the Second Amendment rights of American citizens. When Congress construes a Bill of Rights guarantee broadly, it reflects the interests of the people at large, who influence Congress through the rights of petition and suffrage.

Congress has reaffirmed and embellished the Second Amendment on four occasions. In the Freedmen's Bureau Act of 1866, Congress guaranteed to the freed slaves "full and equal benefit of all laws and proceedings concerning personal liberty, personal liberty, and . . . estate, . . . including the constitutional right to bear arms." Again, in the wartime Property Requisition Act of 1941, Congress prohibited any construction that would "require the registration of any firearm possessed by any individual for his personal protection or sport" or would "infringe in any manner the right of any individual to keep and bear arms."

In the Firearms Owners' Protection Act of 1986, Congress found that "the rights of citizens . . . to keep and bear arms under the Second Amendment to the United States Constitution" required legislation to correct the Gun Control Act and BATF enforcement policies, and enforced this with a prohibition on the registration of firearms owners. And finally, in the Protection of Lawful Commerce in Arms Act of 2005, Congress sought to protect the supply of firearms, declaring that the Second Amendment "protects the rights of individuals, including those who are not members of a militia or engaged in military service or training, to keep and bear arms."

As the branch elected by the people, the U.S. Congress fulfills its proper function when it affirms and protects the constitutional rights of the people. This role is essential to the checks and balances necessary to prevent power from being concentrated in one branch of government. Great weight should be accorded to the repeated determinations by Congress, over a long historical period and in vastly different historical circumstances, that the right to keep and bear arms is a fundamental, individual right that government may not infringe.

Yet while Congress has been working in the twenty-first century to protect the right to arms in the United States, the United Nations has been working to isolate the United States. What the U.N. has done shows the death and suffering that can ensue when the universal human right of self-defense is destroyed.

Chapter 7

U.N. Gun Prohibition: One Country at a Time

The United Nations has not yet succeeded in imposing worldwide gun prohibition, but several countries provide a preview for what the U.N. wants. In these countries, the U.N. has inflicted total gun prohibition, enforced with severe penalties and house-to-house military searches, notwithstanding plain evidence that such a policy leaves innocent families defenseless against violent criminals. These violent criminals often work together with corrupt governments that refuse to protect the innocent. The U.N.'s gun prohibition, and its cooperation with international human trafficking, violates several human rights Declarations and Treaties created by the U.N. itself.

International data show that nations that respect the right of lawful gun ownership have greater freedom, more prosperity, and less violent crime. David Kopel, Carl Moody, and Howard Nemerov examined that data from the fifty-nine nations for which there is available information about per capita gun ownership. The authors investigated the relationships between gun density, freedom, and prosperity. The data showed that "the nations with the highest rates of gun ownership tend to have greater political and civil freedom, greater economic freedom and prosperity, and much less corruption than other nations. The relationship only exists for high-ownership countries. Countries with medium rates of gun density generally scored no better or worse than countries with the lowest levels of gun rates."[1] The three authors acknowledge that disentangling cause and effect can be difficult. One explanation that makes a lot of sense to me is that gun owners acquire a strong sense of personal responsibility and competence, and this attitude helps make them more active in civic life in order to protect all forms of political, civil, and economic freedom.[2]

Don Kates and Gary Mauser studied the homicide and suicide rates for all continental European nations for which data on homicide, suicide, and gun ownership were available. They found that the evidence overwhelmingly contradicted the theory that more guns lead to higher rates of murder or suicide."[3]

Uganda

The international gun banners have invented the phrase "forcible disarmament" as a euphemism for gun confiscation. IANSA and Control Arms complain incessantly about the human rights abuses that supposedly are caused by people owning firearms. Yet the international lobbies are remarkably silent about the human rights abuses that take place when the government decides to round up all the guns.[4]

Here's how "forcible disarmament" works in Uganda. The army targets a village in northern Uganda. The army brings in tanks and helicopter gunships. Then they incinerate the village, sexually torture the men, rape the women, and loot whatever they can find. The army takes whatever guns are found in the charred remnants of the village or whose locations were revealed by torture. Human rights scholar Ben Knighton called the process "ethnocide," since it is used to destroy the particular tribes that have been targeted for "forcible disarmament."[5] Because of what the gun ban groups call a "gun safety" campaign, many thousands of people are now refugees.

Previous dictators in Uganda, such as Idi Amin and Milton Obote, used gun confiscation as part of programs of mass murder. The current gun round-up got started in December 2001, when the United Nations urged the authoritarian government of Yoweri Museveni to initiate "voluntary" disarmament.[6] Fewer than 20 percent of the targeted guns were surrendered, so the army stepped up the program to "forcible disarmament."

The Ugandan government has used U.N. gun control as a pretext, according to David Pulkol, who once served as a director of a Ugandan government intelligence agency;[7] the real purpose of disarmament is government theft of the natural resources of the northern ethnic groups, who are called the Karamojong.

In 2006, the United Nations Development Programme, to its credit, cut off its disarmament funding for Uganda.[8] But UNDP funding resumed in 2007 for "voluntary" gun surrender programs run by various nongovernment organizations (NGOs). But even though Louise Arbour, the then United Nations high commissioner for human rights, criticized the village-burning program, she still provided diplomatic cover, stating that "the decision of the Government to undertake renewed efforts to eradicate illegal weapons in Karamoja is essential."[9]

Kenya

The pastoral tribes of northeastern Uganda also live across the border in Kenya. Like many pastoral peoples around the world, they have long had a high rate of arms ownership. Kilfemarian Gebre-Wold, who used to run a disarmament program in the area, admits that "though many pastoralist households have small arms, the rate of crime and violent incidents is not high in their community . . . the density of weapons does not mean automatically the rise of gun-related violence."[10]

Other NGOs, however, insist that the guns must be taken.[11] According to Oxfam (which is itself a major antigun lobby, and which teamed up with IANSA and Amnesty International to create the "Control Arms" lobby) says that Kenya must have "community arms collection and voluntary arms surrender activities."[12]

The Kenyan arms control laws theoretically allow people to own firearms or bows, with a proper license. In practice, only the rich or the politically powerful can obtain licenses.[13] Although the gun-ban lobbies say that women have a natural instinct to abhor guns, in Kenya "there are anecdotal reports of women defending themselves with guns . . . Women often request ownership of their man's gun if he is killed."[14]

The Kenyan gun confiscation program has been enforced by indiscriminate violence, as the tribespeople continue to resist more than a century of government efforts to take their arms.[15] An example of the violence of gun confiscation was the joint Kenya/Uganda army operation that began in 2005, called "Operation NYUNDO."[16] Kenyan political activist Krop Muroto explains: "No one knows to date how many people were killed in that operation that lasted three months. The community was further devastated by mass killing of their cattle. 20,000 head of cattle were confiscated, rounded up in sheds and starved to death. Among other atrocities . . . the army used helicopter gunships, killed people and destroyed a lot of property."[17]

According to *Reuters*:

Lopokoy Kolimuk, an elder in the dusty and dry village of Kanyarkwat in the West Pokot district, said the soldiers who carried out that mission were wild, beyond humanity. He said many shot Pokots [a people of western Kenya and eastern Uganda] on sight, or forced men to lie on the ground in a line as they ran across their backs. Other men had their testicles tied together and were then made to run away from each other, he said. Women were raped in front of their husbands, sometimes with empty beer bottles.[18]

Operation "Okota" [Collect] began in 2006.[19] The army used tanks and helicopters to attack villages. The government had already announced that it was ready to repeat the atrocities of an infamous 1984 gun confiscation assault on the region, so thousands of people fled.[20]

For the gun prohibitionists who fetishize gun confiscation, the operation was a big success. Seventy firearms were confiscated.[21] To anyone who truly cares about human rights, turning thousands and thousands of people into refugees in order to take a few dozen guns was terrible.

Later that year, the Kenyan government stopped using the military for gun confiscation, and said that it would allow NGOs to take the lead in voluntary gun surrender programs.[22] The Ugandan army continues to enter Kenya, where it loots villages, rustles cattle, and takes guns.[23]

South Africa

South Africa's harsh 2000 Firearms Control Act is a model for the international gun ban movement. As I note in chapter 19, the Axis of Soros has tried to push South African–style laws in Costa Rica and Panama.

The law is the creation of the lobbying organization Gun Free South Africa (GFSA). The group's name shows that the group is committed to the obliteration of a civil right—much like a similar group that might have been called "Church-Free Albania" (when an atheistic communist dictatorship ruled that country) or "Newspaper-Free Kampuchea" (when Cambodia was ruled by the Khmer Rouge), or "Jew-Free Saudi Arabia" (since no Jews are allowed to enter that country).

In *A Nation without Guns: The Story of Gun Free South Africa*, Adèle Kirsten tells the story of how she led GFSA to victory. The introduction is titled "The Art of Breaking the Gun," and is written by Rubem César Fernandes, the executive director of the Brazilian gun confiscation lobby Viva Rio.[24]

GFSA was part of the Axis of Soros from the very beginning. It was and is funded by the Open Society Foundation for South Africa, which is the South African branch of Soros's empire. When Soros and his chief henchwoman, Rebecca Peters, set up the global gun prohibition lobby IANSA, GFSA was a founding member, and on the executive committee; one of GFSA's organizers has risen to the rank of IANSA coordinator for Africa.[25]

The South African law was intended to end decisively the notion of some South Africans that there is a right to own firearms, or to protect oneself with a firearm.[26] It was part of a culture war against white farmers, retaliation for their having failed to fight sufficiently against apartheid, and a means of putting them in their place in the new South Africa by taking away a major tool and symbol of their self-reliance and freedom.

The irony is that it was "the gun lobby" itself that pushed for racial equality during the apartheid period. The South African Gun Owners Association (SAGA) was founded in 1984, in response to a government proposal to restrict the type and number of firearms a person could own. SAGA then worked successfully to change the firearms law so that people of color could be issued licenses. (Unfortunately, nonwhite applicants were sometimes thwarted by police abuse.)[27]

The highly restrictive 2000 law was imposed by the government of South Africa's then president Thabo Mbeki. The Mbeki government violated its very own law in order to help China supply arms to Zimbabwe's genocidal tyrant Robert Mugabe.

The South African law is worth examining in detail, because it is a model for how to disarm people in the guise of enforcing a law that supposedly is based only on "reasonable" regulations.

First of all, to have a gun license, you must pass a test on gun laws. Like voting literacy tests in the Jim Crow era in the United States, these tests are mainly used to prevent people from exercising their rights.

South Africa has eleven official languages, but the test is available in only two of them.[28] You can only take the test at an official test center, which is fine if you live in a big city, but is hard on the half of the population that lives in rural areas.[29] Because South Africa is one of the most crime-ridden nations in the world, intercity travel is extremely dangerous, so a rural person who wants a gun license must risk her life in order to get to the government test center.

If you survive the trip to the test center, and happen to speak one of the test languages, your troubles are just beginning. The Firearms Control Act says that a license "may" be issued for purposes including hunting, target shooting, collecting, or self-defense.[30] Yet the police often refuse to issue licenses, and will not explain why the license was not issued.[31] They abuse the licensing system the same way government officials in places such as New Jersey or California abuse the "may issue" licenses for carrying a defensive handgun: they don't like anyone having guns, so they simply decide that nobody, or hardly anybody, ever has a good enough reason to have a license. For example, a South African businessman who must transport thousands of dollars in cash to a bank for deposit was told that his purpose of protecting himself from being murdered during a robbery was not a "good reason" for having a gun.[32]

Abios Khoele, who is the founder of South Africa's Black Gun Owners' Association, reported, "In our townships, it is not safe at all, especially for people who are taking early transport to work, when it's still dark and they're walking a long distance . . . Those people are sick and tired of crime, and they have no other way of dealing with the situation."[33]

Thanks in part to the gun laws, South Africa is a rapist's paradise. The chance that a South African woman will be raped one or more times during her lifetime is somewhere in the 50 to 80 percent range.[34] Many South Africans believe that raping a virgin is a cure for AIDS, so the rape of children is common. Many rape victims get AIDS and die from it.[35]

Yet the police usually say that a woman's desire to protect herself from rapists is not a good enough reason to have a gun.[36] Over half the members of Black Gun Owners' Association are women; when they apply for a gun license, the police tell them, "Your husband will provide your security."[37] As if women should live by Taliban standards, and never leave the home except when with the husband. A woman who carries a gun without a permit can be imprisoned up to twenty-five years.[38]

If the police do not formally reject your application, it may sit in a pile for years. In the meantime, it is illegal for you to own a gun, or even to retain the gun you already own, since licenses must be renewed every five years.

Deliberately abusive enforcement of the South African firearms law has destroyed the businesses of 90 percent of South Africa's firearms dealers, since their customer base has been decimated.[39] Adèle Kirsten—the Axis of Soros lobbyist who masterminded the 2000 law—explains that 640 out of

720 licensed gun dealers were put out of business; she calls this an important "achievement" that helps in "creating a climate in which gun ownership in South Africa is no longer seen as a norm."[40]

South Africa has one of the worst violent crime problems in the world. For years the government tried to suppress accurate data about crime, and even claimed that violent crime rate was going down. In fact, it is skyrocketing.[41]

The gun prohibition lobbies claim that people should not be allowed to have guns for protection because the government will protect them. As South Africa shows, that is a deadly lie.

The South African government has been an enthusiastic cheerleader for using the United Nations to restrict your Second Amendment rights—an obvious interference in American domestic policy. Yet when the powers of dictators—rather than the rights of free citizens—are involved, the South African government develops a highly scrupulous aversion to U.N. interference.

The government pro-rape policy on gun licenses is matched by a pro-rape foreign policy. At the U.N., South Africa opposed a U.S.-sponsored General Assembly resolution condemning the government use of rape as a political tactic. Although the resolution did not mention any specific countries, the subtext was concern about use of rape by the dictatorships of Sudan and Burma.[42]

The South African government is not only Best Friends Forever with the mass murderer Robert Mugabe; it is also an ardent supporter of the Burmese military dictatorship that has long been persecuting various ethnic groups, such as the Karen. After South Africa voted against Security Council sanctions on Burma, a leader of the largest opposition party in South Africa, Douglas Gibson, asked, "Will South Africa ever meet a dictator it does not like?" If other countries had followed the current South African government's policy of ignoring human rights abuses in other countries, then the racist apartheid regime in South Africa itself would still be in power.[43] Unfortunately for the people of South Africa and the world, the current South African regime is, like its apartheid predecessor, an enemy of human rights.

Cambodia

When Cambodia was a French colony, from 1863 to 1953, the French rulers passed many laws to prevent the Cambodian peasants from arming.[44] On April 17, 1975, a revolutionary war brought the Cambodian communist party to power, and the state of Democratic Kampuchea came into existence. The new government of Pol Pot and his Khmer Rouge perpetrated a reign of terror against unarmed civilians, resulting in the deaths of more than two million people.

On December 25, 1978, an invasion by Vietnam ended Pol Pot's regime, but continued genocide at a slower pace, killing approximately a quarter million people. A period of internecine factional fighting ended on October 23, 1991, when the four warring factions[45] signed the Paris Peace Agreements[46] and invited the U.N. to help restore peace and supervise free elections in the country. The Paris Agreements gave the U.N. a broad mandate to disarm and demilitarize the warring factions, and to improve human rights. UNTAC, the U.N. Transitional Authority in Cambodia, was created.[47]

The terms of the Paris Agreements stipulated that troops from all four factions would be disarmed and demobilized by the U.N., which meant collecting more than 300,000 conventional arms from an estimated 425,000 combatants (203,300 regular army and 220,290 militia).[48] In theory, when that goal was reached, there would be a "neutral security environment as a prelude to activities aimed at creating a neutral political environment,"[49] thereby enabling Cambodians to vote in national elections without coercion. This would represent a major step toward democratization and a humanitarian climate.

The Khmer Rouge ("PDK"), however, refused to disarm, and the remaining factions grew reluctant to proceed with their own disarmament. The phenomenon of "decaying consent" has occurred before in disarmament programs.[50] Leaders of warring factions may sign an agreement, but ground forces refuse to adhere to those agreements when doing so threatens their survival.

The UNTAC program is the *only known instance in which there was an attempt to record empirical data using weapon injuries as an outcome measure after microdisarmament.* David Meddings and Stephanie O'Connor compared the incidence of weapon injuries before and after the UNTAC disarmament.[51] They estimated that "around 25–50 percent" of Cambodia's combatants were "believed to have been disarmed" during the peacekeeping operation. Although a stable government was left in place at the time of departure of the U.N., "the annual incidence of weapon injuries was higher than the rate observed before the peacekeeping operation."[52]

Because of continued violence, the U.N. issued another disarmament imperative just prior to the 1993 election. Yasushi Akashi, the Secretary-General's Special Representative to Cambodia, issued a directive that rendered unlicensed civilian firearm possession illegal as of March 18, 1993, although the Paris Agreements had given UNTAC no legal authority to issue such a decree. Penalties for violation of the U.N. directive included confiscation of arms and imprisonment for a period of six months to three years.[53]

Five years after the U.N.-imposed gun-licensing law, violent crime was still rising in Cambodia.[54] Gun-rights advocates rightly argue that gun-licensing or registration laws can set the stage for gun confiscation, since the government will know where to find all legally owned guns. In Cambodia, gun confiscation followed the U.N.'s gun-licensing fiat. In 1999, the Cambodian government, with U.N. support, banned all firearms, blaming the nation's crime problem on "the large number of guns in circulation, thought to be about half a million."[55] Eventually, the *BBC News* reported, there would be house-to-house searches and a ban on all arms, including firearms previously registered and even arms carried by off-duty police and soldiers.[56]

At the 2001 U.N. Conference on the Illegal Trade in Small Arms and Light Weapons in All Its Aspects, Sar Kheng, Cambodian minister of the interior, said that "illegally held arms" (i.e., all nongovernment arms) were "major obstacles to efforts to reconstruct and rehabilitate the country and to the building of democracy and respect for human rights."[57] He explained:

> The Government of Cambodia has designated management of all arms and explosives as its major task, and has instituted several measures, such as collecting and confiscating all arms, explosives and ammunition left by the war; instituting practical measures to reduce the reckless use of arms; and strengthening the management of weapons registration. Those who possessed weapons during the civil war wish to continue possessing them for self-protection. On the other hand, criminals have no intention of giving up their weapons, because they need them to carry out their criminal offences. However, with assistance from the European Union and from non-governmental organizations (NGOs), there has been some success in raising the awareness of the problem among a majority of Cambodians.[58]

Although the current Cambodian government is not engaged in genocide, it nevertheless has a poor human rights record and is attempting to eliminate the political opposition with threats of violence. And, as the U.N. admitted in its International Drug Control Programme report, Cambodia has become a center for "illicit drug production and trafficking, smuggling and exploitation of human beings, kidnappings, prostitution, illegal gambling, arms trafficking and extortion," and much of this criminal behavior is "protected by Cambodian officials."[59] The government's involvement in the international crime of the trafficking of women for sexual exploitation is an extreme violation of human rights.[60]

The Cambodian people have suffered decades of political and criminal violence. Many Cambodians have personally learned how to use arms for protection against criminals, so it seems doubtful that disarmament plans, even those enforced by government coercion, will persuade the populace to surrender all their arms. As the Working Group for Weapons Reduction in Cambodia (WGWR) survey noted, "it is increasingly common in Cambodian society for people to believe that weapons are needed to protect businesses and homes."[61]

The authors of *Small Arms Survey 2002* admitted, "Most people, while broadly supportive of the weapons collection process, remain reluctant to participate in it themselves so long as the rule of law is not fully established in the country and there is a lack of public trust in the security forces."[62]

The great British philosopher John Locke once explained that the foundation of the people's political sovereignty is their God-given property right to their own bodies.[63] Accordingly, when Cambodians choose to retain their arms so that they may defend themselves and their families against programs of rape and other government-sanctioned violent crimes, they are, in effect, choosing to retain their sovereignty.

The root of the crime problem in Cambodia is the tyrannical government that steals land from peasants, cooperates with organized crime, and enriches itself by participating in the sex-trade enslavement of women and children. It is entirely reasonable for the Cambodian people to want firearms to protect their families and to guard against the recurrence of genocide such as took place the last time they were disarmed.[64]

Unfortunately, yet another disarmament program is being instituted in Cambodia. On January 13, 2003, the Japanese government announced it would provide up to $3.6 million to implement the euphemistically named "Peace Building and Comprehensive Small Arms Management Program in Cambodia."[65] The disarmament program, in the Bakan district, pays for public works construction of medical clinics, schools, roads, or bridges, if the locals surrender a sufficient number of firearms.[66] In other words, if a community does not surrender its only practical means of protecting itself from genocide, common criminals, and government-sponsored criminals, the government will not build any schools, clinics, roads, or bridges.

The rationale for the disarmament program is that "small arms have been sometimes used for criminal objectives, which severely harm the security and social stability of Cambodia, and thus the reduction of arms has been considered as one of the first prioritized social actions toward sustainable peace in Cambodia."[67]

To the contrary, the reduction of civilian arms in Cambodia was the sine qua non for the Khmer Rouge genocide, and continuing efforts to disarm Cambodia's citizens have contributed to the continuing criminal victimization of the Cambodian people by their government.

Coerced community arms surrenders are contrary to the U.N.'s Universal Declaration of Human Rights. A corrupt government that profits from the kidnapping of teenage girls for slavery in the sex trade is grotesquely violating the Universal Declaration, including Article 4 ("No one shall be held in slavery or servitude; slavery and the slave trade shall be prohibited in all their forms"); Article 9 ("No one shall be subjected to arbitrary arrest, detention or exile); Article 13 ("Everyone has the right to freedom of movement and residence within the borders of each state"); Article 16 ("The family is the natural and fundamental group unit of society and is entitled to protection by society and the State"); and Article 23 ("Everyone has the right . . . to free choice of employment . . . Everyone who works has the right to just and favourable remuneration ensuring for himself and his family an existence worthy of human dignity").

In community gun-surrender programs, wealthy foreign organizations tell people, in effect, "We will build you a bridge—if you give up your ability to protect your daughters from sex-trade kidnappers," or "if you give up your ability to protect your families against the genocide and tyranny that occurred here not too long ago." Offering such choices is completely inconsistent with respect for human rights.

Albania

The collapse of several elaborate pyramid schemes in November and December 1996, which impoverished the Albanian people, many of whom lost their entire life savings,[68] led to widespread anarchy and the toppling of the Sali Berisha administration. During the anarchy, "virtually all inmates escaped from the Albanian prisons."[69] The combination of a sudden upsurge in violence and well-placed mistrust of the corrupt Albanian government caused civilians to loot 1,300 armories, removing approximately 550,000 to 1,500,000 arms, plus millions of rounds of ammunition, as well as explosives.[70]

In February 1998, the Albanian government requested aid from the U.N. to retrieve the missing arms. Jayantha Dhanapala, under-secretary-general for disarmament affairs, led a fact-finding mission in Albania in mid-June 1998. The two initial proposals were: (1) the creation of a paramilitary force that would carry out house-to-house searches and confiscation, or (2) a compensated gun surrender program, which the U.N. expected would create an increase in black market gun trafficking into the region.[71]

At first, the U.N. tried a different approach: a voluntary arms collection program that would be linked to building community development projects such as roads, schools, and communications systems, and strengthening the capabilities of local police in order to improve security. There was also an intense public information and education campaign, including TV and radio spots, posters, T-shirts, and concerts.[72]

In 2000, the voluntary program in Gramsch was escalated into national house-to-house gun confiscation. In conjunction with the U.N.'s Weapons in Exchange for Development (WED) program, the Albanian government created a task force of 250 police to visit every household in the country and demand the surrender of arms.[73] During the visit, the head of the family would be expected to hand them over and would sign a document that his home was gun-free. If he were later found to possess arms or ammunition, he would be subject to arrest, prosecution, and incarceration for up to seven years.[74]

The WED program expired in July 2002, as did the amnesty period for voluntary surrender of firearms, yet an estimated 200,000 arms were still unaccounted-for among the civilian population.[75] So a few months before WED was set to expire, the Albanian government enthusiastically embraced another collection program aided by the U.N. On March 12, 2002, the U.N. Development Programme (UNDP) approved the new Small Arms and Light Weapons Control (SALWC) program. Targeting eighteen districts, or about half the country, the program aimed for "the surrender and collection of the greatest number of weapons."[76] Due to a shortage of funding, the SALWC project tried to foster competition in arms surrenders; only the locales most successful in collecting arms would earn public works projects. A new feature of SALWC was "development and establishment of a pilot database project as the basis for a centralized, government-operated weapons control system."[77]

Johan Buwalda, program manager for UNDP's WED program, commented, "It is not only weapons collection. It is also weapons control. So we will assist the police in setting up a database, storing these data, managing the data."[78] In other words, the U.N. was building experience in creating a national gun registry.

Alfred Moisiu, president of Albania, observed that many Albanians were reluctant to disarm: "Most people are not agreeing to hand over the arms, the weapons, because the situation is still not secure here in our country." Moisiu acknowledged that his countrymen believed that unilateral disarmament endangered law-abiding citizens who surrendered their arms, because criminals always will be able to acquire weapons.[79]

It is reasonable for Albanians to be skeptical of the government. As Human Rights Watch reported, in Albania, there is "impunity for police abuse, failures of various government branches to uphold the rule of law, trafficking in human beings, and widespread violations of children's rights."[80]

Organized crime syndicates have trafficked more than twenty thousand Albanian women to Greece for sexual exploitation. Albanian children are also trafficked for what amounts to de facto slavery for the crime syndicates, "to be used in labour, to beg in public places or clean car windows at traffic lights. In other cases, Albanian criminal networks have trafficked babies, which according to the police authorities are sold for US $200."[81]

Rather than persisting in a futile attempt to disarm the public, it would be more effective for government to control police abuses, to pay better attention to fundamental human rights, to spend its resources on required infrastructure, and to reduce the civilian need for arms by protecting the people against slave traffickers.

The coercive disarmament programs, such as military-style house-to-house search-and-seizure, are an assault on human rights. They are characteristic of a police state and have sometimes been precursors of genocide.[82] U.N.-sponsored house-to-house military invasions for gun confiscation violate Article 12 of the Universal Declaration of Human Rights, which states, "No one shall be subjected to arbitrary interference with his privacy, family, [or] home . . . Everyone has the right to the protection of the law against such interference or attacks."

Bougainville

Bougainville is a Pacific island near Papua New Guinea (PNG), with a population of approximately two hundred thousand. Named for French sailor Captain Louis de Bougainville who, in 1768, established trade with the islanders, it is the largest island in the Solomon chain.

For years, Bougainville was controlled by various colonial powers. During World War II, it saw extremely fierce combat, as the last Japanese stronghold in the Solomons. After the war, Bougainville was placed under Australian control as a U.N. Trust territory. Against the wishes of its people, Bougainville found itself ruled by Papua New Guinea (PNG) when PNG gained independence from Australia in 1975, despite the fact that the Bougainvilleans are more closely related to the Solomon Islanders culturally, ethnically, and geographically; PNG lies more than nine hundred kilometers away.[83] In defiance, Bougainville declared itself the independent Republic of the North Solomons fifteen days before PNG gained independence.[84]

In 1960, copper was discovered on Bougainville, and in 1963, the company that eventually evolved into what today is known as Rio Tinto (a leading international mining conglomerate, based in London and Australia) commenced operations.

Land is of utmost importance to the people of Bougainville. Inheritance is maintained through the matrilineal clan system, passing from mother, who is both titleholder and custodian of the tribal land, to eldest daughter.[85]

When, in January 1965, it became apparent that a large open-pit copper mine was to be established, local villagers protested. A hearing was held in the Warden's Court in the town of Kieta,[86] and the court awarded a mining license to Conzinc Riotinto of Australia (a subsidiary of the mining company now called Rio Tinto). Under the court's interpretation of Australian law, what is "on top of the land" belonged to the villagers, but what was underneath—the copper deposits—belonged to the government, and not to the titleholders of the land.

That ruling ran contrary to traditional Bougainvillean ownership. It was also contrary to traditional Anglo-American common law, by which subsurface and mineral rights belong to the owner of the surface land. To the villagers, it was incomprehensible how, after countless generations, the land was no longer theirs.

When the bulldozers came, Bougainvillean landowning women resisted, and lay down with their babies in front of the machines.[87] While Americans sympathized with the brave, unarmed Chinese student who stood in front of a tank in Tiananmen Square, there were no journalists to document similarly brave acts in Bougainville.

Construction of the mine proceeded, accompanied by chemical defoliation of an entire mountainside of pristine rain forest (i.e., the "top of the land" which belonged to the villagers). Huge amounts of toxic mine waste were dumped onto the land and into major rivers. According to a lawsuit filed in November 2000 in the U.S. District Court for the Northern District of California, by 1988,

> the mine . . . dug a crater six kilometers long, four kilometers wide and a half a kilometer deep . . . [It] produced over one billion tons of waste . . . Vast tracts . . . are still barren and devoid of vegetation many years after closure of the mine . . . Thirty kilometers of the river valley system was converted into moonscape . . . What the people of Bougainville see is one of the worst human-made environmental catastrophes of modern times. But the mine turned out to be an enormous source of income for PNG. Rio Tinto gave the PNG government 19 percent of the mine's profits, which at the time, amounted to one-third of the government's income—ample incentive for PNG to overlook environmental damage.[88]

In response, Francis Ona, the son of a dispossessed village chief, formed the Panguna Landowners Association (soon to be known as the Bougainville Revolutionary Army). Ona and his followers shut down the mine on December 1, 1988, using explosives stolen from the mining company to destroy a transmission tower that supplied power to the mine.

In April 1990, the PNG government, with the assistance of the Australian government, imposed a total blockade of the island in an attempt to reopen the mine, and to prevent Ona and the BRA from acquiring arms.[89] Women and children were most affected by the blockade: pregnant women died in childbirth, and young children died from easily preventable diseases. According to the Red Cross, the blockade resulted in the deaths of more than two thousand children in just the first two years of operation.

The blockade of Bougainville—which supposedly ended during a 1994 ceasefire, but which nevertheless continued informally until 1997—was directly responsible for the deaths of an estimated fifteen thousand to twenty thousand people. PNG thus ranks among the more successful mass murderers of the twentieth century, having wiped out 10 percent of the Bougainville population.

Instead of forcing the populace into submission, the blockade had just the opposite effect. In May 1990, Ona declared the independence of the Republic of Meekamui ("the Sacred Island").[90]

Meanwhile, control of Bougainville became even more important economically; an aerial survey in the late 1980s had discovered rich deposits of other minerals, including gold, and even offshore oil.

The U.N. was apprised of events taking place in Bougainville at least as early as 1991. That summer, a BRA delegation to the U.N. Committee hearing in Geneva on the Rights of Minorities and Indigenous Peoples accused the PNG government of numerous atrocities committed against the islanders.[91] Some of these—extrajudicial executions, "disappearances," ill treatment, and arbitrary arrests and detentions, including of women and children—were detailed by Amnesty International.[92]

In his address to the parliament of Rwanda on May 7, 1998, then U.N. secretary-general Kofi Annan apologized: "All of us who cared about Rwanda . . . fervently wish that we could have prevented the genocide . . . In their greatest hour of need, the world failed the people of Rwanda."[93] There was no apology forthcoming for Bougainville, however—just silence, and the determination to disarm the surviving islanders.

To help neutralize the BRA, Papua New Guinea created, funded, and armed the Bougainville Resistance Force (BRF), ensuring its loyalty to the central government, and placed a bounty on Ona's head.

The BRA proved more than a match, however, as they were not only expert guerrilla fighters, but expert in psychological warfare. According to PNG officer Yauka Aluambo Liria, who documented the early years of the Bougainville campaign, it was not long into the fighting that rumors began to spread among the PNG troops about the magical "puri puri" powers possessed by the BRA members from the inner jungles, which enabled them to change into dogs and scout PNG positions, steal weapons, and even kidnap PNG soldiers.[94]

The Bougainville Revolutionary Army even learned how to produce indigenous copies of the M-16 rifle. Completely cut off from imports by the lack of funds and by the blockade, the BRA used materiel and equipment salvaged from mining operations, and materials left on the island after World War II (including thousands of tons of ammunition, and machine-gun parts salvaged from wrecks). Initially, the BRA manufactured crude single-shot firearms, but they soon learned to build more sophisticated guns.[95]

In spite of being isolated from the rest of the world, and lacking friends, funds, and sophisticated armament factories, the BRA prevailed. They outmaneuvered the trained, well-armed soldiers wielding M79 grenade launchers and mortars, and who were backed up by Australian-supplied Iroquois helicopters outfitted with automatic weapons.[96]

Having failed in the military arena, PNG switched tactics. On August 30, 2001, an unrealistic Bougainville Peace Agreement was signed by Bougainvilleans who had strong political ties to PNG.[97] Bougainvilleans loyal to revolutionary leader Francis Ona did not sign. The agreement put a formal end to hostilities, provided for the establishment of an autonomous Bougainville government, and a referendum on full independence from PNG to be held within ten to fifteen years.

The most important part of the Peace Agreement (at least to PNG, Australia, and the U.N.)—and what the independence was utterly contingent upon—was the Rotakas Record of May 3, 2001, an agreement that laid out a "phased weapons disposal plan," and which, upon implementation, would result in complete disarmament of the BRA.[98] Some of its details were reported by Papua New Guinea's *Post-Courier*:

> The weapons disposal plan includes . . . collecting all weapons from ex-combatants and locking them in the containers with robust but simple padlocks. The unit commanders will retain the keys and trunks but allow UN officials to verify the exercise. During the second stage, the weapons would be double-locked in larger

containers with one key held by the local commander and one by the UN . . . After the PNG Security Forces withdraw from each command area the Company Commanders shall deliver arms held by them to one central collection point in each command area . . . The decision on how these weapons should be finally dealt with will be made within one month of the constitutional amendments coming into effect.[99]

In short, this meant that BRA company commanders were no longer in control of their arms. There was also the implied threat that if their arms were not forthcoming, neither would be the independence referendum.

What is the purpose of disarming a people who are headed toward greater autonomy and freedom? Upon independence, disarmament would be a moot point because Bougainville would then be self-governed, and the Bougainvilleans would be free to do whatever they liked, including retaining their arms.

One of the witnesses to the signing of the Bougainville Peace Agreement was New Zealand Foreign Minister Phil Goff, whose country agreed to provide two hundred containers (basically, large trunks) for the storage of arms to be handed in by Bougainvillean ex-combatants. As the first batch of fifteen gun lockers were flown in on November 20, 2001, Goff declared: "The challenge now lies with the Bougainvilleans, particularly ex-combatants, to show their commitment to the Weapons Disposal Plan as expressed in the Bougainville Peace Agreement."[100]

The real challenge, however, was to convince Bougainvilleans who used those arms to halt the plunder of their land to unilaterally disarm. Francis Ona, whose independence movement controlled up to 20 percent of Bougainville, refused to participate in the peace process. The June 11, 1999, *Sydney Morning Herald* quoted a defiant Ona as stating, "There are thousands of homemade weapons hidden in the villages and they will never be handed back until Bougainville becomes independent."[101]

The process of independence moved another step forward on January 23, 2002, when the PNG parliament unanimously voted in favor of constitutional amendments relating to Bougainville. One of these amendments would permit Bougainville to become autonomous under PNG, and the other would permit Bougainville to hold its referendum for independence in ten to fifteen years. Bougainville would be given control of its own foreign affairs, banking system, aviation, and shipping rights. Also, the "legislation allows Bougainville to have its own disciplined forces."[102]

That begs the question: if Bougainville is to have its own "disciplined forces," why should citizens be forced to reacquire firearms, after the second reading in parliament turns the amendments into law?

If peace were the real objective, why not disarm all combatants? Why not disarm, especially, the aggressors—the governments of Papua New Guinea and Australia—instead of only the victims who fought back? Why insist on disarmament first, and postpone a referendum on independence for ten or more years, when independence was clearly the key to a lasting peace? Why should the people of Bougainville believe that once they were disarmed and helpless, the government of PNG would honor its promise ten or fifteen years in the future?

After the signing of the peace agreement, a total of 1,639 guns were registered and placed into locked containers. When it became obvious that the PNG government would not obey the peace agreement, at least two break-ins occurred where the sequestered arms were stored.[103] The first time, 110 weapons were removed. After the second break-in, an additional 360 were discovered missing. As Philip Alpers and Conor Twyford pointed out, "With so much energy being directed at weapons disposal, potential existed for community-wide resentment to develop as other needs were not met, or were met more slowly than expected."[104] That is exactly what came to pass.[105]

It has become clear that both the Australian and the PNG governments are loath to hold the promised referendum on the future of the islanders. The referendum is now promised to take place sometime between

2015 and 2020. This is a violation of the Universal Declaration of Human Rights, which requires that "the will of the people shall be the basis of the authority of government; this will shall be expressed in periodic and genuine elections which shall be by universal and equal suffrage and shall be held by secret vote or by equivalent free voting procedures."[106] The kleptocracy's theft of the resources of the Bougainvilleans, and consequent impoverishment of the people, are inconsistent with the International Covenant on Economic, Social, and Cultural Rights, which recognizes "the inherent right of all peoples to enjoy and utilize fully and freely their natural wealth and resources."[107]

Unfortunately, the collection of firearms—rather than the restoration of human rights, or attention to basic human needs—is the first priority of the U.N. mission on Bougainville. As actually administered, the current "peace" program in Bougainville, like its predecessors, is relentlessly focused on removing arms from civilians and is indifferent to improving the lives of the population, including women and children.

Chapter 8

Mexico

Our American nation is the product of revolution against governments that tried to take away the rights of their subjects, including the right to arms. One of those governments was, of course, the British empire. The other was Mexico, from which the free people of Texas broke away in the Texan revolution.

Everything that has happened since the American Revolution of 1776 and the Texas Revolution of 1835 confirms the wisdom of our revolutionary forebears. Nothing could be more foolish than for modern Americans to squander the gift of freedom that has been bestowed on them. Nothing could be more destructive and dangerous than to let the governments of Mexico or the United Kingdom take away our constitutional freedoms.

Yet the Obama administration is working with both those foreign governments against your Second Amendment rights. The work with the UK takes place mainly at the U.N., in league with the international antigun advocates who are funded by the UK government.

The Mexican government is also active on the United Nations front. A Mexican delegate chaired the U.N. antigun conference in June 2010. Mexico probably won this "honor" because the Mexican government has also been pushing hard in the United States for drastic restrictions on American gun ownership—virtually the whole agenda of the American antigun lobbies.

Before we talk about what the Mexican government is trying to do in the present, let's remember some American history.

Texas was once part of Mexico. The Mexican government encouraged Americans to settle in the vast, thinly populated region of Texas.

But the government of the Mexican republic was taken over by the military dictatorship of General Santa Anna. He trampled on the rights guaranteed by the Mexican Constitution of 1824. The people of Texas peacefully petitioned for Santa Anna to respect their rights, and the rights of other Mexican citizens. But these petitions were rejected, and some of the petitioners imprisoned.

The Revolution began at Gonzales. Santa Anna's government tried to seize a small cannon that the settlers used for protection from Indians. The Texans raised a flag, with the words "Come and Take It."

Those words, by the way, were the same ones that the ancient Greeks had spoken at Thermopylae, when three hundred Spartans defied the Persian invaders who told them to surrender their arms. "*Molon labe!*" ("Come and take them") the Greeks shouted.

For three days the Spartans held off the hordes of Persians at the narrow pass. Although the Spartans were finally defeated, they had saved their nation by giving the Greeks enough time to raise a force to defeat the Persian invaders.

That is exactly what the Texans would do 2,316 years later, at the Alamo. Armed with their personal firearms, swords, and knives, 136 brave Texans in San Antonio resisted Santa Anna's siege from February 23 to March 6, 1836. Like the Spartans, almost all of them sacrificed their lives, and like the Spartans, they saved their nation.

"Remember the Alamo!" cried Sam Houston's volunteers—carrying their personal firearms into battle—when they launched a daring surprise attack on Santa Anna's army at San Jacinto. These Texans were not the professional standing army of Santa Anna; they were the citizen volunteers of Texas, fighting to free their families and their posterity from Mexican tyranny.

The Texans demolished an army twice their size, captured Santa Anna, and won their new nation's independence.

Although today the American and British people are friends, "The Star-Spangled Banner" proudly recounts American valor during the War of

1812, when Americans had to fight Britain again to preserve our independence. The "Texas War Cry" is set to the same tune, and it, too, is an eternal anthem of the right and duty of a free, armed people to defend their hard-won liberty:

> Oh Texans rouse hill and dale with your cry.
> No longer delay, for the bold foe advances.
> The banners of Mexico tauntingly fly,
> And the valleys are lit with the gleam of their lances.
> With justice our shield, rush forth to the field.
> And stand with your posts, till our foes fly or yield.
> For the bright star of Texas shall never grow dim,
> While her soil boasts a son to raise rifle or limb.
> Rush forth to the lines, these hirelings to meet.
> Our lives and our homes, we will yield unto no man.
> But death on our free soil we'll willingly meet,
> Ere our free Temple soiled, by the feet of the foe men.
> Grasp rifle and blade with hearts undismayed,
> And swear by the Temple brave Houston has made,
> *That the bright star of Texas shall never be dim*
> *While her soil boasts a son to raise rifle or limb.*

To recall these words today is not to ignore the great friendship that has grown between the peoples of the United States and Mexico, but to remind us that we must always be vigilant against any foreign government that attempts to infringe our rights.

The dangerous, repressive antigun policies of the United Kingdom nearly led it into disaster. In 1940, France fell to the Nazis, and Hitler began drawing up plans for Operation Sea Lion—the invasion of Great Britain. Yet because of the Firearms Act that Parliament had imposed in 1921, Britain's Home Guard had few guns. The Home Guard instead drilled with umbrellas, canes, spears, pikes, or clubs.

Britain turned to the United States for guns. Here's an advertisement from the November 1940 issue of NRA's magazine the *American Rifleman*:

Send A Gun To Defend A British Home.

British civilians, faced with the threat of invasion, desperately need arms for the defense of their homes. The American Committee for Defense of British Homes has organized to collect gifts of pistols, rifles, revolvers, shotguns, binoculars from American civilians who wish to answer the call and aid in the defense of British homes. These arms are being shipped, with the consent of the British Government, to Civilian Committee for Protection of Homes, Birmingham, England . . . The members of which are Wickham Steed, Edward Hulton, and Lord Davies. You can aid by sending any arms or binoculars you can spare to American Committee for the Defense of British Homes, C. Suydan Cutting, *Chairman* Room 100, 10 Warren Street, New York, N.Y.

Generous Americans donated guns to help defend Great Britain. The National Rifle Association itself supplied seven thousand firearms.

Likewise, American guns helped save Mexican independence. In 1863, the French Emperor Napoleon III overthrew the Mexican government of President Benito Juárez, and installed himself as emperor of Mexico.

Juárez fled to northern Mexico, where he rallied resistance forces. For arms, he turned to the United States. Juárez purchased a thousand Winchester Model 1866 carbines, along with five hundred rounds of .44 rimfire ammunition per gun. Those guns were delivered to Monterey, with "R.M." (Republic of Mexico) inscribed on the frames.

Using those American guns, Juárez won the war, drove out Napoleon III, and saved Mexico as an independent republic, rather than a European colony. His victory is celebrated today as the *Cinco de Mayo*—honoring brave Mexican patriots with their American firearms.

Sadly, the lessons of history were ignored by British and Mexican governments that distrusted their citizens. Great Britain's 1689 Declaration of Right had affirmed that "the Subjects which are protestants may have Arms for their Defense suitable to their Conditions and as allowed by law."

Despite the Declaration of Right, Britain's Parliament has pressed down one terrible law after another on Britain's law-abiding gun owners, making the process of legal gun ownership so difficult that, today, only 4 percent of households contain a legal firearm.

Partly as a result of the gun laws and the government's relentless campaign against the right of self-defense, the U.K. today is a criminal's paradise. According to the United Nations, Scotland is the most violent country in the developed world.[1] Home invasion burglaries (a burglary when the victims are home) are relatively rare in the United States, but are standard in Britain.[2] This is to be expected, since an American home invader is deterred by a very large risk of being shot by the victim, whereas burglars in the UK face no such risk.[3]

Like the British people, the Mexican people are suffering a crime wave partly because their government is violating their constitutional right to arms. The Mexican Constitution provides:

> Article 10. The inhabitants of the United Mexican States have a right to arms in their homes, for security and legitimate defense, with the exception of arms prohibited by federal law and those reserved for the exclusive use of the Army, Navy, Air Force and National Guard. Federal law will determine the cases, conditions, requirements, and places in which the carrying of arms will be authorized to the inhabitants.[4]

Now, this is not a perfect constitutional right. It's not as good as the right in the 1857 Mexican Constitution, which included the right to carry.[5] But the Mexican Constitution does at least protect the right to arms for home defense.

Unfortunately, the Mexican government does not honor even this limited right. The licensing and registration (which must be renewed every year) is an administrative nightmare. There is only one gun store *in the entire country*, and that store is run by the army.[6]

In practice, the only firearm an ordinary Mexican citizen can buy is a .22.

And self-defense? A licensed gun owner may not use a gun for self-defense unless the criminal shoots first. Carry permits are denied to everyone except the wealthy and the politically connected. In a nation of 105 million people, only 4,300 carry licenses.

The Mexican national gun law requires the federal and state governments to conduct public information campaigns to discourage all forms of weapons ownership and carrying. Only sports-related advertising of firearms is permitted. The results? Just what you would expect. Mexico is the kidnapping capital of the world. It's not just the wealthy who are victimized; anyone whose family might be able to pay even a small ransom is at risk.[7]

However, the criminal problem in Mexico that you will hear about most often in the mainstream American media is the drug war. The Mexican government and antigun American media are united in trying to blame American gun owners for Mexico's problems.

Upon taking office in December 2006, Mexican president Felipe Calderón greatly intensified the drug war. He deployed 30,000 soldiers and federal police, and captured some drug lords as well as sixty tons of drugs. Calderón's escalation led to a counteroffensive by the drug lords. Fatalities in the drug war more than doubled, rising to 5,612 in 2008.[8] The large majority of those casualties are drug gangsters, killed either by Mexican law enforcement, or by rival gangsters.

The American government has always gone the extra mile to try to help Mexico with its problem, and to prevent American guns from being acquired by Mexican gangsters. In the 1990s, the BATF initiated Operation Forward Trace. BATF agents conducted wholesale searches of 4473 forms held by FFLs in Southwestern states. BATF compiled name and address lists of buyers (especially, buyers with Hispanic names) who had bought inexpensive handguns or self-loading rifles. BATF then contacted the purchasers and demanded to know where the guns were.

In July 2001, U.S. attorney general John Ashcroft and Mexican attorney general Rafael Macedo de la Concha announced a cooperative law enforcement program, aimed partly at weapons smuggling. Mexican police would provide computerized information about seized firearms to BATF so the Bureau could trace the guns. Ashcroft also assigned U.S. prosecutors in districts bordering Mexico to serve as contacts on gun smuggling cases.

Currently, BATFE is engaged in Project Gunrunner, which deploys a large number of agents near the Mexican border, and which has set up offices in Mexico in order to conduct electronic traces of firearms seized in Mexico.[9]

In the summer of 2008, U.S. Immigration and Customs Enforcement initiated operation *Armas Cruzadas*, a joint project of Customs and Border Protection (CBP), BATFE, and the Drug Enforcement Administration (DEA) to work with Mexican law enforcement to disrupt arms smuggling.

A related law enforcement effort is the Mérida Initiative, which was announced in October 2007. Under the Initiative, the U.S. is providing $1.4 billion to the governments of Mexico and other Central American nations to combat criminal organizations, particularly drug traffickers. Mérida includes efforts to disrupt weapon smuggling and human trafficking. Most of the money goes to buy equipment for Mexican law enforcement. (BATFE's Project Gunrunner has become part of Mérida.)

Other American law enforcement efforts relevant to Mexican gun-running include the 2007 Southwest Border Counternarcotics Strategy, the 2008 National Drug Control Strategy, and the 2007 U.S. Strategy for Combating Criminal Gangs from Central America and Mexico.

Unfortunately, the enormous amount of U.S. funds being sent to Mexico, coupled with the notorious corruption of the Mexican government, gives dishonest Mexican officials every reason to exaggerate their complaints about the United States, and about the problems in Mexico, the better to obtain more money from U.S. taxpayers.

Perhaps the best antismuggling program is the one run jointly by BATFE and the National Shooting Sports Foundation. It's called "Don't Lie for the Other Guy." It teaches firearms store staff how to detect "straw purchasers"—people who are legally eligible to buy firearms and ammunition, but are making the purchase on behalf of someone who is not. Straw purchases are illegal in the United States, and the law was strengthened in 1986, thanks to the NRA's flagship bill of the 1980s: the Firearms Owners' Protection Act. That law protected law-abiding gun owners and gun stores from government abuses, while tightening the laws against gun criminals.

There are a number of cases in which would-be gunrunners in the Southwest have been caught and sent to prison, thanks to conscientious gun store staffers who were on the alert for attempted straw purchases.

President Obama, unfortunately, has teamed up with Mexico's President Calderón for a joint offensive against the Second Amendment.

Traditionally, a new American president's first meeting with a foreign leader is with the prime minister of Canada. But on January 12, 2009, president-elect Obama held a ninety-minute meeting with President Calderón and promised strong action to stop the flow of American guns to Mexico.[10]

American gun control advocates have seized on the Mexican issue to push the same tired agenda of the American antigun lobby, restated as a necessity for American support for Mexico: additional restrictions on gun shows, an expanded ban on so-called assault weapons, more U.S. import bans on allegedly "non-sporting" firearms and magazines, bringing .50 caliber rifles under the National Firearms Act (so that they would be treated like machine guns), a "performance-based standard" for ammunition bans (which would outlaw most centerfire rifle ammunition), repeal of the Tiahart Amendment (which says that federal firearms tracing information can only be used for law enforcement purposes, and not given to groups who want to sue gun owners or gun companies), bullet-serialization, licensing of ammunition sales, and much more.[11]

President Obama, Secretary of State Clinton, Attorney General Eric Holder, and President Calderón have focused on promoting reimposition of the Clinton ban on so-called assault weapons. Some Mexican government officials have also said that the U.S. should register all firearms.

An incessant part of the propaganda campaign is repetition of the claim that 90 percent of Mexican crime guns come from the United States.

But it's just not true. When the Mexican government seizes guns, only a small percentage is turned over to the United States BATFE (which has offices in Mexico) for tracing. Of the guns that Mexico gives to BATFE, a large percentage are indeed traced to the U.S. But that does not provide any evidence that 90 percent of total crime guns in Mexico came from the United States.[12] Why would a Mexican crime gun not be turned over for tracing? To start with, the Mexican government has a registry of every gun purchased in Mexico. So if the serial number shows up in the Mexican registry, there's no point in contacting the U.S. BATFE.

Another reason for not requesting a BATFE trace can be that the gun has no manufacturer mark or serial numbers. For decades, American law has required such identification; but arms manufacturers in China (which are closely allied with the military) manufacture a huge number of unmarked guns for export to criminals, warlords, and rogues all over the planet.

One more reason that Mexican guns might not be traced is that corrupt Mexican law enforcement officials prevent tracing. For example, in 2008, Mexican police in the border town of Reynosa seized 288 "assault rifles"; 428,000 rounds of ammunition; 287 grenades; and a grenade launcher.[13] Yet Mexican authorities refused to let BATFE see the serial numbers in order to investigate how the guns had been trafficked.[14]

Even when a trace is successful, corrupt law enforcement may impede further investigation. For example, February 15, 2007, is known in Mexico as "Black Thursday." That is the day four police officers were murdered in central Mexico by drug gangsters.

The Black Thursday guns were traced to a store in Laredo, Texas. They had been purchased by Raúl Alvarez Jr., then a twenty-eight-year-old resident of Laredo. Alvarez claimed that he had sold the guns to a stranger at a shooting range. BATFE greatly wanted to investigate further, to shut down the trafficking line that had supplied the guns. But BATFE was stonewalled by the Mexican government. The San Antonio *Express-News* reported:

> The ATF wouldn't get much from their Mexican counterparts, who imposed an almost total information blackout about the arrests of 14 suspects, including the alleged shooters. Not even the four widows know what happened to their husbands' alleged killers. The mystery extends to local journalists and municipal police, who are told only the arrested are still in prison but not tried. And, federal authorities have so far refused Express-News interview requests to discuss the case.
>
> The ATF's Elias Bazan, who oversaw the Laredo office at the time, said Mexico's investigators squandered an opportunity to provide the results of their interrogations and any evidence, outside of the guns' serial numbers, that would point to how the weapons were smuggled from the Laredo side.
>
> "We don't have anything from the Mexican government, so we're screwed," Bazan said of his Laredo investigation, which was shut down as a result.[15]

The theory that U.S. gun owners are to blame for the Mexican drug cartels having arms fails to account for the fact that the cartels appear to have plenty of armaments that are not exactly items you can buy at a gun store in Texas or Arizona. In 2007–08, the Mexican government confiscated nearly two thousand hand grenades; other weapons seized include rocket-propelled grenade launchers, rocket launchers, and antitank weapons.[16]

Reporters William La Jeunesse and Maxim Lott explained some of the sources of the Mexican gang weapons:

- — The Black Market. Mexico is a virtual arms bazaar, with fragmentation grenades from South Korea, AK-47s from China, and shoulder-fired rocket launchers from Spain, Israel and former Soviet bloc manufacturers.
- — Russian crime organizations. Interpol says Russian Mafia groups such as Poldolskaya and Moscow-based Solntsevskaya are actively trafficking drugs and arms in Mexico.
- — South America. During the late 1990s, the Revolutionary Armed Forces of Colombia (FARC) established a clandestine arms smuggling and drug trafficking partnership with the Tijuana cartel, according to the Federal Research Division report from the Library of Congress.
- — Asia. According to a 2006 Amnesty International Report, China has provided arms to countries in Asia, Africa and Latin America. Chinese assault weapons and Korean explosives have been recovered in Mexico.
- — The Mexican Army. More than 150,000 soldiers deserted in the last six years, according to Mexican Congressman Robert Badillo. Many took their weapons with them, including the standard issue M-16 assault rifle made in Belgium.
- — Guatemala. U.S. intelligence agencies say traffickers move immigrants, stolen cars, guns and drugs, including most of America's cocaine, along the porous Mexican-Guatemalan border. On March 27, *La Hora*, a Guatemalan newspaper, reported that police seized 500 grenades and a load of AK-47s on the border. Police say the cache was transported by a Mexican drug cartel operating out of Ixcan, a border town.[17]

Because of the reporting by La Jeunesse and Lott, the 90 percent factoid and the American gun control campaign on which it was based were being discredited. Then, the Government Accountability Office rode to the rescue of the Obama administration. A GAO report issued in June 2009 said that the 90 percent figure, or something close to it, was correct.[18]

The GAO report got the kind of media attention you would expect. Yet when you read it, the report presents no additional information to support the 90 percent factoid. Instead, the authors simply say that they talked to Mexican and American law enforcement officials who believe that most of the Mexican guns come from the United States.[19] As Dave Kopel quipped, the report might as well have been titled "Hillary says it. I believe it. That settles it."

Professor George W. Grayson, author of the book *Mexico's Struggle with "Drugs and Thugs,"* calls the factoid a "wildly exaggerated percentage" that is being pushed by President Calderón for purposes of domestic Mexican politics.[20]

It's true, as Mexico's ambassador to the U.S. points out, that most of the guns are found in northern Mexico, near the United States. The simple explanation is that most of the guns are where most of the drug gangs are. The drug traffickers are moving drugs into the United States, where they can be sold to affluent consumers. Drug gangsters are not going to make a lot of money by bringing a very expensive item like cocaine into a very poor country like Guatemala.

On May 20, 2010, Mexican president Felipe Calderón intensified the campaign against American gun rights. Addressing a joint session of the United States Congress, he blamed America for Mexico's problem of violent drug gangs, and asked Congress to reinstate the Clinton-era ban on so-called assault weapons. Calderón claimed that the 2004 sunset of the Clinton gun ban was the direct cause of the current violence in Mexico. In response, many Congresspersons gave him a standing ovation.

According to Calderón, "almost anyone can purchase these powerful weapons." First of all, the so-called assault weapons that were subject to the 1994—2004 Clinton ban were not more "powerful" than other guns. They typically fired intermediate power cartridges. Neither did the banned guns fire faster than other firearms. They fired one, and only one, bullet when the trigger was pulled. Just like every other semiautomatic, or, for that matter, just like a revolver. The Clinton ban was based on superficial cosmetic features, such as whether the gun had a bayonet mount or a folding stock. Such features obviously have nothing to do with the gun's power.

President Calderón was wrong to claim that "almost anyone can purchase" the guns. In fact, every retail firearms sale anywhere in the United States must be approved by the National Instant Check System or its state counterpart. Federal and state laws prohibit millions of persons from owning or possessing firearms—based on convictions for felonies, domestic violence misdemeanors, restraining orders, and many other reasons. The NICS check ensures that such persons are prevented from buying guns.

So if Calderón had been accurate, he would have said, "only persons who have been verified to have a clean record can purchase these ordinary, not-especially-powerful guns."

The Mexican president further claimed: "If you look carefully, you will notice that the violence started to grow a couple of years before I took office in 2006. This coincides with the lifting of the Assault Weapons Ban in 2004."

False. The Clinton gun ban expired in September 2004. Yet the total number of homicides in Mexico *declined* from 12,760 in 2003 to 11,690 in 2004. They remained stable, at 11,732 in 2005, and 11,558 in 2006, and then declined still more in 2007, to 10,291. This low figure in 2007 was far below the figures earlier in the century, when the Clinton ban was in full effect (13,829 homicides in 2000; 13,855 homicides in 2001; 13,144 homicides in 2002).

In other words, the end of the Clinton ban was followed by a sharp decrease in homicides in the Mexico during the subsequent three years.

The surge in Mexican violence started when Calderón escalated the "drug war" there. By 2008, the number of Mexican homicides had soared by 22 percent in a single year, up to 12,577. As a Congressional Research Service report explained: "the government's crackdown, as well as turf wars among rival DTOs [drug trafficking organizations], has fueled an escalation in violence throughout the country, including states along the U.S.-Mexico border."[22]

So if Calderón had spoken accurately, he would have said, "The violence started to grow a year after I took office in late 2006. Falling violence coincided with the lifting of the Assault Weapons Ban in 2004."

The *Economist Intelligence Unit* reported that drug homicides in Mexico doubled from 2007 to 2008, and then rose 30 percent more in 2009.[22] This is inconsistent with Calderón's fingerpointing at the September 2004 sunset of the Clinton ban. Rather, the data show violence rising after Calderón's escalation of the drug war, deploying thirty thousand soldiers and federal police. Calderón's escalation led to a counteroffensive by the drug lords, as well to more turf wars in areas where old gang territories were destabilized.

By the way, according to Calderón himself, 95 percent of the drug war deaths are drug gangsters killed by other drug gangsters.[23] Even so, there are still lots of innocent police officers, journalists, government officials, and other good citizens who have been murdered by the cartels.

No one disputes that *some* of the Mexican crime guns come from the United States. However, the fact that a Mexican crime gun had been manufactured or imported into the United States does not prove that the American retail market is to blame. The United States sells large quantities of guns to the federal Mexican government, and to state and local Mexican governments.

These Mexican government purchases may themselves be a major source of Mexican crime guns. About one-eighth of the Mexican army deserts annually.[24] Many of these deserters take their government-issued automatic rifles with them.

Many of the deserters go to work for higher pay for the drug-trafficking organizations. The *Zetas*, an especially violent gang even by Mexican standards, was founded by Mexican Special Forces deserters.

The *Zetas*, who also recruit from Guatemalan army special forces (*Kaibiles*), have used counterinsurgency tactics to take over various regions from other drug cartels. They have frequently launched grenade attacks on police stations. They deploy weaponry that includes .50 antiaircraft machine guns.

So if a Mexican army deserter is later caught with his M-16, that does not mean that the U.S. civilian gun market is at fault. The same is true for M-16s and other U.S. military weapons that come to the Mexican DTOs after first being legally sold to governments such as Guatemala or South Korea. Marlene Blanco, chief of the Guatemala National Police, says that the police have "lost" at least two thousand guns, including automatic Uzis and AK47s.[25]

Likewise, many U.S. Army M-16 rifles were left behind in Vietnam, and many of them have been sold into the global black market. The May 4, 2010, issue of the Mexico City newspaper *El Universal* reported on the weapons bazaars in Tepito, a Mexico City neighborhood notorious as a place where anyone can buy anything. Anyone with three thousand pesos (less than three hundred U.S. dollars) can buy a gun. A new 9mm pistol is twelve thousand pesos. Hand grenades and assault rifles (fifteen thousand pesos) are only available "on request."

The Tepito black marketers reported receiving wholesale monthly or bimonthly shipments of "revolvers, submachine guns, rifles and grenade launchers."

Significantly, "a percentage of the weapons, the seller said, come from Mexico via Ministry of Defense personnel who provide [them] in part from weapons seized in raids, or stolen from the ministry's own arsenal."

Not only is the Mexican government itself responsible for much of the supply of weaponry in the hands of the cartels; the government is also responsible for the development of smuggling networks. For years, the Mexican government has actively encouraged illegal immigration into the United States. The same human trafficking networks that bring illegal aliens into the U.S. are using their smuggling skills to bring drugs north and guns south. These human trafficking networks never would have developed to such a large size if the Mexican government did not use its U.S. consulates to provide so much support to Mexican illegal aliens in the United States.

The Mexican government gives consular ID cards (with no identity verification) to Mexican nationals in the United States, facilitating their identity fraud and illegal presence here. The Mexican government publishes documents providing advice to illegal aliens, and advice for Mexicans thinking about illegally entering the U.S. With the connivance of the Mexican government, stores near Mexico's northern border operate as outfitting posts for Mexicans preparing for illegal entry.

Mexican border enforcement is a joke. There are plenty of southbound crossings where travelers are subjected to little or no scrutiny, and bringing in a case of ammunition is as easy as pie.

If President Obama were serious about trying to stop the smuggling, rather than just using it as a pretext for pushing restrictions on American gun owners, he could do what Congress has already ordered: build the border fence. Securing our border with Mexico is our right as a sovereign nation. It would not only reduce the rate of illegal immigration; it would make firearms trafficking much more difficult.

Mexico further aggravates its own problems by excessively lenient sentencing for criminals under the age of eighteen. The light punishments have led to the cartels hiring youths as contract killers.[26] Mexico should adopt a policy similar to that of most U.S. states, so that a teenager who deliberately perpetrates a premeditated homicide (such as murder for hire) can be sentenced as an adult, or can at least be given a longer sentence than an ordinary juvenile delinquent.

The Mexican drug trade reaps $25 billion a year in annual *profits* for the Mexican drug cartels, constituting 2 percent of the total Mexican gross domestic product.[27] According to the Mexican government, weapons-smuggling revenues in Mexico are $22 million annually.[28] Thus, the cost of acquiring weapons amounts to less than 1 percent of the cartels' annual profits.

Even if every gun in the United States magically vanished, the cartels have plenty of revenue to acquire firearms on the global black market.

According to the private intelligence analysis company Stratfor, besides the U.S. supply source for guns:

> the cartels also obtain weapons from contacts along their supply networks in South and Central America, where substantial quantities of military ordnance have been shipped over decades to supply insurgencies and counterinsurgencies. Explosives from domestic Mexican sources also are widely available and are generally less expensive than guns.[29]

A Mexican federal government document, *USA-MEXICO Firearms Smuggling* (March 26, 2009) reports that in the previous three years, the government seized 2,804 grenades.

According to the report, the types of arms seized which were among "the highest quantity" were "anti-tank rockets M72 and AT-4, rocket launchers RPG-7, grenade launchers MGL Caliber 37mm., grenade launcher additional devices caliber 37 and 40 mm, 37 and 40 mm grenades, fragmenting grenades."

Arms in "second place" included "rocket launchers and sub-machineguns."

The prevalence of grenades, grenades launchers, submachine guns, and other very powerful weapons in Mexico clearly shows that the Mexican drug trafficking organizations have important sources of weapons other than the legitimate U.S. market. You obviously can't buy a grenade or a machine gun over the counter at a gun store in Tucson or a gun show in San Antonio.

Testifying before the U.S. House Subcommittee on Border, Maritime, and Global Counterterrorism, on July 16, 2009, BATFE stated that the grenades and other military-grade weaponry were coming into Mexico via the southern border with Guatemala.

The Mexican DTOs also rob American gun stores. The *Zetitas* (little Zetas) gang has cells in Houston, Laredo, and San Antonio, and is believed to be carrying out gun store robberies.[30] A gun stolen from Houston by a Mexican gang in 2007 might well end up being seized by Mexican police in 2010, and then traced to the United States.

But that is hardly proof that "lax" American guns laws are to blame for Mexican crime.

In fact, according to BATFE, the average "time to crime" (from lawful sale to seizure by the police) for a U.S. gun traced from Mexico is fourteen years. This suggests that most of the guns were lawfully possessed in the United States, stolen, and eventually sold into a black market that brought them to Mexico. U.S. firearms retailers are not to blame.[31]

Finally, in 2011, the lies began to unravel; new evidence proved beyond doubt that the NRA had been right all along in calling the 90 percent claim a hoax invented for political purposes.

First of all, U.S. diplomatic cables obtained by Wikileaks confirmed that Mexico's southern border with Guatemala was a major source of weaponry for the drug cartels. New reports from the U.S. Department of Justice, from the research firm Stratfor, and from the Woodrow Wilson Center demolished the 90 percent figure and confirmed that Mexico itself, including the Mexican government, was a key supplier of weapons to the *narcotraficantes*. To the extent that U.S. guns were found in Mexico, they were older guns—indicating that they had been stolen and then smuggled south, rather than initially purchased as part of a gun-running operation.

But then there was the revelation of a major source of new U.S. firearms going directly to Mexican criminals. That source was the Bureau of Alcohol, Tobacco, Firearms and Explosives (BATFE), whose "Fast and Furious" program channeled twenty-five hundred firearms from licensed firearms dealers into the hands of smugglers and other criminals.

New Research

Licensed Americans firearms dealers are not breaking the law.[32] BATFE conducted more than two thousand inspections of licensed firearms dealers in the border states, and the result was a license revocation for only two dealers; even those license revocations for which the reasons are not publicly available did not result in any criminal charges.

Several secret U.S. State Department cables, made public by Wikileaks, reflect State Department knowledge that American firearms stores are not a major source of weapons for Latin American drug cartels. Originally reported in the Mexican newspaper *La Jornada*, the cables reveal that about 90 percent of the Mexican cartels' heavy weaponry is smuggled via Mexico's southern border from Guatemala, where the smugglers operate with impunity. The 577-mile Mexico-Guatemala border is patrolled by only 125 Mexican immigration officers. In contrast, as one cable noted, there are 30,000 U.S. Customs and Border Patrol officers for the 1,926-mile Mexican border.[33]

In other words, if we assume that each border officer works an eight-hour shift, at any given time there are more than five U.S. officers per mile on the Mexico/U.S. border, and only one Mexican officer per fourteen miles on the Mexico/Guatemala border. If you were a smuggler, which border would you pick?

While the global black market is supplying the Mexican cartels' weaponry, a significant part of it originates in Central America. The U.S. embassy in Guatemala reported that it "has received new information indicating rogue elements within the Guatemalan army are selling military-grade weapons and munitions to narcotraffickers . . . The involvement of Guatemalan military officers in the sale of weapons to narcotraffickers raises serious concerns about the Guatemalan military's ability to secure its arms and ammunition."[34] Likewise, a cable from the State Department headquarters in Washington to the U.S. embassy in Honduras explained that the U.S. government "has become aware that light antitank weapons (LAWs) and grenades supplied to Honduras under the Foreign Military Sales program were recovered in Mexico and Colombia."[35]

Reporting by William La Jeunesse of Fox News explained that many of the machine guns, grenades, and plastic explosives used by the Mexican cartels do originate in the United States. But their source is not gun shows in Texas or gun stores in Arizona. Rather, the source is the United States government. He detailed the three key paths that take the weapons from America to the cartels:

The first is direct deliveries to the Mexican military, and to other Latin American militaries, by the U.S. Department of Defense. The legal term for these, according to the U.S. Department of State, is "foreign military sales."

Second, the Mexican government orders arms directly from American suppliers. These are called "direct commercial sales." For example, in fiscal year 2009, the Mexican government bought $177 million in U.S. weaponry, including $20 million worth of automatic and semiautomatic firearms.[36]

Third, the supply of new firearms is augmented by older ones owned by the militaries of Honduras, Guatemala, and Nicaragua. The arms in these arsenals include not only American ones, but also Kalashnikov machine guns.

Whether owned by government of Mexico or other Central American governments, the arms often end up being resold to the cartels. Sometimes they are taken by individual Mexican soldiers who are deserting to work for the cartels, but the larger volume comes from bulk sales by corrupt military officers.[37] A November 2009 cable from the U.S. Embassy in Mexico suggested that once arms are transferred from Mexico's army (which controls almost all the imports) to Mexican state governments, state governments are lax about keeping tabs on the weapons.[38]

Stratfor, a research organization that uses open-source intelligence, noted the seizure of an in-transit cartel arsenal from a semitrailer near Nuevo Laredo on March 25, 2011, right across the Rio Grande from Laredo, Texas. In the cache were a pair of M249 machine guns (currently used by the U.S. military) and an M1919 (a machine gun used by the U.S. army decades ago).

You certainly can't buy either of those at a gun store or gun show. Also in the cache was a Russian-made RPG-7 rocket-propelled grenade launcher, which is used by the Mexican army, including special forces.

Stratfor concluded that "the bulk of the military ordnance was probably acquired from the Mexican military, and not smuggled into Mexico from Texas."[39]

Another Stratfor report observed that "the international media and Mexican politicians almost exclusively have focused on the flow of arms from the United States southward into Mexico." While acknowledging that rifles and handguns are smuggled south, Stratfor explained that many come from elsewhere; for example, the "large majority of fragmentation grenades" used by the Mexican cartels are South Korean–made M57s.

Stratfor explained that for half a century, Latin America had been rife with civil wars and insurgencies, but all these had now ended, except in some regions of Colombia and Peru. As a result, there are vast supplies of surplus military weapons available for the black market. In addition, newer arms, still in use by national militaries, are made available by corrupt officers. So why does the Mexican government point its finger at American firearms retailers? Stratfor explains:

> The lopsided Mexican government focus on the U.S. flow largely has resulted from a desire for political gain and funding. In contrast to the U.S. government, the governments of Guatemala and El Salvador have a hard enough time keeping a lid on their own domestic security situation. They have very little to offer in the way of countering this weapons flow. (In some cases, corrupt officials in those two Central American countries stand to gain from these illegal sales.) The United States, however, has much to offer in terms of funding and other programs (such as the Bureau of Alcohol, Tobacco, Firearms and Explosives' eTrace program), and therefore Mexico makes every attempt to keep attention

on the weapons-flow issue focused on the flow south from the United States.[40]

The definitive dismantling of the anti-American gun hoax came in a February special report, *Mexico's Gun Supply and the 90 Percent Myth*.[41] Based on 2008 data, Stratfor found that fewer than 12 percent of guns seized by the Mexican government could be traced to the United States, explaining that the 90 percent figure "is more political rhetoric than empirical fact."

Stratfor observed that "the Mexican government has tried to deflect responsibility for the cartel wars away from itself and onto the United States. According to the Mexican government, the cartel wars are not a result of corruption in Mexico or of economic and societal dynamics that leave many Mexicans marginalized and desperate to find a way to make a living. Instead, the cartel wars are due to the insatiable American appetite for narcotics and the endless stream of guns that flows from the United States into Mexico and that results in Mexican violence."

Yet "In fact, the 3,480 guns positively traced to the United States equals less than 12 percent of the total arms seized in Mexico in 2008 and less than 48 percent of all those submitted by the Mexican government to the ATF for tracing. This means that almost 90 percent of the guns seized in Mexico in 2008 were not traced back to the United States."

Why did so few of the Mexican gun seizures result in a successful trace to the United States?

The remaining 22,800 firearms seized by Mexican authorities in 2008 were not traced for a variety of reasons. In addition to factors such as bureaucratic barriers and negligence, many of the weapons seized by Mexican authorities either do not bear serial numbers or have had their serial numbers altered or obliterated. It is also important to understand that the Mexican authorities simply don't bother to submit some classes of weapons to the ATF for tracing. Such weapons include firearms they identify as coming from their own military or police forces, or guns that they can trace back themselves as being sold through the Mexican Defense Department's Arms and Ammunition Marketing Division (UCAM). Likewise, they do not ask ATF to trace military ordnance from third countries like the South Korean fragmentation grenades commonly used in cartel attacks.

In short, "there is no evidence to support the assertion that 90 percent of the guns used by the Mexican cartels come from the United States— especially when not even 50 percent of those that were submitted for tracing were ultimately found to be of U.S. origin."

So where do the Mexican crime guns come from? It depends on the type of gun.

The first category of weapons encountered in Mexico is weapons available legally for sale in Mexico through UCAM. These include handguns smaller than a .357 magnum, such as .380 and .38 Special.

A large portion of this first type of guns used by criminals is purchased in Mexico, or stolen from their legitimate owners. While UCAM does have very strict regulations for civilians to purchase guns, criminals will use straw purchasers to obtain firearms from UCAM or obtain them from corrupt officials. Cartel hit men in Mexico commonly use .380 pistols equipped with sound suppressors in their assassinations. In many cases, these pistols are purchased in Mexico, the suppressors are locally manufactured and the guns are adapted to receive the suppressors by Mexican gunsmiths.

Some of these handguns, ranging in caliber from .22 to .380, did come from the U.S. "There are a lot of cheap guns available on the U.S. market, and they can be sold at a premium in Mexico . . . Still, the numbers do not indicate that 90 percent of guns in this category come from the United States."

The next category is guns that Mexican civilians are not allowed to own, such as .357, 9mm, and .45 handguns, and semiautomatic rifles. These are "obtained from deserters from the Mexican military and police, purchased from corrupt Mexican authorities or even brought in from South America." The semiautos "are often converted by Mexican gunsmiths to be capable of fully automatic fire."

Notably, Mexican criminals are not the only purchasers for these smuggled arms. "There are many Mexican citizens who own guns in calibers such as .45, 9 mm, .40 and .44 magnum for self-defense—even though such guns are illegal in Mexico."

The final category of weapons, explained Stratfor, comprise those that were not available to the civilian market in the U.S. or in Mexico. In other words, "military-grade ordnance," such as "hand grenades, 40 mm grenades, rocket-propelled grenades (RPGs), automatic assault rifles and main battle rifles and light machine guns."

These are supplied by "the international arms market—increasingly from China via the same networks that furnish precursor chemicals for narcotics manufacturing—or from corrupt elements in the Mexican military or even deserters who take their weapons with them."

The fundamental problem is that "the same economic law of supply and demand that fuels drug smuggling into the United States also fuels gun smuggling into Mexico. Black market guns in Mexico can fetch up to 300 percent of their normal purchase price—a profit margin rivaling the narcotics the cartels sell." So even if it were somehow possible to hermetically seal the U.S.-Mexico border and shut off all the guns coming from the United States, the cartels would still be able to obtain weapons elsewhere—just as narcotics would continue to flow into the United States from other places."

Stratfor's rejection of the 90 percent hoax is consistent with a November 2010 report from the U.S. Department of Justice, Office of Inspector General. Under the scrutiny of the inspector general, BATFE admitted that "the 90% figure cited to Congress could be misleading because it applied only to the small portion of Mexican crime guns that are traced."

The report revealed that 26 percent of Mexican trace requests could not be completed due to serial number errors.

Further, of the firearms that BATFE could trace, 75 percent had been sold more than five years ago, and only 18 percent had been sold within the previous three years. Indeed, the average age from a gun traced from Mexico was fourteen years.[42]

BATFE uses the so-called time to crime (the time from when a firearm is sold at retail until the time a trace is requested) as a rough guide to whether the firearm was bought for criminal purposes. If a gun was used for a crime shortly after it was sold at retail, BATFE believes that it is relatively more likely that the gun was originally purchased by a criminal, a straw man, or a trafficker. If the "time to crime" is lengthy, then it is relatively more likely that the gun was legally purchased, later stolen, and then sold into the black market.

So with American guns in Mexico being an *average* of fourteen years old, BATFE's own data indicate that most of those guns were probably stolen from lawful owners, rather than bought by agents of the cartels.

Not long ago, the Woodrow Wilson Center for International Scholars was touting the claim that Mexico's crime problem was America's fault. But the accumulation of evidence apparently convinced even the Wilson Center to issue a new report. Among the findings in the report:

ATF agents say they can use only about eight percent of Mexico's firearm trace requests to initiate investigations, in part because many of the trace requests lack basic identification data and were purchased in the United States more than five years ago.[43]

And:

Mexico has submitted a total of 78,194 firearm trace requests to the United States from FY 2007 to FY 2010. During approximately the same time frame, President Calderon said Mexico had seized about 90,000 arms. Looking at these numbers, it may appear Mexico is providing ATF with information on a large number of the firearms it has seized since the start of the Calderon Administration, but ATF now reports that tens of thousands of the trace requests are duplicates. In some cases, ATF has received information on the same firearm up to five times as Mexican police, a crime lab, the military, and the Attorney General's office all write down information on the same firearm, and the individual in the Attorney General's office in Mexico City submits trace requests on all of them.[44]

BATFE justifies its ever-expanding budget by claiming that it is dedicated to solving the problem of high-volume firearms trafficking. Yet as demonstrated in research by Professor Gary Kleck of Florida State University, less than 1 percent of criminal guns are supplied by high-volume traffickers (250 or more guns per year). The black market is instead supplied with guns stolen during burglaries, guns purchased from criminals' friends, and other low-volume sources.[45]

Blaming law-abiding American gun stores and gun owners for Mexico's crime problem may make political sense for Mexican president Felipe Calderón and American president Barack Obama, but it's not the truth.

Operation Fast and Furious

In 2011, it was revealed that one major organization *was* complicit in the shipment of more than twenty-five hundred new guns into the hands of Mexican criminals.[46] That organization was the Bureau of Alcohol, Tobacco, Firearms and Explosives. BATFE's "Operation Fast and Furious" deliberately allowed firearms to go south, and urged American firearms dealers to sell guns to people who were obvious criminals or straw purchasers.

Fast and Furious was run out of BATFE's Phoenix office. A similar gun-running operation was conducted in Tucson. Called "Wide Receiver," it, too, was under the control of the Phoenix office.[47] (Instead of repeating the names for both operations, I will just refer to "Fast and Furious.")

Among the results of this hideous perversion of law enforcement was the December 14, 2010, murder of U.S. Border Patrol officer Brian Terry by illegal alien Mexican criminals. Two guns from Fast and Furious were recovered at the murder scene. Confidential BATFE sources say that many other Fast and Furious guns have been found at crime scenes in Mexico.[48] Mexican congressman Humberto Trevino says that Fast and Furious guns have been used in 150 murders and other shootings in Mexico.[49]

In February 2011, BATFE agent John Dodson, concerned about the death of agent Terry, came forward and revealed that BATFE's Phoenix office had a plan—which was opposed by several agents—to allow guns to "walk" south over the Mexican border.

Licensed firearms dealers were reluctant to participate in the BATFE's program to sell firearms to obvious straw purchasers and other suspicious buyers. As one dealer wrote in June 2010, "I shared my concerns with you guys that I wanted to make sure none of the firearms that were sold per our conversation with you and various ATF agents could or would ever end up south of the border or in the hands of bad guys." The dealer explained: "I want to help ATF with its investigation but not at the risk of agents' safety because I have some very close friends that are US Border Patrol agents."[50]

BATFE assured the dealers that "safeguards were in place" to keep the guns from going into Mexico or from being used in crimes. As Iowa senator Charles Grassley, ranking Republican on the Senate Judiciary Committee, later observed, those assurances were "untrue."[51] Among the dealers who did not want to participate in Fast and Furious was the dealer who sold the firearms that would eventually be found at the scene of Agent Terry's murder. The U.S. Attorney's office had told him to continue participating.[52]

According to Dodson, there were seven BATFE agents on the Phoenix Fast and Furious task force, four of whom raised strong objections.[53] David Voth, the supervisor of Phoenix Group (VII), sent a memo ordering the dissenters to fall in line:

> It has been brought to my attention that there may be a schism developing amongst the group. Whether you care or not people of high rank and authority at HQ are paying close attention to this case

and they also believe we [Phoenix Group VII] are doing what they envision the Southwest border groups doing. It may sound cheesy but we are "The tip of the ATF spear" when it comes to Southwest Border Firearms Trafficking. We need to resolve our issues at this meeting. I'll be damned if this case is going to suffer due to petty arguing, rumors or other adolescent behavior. I don't know what all the issues are but we are all adults, we are all professionals and we have the exciting opportunity to use the biggest tool in our law enforcement toolbox. If you don't think this is fun you're in the wrong line of work—period! This is the pinnacle of domestic U.S. Law enforcement techniques. After this the tool box is empty. Maybe the Maricopa County Jail is hiring detention officers and you can get paid $30,000 (instead of $100,000) to serve lunch to inmates all day. We need to get over this bump in the road once and for all and get on with the mission at hand. This can be the most fun you have with ATF, the only one limiting the amount of fun we have is you.

A particularly egregious example of such "fun" involved Jaime Avila, who bought the two rifles found at the scene of Agent Terry's death. According to a letter from Senator Grassley to Alan D. Bersin, the commissioner of U.S. Customs and Border Protection (CBP):

CBP officials allegedly stopped Jaime Avila near the border in the spring or summer of 2010. He allegedly had the two WASR-10 rifles in his possession that were later found at the scene of Agent Brian Terry's murder, along with over thirty additional weapons. CBP officials contacted ATF or an Assistant United States Attorney who allegedly instructed CBP to allow Avila [to] proceed without seizing the weapons.[54]

Besides strongly encouraging licensed firearms dealers to conduct illegal sales, BATFE was apparently engaged in its own illegal sales. According to a BATFE agent, BATFE undercover agents personally supplied Mexican gunrunners with firearms. The stated purpose was to gain the trust of the Mexican gangs, but things did not work out very well. For example, after delivering a pair of .50 caliber machine guns to the gangsters, BATFE promptly lost track of the machine guns after they entered Mexico.[55]

Information about Fast and Furious was apparently hidden from BATFE agents in Mexico. Even BATFE's head of Mexican operations, Darren Gil, was mostly kept in the dark. Gil says that when he raised concerns, BATFE told him that Fast and Furious was known to BATFE acting director Kenneth Melson and had been approved by the U.S. Department of Justice, the cabinet department of which BATFE is a component. Although Gil's authorization was required for any BATFE operation that allowed guns in Mexico, his authorization was never sought, and BATFE locked him out of computer files, apparently to prevent him from discovering what was going on.[56]

Gil, who retired in December 2010 partly because of his objections to Fast and Furious, warned that "the Mexicans are gonna have a fit when they find out about it." He worried that "at some point, these guns are gonna end up killing either a government of Mexico official, a police officer or military folks, and then what are we gonna do?"[57]

Phoenix BATFE agent John Dodson gave similar warnings: "I specifically asked one time, 'are you prepared to go to the funeral of a Border Patrol agent . . . are you prepared for that fact because it's only a matter of time before that happens.'"[58]

Everything that Gil and Dodson warned about came to pass. Border Patrol agent Terry was murdered. The Mexican government is considering criminal prosecution of BATFE agents there, even though those agents were never informed about Fast and Furious. As Gil explained, the Mexican "government's looking at (ATF agents) potentially bringing weapons into their country, which in many cases is an act of war." He charges that BATFE executives "are leaving my guys out in Mexico alone, and they're not doing the right thing."[59]

At a May 4 Senate Judiciary Committee hearing, Senator Grassley pointed to a BATFE memo showing that the Bureau had allowed criminal straw purchasers, believed to be working for the Mexican cartels, to purchase 1,608 guns. (As noted previously, the total number of Fast and Furious guns appears to be as high as 2,500.) Of the guns acknowledged in the memo, 179 were later recovered in Mexico, 130 in the U.S., and the remainder presumably are in the hands of the criminals who had hired the straw purchasers.[60]

To put this in perspective, in 2010, U.S. Immigrations and Customs Enforcement seized approximately 778 Mexico-bound firearms, setting a new record.[61] So BATFE's contribution to cartels' arsenals was not insignificant.

The effect on U.S.-Mexico relations has been disastrous. In March 2011, the U.S. ambassador, Carlos Pascual, resigned.[62] "Several sources close to diplomatic circles inside Mexico tell CBS News that from Mexico's viewpoint, the ATF 'gunwalking' scandal was the final straw in a series of controversies," the network reported.[63] Fast and Furious provides a handy cudgel for Mexico's radical leftists to oppose law enforcement and national security cooperation with the United States.[64]

To serve as BATFE's special attaché to the Mexican government, BATFE was planning to replace Gil with William Newell, the special agent in charge who ran Fast and Furious.[65] Those plans were apparently shelved due to the exposure of Fast and Furious, and Newell was transferred to BATFE's offices in Washington.

As I observed while this scandal was breaking open, our government has been willing to let people die to advance their assault on the Second Amendment. Our southern border proves it. When BATFE officials *order* lawful gun dealers to make illegal sales, that's corrupt. When BATFE authorizes and watches thousands of guns walk across the border and fall into the hands of Mexican drug cartels, that's not just bizarre law enforcement; it's government-sanctioned gunrunning. When does it stop being law enforcement and start being a criminal enterprise? Innocent people are dying. It makes no sense at all.[66]

"A cover-up at the highest level of Justice"

In the media, investigation of Operation Fast and Furious was spearheaded by CBS News reporter Sharyl Attkisson.[67]

After CBS News ran its first report, on February 22, BATFE's Scot L. Thomasson, chief of the Public Affairs Division, swung into action. He sent a memo to all BATFE Public Information Officers, asking them to "lessen the coverage of such stories in the news cycle by replacing them with good stories about ATF." He requested: "Please make every effort in the next two weeks to maximize coverage of ATF operations/enforcement actions/arrests at the local and regional level" in order to displace public attention to the "negative coverage by CBS News."

As he noted, "Fortunately, the CBS story has not sparked any follow up coverage by mainstream media and seems to have fizzled."[68]

He was right about the national media, most of which continues to ignore the BATFE scandal. But Congress has not been so supine.

The chairman of the House Committee on Oversight and Government Reform, Pro–Second Amendment Republican Daryl Issa of California, launched an investigation into "Fast and Furious." And veteran Iowa Republican senator Charles Grassley, the ranking member of the Senate Judiciary Committee, is conducting his own investigation.

As soon as Congress took action, BATFE management wrote a memo ordering agents not to talk to Congressional staff.[69] The reaction against agents who cooperated with Congress was swift. As one news report detailed, "An unidentified ATF employee alleged that he was 'called to the carpet' by supervisors, accused of lying and ordered to write down everything that was said in meetings that were held with Senate staffers conducting an inquiry."[70]

As I write this chapter, the Obama administration has attempted to stonewall the congressional investigators. Hillary Clinton's Department of States has thus far refused to comply with requests from Senator Grassley and Representative Issa for documents about her department's knowledge of "Fast and Furious"—particularly about the exchange of information in the summer of 2010 between the Department of Justice and the U.S. ambassador in Mexico.[71]

BATFE acting director Kenneth Melson refused to testify before the Senate Foreign Relations subcommittee on Western Hemisphere, Peace Corps and Global Narcotics Affairs—even though BATFE's gunrunning program has caused a disaster in U.S.-Mexico relations.[72]

BATFE and its parent, the Department of Justice, have thus far defied and delayed answering subpoenas. For example, BATFE and Melson refused to produce *any* documents in response to a March 2011 request, and later a subpoena from the House committee. Likewise, the DOJ has ignored since January 2011 a document request from Senator Grassley. The DOJ asserts that allowing Congress to see the documents would interfere with DOJ's own investigation.

An exasperated Chairman Issa explained that DOJ has no legal basis for its refusal:

> The Department's internal policy to withhold documents from what it labels pending criminal investigations may not deprive Congress from obtaining those same documents if they are pertinent to a congressional investigation—particularly in a matter involving allegations that reckless and inappropriate decisions by top Justice Department officials may have contributed to the deaths of both U.S. and Mexican citizens.

He pointed out that Supreme Court case law plainly refutes the DOJ's assertion that they can choose not to obey a congressional subpoena for documents. He continued:

Efforts by the Department of Justice and ATF to stonewall the Committee in its investigation by erroneously, but matter-of-factly, citing an internal department policy as a preventative measure for denying access to documents have only enhanced suspicions that such officials have played a role in reckless decisions that have put lives at risk. The Committee continues to pursue this matter vigorously, in part, because concerned individuals have indicated they do not have confidence in the Department's ability to review the actions of its own top officials.

Further,

Even if a legal basis did exist for withholding documents, the first step in evaluating this argument and the basis for a meaningful conversation between the Committee and the Department of Justice would be the production of a log of documents responsive to the subpoena with a specific explanation as to why you cannot produce each document.

Yet "the Department has failed to provide any such log."[73] Eventually, BATFE officials partially responded to Issa's subpoena, after he threatened to hold them in contempt of Congress, but the documents were heavily redacted. Issa complained: "So they've made no sufficient response to our subpoena. We consider that it continues to be a cover-up at the highest level of Justice." As a committee chairman, Issa has subpoena power, but as a ranking minority member, Senator Grassley does not. Accordingly, in May, Grassley threatened to use the Senate rules to hold up Obama administration nominations unless the documents he requested are produced.

Ludicrously, DOJ spokeswoman Tracy Schmaler asserted that DOJ "made clear to law enforcement agencies and prosecutors working along the border that no one should allow guns to illegally cross."[74] DOJ did not write such a memo until March 2011, after "Fast and Furious" had been exposed.[75]

DOJ made similar implausible denials in a February 4, 2011, letter to Senator Grassley, insisting that the whistleblower claims were "false" and claiming that "ATF makes every effort to interdict weapons that have been purchased illegally and prevent their transport to Mexico." In a May 2, 2011, letter to Grassley, DOJ stood its ground: "It remains our understanding that ATF's Operation Fast and Furious did not knowingly permit straw buyers to take guns into Mexico."[76]

Who made the decisions?

How high up does the responsibility go for Fast and Furious? You can start with Obama's appointed United States attorney for Arizona, Dennis Burke. A January 2010 BATFE memo states that Burke "fully supports" Fast and Furious. The memo also noted that the gun trafficking being allowed by BATFE was at an unusually high pace: "This blitz was extremely out of the ordinary."[77]

Burke is an Obama-Clinton insider. Eric Holder appointed him to the Attorney General's Advisory Committee, and made him chair of Attorney General's Subcommittee on Border and Immigration Law Enforcement. From 2003 to 2008 he was chief of staff to Arizona governor Janet Napolitano. When she became secretary of the Department of Homeland Security, he became her senior adviser. Before that he was assistant attorney general for legislative affairs for Bill Clinton's attorney general Janet Reno, and was senior policy analyst at the Clinton White House Domestic Policy Council.

The buck doesn't stop with Attorney General Holder's top adviser on border issues. Back in the D.C. headquarters known as "Main Justice," Lanny Breuer, who runs the DOJ's Criminal Division, not only knew about Fast and Furious; he approved wiretaps to facilitate the peration.[78] Breuer had previously served as special counsel to the Clinton White House, and helped defend Clinton during his impeachment trial.

The Department of Justice asserts that just because Breuer knew about Fast and Furious, and approved wiretaps for it, that does not mean that he "approved" of the operation."[1]

While BATFE and the U.S. Department of Justice have been stonewalling congressional investigators, it is becoming increasingly clear that responsibility for Fast and Furious goes at least as high as Attorney General Eric Holder, who has proven himself unfit to serve as U.S. attorney general— just as the NRA warned in January 2009.

Finally, on May 2, 2011, Attorney General Holder himself testified before the House committee. Chairman Issa pointed out that "the Justice Department is basically guilty of allowing weapons to kill Americans and Mexicans."

Holder retorted that blaming his department of Agent Terry's death was "offensive."[80]

"But what if it is accurate, Mr. Attorney General?" Issa responded.

Holder testified to the House Committee that he had only learned about Fast and Furious a few weeks before. Yet Senator Grassley had met personally with Holder on January 31, and hand-delivered to him letters that Grassley had written to BATFE acting director Melson on January 27 and 31, directly asking about the gunrunning scandal. Further, Grassley had sent follow-up letters to Holder on February 9, February 16, and March 3.[81]

When Holder was asked how guns were allowed to "walk" into Mexico, he answered, "I frankly don't know." With that statement, Holder is either covering up the crimes committed, or he's incompetent. Either way, he can't be trusted with the powers of the attorney general, the law enforcement he commands, the sanctity of the Second Amendment, or the lives of federal agents.

As I told the NRA membership at the annual meeting in Pittsburgh this spring, "Eric Holder said he didn't know about the operation. He's the U.S. attorney general. He's supposed to be in charge, and he didn't know? Who's minding the store over at the Justice Department? Because if Holder didn't know, Holder's got to go."

While much of the national media has ignored or downplayed the Fast and Furious scandal, an editorial in *Investor's Business Daily* asked, "Is Obama a Gunrunner?" Describing Fast and Furious as "at best embarrassing and at worst an unconscionable dereliction of duty," the editorial agreed with me that Eric Holder should resign, and concluded that "Operation Gunrunner should be the 'smoking gun' that makes it happen."[82]

The defenders of Fast and Furious claim that BATFE was engaged in a sophisticated operation to follow the guns into Mexico, and then discover a "Mr. Big" who was running the smuggling operation. BATFE's assistant director in charge of field operations, Mark Chait, said that he personally decided to implement Fast and Furious because prosecutions of low-level straw purchasers were going nowhere in terms of cracking the gun-smuggling cartel operations.[83]

Perhaps if BATFE had worked with dealers to implant hidden transponders in guns that would be sold to straw purchasers, the guns might have shown the path to Mr. Big. Indeed, that was what BATFE began to do starting with a 2005 pilot program in Laredo, Texas, that was later expanded. Straw purchasers would be given guns with secret electronic tracking devices. The purchasers would then be monitored, and BATFE would make arrests. But in late 2009, the Obama administration reversed the Bush policy of stopping the guns before they entered Mexico. Under the Obama system, guns would be allowed to be taken over the border.[84]

Holder has ordered an inspector general from the DOJ to conduct an investigation of Fast and Furious. But we already know that the Obama administration has fired inspectors general who reveal Obama administration malfeasance. We also know that the reason that BATFE agent John Dodson was forced to blow the whistle on Fast and Furious was because the DOJ inspector general ignored his attempts to tell them about the problem.[85] And Holder is using the DOJ's internal review as a pretext to hide information requested by Congress.

What about President Obama? Interviewed by Univision's Jorge Ramon on March 23, President Obama said that he "did not authorize" Fast and Furious and that he "was not informed" about it.[86] That stonewalling speaks volumes about his broken promises to give Americans an open, transparent, and accountable government.

The Obama/Brady Counterattack

Much of the national media remain impervious to the facts, and continue to regurgitate the 90 percent propaganda from the Obama administration and the gun prohibition lobbies. For example, the *Washington Post* still asserts that the Mexican drug gangs are "snapping up the military-style machine guns available in U.S. gun shops," as if fully automatic firearms were sold over the counter at gun stores. That hasn't been legal since the National Firearms Act of 1934.

While perpetrating a cover-up, the Obama administration continues to use Mexico as a pretext to impose more gun control. On March 30, 2011, Sarah and James Brady visited the White House to confer with the administration's "point man" on gun control, Steve Croley. President Obama himself stopped by. According to Mrs. Brady, he wanted "to fill us in that it [gun control] was very much on his agenda." He told the Bradys, "I just want you to know that we are working on it," and "We have to go through a few processes, but under the radar."[87] Or as the *Huffington Post* reported, "the Obama administration is exploring potential changes to gun laws that can be secured strictly through executive action, administration officials say."[88]

That is one promise that Barack Obama is keeping. BATFE announced that it wanted to create a new "emergency" requirement to register rifle sales, supposedly because of the problems in Mexico.

BATFE wants to require that every time a person in a state that borders Mexico purchases two or more semiautomatic centerfire rifles that use detachable magazines within five days, the store would be required to send BATFE a report of the sale. So if you buy your nephew a Remington 7400 deer rifle on Monday, and then buy yourself a Winchester 1907 for your collection on Friday, your name will be kept on a permanent government registration list. Although supposedly aimed at guns going to Mexico, the BATFE proposal also covers collectible "curios and relics"—not exactly the type of firearm usually sought by drug gangsters.

BATFE's plan is illegal. By statute, Congress has created a system for reporting people who purchase two or more handguns from a store within a five-day period. The "multiple sales report" is sent to local law enforcement, and to BATFE. Local law enforcement is supposed to destroy the records within twenty days (unless the sale was illegal), but BATFE can keep its records forever (18 U.S. Code section 923(g)(3)). As of 2010, BATFE had accumulated about 4.2 million handgun multiple sales reports. So when Congress wanted to create a system for multiple sales reporting, it did so. Congress decided that there should be no such reports for long guns.

Yet the Obama BATFE is attempting to use the manufactured crisis of American guns in Mexico as an excuse to impose regulations for multiple sales reporting for semiautos in the border states. Most likely, long gun registration in the border states would be used as the foundation to eventually expand the reporting and registration requirement to all long gun sales throughout the United States. This is exactly what the Brady Campaign is pushing for.[89]

The Brady "research" center even twisted Agent Terry's murder into a justification for the Brady/BATFE agenda. In a May 2011 report, the Brady Center noted Agent Terry's death, and then wrote:

> The shooting has engendered controversy, as it is alleged that federal prosecutors and ATF permitted 1,998 guns to be purchased and retained by suspected straw buyers in the hope that a major case could be built. While the truth of those allegations are disputed and unconfirmed. it [sic] is undisputed that if firearms laws were stronger by prohibiting multiple sales and requiring

responsible sales practices, these gun sales could not have been legally completed.[90]

What nonsense! Although BATFE and DOJ continue to cling to their preposterous denials that no guns were allowed to walk across the border, the facts plainly show otherwise.[91]

And the Brady claim about multiple sales reports—talk about chutzpah! Firearms dealers in the Southwest were already voluntarily calling BATFE to warn about suspicious customers who wished to purchase multiple firearms. The dealers didn't want to make the sales, but BATFE told them to go ahead anyway. The very dealer who sold the guns used by criminals who murdered agent Terry had personally tried to opt out of BATFE's guns-for-criminals program, but Obama's U.S. attorney assured him that everything would be fine. If BATFE and the Obama administration will pressure dealers to make multiple sales to obvious straw purchasers, it is outrageous for the Brady gang to pretend that a multiple sales report submitted several days after the sale would have saved Agent Terry.

The one thing that multiple sales reports really are good for is building a centralized national gun registration list, and the one thing a centralized gun registration is good for is gun confiscation.

In Congress, the NRA is hard at work to attach appropriations riders that will block BATFE from implementing its gun registration scheme. We'll pursue any avenue to block this scheme in the Congress or in the courts.

Mexico's planned lawsuit

Meanwhile, the Mexican government is understandably furious about Operation Fast and Furious. But anger at BATFE's malfeasance is not slowing down the Mexican government's assault on American gun ownership. Mexico's ambassador to the United States suggested that American gun stores could be called "providers of material support to terrorists."[92]

On November 2, 2010, the Mexican government retained the New York City and Austin, Texas, law firm of Reid, Collins & Tsai to make plans for lawsuits against American gun manufacturers.

It's particularly ironic that President Calderón's government would plan a suit against American manufacturers since their trade association, the National Shooting Sports Foundation, has for years operated a program called "Don't Lie for the Other Guy," which educates consumers about the severe legal penalties for making a straw purchase, and teaches firearms retailers how to spot straw purchasers. Perhaps Calderón ought to sue BATFE instead, for forcing retailers to allow sales to straw purchasers.

You may wonder how a Mexican lawsuit could possibly succeed, since the Protection of Lawful Commerce in Arms Act (PLCAA), passed by Congress in 2005, prohibits such baseless lawsuits in all state and federal courts.

Well, to start with, the Mexican government could bring a lawsuit in a *Mexican* court. The PLCAA doesn't apply to courts in other nations. A Mexican court could decide that it has jurisdiction over the American manufacturers, because the manufacturers have voluntarily done business in Mexico, maybe even by selling firearms to the Mexican military or police.

Or, as discussed in chapter 3, a suit could be brought in the World Court (which is located in the Netherlands) or the Inter-American Court of Human Rights (located in Costa Rica). Such suits would probably require some cooperation and consent by the United States government, and the Obama administration could decide to help out.

Perhaps most ominously, the Mexican government could launch a frontal assault on the Protection of Lawful Commerce in Arms Act. The Mexican government and their lawyers would carefully look for an American jurisdiction stacked with plenty of antigun judges. Then they would file the suit and ask the court to declare the PLCAA unconstitutional.

The Brady Campaign has been calling the PLCAA unconstitutional ever since its enactment. Brady Campaign lawyers have repeatedly attempted to void the PLCAA, but their arguments have failed in the courts.

As a practical matter, a suit by the government of Mexico may get a much more sympathetic hearing than a suit by a gun-ban group that has virtually no grassroots support. It is rare for foreign governments to appear as plaintiffs in American courts. There may never have been a lawsuit in which the foreign government complains that the actions of some American businesses are putting the very survival of that foreign nation in jeopardy.

Every American judge knows that the stability of the Mexican government is of paramount national interest to the people of the United States, and that if the cartels succeed in turning Mexico into a narco-state, the result will be a disaster for the United States.

So Mexican claims would get the most careful attention from any judge, and might convince some judges to bend the law as far as necessary in order to save the Mexican government.

Whatever happened in the trial court, the Mexican lawsuit would be designed to make its way to the United States Supreme Court. By the time the case got to the Supreme Court, President Obama may have had time to appoint one more antigun justice, creating a five-justice antigun majority.

The Obama-dominated Supreme Court could throw out the PLCAA, and thereby open the floodgates to lawsuits designed to destroy America's firearms manufacturers. American gun manufacturers would be destroyed by litigation costs not only from Mexico, but also from a fresh round of lawsuits filed by antigun politicians and the gun prohibition groups.

Will the Mexican government overcome its massive problem with law enforcement corruption and someday shut down the cartels? It is hard to say. It seems unlikely that the situation is going to get a lot better anytime soon.

So while President Obama dithers and delays and finds excuses not to build the fence, American gun owners will continue to face demands for restrictions on their rights, in order to fix the problems in Mexico that are supposedly America's fault.

Because the cartels will always have all the money they need to buy all the guns they want, nothing that is done to American gun owners will disarm the Mexican cartels. So as soon as one set of restrictions is forced onto Americans, and the Mexican cartels remain well armed, the failure of one set of restrictions will be quickly followed by demands for more.

Chapter 9

Peacekeepers, Rapists, and Gunrunners

The U.N. never tires of proclaiming its strong opposition to illegal gunrunning and to sexual violence. However, the U.N. does not do much to punish its employees who run guns and perpetrate sexual assaults, including the rape of children. The U.N. "Peacekeepers" are the organization's global army; when they commit the crimes that made America's Founders so wary of standing armies, the U.N. response is a cover-up.

Corrupt and Expensive

With more than one hundred thousand soldiers in eighteen nations, the U.N. has more deployed troops than any nation except the United States.[1] Although the U.S. pays 22 percent of the general U.N. budget, American taxpayers pay 27 percent of the "peacekeeping budget."[2] The Department of Peacekeeping Operations (DPKO) spends more than $7 billion a year.[3]

An audit of a billion dollars of procurement of the DPKO found that at least $265 million had been lost in waste and fraud.[4] A separate audit of peacekeeping in Sudan found tens of millions of dollars of money wasted, and strong evidence of fraud and corruption.[5]

The DPKO's largest food services contractor paid tens of millions of dollars to settle a suit alleging that the company, in conjunction with corrupt U.N. officials, had engaged in racketeering and bid-rigging to win U.N. contracts.[6] Appointments of positions of responsibility in DPKO are often based on "political pressure, favoritism, and cronyism . . . resulting in institutional weaknesses and a staff that is less than ideally equipped to complete the required tasks," the Heritage Foundation reports.[7]

Gunrunning in the Democratic Republic of the Congo

The Democratic Republic of the Congo (DRC) has been the site of civil wars, and, often, foreign invasions ever since it gained independence from Belgium in 1960. Many Congolese have to believe that "of all the bad governments we had, the Belgian colonists are still the best."[8]

Thanks to abundant natural resources, including vast mineral wealth, the DRC ought to be one of the richest countries in the world. Instead, its people are among the poorest.

The current war going on in the DRC involves a dizzying variety of warlords in the eastern part of the country, a central government in Kinshasa that (like all of its post-Belgian predecessors) has never exercised real sovereignty over the whole country, and a national army that is only sometimes under the command of the central government.

The United Nations has sent peacekeeping troops into the DRC, along with many aid workers. The whole enterprise is known as MONUC, for its French acronym.

One thing that the U.N forces are not particularly interested in is fighting the warlords. The *Inner City Press*, a New York City newspaper that follows the U.N. closely, reported: "In the Congo, MONUC has an air force and peacekeepers everywhere, except when called on to engage rebel groups like the CNDC—then they stand down and return to their bases, with good food and even surfing."[9] The *Inner City Press* elaborated in another article:

It has emerged that during the fighting in December [2007] in North Kivu in which the forces of renegade Tutsi general Laurent Nkunda soundly thrashed the Congolese Army, the UN Peacekeeping battalion in the area, Indian nationals, stood down and did not fight. Worse, the orders to take no chances are said to have come from New Delhi, which continues to cash big UN checks for providing peacekeepers to UN mission[s]. But what's the value, in a place like Eastern Congo, if the troops refuse to fight?[10]

According to a report by Doctors Without Borders, on November 1, 2008, the terrorist Lord's Resistance Army launched an attack on civilians in the northeastern DRC. The U.N. Peacekeepers remained inside their base near the town of Dungu while hundreds of civilians were slaughtered. The Peacekeepers also failed to evacuate wounded victims.[11]

The United Nations Security Council has imposed an embargo on the transfer of arms to warlords in the eastern Democratic Republic of the Congo. Yet the warlords remain well armed, thanks to guns supplied by China, Rwanda, and Sudan, among others.[12] In fact, United Nations peacekeepers in the DRC itself were caught selling guns to the warlords.

In May 2007, British Broadcasting Corporation reporter Martin Plaut broke the story that "Pakistani UN peacekeeping troops have traded in gold and sold weapons to Congolese militia groups they were meant to disarm."[13] The particular warlords, the so-called Nationalist and Integrationist Front, have been accused of war crimes and genocide, making the supplying of arms to them particularly heinous.

A follow-up story by Plaut reported on a secret internal U.N. report confirming the existence of a guns-for-gold smuggling network involving Pakistani peacekeepers.[14] (Ivory was also smuggled.)[15]

Facing demand for a public investigation, the U.N. announced in April 2008 that there was no problem. Jean-Marie Guéhenno, the under-secretary-general for Peacekeeping Operations, announced, "The investigation has found no evidence of gun smuggling. But it has identified an individual who seemed to have facilitated gold smuggling."[16] The report said that the gold smuggling was part of an operation involving an Indian business based in Kenya.[17]

Alan Doss, the present head of the United Nations mission in the Congo, said that the allegations of arms smuggling had not been proven.[18] Doss's predecessor at MONUC, William Lacy Swing,[19] had been even firmer: "This I can categorically deny."[20]

The BBC's Plaut explained the real story:

> There are indications that the UN covered up what was taking place for political reasons . . . UN insiders the BBC has spoken to tell us this aspect [gun smuggling] of the UN report was suppressed for political reasons—it was simply too difficult to accuse Pakistan of re-arming known killers, since Pakistan is the largest troop contributor to the UN, providing 10,000 troops across the world.[21]

From the U.N.'s point of view, it seems that you can't admit that the cops are in league with the criminals, because that might make the cops unhappy.

The facts strongly suggest that Pakistani peacekeepers armed the warlords. Ammunition manufactured in Pakistan was confiscated from warlords.[22] Uganda's defence minister Crispus Kiyonga charged that MONUC had rearmed rebels.[23] Internal U.N. reports showed that the U.N.'s Office of Internal Oversight Services (OIOS) in February had dismissed the evidence of DRC gunrunning.[24]

Human Rights Watch (HRW) pointed out that the U.N.'s self-exoneration "report" was a cover-up:

> We are, however, disappointed by the apparent narrowness of the report's conclusions, the lack of transparency in the process, the slow progress of the investigation, and most important, the continuing lack of accountability. You told the British Broadcasting Corporation (BBC) on July 13 that this matter is "now closed." Yet no individual has yet been held accountable despite findings by

OIOS, the investigative arm of the United Nations, that illegal behavior by at least one Pakistani officer had occurred.[25]

The U.N. had claimed that only one peacekeeper had done anything wrong. HRW considered this quite implausible: "It is our view that the assistance provided by Pakistani peacekeepers went well beyond one individual."[26] Further, as HRW pointed out, "The slow process in carrying out this investigation and the continued lack of action raises important questions about how the UN investigates itself."[27] And besides, there were lots of other problems involving MONUC peacekeepers:

> We note in this connection that the allegations against the Pakistanis are just one of a series of allegations that have emerged in recent months. These include allegations of gold trading by Indian peacekeepers in North Kivu, the alleged killing of two Congolese detainees and the beating of others by Bangladeshi peacekeepers in Ituri in February 2005, and ongoing allegations of sexual exploitation, among others. As far as we are aware, nobody has been prosecuted in connection with most of these cases.[28]

HRW's suspicions about a cover-up were confirmed by U.N. staff. The DRC investigation had been conducted by the OIOS. Matthias Basanisi, who was the deputy chief investigator for the Congo, published an article explaining that the OIOS had produced a whitewash, had ignored evidence of gunrunning, and had removed him from the investigation in 2007 when he refused to cooperate in the cover-up.

In the *New York Times*, Basanisi wrote:

> I was the investigator in charge of the United Nations team that in 2006 looked into allegations of abuses by Pakistani peacekeepers in Congo and found them credible. But the investigation was taken

away from my team after we resisted what we saw as attempts to influence the outcome. My fellow team members and I were appalled to see that the oversight office's final report was little short of a whitewash.

The reports we submitted to the office's senior management in 2006 included credible information from witnesses confirming illegal deals between Pakistani peacekeepers and warlords from the Front for National Integration, an ethnic militia group notorious for its cruelty even in such a brutal war. We found corroborative information that senior officers of the Pakistani contingent secretly returned seized weapons to two warlords in exchange for gold, and that the Pakistani peacekeepers tipped off two warlords about plans by the United Nations peacekeeping force and the Congolese Army to arrest them. And yet, much of the evidence we uncovered was excluded from the final report released last summer, including corroboration from the warlords themselves.

[F]ormer colleagues of mine who recently investigated similar allegations against Indian peacekeepers in Congo are worried that some of their most serious findings will also be ignored and not investigated further.[29]

The OIOS responded that Basanisi had not provided evidence of gunrunning, but merely allegations.[30]

The *Washington Post* reported that it has obtained a summary of "internal documents, e-mails and eyewitness testimony" that showed that the smuggling operation was far more extensive, and the crime far more serious, than the U.N. report had claimed. The *Post* explained:

Pakistani commanders established commercial links with two Nationalist and Integrationist Front leaders, Gen. Mateso Nyinga—known as Kung Fu—and Col. Drati Massasi—known as

Dragon—as early as spring 2005, according to accounts by a U.N. interpreter and the two militia leaders.

The illegal trade continued with commanders of the Congolese armed forces after the militia was driven from the area in October 2005 and its two commanders were jailed, according to testimony from a Congolese officer and other internal documents.

. . . One Pakistani commander, Maj. Ali Zaman, supplied the militia with weapons so it could protect the Pakistani troops and promised to tip the militia off before raids by government forces, according to the sources.

. . . [N]yinga and Massasi, meanwhile, issued a handwritten confession from their jail cells in May. They said they facilitated the Pakistanis' participation in the gold trade and received arms to protect the Pakistani zone from attacks . . . The note was delivered to Human Rights Watch and others by a source close to the two militia leaders, according to Van Woudenberg.[31]

The quantity of guns supplied by the Pakistani peacekeepers was probably low compared to how many guns the U.N. ended up providing to the DRC warlords by another channel. Since the late 1990s, the U.N. has been working to disarm the citizens of Albania, even though the often-corrupt Albanian government is unable to protect the people of that mountainous nation.[32] After the U.N. helped the Albanian government collect more than a hundred thousand guns, the government then sold the guns on the international black market, where the Rwandan government bought large quantities, and then delivered them (in violation of a Security Council arms embargo) to warlords in the DRC.[33]

Sexual Abuse in the Democratic Republic of the Congo

U.N. "peacekeepers" and staff have perpetrated sexual abuse of women and children, a problem that was covered up by the U.N. itself, despite then secretary-general Kofi Annan's self-serving protestations to the contrary.[34]

Although Kofi Annan had long tolerated a culture of rape in the Department of Peacekeeping Operations, the negative publicity about the DRC peacekeepers became a serious public relations problem for the United Nations. If my book *The Global War on Your Guns* played some role in putting pressure on the U.N., I'm glad it did. Certainly that book, with more than a hundred thousand copies sold, was the biggest-selling book that exposed the problem.

So the U.N. once again announced a policy of "zero tolerance" for rapes by peacekeepers and for sexual relations with underage girls. It would be nice if the U.N. had been against rape all along, but better late than never.

At headquarters in New York, there do appear to be some staffers who are taking the anti-rape policy seriously.[35]

The French government prosecuted Didier Bourget, the MONUC employee who ran a child pornography and rape ring. He is currently in prison for raping young girls when he was working in the DRC and the Central African Republic between 1998 and 2004.[36] Bourget must feel like the unluckiest man in the world; he is one of the very few U.N. rapists who has ever been sent to prison.

But out in the field, abuses appear to be continuing. A 2006 investigation by the U.N.'s OIOS found 217 allegations of sexual abuse by DRC peacekeepers. The report said many of the allegations were credible, and that sexual assault by peacekeepers appears to be "frequent and ongoing." According to the report, "One victim informed (investigators) that she had received a message from a peacekeeper that he would 'hack them' if he ever saw them again." Ten of the alleged victims, all under eighteen, lived in a liquor store that also operated as a house of prostitution.

However, the OIOS could establish proof against only one of the seventy-five peacekeepers who had been accused.[37]

In 2008, the Indian army, which supplies many of the U.N. peacekeeping troops, announced that it had opened an investigation of at least a hundred Indian peacekeepers participating in a child prostitution ring, involving both girls and boys, in Goma, the capital of the North Kivu province in the eastern DRC.[38]

The *New York Times* reports that "the United Nations already considers eastern Congo the rape capital of the world"[39] (although South Africa, thanks to its new gun law, is vying for that infamous title). In the recent past, there have been a huge number of rapes of men. Most of the Congo rapes are perpetrated by the warlord armies or other criminals, but according to the *Times*, "One mother said a United Nations peacekeeper raped her 12-year-old boy. A United Nations spokesman said that he had not heard that specific case but that there were indeed a number of new sexual abuse allegations against peacekeepers in Congo and that a team was sent in late July to investigate."[40] Jessica Neuwirth, president of the New York–based organization Equality Now, told the U.N. that women in the DRC ask, "What good is that [U.N.] presence to us, when we continue to be kidnapped and raped?" Neuwirth said that "the 200,000 women who have been raped in the DRC are expecting more concrete and timely results. They are asking me to present their petition to you. We must therefore take action. What can we do?"[41]

Feminist author Eve Ensler wrote:

While the number of criminal prosecutions has risen marginally, only low-ranking soldiers are being prosecuted. Not a single commander or officer above the rank of major has been held responsible in all of Congo. Rapes by the national army are increasing, too. MONUC, the U.N. peacekeeping mission, is not only allowing perpetrators to go unpunished but is also providing logistical support to them for their movements in the field.[42]

The *Inner City Press* reported:

The pandemic of rape of women in the Democratic Republic of
the Congo has many complex causes but these include the United
Nations, according to Doctor Roger Luhiriri of the Panzi Hospital
in Bukavu in Eastern Congo. Doctor Luhiriri noted that "at first
MONUC was an observer mission, then they sent troops. . . . He
gave an example, saying the rebel General Laurent Nkunda and
one of his colonels mutinied in Bukavu and, in presence of the
UN, his group engaged in rape. All were present," he said, adding
that "the UN contributes to rape in Eastern Congo, it has changed
from a mission of peace to a mission war, a shame for the UN."[43]

Not that MONUC never helps anyone. In 2009, MONUC
provided an airlift so that two doctors could provide diabetes treatment to
Major General Sylvestre Mudacumura, the warlord in charge of the FDLR (a
group led by Rwandan genocidaires who have been operating in the DRC,
and whom MONUC is supposed to be suppressing).[44]

MONUC was not quite so speedy in responding to reports of
mass rapes of 154 women in August 2010 in a village twenty miles from a
peacekeeper base. The U.N. initially claimed that it had no knowledge until
weeks later, but this turned out not to be true.[45]

Karl Steinacker, who worked for the U.N. in the Congo until 2009,
explains the problem: "There is a general state of incompetence, which is
linked to apathy."[46]

According to a report by a U.N.-created Group of Experts,
MONUC is a failure. Indeed, its support for the Congolese national army
is making things worse, because that army is itself a massive perpetrator
of atrocities against the civilian population—not surprisingly, since many
army commanders were formerly independent warlords. Another report, by
Human Rights Watch, concluded that MONUC's support for the Congolese
army constitutes violations of the laws of war.[47]

West Africa

U.N. peacekeepers arrived in Liberia in 1996. Most were from Nigeria, and they reportedly encouraged nine- or ten-year-old girls from a nearby refugee camp to have sex with them, in exchange for rice or a bit of cash. Ghanian peacekeepers did the same, except they would give the little girls an entire can of rice, rather than just a handful. As a result, the girls started coming to the Ghanian camp instead of the Nigerian one.

"One day dead little girls started appearing on the path from the displaced persons camp to the Ghanian camp . . . The girls had been decapitated and their heads inserted inside their nine-year-old genitals." A U.N. investigator concluded that the Nigerians were warning the girls to not go to the Ghanian camp for the extra food.

"And these are the peacekeepers," the authors of *Emergency Sex and Other Desperate Matters* note.[48] The book recounts an incident in which Liberian refugees were fleeing from a rebel army until U.N. peacekeepers intercepted them and told them to stay put in a village. Then the peacekeepers withdrew, leaving the refugees behind to be soon slaughtered by the rebels. Further south, the peacekeepers refused to allow any refugees to flee through U.N. defensive lines, thereby leaving the refugees nowhere to escape the rebels.[49]

The sexual abuse in Liberia was hardly atypical. A 2002 report by Save the Children detailed how staff from more than forty international "aid" agencies—including from the United Nations High Commissioner for Refugees (UNHCR)—raped and sexually abused refugees in Liberia, Sierra Leone, and Guinea. The report also accused the U.N. of trying to cover up the problem.[50]

In 2001, the United Nations High Commissioner for Refugees and Save the Children conducted a joint investigation of the abuses. They found widespread problems, including "humanitarian" workers who refused to give out food or supplies unless the refugees submitted to sex. The report, a draft of which was released in February 2002, contained extensive recommendations.[51] By October 2002, the High Commissioner for Refugees could point to a long list of reforms that had been implemented.[52]

But in March 2005, the *Washington Post* reported on a February 8, 2005, internal U.N. letter, which stated that in Gbarnga, Liberia, "girls as young as 12 years of age are engaged in prostitution, forced into sex acts and sometimes photographed by U.N. peacekeepers in exchange for $10 or food or other commodities." Further, the letter reported that in Robertsport, Liberia, community leaders said that U.N. peacekeepers were "using administrative building premises and the surrounding bush to undertake sex acts with girls between the age of 12–17."[53]

Liberia

In May 2006, Save the Children U.K released a report finding that U.N. peacekeepers, as well as other aid workers, were sexually exploiting girls as young as eight years old. Based on interviews with more than three hundred people, "all of the respondents clearly stated that the scale of the problem affected over half of the girls in their locations."[54] The U.N. office in Liberia said that it had been notified of only eight cases of sexual abuse, and that one staff member had been suspended.[55]

Sudan

As in the Democratic Republic of the Congo, the U.N. peacekeeper command in Sudan seems uninterested in using soldiers for anything involving soldiering. Food rations for the refugees in Darfur had to be cut in half because the U.N. would not use its peacekeepers in Sudan to protect U.N. World Food Program trucks from hijackers.[56] In September 2010, the peacekepers refused to go to a site, the Tabaret Market, to rescue victims who were dying in the streets after having been attacked by Janjaweed thugs. The

U.N. commanders decided not to act unless the Sudanese government (that is, the sponsor of the Janjaweed) granted permission.[57]

In January 2007, the *Daily Telegraph*, one of the leading newspapers in the United Kingdom, reported that the peacekeepers for the U.N. Mission in Southern Sudan (UNMIS), raped and sexually abused children as young as twelve. The abuse appears to have begun shortly after the U.N. arrived there, and was documented in July 2005 by an internal U.N. report prepared by UNICEF. Contacted by the *Telegraph*, the British regional coordinator said that the claims were unsubstantiated, and not supported by medical evidence.[58]

Ivory Coast

In 2007, the United Nations opened an investigation into sexual abuse in the Ivory Coast, allegedly perpetrated by Moroccan soldiers. The abuse was said to have involved girls under age eighteen, to have left some of the girls pregnant, and to have victimized about a hundred girls in the months before the investigation began.[59]

Before the 2007 scandal came to light, the U.N. from 2005 to 2007 had repatriated or dismissed seventeen peacekeepers in the Ivory Coast.[60] There were also allegations that the leadership of the U.N. mission in the Ivory Coast had been told about the widespread problem but did nothing about it. The mission refused to answer media questions about the allegation.[61]

A 2008 report by Save the Children studied the Ivory Coast and Haiti and found many instances of peacekeeper sexual abuse. For example, the BBC reported one incident involving Pakistani soldiers:

A 13-year-old girl, "Elizabeth" described to the BBC how 10 UN peacekeepers gang-raped her in a field near her Ivory Coast home. "They grabbed me and threw me to the ground and they forced themselves on me . . . I tried to escape but there were

10 of them and I could do nothing," she said. "I was terrified. Then they just left me there bleeding." No action has been taken against the soldiers.[62]

Haiti

U.N. peacekeepers in Haiti severely beat two Haitian policeman in the capital, Port-au-Prince, because the peacekeepers (for some unknown reason) told policemen to leave the area. Among those who joined in the attack were ten Brazilian peacekeepers.[63]

In 2007, 108 Sri Lankan peacekeepers were sent home after an investigation found that they had patronized prostitutes, some of them as young as thirteen. The soldiers amounted to about a tenth of the Sri Lankan force, and were said to face possible court-martial.[64]

The Sri Lankan case is an example of some progress that has been made. U.N. agreements with Troop Contributing Countries now require the countries "to bring the full force of their legal sanctions to bear" on troops who commit crimes, although the requirement is difficult to enforce.

Unlike in the past, once the U.N. notifies a country of an alleged crime, the U.N. now offers the assistance of the U.N.'s Office of Internal Oversight Services to investigate the crime. The Sri Lankan government accepted this assistance.[65]

One Haitian girl said she had been raped when she was fifteen. "I thought they came to protect us. I never thought they could abuse me in this way." The U.N. said that it had investigated her charges and found no substantiating evidence. Her lawyer responded that the investigation was a whitewash, and the U.N. had not given the final report to either him or the victim.[66]

As reported in the *Los Angeles Times*:

"The Sri Lankan case is the one we are hearing about now, but it's not the only one," said Olga Benoit of Haitian Women's Solidarity, recalling two Pakistani peacekeepers who were expelled two years ago for raping a mentally ill woman in Gonaives and a French policeman disciplined for keeping a prostitute captive . . . Anecdotal reports on the Sri Lankan scandal indicate girls in their early teens were often involved, and that in the poorest areas of the capital the going rate for sex was a dollar.[67]

A fourteen-year-old girl said she had been raped inside a U.N. naval base; according to the BBC, "Despite detailed medical and circumstantial evidence, the allegation was dismissed by the UN for lack of evidence."[68]

After the May 2008 report by Save the Children, the chairwoman of the Haitian Lawyers Leadership Network said, "In Haiti, children as young as six were sexually abused by peacekeepers and aid workers, according to the report; and by the lack of media coverage it would seem that the world doesn't care." She continued: "Those of us on the ground in Haiti have been saying these things for years, but this report has credibility because of the group putting it out.[69]

The Sri Lankan government has not provided information to the the public about what discipline had been imposed on the peacekeepers. The U.N. had promised to be transparent, and to create a website providing information about the Sri Lankan abuse. But no website is yet online.[70] *Wall Street Journal* reporters found that twenty-three soldiers had been convicted by a military court in Sri Lanka, and as a result, three of them were forced out of the military.[71]

Brian Conconnon, director of the Institute for Justice and Democracy in Haiti, contends, "What the UN Mission in Haiti is doing is not a mission of stabilization." Instead, "it is a mission that engages in operations of massacres, assassinations and alleged sexual abuse of women and children more so than activities of reconstruction and peacekeeping."[72]

Save the Children accused the U.N of "endemic failure" to deal with the abuse.[73]

Reform?

Throughout late 2004 and the first part of 2005, the U.N. bureaucracy issued numerous promises of reform, for "zero tolerance" for sex abuse, and so on,[74] but after leading his own investigation, Jordan's Prince Zeid al-Hussein told the media in 2005 that the U.N. member states were uninterested in real reform. "The entire responsibility for this mess is with the member states." His calls for reform were met with what he called "utter silence." He scheduled meetings to discuss reform, and no one would attend.[75] Prince Zeid explained to the Security Council that the U.N. had been covering up abuses by peacekeepers ever since its inception sixty years ago.[76]

Today, as before, the worst thing that is likely to happen to a U.N. peacekeeper who sexually abuses someone is that he will be sent home. As before, hardly any of the few peacekeepers who are sent home are punished, or even charged.[77]

Criminal prosecutions are extremely rare. Many countries have no criminal law regarding a soldier's rape that is perpetrated outside the country. Home-country prosecutors may have great difficulty in gathering sufficient information for a conviction.

Prosecutions in the country where the rape occurred are legally impossible, since U.N. troops have legal immunity. (Although the U.N. could, if it wanted to, waive the legal immunity.) Unfortunately, few U.N. peacekeeping deployments take place in nations that have functioning judicial systems.

One of the coauthors of *Emergency Sex and Other Desperate Measures: A True Story from Hell on Earth*, which detailed the incompetence and abuses of U.N. peacekeepers, was New Zealand doctor Andrew Thomson. Although he had worked for the U.N. for twelve years and his contract had been renewed annually, he was terminated without explanation.[78]

Another coauthor, Kenneth Cain, left the U.N. in 1996. Cain explains that most U.N. employees come from a corrupt national elite that can get away with anything, as long as they do not offend someone more powerful. At the U.N., they have created a similar culture. "They are perfectly happy to release documents that promise or imply efforts to reform—and time after time it dies before the ink is dry . . . The United Nations promulgates human-rights standards to the whole world. But when you try to hold them to the very same standards, it's impossible."[79]

Rape, kidnapping, human trafficking, and pederasty committed by peacekeepers are violations of human rights standards created by the U.N., including the Convention on the Rights of the Child, Convention on the Elimination of All Forms of Discrimination against Women, and the Universal Declaration of Human Rights.

Anne Bayefsky, editor of the "Eye on the U.N." project at Touro Law School, argues that:

> the U.N. officially has a policy of "zero tolerance" but the reality is that it's cognizant of these abuses for years . . . The United Nations knows its peace operations are plagued with sexual exploitation and abuse and every once in a while, they produce another report saying "we really have to ensure the zero tolerance policy is implemented," yet the problem occurs over and over again so it's clearly not being implemented."[80]

At the very least, the U.N. could follow the recommendations of its own 2005 report by docking the pay of soldiers who perpetrate sexual abuse, and setting up a fund to assist the women and girls who are impregnated by U.N. soldiers.[81]

Another step would be to stop using troops from countries, such as Nepal, which practice systematic torture or abuse.[82] The U.N. could also choose to take peacekeeping troops only from countries with good records of prosecuting peacekeeping troops who commit crimes against civilians.[83]

One simple step might be for the U.N. to have a review process for soldiers who are slated for U.N. peacekeeping assignments. At the least, the review might screen out some soldiers who have convictions for sexual assault. However, the U.N. has refused to set up such a process.[84]

The U.N. is creating a new internal justice system for U.N. personnel. But secretary-general Ban Ki-moon has rejected the recommendation of an U.N. expert panel that the system include peacekeepers. So the soldiers will remain subject only to whatever sanction, if any, their own country decides to impose for rape perpetrated in the Third World.[85]

Meaningful reform is unlikely. Developed countries do not like to contribute peacekeepers because of the cost. Besides, some soldiers from freedom-loving nations are understandably reluctant to serve under a U.N. command. So the countries that supply large numbers of peacekeepers tend to be those who pay their soldiers poorly.[86] The governments of those countries make a profit in renting out their soldiers to the U.N. The leading troop-contributing countries are, in order: Pakistan, Bangladesh, India, Nigeria, Nepal, Ghana, Jordan, and Rwanda.[87] None of them are known for treating women well.

Actor and gun control activist George Clooney, who joked viciously about Charlton Heston suffering from Alzheimer's disease, is an official U.N. "messenger of peace." In 2008, he appeared in a commercial for the U.N. peacekeepers, telling viewers that "the UN has more than 100,000 peacekeepers on the ground in places that others can't, or won't, go, doing things that others can't, or won't, do."[88]

The truth is that what the U.N. peacekeepers "won't do" is fight. What they don't do is stop raping children. And what the U.N. doesn't do is take meaningful action to stop the global abuses perpetrated by its standing army.

Chapter 10

United Nations Corruption

The United Nations brags that it spends $30 billion a year.[1] American taxpayers pay for more than $5 billion of that, required to fork over 22 percent of the U.N.'s budget.[2] U.N. spending has been growing rapidly; it has nearly tripled since 1999. The 2008–09 biennial budget grew 25 percent larger than the 2006–07 budget,[3] and the 2010–11 budget grew 18 percent above that.[4] The United Nations Association (a private pro-U.N. organization) celebrated the good news: "Need a Job? UN Payroll Is a Bright Spot in Bleak Times."[5] This is good news for the fortunate few on the U.N. gravy train, but bad news for the struggling American taxpayers who subsidize them. A deeply corrupt organization, the U.N. spends enormous sums of U.S. taxpayer money on waste, fraud, and abuse.

Oil-for-Food

The U.N. Oil-for-Food program was supposed to aid the poor people of Iraq; instead, it was used to help dictator Saddam Hussein oppress and murder the Iraqis, protect himself by bribing foreign governments, and finance terrorism against Americans.

After the 1991 Gulf War, Saddam Hussein agreed to a cease-fire on the part of coalition forces—which could have easily deposed his criminal regime—in exchange for complete dismantlement of his weapons of mass destruction (WMD) program. The burden was explicitly on Saddam to prove that he had disarmed. He was given a fifteen-day deadline to declare all of his WMD facilities and weapons, and required to "unconditionally accept" total destruction of his WMDs.[6]

Saddam thumbed his nose at one U.N. resolution after another, and never complied with the U.N.'s repeated disarmament demands. The economic sanctions imposed as a result of his invasion of Kuwait had little impact on Saddam personally. As head of what was in effect an organized criminal gang that looted Iraq, he always made sure there was enough money to pay for his palaces and luxuries. The sanctions did, however, put a crimp in his WMD plans, and in his efforts to rebuild the Iraqi military. The sanctions also had a significant impact on the ordinary people of Iraq.

The United States supported a U.N. proposal for a strict policy to allow some oil sales by Iraq, with the revenue being carefully monitored to ensure that it was spent for the benefit of the Iraqi people, and not for Saddam. The dictator rejected the proposal out of hand.

In 1996, the U.N. caved in, and created the Oil-for-Food program (OFFP). Although ostensibly meant to help Iraqis, it was almost instantly taken over by Saddam, to finance his dictatorship and to extensively bribe foreign governments, and the U.N.[7] The bank chosen to administer the program was a Parisian institution that was already a major holder of Saddam's government accounts.[8] Saddam was allowed to be the exclusive decision maker on who would get oil contracts, and contracts to supply goods to Iraq. Within the U.N., it was "assumed from the beginning that Iraq would corrupt it [OFFP] from the start."[9] A U.S. House International Relations subcommittee concluded:

> Once firmly ensconced as gatekeeper of contracts, Saddam Hussein's strategy of corrupting the program was relatively simple and was achieved by a number of means: fraudulent orders for humanitarian goods paid for, but never delivered; a partial delivery of humanitarian goods with proceeds shared among regime elements; goods shipments with obscure descriptions to hinder timely inspections; overpricing of humanitarian goods designed to hide kickbacks; after sale service fees of as much as 30%, a portion

of which was paid as a kickback; overcharging for shipping costs and outright theft of goods destined for the Iraqi people.[10]

The U.N. staff in Baghdad knowingly allowed itself to be infiltrated by Saddam's intelligence service, and permitted their communications with the outside world to be monitored by Iraqi intelligence. Rather than forcing Iraq to comply with U.N. resolutions, the U.N. Baghdad staff acted as a public relations arm for the dictator—demanding that sanctions be lifted even though Saddam was still in violation of every U.N. resolution. The few conscientious U.N. employees who did speak up were quashed by the management and told that they were spies.[11]

Benon V. Sevan was appointed by Kofi Annan in October 1997 as executive director of the Iraqi OFFP. Sevan actively obstructed all inquiries into corruption.[12] It later turned out that Sevan was being bribed by Saddam, from whom he received special oil allocations for 13 million barrels.[13]

When the United States and Britain slowed down U.N. processing of OFFP contracts, so they could be examined more carefully, Annan objected.[14]

According to the U.S. General Accounting Office, Saddam reaped $10.1 billion from OFFP[15] and used OFFP to acquire materials that were ostensibly for civilian use, but were in fact used to build up his weapons programs.[16]

Among the uses to which Saddam put the OFFP revenues were twenty-five-thousand-dollar rewards to the families of Palestinian terrorist bombers.[17] He was very public about his reward payments to the terrorists, yet his funding of terrorism never received the slightest condemnation from the U.N.

Other revenues from OFFP corruption appear to have funded the terrorist insurgents currently fighting against the elected Iraqi government and its coalition allies.[18] Stated another way, the U.N. facilitated Saddam's acquisition of the enormous funds that are still paying for the killers of U.S. troops.

By early 1998, the Saddam regime had stepped up its defiance of U.N. weapons inspectors. Kofi Annan's response before the Security Council on February 1, 1998, was to ask that OFFP be doubled.[19] After praising Saddam as "a man I can do business with,"[20] Annan resolved the inspections crisis by making a deal with Saddam that U.N. inspectors would be accompanied by diplomats, including some friendly to the dictator. These diplomats gave the Iraqis advance warning of inspections, so suspicious WMD facilities could be cleared before the inspectors arrived. Annan's staff condemned the U.N. inspectors as "cowboys" who had been insufficiently deferential to the Saddam government's feelings.[21]

By 2000, the corruption in OFFP had grown to an enormous size. At the same time, Annan bragged to the Security Council that he had reformed OFFP to make it transparent.[22] Yet, when investigators pored over records of the Saddam regime, they discovered that Saddam had given Benon Sevan vouchers for millions of barrels of oil.[23] They also discovered that kickbacks had been paid to more than two thousand companies, with businesses from France, Russia, and China receiving preferential treatment.[24]

Vladimir Zhirinovsky (deputy chair of Russia's parliament, the Duma); France's former U.N. ambassador Jean-Bernard Merimee; and George Galloway (a pro-terrorist, viciously anti-American member of the British Parliament) also received Iraqi OFFP bribes.[25]

Annan at first resisted making any U.N. documents available to outside investigators. Under enormous pressure from Congress, Annan ultimately allowed outside access to the documents. But first, Annan's chief of staff, S. Iqbal Riza, directed the shredding of thousands of papers related to OFFP.[26]

Nobody at the U.N. got fired because of Oil-for-Food. Benon Sevan fled Cyprus to live in a penthouse, where he is safe from extradition to the United States for a 2007 indictment in federal court. The U.N. keeps on sending him his pension there, and has refrained from even mildly suggesting that he ought to return to the U.S. to face the charges.[27]

The exposure of Oil-for-Food did lead to many promises of United Nations reform, few of which were kept.

The Cotecna Connection

Cotecna is a Swiss company that was interested in acquiring a U.N. contract to monitor the OFFP spending. Kofi Annan had friends at Cotecna, and he asked them to help find work for his son, Kojo.[28]

Kojo Annan was paid $400,000 by Cotecna. He had been hired to help them obtain a multimillion-dollar contract, which he did, and yet he was kept on the payroll even after the contract had been awarded.[29] Kofi Annan later claimed that he had no idea that Kojo had gotten a job with Cotecna.[30] He also claimed that he thought his son's involvement in Cotecna had ended in 1999, even though Kojo was still on the payroll in 2004. When the scandal broke, Benon Sevan (understandably) ordered Cotecna not to cooperate with investigators.

Annan has claimed that he received an "exoneration" by the Independent Inquiry Committee (IIC) that was headed by Paul Volcker.[31] In fact, Robert Parton, a former FBI agent who was the senior investigator of Annan's participation in the OFFP, stated that Annan lied.[32] The Volker Committee was supposed to fully investigate the Oil-for-Food corruption. But according to a U.S. House of Representatives International Relations subcommittee, Parton stated that Volcker and the other senior members were "unwilling to reach any conclusion that would result in significant adverse consequences for the secretary-general."[33]

The International Relations subcommittee concluded that the problems of OFFP are not aberrational, but are endemic and the inevitable result of the U.N.'s structure:

> The U.N.'s capacity to punish wrongdoing within its ranks also suffers from a lack of a functioning independent administrative

justice system, allowing crimes or malfeasance to go unpunished, and when cases are brought up, they frequently are riddled with procedural errors such that many are overturned on appeal by the United Nations' own supreme tribunal. Each of the deficiencies detailed in this report has individually and collectively contributed to the culture of impropriety and the lack of accountability that undergirded the oil-for-food era. The very fact that the IIC had to be created is a sign of the U.N.'s inability to investigate and expose its own wrongdoing.

Problems associated with the OFFP are not isolated or unique to that particular U.N.–administered program. The OFFP, and the myriad of problems associated with it, are symptomatic of a pervasive mismanagement and failure of leadership at the U.N.

Among the management and organizational weaknesses are a lack of appropriate and effective internal or external independent oversight (including both audit and investigations); the near absence of adequate internal controls within the Secretariat [the office of the Secretary-General]; and a lack of appropriate and modern accountability mechanisms, including a functioning whistleblower protection policy; a code of ethics; an ethics training and certification regime; a financial disclosure process and policy; and a freedom of information policy. "In addition to being decades behind other public institutions in its business processes, internal controls, and accountability mechanisms, the U.N. suffers from a lack of proper leadership and commitment to excellence by the organization's senior most leadership."[34]

Construction Spending

Suppose that the government hired somebody to shovel taxpayer dollars into the East River, near the United Nations headquarters. That would be a colossal waste of money. But it would be rather thrifty compared to the U.N.'s renovation and expansion of its New York City headquarters.

U.S. taxpayers will end up picking up the tab for at least $400 million of this project, whose costs have risen from $1.2 billion to $2 billion, and may still climb. Not to mention all the additional money dumped into the project by the taxpayers of New York City and New York State.

There's no dispute that the U.N. headquarters building, originally constructed in 1952, needs renovation. Over the last half century, the U.N. has failed to perform the basic maintenance and upgrades that would be expected of any responsible building owner. So now, the building is a mess and needs a massive overhaul.

Back in 2005, the U.N. was saying that the renovation would cost $1.2 billion. Donald Trump, who knows a lot about construction projects in Manhattan, testified before the U.S. Senate and said that the U.N.'s cost estimates were wrong. First of all, he explained, $1.2 billion was far too high; a competent real estate developer could do the project for $700 million.

But the U.N.'s core competence is spending other people's money. With costs up to $2 billion already, and plenty of time for more cost overruns before the planned completion of construction in 2013, U.N. officials say that the spending is so high because renovation costs more than building something new. "Anyone who says that building renovation is more expensive than building a new building doesn't know the business," Trump retorted. "It only costs a fool more money."[35] But the U.N. officials are not fools. It's not their money they are spending. It is yours.

After calling the U.N.'s cost proection the result of "incompetence or fraud," Trump put his money where his mouth is. He offered to finish the project for what he said the price should be. Secretary-general Kofi Annan refused even to meet with Trump to discuss the offer.[36] Trump called the U.N. headquarters project "the most ridiculous construction development I have ever witnessed."[37]

The U.N.'s construction management system seems almost deliberately geared to facilitating waste, fraud, and abuse. The United States government's Government Accountability Office (GAO) has written two reports that dissect the problem. The report *United Nations: Internal Oversight Controls and Processes Need Strengthening* notes that the U.N.'s Office of Internal Oversight Services (OIOS) is supposed to monitor the rest of the U.N. to prevent fraud. But in practice, this rarely works.[38]

Another GAO report, *United Nations: Weaknesses in Internal Oversight and Procurement Could Affect the Effective Implementation of the Planned Renovation*, examines the headquarters renovation.[39] Both GAO reports explain that in order to audit a U.N. agency, OIOS needs to get permission from that agency. To fund the audit, OIOS needs to get the target agency to pay for the audit.

This is like saying that the police can only investigate a suspected organized crime gang when the gang agrees to an investigation. Plus, in order to pay for the investigation, the police would need to ask the gang for money. This is not exactly a formula for tough investigations that will uncover high-level corruption.

The problems at OIOS are systemic, and not limited to construction oversight. An internal audit of OIOS itself found that "OIOS suffers from an ineffective and unclear structure, lack of independent budget and limited to no administrative support . . . poor management, conflicts at the senior management level, lack of communication . . . lack of standard operating procedures and constant disagreements with regard to the scope of some of the investigative procedures of the division. This has obviously resulted in instability, high turnover rates and non-optimal working conditions for investigators."[40] OIOS chief Inga-Britt Ahlenius refused to release the audit report, although it was eventually leaked to the media.[41]

In American governments, one important part of the checks and balances to promote honesty is that contract bidders who have been rejected can make a protest. So if two construction companies submit a bid to build an elementary school, and Company A wins the contract but Company B thinks that bribery or falsification was involved, Company B can protest. This is helpful, because Company B has a greater incentive than anyone else to be watchful for problems in the contract award process. The U.N., however, has no independent bid protest process.[42]

Not that all the cost overruns at the U.N. are due to corruption. Simple incompetence is also an important factor, since the U.N.'s Procurement Service staff has not been fully trained to know the U.N.'s own procurement rules.[43]

Thus, the GAO report on headquarters construction warned of "numerous weaknesses" that were making the renovation project "highly vulnerable to waste, fraud, and abuse."

But in the U.N., even raising these issues is considered outrageous. Mark Malloch Brown (who was Kofi Annan's right-hand man, and also happened to be George Soros's best friend at the U.N.) lashed out at the United States for being the only nation not to fully support the headquarters renovation. Brown blamed "unchecked U.N.-bashing" in U.S. domestic politics. Annan said that he agreed.[44]

If the National Rifle Association telling the truth about the U.N. has helped make American politicians a little more hesitant about dumping American taxpayer dollars into the money pit at U.N. headquarters, I'm glad we did so.

Brown, who is British, excoriated Rush Limbaugh and Fox News for putting the U.N. in a bad light. Brown pronounced the radio host's name "Lim-bow," which indicated that Brown had never actually listened to *The Rush Limbaugh Show*, and probably had very little idea about the show's content. As for Fox News, you will see its reporting cited frequently in the endnotes of this chapter and other chapters; that is because Fox News—like the *Washington Post*, the *Wall Street Journal*, and the Inner City Press—has done excellent reporting that exposes the corruption and mismanagement at the United Nations. Of course, Brown did not—and could not—point to any factual error in any of the U.N. reporting by Fox News.

After U.S. ambassador John Bolton criticized Brown, John Podesta (Bill Clinton's former chief of staff, who now runs a think tank funded by George Soros) rushed to the defense of his fellow Sorosite, and lashed out at Bolton.[45]

With the New York headquarters years away from completion, and the spending already hundreds of millions of dollars too high, the U.N. is getting ready for another palatial renovation. This one is for its office in Geneva, Switzerland, at the Palais des Nations.[46] It is expected to cost more than a billion dollars.[47] That's more than twice what it would cost to construct a new building from the ground up. By the way, a billion dollars is more than UNICEF spends on humanitarian action in an entire year! A billion dollars would be enough to create potable water supplies for 22 million families in Africa.

Claudia Rosett, formerly a writer with the *Wall Street Journal* who penned numerous exposés of U.N. malfeasance, now works for the Foundation for the Defense of Democracies. She calls the Palais des Nations boondoggle "outrageous," but notes that it "is entirely consistent with their spending habits worldwide for years."[48]

Not that the United Nations has forgotten Africa. Secretary-General Ban Ki-moon has promised to upgrade the U.N. offices in Nairobi, Kenya, to the same level as their offices in Geneva and Vienna. Unsurprisingly, the current construction projects at the U.N.'s Gigiri complex in Nairobi are poorly managed and wasting money.[49]

Lost Art

The United Nations wants to register your guns in regional gun registries. But the U.N. cannot even keep the valuable artwork it owns in its own buildings. A dozen or more valuable artworks have gone missing from the New York City headquarters. These include a bronze sculpture by Jose de Rivera, and an ancient Mayan stone head. The U.N.'s Office of Internal Oversight Services reported that no one was responsible for guarding, cleaning, or insuring the artwork, which was now "lost." Assistant secretary-general Michael Adlerstein retorted that the art was not lost. It was just "unaccounted" for.[50]

If Alderstein really thinks that the missing art is "unaccounted" for rather than stolen, then the solution is simple. He could just send a memo to all employees in the NYC headquarters building: "To all staff: If you have recently seen a stone Mayan head in the building, please inform me right away." Then, presumably, someone will tell Alderstein, "Oh yes. There's a stone Mayan head in the copy room on the 37ᵗʰ floor. We've been using it as a table for the fax machine." Actually, once the staff started looking for the missing artwork, they did find one item, a painting that still hung safely on a wall on the 22ⁿᵈ floor.[51]

Alderstein, by the way, is in charge of the $2 billion "Capital Management Plan" to renovate the U.N. headquarters.

Corruption and Waste

Corruption accounts for a very significant share of the U.N. budget. The U.S. comptroller general testified to Congress in that the U.N. had lost hundreds of millions of dollars due to corruption.[52] U.N. elections "are usually tainted by politics, bribery, cheque book diplomacy and subtle donor threats (to cut off aid)."[53]

People all over the world, especially Americans, responded generously to help the victims of the tsunami that devastated South Asia in December 2004. The United Nations was peeved, called the United States "stingy," and demanded that the U.N. be in charge of all relief efforts. Fortunately, President Bush did not go along. Although the U.N. had promised that its relief spending would be transparent, trying to figure out where the U.N.'s money is going is like trying to follow a black bird on a dark night.

The *Financial Times* made a valiant effort. To the extent that the spending could be tracked at all, the U.N. tsunami spending had an overhead triple the level of private charities, thanks to indulgences on luxury hotels and the like.[54]

Many of the U.N. staff in Haiti have been housed on a gigantic passenger vessel dubbed the "Love Boat" by U.N. employees. The boat, the *Ola Esmeralda*, is owned by a Venezuelan company with close ties to dictator Hugo Chávez. The U.N. paid rent of $72,500 per day—about twice the standard market rate for such a rental.[55] (Chávez, by the way, who has been destroying Venezuela's democracy and crushing the free press, was in 2006 awarded the José Marti International Prize by the U.N. Educational, Scientific, and Cultural Organization, for his contributions to the "struggle for liberty." Fittingly, the prize was personally presented by Fidel Castro.[56])

Guido Bertucci, who ran the U.N. department[57] that is supposed to promote good governance in nations around the world, was caught falsifying documents and misspending funds by the Office of Internal Oversight Services.[58] Yet his boss did nothing about it.

Bertucci eventually resigned from the U.N., thereby insulating himself from any punishment other than a note in his personnel file. If the U.N. were serious about disciplining high-level employees for malfeasance, the U.N. could have refused to accept the resignation, or could have put him on leave, which would have allowed more serious actions to be taken.[59] Shortly after his resignation, the U.N. invited him to be a speaker at a major U.N. conference.[60]

Bertucci maintained his innocence and blamed the Greek staff for incompetence, particularly chief technical adviser Panos Liverakos, whom Bertucci had fired. Liverakos said that he was fired by Bertucci because he "blew the whistle on him."[61] Bertucci responded that if his actions are criminal, then "maybe every single manager of the U.N. should be indicted."[62] Which might be going too far, since not every U.N. manager is corrupt. But the U.N. certainly has shown little interest in doing anything about the ones who are.

The son-in-law of secretary-general Ban Ki-moon has been rather mysteriously rising in the ranks of the U.N. system, coincidentally at a time when the secretary-general gave his son-in-law's latest patron greater freedom to make high-level staffing decisions on his own. The son of secretary-general Kofi Annan's chief of staff benefited from similar treatment, with payments to him being laundered through a middleman to avoid scrutiny. The U.N. has repeatedly refused to answer questions from the Inner City Press about the Secretary-General's apparent collaboration in nepotism.[63]

Nicaragua's Miguel d'Escoto Brockmann is a radical Communist, a vehement anti-American, and served as president of the U.N. General Assembly. (He was succeeded in 2009 by the Libyan Ali Adbussalam Treki.) Apparently applying the Marxist rule "From each according to his ability, to each according to his needs," d'Escoto Brockmann decided that his relatives needed some high-paying jobs. So he hired his nephew as an economics advisor, and his niece as deputy chief of staff. He, too, refused to answer press questions about nepotism.[64]

Reform, Not

I've already said it, but I want to say it again for emphasis: there a lot of good people among the seventy thousand who work for the U.N.[65] Some of them have worked very hard to try to clean up the U.N. Unfortunately, their successes tend to be temporary, since the U.N.'s forces of sleaze are so much more powerful.

For example, the U.N.'s Iraq Oil-for-Food program was eventually exposed as one of the largest programs of corruption in world history, giving Saddam Hussein more than $10 billion of illegal revenue[66] (which, of course, he used to kill Iraqis, fund international terrorism, and to kill soldiers from America and its allies). So in 2006, the U.N. set up a special Procurement Task Force that was supposed to look into corruption in U.N. contracting.

The unit did a great job. They found $630 million of apparently corrupt contracts. The investigations led to two criminal convictions, to discipline of seventeen more U.N. employees, and to forty-five companies being removed or suspended from U.N. contracting.[67]

The task force also found that Gary K. Helseth, a U.N. official in charge of more than a billion dollars in reconstruction funds for Afghanistan, stole nearly half a million dollars to pay for his luxury lifestyle, including first-class tickets to Las Vegas.[68] But as an October 2008 report by the task force stated: "It is a matter of concern that the task force's recommendations for recovery actions—supported by documentary evidence of fraud, corruption and misappropriation of funds resulting in losses and damages—have not been vigorously pursued."[69]

Summarizing the report for a U.N. budget committee, OIOS head Inga-Britt Ahlenius stated that the report revealed a "serious problem" of lack of effective internal controls in the U.N. that made it "open to waste, abuse, fraud and corruption." She observed, "Historically the (U.N.) organisation has been slow and even resistant to hold culprits accountable—and not proactive in seeking to recover damages caused by corrupt conduct."[70]

All this was more than enough for the U.N. The task force's mandate expired on January 1, 2009, and was not renewed. Shortly before the mandate expired, the Procurement Task Force had issued four new reports, on twenty different confirmed schemes of corruption.[71] Because of the shutdown, 175 pending investigations were thwarted.[72] As one U.N. insider explained, "The U.N. does not like embarrassing stories to come out about fraud and abuse."[73] Leading the effort to kill the Procurement Task Force were Russia and Singapore: both of the criminal convictions that had resulted from the task force investigations were of Russians, and a Singapore U.N. official was caught by the task force. Russia was also worried about the task force's investigations of Russian corporations.[74]

Likewise involved in shutting down the Task Force was the Group of 77.[75] The G77 calls itself a group of "developing" countries, which forms an alliance that often controls the U.N. by sheer numbers. The term "developing" is a misnomer, since many of the countries are economically stagnant because they are under the thumb of dictatorships whose main objective is looting their own nations. (A few democracies do belong.) The G77 now comprises

130 nations. At the U.N. in 2009, the head of the G77 was Sudan. In the interest of honesty, the G77 would be better named "the International League of Kleptocracies" (ILK).

The temporary task force had been a part of the U.N.'s permanent Office of Internal Oversight Services (OIOS). But as explained above, the OIOS is often ineffectual. U.N. management has been working hard to prevent the temporary investigators from the special task force getting permanently hired by OIOS—because the investigators have expertise in contract fraud which OIOS does not. Russia was especially hard-nosed about making sure that task force head Robert Appleton did not continue his work.[76]

With the task force out of business, the U.N. in the next year did not complete an investigation of a single significant cause of fraud or corruption.[77]

From 2006 to 2010, the job of director of the investigative division of OIOS was left vacant. The investigators were ordered not to open new cases about U.N. contractors or former U.N. staff. They were further told to close down or abandon existing investigations.[78]

Appleton, by the way, had applied to be head of investigations at OIOS. A panel of non-OIOS employees unanimously recommended him for the job, ahead of seventy-two other applicants. Then, the secretary-general's "Senior Review Group" stepped in to block the appointment, and insisted that the whole hiring process be started over. They claimed that since all four finalists had been American males, the process had violated U.N. rules about gender and geographic diversity.[79] Not to mention the unwritten rules against uncovering corruption at the U.N.

Ban used the same gender pretext to thwart the appointment of a strong director of the U.N.'s Joint Inspection Unit, whose inspectors had been uncovering mismanagement of the $10 billion that the U.N. spends on procurement.[80]

In July 2010, Inga-Britt Ahlenius stepped down after five years as undersecretary-general of the Office of Internal Oversight Services. Her final act was to send a scathing fifty-page memo to Ban Ki-moon detailing his record of "undermining" OIOS. She told Ban: "Your actions are not only deplorable, but seriously reprehensible."[81]

The inauguration of President Obama coincided with the end of efforts by the U.S. delegation to the U.N. in pushing for financial reform and transparency.[82] Making matters worse, in the U.S. Senate, antigun, pro-U.N. Al Franken has replaced Minnesota senator Norm Coleman, who led the Senate investigation of the Oil-for-Food scandal. Franken has, unsurprisingly, displayed no interest in doing anything about the massive thefts of U.S. taxpayer dollars that are routine in the U.N.

Under the George W. Bush administration, the U.S. had withheld some its U.N. payments, as leverage in trying to force budgetary reform, transparency, and reductions in corruption. The Obama administration promptly reversed course, paid all the arrears, and left the U.S. helpless to push for reform.[83]

Even an attempt to improve the efficiency of the $778 million U.N. office in charge of organizing meetings (the Department of General Assembly and Conference Management) ended with "no progress or change," according to an OIOS report. As the OIOS noted, assessing progress was difficult because financial records were "compromised" through "retrospective adjustment." That's a polite way of saying that the financial records were changed in order to conceal waste and fraud.[84]

Former secretary-general Kofi Annan, who had played a key role in facilitating the Oil-for-Food program, and whose cronies made themselves rich with its corruption, did propose some timid reforms in U.N. management. These reforms were rejected by the U.N. budget committee. Most the countries that actually pay for the U.N. voted for the reforms. But they were outvoted by nations that, all combined, pay only 12 percent of the U.N. budget.[85] For them, U.N. money is free money. Most of these countries are themselves corrupt dictatorships, so the U.N. is accurately seen as a treasure trove for them and their cronies to loot. These kleptocracies even wrote Kofi Annan a letter telling him to stop talking about U.N. reform.[86]

Annan's successor, Ban Ki-moon, made his personal finances public, and got rid of entrenched staff in his own office. "I tried to lead by example," he said, but "nobody followed." At an August 2008, closed-door meeting with top U.N. staff, held in Turin, Italy, the secretary-general said, "We all know the U.N. is a huge bureaucracy . . . Then I arrived in New York. There is bureaucracy, I discovered—and then there is the U.N." A reporter who learned about the speech from people who had been in the room summarized it as blasting the U.N.'s top officials for "crippling the world body through a combination of self-interest, petty squabbling and egoism."[87]

Whistleblowers

The U.N. is a very abusive employer, at least according to a report of three international jurists who studied the world body. The report found that the U.N. is "in breach of its own human rights standards because of the unfair way it treats its own employees."[88] The investigators who produced the report were hired by the U.N. employees union, but the record of how the U.N. treats whistleblowers lends credence to it.

Charmine Koda was the director of the U.N. Information Center in Tokyo. She found extensive financial misdealing at the Center, such as falsified invoices for services that had not yet been delivered. She reported the problems to the Department of Public Information, which is in charge of the Information Centers. After the Department did nothing, she informed the Office of Internal Oversight Services. Apparently in retaliation, some of her authority over the Tokyo Information Center was removed. She filed a complaint alleging harassment by the person who was then the second-ranking person in the Department of Public Information. The U.N. asserted that she was not entitled to the institutional protections for whistleblowers, since it was her job to report problems. There is nothing in the U.N.'s whistleblower rules that supports the ruling. Koda left the U.N. a little while later, and in 2008 wrote an exposé.[89]

A U.N. official with twenty years' experience, James Wasserstrom, blew the whistle on mismanagement and possible kickback corruption in U.N. energy projects in Kosovo. The U.N. responded by opening an investigation of Wasserstrom, and decided that his job would be eliminated. Then, when he was leaving Kosovo, U.N. police detained him at the border and seized his U.S. passport. They searched his apartment in Pristina, Kosovo, and took his computer.

According to Wasserstrom, the U.N. "uses the whistle-blowing program to get its most ethical staff to stick their heads above ground in order to chop them off." "The U.N. isn't serious about cleaning up its act," he says.[90]

At the U.N. office in Geneva, Switzerland, Cynthia Brzak complained of sexual harassment by Ruud Lubbers, who at the time was head of the U.N. agency for refugees. Her complaint resulted in an OIOS investigation, and a secret report that Lubbers had engaged in "serious acts of misconduct." Yet secretary-general Kofi Annan wrote an official letter to Brzak, asserting that her complaints could not be "sustained."

After someone leaked the report to the media, Lubbers resigned. Brzak says that she suffered from retaliation, including threats that she would be fired.[91]

Another U.N. employee was suspected of having informed the Inner City Press about problems in U.N. Medical Services. The U.N. broke into her e-mail and scoured it to see if she had communicated with the newspaper. When the Inner City Press asked the U.N. if the e-mail spying was legal, the U.N. refused to answer.[92]

The United Nations Dispute Tribunal was created in July 2009 to provide a formal mechanism, with neutral judges, for adjudication of disputes involving U.N. employees. The Tribunal was seen as a welcome reform, because U.N. employees have no rights to sue under the labor laws of the United States, or of any other nation where the U.N. operates. However, Secretary-General Ban and the rest of top U.N. management have undermined the Tribunal by refusing to turn over personnel records necessary to the resolution of a case, and thus directly defying orders from the U.N.'s own judges.[93]

The U.N. Dictators Program

The flagship agency of the U.N. is the United Nations Development Programme (UNDP).[94] It is supposed to help the development of backward nations. But it is a cesspool of corruption. And it is perhaps the most destructive antigun agency within the U.N.

The UNDP spends $9 billion a year and generally directs other U.N. agencies that are working in the same part of a nation as UNDP. The United States voluntarily gives UNDP $250 million a year, above and beyond the U.S. dues payments to the U.N.[95]

The UNDP in Afghanistan had a contract with the U.S. Agency for International Development (USAID). After the contract expired, the UNDP took $1.7 million from a bank account that had been set up for USAID to pay for UNDP projects. The money was removed without USAID's consent. The UNDP claimed that the money was for services previously rendered, but would not supply the necessary documentation, or allow UNDP staff to be interviewed by U.S. investigators.[96] The U.N. has refused to answer press questions about the issue.[97]

The UNDP pushed to allow its chief operating officer to write checks on his own discretion, for any amount of money, without the normal budgetary approval process. At the time, UNDP could was already able to write checks up to $50,000 without authorization or supervision.

The UNDP pointed out that UNICEF and the World Food Program (WFP) already had unlimited power to write unsupervised checks. It was telling that UNDP is angling to get the same unlimited spending power as the WFP shortly after a scandal in which the WFP paid $90 million to contract employees, in violation of U.N. rules for paying contractors. Although the WFP's abuse of power was condemned by a U.N. budget oversight committee (the Advisory Committee on Administrative and Budgetary Questions), the WFP staff and governing board ignored the criticism. With unlimited spending, UNDP would have been able to pay off plaintiffs in lawsuits against the UNDP, without the plaintiffs' claims becoming known to the public.[98] Fortunately, the request for unlimited spending power was rejected; instead, the spending limit was raised to $75,000.[99]

The UNDP spends $2.6 billion annually just on procurement. Yet a secret internal audit revealed that UNDP's procurement system is in chaos, with a dysfunctional bidding process, a paperwork mess, the inability even to make proper evaluation of major technology purposes, and an "apparent conflict of interest" in which procurement personnel are in charge of uncovering problems with procurement.[100]

Lax on stopping corruption, the UNDP is particularly tough on anyone who blows the whistle on them. According to the U.N. Ethics Office, the UNDP procedures for investigations deprive whistleblowers of due process, and refuse to allow them to tell their story.[101] In Somalia, U.N. employee Ismail Ahmed exposed bid-rigging by the UNDP. The OIOS wanted to investigate, but UNDP blocked them.[102] The UNDP has opted out of the jurisdiction of the U.N. Ethics Office, and promised that it will be its own ethics monitor.[103]

The corruption at UNDP is much more harmful than simply wasting the money of the taxpayers around the world. UNDP corruption has helped to support the tyrannies in North Korea and Burma. No wonder some people say that a more accurate name for the UNDP would be the "U.N. Dictators Program."[104]

Cash for Kim

"Cash for Kim" is the name for the massive scandal of UNDP assistance to the maniacal Kim Jong-Il regime in North Korea. The North Korean dictatorship could not continue to exist without supporting the lavish lifestyles of the top Communist Party functionaries. A variety of financial sanctions on North Korea have made acquiring luxury goods more difficult, so hard currency is almost essential to the regime maintaining its power. The UNDP's office in Pyongyang came to the regime's rescue, illegally supplying it with hard currency.

The UNDP flagrantly violated U.N. internal regulations. The UNDP also flagrantly violated U.N. Security Council resolutions that were trying to stop North Korea's nuclear weapons production program.

So consider this: the very same U.N. entity that is at the forefront of taking away guns from ordinary, decent people all over the world was *also* at the forefront of using your tax dollars to support North Korean production of nuclear weapons.

If you had wanted to set up a program designed for corruption, you could hardly do better than the UNDP's North Korean office. The UNDP allowed the North Korean regime to handpick many of the employees, including key managers. The assistant to the head of the UNDP office, and the technology officer (who was in charge of all the computers and communications), and the program officers to oversee UNDP projects in North Korea, and the finance officer were all North Korean nationals chosen by the North Korean dictatorship.[105]

In violation of UNDP rules, the employees were paid in hard currency and also given supplemental pay in hard currency. The North Korean government may have taken much of the employees' salaries for itself.[106]

The finance officer wrote the UNDP checks. In violation of common-sense anti-fraud standards (and the UNDP's own rules) she was also the person who balanced the checkbook.[107] Thus, she had a completely free hand to loot the UNDP checking account, and use it to pass money to the Kim regime. When the U.N. finally conducted a serious investigation, the North Korean regime refused to let U.N. inspectors enter the country or talk to the finance officer. So the investigators could never examine any of the originals or copies of the $16.6 million of canceled checks.[108]

Some, or many, or most of the checks may have been made out to "cash." The inspectors did study a sample of alleged payments based on the check register. In 78 percent of the sample, it was impossible to verify the signature on the payment receipt. On the other 22 percent, there was no signature on the receipt.[109]

Because of international economic sanctions against North Korea, it has been tough for the regime to get money out of the country. The UNDP helped, letting North Korea use UNDP accounts to transfer funds to money laundering centers such as Macau.[110]

In sum, the UNDP in North Korean disbursed $23.8 million of its own money and money spent for other U.N. entities. Almost all the spending was in hard currency, of which the Kim regime *directly* received about $9.12 million, according to the investigator's estimate.[111] How much was given indirectly to the Kim regime (by individuals or organizations who then passed some or all of the money to the regime) is unknown.

None of this was a sudden development. Internal UNDP audits since 2001 had revealed the problems,[112] but UNDP management ignored the audits, and attempted to prevent any of the members of the UNDP governing board from learning about them.[113]

Yet even after the scandal began to come to light, in 2007, UNDP officials told a U.S. Senate subcommittee that the UNDP had given "no more than $380,000" to the North Korean government.[114] A Senate subcommittee investigation revealed that UNDP gave money to North Korean fronts that were involved in the international proliferation of nuclear weapons and conventional arms.[115]

What was not previously known, at least to outsiders, was how extensively other U.N. entities illegally passed hard currency to the dictatorship. UNDP offices outside of North Korea spent between $9.5 million to $27.4 million, with an unknown amount going to the Kim regime.[116]

Another $381 million was spent for the Agriculture Recovery and Environmental Protection (AREP), Cooperation Framework, which raised money from private donors hoping to save the people of North Korea from starvation.[117] As the lead agency on the ground in North Korea, UNDP was part of the Agriculture program, and no one knows how much of this money may have been seized by the Kim regime. The U.N. auditors did not attempt to find out.[118]

Counterfeiting is one of the North Korean regime's main economic activities. For more than a decade, the UNDP's safe in Pyongyang stored counterfeit United States $100 bills. The counterfeits were dutifully listed in annual audit reports, but senior UNDP officials claim they had no knowledge. Nobody bothered to tell the United States about the trove of counterfeit American money. [119]

The UNDP also provided North Korea with dual use military-civilian technology, suitable for North Korea's nuclear weapons development. [120] There were ninety-five items acquired this way, in violation of U.S. laws about the export of dual use technologies. These included high-technology equipment for nuclear and missile programs.

When making the purchases, the UNDP sometimes conveniently failed to disclose that the equipment would be used by North Koreans, not by foreign UNDP staff. In one case, another U.N. agency falsely told a Dutch exporter that the equipment was for the Pyongyang UNDP office, when in fact it was slated for a distant rural location. The UNDP made essentially no effort to ensure that the dual-use goods were not used for military purposes, or even to keep files of the records on what kind of uses were allowed. [121]

Some of the technology transfers took place even after a pair of 2006 Security Council resolutions imposed a global embargo on the transfer of military goods to North Korea. [122]

The UNDP refused to answer U.S. questions about technology transfers; at other times, UNDP claimed that the only technology transferred was harmless stuff like "rice husk removers." [123]

With North Korean technology officers able to monitor all communications, it was impossible for anyone in Pyongyang to tell the world what was going on. An investigation by the U.S. Congress found that the U.N. Development Programme has not objected to the North Korean government searching the homes of UNDP staff and spying on all their communications. [124]

Finally, a very brave whistleblower, operations manager Artjon Shkurtaj, was able to leave North Korea and warn the world. The UNDP program in North Korea was shut down. At that point, the UNDP took all the dual-use military equipment it owned—and gave it to the North Korean government![125] This was another UNDP violation of the Security Council resolutions against supplying military equipment to the North Korean dictatorship.

As usual when the U.N. gets caught, there were promises of tough reform. The secretary-general promised a full audit of the U.N. This got scaled back to an audit of only the UNDP in North Korea, and the auditors were not even allowed to enter the country.[126] Although the audit detailed much of what had gone on, it concluded that nobody had done anything wrong. The only problem was poor communication between the UNDP Pyongyang office and the rest of the UNDP.[127]

Actually, one person did get in trouble because of Cash-for-Kim: the whistleblower. Artjon Shkurtaj had been a contract employee. He had been offered a permanent job, but after he blew the whistle, the offer was rescinded on the grounds that UNDP wanted to hire a woman. The person who eventually got the job was a man.[128]

After the exposure of the Oil-for-Food food scandal, the U.N. had hired its first ethics commissioner, Robert Benson. But Benson was apparently unable to prevent the U.N. bureaucracy from punishing Shkurtaj.[129]

In January 2009, the UNDP announced it would resume operations in North Korea, promising that it would be more careful this time, and, for example, would not give "cash advances to the government." Instead of hiring whomever the North Korean tyranny said, the UNDP would now pick from a list of three potential employees handpicked by the North Korean tyranny.[130]

A few months later, the U.N.'s World Food Program was caught spending $130 million in transportation costs for shipping food into North Korea. A shipping expert called the rates "absolutely ridiculous," and said that they were about double what the current market rate should be for sea shipments from China to North Korea. The shipping carriers all happen to be owned by the North Korean government, and thus the U.N. continues to enrich the North Korean regime. The World Food Program also enriches itself with this corrupt bargain. The WFP collects from the U.N. budget a 7 percent premium on operational costs. So the more the WFP wastes on high shipping expenses, the more money the WFP receives for itself. A good deal all around, except for the starving people of North Korea, and the American and other taxpayers who pay for the WFP.[131]

The U.N. Development Programme currently has programs in Iran, Syria, and Zimbabwe. Given what happened in North Korea, it is hard to feel confident that the UNDP is not also aiding those regimes in acquiring weapons technology, and in enriching themselves so as to perpetuate the tyrannies.[132] Indeed, UNDP has already helped Iran diplomatically by choosing the Islamic Republic of Iran as chair of its executives board for 2009.[133] That's the board that is supposed to supervise UNDP and prevent corruption.

The UNDP has heavily funded the dictatorship in Burma, allowing money that was meant for helping the Burmese people to be diverted into a currency exchange program that enriched the military dictators.[134] The UNDP came into Burma with dollars, but, starting in 2006, in order to spend the dollars, they had to be converted into kyat, the Burmese currency. The UNDP bought "Foreign Exchange Certificates" through the government-controlled Myanmar Foreign Trade Bank. The exchange rate was ridiculously bad, so that of every dollar the UNDP exchanged, the Burmese dictatorship made a profit for itself of 15 to 25 percent.[135] Stated another way, 15–25 percent of UNDP spending in Burma was a no-restrictions gift to the dictatorship.

Between 2002 and 2006, the UNDP spent more than $74 million in Burma, including more than $33 million in 2006.[136] Because the UNDP is in charge of foreign exchange transactions for the U.N., the U.N. spending by other agencies for relief from the devastating Cyclone Nargis, which hit Burma in May 2008, lost at least $10 million in exchange transactions; the money went into the pockets of the military dictatorship.[137]

The Burmese/UNDP scheme was exposed by Matthew Russell Lee, of the Inner City Press, a year before the cyclone hit.[138] U.N. officials denied that there was any problem, or any losses.[139] An internal U.N. memo, written after the cyclone, revealed that the U.N. did know about the problem; yet two weeks later, the U.N. asked the world for an extra $300 million—for Burma—without disclosing that at least $60 million of the money donated for cyclone relief would be stolen by the Burmese dictatorship.[140]

Because of financial sanctions on Burma, the UNDP has probably been the largest supplier of hard currency to the dictatorship. [141]As in North Korea, the UNDP has allowed the Burmese dictatorship to choose the local staff hired by UNDP. [142]

Why is the UNDP such a mess? It is not unreasonable to suggest that some of the blame lies with Mark Malloch Brown, administrator of the UNDP from 1999 to 2005. Thereafter, Brown rose to *Chef de Cabinet* to secretary-general Kofi Annan, and then to deputy secretary-general. From 2007 to 2009 he served in the cabinet of United Kingdom prime minister Gordon Brown, as minister of state at the Foreign and Commonwealth Office (FCO) for Africa, Asia and the United Nations.

Throughout his tenure in the United Nations and the United Kingdom, Brown has had a very close relationship with George Soros. Back in 1993–94, Brown served on the Soros Advisory Committee on Bosnia. In May 2007, he was appointed vice president of Soro's Quantum Fund, vice chairman of Soros Fund Management, and vice chairman of Soros's Open Society Institute.[143]

According to Brown, Soros and UNDP "collaborate extensively."[144]

At the U.N., Brown was a key obstructionist against U.S. reform efforts.[145] His defenses of the U.N. corruptocrats rose to a level of ludicrousness not seen since the days when "Baghdad Bob" (Saddam Hussein's information minister) was holding press conferences in March 2003, announcing that Saddam's army was defeating the Coalition invaders.

"Manhattan Mark" claimed that the Volcker investigation of Oil-for-Food had "fully exonerated" Kofi Annan. Actually, Volcker found that Annan had known about the misuse of Oil-for-Food since 2001, but had never informed the Security Council or the public.[146] Manhattan Mark declared, "Not a penny was lost from the organization."[147] In fact, an internal audit by the U.N. itself admitted that more than half a billion dollars had been lost.[148]

Like Soros, CNN founder Ted Turner has also been giving huge sums to the United Nations and related organizations, including sums that are used for lobbying Congress. For a while, Brown was in charge of the Turner-U.N. collaboration. According to journalist Claudia Rosett, "Asked in a recent interview about the dangers of collusion between big business and a public institution like the U.N., Mark Malloch Brown declared indignantly that the U.N. was doing 'God's work,' and walked out."[149]

Whether or not Brown and the U.N. are doing God's work, they are surely doing George Soros's work. In Soros's mind there really is not much difference between the two, as I explain in chapter 19.

Soros's work here on earth includes banning guns, and so does the work of the UNDP. In a practical sense, the UNDP may be the most important U.N. antigun agency.

When an American thinks of "United Nations," the image that is likely to come to mind is the headquarters building in New York City. Unless you live or work in midtown Manhattan, the U.N. seems far away. In the Third World, however, the U.N. is a much more common presence. The UNDP has operations in 166 countries.[150] Because the UNDP has so many "boots on the ground" so much of the time, other U.N. agencies that come into a country tend to fall under the leadership of UNDP. So do many other non-U.N. international aid organizations.

Now, when Mark Malloch Brown took over the UNDP in 1999, the agency had scant involvement with firearms policy. By the time he left, UNDP had been turned into a global gun control organization. Want some clean drinking water for your village? Sure, the UNDP says; we'll build that well just as soon as everyone in town gives all their firearms to the government. It's blackmail of some of the world's most vulnerable people—forcing them to surrender their only means to defend their families, in exchange for assistance with other necessities of life.

The UNDP propagandizes extensively for gun control. It even publishes a book, the *How to Guide: Small Arms and Light Weapons Legislation*, which tells governments about the minimum kinds of gun controls they should impose.[151]

The guide for controls on civilians is based on the principle that "the possession and use of weapons is a privilege that is conditional on the overriding need to ensure public safety."[152] They want registration for all guns, and licensing for all gun owners. Every gun owner should be required to provide a "good reason" showing "genuine need" for the gun. The UNDP does not like the idea of defensive gun ownership, but "if personal protection is permitted as a good reason, applicants should prove to the police that they are in genuine danger that could be avoided by being armed."[153]

The UNDP takes arms rationing ("one gun a month") to its intended conclusion: "Number of firearms allowed . . . Someone may have a good reason to possess a single firearm, but the law should not assume that this same reason automatically justifies a second one, or a third. Each time good reasons should be proven, taking into account the firearms already possessed. In addition, there should be an upper limit for the number of firearms possessed."[154]

The "checklist of elements" for gun control laws includes the following:

- No military style weapon should be possessed by civilian. [*sic*]
- A valid firearms license should be shown every time ammunition is purchased, and dealers should record the quantity and information on the purchaser.
- Limits can be placed on the amount that can be purchased in a month, as well as a limit on the amount of ammunition that can be stored.

- Restriction should be placed on the possession of firearms in public places. A license to carry a firearm for an exception and limited period can be granted under the law.
- Inspections of storage facilities [that is, your home] can be built into the process of registering a firearm.[155]

The UNDP (along with the secretary-general, and along with the international gun ban lobbies) claims that the antigun agenda is necessary because the proliferation of firearms causes economic underdevelopment.[156] This is just not true, as David Kopel, Paul Gallant, and Joanne Eisen have shown in their article "Does the Right to Bear Arms Impede or Promote Economic Development?"[157] Examining Latin America and sub-Saharan Africa—with particular attention to Kenya and Zambia—the three authors show that development failure long predated the proliferation of arms in those areas. The collapse of the Soviet empire in the late 1980s did result in many Warsaw Pact arms—particularly AK-47-type rifles—being sold into the Third World. However, sub-Saharan Africa and much of Latin America had made themselves into an economic mess long before.

Kopel, Gallant, and Eisen trace the development problems to the tremendous corruption in those areas, and to the lack of property rights. They point out that in Africa, the problems have been made much worse by malaria—which the U.N. is aggravating by coercing nations not to use DDT for mosquito control. (Indiscriminate use of DDT can be harmful to birds, but spot applications in stagnant water pools cause little risk to birds, and could literally save millions of human lives.)

AIDS is another huge cause of economic disaster, in part because so many people of working age are killed by it. That problem has been significantly worsened by governments skimming off much of the money Western nations have donated for AIDS relief and medicines. Kopel, Gallant, and Eisen point out that the U.N.'s gun obsession offers corrupt governments a convenient way to blame outsiders for underdevelopment, when in truth, the major cause is that those same governments exist mainly to steal from the working people of those nations.

Burma

In 2008–09, Burma was chosen to be one of the twenty-one vice-presidents of the General Assembly.

In 2008, five opposition leaders in Burma delivered a letter to the UNDP office in Burma, asking secretary-general Ban Ki-moon not to accept the military dictatorship's draft constitution. But the UNDP failed to deliver that letter to the secretary-general's office in New York.[158] Similarly, the UNDP office in Burundi, Africa, had failed to let New York know about a letter from forty-six opposition leaders asking the U.N. for protection from death threats. Two weeks later, someone threw hand grenades into the homes of four of the dissident legislators.[159] U.N. mail delivery seems to be somewhat better when the sender is an anti-American terrorist; as I note later in the chapter on terrorism, a U.N. agency in Gaza delivered a letter from Hamas to Senator John Kerry.

A report from the Karen Human Rights Group (the Karen are one of the Burmese ethnic groups persecuted by the junta) charged several other U.N. agencies with complicity in human rights abuses in Burma:

UNICEF, the UN Development Programme (UNDP), UNAIDS . . . all provide funding for the Myanmar Maternal and Child Welfare Association, a coercive parastatal agency controlled by the SPDC and implicated in widespread extortion as part of its vigorous recruitment drive . . . In some areas villagers have been led to believe that access to UNICEF-funded polio inoculation programmes requires that they enlist in the Myanmar Women's Affairs Federation, another coercive parastatal organisation involved in similar coercive recruitment practices and demands for money. The Food and Agricultural Organisation (FAO) of the United Nations has paid the SPDC US$ 14 million to carry out an "oil crop cultivation programme"; disregarding the manner in which the SPDC implements such agricultural programmes. The nation-wide compulsory castor and jatropha cultivation scheme, for example, for which the SPDC may be diverting the FAO funds has involved widespread forced labour and extortion, and aims to produce biofuel for military use. The United Nations Economic and Social Council for Asia Pacific (UNESCAP) has been supporting the SPDC in the development of the "Asian Highway"—a transnational network of roads which, in Karen State, has involved land confiscation and the forced labour of local villagers, all without compensation.

The report said that the U.N. agencies had refused to answer questions about whether they knew about the human rights abuses in the projects they were funding.[160]

Conclusion

Instead of spending more than $5 billion a year on the United Nations, the United States could take that money and provide clean drinking water to more than a hundred million families in Africa. Or instead of throwing money at the UNDP to subsidize North Korean and Burmese dictators and other gun grabbers, the U.S. government could stop voluntarily giving a quarter billion of your tax dollars every year to UNDP. That would be enough to provide clean water to more than four million additional families every year.

Giving water to the thirsty is much better than giving Kim Jong-Il technology for light-water nuclear reactors; and it is better to give water than to make people give up their right of self-defense in order to get some water.

273

Putting the American tax money that is currently wasted or misused by the UNDP into global clean water projects would be a wonderful humanitarian project, and completely in the spirit of the noble aspirations of United Nations founders. Almost everyone would be better off—except for the U.N. den of thieves.

Chapter 11

United Nations and Genocide: A Historical Perspective

The United Nations was founded to prevent the recurrence of global disasters such as World War II and, in particular, to prevent future tyrants from emulating the genocides perpetrated by Adolf Hitler and Hideki Tojo.

In 1948, the United Nations General Assembly adopted the Convention on the Prevention and Punishment of the Crime of Genocide, which was ratified by enough states in 1951 that it became binding international law.[1] The Convention not only outlaws genocide; it also forbids any government from assisting genocide in any way. Further, the Genocide Convention requires signatory states to act to stop genocides in progress.

Yet despite the promising start, the U.N. has proved almost entirely useless in preventing crimes against humanity. Indeed, it has barely ever tried, and its agenda to ensure that victims are disarmed and defenseless can only lead to future genocides.

University of Hawaii political science professor R. J. Rummel, the world's leading statistical scholar of mass murders by governments, estimates that during the twentieth century, governments murdered approximately 169,198,000 victims. That does not include people killed by warfare; if you add war deaths, the death by government total rises by 33 million. Indeed, dictatorships are the major cause of violent death in the world, far exceeding all other causes.

Professor Rummel's book, *Statistics of Democide: Estimates, Sources, and Calculations on 20th Century Genocide and Mass Murder*, includes data on mass murders throughout the twentieth century. These are *some* of the genocides that took place between 1946 and 1987, after the creation of the U.N.:

In Asia[2]

- Vietnam (1,678,000)
- North Korea (more than 2 million)
- Pakistan (1,503,000, mainly from West Pakistan's 1971 mass murder of more than a million Bengalis and Hindus in East Pakistan, which is now the independent nation of Bangladesh)
- Iraq (the 1966–88 murder of more than 100,000 Kurds and southern Shiites)
- Communist China (73 million)
- Cambodia (by the Khmer Rouge from 1975 to 1979: 2,035,000; by the Vietnamese-allied military government that took power afterward: 230,000)
- Afghanistan (by the Communist government that took power in a 1978 coup: 237,000)
- Soviet Union (22.485 million; as with other countries on this list, the figure is only for murders from 1946 onward, after the U.N. had been created)
- Indonesia (1965: 509,000 communists and ethnic Chinese)
- East Timor (1975–98: 150,000 killed by the Indonesian government)

In Europe[3]

- Poland (885,000 from 1945 to 1948)
- Czechoslovakia (185,000)
- Romania (435,000)
- Bulgaria (185,000)
- Yugoslavia (1,072,000 from 1944 to 1987, under the Tito dictatorship; in the 1990s, about 25,000–100,000 murdered in Bosnia-Herzegovina)

In Africa[4]

- Ethiopia (725,000, by the communist dictatorship that took power in 1974)
- Rwanda (600,000 to 1,000,000 Tutsi and moderate Hutus killed in 1994)
- Uganda (301,000 by Idi Amin; 262,000 after Amin)
- Burundi (1967–87 murders of Hutus, 150,000)
- Sudan (starting in 1955 and continuing to the present: murders of non-Arab Africans, Christians, and animists, more than one million)

Professor Rummel summarizes the statistics: from 1945 through 1987, about 114 million people were murdered by governments. Of those 114 million, about 104 million were killed by Communism, a political system that imposed repressive gun laws wherever it obtained power. Rummel estimates that since 1987, between 3 million and 6 million more people have been mass-murdered by governments.[5]

To read this list of genocides is to read a list of U.N. failures. Never, anywhere in the world, in the U.N.'s six-plus decades of existence, has it acted to stop a genocide in progress. To make matters worse, the U.N. has become, in practice, a genocide enabler. Formerly, tyrants preparing for genocide carried out civilian disarmament themselves. Now, genocide perpetrators have U.N. assistance in disarming their victims.

Rwanda

Not too long ago, the U.N. facilitated the genocide against the disarmed people of Rwanda,[6] a nation that had been ruled since 1973 by the dictator Juvénal Habyarimana, a member of the majority Hutu tribe. The Tutsi minority comprised about 10 to 15 percent of the population.

Rwanda had an ideal gun control system by U.N. standards: a 1979 law nearly completely outlawed civilian gun possession. Of course, the government still had guns, and every family had a machete—an essential daily tool for the small farming villages where almost all Rwandans lived.

Years of oppression drove the many Tutsi and moderate Hutus to join the Rwandan Patriotic Front (RPF), a group of rebel militias that operated out of nations bordering Rwanda.

The Rwandan government had long been calling for killing the Tutsis and, ever since achieving independence from Belgium in 1959, had carried out many mass murders of Tutsis, as well as many other forms of ethnic persecution. In 1992, President Habyarimana escalated the rhetoric even further, with insistent calls for Tutsi extermination. His propaganda was reinforced by two major radio stations; Radio Rwanda and Radio Milles Collines constantly called the Tutsis "cockroaches" and called for their extermination in songs and "comedy" routines.

All of the several Hutu political parties had one thing in common: their platforms demanded the killing of Tutsis, in meticulous and explicit detail.[7] At political rallies and meetings, Hutus were told to stop being friends with Tutsis, or sharing farm work with them, because one day the Hutus would have to kill the Tutsis.[8]

In 1990, the Habyarimana clan had formed a group of organized violent gangs called the *interahamwe*, founded on the principle of hatred of Tutsis and obedience to the Habyarimana dictatorship. (Foreign observers refer to these gangs as "militias," but they obviously had nothing in common with legitimate militias, created for community self-defense.)

After an April 1993 visit to Rwanda, the U.N.'s special rapporteur of the Commission on Human Rights documented the extensive massacres and other killings of Tutsis that were taking place. He did not conclude that the massacres constituted genocide, but did raise the possibility. His report was "largely ignored" by the United Nations.[9]

278

U.N. peacekeepers were sent to Rwanda late that year. On January 11, 1994, the head of the U.N. mission in Rwanda, Canadian general Roméo Dallaire, send an urgent message to the U.N. headquarters in New York. The message was directed to the Department of Peacekeeping Operations, headed by Kofi Annan.

Dallaire reported what he had learned from an informant, who had been put in touch with Dallaire by a "very, very important government politician." A large organized gang called the Hutu *interhamwe* was receiving training in Rwandan government army camps. The *interhamwe* were being prepared to register all Tutsi in the region of Kigali, the capital city.

The informant suspected that the purpose of registering Tutsis was "for their extermination." He also knew where the *interhamwe* had huge caches of arms, and he offered to tell the U.N., so the peacekeepers could seize them. Dallaire informed Annan's office that he intended to seize the caches that were about to used for genocide.

Annan's office had every reason to believe Dallaire. The personal representative of the U.N. secretary-general had cabled Annan's office to say that he had met with the prime minister designate of Rwanda, who had "total, repeat total confidence in the veracity" of the informant. The previous year, the U.N. had received reports of two thousand Tutsis being murdered. The U.N. Human Rights Commission, in a 1993 investigation of Rwanda, had warned that the nation was at risk of genocide. Senior Rwandan military officers had written to General Dallaire in December 1993 to tell him about a plan to mass murder Tutsis. And a Hutu radio station was broadcasting intense hate propaganda, inciting the Hutus against the Tutsis.

Despite all the evidence, Annan's assistant in New York, Iqbal Riza, ordered General Dallaire to leave the arms alone, and chastised him for even thinking of seizing them. Instead, he was ordered to pass along his information only to the U.S., French, and Belgian embassies, and to the president of Rwanda.

In February, Dallaire's office cabled New York again, warning of "catastrophic consequences" if the peacekeepers stood idle. Again, Annan's office ordered Dallaire to stand down.

The genocide began on April 6, 1994, perpetrated by the *interahamwe* and the Rwandan army. Almost all the killers used machetes, although a few used spears, clubs, or bows. The Rwandan army and the *interahamwe* used firearms, including machine guns, for crowd control, but hardly ever for actual killing. Sometimes educated people who had been especially vociferous in agitating for genocide would be given a gun by the government so they could kill without getting blood on their clothes. As the genocide spread nationwide, it was carried out by entire Hutu villages, which would assemble every morning and spend the day murdering and looting. Sometimes the army or the *interahamwe* led them, but more often they were on their own.[10]

On April 7, the killers struck the Rwandan prime minister, her five children, and the ten Belgian soldiers who were guarding her. After the Belgians surrendered, the entire contingent was murdered.

In the first few days, tens of thousands of Tutsis and moderate Hutus were slaughtered. General Dallaire cabled the U.N. to ask for reinforcements and the authority to take forceful action against the genocide. Annan's department replied that Dallaire should do nothing that would "compromise your impartiality." As Dallaire later explained, if the U.N. peacekeepers in Rwanda had been joined by three hundred U.S. Marines and nine hundred French soldiers (a force the French eventually sent in June), the genocide could have been stopped.

The U.N. ordered Dallaire to focus solely on evacuating foreigners, with the explicit instruction "no locals." Annan and his staff did not want to compromise their neutrality by helping the genocide victims.

In response to the U.N. evacuation of foreigners only, the radio stations told the Hutu mobs, "The foreigners are departing. They had material proof of what we are going to do, and they are leaving Kigali. This time around they are showing no interest in the fate of the Tutsis." The U.N. evacuation further emboldened the killers.[11]

Early on in the genocide, thousands of Rwandan civilians had gathered in areas where U.N. troops had been stationed, thinking they would be protected. They were not. When the U.N. forces departed, Hutu mobs moved in to slaughter all the Tutsis left behind.

If the Rwandans had known that the U.N. troops would withdraw, they would have fled, and some might have survived. "The manner in which troops left, including attempts to pretend to the refugees that they were not in fact leaving, was disgraceful," an independent report later concluded.[12]

By the end of April, one hundred thousand Rwandans had been murdered. But at the Security Council in New York, the Clinton administration joined other nations in refusing to use the word *genocide*, because admission that *genocide* was taking place would create a legal obligation on the U.N., the United States, and other nations to try to prevent it.

Eventually, the U.N. authorized the dispatch of nine hundred French soldiers, who in late June occupied a quarter of the country and began running the country in collaboration with the Rwandan Hutu government that had perpetrated the genocide.

The genocide ended on July 4, 1994, when the Hutu government was ousted by the RFP militias of Tutsis and moderate Hutus. There were eight hundred thousand Rwandans, mostly Tutsi, dead. The 103 days of murder were the fastest genocide in world history.

The main impact of the French who had been dispatched by the U.N. was to cover the retreat of the murderous Hutus into the Democratic Republic of the Congo.[13] The disarmed civilian population had been left to die by the U.N.; the mass murders ended because of the genocidal regime was overthrown by forces of arms—by what the U.N. condemns as "illegitimate" arms because they are possessed by "non-state actors."

It was later discovered that the U.N. was not just a do-nothing observer of the Rwanda genocide. Callixte Mbarushimana, a staffer with the U.N. Development Programme, actually "lent vehicles and satellite telephones of the UNDP to military officers, and he also used the UNDP vehicles to facilitate his own contribution to the killings"—as later admitted on a U.N. website. According to a U.N. document, he played a role in "the death of UNDP's National Personnel Officer, Ms. Florence Ngirumpatse, and a number of refugees in the residence where they had taken refuge." Yet the United Nations continued to employ Mbarushimana until 2001. The Inner City Press reported, "The UN has yet to answer when it knew what it came to know about Mbarushimana, and what actions if any it took on what it knew."[14]

Kofi Annan repeatedly interfered with and obstructed investigations about the handling of the Dallaire cable. When a Belgian commission began investigating the Rwanda genocide, Annan forbade Dallaire to testify, because the testimony was not "in the interest of the organization."[15]

Srebrenica

"The spread of illicit arms and light weapons is a global threat to human security and human rights," insists Annan.[16] It would be far more accurate to say, "The U.N.'s disarmament policy is a global threat to human security and human rights." It was the U.N.'s lethal policy that was directly responsible for the deaths of thousands of innocents in Srebrenica, Bosnia, in 1995. A future of U.N. gun control is a future filled with thousands more Srebrenicas.

Srebrenica was the best-known atrocity in a genocide campaign run by Yugoslav president Slobodan Milosevic and facilitated by the U.N. Located near the eastern border of Bosnia-Herzegovina, the silver-mining town of Srebrenica was once part of the Republic of Yugoslavia. Yugoslavia had been created by the Treaty of Versailles in 1919, and until the country broke up in 1991, it was the largest nation on the Balkan peninsula, composed of six republics: Serbia, Croatia, Bosnia-Herzegovina, Macedonia, Slovenia, and Montenegro, as well as two provinces, Kosovo and Vojvodina.

Yugoslavia was turned into a Communist dictatorship in 1945 by Marshal Tito, whose iron hand kept ethnic tensions in check until his death in 1980. His successors feared civil war, so a system was instituted according to which the collective leadership of government and party offices would be rotated annually. But the new government foundered, and in 1989, Serbian president Milosevic began reimposing Serb and Communist hegemony. Slovenia and Croatia declared independence in June 1991.

Slovenia repelled the Yugoslav army in ten days, but fighting in Croatia continued until December, with the Yugoslav government retaining control of about a third of Croatia. Halfway through the Croat-Yugoslav war, the U.N. Security Council adopted Resolution 713, calling for "a general and complete embargo on all deliveries of weapons and military equipment to Yugoslavia" (meaning Yugoslavia, plus Croatia and Slovenia).[17] Although sovereign nations are normally expected to acquire and own arms, Resolution 713 redefined such weapons as "illicit" in the eyes of the U.N.

It was universally understood that the Serbs were in control of most of the Yugoslavian army's weaponry, and that the embargo therefore left them with military superiority. Conversely, even though the embargo was regularly breached, it left non-Serbs vulnerable. The U.N. had, in effect, deprived the incipient countries of the right to self-defense—even though every nation is guaranteed a right to self-defense by Article 51 of the U.N. Charter.[18]

Macedonia seceded peacefully from Yugoslavia in early 1992, but Bosnia-Herzegovina's secession quickly led to a three-way civil war between Bosnian Muslims ("Bosniacs"), Serbs (who are Orthodox), and Croats (who are Roman Catholic). The Bosnian Serbs received substantial military support from what remained of old Yugoslavia (consisting of Serbia and Montenegro, and under the control of Slobodan Milosevic).

Security Council Resolution 713 now operated to make it illegal for the new Bosnian government to acquire arms to defend itself from Yugoslav aggression. This was rather ironic, since Bosnia did not even exist as an independent nation when Security Council Resolution 713 was passed in

1991. But since Bosnia had declared independence from Yugoslavia, and Yugoslavia's murderous government was subject to the U.N. arms embargo, the U.N. insisted that the embargo also applied to Bosnia.

The Bosnian Muslims were told that they did not need arms of their own; instead, they would be protected by U.N. and NATO peacekeeping forces.[19] Bosnia-Herzegovina president Izetbegovic "was in favour of the UNPROFOR [United Nations Protection Force] proposal, which, as he understood it, meant that the Bosniacs would hand their arms over to UNPROFOR in return for UNPROFOR protection."[20]

Creation of "safe areas" pursuant to Resolution 819, which was adopted by the Security Council in April 1993, also proved disastrous. Safe areas were "regions, which should preferably be substantially free of conflict beforehand, where refugees could be offered a 'reasonable degree of security' by a brigade of peacekeeping troops."[21]

The concept of a safe area, however, was a pacifist fantasy, with little resemblance to the reality on the ground. Even the U.N. forces were not safe; they could not protect themselves, let alone anyone else. In fact, the U.N.'s so-called peacekeepers were so inept and passive that the Bosnian Serbs often took them hostage, sometimes by the hundreds, in a single operation.[22] The U.N. hostages would then be used by the Bosnian Serbs to deter the U.N. and NATO from taking more aggressive action.

The first, and so far only, contested case involving the scope of the duty to prevent genocide was *Bosnia v. Yugoslavia*, in which Bosnia sued Yugoslavia in the United Nations' International Court of Justice (ICJ).[23] In April 1993, the International Court of Justice ruled, with only one dissenter, that Yugoslavia was perpetrating genocide, and ordered it to stop.[24] Of course Yugoslavia ignored the court order.

A few months later, Bosnia brought forward additional legal claims, including a request to have the U.N. embargo declared illegal, as a violation of the Genocide Convention. The majority of the ICJ dodged the question, stating that it had no jurisdiction over the Security Council's embargo.

Judge Elihu Lauterpacht, wrote a separate opinion, which was the first international court opinion ever to address the legal scope of the Genocide Convention's affirmative duty "to prevent" genocide. Judge Lauterpacht cited the findings of a special rapporteur about the effect of the arms embargo, and pointed to the "direct link . . . between the continuation of the arms embargo and the exposure of the Muslim population of Bosnia to genocidal activity at the hands of the Serbs."[25]

Normally, Security Council resolutions are unreviewable by the ICJ; however, Judge Lauterpacht ruled that the prevention of genocide is *jus cogens*, or "compelling law."[26] This is a technical international law term for a law that overrides all conflicting laws. He concluded that the Security Council arms embargo became void once it made U.N. member-states "accessories to genocide."[27]

Formal repeal of the Security Council embargo was impossible because Russia threatened to veto any action harmful to its client-state Serbia. However, Judge Lauterpacht's opinion stated that the U.N. embargo was already void, as a matter of law, the moment it came into conflict with the Genocide Convention.

By summer 1995, the population of Srebrenica, a designated safe area, had swelled with refugees. By the time of the massacre, it was an island of Bosniacs in Bosnian Serb territory, an island the U.N. had sworn to protect.

But the U.N. would not honor its pledge. As the BBC later reported, "A former U.N. commander in Bosnia has told a Dutch parliamentary inquiry into the Srebrenica massacre that it was clear to him that Dutch authorities would not sacrifice its soldiers for the enclave."[28]

And, indeed, on July 11, 1995, Bosnian Serb forces entered Srebrenica without resistance from Bosniac or U.N. forces; not a shot was fired. (The Bosniac general in Srebrenica had recently been recalled by his government, leaving the Bosniac forces leaderless.) The peacekeepers ignored the pleas of the Muslims in the camp not to abandon them.[29]

Ethnic cleansing and genocide followed. The men and boys were separated from the women, then taken away and shot.

Knowing that remaining in the U.N. safe area would mean certain death, some ten thousand to fifteen thousand Bosniac males fled into the surrounding forests, escaping to the Bosniac-held town of Tuzla. Only about three thousand to four thousand were armed, mostly with hunting rifles. These were the men who survived what has since become known as the six-day "Marathon of Death."[30]

And the rest? Laura Silber and Allan Little, in their book *Yugoslavia: Death of a Nation*, describe the slaughter in the forest: "Some were killed after having surrendered, believing the U.N. would protect them . . . Serb soldiers, some even dressed as U.N. peace-keepers driving stolen white U.N. vehicles, would guarantee the Muslims' safety. Then they would shoot."[31] In this way, more than seventy-five hundrd men and boys were killed.

The Srebrenica massacre was Europe's worst atrocity since World War II, but it was only one small part of the genocide and ethnic cleansing of Bosnia. Approximately two hundred thousand people were killed; another million became refugees.[32]

Three months after the massacre at Srebrenica—lightning speed for the U.N.—a unanimous Security Council rescinded its arms embargo against the nations of the former Yugoslavia.[33]

Who was responsible for the Srebrenica genocide and the rest of the genocide in Bosnia? Primarily, of course, the Yugoslav government and its Bosnian Serb allies. Many of the perpetrators have been prosecuted before the International Criminal Tribunal for the Former Yugoslavia (ICTY) at the Hague.[34] Bosnian Serb general Radislav Krstic, the senior commander of the Srebrenica genocide, was found guilty by the ICTY on August 2, 2001, and sentenced to a forty-six-year prison term.[35] (The ICTY has no death penalty.)

Ex-Yugoslav president Slobodan Milosevic was among the former leaders prosecuted for genocide and for crimes against humanity. As his four-year trial for those crimes was drawing to a close, Milosevich was found dead in his cell at the U.N. detention center in the Hague on March 11, 2006.

A large share of the blame for Srebrenica was placed on the Dutch government and ill-prepared Dutch peacekeepers, as detailed in an April 2002 report by the Netherlands Institute for War Documentation.[36] Dutch prime minister Wim Kok and his entire cabinet resigned in shame a week later.

The Convention on Genocide makes "complicity in genocide" a punishable act.[37] The U.N.'s reflexive attempt at disarmament prior to the massacre at Srebrenica might be said to fulfill the definition of complicity: "a state of being an accomplice; partnership in wrongdoing."[38] Even if not legally complicit, the U.N. undeniably functioned as a facilitator of genocide.

The U.N. was hardly ignorant of the murderous Serb intent. Prior to Srebrenica, the U.N. knew about other mass killings committed by the Serbs against the Bosniacs between 1991 and 1994. One of the largest took place in April 1992 in the town of Bratunac, just outside Srebrenica; approximately 350 Bosnian Muslims were tortured and killed by Serb paramilitaries and special police.[39]

The U.N. was fully aware of Milosevic's designs for a "Greater Serbia" (incorporating portions of Bosnia), and was also fully aware of the disparity in military capabilities between Milosevic and his intended victims.

In short, the U.N. was aware of Milosevic's propensity for ethnic cleansing and had ample reason to know that its actions would create a situation ripe for genocide. The atrocities at Srebrenica could not have been perpetrated by the Serbs on such a grand scale had not the U.N. and its policies first prepared an enclave of victims, most of them disarmed.

If the U.N. were genuinely interested in protecting people from genocide, then the person who supervised the incompetent, genocide-facilitating actions of the organizaton's so-called peacekeepers would be fired. During the Srebrenica genocide, the U.N. undersecretary-general for Peacekeeping Operations was Kofi Annan.

The only consequence he suffered for his deadly incompetence was being promoted to secretary-general, and then being awarded the Nobel Peace Prize on December 10, 2001.

In 1998, three years after the Srebrenica massacre, he did offer an apology:

> The United Nations . . . failed to do our part to help save the people of Srebrenica from the Serb campaign of mass murder . . . In the end, the only meaningful and lasting amends we can make to the citizens of Bosnia and Herzegovina who put their faith in the international community is to do our utmost not to allow such horrors to recur. When the international community makes a solemn promise to safeguard and protect innocent civilians from massacre, then it must be willing to back its promise with the necessary means. Otherwise, it is surely better not to raise hopes and expectations in the first place, and not to impede whatever capability they may be able to muster in their own defense.[40]

The apology would have been meaningful if Annan had changed the policies of the U.N., rather than continuing to impose the same morally bankrupt ones that led to genocide in Bosnia. In fact, just months after the show of contrition, he and the U.N. were back at work preventing prospective genocide victims from defending themselves, this time in East Timor.

In 2007, a group called "Mothers of Srebrenica," representing survivors and widows of the massacre, brought suit in a Dutch court against the government of the Netherlands, and the United Nations. A trial court allowed the suit to go forward, but an appeals court blocked it. The appellate court ruled that the United Nations had "absolute immunity" based on international law.

"That the UN has unlimited immunity even if a genocide happens, we can't accept," said plaintiffs' lawyer Alix Hagedorn. The plaintiffs argue that the Convention on the Prevention and Punishment of the Crime of Genocide (a treaty created by the U.N. in 1948) means that the U.N. has a legal obligation to prevent genocide, and that there must be a legal remedy for the relatives of genocide victims when the U.N. refuses to fulfill its obligation.

Even if the U.N. does have legal immunity, it can waive immunity if it chooses, and has sometimes done so, such as in cases where the U.N. has allowed some of its officials to be criminally prosecuted for corruption. When the Inner City Press asked U.N. staff lawyer Nicolas Michel if the U.N. had considered waiving immunity in the Dutch case, "he said he [didn't] have to [explain], and that he should not be taped." The reporter concluded that the operating principle for the U.N. was "Impunity breeds contempt."[41]

In 2010, German artist Philip Ruch created a monument to the Srebrenica victims. The "Pillar of Shame" consists of more than eight thousand pairs of shoes, one pair for each victim. Surrounded by wire mesh, the piles of shoes are nearly nine yards high. If you look at the Pillar of Shame from a distance, you will see that it spells out "U.N." Ruch says he hopes that the Pillar of Shame will be a "warning for all future U.N. employees never again just to stand by when genocide unfolds."[42]

East Timor

Slightly larger than the state of Maryland, the island of Timor lies in Southeast Asia, four hundred miles northwest of Australia. The Portuguese first visited the island in the early 1500s. Beginning in the eighteenth century, the Dutch competed with the Portuguese for control of Timor. In the middle of the nineteenth century, they divided the island between them. When the Dutch East Indies gained independence in 1949 as the nation of Indonesia, West Timor was absorbed into Indonesia, and Portugal retained the eastern part of the island as its colony.

Portuguese occupation of Timor was characterized by the exploitation of its people through oppressive taxation, forced labor, and other human rights abuses. Portugal's harsh treatment of the Timorese led to widespread resentment, and, eventually, violent rebellion. Although Portugal was able to suppress the rebellions, resistance continued.

Portugal's fascist government was toppled on April 25, 1974, by the Carnation Revolution, a relatively nonviolent military coup. The new government in Lisbon was dedicated to democracy and to the decolonization of Portugal's overseas territories.

Thirsting for freedom, the Timorese leadership began preparing for liberation. Kay Rala Xanana Gusmao (now the president of Timor) recalled, "Our only ideology was *ukun rasik an*, self-determination." He believed the only choice the Timorese had was between freedom and "total extermination." It was only by defying a United Nations gun-control campaign that the Timorese won their freedom, and avoided total extermination.

When Portugal officially abandoned its colonies in 1975, East Timor declared independence. But a few days later, on December 7, Indonesia invaded. Within six months, there were thirty-five thousand Indonesian troops in East Timor, and ten thousand more were standing by in West Timor.

The armed occupation lasted twenty-four years. In an attempt to bring East Timor to its knees, Indonesia resorted to forced sterilization (paid for by the World Bank), mass starvation, rape, murder, torture, and conventional and napalm bombing directed at isolated villages, most of which were leveled to the ground.[43]

Between 1975 and mid-1999, more than two hundred thousand East Timorese—a third of its preinvasion population of seven hundred thousand—had been killed. The overwhelming majority of casualties were civilians. It is estimated that a hundred thousand East Timorese were killed by Indonesian troops just in the first year of the invasion. That, combined with the twin policies of forced sterilization and the migration of Indonesians into East Timor, led observers to conclude that Indonesia intended ethnic cleansing for the Maubere people.[44]

What did the U.N. do? In effect, it did nothing. Toothless resolutions decreed that Indonesia should withdraw from East Timor. There were no sanctions. The U.N. refused to use the word *genocide* to describe the rampant murder that was being perpetrated in East Timor.

In effect, the U.N. response to the Indonesia's genocide in East Timor was to pass a sternly worded resolution warning that if Indonesia did not stop, it would pass another sternly worded resolution—all of which was consistently ignored by Indonesia.

Even so, Timorese resistance stiffened. What the East Timorese people needed were loaded firearms, not empty words from the U.N. In spite of the resources expended by Indonesia to prosecute the war—a cost of up to $1 million (U.S.) per day—the Armed Forces for the National Liberation of East Timor (*Falintil*) waged a successful guerrilla campaign, using arms left over from the days of Portuguese rule, or stolen from Indonesian troops.

In the eyes of the U.N., once those arms fell into the hands of *Falintil*, they crossed the line from what the U.N. defines as "licit" guns, into "illicit" guns.

It is here that the hypocrisy and inconsistency of U.N. policy becomes apparent. The U.N. equates "licit gun" with "government gun," and "illicit gun" with "antigovernment gun." As Charles Scheiner, national coordinator for the East Timor Action Network, correctly pointed out, however, "The guns used by the Indonesian military to kill two hundred thousand East Timorese civilians were almost all 'legal' [but] the line between legality and illegality is irrelevant to the victims."[45]

That line in the sand—distinguishing licit from illicit—legitimizes possession of firearms owned by governments and people approved by those governments, rendering firearm possession by all others illegitimate. Yet it was illegitimate transfers that armed *Falintil*. Measured against U.N. standards, the *Falintil* guerrillas—as "non-state actors"—were in unlawful possession of the firearms they used to defend their country and their people when there was no one else to do so. Similarly illegitimate by that same U.N. standard was the French Underground that resisted the Nazis, almost every anticolonial movement in the world, and the American Revolution.

According to the U.N. Institute for Disarmament Research, "the ready availability of weapons makes it far too easy for substate groups to seek remedy for grievances through the application of violence."[46]

In other words, the U.N. lamented that it was "far too easy" for *Falintil* to resist Indonesia's genocide. Although the U.N. did offer resolutions telling Indonesia to get out of East Timor, those words were meaningless without the force supplied by *Falintil's* illicit arms.

James F. Dunnigan, military historian and editor of StrategyPage.com, pointed out why *Falintil*—a guerrilla army comprised of both men and women, equipped with only small arms and support from the civilian populace—prevailed against the might of Indonesia: "The basic idea behind guerilla war is to keep your force intact, not to fight the enemy. Guerillas who keep those priorities straight are successful. The East Timor separatists used a sound strategy, and eventually, the situation became intolerable for the occupying power . . . That was how the American Revolution was fought. Washington didn't have to win, or even fight, battles, he just had to keep the Continental army intact until the British parliament got tired of paying for the North American war."[47]

In 1999, the Indonesian government, headed by B. J. Habibie, finally agreed to an East Timorese vote on self-determination: autonomy under Indonesian rule, or complete independence.

Indonesia, though, had merely changed tactics. The *Sydney Herald* (April 29, 1999) detailed Indonesia's "three-pronged attempt" to sabotage the referendum process: "to first destabilize the situation in East Timor sufficiently to prevent a referendum; second, to terrorise the population sufficiently to ensure a pro-integration outcome in case a referendum takes place; and third, to 'Timorise' the conflict by presenting to the world a picture of 'warring Timorese factions.'"[48]

So the Indonesian military set about training militias in East Timor.[49] These bore no resemblance to the American model our Founding Fathers had in mind, our well-armed citizenry that provides homeland security. Indonesia's militias consisted of armed gangs of thugs, perpetrating mayhem and rape, and intimidating anyone believed to be in support of independence. While Jakarta tried to cast *Falintil* as the cause of continued violence in East

Timor, it was evident that the violence was orchestrated by the Indonesian army and its militia thugs.[50]

In April 1999, Indonesian Foreign Minister Ali Alatas demanded that the East Timorese give up their arms as a precondition for peace.[51] East Timor resistance leader Xanana Gusmao refused. He reiterated that *Falintil* guerrillas were never involved in acts of terrorism but had always acted in self-defense. They should therefore be treated as "an army of liberation and not as a band of bandits." He did, however, agree to a U.N.-brokered compromise between East Timor and Jakarta: *Falintil* and the Indonesian militias were to refrain from carrying arms except in designated areas called "cantonments."[52]

While *Falintil* remained passive in accordance with the truce, the Indonesian military continued to encourage militia misbehavior, leaving the undefended East Timorese populace easy prey.[53] Because independence depended on the referendum, which in turn depended on the cantonment of *Falintil*, East Timorese leaders had no choice.

On May 5, 1999, agreements were signed allowing the referendum to go forward, and on June 11, U.N. Resolution 1246 formally established the U.N. Mission in East Timor (UNAMET) for the purpose of organizing and supervising the referendum process.[54] The "responsibility . . . to maintain peace and security in East Timor . . . in order to ensure that the popular consultation [the vote] is carried out in a fair and peaceful way and in an atmosphere free of intimidation" was placed on the Indonesian government.[55]

Remember, all this was taking place just a few months after Kofi Annan had apologized for the U.N.'s failure to protect the disarmed genocide victims in Bosnia.

Now, after decades of genocide perpetrated by Indonesia against the Timorese, the ever-helpful U.N. insisted that the vast majority of the Timorese people be deprived of armed protection. They were supposed to rely on the Indonesian government to protect them.

The Indonesian army and its militias, with a long record of broken promises of nonaggression, now had a monopoly of power in East Timor, and their terror campaign persisted. One knowledgeable Western security expert predicted, "If independence wins, these autonomy guys will go berserk."[56]

On August 30, 1999, the referendum was held. The turnout was huge, and the vote was 78.5 percent for independence.[57] *Falintil* remained in cantonment, muzzled.

Until the eve of the referendum, the Indonesian military and police continued to promise to curb the violence and to honor a free vote. And as predicted, once East Timor voted to cut its ties with Indonesia, the Indonesian military set loose their vengeful militias on a defenseless populace. They hunted down independence supporters and their families, and torched villages.

According to the *New York Times*, one militiaman said that his orders were "to kill anyone on the street who stood for independence." And, he added, "if they could not hold onto East Timor, they would leave behind a wasteland devoid of schools, society, structure or a population."[58]

Falintil remained passive, in compliance with U.N. orders.[59]

The extraordinary restraint exhibited by *Falintil* during the ensuing chaos earned high praise from U.N. officials: "Throughout all this emergency they have not moved. The Indonesians want them to come out and attack so they can blame the chaos on *Falintil*."

As the world took notice, international pressure was finally brought to bear on Jakarta. Three weeks after the referendum, the first wave of Australian, New Zealand, and British troops—the core of the U.N. peacekeeping force—arrived in Dili, the capitol of East Timor. Within a week, three thousand troops had arrived, with a final target of eight thousand.[60]

It was good these Australian, New Zealand, and British troops finally arrived to stop the Indonesian depredations. But it is difficult to think of any good reason why the people of East Timor should have been forced to meekly submit to three weeks of mass murder, rape, and pillage while people in other countries pondered what to do. It was the U.N.'s obsession with disarmament that allowed the murder, rape, and pillage.

University of Minnesota law professor Barbara Frey, the U.N.'s special rapporteur on how small arms are used in human rights violations and a member of the international gun prohibition lobby IANSA, wrote, "While male-dominated society often justify small arms possession through the alleged need to protect vulnerable women, women actually face greater danger when their families and communities are armed."[61]

To see how catastrophically and callously wrong Frey is, one need only consider the examples detailed in this book: the women and girls raped, kidnapped, and murdered in East Timor, Rwanda, Bosnia, Kosovo, Albania, Liberia, Sierra Leone, and the Congo—because neither they nor anyone else in their families had a firearm to protect them. Because they were disarmed at the behest of the U.N. And quite often, the criminal perpetrators were U.N. staff and peacekeepers.

After the Commonwealth troops arrived, the U.N. again ordered *Falintil* to disarm completely. Again, they refused. Recognizing the high cost of confiscating *Falintil's* arms, U.N. peacekeepers backed off; on October 5, 1999, Australian army colonel Mark Kelly, spokesman for the international peacekeeping force Interfet, made a face-saving statement: "The ongoing discussions we will have with the *Falintil* leadership will look towards the eventual disarming. We have got a requirement to disarm those people under our [U.N.] mandate."[62]

By December, it was decided that *Falintil* would be transformed into East Timor's "legally constituted police force."[63] If the U.N. could not disarm *Falintil*, then the group could be legitimized in U.N. eyes by morphing it into the East Timor Defence Force.

On February 1, 2001, the *Falintil* guerrilla force became the world's newest internationally recognized army. Its mission was declared by its new commander, Brigadier-General Taur Matan Ruak: "to guarantee the defence of our homeland, of the new sovereign state of Timor, fully respecting the new democratic institutions and the political representatives democratically elected by our people."[64] Meanwhile, the U.N. continued to work toward its goal of total gun prohibition for civilians. As a price of independence, the Timorese were forced to accept Regulation Number 2001/5, On Firearms, Ammunition Explosives and Other Offensive Weapons in East Timor, enacted into law on April 23, 2001, by the U.N. Transitional Administration in East Timor (UNTAET).[65] The U.N.'s determination to disarm civilians finally prevailed.

The disarmament-minded U.N. promised to provide security guards to protect East Timor's president. But during a February 11, 2008, assassination attempt, the U.N. guards behaved like "cowards," according to the president's brother. He "accused them of hiding from bullets while he cradled the President's head in his arms." He said, "I believe the UN security operators failed completely."[66] The president survived, but the incident shows that the U.N. does not even keep its promise to protect a head of state. The idea that ordinary people can give up their guns and count on the U.N. to protect them is suicidal.

Sudan

In September 2004, the United States government explicitly invoked the Genocide Convention to call upon the U.N. to stop the genocide in Sudan. The call by the U.S. was the *only* time any party to the Genocide Convention has ever invoked the Genocide Convention to call upon the U.N. Security Council to take action against a genocide.

Did the U.N. then stop the genocide in the Sudan? Of course not. Did the organization even use the word *genocide* to describe the genocide in the Sudan? Of course not. Did the U.N. respond to the mass murder of unarmed civilians by pushing for more gun control? Of course.

In 1989, Sudan's elected government was overthrown in a military coup by the National Islamic Front, which created a racist, Islamist tyranny in Khartoum. The Institute for the Study of Genocide reported that, "animated by a radical Islamism and a sense of Arab racial superiority, the movement engaged in genocide almost from the time it seized power."[67] Now, genocide in Sudan continues "by force of habit."[68]

The first genocide was perpetrated against the people of the Nuba Mountains, in central Sudan. Afterwards, the Arab Sudanese dictatorship carried out genocide against the Christian and animist black Africans who live in southern Sudan, killing about 2.2. million, and driving 4.5 million from their homes.[69] Victims who were not killed were often sold into slavery. Rape was used extensively as an instrument of state terror.

Fortunately, rebel groups among the south Sudanese had arms. Although there were not enough arms for the innocent civilians to protect themselves, the southern rebel groups were able to keep up an armed resistance. Under intense pressure from President George W. Bush, the Khartoum government finally accepted a cease-fire in late 2004. The government has promised that in 2010, the south Sudanese will be able to vote on a referendum for independence. But never have the Khartoum dictatorship's promises been of any value.

The referendum has been put off until 2011, and today, it is not clear whether the peace agreement will hold; the leader of the southern rebels, who was supposed to become vice president of Sudan, died in a suspicious helicopter accident in the summer of 2005.

While armed rebels have, at least temporarily, stopped the genocide in south Sudan, the situation is even worse in western Sudan. The three states of western Sudan are collectively known as "Darfur." As in the south, much of the population is black African. Unlike in the south, the black Africans of Darfur are Muslims.

Also inhabiting Darfur are Arab nomads, who have a long-standing conflict with black African pastoralists there. The Arabs consider the blacks to be racially inferior and fit only for slavery. "Beginning in the mid-1980s, successive governments in Khartoum inflamed matters by supporting and arming the Arab tribes, in part to prevent the southern rebels from gaining a foothold in the region . . . Arabs formed militias, burned African villages, and killed thousands. Africans in turn formed self-defense groups, members of which eventually became the first Darfur insurgents to appear in 2003."[70]

These so-called Janjaweed (literally, "evil men on horseback" or "devil on a horse") militias are like the terrorist gangs created by the Indonesian government—little different from state terror organizations such as Hitler's SS or Stalin's NKVD.

Because of the abuses of the tyrannical Islamist government in Khartoum, two movements seeking independence for Darfur were created in February 2003: the Sudan Liberation Army (SLA), and the Justice and Equality Movement (JEM). In April 2003, the rebels successfully attacked a government airfield, provoking massive retaliation by the Khartoum government.[71]

The Janjaweed have caused the deaths of up to four hundred thousand black Sudanese, have raped many thousands, and have forced two million black Sudanese into refugee camps.[72] "When the Janjaweed attack, they do unmistakably hurl racial abuse at their victims, alleging in particular that Africans are born to be slaves: 'Slaves, run! Leave the country. You don't belong; why are you not leaving this area for Arab cattle to graze?'"[73]

The Janjaweed attacks on villages were supported with aerial bombing by the Sudan Air Force.[74] There were no reports of response to these attacks from villagers or from the JEM or SLA. The rebel groups did not appear to have anti-aircraft weapons, such as surface-to-air missiles. The rebels did, however, possess small arms and light weapons, including firearms.[75]

Salah Gosh, head of Sudan's national security, admitted that the government, indeed, bombed the villages, noting: "The [rebel] militia are attacking the government from the villages. What is the government going to do? It will bomb those villages."[76] Notably, the majority of villages bombed were villages where there were no armed rebels.[77] Thus, the destruction of the villages should be seen not as an overzealous form of counterinsurgency warfare, but rather as a deliberate attempt to destroy an entire society. The ethnic cleansing of Darfur had been so thorough that, literally, there were no villages left to burn.[78]

Although ethnic cleansing is not uncommon where the population supports an antigovernment insurgency, it can also lead to deaths of innocent civilians on a large scale. Intentionally targeting civilians has long been recognized as a violation of the laws of warfare. An Amnesty International report noted: "International law also makes it clear that use of such tactics does not provide the other side with a license to kill civilians."[79]

The Sudanese government tells the international community that the central government is not responsible for the Arab versus African violence in Darfur. However, Human Rights Watch observed that "government forces not only participated and supported militia attacks on civilians, they also actively refused to provide security to civilians seeking protection from these militia attacks."[80]

Despite promises from the Sudanese government, the attacks on Darfur grew even worse in early 2005. The U.S. Department of State reported that brutal attacks were still occurring, and that "attacks on civilians, rape, kidnapping and banditry actually increased in April."[81] According to the *Sudan Tribune*, "Attention to Darfur's staggering death toll—which has grown to approximately 400,000 over the course of more than two years of genocidal conflict—has increased in the past several months."[82] U.N. undersecretary for humanitarian affairs Jan Egeland warns that the death rate might increase to 100,000 per month if the humanitarian relief collapses.[83]

Egeland noted, "The only thing in abundance in Darfur is weapons."[84] However, these arms are distributed unevenly among Darfur's population. Despite the U.N. arms embargo,[85] Sudan has been funding its arms buildup using income from its oil sector to supply the Arab militia friendly to Khartoum.[86] According to Amnesty International, the Janjaweed are so well supplied that the majority of them have five or six guns per person.[87]

But in Sudan, it is virtually impossible for an average citizen to lawfully acquire and possess the means for self-defense. According to the national gun-control statutes,[88] a gun licensee must be older than thirty, must have a specified social and economic status, and must be examined physically by a doctor. Females have even more difficulty meeting these requirements because of social and occupational limitations.

When these restrictions are finally overcome, there are additional restrictions on the amount of ammunition one may possess, making it nearly impossible for a law-abiding gun owner to achieve proficiency with firearms. A handgun owner, for example, can only purchase fifteen rounds of ammunition a year. The penalties for violation of Sudan's firearms laws are severe and can include capital punishment.

The U.N. and the international gun-prohibition groups complain that Sudan's gun laws are not strict enough—but the real problem with the laws is that they have been—and are—enforced arbitrarily. A U.S. Department of State document stated: "After President Bashir seized power in 1989, the new government disarmed non-Arab ethnic groups but allowed politically loyal Arab allies to keep their weapons."[89] Meanwhile, there are many reports that the Arab militia have been armed and supplied by the government in Khartoum.[90]

After a village has been softened up by government air bombardment, the Janjaweed enter and pillage, killing and raping in order to displace the population and steal the land.[91]

Amnesty International reported the testimony of a villager who complained, "None of us had arms and we were not able to resist the attack."[92] One underarmed villager lamented, "I tried to take my spear to protect my family, but they threatened me with a gun, so I stopped. The six Arabs then raped my daughter in front of me, my wife and my other children."[93]

In cases when the villagers were able to resist, the cost to the marauders rose: Human Rights Watch reported that "some of Kudun's residents mobilized to protect themselves, and 15 of the attackers were reportedly killed."[94]

The *Pittsburgh Tribune-Review* asked a U.S. State Department official why there were no reports of the Darfur victims fighting back. "Some do defend themselves," he explained. But he added that the perpetrators have helicopters and automatic rifles, whereas the victims have only machetes.[95]

A teenage girl with a gun might not be the ideal soldier. But she is certainly not the ideal rape victim. It is not particularly difficult to learn how to use a firearm to shoot a would-be rapist from a distance of fifteen or twenty-five feet away. With an AK-47 type rifle, which is plentiful in some areas of the Third World, self-defense would be quite easy. Would every one of the Janjaweed Arab bullies who enjoy raping African girls be brave enough to dare trying to rape a girl who was carrying a rifle or a handgun?

The *Tribune-Review* asked an Amnesty International representative, Trish Katyoka, whether the Darfur victims should be armed.[96] Her response is worth analyzing sentence by sentence.

She began: "We at Amnesty International are not going to condone escalation of the flow of arms to the region." The answer is not surprising. In the last decade, Amnesty International has become a leading worldwide advocate for total gun prohibition—a stance contrary to its declared policy of opposing government abuses of human rights.

Amnesty International is a member of George Soros's gun prohibition group IANSA (International Action Network on Small Arms). Along with IANSA and Oxfam, Amnesty International created another gun prohibition lobby, Control Arms.

"You are empowering (the victims) to create an element of retaliation," the AI representative insisted. Her answer shows a serious confusion about self-defense. "Retaliation" is taking revenge for a misdeed after the fact. Self-defense is prevention of an imminent, unlawful, violent attack. Protecting a girl from an imminent gang rape has nothing to do with retaliation.

"Whenever you create a sword-fight by letting the poor people fight back and give them arms, it creates an added element of complexity. You do not know what the results will be." Ms. Katyoka summarized: "Fighting fire with fire is not the solution to genocide. It is a dangerous proposition to arm the minorities to fight back."

According to the Institute for the Study of Genocide, there is no reason to believe that the Darfur genocide will ever stop; the U.N. sent several thousand African Union troops to protect the international aid workers (but not to protect the Darfuris), and the AU force has proven incapable of even protecting the aid workers. Many Darfuris are now starving to death and dying of epidemics in remote refugee camps that the Sudanese dictatorship has cut off from all outside supply.[97] The IGS argues for NATO intervention, which appears to have no likelihood of ever taking place—and is especially unlikely in light of the French government's current, lucrative commercial arrangements for oil extraction in Sudan.

The U.N.'s actions are patently ineffectual. The Security Council "demanded" that the Khartoum tyranny disarm the Janjaweed, and the Khartourm dictators replied that they would not.

In March 2004, the U.N. Humanitarian Coordinator for Sudan, Mukesh Kapila, spoke the truth by stating, "The only difference between Rwanda and Darfur is the numbers involved." Rejecting Sudanese government claims that Darfur is simply in a state of civil war, with some civilians being accidentally injured therein, Kapila stated that Darfur "is more than just a conflict, it is an organized attempt to do away with a group of people." In response, the Sudanese government demanded that the U.N. get rid of Kapila, and the U.N. acceded, forcing him to resign.[98]

The Security Council's toothless demand, its referral to the International Criminal Court, and its authorization of the pathetic African Union force to protect only foreigners in Darfur might be regarded as feeble— but at least well-intentioned—efforts to try to take small steps against the genocide.

But the actions of the U.N. secretary-general appear to be of a different character altogether. Some of the Darfur refugees are currently being held in what the Institute for the Study of Genocide calls "concentration camps run by Janjaweed and Sudanese army guards, where murder and rape are standing orders."[99]

With the Sudan dictatorship already killing people in concentration camps, Secretary-General Annan's solution was . . . more concentration camps! In 2004, the special representative of the secretary-general signed a Sudanese government plan for the creation of safe areas where the Darfuris would be "guarded" by the Sudanese army—the same Sudanese army that has been carrying out genocide against these same Darfuris, who are now refugees only because the Sudanese army abetted the Janjaweed in burning down all the Darfuri villages.

The special representative of the secretary-general who signed the safe areas plan was Jon Pronk, who in 1995 was the Dutch Development Cooperation minister, with authority over the safe areas scheme in Bosnia that led to eight thousand Bosnians being murdered by the Serbs while the Dutch peacekeepers stood idle.[100]

Eric Reeves, a scholar with the Institute for the Study of Genocide, predicts that a new genocide will begin against the people of oil-rich eastern Sudan.[101]

If the Darfuris in the refugee camps possessed firearms, the refugees would hardly be able to march on Khartoum and overthrow the government, but they would be able to drive off the Janjaweed who come to a camp for plunder, murder, and rape.

Interestingly, the U.N. has, on at least one occasion, admitted that some communities in the world have survived only because they were armed. However, the U.N. views this as a problem to be solved, not something to be celebrated. A 2002 U.N. book setting out future global gun control plans explained the need for "long-term strategies to reverse the culture of violence and gun dependency through strategic education and socio-economic development projects in communities that are dependent on arms traffic *or that survive due to their access to and/or use of small arms.*"[102]

When Ban Ki-moon took over as secretary-general on January 1, 2007, he promised that he would make Darfur the U.N.'s top priority. Yet even now, as President Barack Obama's U.N. ambassador Susan Rice has stated, Darfur is the victim of an "ongoing genocide."[103]

The U.N. Security Council did tell the International Criminal Court to open a case against the Sudanese government leaders for the crimes in Darfur. As a compromise, the case referral was for "crimes against humanity" rather than genocide. (Sudan's U.N. patron and protector, China, allowed the compromise referral to pass, since China at the time was focused on its international image during the period leading up to the Beijing Olympics.) The Sudanese government responded by expelling many foreign aid workers from Darfur, so some critics said the ICC referral had been counterproductive. Supporters of the referral countered that it might have a deterrent effect on other regimes contemplating genocide. The referral did show that the U.N. was at least trying to do something about Darfur.

Before Ban took the helm, the only foreign forces in Darfur were some African Union troops who had no mandate to protect civilians, only to protect aid workers. Thanks in part to Ban, those soldiers are supplemented by U.N. peacekeepers, who are (relatively speaking) more capable, and who were given a mandate to also defend civilians. It was a respectable plan, but it has not worked out well.

The build-up of the U.N. forces has been very slow. One reason is that African nation troops are given preference; many African governments are torpid about doing anything helpful, and besides, they also want to maintain a friendly relationship with the genocidal butchers of Khartoum. In addition, the U.N. deployments depend, to a degree, on the tyrants' permission, and the Khartoum killers have not exactly put U.N. troop deployment permissions on the top of their "to-do" list.[104]

Meanwhile, Secretary-General Ban Ki-moon is seeking reelection to a second four-year term, reports the *Economist*. "Partly for that reason, say UN-watchers, he tries not to offend China over the conflict in Darfur, and over efforts by the International Criminal Court to arrest Sudan's president, an ally of China's, on war-crimes charges."[105]

Indeed, Ban is so desperate not to offend the Sudanese dictatorship that he uttered not a word of protest when U.N. workers were expelled from Sudan because they had been passing out rape detection kits.[106]

Considering how many million people did not survive the genocides of the last sixty years while the U.N. did nothing effective to save those disarmed victims, the U.N. should focus on protecting disarmed victims, rather than on disarming the communities that found a way to "survive due to their access and/or use of small arms."

Abandoned by the world, the people of Sudan have every moral right, every right under natural law, and every right under the Universal Declaration of Human Rights and other international human rights instruments to use firearms to save their lives. That the international gun prohibition movement would deny the right to possess defensive arms even by the victims of genocide, and even when the rest of the world has forsaken those victims, seems to me clear evidence that the international gun prohibition is neither "pro-life" nor "pro-choice," but is instead morally blinded by its obsessive hatred of guns and gun owners. The U.N. is complicit in genocide, and the international gun haters are complicit in evil.

Zimbabwe

Back in 2001, David Kopel, Paul Gallant, and Joanne Eisen predicted that Zimbabwe was "ripe for genocide," and they observed that the gun control system made genocide possible.[107] Unfortunately, their prediction was accurate.

Zimbabwe used to be a British colony called "Rhodesia." In 1965, a white-led government declared independence in order to preserve white rule. The new nation instantly became a global pariah. In 1972 various black groups began an effort to overthrow the white government of Ian Smith. Eventually, the government agreed to a power-sharing arrangement with the black majority in 1979, and Bishop Abel Muzorewa, who was black, was elected president.

However, international pressure, including pressure from Jimmy Carter, led to new elections in 1980; Robert Mugabe, leader of one of the military factions, stole the election by terrorizing his opponents.

Mugabe has held power in Zimbabwe ever since. Although the usual crowd of useful idiots extolled Mugabe as a symbol of the new Africa, Mugabe (whose close relationship with communist tyrannies was well-known long before he took power) sent his North Korean-trained forces in the central states of Midlands and Matabeland in 1983 for mass murder, rape, torture, and kidnapping.[108]

From time to time, Zimbabwe has held elections, but Mugabe has unquestionably stolen the last two, in 2002 and 2008. In 2000, he began to drive the nation's economy off a cliff by seizing farms that belonged to white people and giving them to political cronies.[109] His wife, Grace, was given a farm that had belonged to an elderly couple; she turned it into her weekend vacation home. He ignored a ruling by the Zimbabwe Supreme Court that the land seizures were illegal.[110]

The Mugabe regime has much in common with the Nazis. Like Hitler, Mugabe blames the British for the suffering that he himself has inflicted on his nation. Mugabe's right-hand man, the late Chenjerai Hunzvi, adopted the nickname "Hitler."[111] Hitler Hunzvi warned: "Anyone who resists the farm takeovers will end up six feet under." Unsurprisingly, Hitler Hunzvi thought that Adolf Hitler had been treated unfairly by "Western propaganda," and that Great Britain, not Nazi Germany, was the real embodiment of evil.[112]

Robert Mugabe and Hitler Hunzvi sent terrorist gangs to gang-rape women and girls in villages that had supported the opposition party, the Movement for Democratic Change (MDC). The gangs have kidnapped thousands of victims and kept them in government concentration camps as sex slaves.[113]

Once known as the breadbasket of Africa, Zimbabwe now is a basket case. For years, the people have been suffering from famine. The food shortage is not mainly caused by the weather. Even during a drought back in 1992, Zimbabwe's rich land produced a surplus of food for export. Rather, the famine may be the result of a decision to wipe out much of the population—of "taking the system back to zero" as Zimbabwe's henchmen called it.[114]

"We would be better off with only six million people," said the organization secretary of Mugabe's political party. Didymus Mutasa, head of the secret police, agreed: "We would be better off with only six million people, with our own people who support the liberation struggle. We don't want all these extra people."[115]

Election theft, government rape camps, farm confiscation, and genocide by starvation—all were made possible by gun control. Ian Smith and Robert Mugabe both inherited the 1957 Rhodesian Firearms Act. That Act made it impossible for anyone to acquire a firearm without the firearm being recorded by the government, since all firearms transactions must be routed though a government-licensed dealer. This is what George Soros's gun confiscation queen, Rebecca Peters, told the Million Mom March they must demand, in order to receive funding from Soros. The MMM's director, Donna Dees-Thomases, recounted that "to hear Rebecca explain it, without licensing and registration, all of the other laws proposed or already on the books were difficult to enforce."[116]

Among the laws that registration makes possible is gun confiscation, as Peters herself well knew, for she was the mastermind of Australia's confiscation of more than seven hundred thousand firearms in 1996–97.

So, too, in Zimbabwe. In 2000, gun licenses were revoked, with the purpose of taking self-defense guns from the white farmers.[117] Then Mugabe launched house-to-house searches for any guns that might not be known to the government:

> Zimbabwe's white farmers came under renewed pressure yesterday as squads of up to 20 police searched at least 200 properties for illegal weapons . . . Chen Chimutengwende, the Information Minister, confirmed that police had orders to scour all 4,000 white-owned farms for unlicensed firearms [and] ammunition. Said one farmer about such an incident on a nearby farm, "Every single square inch of the farmhouse was searched. They even looked

under the knickers." The story noted that "the police retreated looking 'disappointed' after failing to find any illegal weapons."[118]

The tyrant then armed his mobs of domestic terrorists: "Senior Zimbabwe Republic Police (ZRP) officers have clandestinely released firearms from the police armoury to independence war veterans . . . to unleash violence and terror on white-owned commercial farms and against members of the opposition."[119]

In the midst of the firearms and gun confiscations, one farmer explained:

Police may inspect weapons and licenses any time. The big deterrent to shooting anyone, even in self-defense, is that a murder charge is automatic, and the onus is now on you to prove innocence or reduce the charge . . . And whatever, you are in the wrong. Better to have a black security guard with a weapon. Ninety percent of black Zimbabweans are good people and just want to get on and make a living. The lunatic fringe of racist and get-rich-quickers are killing the country.[120]

With the reign of terror in progress, Mugabe ordered a national firearms "audit." The remaining gun owners (obviously not including the government's gangsters) were ordered to take their firearms certificates to a police station, to verify the number and type of guns owned. The pretext was rising crime, although the obvious purpose was the consolidation of tyranny.[121]

The farm confiscations were also devastating for wildlife. According to Zimbabwean environmental scholar Brian Gratwicke, "Eighty percent of 250,000 head of game that lived on privately owned commercial farms have been poached by land invaders—often with the encouragement of senior ZANU-PF [Mugabe's political party] officials who wanted to wrest control of the farms from their rightful owners."[122] Government officials are active poachers.[123]

In 2005, the government announced a "clean-up" campaign, to make people homeless. This time, the victims were not the white rural land owners, but black people in the cities. Gun confiscation was part of the program, as explained by ZimOnline, a dissident news service based in South Africa:

> Police at the weekend said they were revoking licences for all automatic rifles and some types of pistols and said civilians owning such weapons had until today to surrender them . . .
>
> But sources at police headquarters in Harare said the move was just precautionary to ensure such weapons could not be used by civilians should tension gripping Zimbabwe in the wake of the government's clean-up exercise erupt into public violence. "The ban is targeted at all automatic weapons which the government fears could pose a security threat in the country should the civil strife in Zimbabwe turn violent," said a source, who did not want to be named for fear of victimization . . . Zimbabwe's security forces have been on high alert since the government launched a "clean-up" campaign last month that has left close to a million people without shelter after their shanty homes were demolished.[124]

The "clean-up" program was called Operation Murambatsvina ("drive out the filth"). It forced two million destitute people from their urban homes, back into the countryside, with no means of support, because the government wanted them "re-ruralized." Some of the victims had come to the cities to try to make a living after the farm confiscation program destroyed their employment.[125]

At the U.N., Anna Tibaijuka, head of UN-Habitat, wrote a report exposing Mugabe's lies and condemning the evictions. Her apparent reward for this good deed was that Secretary-General Ban Ki-moon terminated her employment at the U.N. when her Habitat appointment expired in 2010.[126]

The *Sunday Times* of London reported in January 2007: "A vast human cull is under way in Zimbabwe, and the majority of deaths are a direct result of government policies. Ignored by the UN, it is a genocide perhaps 10 times greater than Darfur's and more than twice as large as Rwanda's."

The *Times* explained that Zimbabwe's population had fallen from 18 million to fewer than 11 million." Perhaps three million had fled to other countries, mainly South Africa. The remainder may be genocide victims. The seizure of the farms by Mugabe's cronies caused the collapse of food production. So the government launched Operation Maguta ("live well"): "Under Maguta, the army descends on villagers on communal land to compel them to grow maize and sorghum, which they must then sell to the army-run Grain Marketing Board. In Matabeleland, where maize does not grow well, the army has gone in hard, beating peasants who resist, raping women, chopping down orchards and tearing up vegetable patches."[127]

The *Sunday Times* explained that:

> the evictions had the effect of collapsing the economy and cutting the food supply far below subsistence level in every subsequent year. Yet Zimbabwe does not even get on to the UN agenda: South Africa's President Thabo Mbeki, who has covered for Mugabe, uses his leverage to prevent discussion. How long this can go on is anyone's guess. Mugabe—and, to a considerable extent, Mbeki—have already been responsible for far more deaths than Rwanda suffered, and the number is fast heading into realms previously explored only by Stalin, Mao and Adolf Eichmann.[128]

The inflation rate rose to 231 million percent, and the unemployment rate to 80 percent.[129] Cholera is spreading. Millions of people need food aid.[130] But the government prevents foreign organizations from distributing food; the government takes the food and gives it only to areas that have voted for the Mugabe regime.[131]

To say that the United Nations has done nothing would be inaccurate. The U.N. has been an active facilitator of the genocide and tyranny. As in Burma and North Korea, the U.N. has knowingly exchanged foreign hard currency with the Mugabe regime at a rate that has made Mugabe a huge profit. (The U.N. said that it stopped doing this in 2008, after Mugabe stole $7 million from the U.N. Global Fund to Fight AIDS, Tuberculosis and Malaria.) As usual, the U.N. refused to answer press questions about the currency exchange subsidy to the regime.[132]

In 2007, the U.N. Commission on Sustainable Development (CSD) elected Zimbabwe as its chair. According to the U.N., sustainable development is "development that meets the needs of the present without compromising the ability of future generations to meet their own needs." The U.N. says that "good governance within each country and at the international level is essential for sustainable development" and "peace, security, stability and respect for human rights and fundamental freedoms . . . are essential for achieving sustainable development and ensuring that sustainable development benefits all."[133]

Zimbabwe plainly exemplifies the opposite. Because of Mugabe, Zimbabwe now has the world's lowest life expectancy.[134] Journalist Claudia Rosett, noting that Zimbabwe is far from the only thugocracy on the Commission, suggested that a better name would be the "U.N. Commission on Sustainable Dictatorships."[135]

Because the Zimbabwean chairman, Francis Nhema, has played a leading role in the oppression of the people of Zimbabwe, he is the subject of a European Union travel ban. Asked about the controversy regarding his selection, Nhema answered, "At the end of the day the majority rules as democracy does."[136] An impressively brazen answer for the representative of a regime that has been stealing elections since Jimmy Carter was president.

Nhema, by the way, got a twenty-five-hundred-acre farm thanks to the land confiscation. It now lies mostly idle.[137]

Zimbabwe has also been given a seat on the executive board of the U.N. World Food Program.[138] It was also put on on the executive board of UNICEF,[139] and on the governing council of the U.N. Human Settlements Program (UN-HABITAT).[140]

Despite the European Union travel ban on Mugabe and his cronies, Mugabe was able to take a luxury trip to Rome to attend a U.N. Food and Agriculture Organization summit on food security. "This is the person who has presided over the starvation of his people. This is the person who has used food aid in a politically motivated way," protested Australian foreign minister Stephen Smith. "So Robert Mugabe turning up to a conference dealing with food security or food issues is, in my view, frankly obscene."[141] At the Rome conference, Mugabe was allowed to give a speech blaming Zimbabwe's problems on Britain, and nobody from the U.N. criticized him for starving millions.[142]

At the U.N., the Mugabe regime has been protected by China and South Africa. Questioned about South Africa's role in defense of the Mugabe tyranny, South Africa's U.N. ambassador, Dumisani Kumalo, shot back, "We do not apologize for having very strong, long relationship with Zimbabwe." He added, "There are a lot of people in Zimbabwe who died for me to stand up here as ambassador."[143] And there are many more people in Zimbabwe, millions in fact, who have died because of the South African government stands in solidarity with Mugabe and genocide. Sudan's U.N. ambassador Abdalmahmood Abdalhaleem Mohamad said South Africa "is a great nation; it's a role model for us."[144]

Secretary-General Ban Ki-moon is apparently intimidated by Mugabe. According to the *Economist*, "After a tough word with Robert Mugabe produced a tongue-lashing in return, say insiders, Mr Ban did his darnedest never to upset Zimbabwe's despot again."[145]

There is no U.N. arms embargo against Zimbabwe's tyranny, or any other form of sanctions. At the 2006 U.N. antigun conference, Zimbabwe's delegate was a retired military officer who happened to be one of the most notorious arms smugglers in Africa.[146] He bragged to the United Nations about the strict gun controls that Zimbabwe's government imposed on the people:

> May you allow me to share with you some of our water tight measures in the control of small arms and light weapons . . .
>
> If any individual has to acquire a small arm, be it for self protection or sports, the process is very strict that only a determined individual would ever go through the thorough vetting system . . .
>
> Our control system has proven that no arms can be trafficked into the country without an official permit. [Our country] has banned the sale and possession of self-loading rifles and individuals [*sic*] and security campanies [*sic*].
>
> Mr President allow me to conclude by saying [our country] has ratified the SADC [South African Development Community] protocol on firearms, ammunitions and other related materials. In line with the SADC protocol an implementation national action plan 2006–2009 is now in-place.[147]

No speaker at the United Nations conference pointed out that Zimbabwe's delegate was a professional arms smuggler, or that the very laws that he extolled had been used by that delegate's government for genocide.

Mugabe stole another election in 2008, and South African president Mbeki backed him up again. Finally in January 2009, Mugabe agreed to a "power-sharing" arrangement in which opposition political forces would be allowed some of posts in government, with the Mugabe group retaining control of the military, police, and the judicial system. But little has changed in Zimbabwe, and even if the new prime minister, Morgan Tsvangirai, were actually to take real power tomorrow, millions of people are already dead, thanks to the genocide that was made possible by gun control and by the collaboration of the United Nations.

Chapter 12

More Gun Control for Genocide Victims

While unwilling to say the word *genocide* about Sudan, the United Nations is very vocal about gun control in places like Sudan, saying we need a lot more of it. The U.N. has been promoting regional gun prohibition plans around the world.

In the Great Lakes and Horn of Africa regions, the prohibition plan is "the Nairobi Protocol for the Prevention, Control and Reduction of Small Arms and Light Weapons in the Great Lakes Region and the Horn of Africa."[1] The protocol was signed on April 21, 2004, by representatives of eleven nations: Burundi, Democratic Republic of the Congo, Djibouti, Eritrea, Ethiopia, Kenya, Rwanda, Seychelles, Sudan, Uganda, and Tanzania.[2]

Of the signatories, only Eritrea (which won independence in 1991 in a revolutionary war against Ethiopia) has been democratic for at least half its existence as an independent nation. The majority of signatories of the Nairobi Protocol have witnessed genocide in their nations within the last several decades, including the current genocides being perpetrated in the Democratic Republic of the Congo, Ethiopia, and Sudan.

To prevent genocide, the U.N. should encourage the dictatorships of East Africa to respect human rights, but instead it pushes for more stringent gun controls on the people of Rwanda, and on people in other nations targeted for genocide.

In the U.N.-sponsored Nairobi Protocol, the genocidal and dictatorial governments of East Africa, together with a few nominally or actually democratic governments, promised to incorporate in their national laws the prohibition of civilian possession of small arms. Terms included:

- The total prohibition of civilian possession of semiautomatic rifles;
- Centralized registration of all civilian-owned small arms;
- Competency testing of prospective small arms owners;
- Restrictions on owners' rights to relinquish control, use, and possession of small arms; and
- Restriction on the number of small arms that may be owned.[3]

The protocol also requires "heavy minimum sentences for . . . the carrying of unlicensed small arms," as well as programs to encourage citizens to surrender their guns, widespread searches for firearms, and educational programs to discourage gun ownership.[4]

In other words, the U.N. is successfully pushing for gun control in four East African nations with *current, ongoing* genocides, and in several others with recent histories of mass murder. Quite plainly, the U.N. believes that resisting an actual genocide in progress is not a sufficient reason for someone to want to own a gun.

A set of mandatory antigun laws—mostly similar to East Africa's Nairobi Protocol—is also being pushed in southern Africa, for the nations in the Southern African Development Community (SADC).[5] The large majority of the fourteen governments that have signed the U.N. antigun protocol are notoriously corrupt.[6] Few of them are democratic. Two of them—Zimbabwe and Congo—are the sites of genocides currently taking place. The U.N. has not stopped the genocides—but it has worked to make sure that the victims are defenseless.

The implementation of SADC is being coordinated by the Southern African Regional Police Chief's Co-operation Organization (SARPCCO). Its secretariat (headquarters) is in Harare, Zimbabwe.

ECOWAS

Over in West Africa, the U.N. is promoting an even more extremist antigun agenda among the Economic Community of West African States (ECOWAS). The ECOWAS Convention on Small Arms and Light Weapons, Their Ammunition and Other Related Materials is approximately similar to the Nairobi or SADC Protocols, in that it permits states to allow personal firearms ownership, if they choose, as long as they have licensing, registration, a maximum number of guns that be owned, etc. The Convention went into force on September 29, 2009.

Sixteen nations make up ECOWAS. In two of them—Mali and Niger—the Tuareg tribesmen of the desert north successfully took up arms to defend themselves against the depredations of the kleptocracy based in the capital city. Because the Tuareg were able to defend their rights with arms, they were able to force governments in the southern capital to stop stealing foreign food aid, which was supposed to be sent to starving people in the north.[7] The ECOWAS Convention, if successful, will ensure that starving people in West Africa will never again be able to take up arms against such corrupt governments.

In Liberia in the 1990s, two sides of the army fought a civil war and perpetrated what was called "attempted genocide" against civilians in tribes that supported the other faction.[8] U.N. peacekeepers prevented innocent civilians from fleeing, and then abandoned them so that they were mass murdered. Now the U.N. is making sure that Liberians will never have arms for self-defense.

In Nigeria, the nation's Christians and animists are under constant attack by violent Islamist extremists funded by pro-terrorist Arab groups. For example, in November 2002, Muslim rioters killed more than two hundred Christians in anger over an article in a Lagos newspaper that said that Mohammad would have wanted to marry a Miss World contestant. When the Nigerian government refused to protect the Christians, the Most Reverend

John Olorenfemi Onaiyekan, Nigerian archbishop, told Nigerian Christians: "It is a Christian duty to protect yourselves."[9]

But the good people of Nigeria will be unable to, as the ECOWAS Convention will ensure that law-abiding citizens cannot obtain defensive arms.

Under the Utopian vision of the U.N. and gun prohibition groups such as IANSA, citizens need not protect themselves, because the government will. But in Nigeria, the government refuses to protect people—and in many other countries of Africa, it is the genocidal government from which people need protection.

As for relying on the U.N. for protection, the situation hasn't improved since 1994, when the U.N. forces fled in Rwanda, or 1995, when the U.N. forces fled in Bosnia. In both countries, the U.N. lured unarmed victims to "safe" areas, then abandoned them, turning them into easy prey for genocide.

Let's look at what happened in Sierra Leone—another ECOWAS country where the U.N. wants to disarm every innocent civilian.

In May 2000, Sierra Leone "nearly became the U.N.'s biggest peacekeeping debacle" as Dennis Jett explains in his book, *Why Peacekeeping Fails*. Five hundred U.N. "peacekeepers" were taken hostage by rebels of the Revolutionary United Front (RUF).[10] The RUF has been described by Human Rights Watch as a "barbarous group of thugs" who "lived off the country's rich diamond fields and terrorized the population with its signature atrocity of chopping off arms and hands of men, women, and often children."[11]

Jett continues: "The RUF troops are unspeakably brutal to civilians, but will not stand up to any determined military force. Yet the U.N. peacekeepers, with few exceptions, handed over their weapons including armored personnel carriers and meekly became prisoners." It was only the deployment of Britain's troops to the former colony that saved civilian lives and averted a "complete U.N. defeat."

As the U.N. aims to disarm the citizens of sub-Saharan African, it is targeting the victims of some of the world's worst tyrannies and dictatorships. Of the sub-Saharan counties, only eight are rated "free" by the Freedom House annual report, *Freedom in the World 2009*. Another twenty-three are "partly free"—mostly dictatorships in which government abuse is significant but not always pervasive. And sixteen are rated "not free."[12]

The Universal Declaration of Human Rights recognizes the fundamental right of people victimized by tyrannies to revolt against the government that is destroying their inalienable human rights. Instead, the U.N. would disarm the victims of government abuse, leaving them defenseless against governments that pose a significant danger of genocide.

The Human Rights Alternative to Genocide

In an article in the *Notre Dame Law Review*, David Kopel, Paul Gallant, and Joanne Eisen argue that genocide victims have a fundamental human right to possess arms, under international law. They point out that nearly every nation in the world has signed the Convention on the Prevention and Punishment of the Crime of Genocide.[13]

The Convention states: "The Contracting Parties confirm that genocide, whether committed in time of peace or in time of war, is a crime under international law *which they undertake to prevent* and punish."[14] International law is clear that the duty to prevent is real, and is entirely distinct from the duty to punish.[15]

The Genocide Convention prohibits more than the direct killing of humans. Other actions—if undertaken with genocidal intent—can constitute genocide. For example, rape would not normally be genocide, but if a political or military commander promoted the widespread rape of a civilian population—with the intent of preventing normal reproduction by that population—then the pattern of rape could constitute genocide.[16]

Similarly, though many governments do not provide their citizens with minimal food rations or medical care, such omissions are not genocide. On the other hand, if a government eliminated food rations to a particular group but not to other groups, and the change in rations policy was undertaken with the intent of exterminating that group by starvation, then the government's termination of food aid could constitute genocide.[17]

Thus, if a government enacted or applied arms control laws for the purpose of facilitating genocide, then the government's actions would constitute genocide.[18] The Universal Declaration of Human Rights, which was adopted by the U.N. in 1948, never explicitly mentions "genocide," but a right to resist genocide is an inescapable implication of the rights the Declaration does affirm.

First, the Declaration affirms the right to life.[19] Of course, the right to life is recognized not just by the Universal Declaration, but also by several other international human rights instruments.[20]

Second, the Declaration affirms the right to personal security.[21] The right of self-defense is implicit in the right of personal security, and is explicitly recognized by the European Convention on Human Rights[22] and by the International Criminal Court.[23]

The preamble of the Universal Declaration of Human Rights recognizes a right of rebellion as a last resort: "Whereas it is essential, if man is not to be compelled to have recourse, as a last resort, to rebellion against tyranny and oppression, that human rights should be protected by the rule of law."[24] The drafting history of the Universal Declaration clearly shows that the preamble was explicitly intended to recognize a preexisting human right to revolution against tyranny.[25]

Finally, Article 8 of the Universal Declaration states: "Everyone has the right to an effective remedy."[26] The Universal Declaration therefore comports with the long-established common-law rule that there can be no right without a remedy.[27]

Thus, the Declaration recognizes that when a government destroys human rights and all other remedies have failed, the people are "compelled to have recourse, as a last resort, to rebellion against tyranny and oppression." Since "everyone has the right to an effective remedy," the people necessarily have the right to possess and use arms to resist tyranny, if arms use is the only remaining "effective remedy."[28]

The Anglo-American legal tradition supports the right to armed resistance among the "general principles of law recognized by civilized nations." For example, the U.S. Supreme Court noted that the right to arms, like the right to peaceably assemble, is not created by positive law, but rather derives "'from those laws whose authority is acknowledged by civilized man throughout the world.' It is found wherever civilization exists."[29]

William Blackstone's *Commentaries* on the common law, published in 1765, are by far the most influential legal treatise ever written, and were regarded as an essential part of the foundation of the common law throughout the English-speaking world and in the one-third of the globe where British law ruled. The *Commentaries* are part of the common-law heritage of any present or former British colony or member of the Commonwealth of Nations.

In the explanation of human rights under the common law, Blackstone first described the three primary rights: personal security, personal liberty, and private property. He then explained the five "auxiliary rights" that protected the primary rights:

> The fifth and last auxiliary right of the subject, that I shall at present mention, is that of having arms for their defence suitable to their condition and degree, and such as are allowed by law . . . and it is indeed a public allowance under due restrictions, of the natural right of resistance and self preservation, when the sanctions of society and laws are found insufficient to restrain the violence of oppression.[30]

When a government is perpetrating genocide—"when the sanctions of society and laws are found insufficient to restrain the violence of oppression"— that is exactly when people most need—and have a fundamental human right to possess—"arms for their defence."

More U.N. Gun Control, More Genocide

Holocaust historian Abram L. Sachar observes that "the difference between resistance and submission depends very largely upon who was in possession of the arms that back up the will to do or die."[31] He is hardly alone. In 1967, the International Society for the Prevention of Crime held a Congress in Paris on the prevention of genocide. The Congress concluded that "defensive measures are the most effective means for the prevention of genocide. Not all aggression is criminal. A defense reaction is for the human race what the wind is for navigation—the result depends on the direction. The most moral violence is that used in legitimate self-defense, the most sacred judicial institution."[32]

I believe that it is time to make "Never Again!" a reality, and not just a slogan. Half a century after the international community made the Genocide Convention into binding international law, overt genocide is being perpetrated in half a dozen countries in Africa. As with every other genocide in the last half-century, the U.N. refused to take meaningful action to stop it.

Philosophy professor Samuel Wheeler observes:

It is hard to see how a United Nations interested in the safety of persons rather than nations could hold that disarming the citizenry is a good idea. In none of the deadly sequence of genocides and citizen-slaughters that have characterized the Third World in the eighties and nineties have ordinary citizens been better off for having been helpless before the assaults of government agents . . . It is hard to avoid the conclusion that the United Nations initiative [of disarmament] is concerned with the interests of nation-states rather than the interests of people. It would be unkind to speculate about the post-colonial attitudes that block consideration of the possibility of directly arming the citizens of the turbulent regions of Africa and Asia that have been the locus of recent genocides.[33]

If you follow the U.N.'s plan to ban civilian firearms ownership then you eliminate the most effective deterrent to genocide.

Civilians with light arms cannot necessarily overthrow a well-entrenched and well-armed regime, but even the most powerful governments find it very difficult to perpetrate genocide against armed populations. The historical record is clear about how very rare it is for genocide to be attempted—let alone succeed—against an armed populace. If every family on this planet owned a good-quality rifle, genocide would be on the path to extinction.

It would be difficult to find an organization whose work has facilitated government mass murder of more people, in more diverse locations around the world, than the U.N. has in two decades. If the U.N.'s global gun prohibition campaign succeeds, genocide will become even more common.

After Kopel, Gallant, and Eisen published an article about the genocide in Bosnia, an American soldier sent them an e-mail, which Dave Kopel shared with me. That serviceman wrote:

> In 1999 I spent a year with the peacekeeping mission in Bosnia. I was stationed in the former "safe" area Gorazde. I learned a lot about that war and how the civilians were massacred. One day we were discussing guns and private ownership. In response to the statement that the U.N. believes only the police and military should have guns, a Bosnian exasperatedly asked: "Who do you think slaughtered everyone?"[34]

Chapter 13

The "Table for Tyrants": The U.N. vs. Human Rights

In the Charter of the United Nations, the member states pledge "to reaffirm faith in fundamental human rights, in the dignity and worth of the human person, in the equal rights of men and women." Long ago, the United Nations upheld that pledge by creating the Universal Declaration of Human Rights, which affirms that "it is essential, if man is not to be compelled to have recourse, as a last resort, to rebellion against tyranny and oppression, that human rights should be protected by the rule of law." Then, to protect human rights, the United Nations created the Commission on Human Rights, and made Eleanor Roosevelt its first chair.

Fighting Western Attempts to Fight Terror

After the July 2005 terrorist attacks on London, the British government announced plans to use its existing legal powers to deport resident foreigners who encouraged or glorified terrorism. The U.N. promptly objected.

Manfred Nowak, the U.N. Commission on Human Rights' special rapporteur on torture, threatened to have Britain brought up before the U.N. General Assembly for human rights violations. Nowak's argument was that some of the deported terrorist inciters might be tortured in the country to which they would be deported, notwithstanding assurance from the recipient country.[1]

The U.N. is also against killing terrorists. Consider Abdel Aziz al-Rantissi and Sheikh Ahmad Yassin.[2] Yassin, the head of the terrorist organization Hamas, was killed in early 2004 by the Israeli Defense Forces. He was succeeded by al-Rantissi, who promptly called for more terrorism:

"The doors are wide open for attacks inside the Zionist entity."[3] He had repeatedly called for the murder of Jews "everywhere."[4] After four weeks as head of the terrorist entity, al-Rantissi was killed by the Israeli army.

The U.S. government had named both Yassin and Rantissi as Specially Designated Global Terrorists. In 2003, the Bank of England froze al-Rantissi's assets because, they said, "the Treasury have reasonable grounds for suspecting that" al-Rantissi may "facilitate or participate in the commission of acts of terrorism . . . or may be a person who commits, facilitates or participates in such acts."[5]

Kofi Annan, however, indignantly denounced the death of Yassin: "The Secretary-General strongly condemns Israel's assassination . . . extrajudicial killings are against international law."[6] Annan likewise deplored the "assassination of al-Rantissi."[7]

Despite Annan's malicious claims, the killings of the Hamas leaders were entirely proper under international law. Hamas has declared itself to be in a state of war with Israel, and vows that it will never cease the war until Israel and the Jews are exterminated.

"Hamas" is an Arabic acronym for "Islamic Resistance Movement." The group's founding charter is explicit:

> Israel will exist and will continue to exist until Islam will obliterate it, just as it obliterated others before it . . . There is no solution for the Palestinian question except through Jihad.[T]he Islamic Resistance Movement aspires to the realisation of Allah's promise, no matter how long that should take. The Prophet, Allah bless him and grant him salvation, has said:
>
> "The Day of Judgement will not come about until Muslims fight the Jews (killing the Jews), when the Jew will hide behind stones and trees. The stones and trees will say O Muslims, O Abdulla, there is a Jew behind me, come and kill him. Only the Gharkad tree, would not do that because it is one of the trees of the Jews."[8]

In a war, the soldiers on one side are not required to capture the leaders on another side and take them back home for a civil trial. In a war, the military on one side may attempt to kill the military on the other side. Hamas, however, violates the rules of war, because its primary targets are civilians, rather than soldiers.

Israel obeys the laws of war by targeting combatants and attempting to minimize civilian casualties. This is precisely what Israel did when it killed Yassin and al-Rantissi.[9]

Nevertheless, the U.N. Human Rights Commission was so unnerved that it convened in a special sitting and for three hours flailed at Israel for killing the terrorist masterminds, before voting 31 to 2 to condemn it.[10] Shortly thereafter, the Commission adopted another one of its resolutions with code words urging terrorism against Israel, lauding "the legitimacy of the struggle [against] foreign occupation by all available means, including armed struggle."[11]

Civilized nations fight terrorism by preventing terrorists from entering the country, yet that, too, is forbidden by the U.N. The International Court of Justice (ICJ) was established by the U.N. in 1945 to hear disputes between states. For example, if two countries have a disagreement about the interpretation of a fishing treaty, they can ask the ICJ to hear the case.

After suffering years of suicide bombings and other terrorism, Israel began building a security fence to protect itself from violent attacks. Even before the fence was completed, it reduced terrorist attacks by 90 percent.[12]

On July 9, 2004, the ICJ ruled the security fence illegal.[13] The court acknowledged that Israel faced a problem of "violence," but it refused to describe the violence as terrorism. After the ICJ decision (which, as a matter of international law, is nonbinding and merely advisory), the General Assembly insisted by a vote of 150 to 6 that Israel remove the security fence from the West Bank.[14] The U.N. followed up in March 2005 with a two-day International Meeting on the Question of Palestine, damning Israel for building the fence.[15]

It should be noted that Spain, Turkey, Saudi Arabia, and India have also built defensive structures in disputed territories, and the U.N. has never voted to condemn those actions.

The U.N. is the place where state sponsors of terrorism applaud themselves for their opposition to terrorism. It is the place where the liberation of Afghanistan from Osama bin Laden and the Taliban can be denounced as terrorism. It is the place where the worst human rights violators in the world—tyrannical rulers of countries where there is no such thing as a fair trial—can froth with anger about the killing of terrorist commanders without a trial.

The U.N. produces enormous quantities of paper announcing its opposition to terrorism—yet produces even larger quantities of propaganda in favor of terrorism. It funds, or has funded, terrorists all over the world, including al-Qaeda, Fidel Castro, Hamas, Hezbollah, Islamic Jihad, Iran, North Korea, the Taliban, and Saddam Hussein. The U.N. talks to the Western media about celebrating diversity and global understanding, but it collaborates with and covers up for terrorists. It actively prevents settlement of the Arab-Israeli conflict. It funds vicious hate propaganda and allows its refugee camps and schools to be used as terrorist bases and bomb factories.

In the next chapter I will explain how the U.N. has promoted terrorism against the U.S. by giving money to bin Laden, by giving World Bank money to governments that sponsor anti-American terrorism, and by taking up the propaganda line that American resistance to terrorism is evil.

The subsidies to anti-American terrorists, and the attempt to delegitimate America's right of self-defense, were not invented out of thin air. Rather, they were founded on decades of practice in doing the same thing—on a much larger scale—to Israel. In effect, U.N. policies aiding terrorism and demonizing resistance to terrorism have been perfected in their use against Israel, and are now being deployed against the U.S. During the 1930s, far too many people in Britain, France, the U.S., and other democracies failed to realize that what Hitler was doing to the German Jews was in fact a direct attack on their own personal security. What tyrants and terrorists do to minority groups often foreshadow what will be done to larger groups. Aggressors first go after the victims who seem to be the easier targets, and then work their way up to other targets. U.N.-sponsored aggression against the Jews and Israel has, in fact, led to U.N.-sponsored aggression against America. As Harvard's Ruth Wisse explains:

> A society's deflection of energy to anti-Semitism is a sign of its political demoralization; the more it whips up frenzy against the Jews, the more it requires going to war to release that frenzy. The rise of anti-Semitism at the U.N. correlates with the rise of the politics of resentment against what the Jews represent—an open and democratic society, the ethic of competition and individual freedom.[16]

No one agrees with every aspect of Israeli policy—or with every U.S. policy, for that matter. Both nations thrive as contentious democratic societies, where citizens are free to express their disagreements on all sorts of issues.

But Israel is the canary in the coal mine, and there is a direct link between the U.N.'s long-standing assistance to terrorist war on Israel and the U.N.'s more recent assistance of terrorist war on the U.S.

If you think that unresolved tensions between Israel and the Arabs are part of the cause of global terrorism today, then consider which global organization has done the most to cause, rather than solve, those problems.

When the U.N. should take firm action against terrorism—as in the International Atomic Energy Agency's duty to prevent terrorist Iran from building nuclear weapons to attack the U.S., Israel, and England—it dithers and lets the terrorists move forward.

U.N. Commission on Human Rights Changes in Name Only

For many years, the U.N. Commission on Human Rights acted so outrageously that even U.N. leaders realized that the Commission was harming the U.N.'s credibility. The Commission had encouraged terrorist bombings of Israeli civilians, ignored the ongoing slave trade in Libya and Sudan, and refused to criticize the Zimbabwe genocide.[17] Moreover, the 2001 Durban racism conference was run by the Commission, and had turned into an orgy of race-hatred, anti-Americanism, and anti-Semitism. (President Obama in 2009 gave the Presidential Medal of Freedom to Mary Robinson, the antigun campaigner and former United Nations High Commissioner for Human Rights who had allowed the Durban conference planning to be taken over by the hate groups.)

In 2005, the Commission turned itself into an utter mockery by choosing as its chairman an employee of Moammar Qaddafi's tyrannical regime in Libya.[18]

Secretary-general Kofi Annan was forced to admit, "We have reached a point at which the commission's declining credibility has cast a shadow on the reputation of the United Nations system as a whole, and where piecemeal reforms will not be enough."

So the Commission on Human Rights had to go. Delegates from the G-77, which was chaired in 2009 by Sudan, complained to Annan. They liked the Commission just the way it was: as a forum for bashing the West, inciting terrorism against Israel, and doing nothing about the human rights violations perpetrated by the kleptocracies that keep the "underdeveloped" nations underdeveloped. Annan explained to them that the Commission had to go. Annan then said he would ensure that any changes would be merely cosmetic.

He kept his promise. The Commission on Human Rights was abolished, and in March 2006, the new Human Rights Council was created. On the new Human Rights Council, there is no requirement that a country meet minimal standards for human rights, or have a democratic form of government.[19] A country can be elected to the Human Rights Council even if it is currently under Security Council sanctions for human rights violations.[20] The new HRC actually worsened the key problem of the old Commission: selection of members according to regional groups, which means that the Organization of the Islamic Conference and the African dictatorships can stack the HRC with dictator-friendly delegations.[21]

The Sorosphere was quick to extol the new Human Rights Council as yet another example of the great reforms being implemented at the U.N. Morton Halperin, who runs Soros's Open Society Institute, delivered a May 2006 report praising the HRC, and repeated that praise later in testimony to Congress.[22]

As a token gesture of reform, HRC candidates are now required to pledge that they will protect human rights. Yet in May 2009, Saudi Arabia and Kyrgyzstan had both the nerve and the honesty not to make the pledge. They were elected anyway.[23] Joining these dictatorships as winners in the May 2009 elections for HRC membership were China, Cuba, and Russia.[24] Based on ratings from Freedom House, countries that are "free" are, once again, a minority on the HRC.[25]

In 2010, the dictatorial regimes of Libya and Angola were elected to the HRC. So was Uganda, where the government kills and rapes people, and burns down villages, for the ostensible purpose of carrying out U.N. gun control. Cuba became HRC vice president. Freedom House reported that only five of the fourteen countries elected to the HRC in 2010 had human rights records that made them "qualified" to sit on a genuine human rights body.[26]

Strong American lobbying did thwart Iran's bid for a spot on the HRC, but the price was that Iran was instead selected for the U.N. Commission on the Status of Women (CSW)—a disgusting reward for one of the most misogynistic tyrannies in the world. Iran will, however, fit right in, since the CSW never condemned any nation by name—except, of course, for Israel.[27]

The HRC has an advisory committee that is supposed to provide expert advice on human rights law. For chair of the advisory committee, the HRC chose Miguel Alfonso Martinez, a representative of the totalitarian Castro regime. For the three vice-chairs, they picked two representatives of dictatorships (Vladimir Kartashkin of Russia, and Mona Zulfikar of Egypt), plus one from democratic South Korea.[28] In 2010, Miguel D'Escoto—the America-hating Communist representative of the Sandinista regime in Nicaragua—was appointed to the advisory panel.

As envisioned by Eleanor Roosevelt, the U.N.'s Human Rights body would be a great protector of civil liberties. Yet the HRC is now at the global forefront of suppression of freedom of speech. In reaction to the publication Danish newspaper cartoons that criticized Islamic terrorism (and that violated the rule of some but not all Muslims against drawings of Muhammad), the HRC passed a resolution expressing its "deep concern at attempts to identify Islam with terrorism, violence and human rights violations." The resolution said that "freedom of expression . . . may therefore be subject to certain restrictions . . . necessary for the respect of the rights or reputations of others."[29]

The HRC legal experts committee told Great Britain that the nation has a problem with "negative public attitudes towards Muslim members of society." Accordingly, the government "should take energetic measures to eliminate this phenomenon and ensure that authors of such acts of discrimination on the basis of religion are adequately deterred and sanctioned."[30] In other words, the government should punish people who have the "wrong" attitudes about Islam.

On June 16, 2008, the Human Rights Council prohibited any criticism of Sharia law. HRC president Doru Romulus Costea (Rumania) imposed the ban, which applies to all HRC meetings, because an Islamist delegate had complained about a three-minute HRC presentation by the Association for World Education and the International Humanist and Ethical Union. The presentation had called attention to the human rights violations of female genital mutilation, the stoning of women, and "honor" murders of women.[31]

Likewise forbidden is pointing out what Islamic terrorist groups believe. On January 24, 2009, the HRC devoted its meeting to berating Israel for defending itself against terrorist attacks launched from the Gaza Strip. Gaza is ruled by the terrorist organization Hamas. At the HRC meeting, David Littman, a representative of the World Union of Progressive Judaism (a consortium of various Jewish liberal groups, including American Reform Judaism), attempted to quote from the Hamas Charter, which states: "Israel will exist and continue to exist until Islam will obliterate it, just as it obliterated others before it." He explained that Israel's defensive actions against the attacks from Gaza needed to be understood in the context of self-defense against an enemy devoted to the extermination of Israel. He urged that the HRC fulfill its duties under the Genocide Convention to take action against a government with an avowed intention of genocide.

The HRC president repeatedly tried to stop Littman from speaking, leading him to remark, paraphrasing Shakespeare, "There is a general malaise in the air, a feeling that something is rotten in the state of this council."

In retaliation, Cuba, Qatar, Sudan, Egypt, and China attempted to revoke the U.N. Non-Government Organization (NGO) status of the World Union of Progressive Judaism. The group has been a U.N.-recognized NGO since 1972, and is thereby allowed to enter the U.N. building, to observe some U.N. meetings, and to speak at some of those meetings. The World Union avoided expulsion only by apologizing (for having dared speak truth to power).[32]

In March 2008, the HRC ordered a special rapporteur to report on cases "in which the abuse of the right of freedom of expression constitutes an act of racial or religious discrimination."[33] By this the HRC means things such as the Danish cartoons that criticized Islamic terrorism, rather than the speeches of Iran's president that incite anti-Semitism and promote genocide and terrorism. The HRC has also enacted a resolution against "defamation" of religion. The resolution was later enacted by the full General Assembly; the resolution mentions only one religion, Islam, and, if it became international law, would outlaw criticism of Islam.[34]

The World Association of Newspapers and World Editors Forum represents eighteen thousand newspapers around the world. At the 2008 Congress in Gothenburg, Sweden, the group protested the HRC's "repeated efforts to undermine freedom of expression."[35]

When not busy violating human rights itself, the Human Rights Council has shown little interest in doing anything about human rights violations by dictatorships. Indeed, the new Human Rights Council has proven to be worse that the old Commission on Human Rights. The new Council abolished previous Human Rights Commission investigations of human rights abuses in Belarus, Cuba, the Democratic Republic of the Congo, Liberia, Iran, Kyrgyzstan, Turkmenistan, and Uzbekistan.[36] The Council has continued the practice of the Commission of doing nothing about the genocide in Zimbabwe.[37]

Of the twenty "worst of the worst" human rights disasters, as identified by Freedom House in 2007, the HRC has adopted no resolution or decision regarding nineteen of them: Belarus, Burma, China, Tibet (occupied by China), Ivory Coast, Cuba, Equatorial Guinea, Eritrea, Laos, Libya, Western Sahara (occupied by Morocco), North Korea, Chechnya (Russia), Saudi Arabia, Somalia, Syria, Turkmenistan, Uzbekistan, and Zimbabwe.[38]

The Council has engaged in some timid activity regarding Sudan— noting the existence of problems there, praising the Sudanese government for its supposed cooperation with the U.N., and carefully refraining from any condemnation of Sudan's genocidal tyrants. (The same guys against whom the U.N. Security Council ordered the International Criminal Court to open up a criminal investigation for crimes against humanity.)

The one country that the HRC does get really upset about, all the time, is Israel. The HRC has adopted more anti-Israel resolutions than resolutions criticizing all other nations combined.[39] In fact, 80 percent of its country-specific resolutions have been against Israel.[40] The HRC condemns Israel for fighting against Hamas in Gaza, but does not criticize Hamas for launching the thousands of rocket attacks on civilians that made Israel's counterattack necessary.[41]

While Israel was fighting Hamas in Gaza, the Sri Lanka government (which is Buddhist) was engaged in a final offensive to wipe out the Tamil Tiger rebels (who are mostly Hindu). Palestinian civilian casualties were several hundred, almost all the result of Hamas using civilians as human shields, in violation of the laws of warfare. Civilian casualties in the Tamil-controlled areas were seven thousand or more. The HRC resolution on Gaza "strongly" condemned Israel, accused it of "aggression" and grave "violations," and demanded an immediate Israeli withdrawal. The name of the aggressor ("Hamas") was not even mentioned, let alone criticized for launching thousands of rocket and mortar attacks on civilians.

As for Sri Lanka, the HRC adopted a resolution sponsored by the Sri Lankan government, commending the government for its humane treatment of civilians (although many international observers had reported to the contrary), and condemning the Tamil Tigers for attacking civilians.[42] Louise Arbour, formerly the U.N. high commissioner for human rights, charged that the U.N. was "close to complicit" in war crimes perpetrated by the Sri Lankan government.[43]

The hypocrisy of the U.N. in general and the HRC in particular, is highlighted by the contrasting approaches to the so-called Occupied Palestinian Territories and Tibet. Israel ended up controlling the territories because their former owners, Egypt and Jordan, went to war with Israel in 1967. Neither country wants them back. Tibet, in contrast, is under the Chinese thumb because Mao Zedong launched an unprovoked invasion in 1951.

More than a million Tibetans have died because of the Chinese occupation. Freedom of religion, speech, and press is entirely suppressed. Israeli settlements (which were withdrawn from Gaza in 2005) in the disputed West Bank territories are trivially small compared to the Han Chinese settlements in Tibet, which have made the Tibetans a minority in their own nation. The Tibetan leadership in exile has repeatedly asked to live in peace with the Chinese, and has even offered to accept Chinese rule as long as Tibetan local autonomy is respected.

Journalist Joseph Klein, who frequently investigates the U.N., summarizes:

> Israel is the constant target of vitriol from the UN Human Rights Council on which China sits along with other serial human rights violators. Indeed, while China has gotten away with regularly breaching the 1949 Fourth Geneva Convention, which is supposed to protect Tibetan civilians living under Chinese occupation from being deliberately targeted for violence. Israel is regularly accused by U.N. bodies of violating this same Convention whenever it tries to contain Palestinian terrorism against Israeli citizens. China also has escaped any reproach for its repeated violations of the Universal Declaration of Human Rights, International Covenant on Civil and Political Rights and International Covenant on Economic, Social and Cultural Rights, which recognize that freedom of religion is a basic human right.[44]

Durban II

The encore to the 2001 Durban conference was an April 2009 "review conference" in Geneva, Switzerland, on "Racism, Racial Discrimination, Xenophobia and Related Intolerance." The original conference in Durban, South Africa, had been organized by the old Commission on Human Rights, and the 2009 conference was organized by its even-worse successor, the new Human Rights Council.[45] Since the 2009 event was a follow-up to the 2001 hatefest in Durban, most of the media dubbed it "Durban II." The name led to protests from the South African representative, who resented having his country linked to the 2009 fiasco.

It was not hard to foresee trouble. During a public planning meeting in Geneva, regarding freedom of expression and "defamation" of religion, delegates from Muslim and African countries ordered a television crew from the French-German culture channel ARTE kicked out of the room.[46]

Nongovernment organizations representing persecuted groups such as the Tibetans, Tamils, or the Dalits (a low-caste group in South Asia) were prevented from attending Durban II.[47]

To deliver the opening address for Durban II, the HRC picked Iranian president Mahmoud Ahmadinejad, who lived down to expectations by calling Israel the most racist country in the world.[48]

During the conferences, when NGOs brought up Ahmadinejad or the plight of the Tibetans or Berbers (indigenous tribes of northwest Africa, currently persecuted by the Arab-ruled governments of the region), they would be interrupted by calls for a point of order from countries such as Libya, China, Iran, and South Africa. Meanwhile, nobody stopped speakers from comparing Israelis to Nazis, or asserting truther fantasies such as "9/11 is an unexplained mystery blamed on Arabs."[49] (Despite the U.N.'s pre-Conference promise that "hate speech and ethnic insults will be barred."[50])

At the end, Navanethem Pillay, the U.N. high commissioner for human rights and secretary-general of Durban II, announced with a straight face that Durban II had been "a celebration of tolerance and dignity for all."[51]

The Durban II "outcome document" was a road map for the destruction of human rights. It repeatedly misused cultural diversity/identity/respect to negate the U.N.'s founding principle of universal human rights.[52] So, for example, although the U.N. at its foundation and many times thereafter has affirmed the equality of women, the universal principle of equality is supposed to be understood in a cultural context, so that it is somehow permissible to execute women who are rape victims, or mutilate the genitals of infant girls.

Thor Halvorssen, founder of a genuine human rights organization, the Oslo Freedom Forum, pointed out that the Durban II conference had nothing to say about the following: the genocide and racial and religious persecution in Sudan; the persecution of Tibetans by the occupying Chinese army; the modern slavery in the sugarcane fields of the Dominican Republic or in Arab and Muslim countries; and the racial/ethnic/religious persecution and human rights violations in Belarus, Bolivia, Burma, Cuba, Egypt, Equatorial Guinea, Russia, Venezuela, and Zimbabwe.[53]

The "outcome document" said that slavery, the slave trade, and genocide should never be forgotten.[54] Except that when they are perpetrated today, they apparently can be ignored.

Special Rapporteurs

A "special rapporteur" is a type of expert who is selected by an international organization to provide advice. The United Nations makes extensive use of special rapporteurs. Sometimes, the U.N. picks fair-minded experts. Other times—and especially at the HRC—the special rapporteurs appear to have been picked primarily for their expertise in promoting an anti-freedom, anti-America agenda.

For example, the HRC's "Special Rapporteur on the (so-called) "Occupied Palestinian Territories" is Richard Falk. He is a fellow traveler with the despicable "truther" movement, which claims that the September 11 attacks were planned by the Bush administration. Falk shies away from saying that the truthers are correct, but says that there has been a cover-up that must be investigated. Falk penned an admiring preface to truther David Ray Griffin's *The New Pearl Harbor: Disturbing Questions about the Bush Administration and 9/11.*

When the terrorist organization Hamas took over Gaza in June 2007, Falk reacted by asking the world to "start protecting the people of Gaza" from Israel. He urged that the U.N.'s International Court of Justice at the Hague investigate "whether the Israeli civilian leaders and military commanders responsible for the Gaza siege should be indicted and prosecuted for violations of international criminal law."[55]

Because Hamas is in a state of war with Israel, Israel has every legal right under international law to blockade the Hamas territory to prevent Hamas from importing more weapons and munitions. Because Hamas attempts to use the shipment of civilian products to smuggle weapons of war,

Israel likewise has the right to interdict all such shipments, and to inspect them to ensure that they do not contain arms.[56]

Falk, however, accuses Israel of a "crime against humanity" and "apartheid" for exercising its rights under international law.[57]

Falk's long-standing campaign to allow Hamas to import weapons received a major boost in May 2010, when an organization known as Turkish IHH attempted to run the blockade.[58] According to France's top counterterrorism investigative magistrate, Jean-Louis Bruguiere, the IHH assisted the al-Qaeda millennium bombing plot against Los Angeles in 1999.[59] The French investigation also revealed that IHH was linked to al-Qaeda in Milan, Italy, and to Algerian terrorists in Europe, and that IHH recruited Islamic terrorists to send to Bosnia, Chechnya, and Afghanistan. The IHH forthrightly admits that it supports Hamas.[60] That didn't stop the U.N. from granting IHH status as an official U.N. Non-Government Organization. (Indeed, a Saudi NGO, the International Islamic Relief Fund, remains in good standing as a U.N. NGO, even though the U.N. itself had identified two of its branches as providing aid to al-Qaeda.)[61]

Laden with terrorists and armed with pistols, knives, and other weapons, the IHH flotilla set off to break the Israeli blockade, ostensibly to deliver humanitarian aid to Gaza.[62] The Israelis offered to allow all humanitarian goods into Gaza, provided that they were offloaded at a port where Israel could inspect them, to make sure no arms were being smuggled. But the purpose of the flotilla was not to help the Gazans; it was to set a precedent of breaking the blockade, and thus facilitate arms deliveries to Hamas.

Back in the United States, propaganda for the terrorist flotilla was being provided by Fenton PR Communications.[63] Fenton, which receives grants from the antigun Joyce Foundation, has a long record of public relations services for Communist dictators, extreme-Left causes, and antigun organizations such as the Tides Foundation. Fenton has participated in "political campaigns against the death penalty and gun-ownership rights."[64] For example, in Fenton's report on its past twenty-five years of work, the very first item for which it took credit was "refram[ing] the conversation" by characterizing "gun violence as a health epidemic." Thus Fenton credits itself for having "helped move the debate beyond the Second Amendment."[65]

The Israelis intercepted the flotilla, and minimized the use of force, so the initial boarding crews used only paintball guns. The terrorists attacked with all their weapons; the Israelis defended themselves, and several of the so-called peace activists were killed or wounded.

The United Nations, the mainstream media, and the rest of the anti-Israel cabal worked themselves into predictable hysterics. The U.N. Human Rights Council opened up another "investigation" of Israel, while the office of the U.N. secretary-general opened up a second one, at the urging of President Obama.

All this was undoubtedly a dream come true for special rapporteur Richard Falk.

Another one-sided "investigation" was set up by the HRC regarding Israeli military actions in Gaza in late 2008 and early 2009. After Israel completely withdrew from Gaza in 2005, Palestinian terrorists immediately began launching rockets and mortars at Israel; the bombardments were not aimed at military targets, but at civilians, and were therefore war crimes. In 2007 the Gaza government was taken over by Hamas, which the United States has designated as a terrorist organization. Finally, Israeli counterattacked in December 2008. Throughout the war, Hamas used human shields for its artillery and fighters, and located its headquarters and bases in hospitals, schools, and other civilian facilities; this, too, was unquestionably a war crime.

The Human Rights Council, however, commissioned an investigation of international law violations during the Gaza war, and ordered that the inquiry examine only the supposed illegality of Israeli actions, while ignoring actions of Hamas and the other terrorist groups in Gaza.[66] To run the inquiry, the HRC then picked four "commissioners" all of whom had previously made statements expressing outrage at Israel for the conduct of the Gaza war.[67]

To no one's surprise, the inquiry, known as the Goldstone Report, claimed that Israel had committed war crimes, downplayed Israel's right of self-defense, glossed over Hamas terrorism, asserted that there was no evidence that Hamas used human shields, and urged that the International Criminal Court begin prosecuting Israelis.[68]

The U.N. then commissioned a follow-up report commission, to be headed by an anti-Israel German who had once worked as a lawyer for the terrorist Yasser Arafat.[69]

If the U.N. had an agenda to eliminate the state of Israel by first delegitimizing its existence, one would expect the U.N. to be doing exactly what it has been doing, especially at the HRC.[70]

Former U.S. ambassador to the U.N. John Bolton explained the bigger picture:

> The Goldstone Report has important implications for America. In the U.N., Israel frequently serves as a surrogate target in lieu of the U.S., particularly concerning the use of military force pre-emptively or in self-defense. Accordingly, U.N. decisions on ostensibly Israel-specific issues can lay a predicate for subsequent action against, or efforts to constrain, the U.S. Mr. Goldstone's recommendation to convoke the International Criminal Court is like putting a loaded pistol to Israel's head—or, in the future, to America's.[71]

More broadly, the U.N.'s concerted campaign to deny Israel and the United States their rights of national defense can be understood as related to the U.N. campaign to destroy your right of personal self-defense.

Much as the Goldstone Report has done to legitimize terrorists, and undermine democratic nations' resistance to terrorism, it's difficult for anyone to claim to have done more to spread malicious propaganda than Jean Ziegler, the U.N. special rapporteur on the right to food.[72] Ziegler is a Swiss socialist politician who uses his U.N. position to push extremist anti-American policies.

According to the U.N.'s Food and Agricultural Organization (FAO), there are seventeen countries that suffer from man-made (i.e., government-caused) food emergencies. Ziegler has mildly criticized two: Sudan (which is carrying out genocide) and Burundi.[73] Fifteen other countries perpetrating death by starvation have never been the subject of a critical word from Ziegler: Burundi, Central African Republic, Chad, Democratic Republic of the Congo, Republic of the Congo, Cote d'Ivoire, Eritrea, Guinea, Haiti, Liberia, the Russian Federation (Chechnya), Sierra Leone, Somalia, Tanzania, and Uganda.

Ziegler reserves much harsher language for the U.S., which he calls an "imperialist dictatorship." He also has attacked President George W. Bush as "the Pinochet [the former dictator of Chile] who sits in the White House."[74]

After September 11, Ziegler made the preposterous claim that U.S. military action against the Taliban would cause "apocalyptic" results, that would lead to "the end for the Afghan nation."[75] Ziegler would also claim that the coalition liberation of Iraq violated the food rights of Iraqis.[76] An actual violation of Iraqi rights was the theft by Saddam Hussein's regime and its U.N. accomplices of Oil-for-Food money intended to pay for food for Iraqi civilians. Ziegler has never complained about this well-documented violation of rights.

Ziegler is also a huge fan of Cuban tyrant Fidel Castro, a state sponsor of terrorism, and Ziegler claims that the U.S. economic embargo of Cuba is "genocide." Ignored is Castro's corrupt control of the Cuban economy, which he has used to make himself one of the richest men in the world. Ziegler is not alone at the U.N. in his admiration of Cuba's Marxist dictatorship. Recently, for only the second time in history, movie crews were allowed inside the U.N. General Assembly, when Kofi Annan authorized the filming of *Che*, which glorifies Che Guevara. According to the Free Society Project's Truth Recovery Archive, Guevara, while commander of Castro's Cabana prison from 1957 to 1959, ordered the executions of (and often personally executed) more than two hundred Cubans.[77]

On December 21, 1988, Libyan dictator Moammar Qaddafi launched what was then the deadliest attack in history against American civilians. His agents blew up Pan Am flight 103, murdering 189 Americans, and 81 people from twenty other countries. The next year, Ziegler participated in the founding of the Moammar Khadaffi Human Rights Prize (aka the Al-Gaddafi International Prize for Human Rights).[78] In 2002, Ziegler himself won the prize.[79] He shared the prize with, among others, Holocaust denier Roger Garaudy. Two years later, while serving as the U.N.'s special rapporteur, Ziegler helped found the explicitly anti-American magazine *L'Empire*, which denounces the war on terrorists.[80]

Ziegler was appointed special rapporteur by the Commission on Human Rights and seamlessly made the transition to being special rapporteur to the new, supposedly reformed Human Rights Council. At the end of his special rapporteur term in 2008, the HRC elected him a member of its advisory committee.

The Human Rights Commission/Council and the Gun Issue

On the gun issue, the Human Rights Commission/Council chose, as it has on so many other issues, a "special rapporteur" who was opposed to human rights. Remember that the old Human Rights Commission was recognized as a public disgrace even by Kofi Annan. In 2002, that disgraceful commission chose University of Minnesota law professor Barbara Frey as its special rapporteur on human rights violations committed with small arms and light weapons. The Human Rights Commission framed its mandate narrowly: Frey was supposed to look at preventing the use of firearms to perpetrate human rights violations. She was not to inquire into the use of firearms to protect people from human rights violations. Nor was she to examine where firearms laws were ever enforced in ways that violate human rights.[81]

Thus, the Frey investigation was similar to other "investigations" ordered by the HRC. There is no indication that Frey had any objection to entering into this biased antigun research. Why would she? She is a member of IANSA, the international gun prohibition lobby funded by George Soros.

Frey did her part for the Axis of Soros. Besides producing various papers and studies, she joined a strategy meeting in Brazil in March 16–18, 2005, to help the advocates of the planned October 2005 referendum on gun prohibition there. The strategy meeting was funded by UNESCO.

When the new Human Rights Council replaced the old Human Rights Commission, the new Council used the transition to eliminate the special rapporteurs who had actually promoted human rights, such as by investigating human rights abuses in Belarus. The Council kept on the rapporteurs who promoted the inhumane anti-rights agenda, such as the anti-Israel rapporteur and the far Left extremists such as Jean Ziegler.[82] Special Rapporteur Frey made the transition to the new Council seamlessly.

In early July 2006, the United Nations antigun conference ended without a new legally binding global antigun treaty. The gun prohibition lobbyists were bitterly disappointed. On July 27, 2006, Frey launched the counteroffensive, announcing that extremely repressive gun control, as well as prohibition on most uses of firearms for self-defense, was *already required* by international law. So she said in her special rapporteur report.[83]

Less than a month later, her report was officially adopted by the United Nations, as a statement of mandatory international law that overrides all national constitutions and law. Like the old Commission on Human Rights, the new Human Rights Council has a subcommission on the Promotion and Protection of Human Rights. On August 21, 2006, the Subcommission endorsed the Frey Report in toto, and wrote a list of what it said that governments were supposed to do.[84] Here's some of what the U.N. ordered, along with my explanation in [brackets]:

PRINCIPLES ON THE PREVENTION OF HUMAN RIGHTS VIOLATIONS COMMITTED WITH SMALL ARMS

Solemnly proclaims the human rights principles set forth below, formulated to assist Member States in their task of ensuring and promoting the proper action by State agents, especially law enforcement officials, with respect to their unequivocal role to protect the right to life, liberty and security of the person, as guaranteed in the Universal Declaration of Human Rights and reaffirmed in the International Covenant on Civil and Political Rights, and urges that every effort be made so that the principles become generally known and respected. [Claims that the antigun agenda is required by existing human rights law.]

8. State agents, including law enforcement officials, shall not use small arms against persons except in self-defence or defense of others against imminent threat of death or serious injury, to prevent the perpetration of a particularly serious crime involving grave threat to life, to arrest a person presenting such a danger and resisting their authority, or to prevent his or her escape, and only when less extreme means are insufficient to achieve these objectives . . .

[Police cannot use guns against criminals who are perpetrating or escaping from crimes, unless the crime itself involves "grave threat to life." In other words, if the rapist is fleeing the scene of the crime, and he has not killed the victim, the police cannot shoot him in order to prevent his escape.]

PRINCIPLES ON THE PREVENTION OF HUMAN RIGHTS VIOLATIONS COMMITTED WITH SMALL ARMS

B. Due diligence to prevent human rights abuses by private actors

10. In order to ensure the protection of human rights by

preventing small arms violence by private actors, Governments shall enact licensing requirements to prevent possession of arms by persons who are at risk of misusing them. Possession of small arms shall be authorized for specific purposes only; small arms shall be used strictly for the purpose for which they are authorized. Before issuing a licence Governments shall require training in proper use of small arms, and shall take into consideration, at a minimum, the following factors: age, mental fitness, requested purpose, prior criminal record or record of misuse, and prior acts of domestic violence. Governments shall require periodic renewal of licences. [All gun owners must be licensed, and must re-apply for a license to continue to own the gun. The license must allow the use of the gun only for a particular purpose, and not for general lawful purposes.]

11. Governments shall ensure that proper controls are exercised over the manufacturing of small arms through incorporation into national law and by other measures. For the purpose of identifying and tracing small arms, Governments shall require that at the time of manufacture, each small arm has a unique permanent mark providing, at a minimum, the name of the manufacturer, the country of manufacture and the serial number.

12. Governments shall ensure the investigation and prosecution of persons responsible for the illegal manufacture, possession, stockpiling or transfer of small arms. Governments shall impose penalties for crimes involving the misuse of small arms, including to commit domestic violence, and for the unlawful possession of small arms. [If you have a gun without having a license, the government must punish you.]

13. With the cooperation of the international community, Governments shall develop and implement effective disarmament, demobilization and reintegration programmes, including the effective collection, control, storage and destruction of small arms, particularly in postconflict situations. Governments should take steps to encourage voluntary disarmament. Governments should implement public awareness and confidence-building programmes, in cooperation with civil society and nongovernmental organizations, to prevent a return to armed violence and to encourage alternative forms of dispute resolution. Governments should incorporate a gender perspective in their peacekeeping and public awareness efforts to ensure that the special needs and human rights of women and children are met, especially in post-conflict situations. [Governments should encourage people to surrender their guns.]

14. Governments shall prohibit international transfers of small arms which would violate their obligations under international law, including in circumstances in which such arms are likely to be used to commit serious human rights violations. [Governments must ban international sales of guns to countries that violate human rights. In U.N.-speak, this means the United States and Israel.]

15. In light of the obligation of a State, under international human rights law, to prevent human rights violations, States are required under international law to provide, upon request, assistance, for the purposes of judicial proceedings in other States, in the provision of information regarding the ownership or purchase of small arms and light weapons in the former State. [If gun companies or gun owners are sued or criminally prosecuted in a foreign court, the U.S. government must give the foreign court

information about the defendant's firearms ownership or purchases in the United States.]

The Frey Report and its endorsement by the HRC is precisely what gun prohibitionists such as Harold Koh (the U.S. State Department's new top lawyer) and his fellow transnationalists can use to assert that the United States *already* has an international legal obligation to impose extremely repressive gun laws.

The new Arms Trade Treaty being drafted by the United Nations is supposed to outlaw arms transfers to countries that violate human rights. The standards of the Human Rights Council claim that an international embargo on the sale of arms (and of raw materials that can be used to make them) is mandatory for countries that are serious violators of human rights. By the Frey/HRC standards, American gun laws are in gross violation of human rights standards. According to Frey and the U.N., it is a violation of international human rights law if the government does not adopt the following gun control system:

- All gun owners must be licensed.[85]
- The license must be renewed periodically.
- To acquire a license, a person must meet training criteria.
- The license must be for a specific purpose, and other uses of the licensed gun must not be allowed. (E.g., if the license is to use the gun for duck hunting, then the licensed gun may not be used for self-defense.)

Simply put, this means that the gun control laws of every American state are insufficiently strict, even the laws of New York City and pre-*Heller* Washington, D.C.

For example, in New York City, you need a license to own a long gun, but once you have the license, you can use the gun for any lawful purpose.

You can go hunting with it on Saturday, take it to target practice on Tuesday, and if someone attacks you on Thursday, you can use the gun for lawful protection against the attacker. (D.C. has a registration system that functions the same as a license; pre-*Heller*, D.C. would have allowed use of the long gun for self-defense in a place of business, but not in the home.)

Thus, even New York City and the District of Columbia violate the U.N. mandate that "possession of small arms shall be authorized for specific purposes only; small arms shall be used strictly for the purpose for which they are authorized."

Only a few states require licenses for handguns, and hardly any do so for long guns. No state (except New York for handguns) requires that the license applicant specify a particular purpose for which the gun will be used. Rather, the American principle is that if you can legally own the gun, you can use it for all lawful purposes. (Of course, carrying the gun in a public place may require a separate license.)

The U.N. also says, "Governments should take steps to encourage voluntary disarmament." This means that waste-of-money programs such as gun "buy-backs" (as if the government had been the original owner of the gun) would be legally mandatory. And government programs that *encourage* gun ownership (such as state fish and wildlife programs that promote responsible hunting) might be illegal.

In short, according to the United Nations, almost every firearms sale in the United States is an illegal violation of human rights.

Bad as Frey's gun control agenda is, her pronouncements against self-defense are even worse. These, too, have been declared to be international law by the U.N. Human Rights Council's subcommission. According to Frey:

> No international human right of self-defence is expressly set forth in the primary sources of international law: treaties, customary law, or general principles. While the right to life is recognized in virtually every major international human rights treaty, the

principle of self-defence is expressly recognized in only one, the Convention for the Protection of Human Rights and Fundamental Freedoms (European Convention on Human Rights), article 2.[86]

Frey's report specifically cites and disagrees with a Kopel/Gallant/ Eisen article saying that people have a right to self-defense against genocide.[87] Like IANSA, she denies that people have a responsibility to protect themselves: "It is the State that must be responsible—and accountable—for ensuring public safety, rather than civilians themselves."[88]

Thus, according to the U.N. and Frey, international law requires that governments drastically constrict the circumstances when self-defense is allowed. Generally speaking, in the United States armed self-defense is allowed *at least* when you are the victim of a major violent felony attack and you reasonably believe that no lesser use of force would protect you. States vary about whether you must first retreat from your home or from a public place, whether force can be used to defend third persons (or only some third persons, such as family members), or whether your decision to use a gun can be second-guessed by a prosecutor who would claim that you should have used your fists instead.

But even in the most restrictive American jurisdictions, the law is clear that firearms can sometimes be used for self-defense against someone who is trying to rape you, or someone who is trying to commit mayhem (that is, permanently injure you, such as by cutting off a limb), or someone who is perpetrating an armed robbery.

Frey and the U.N., however, declare that all this is illegal: firearms can be used for self-defense *only* against a deadly threat. In other words, if the carjackers are going to gang-rape you, torture you, and cut off your feet, but not kill you, then if you use a gun against them, you are violating *their* right to life.[89] Guns "may be used defensively only in the most extreme circumstances, expressly, where the right to life is already threatened or unjustifiably impinged," insist Frey and the U.N.[90]

Harold Koh says that the federal courts should allow lawsuits based on violations of any international human rights treaty the U.S. has ratified. The United States has ratified the International Covenant on Civil and Political Rights. This treaty protects the right to life.[91] According to Frey and the U.N., it is a violation of this particular treaty (and all other treaties that protect the right to life) if the government allows you to shoot a rapist.

Thus, when we put the Koh and Frey/U.N. rules together, if you shoot the rapist, his relatives can sue *you*, because you violated his right to life. The U.N. rule is that guns may be used only if you think someone is going to kill you. Using guns for self-defense against rape (or mayhem, torture, carjacking, and armed robbery) is a violation of the criminal's rights.

The U.N. and Frey apply the same restrictions to law enforcement officers, except that they can shoot a murderer who is escaping or resisting arrest. Like civilians, they cannot shoot a rapist or other nonmurderous criminal in order to thwart the crime, or to effect an arrest or stop an escape.[92]

Overriding the Constitution

You may have wondered how the Frey/U.N./IANSA antigun, anti-self-defense mandate could claim priority over the constitutions of the United States (and other countries) that explicitly protect the right to arms, and the approximately two dozen national constitutions that recognize the right of self-defense. They have an answer:

Under international law, a *jus cogens* is a law that overrides everything else to the contrary.[93] Frey and her friends argue that many international treaties recognize a right to life. (This is true.) From this unremarkable point, she asserts that in order to respect the right to life—and to avoid violating the criminal's right to life—all governments are required to implement her antigun and anti-self-defense agenda.[94]

Like most of what Frey and the Human Rights Commission claimed, the assertion about restricting self-defense being a *jus cogens* was a pure fabrication. It is contradicted by a report of the U.N.'s International Law

Commission acknowledging that self-defense is one of the "most frequently cited examples" of *jus cogens*.[95]

Frey complains that the "regulation of civilian possession of firearms remains a contested issue in public debate—due in large part to the efforts of firearms manufacturers and the United States of America–based pro-gun organizations." It is an honor for the National Rifle Association to earn the wrath of human rights opponents. However, Frey's real problem, legally speaking, is not the NRA, but the mountain of genuine international law that she refused to acknowledge in her report.

Origins of International Law

International law has its origins in middle centuries of the second millennium, in Europe. It was there that scholars first articulated universal legal rules to govern the conduct of nations. These scholars were mainly concerned with the conduct of warfare. They built their legal system to govern warfare by extrapolating from what they recognized as the universal, natural right of personal self-defense.

The story is told in great detail in the Brigham Young University *BYU Journal of Public Law* article "The Human Right of Self-Defense," by David Kopel, Paul Gallant, and Joanne Eisen. It is worth summarizing some highlights here, because the U.S. Constitution itself makes reference to international law.[96] So it is important to understand the true international law that the Founders recognized, in contrast to the witch's brew of anti–human rights "law" that is concocted by Barbara Frey, Harold Koh, the Human Rights Council, and the rest of the "transnationalists" in the Axis of Soros.

Professor of theology (including philosophy) at the University of Salamanca in Spain, Francisco de Vitoria (1486–1546) was in his time the most prestigious professor in the world. His classroom (for which lectures were open to the public) was known as "the cradle of international law."[97]

Vitoria addressed the most important international law controversy of his day: the Spanish conquest of the New World. He demolished every argument that Christians had any right to conquer non-Christians just because of religion. He insisted that everyone—including Mexican Indians and Muslim Turks—had a natural right of self-defense. To deny that right would place the world in "utter misery, if oppressors and robbers and plunderers could with impunity commit their crimes and oppress the good and innocent, and these latter could not in turn retaliate upon them."[98]

The fact that self-defense by innocents is legally and morally just, wrote Vitoria, leads inescapably to the rule that the deliberate killing of innocents is unjust, regardless of whether that killing is perpetrated by a person or by a nation. "Hence it follows that even in war with Turks it is not allowable to kill children. This is clear because they are innocent. Aye, and the same holds with regard to the women of unbelievers."[99]

Thus, innocent Muslims or Indians had a right of self-defense against attacks by Christians; a child had a right of self-defense against a father who was trying to murder him; and citizens had a right to self-defense against a murderous government.

Vitoria was the founder of the philosophical group known as the School of Salamanca. Perhaps the greatest of all the succeeding philosophers in this school was Francisco Suárez (1548–1617). He, too, is recognized as a founder of international law.[100]

Suárez called self-defense "the greatest of rights."[101] Because self-defense is part of the natural law, no government may abolish it, he wrote.[102]

Like the Americans who created the Second Amendment, Suárez understood that "the state" is not the same thing as "the government." If a king became a tyrant, then "the state" could depose the tyrant, because of "natural law, which renders it licit to repel force with force."[103] (The "repel force with force" principle is from ancient Roman law.[104])

Suárez's rule that "the state" can remove tyrannical government was an application of his principle that a prince could have legitimate power only if the people had bestowed that power upon him.[105]

The same point is made in the greatest paragraph of political philosophy ever written, paragraph 2 of the Declaration of Independence, that governments "deriv[e] their just powers from the consent of the governed." Suárez and Thomas Jefferson alike show why most of the government delegations at the United Nations are illegitimate: these delegations do not represent governments who derive their just powers from the consent of the governed. To the contrary, these self-said "governments" are nothing more than gangs of thieves who rule by force.

Suárez, a Catholic, had a great influence on Protestants. As British historian Lord Acton put it, "the greater part of the political ideas" of John Milton and John Locke "may be found in the ponderous Latin of Jesuits who were subjects of the Spanish Crown," such as Suárez.[106] Like Vitoria, Suárez was a key source for Hugo Grotius (1583–1645), the greatest international law philosopher of all time.[107]

Grotius's masterpiece *The Rights of War and Peace* has "commonly been seen as the classic work in modern public international law, laying the foundation for a universal code of law."[108] The book was "the first authoritative treatise upon the law of nations, as that term is now understood."[109] "It was at once perceived to be a work of standard and permanent value, of the first authority upon the subject of which it treats."[110]

Needless to say, Barbara Frey's U.N. reports never even acknowledge that the book exists.

Grotius wrote *The Rights of War and Peace* in order to reduce the barbarism of warfare, and in particular to stop attacks on noncombatants. His legal system was built on natural law. "Two principles were uppermost: self-defense and self-preservation."[111] He argued that self-defense is manifestly natural, since animals, like even a human baby, have an instinct of self-defense.[112] Without self-defense, civilized society would be impossible, and "human Society and Commerce would necessarily be dissolved."[113]

According to Grotius, it was just and lawful to defend oneself against attempted homicide, rape, mayhem, or robbery.[114]

The American Founders, who were mostly Protestants, did not know Suárez and Vitoria directly, but absorbed their ideas through the mediation of Grotius and others. Also well-known to the Americans, and second only to Grotius as a founder of international law, was Samuel Pufendorf, a Swede, who was the world's first professor of international law.

Among the many libels that antigun media spread against gun owners is the notion that they are social isolates. Yet the very existence of groups such as the National Rifle Association—with four million members—shows the opposite. The NRA is successful because, as Pufendorf observed, humans are naturally inclined toward peaceful cooperation.

The happy state of peaceful cooperation, Pufendorf explained, depends on the right of self-defense, so that people can live together socially. To ban the use of force in self-defense would turn "honest Men" into "a ready Prey to Villains."[115] "So that, upon the whole to banish *Self-defence* though pursued by *Force*, would be so far from promoting the Peace, that it would rather contribute to the Ruin and Destruction of Mankind."[116] Pufendorf thought it ridiculous to claim "that the *Law of Nature*, which was instituted for a Man's Security in the World, should favor so absurd a Peace as must necessarily cause his present Destruction, and would in fine produce any Thing sooner than *Sociable* life."[117]

Destroy the Right to Self-Defense and Destroy Society

Modern South Africa and the United Kingdom are two of the many places where the destruction of the right of self-defense is leading to the destruction of society itself. To walk six blocks in downtown Johannesburg in broad daylight can be risking one's life. To go out at night in Liverpool and Birmingham is to expose oneself as helpless prey to criminal gangs and mobs of drunken louts. So decent people retreat. They hide behind barbed-wire fences and iron gates, and if they want to go "out," they must take a taxi, or spend their time in an inner courtyard of their home.

Unlike Frey (and the government of the United Kingdom), Pufendorf did not demand that a victim must use only arms proportionate to those of the attacker.[118] Pufendorf thought that deadly force could be used against attempts to inflict mayhem or other nonlethal injuries, as well as against rape, assault, or robbery.[119] Conversely, deadly force could not be used to redress an insult to one's honor, or to punish criminals after the fact.[120]

Pufendorf agreed with Grotius that entering into a social compact did not mean that the people gave up the right to resist tyranny, for no one would choose "certain Death" by surrendering the right to "oppose by Arms the unjust Violence of their Superiors."[121]

Jean de Barbeyrac, the most influential translator of Pufendorf and Grotius, added his own commentary saying that if a government attempted to impose a uniform religion, and to deprive people of their freedom of religious conscience, then "the People have as natural and unquestionable a Right to defend the Religion by Force of Arms . . . as to defend their Lives, their Estates, and Liberties."[122]

The principle articulated by Barbeyrac is one reason that the First Amendment right of free exercise of religion and the Second Amendment right to arms are placed next to each other in our Constitution.

The international law philosopher who was most directly influential on the American Founders was probably Emmerich de Vattel (1714–1767). His work, *The Law of Nations; or, Principles of the Law of Nature, Applied to the Conduct and Affairs of Nations and Sovereigns*, was founded on Grotius.[123] Today, when we want to know about international law as understood by the American Founders, Vattel is often the first source to be consulted.

Like his predecessors, Vattel recognized self-defense as a right and a duty: "Self-preservation is not only a natural right, but an obligation imposed by nature, and no man can entirely and absolutely renounce it."[124] That right could be exercised whenever the government failed to protect an individual; the right extended to protection from rape and robbery (and not, as the Frey and the U.N. claim, only to homicide).[125]

The right also included a collective right of self-defense against a tyrant, for a tyrant "is no better than a public enemy against whom the nation may and ought to defend itself."[126] Of course Vattel—like his predecessors, and like the American Founders—could distinguish between a just, collective, people's uprising against a tyrant, versus the demented and wicked attempt by one or a few people to murder a government official in a democracy.

Fortunately, our American Constitution provides an additional check against self-deluded evildoers who think they have a private right to start a revolution. Under the Second Amendment, the use of armed force against an allegedly tyrannical federal government could be legal only if that use of force were explicitly authorized by state governments. This is the scenario sketched out by James Madison in *The Federalist* number 46. Thomas Jefferson made the same point in his 1811 letter to Destutt de Tracey, adding that if a state legislature were prevented from meeting, then a special state convention would take its place.

In the BYU article, Kopel, Gallant, and Eisen go on to show that the right of self-defense (including the community right and duty of self-defense against tyrants) is protected by many national constitutions, and recognized by the major legal systems of the past and present. They argue that the right to self-defense necessarily implies a right to arms, based on the legal maxims "When the law grants anything to any one, all incidents are tacitly granted"[127] and "When the law gives a man anything, it gives him that also without which the thing itself cannot exist."[128] Thus, the right to publish a newspaper implies a right to buy and possess printer's ink.

Some people (such as martial arts experts) may be able to defend themselves without using arms, but most people cannot. An elderly woman attacked in her home by three young, tough invaders cannot be expected to protect herself without arms. Firearms are, of course, the ideal defensive weapons. They allow a smaller person to defend herself at a distance from a group of larger, stronger attackers.

Accordingly, if the Human Rights Council were actually interested in defending human rights—rather than making things easier for dictatorships—the Council would be exploring whether the universal, natural, and inalienable right of self-defense should be understood to imply a right to the possession of defensive arms, especially in the home.

Conclusion

In 1948, before the United Nations had been taken over by dictatorships, Eleanor Roosevelt headed the Commission on Human Rights. The U.N. was debating what would become the Universal Declaration of Human Rights (A declaration that acknowledges the right of revolution against tyranny). Mrs. Roosevelt warned that dictatorships were trying to pervert human rights language to inhuman purposes.

Speaking at the Sorbonne, in Paris, she declared: "We must not be deluded by the efforts of the forces of reaction to prostitute the great words of our free tradition and thereby to confuse the struggle." She said that "democracy, freedom, human rights have come to have a definite meaning to the people of the world, which we must not allow to so change that they are made synonymous with suppression and dictatorship."[129]

Sad to say, Mrs. Roosevelt's fears have come to pass. Today, the misnamed Human Rights Council prostitutes the great words of our free traditions and makes them synonymous with dictatorship, genocide, ethnic persecution, suppression of freedom of speech and religion, confiscation of arms, and denial of "the greatest of all rights," the right of self-defense.

Vaclav Havel, the former president of the Czech Republic, who was one of the leaders of the dissident movement when his nation was ruled by Soviet puppets, calls the HRC "a table for tyrants."[130]

Florida Congresswoman Ileana Ros-Lehtinen, who chairs the House Foreign Affairs Committee, introduced in the 111th Congress the U.N. Transparency, Accountability and Reform Act, a bill to withhold U.S. funding to the U.N. until some long overdue reforms are made. Regarding the HRC, she proposes suspending U.S. taxpayer support for that body as long as the HRC contains any member that the Secretary of State has determined to have "repeatedly provided support for acts of international terrorism" or which the president of the United States "has designated as a country of particular concern for religious freedom."[131]

Representative Cliff Stearns (R-FL) also introduced legislation in the 111th Congress to simply cut off American taxpayer funding for the HRC.[132] In the unlikely event the HRC were significantly improved, funding could be restored.

A U.S. funding cut-off is appropriate, because recent history shows that the United Nations has obstructed every effort at genuine reform of the Human Rights Council/Commission. The Axis of Soros will continue to use the so-called Human Rights Council to prostitute the language of human rights, and to advance an agenda of disarmament and destruction of human rights. I promise you that the National Rifle Association will follow in the footsteps of America's Founding Fathers in defense of human rights. We will fight alongside our Allies of Freedom, and we will never surrender.

Chapter 14

The U.N. and Terrorism: A Blood and Money Trail

The actions of the United Nations regarding terrorism run the gamut from useless to deadly: the U.N. denounces U.S. antiterrorism efforts, while at the same time it foments terrorism and contributes direct financial and material support for terrorism in the Middle East. U.N. officials mouth the right words about terrorism, but the world body does virtually nothing concrete to combat escalating violence.

Several governments that are state sponsors of terrorism are U.N. members in good standing. The U.S. State Department has officially named five such governments currently: Iran, Syria, North Korea, Sudan, and Cuba.[1]

Syria has the longest record as a named state sponsor of terrorism—since 1979. Sudan is the most recent nation, so designated in 1993. Yet whether a regime has been a notorious sponsor of terrorism for more than a decade or for a quarter century does not matter to the U.N. Criminal, terrorist regimes are treated like any member state, granted seats and sometimes leading roles on U.N. committees and commissions dealing with terrorism, human rights, and Middle East issues. Notably, terrorist states have repeatedly been members of the Security Council.[2]

At the U.N., the terrorist coalition is so strong that it can block meaningful action against terrorism. Often, the coalition is able to use the U.N.—especially in the Middle East—to propagandize in its favor and to provide funding directly and indirectly. The terrorists-in-good-standing at the U.N. are often supported by other member states—including China, Russia, and many of the Arab and African states.

Since U.S. taxpayers provide 22 percent of the U.N.'s budget, vast amounts of American tax money collected from people like you and me have been used by the U.N. to pay for suicide bombers, schools that incite children to become terrorists, and a relentless stream of hate propaganda.

U.N. Money for Osama bin Laden and Other Terrorists

A few weeks after the September 11, 2001, attacks, the British Broadcasting Corporation announced: "A BBC investigation has revealed that the United Nations funded the work of a charity believed by the United States to be a front organization for Osama Bin Laden."[3] The charity was the Muwafaq (Arabic for "blessed relief") Foundation, located in Sudan, to which the U.N. donation was made in 1997. The Sudanese government was then (and is now) a notorious state sponsor of terrorism and an ongoing genocide perpetrator. Yet the U.N. apparently had little interest in checking the bona fides of the government-approved "charity" operating out of the same nation that had harbored Osama bin Laden until 1996.[4]

The U.S. Treasury Department explained that the Muwafaq "charity" was used as a front by Saudi Arabian businessmen to deliver money to bin Laden.[5] In November 2001, the Treasury Department stated:

> The Muwafaq Foundation provided logistical and financial support for a *mujahidin* battalion in Bosnia. The Foundation also operated in Sudan, Somalia, and Pakistan, among other places. A number of individuals employed by or otherwise associated with the Muwafaq Foundation have connections to various terrorist organizations . . . The Muwafaq Foundation also provided support to Hamas and the Abu Sayyaf Organization in the Philippines . . . The Muwafaq Foundation also employed or served as cover for Islamic extremists connected with the military activities of Makhtab Al-Khidamat (MK) [a group that later merged into al-

Qaeda] . . . A number of NGOs, formerly associated with the MK, including Muwafaq, also merged with al-Qaeda.[6]

The BBC reported that Charles Shoebridge, a retired British antiterrorism intelligence officer, said that the U.N. was in a good position to have looked into the credentials of the charities to which it gave money. "You would have thought that an organisation like the U.N. would have access to a certain amount of information from its constituent members' intelligence services," he added.[7]

"The fact that the U.N. has been so easily duped will no doubt cause great unease within the international community," concluded the BBC report. "Not only would it have allowed terrorists to masquerade under a cloak of decency—it actually provided hard cash with which they could fund their cause."[8]

The BBC's prediction turned out to be incorrect. The "international community"—at least the international community that runs the U.N.—kept up business as usual. Which is to say, the U.N. kept on funding terrorism.

The amount the U.N. gave to bin Laden wasn't much, at least by the U.N.'s profligate standards for spending other people's money. The Sudanese "charities" got $1.4 million, and the BBC investigator apparently did not discover how much of that money was delivered to bin Laden's charity. We do know that the 1997 gift came at a time when al-Qaeda was hurting for money. One of al-Qaeda's top employees quit in 1996 because he was only being paid $500 a month.[9]

But the money that the U.N. gave Osama bin Laden is a pittance compared to its funding of some other terrorists.

Oil-for-Terrorism

The largest financial program in U.N. history, the Iraqi Oil-for-Food program, was corrupted right from its start in late 1996, with U.N.

knowledge and acquiescence. Upon taking office as secretary-general on January 1, 1997, Kofi Annan announced a "reform" that consolidated the two small U.N. programs related to Oil-for-Food. (One program had been for sanctions; the other program for trade allowed under the Oil-for-Food exemption to the sanctions.) The two programs were merged into a massive and permanent Office for Iraqi Programmes, that Annan made part of the Office of the Secretariat. This would allow him to grow the program, under his control, to enormous size, and to limit the Security Council merely to reviewing the dissimulating reports he provided every six months.

From the beginning, Saddam Hussein lined his pockets with money intended to help poor people in Iraq and used the money to finance his military and secret police. Moreover, he used the money to stow away cash and weapons for the terrorists now determined to overthrow the democratically elected government of Iraq, murder Iraqi civilians by the thousands, and kill American and other coalition soldiers.

In January 2006, the *Weekly Standard*'s Stephen Hayes reported on Hussein's government documents that had been seized and translated. They show that Saddam's government—which, remember, was being funded by U.N. corruption—trained two thousand terrorists every year at Iraqi bases.[10]

U.N. corruption ran all the way to the top—to the son of Secretary-General Kofi Annan, and to the man, Benon Sevan, whom Annan appointed to run the Oil-for-Food. (Sevan, of course, fled to Cyprus, which has no extradition treaty with the U.S.) We also know that Saddam used his U.N. revenue to pass out huge bribes to high-ranking officials in the French and Russian governments. The Volcker Commission investigation found that both Kofi Annan and deputy secretary-general Louise Fréchette (a leader of the U.N. antigun campaign and the direct supervisor of Benon Sevan) were "informed of the issue of kickbacks, but remained passive."[11]

Now that some of the Oil-for-Food documents have been made public, we understand that it was impossible to expect that the U.N. would ever authorize force against Saddam—even though he flouted seventeen Security

THE U.N. AND TERRORISM

Council resolutions demanding proof that he had disarmed and that he allow unhindered U.N. inspections. Thanks to the corrupt program set up by Kofi Annan, Saddam bribed the U.N. itself, and bribed permanent members of the Security Council, who threatened to veto any resolution approving the use of force. After the coalition liberated Iraq, Annan sniffed that the U.S.-led invasion was "illegal" because it was not authorized in advance by the U.N.[12]

Annan's sniping about the "illegality" of the liberation of Iraq was delivered in September 2004, in a transparent attempt to influence U.S. public opinion in favor of Massachusetts senator John Kerry, the antigun extremist who wanted to subject U.S. policies to what he called the "global test."

The week before the election, the U.N. launched an "October surprise." Mohammad ElBaradei, the Egyptian head of the U.N.'s International Atomic Energy Agency, told the *New York Times* that 350 tons of explosives had gone missing from the Al Qaaqaa munitions depot in Iraq. The media jumped on the story, and the Kerry campaign launched ads on the missing explosives so quickly that it was difficult to believe that Kerry and media (and perhaps the U.N.) were not working in coordination.

ElBaradei's wild claims were quickly disproven, but it was not the first time, nor the last, that the U.N. would attempt to interfere with America's right to choose how to defend itself in the war on terror.

Terror-Funding Banks

Two major multinational institutions enable developed nations to make economic development loans and grants to the Third World: the International Monetary Fund (IMF) and the World Bank. The IMF is not part of the U.N., but the World Bank is. Funding from these institutions (in other words, funding from taxpayers in countries such as the U.S.) often does much more harm than good, since corrupt third-world governments use the funding to enrich themselves and to strengthen their grip on national power.[13]

Three weeks after the September 11, 2001 attacks, a Heritage Foundation paper titled "Stop Subsidizing Terrorism" detailed IMF and World Bank support of terrorist governments.[14] Of the countries that the U.S. named as state sponsors of terrorism, Iran has received $625 million from the IMF and World Bank (even though it is a wealthy, oil-rich country); Syria has received $265 million; and Sudan has received $1.8 billion. When ruled by the Taliban, Afghanistan received $230 million.[15] The governing "Articles of Agreement do not allow those institutions to prohibit lending to countries that undermine international peace and stability by supporting foreign terrorist organizations," Heritage noted.

Citing public documents covering 1998–99, the Heritage Foundation also pointed out that other U.N. agencies had given millions of dollars to terrorist regimes. The Office of the U.N. High Commissioner for Refugees gave money to Libya and Iran, while the U.N. Relief and Works Agency for Palestine Refugees in the Near East gave to Syria.

The World Bank also provides funding to terrorist training centers through "investments" (that is, donations) to several Palestinian universities, all of which have official student chapters of the terrorist organization Hamas.[16] These student chapters have been, and will continue to be, the training grounds for the next generation of terrorists and their propagandists.[17]

At Al-Najah University, a World Bank beneficiary, the student chapter of Hamas celebrated the terrorist bombing of a Sbarro pizzeria in Israel by constructing a mock pizza parlor and filling it with images of severed body parts.[18]

The World Bank does not seem to mind glorifying terrorists. One of its projects was paying for the "development of the Dalal Mughrabi Street" in Gaza. Dalal Mughrabi was a terrorist for the Palestine Liberation Organization who hijacked a bus in 1978 and murdered thirty-six Israelis and American photographer Gail Rubin.[19]

The U.N. General Assembly has granted Observer status to the Islamic Development Bank Group (IDB).[20] Observer status allows an organization to speak at General Assembly meetings, and to sponsor and sign resolutions. The IDB has administered incentive funds to promote homicide bombing. The Al-Quds Intifadah Fund and the Al-Aqsa Fund were created by the Arab League in 2000 to pay rewards to the families of bombing perpetrators. The IDB disbursed the rewards based on instructions from the donor countries.[21]

The IDB also disburses Saudi funds from Saudi prince Salman Ibn Abd Al-Aziz's Popular Committee for Assisting the Palestinian Mujahideen, and Prince Nayef's Support Committee for the Al-Quds Intifada.[22] As Anne Bayefsky of Eye on the UN wrote, the IDB's General Assembly observer status gives it "extraordinary global access to policymakers for an entity linked to terrorist."[23]

In March 2008, U.N. Security Council Resolution 1803 warned all nations "to exercise vigilance" over banks based in Iran. The Resolution specifically identified Bank Melli, which is owned by the government of Iran, as a tool that finances Iran's development of nuclear weapons. Incredibly, the U.N. Children's Fund (UNICEF) continues to keep an account in Iran at that bank, and to transfer money from that Iranian bank to Gaza, which is controlled by the Iranian-funded terrorist organization Hamas. UNICEF also keeps millions of dollars at the Iranian-government-owned Bank Tejart, which the U.S. government has placed under sanctions for its role in facilitating Iranian state terrorism.[24]

Pakistan Earthquake Relief Funds Aid Terrorists

After a devastating earthquake in Pakistan in October 2005, the United Nations rushed in with money. Some of that money went to two terrorist organizations: the Al Rashid Trust (which is believed to provide financing to al-Qaeda, and is on the U.N.'s own sanctions list) and Jamaat ud Dawa (which is on the U.S. sanctions list, and is believed to be affiliated with the Kashmir terrorist group Lashkar-e-Toiba).

The U.N. told critics that it was just supplying aid to help the earthquake victims, but the BBC reported this about the terrorist groups:

> The aid they got from international agencies—have really boosted their position locally. One Jamaat leader told us that people were now trusting them with their children—they hadn't before the earthquake—and they had actively recruited hundreds of children left orphaned or fatherless. He said they had already sent 400 such children under the age of nine to board at their madrassas, or religious schools, some hundreds of miles from their homes.[25]

One such madrassa, in the town of Mansehra, was originally set up with aid from United Nations International Children's Fund, UNICEF. The BBC found the primary school children singing a song: "When people deny our faith, ask them to convert and if they don't, destroy them utterly."[26]

Food, Starvation, and U.N. Celebration of Dictators

Robert Mugabe, the Marxist tyrant of Zimbabwe, has stolen elections, destroyed the free press, and squelched the judiciary, and his regime is engaged in a campaign of genocide against the people of Zimbabwe by starving them to death.[27] In 2005, he bulldozed huge zones of the capital city of Harare, where many opponents of his regime lived, leaving hundreds of thousands of destitute victims homeless and starving.

Mugabe destroyed Zimbabwe's food economy by confiscating land from white farmers, which he gave to his political cronies under the specious pretext of "land reform." Mugabe has long carried out a gun control program to ensure that no one can resist his tyranny and genocide.

So how did the U.N. Food and Agriculture Organization (FAO) celebrate its sixtieth anniversary on October 17, 2005? It invited Robert Mugabe to come to the celebration in Rome. Since Mugabe was on U.N. business, he was allowed to ignore a European Union (E.U.) ban on his travel.

Mugabe delivered a speech on his "land reform" program before a U.N. organization that is supposed to be *fighting*, not causing, world hunger.

At the anniversary celebration, the FAO also bestowed its Agricola Medal on Brazil's notoriously corrupt president Lula da Silva, who a week later would lose his campaign to outlaw gun ownership in Brazil, and who also advocates a global U.N. tax on guns.

Mugabe and an entourage of more than sixty showed up again at the 2009 FAO conference in Rome. Again, he praised himself for stealing land from farmers. Because Mugabe and most of his entourage are subjects of European Union travel sanctions, the U.N. provided an opportunity for the Zimbabwe kleptocracy to go on European shopping sprees with the money they had looted from the people of Zimbabwe.[28]

Meanwhile, in Somalia, the U.N.'s World Food Program (WFP) pays money to food distributors who work closely with radical Islamist and terrorist groups, and which allow food aid to be stolen by the groups. Up to half the food aid sent to Somalia has been stolen by the Islamists or other participants in the Somali web of corruption. When the WFP's misspending was revealed, the WFP promised that it would end its relationship with the distributors, but within weeks signed new contracts with those same distributors.[29]

Hezbollah

As our nation engages terrorists around the world, U.N. "peacekeepers" are actually working side by side with Hezbollah, a Lebanese Islamic terrorist group that used truck bombs to kill 241 marines in their barracks in Lebanon in 1983. Hezbollah also kidnapped and tortured to death Marine Colonel William R. Higgins and the CIA station chief in Beirut, William Buckley.

The U.S. State Department states that Hezbollah (Arabic for "Party of God") is responsible for two bombings of the U.S. Embassy in Beruit, the kidnapping of more than thirty Westerners, and hijacking TWA flight 847 (Athens to Rome) in 1985. Hezbollah has been designated as a terrorist organization not only by the U.S., but also by the EU and many democratic governments.

At the level of rhetoric, U.N. secretary-general Kofi Annan is a staunch opponent of terrorism.[30] Yet when the U.N. Security Council was considering a 2005 resolution to tell Syria to remove its troops from Lebanon, Annan was asked whether Hezbollah should be disarmed.[31] Annan answered: "We need to recognize that they are a force in society that one will have to factor in as we implement the resolution."[32] The Security Council did adopt Resolution 1559, which ordered Syria out of Lebanon, and ordered that Hezbollah be disarmed. Yet the secretary-general's special envoy to Lebanon, Terje Roed-Larsen, acknowledged that disarming Hezbollah was not part of his "action agenda."[33]

The announcement of the secretary-general and his special envoy that Hezbollah—even when armed in violation of a Security Council resolution and when engaged in terrorism—is entitled to consideration is hardly consistent with Annan's generalities about terrorism, such as: "It should be clearly stated, by all possible moral and political authorities, that terrorism is unacceptable under any circumstances, and in any culture."[34] Except sometimes.

Early in 2005, Annan sent his special envoy Lakhdar Brahimi to attend the funeral of Rafik Hariri, the former Lebanese prime minister who was assassinated because he spoke out against Syria's colonization of Lebanon. While in Lebanon, the U.N.'s special envoy also met with the head of Hezbollah, Sheikh Mohamed Hussein Fadlallah—a man whom diplomats from the U.S. and other freedom-loving countries resolutely refuse to dignify with an official diplomatic visit.[35]

The Security Council ordered an investigation of the assassination of Hariri. When the report was completed, Annan ordered that portions be blacked out before being released to the public. Those portions showed—when the full report was leaked—that the trail of responsibility for the assassination stretched all the way to the brother-in-law of Syrian tyrant Bashir Assad.

U.N. Interim Force in Lebanon

In 1982, Israel invaded Lebanon, in order to stop attacks on Israel from Hezbollah and PLO bases there. In 1990, Israel withdrew from Lebanon, in compliance with Security Council Resolution 425. The U.N. deployed peacekeepers—the U.N. Interim Force in Lebanon (UNFIL)—to prevent incursions from one nation into another. Yet in practice, UNFIL has turned into an ally of Hezbollah and an active enemy of Israel.

The so-called peacekeepers of UNFIL do not interdict Hezbollah terrorist attacks on northern Israel.[36] Instead, UNFIL allows Hezbollah to take up positions that are adjacent to the UNFIL peacekeepers.[37] Moreover, UNFIL has established a permanent dialogue with the terrorist organization.[38] As one Israeli leader summarized, "The U.N. is in fact collaborating with a terrorist organization."[39] UNFIL's most notorious collaboration with terrorists involved the kidnapping and murder of three Israeli soldiers, and the subsequent cover-up. On October 7, 2000, Hezbollah terrorists entered Israel, attacked three Israeli soldiers on Mount Dov, and abducted them to Lebanon. The kidnapping was witnessed by several dozen UNFIL soldiers who stood idle.[40] One of the soldier witnesses described the kidnapping: the terrorists set off an explosive that stunned the Israeli soldiers. Clad in U.N. uniforms, the terrorists called out, "Come, come, we'll help you."

It appears that at least four of the UNFIL peacekeepers, all from India, received bribes from Hezbollah in order to assist the kidnapping by helping them get to the kidnapping spot and find the Israeli soldiers.[41] Some of the bribery involved alcohol and Lebanese women.[42]

But there is evidence of far greater payments by Hezbollah to the UNFIL Indian brigade, including hundreds of thousands of dollars for assistance in the kidnapping and cover-up.[43] The U.N. cover-up began almost immediately.

The Beruit *Daily Star* reported the story as told by a former officer of the Observer Group Lebanon (OGL), which is part of the U.N. Truce

Supervision Organization (UNTSO): "A few hours after the kidnapping, UNTSO learned that two abandoned cars had been discovered. One was a white Nissan Pathfinder with fake U.N. insignia; it had hit an embankment because it was being driven so fast that the driver missed a turn. The other was a Range Rover; it was missing a tire rim, and was still running when it was discovered."[44]

Rather than using the very recently abandoned vehicles as clues to rescue the kidnap victims, the U.N. initiated a cover-up. Eighteen hours after the kidnapping, a team of OGL and the Indian UNFIL began a videotaped removal of the contents of the cars.[45]

The UNTSO officer told the *Daily Star* that the U.N. ordered its personnel to destroy all photographs and written reports about the incident.[46]

Did the U.N. provide the Israelis with the automobile contents, or the videotape, both of which might have helped the Israelis rescue the kidnap victims? Of course not.

Israel found out about the videotape and demanded that the U.N. let Israeli investigators see it. Kofi Annan and his special envoy first denied that any videotape existed, but nine months after the kidnapping, on July 6, 2001, the U.N. admitted that it had the videotape. Annan ordered an internal U.N. report, which was led by U.N. undersecretary-general Joseph Connor. (Connor was later implicated in the Oil-for-Food scam.) The report revealed that the U.N. had two additional videotapes, one containing still photographs from the kidnapping itself.

Even after admitting the existence of the first videotape, Annan refused to allow Israel to view it, claiming that doing so would undermine U.N. neutrality. The U.S. House of Representatives thought differently. On July 30, 2001, it passed, on a 411 to 4 vote, a resolution urging the U.N. to allow Israel to see the videotape.[47] Annan relented, but only under the condition that the tape be edited so as to hide the faces of the Hezbollah perpetrators.[48]

On January 29, 2004, the bodies of the murdered Israelis were returned to Israel by Hezbollah, as part of a prisoner exchange.

UNIFIL and Hezbollah

Year after year, Hezbollah built fortifications, and placed rocket launchers in homes, schools, and mosques. Hezbollah terrorists conducted training with the Iranian Revolutionary Guards. These actions were far too extensive to be concealed. Indeed, not only did the U.N. and Hezbollah flags fly side by side; the U.N. Interim Force in Lebanon (UNIFIL) and Hezbollah shared water and telephones. At the least, UNIFIL should have formally notified the Security Council about what was going on, which was a flagrant violation of the Security Council's resolutions regarding Lebanon.[49]

Hezbollah's takeover of southern Lebanon, thanks in part to the negligence and complicity of the United Nations, resulted in the opposite of what "peacekeeping" is supposed to accomplish. Hezbollah used its Iranian- and Syrian-supplied weapons to launch relentless rocket attacks on northern Israel. The rockets were not aimed at military targets, but instead at civilians, for the purpose of terrorism. Then, in 2006, Hezbollah crossed the border and kidnapped three Israeli soldiers. So after years in which UNIFIL had done no peacekeeping in Lebanon, Israel finally acted to protect itself, and invaded Lebanon to take on Hezbollah directly.

During the war, UNIFIL acted as an intelligence service on behalf of Hezbollah. The UNIFIL forces in southern Lebanon were of course in an excellent position to observe activities by both the Israelis and Hezbollah. UNIFIL published daily online reports of Israeli military activities, including the precise locations of Israeli structures and troops. Information was a fresh as thirty minutes, and never older than twenty-four hours. In contrast, there were *zero* postings about specific Hezbollah locations. The only information about Hezbollah was useless generalities, such as that Hezbollah "fired rockets in large numbers from various locations."[50]

The United Nations also acted as a de facto propaganda mouthpiece for the terrorists. For example, the U.N. Humanitarian Coordinator in Lebanon, David Shearer, insisted that the Israeli Defense Forces stop all interference with supply routes that were being used to convey humanitarian relief. Yet Shearer had no criticism of Hezbollah for making those supply routes legitimate military targets by using them to transport weapons and fighters. In essence, the U.N. rewarded Hezbollah's tactic of turning the Lebanese people into human shields.[51]

Annan and the rest of the U.N. cooperated with Hezbollah's human shield strategy by turning U.N. forces themselves into human shields for the terrorists. Although UNIFIL itself was forbidden to take any military actions, the UNIFIL forces were left in the combat zones, allowing Hezbollah forces to launch rockets from adjacent positions.[52]

On July 25, 2006, Israeli artillery hit a United Nations *Observer* post in Khiyam, Lebanon. Annan proclaimed himself "shocked and deeply distressed by the apparently deliberate targeting by Israeli Defence Forces."

The U.N. assistant secretary-general for peacekeeping operations, Jane Holl Lute, told the media that "no Hezbollah activity was reported in the area"; other U.N. sources made similar claims.[53]

Then the truth came out. One of the peacekeepers had been Canadian major Hess von Krudener. A week before his death, he had sent an e-mail reporting, "The closest artillery has landed within two metres of our position." He explained, "This has not been deliberate targeting, but has rather been due to tactical necessity. Please understand the nature of my job here is to be impartial and to report violations from both sides without bias. As an Unarmed Military Observer, this is my raison d'être." One of the recipients of the e-mail was Canadian major general Lewis MacKenzie. As MacKenzie observed, "What he is saying translates roughly as: 'Hezbollah soldiers were all over his position and the IDF were targeting them. And that's a favorite trick by people who don't have representation in the UN. They use the UN as shields knowing that they can't be punished for it."[54]

UNIFIL's commander, General Alain Pellegrini, told the media that Hezbollah was "taking the cover of villages or U.N. positions to act, hoping this proximity to people will be a problem to [Israeli troops] when they have to respond." Indeed, Hezbollah had just launched rockets from a position next to UNIFIL bases four times within a recent twenty-four-hour period.[55]

The very same day that the Israeli shell had hit the UNIFIL outpost, Hezbollah attacked and damaged a U.N. convoy. Kofi Annan uttered not a word of protest.[56]

UNRWA: The Mother of Terrorism

If the U.N. Relief and Works Agency for Palestine Refugees in the Near East (UNRWA) were a private organization, the fair application of existing U.S. law would result in UNRWA being classified as a Foreign Terrorist Organization (FTO) by the U.S. State Department, and its assets frozen by all governments committed to fighting terrorism. Briefly put, an organization is "engaged in terrorist activity" if it knowingly transfers funds to terrorists, knowingly allows its facilities to be used for terrorism, or provides other material support to terrorists.[57]

To be sure, UNRWA is not an *exclusively* terrorist organization in the sense that al-Qaeda is. Al-Qaeda has no activities other than terrorism and terrorist propaganda.

UNRWA, however, willingly accepts large sums of money from known terrorist finance organizations and knowingly distributes large sums of money to them. Its property is used for terrorism, including bomb making, and it intentionally finances massive amounts of hate propaganda designed to incite terrorism. A great deal of UNRWA's material support for terrorism is given to Hamas, which is itself designated a FTO by the U.S. government.[58]

With a 2008 budget of 541.8 million, including $148 million from U.S. taxpayers, UNRWA is the largest Western-funded organization for the support of terrorism.[59]

James Lindsay was UNRWA's legal adviser from 2000 until 2007, and general counsel from 2002 to 2007. Although he remains supportive of UNRWA's mission, he authored a whistleblowing report, titled *Fixing UNRWA: Repairing the UN's Troubled System of Aid to Palestinian Refugees.*[60] He noted UNRWA's standard role as a propaganda service for terrorists:

UNRWA's support of Palestinian views was notable throughout the second intifada. Although it issued mild, pro forma criticisms of Palestinian attacks (most of which were clearly war crimes), the agency put more effort into criticizing Israeli counterterrorism efforts (which were condemned using language associated with war crimes, though any such crimes were far from proved. This trend has endured well beyond the intifada. In a typical example, Palestinians in Gaza launch a terrorist attack against Israelis—often a rocket strike on civilians, a war crime. This leads to an IDF attack on the terrorists, during which Palestinian civilians (among whom the terrorists place themselves) are killed or injured. UNRWA then lodges a protest condemning "Israel's disproportionate, indiscriminate and excessive use of force, as well as the firing of rockets from Gaza into Israel, naming the aggressor only as an afterthought. If, however, there is no Israeli military response, the Palestinian terrorism normally passes without UNRWA comment.[61]

Similarly, UNRWA's then commissioner general Karen Koning AbuZayd castigated Israel for its blockade of Gaza. Israel allows the import of food and other essentials, but prohibits the import of weapons—since Gaza's government is run by Hamas, which is in a declared state of war with Israel. Of course, the necessity of inspecting shipments of foods to prevent the smuggling of hidden bombs and other weapons necessarily slows the pace of imports.

AbuZayd complained, "In all of our years of working in conflict situations, even with so-called 'rogue states,' of all the interlocutors we've worked with, the Israelis are the most intransigent."[62] Yet she ignored the intransigence of Hamas and other terrorists.

Israel completely withdrew from Gaza in 2005. The terrorists used the withdrawal as an opportunity to intensify their rocket barrage on Israeli border towns. From time to time, Israel would launch raids against the terrorists. U.N. undersecretary-general for humanitarian affairs John Holmes described this as "a vicious cycle of violence"—as if there were no moral distinction between criminal aggression and self-defense.[63] This amounts to a broader application of the Soros/IANSA principle of moral equivalence between armed criminals and armed crime victims.

Finally, on December 27, 2008, Israel took the war to the Gaza terrorists in Operation Cast Lead. UNRWA consistently mimicked the key Hamas position: the Israelis should immediately stop fighting and withdraw, with no requirement that Hamas cease its rocket and mortar attacks on Israeli towns.[64]

In having a cooperative relationship with Hamas, whose own charter calls for the destruction of Israel and the killing of all Jews, UNRWA is not out of step with the rest of the United Nations. Kofi Annan's press spokesman refused to say that Hamas is a terrorist organization.[65] In fact, the UN Division for Palestinian Rights supports Palestinian terrorism in general, and Hamas in particular.[66]

UNRWA has twenty-four thousand employees, 99 percent of them Palestinian, making it by far the largest United Nations organization in size of permanent staff.[67]

The Terrorist Welfare State

Writing in *Forbes*, journalist Claudia Rosett calls UNRWA's dominion "a UN-supported welfare enclave for terrorists." She points out that UNRWA now serves more than 4.6 million "refugees." Few of them are refugees by the normal meaning of the word as applied by the U.N. High Commissioner for Refugees: people who have been forced to leave their homeland, and who have not found a safe place to live elsewhere permanently.[68] Instead, most of UNRWA's so-called refugees are descendants of people who left Israeli two or three generations ago, and many of them are now citizens of other countries.[69]

In Gaza, 70 percent of the population is classified as "refugees" by UNRWA.[70] This means that they receive free food and free housing, free medical care, and free education.[71] There is no work requirement for any of these benefits.

Many of these "refugees" are housed in squalid camps run by UNRWA. Since Israel completely withdrew from Gaza in 2005, there is no good reason why people should still be housed in camps. A humanitarian aid program for them would help them establish permanent housing.

Sadly, UNRWA is run for the purpose of ensuring that the "refugee" problem is never solved, so Arab dictatorships can continue to use it in their anti-Israel campaign. So the Palestinians are kept in the camps, with UNRWA continuing to make the absurd promise to them that they will one day "return" to Israel—a nation in which most of them have never lived or visited.[72]

Thus, as George Mason law professor Peter Berkowitz points out, "by providing welfare instead of work, the UNRWA has created incentives for Palestinians to remain dependent on the very international organization that is premised on resisting compromise with Israel."[73]

James Lindsay has written that "no justification exists for millions of dollars in humanitarian aid going to those who can afford to pay for UNRWA services." He believes that the most important reform is "the removal of citizens from recognized states—persons who have the oxymoronic status of 'citizen refugees'—from UNRWA's jurisdiction."[75]

UNRWA: Funded by U.S. Taxpayers

As the largest donors to the UNRWA, U.S. taxpayers pay about a third of UNRWA's budget, giving the organization more than $100 million per year.[75] Since 1950, U.S. taxpayers have given UNRWA more than $2.5 billion.[76] Saudi Arabia, Kuwait, and the smaller Gulf States contribute a combined total of about 2 percent of UNRWA's budget. Other Arab nations, such as Libya, Egypt, Syria—which constantly profess concern for the well-being of the Palestinians—contribute little or nothing.[77]

UNRWA also receives substantial terrorist funding—making it apparently the only U.N. agency that not only gives money to terrorists, but also gets money from them. According to the U.S. Department of the Treasury, a "charity" known as the Islamic African Relief Agency (IARA) transferred millions of dollars to Osama bin Laden's terrorist networks. In October 2004, the Treasury froze IARA's assets. IARA's energetic head, Mubarak Hamed, has been charged with raising $5 million for bin Laden in just a single fund-raising swing through the Middle East in 2000. One of IARA's subsidiaries, the Islamic American Relief Agency, gave UNRWA $510,000.[78]

Another UNRWA donor—of $5,076,000—is the Islamic Development Bank, which also created the Al Aqsa Fund. This Fund has been declared by the U.S. Treasury Department to be a Specially Designated Global Terrorist (SDGT) entity because it funnels money from donors in the Persian Gulf to the terrorist organization Hamas.[79]

In UNRWA's public records, you will find something called the "Saudi Committee," that has given UNRWA $1,640,000. The reported name is a deceptive condensation of the Saudi Arabia Committee for Support of the Intifada Al Quds. (Al Quds is the Arabic name for Jerusalem.) The Saudi Committee is believed to contribute funds for Hamas suicide bombing.[80]

The government of Syria, designated by the U.S. State Department as a state sponsor of terror, has created an organization called the Syrian Arab Popular Committee. It sponsors rallies in Syria and Lebanon demanding the extermination of Israel. The committee has also given $3,538,276 to UNRWA.[81]

Why is UNRWA such an appealing, and willing, recipient of terrorist funding? Part of the answer goes back to UNRWA's creation in 1949 to help settle Palestinian refugees who fled Israel after five Arab nations (with substantial Palestinian military support) started and lost a war to destroy Israel in 1948–1949.[82] The expectation was that once UNRWA helped solve the Palestinian refugee problem, the agency would cease to exist.[83] Accordingly, UNRWA developed a bureaucratic imperative that virtually ordained that refugees would never resettle. More than fifty-six years after UNRWA was created, refugees are still living in UNRWA's camps—the only refugee population in the world whose status has persisted for more than half a century.

The Arab governments, except for Jordan, exacerbate the problem by denying resident Palestinians even miminal rights. For example, in Lebanon, Palestinians are prohibited from practicing professions such as medicine, law or engineering. They are forbidden to own property. They cannot leave their own town without a special permit. All other foreigners in Lebanon are allowed to use the health-care system, but not Palestinians.[84] Yet the so-called supporters of Palestinian rights, such as former president Jimmy Carter, self-righteously accuse Israel of "apartheid"—even though Arab Israelis have the same full set of civil rights as Jewish Israelis. Carter, the U.N., Soros, and the rest of the Israel-haters rarely seem to utter a word of criticism about how Arab governments treat those Palestinians.

The creation of UNRWA has turned out to be a catastrophe. The Palestinians are the people who have been most victimized by UNRWA, although the Israelis have also suffered immensely. Because the suffering of Palestinians has been used so effectively by terrorists to build support for attacks on the U.S., Americans are also victims of UNRWA.

UNRWA'S Financial Aid to Hamas

Hamas (an acronym for "Islamic Resistance Movement") has been designated a FTO by the U.S. State Department. The terrorist designation is richly deserved. Hamas has launched hundreds of terrorist attacks, including many of the most infamous suicide bomb attacks.[85]

Where does Hamas get its money? A great deal of the terrorist money comes from UNRWA—and, therefore, from U.S. taxpayers. UNRWA's relationship with Hamas is so notorious that Congress enacted a specific requirement that UNRWA screen out beneficiaries (including UNRWA employees) who are members of Hamas or other terrorist organizations, or who have received terrorist training. *Only* if UNRWA performs such screening is UNWRA eligible for U.S. foreign aid.[86]

When the U.S. government's General Accounting Office (GAO) asked UNRWA if it was performing the required screening, UNRWA admitted that it was not.[87] The then head of URNWA, Commissioner-General Peter Hansen, told the Canadian Broadcasting Corporation (CBC): "I am sure that there are Hamas members on the UNRWA payroll, and I don't see that as a crime."[88] It may not be a crime according to the U.N., but it is illegal under U.S. law for UNRWA to receive U.S. aid, until UNRWA stops knowingly employing Hamas.

UNRWA is so blatantly contemptuous of the U.S. requirements that when six houses were accidentally "destroyed during bomb-making activities," UNRWA declared that there was insufficient evidence to cut the families off from UNRWA benefits.[89]

Worse, UNRWA allows its staff to openly participate in terrorist organizations, including Hamas. As one Israeli official observed, "As long as UNRWA employees are members of Fatah, Hamas, or PFLP [Popular Front for the Liberation of Palestine], they are going to pursue the interests of their party within the framework of their job . . . Who's going to check up on them to see that they don't? UNRWA? They are UNRWA."[90]

Indeed, Hamas openly controls the UNRWA employees' union, including the executive council. UNRWA employees are so pro-Hamas that the Hamas candidates won 90 percent of the vote in the union elections and have won every UNRWA union election since 1990.[91] UNRWA Commissioner-General Hansen has admitted that Hamas runs the UNRWA union.[92] Hamas members are required to pay a portion of their salaries to Hamas, and thus UNRWA salaries provide a substantial portion of Hamas's revenue.[93]

The GAO, in an investigation of UNRWA, pointed to more cases in which UNRWA engaged in terrorist activity:

- A UNRWA employee convicted of throwing firebombs at a public bus.
- A UNRWA employee who was a member of Islamic Jihad and was convicted of possession of explosives. Islamic Jihad has been designated a FTO by the U.S. State Department.
- A UNRWA employee who was a member of Hamas and was convicted of supplying chemicals to a bomb maker.

Between 2001 and 2004, seven UNRWA employees were convicted of participation in terrorist activities.[94] Nevertheless, UNRWA brazenly lies about its role in terrorism. UNRWA commissioner-general Peter Hansen told the GAO that "UNRWA has no evidence that would justify denying beneficiaries relief or humanitarian aid owning [sic] to terrorism."[95] What Hansen's doublespeak really means is that even when the evidence is undeniable—such as bomb makers accidentally blowing up their own houses—UNRWA pretends that the evidence does not exist, and continues to give money to known terrorists.

UNRWA itself acts as a Foreign Terrorist Organization, under the standards of U.S. law, by providing safe houses to terrorists. In 2002, Hamas terrorists murdered twenty-nine people at a hotel in the town of Netanya. Israel finally decided to take action against the terrorist bases—the UNRWA camps where terrorists concealed themselves in the civilian population.

The most notorious of these camps was Jenin, near Israel's border. Two weeks after September 11, 2001, the head of Tanzim (a terrorist subdivision of Yassir Arafat's Fatah) was informed that

> of all the districts, Jenin boasts the greatest number of fighters from Fatah and other Islamic national factions. The refugee camp is rightly considered to be the center of events and the operational headquarters of all the factions in the Jenin area—as the other side calls it, a hornets' nest. The Jenin refugee camp is remarkable for the large number of fighting men taking initiatives in the cause of our people . . . It is little wonder, therefore, that Jenin is known as the capital of the suicide martyrs.[96]

Jenin was hardly UNRWA's only major terrorist base, and the seizure of the UNRWA camps has revealed massive evidence—including documents and weapons—of UNRWA's material support for terrorism. UNRWA, however, claims that it has no control over its own camps, because is has no "police force, no intelligence apparatus and no mandate to report on political and military activities."[97] This is nonsense. UNRWA claims "official" ownership of the camps, and precisely demarcates their boundaries and buildings. When the owner of house in one of the camp dies, he cannot bequeath the house to his children. As one UNRWA official put it, "This is not his property, it's our property."[98]

UNRWA Proterrorism Education

UNRWA runs a massive school system, including 266 schools with 242,000 students just in the West Bank and Gaza. UNRWA schools are used as bomb-making centers, as terrorist hideouts, as ammunition depots for terrorists, as offices for terrorist organizations, and for "youth clubs" that are actually terrorist cells.[99]

When then commissioner-general Hansen spoke at a 2004 conference at the Van Leer Jerusalem Institute, he was questioned about UNRWA camps serving as terrorist bases. Hansen asserted that the claims were "made up" in order "to delegitimize" UNRWA. "There hasn't been a single case documented," he declared. When Hansen said the word "terrorism," he used finger quotes.[100]

The claim that there has not been "a single case documented" is an outrageous lie, since several UNRWA employees have been convicted of terrorism, massive terrorist weapons caches have been found in UNRWA camps, and UNRWA camps openly and frequently conduct terrorist recruitment indoctrination.[101]

But the essence of his answer was the finger quotes around "terrorism." Quite plainly, Hansen rejected the idea that what UNRWA, Hamas, and related groups do is terrorism. The definitional problem is not unique to Hansen (who left UNRWA in March 2005);[102] rather it is endemic at the U.N.

Hamas controls all eleven seats on the governing board for the UNRWA teacher's union in Gaza, and has run the union since 1993.[103] Reportedly, Hamas operative Suhil el-Hindi has control of teacher employment and the curriculum at UNRWA schools and summer camps.[104]

At the UNRWA camp in Kalandia, in the West Bank, Israelis captured a school notebook bearing the UNRWA emblem on the back cover—along with a photo of a masked gunman. The notebook profiled so-called martyrs of "the Star Team" who perpetrated terrorist bombings.[105] UNRWA named a youth soccer tournament in honor of Abu Jihad, who, as second-in-command to Yasser Arafat, carried out numerous terrorist attacks, including a 1978 bus hijacking in which his forces murdered thirty-seven civilians.[106]

Almost all post-2000 suicide bombers have come from the West Bank, mainly because (until Israel built its security fence) they had a much easier time getting in to Israel than did other terrorists. About 25 to 30 percent of Palestinian students in the West Bank are educated in UNRWA schools. Yet these schools have produced about 60 percent of the homicide bombers.[107]

According to Lindsay, "teachers in UNRWA schools were afraid to remove posters glorifying 'martyrs' (including suicide bombers) for fear of retribution from armed supporters of the 'martyrs.'"[108]

Awad al-Qiq was the deputy headmaster at UNRWA's Rafah Prep Boys School in Gaza, where he had taught science for eight years. He was also the head rocket and mortar builder for Islamic Jihad, and was killed in an airstrike on his bomb factory, a short distance from the school. He was buried wrapped in an Islamic Jihad flag. The group said that he was the "martyr" who had been "chief leader of the engineering unit"; they fired some rockets into Israel in his honor.[109] UNRWA spokesman Christopher Gunness asserted, "We have a zero-tolerance policy towards politics and militant activities in our schools. Obviously, we are not the thought police and we cannot police people's minds."[110]

So as the Global Research in International Affairs Center observed, "Qiq was thus simultaneously building weapons for use in attacking Israeli civilians while indoctrinating his students to do the same thing. Islamic Jihad did not need to pay him a salary for his military and militant activities since the UN, and American taxpayers, were already doing so."[111]

Another UNRWA schoolteacher was Issa al-Batran, who when not teaching school was a senior Hamas commander, until he was killed by an Israeli airstrike.[112]

At a 2005 ceremony honoring teachers at UNRWA's school in Khan Yunis, in Gaza, the speaker proudly listed five teachers from that school alone who had died as *shahids* (martyrs) while serving as terrorists.[113]

James Lindsay proposes to "allow the UN Educational, Scientific and Cultural Organization (UNESCO), or some other neutral entity, to provide balanced and discrimination-free textbooks for UNRWA initiatives."[114] Some U.S. Congresspersons have introduced a resolution for all UNRWA educational materials to be made available on the Internet.[115] U.S. pressure, including from then senator Hillary Clinton, has led UNRWA and the Palestinian Authority to adopt some new textbooks, but even these new textbooks call for religious war for the destruction of Israel, and incite children to seek death in "martyrdom."[116] When Hamas demanded that all textbooks exclude any mention of the Holocaust, UNRWA meekly submitted.[117] In short, UNRWA schools will continue to be hate academies as long as they remain under the political control of Hamas and similar groups.

Offensively Armed Refugee Camps

In Lebanon, the Nahr al Bared UNRWA camp (housing approximately sixty thousand people) was taken over by an al-Qaeda affiliate named Fatah al-Islam. UNRWA officials knew about the takeover for months, but did nothing about it. "Somebody hasn't been doing their job," complained UNRWA commissioner-general Karen AbuZayd. She was referring to Palestinian gunmen whom UNRWA hires as camp security guards. She should have looked at herself and her own top staff, since UNRWA, as usual, failed to inform the United Nations Security Council about its knowledge of terrorist group activity.[118]

Fortunately, the Lebanese government, which is timid about Hezbollah, took a more pro-active approach regarding the al-Qaeda group. The Lebanese Army invaded the Nahr al Bared camp and used all the force necessary to destroy the terrorists, even though the terrorists employed human shields.

U.N. Security Council Resolution 1208, enacted in 1998, prohibits the militarization of refugee camps.[119] It was a response to problems in Africa at the time. UNRWA has, obviously, made essentially no effort to obey Resolution 1208 regarding its own camps.[120]

UNRWA Commissioner-General AbuZayd admits that Resolution 1208 is legally binding, but says that it is not her problem. She argues that 1208 "requires action to be taken by the authorities where the camps are located, not by the humanitarian agencies." The text of the resolution, however, says otherwise.[121]

"We don't run camps; that is the responsibility of the sovereign governments and authorities wherever the camps are based," she adds. "It's like asking, 'What has Bethesda Hospital done to combat street gangs in Washington, D.C.?' We do send situation reports to the U.N.'s security department and the Office of the Secretary-General; these are simple, straightforward factual accounts of clashes and other incidents."[122]

Nonsense. The proper analogy would be the responsibility of Bethesda Hospital for allowing terrorists to set up military headquarters inside the hospital building, and to launch rockets from that building, using the patients and doctors as human shields. UNRWA has the responsibility to keep terrorists from using its own buildings.

Is Reform of UNRWA Possible?

James Lindsay's reform suggestions for UNRWA are sensible, and it would be wonderful if they were implemented. However, the political reality of the United Nations is that significant reforms of UNRWA are impossible. For more than half a century, UNRWA has been the tool of Arab dictatorships whose objective is a permanent state of war with Israel. Of all the victims of UNRWA, the greatest victims have been the millions of Palestinians whose dreams UNRWA has stifled and perverted.

Simply put, UNRWA should be abolished. Its functions should be transferred to the United Nations High Commissioner for Refugees (UNHCR), which is in charge of helping refugees in other nations. The UNHCR's objective is swift action to help the true refugees find permanent new homes; in contrast, UNRWA has kept generation after generation in a "refugee" limbo, based on the fiction that they will one day "return" to Israel—a nation in which most of the so-called refugees have never lived.

For nearly six decades, the United States has been paying for a program whose very purpose is to obstruct Arab-Israeli peace, and which foments and subsidizes terrorism.

The U.N.'s obsession with the Palestinian "refugees" (who are only refugees today because for sixty years the U.N. has made sure that they stay refugees) is ridiculous and unfair. When 230,000 Haitians were killed in an earthquake, the U.N. spent $10 million helping them. When at most 1,300 Gazans died during Operation Cast Lead—in a war their government had provoked by massive shelling of civilians in a neighboring country—the U.N. showered Gaza with $200 million in additional lucre for the terrorist welfare state. Even the United States government, which generously provided $700 million to Haiti, gave $900 million extra to Gaza. Why should Gaza, which is in a perpetual state of terrorist war against a neighboring country, keep getting so much money to repair the problems their own government has caused, while Haiti, which is neither run by terrorists nor at war with anyone else, receives so much less?[123]

Until UNRWA is terminated and its functions taken over by UNHCR, United States taxpayer funding should terminate. There is a much better use for that money: While the dictatorships that run the U.N. beat their breasts with feigned concern about the refugees who live near Israel, the U.N. has done almost nothing for the three million refugees who have fled from the genocide in Zimbabwe.[124]

It would be better for everyone—including the Palestinians who have spent decades stuck in UNRWA's welfare hellhole—if the United States immediately ceased all funding for UNRWA, and instead directed the money to the relief of the Zimbabwe refugees.

Canada, which for many years made huge voluntary donations to UNRWA, announced in early 2010 that it would cut off all its funding for UNRWA, and instead give the money to nongovernment organizations that actually help Palestinians.[125]

Antiterrorism Treaty

At the verbal level, the U.N. may appear tough on terrorism, having adopted many different antiterrorism treaties and conventions. But although there is a 1997 International Convention for the Suppression of Terrorist Bombing, UNRWA houses and schools serve as terrorist bomb-making centers. Although there is the 1999 International Convention for the Suppression of the Financing of Terrorism, the World Bank and other U.N. entities finance state sponsors of terrorism, and terrorist organizations such as Hamas. Although there is the 2005 International Convention Against Nuclear Terrorism, which supplements the 1970 Treaty on the Non-Proliferation of Nuclear Weapons, responsible U.N. agencies have done nothing meaningful to prevent the terrorist states of Iran and North Korea from attempting to build nuclear weapons, just as they did nothing to stop Saddam Hussein's nuclear program in the 1970s and 1980s.

There are U.N. treaties against hijacking, against violence at airports, against violence toward diplomats, against hostage taking, and against interference with maritime navigation. Nonetheless, the U.N. has for more than three decades honored and extolled Yasser Arafat and his terrorist PLO—the man and the group that invented the modern practice of terrorist airplane hijacking, who murdered numerous diplomats, kidnapped countless hostages, and hijacked the cruise ship *Achille Lauro*.

Nor has the U.N.'s tough talk about terrorism led to meaningful action. In 1999, Security Council Resolution 1267 created a sanctions committee that was supposed to name governments that assisted al-Qaeda and the Taliban financially, failed to freeze their assets, or allowed them to use the state's territory.[126] The committee has never been able to agree to name any government that violated Resolution 1267.[127]

On September 28, 2001, Security Council Resolution 1373 ordered all states to combat terrorism. The Resolution created a Counter-Terrorism Committee (CTC), which was supposed to receive mandatory reports from states about their antiterrorism measures. Yet the CTC has never named any state sponsor of terrorism, not has it named any individual or group as terrorist.[128]

In 2005, Kofi Annan urged the U.N. to adopt a comprehensive antiterrorism treaty. Sometimes called "the mother of all treaties," it was supposed to provide a wide-ranging global program against terrorism.[129] However, all 191 U.N. members have a seat on the treaty working group,[130] which means that the state sponsors of terrorism, and their allies, are solidly represented. The effort to negotiate the treaty collapsed in December 2005 because of the absence of agreement over a definition of terrorism.[131]

Kofi Annan, to his credit, pushed for compromise language: "Any action constitutes terrorism if it is intended to cause death or serious bodily harm to civilians or noncombatants with the purpose of intimidating a population or compelling a government or an international organization to do or abstain from doing any act."[132]

It was all for naught. Even though the U.N. has many official declarations against terrorism, the absence of a definition means that any terrorist, including terrorist states such as Syria, can simply define terrorism as something done only by their political enemies. Thus, Syria can proudly declare its opposition to all forms of terrorism.[133]

Some of the leaders of the pro-terrorist bloc have also argued that the treaty should prohibit "state terrorism."[134] State terrorism is certainly a real phenomenon, and Syria is one of its prime practitioners. But U.N. advocates of the "state terrorism" language in the draft treaty are not after stopping genuine state terrorism, but creating a new cudgel with which to bash the U.S. for liberating Iraq and Afghanistan, and to bash Israel for defending itself against terrorists.[135]

Nuclear Weapons for Terrorists

Imagine "a world without America." Such a world is "attainable, and surely can be achieved." This was the vision of Iranian president Mahmoud Ahmadinejad, speaking on October 26, 2005, at the World without Zionism conference in Tehran, where he called for the extermination of Israel. His chief adviser has announced, "We have established a department that will take care of England," and "England's demise is on our agenda."[136]

Most Americans still can't pronounce Ahmadinejad's name, but almost everyone saw him on television back in 1979, as one of the ringleaders of the hostage-taking at the American embassy in Tehran. Now he rules a theocratic tyranny that is rapidly developing the ability to engage in nuclear warfare. With Iran's long-standing ties to Hezbollah and other terrorist groups, he will soon have the means to deliver a nuclear device to a target, without the device being traceable to Iran.

The U.N. International Atomic Energy Agency (IAEA), based in Vienna and run by a thirty-five-member board of governors, is supposed to be about the business of stopping nuclear weapons proliferation; yet one member of the board of governors was Pakistan, which illegally developed its own atomic bombs and recklessly sold nuclear technology on the world black market, including to North Korea. Other pro-terrorist nations which have been to the board include Cuba, Syria, and Belarus.

For years, the IAEA, like the European Union, has been engaged in fruitless negotiations, pleading with Iran to give up its nuclear weapons program. In September 2005, the IAEA finally admitted the obvious, and declared that Iran was violating its obligations under the Nuclear Non-Proliferation Treaty, which has been in force since 1970. Yet it took until January 2006 for the IAEA to even consider referring Iran's violation to the U.N. Security Council, even though IAEA was required by its own statute to make a referral.[137] Kofi Annan, meanwhile, worked furiously to prevent the Security Council from looking into Iran's nuclear weapons development.[138]

The IAEA's inaction regarding the Iranian nuclear weapons program is reminiscent of its prior inaction about the Iraqi nuclear weapons. In the late 1970s, Saddam Hussein began developing a nuclear weapons program (under the pretext of building a civilian nuclear power industry in the oil-rich nation). The IAEA did nothing, and ultimately Israel ended the program by bombing the Osirik nuclear reactor in 1981.

Saddam was persistent. By 1991, as the IAEA would later admit, he was within twelve to eighteen months of being able to build a nuclear weapon.[139] Losing the Gulf War proved a big setback to his plans. He was still trying, apparently unsuccessfully, when he was finally deposed in 2003.

Saddam's best friend, the Syrian dictatorship, has been busy on its own nuclear weapons program. As the IAEA admits, the Syrians have been stonewalling IAEA inspectors, and Syrian explanations of the uranium traces that the IAEA did find are implausible. Yet IAEA continues to refuse to refer Syria's nuclear weapons program to the U.N. Security Council for potential Council action.[140]

Regarding Iranian nuclear terrorism—as with so many terrorism and genocide issues—the U.N. declares that it is the only entity with the legitimate right to authorize forceful action. Then, by refusing to authorize forceful action, it in effect gives the terrorists and genocidaires limitless freedom to carry out their evil plans.

The U.N. and the Iranian Dictatorship

The United Nations Security Council has embargoed the export of nuclear weapons materials to Iran. So although the Security Council could be criticized for not doing enough regarding Iran, it has at least done some good.

The more serious problem is how much of the rest of the United Nations actually *helps* the terror-sponsoring Iranian dictatorship. As I noted in the chapter on U.N. corruption, Iran has chaired the executive board of the United Nations Development Programme.

George Soros's man at the U.N., deputy secretary-general Mark Malloch Brown, was a top global apologist for the regime. He brushed off Iran's nuclear weapons program and its supplying of arms to the Hezbollah terrorists as just an expression of the regime's desire for "a normalization of its relationships and to be brought back into the international community."[141]

When the Iranian dictatorship stole the 2009 election and then unleashed weeks of murderous violence on the pro-democracy forces there, secretary-general Ban Ki-moon spent the first weeks just saying that he was aware of the situation, and monitoring it. Finally, his office put out a written statement that he was "dismayed."

In contrast, when Israel counterattacked the terrorists in Gaza in late December 2008, Ban went into what his spokeswoman called "around-the-clock efforts with world leaders" to try to make the Israelis stop. Ban proclaimed that he was "deeply dismayed" and "deeply alarmed." He called Israeli actions "outrageous, shocking and alarming" and said he was so "appalled" that he could not even describe how he really felt.[142] These latter comments were in response to U.N. claims that Israel had shelled a U.N. school; as it turned out, the claims were false.

The United Nations Human Rights Council picked Iran's president Mahmoud Ahmadinejad to deliver the opening address at its 2009 Durban II conference on racism, where Ahmadinejad delivered a racist diatribe against Israel.

The Food and Agriculture Organization allowed Ahmadinejad to deliver a speech at its 2009 conference in Rome, where he blamed global hunger on Western democracies.[143]

The U.N. Human Rights Council—which is even more hostile to human rights than was its disgraced predecessor the Commission on Human Rights—has terminated the investigation of human rights abuses in Iran.[144]

A report by Brett Schaefer and Steven Groves of the Heritage Foundation provides a litany of Iran's violations of the terms of its U.N.

membership. The U.N. Charter demands that all member states be "peace loving" and that they "shall refrain in their international relations from the threat or use of force against the territorial integrity . . . of any state."[145]

Yet the Iranian regime repeatedly calls for the destruction of Israel, and supplies arms to Hezbollah and Hamas in their own wars to exterminate the Israelis. The Iranian dictatorship has provided refuge to top leaders of al-Qaeda.[146] It has armed al-Qaeda and other terrorists in Iraq.[147]

All in flagrant violation of numerous U.N. Security Council resolutions on terrorism and the Middle East.[148]

Yet this rogue regime, which is building offensive nuclear weapons, won reelection as vice-chair of the U.N. Disarmament Commission.[149] This also happens to be the U.N. body in charge of the global antigun campaign.

If the U.N. acted according to its own charter, Iran should have been expelled long ago, and the Security Council should have authorized all nations to take whatever forceful action is necessary to stop the regime's international terrorist aggression.[150]

The Lebanese terrorist organization Hezbollah is the vanguard of Iran's global war. Israelis are not the only victims. Hezbollah perpetrated the 1983 bombing of the U.S. embassy in Beirut (sixty-three dead), the bombings of U.S. and French barracks in Lebanon that same year (more than three hundred dead), the 1985 hijacking of a TWA airliner, and the 1994 bombing of a Jewish community center in Argentina (eighty-five dead).[151]

The commander of these terrorist attacks was Imad Mughniyah, who was killed (presumably by Israel) in Damascus on February 12, 2008. Iranian Revolutionary Guards general Mohammad Ali Jaafari sent Hezbollah a condolence note, predicting the imminent disappearance of "the cancerous bacterium called Israel." The Iranian general was upset, since Mughniyah had worked closely with Iran in joint training exercises of the Iranian Revolutionary Guard and Hezbollah, and in global terrorism attacks.[152]

In an interview on Iranian television, Hezbollah's terrorist chieftain, Sheik Hassan Nasrallah, proclaimed his utter subservience to his Iranian masters: "We are ready to be torn apart, spliced into tiny pieces, so that Iran will remain exalted . . . I am a lowly soldier of the Imam Khamenei. Hezbollah youths acted on behalf of the Imam Khomeini."[153]

Self-Defense Is Not a Privilege

The ultimate conflict of our times—a conflict that the U.N.'s pro-terrorism actions force us to confront directly—is between civilization and barbarism. We know the Second Amendment protects our right to self-defense—including self-defense against tyrants and terrorists. This right was not invented by the American Founders, but instead has roots that are as old as civilization itself. Ancient Greece and Rome recognized the right. The right has been expounded by Jewish scholars studying the Torah and Talmud, and by Christian scholars explaining self-defense as part of the natural law that God inscribes on every human heart. It is a right extolled by Confucius and by the great Taoist philosophers of ancient China. And it is a right recognized for many centuries by the great scholars of legitimate (and antiterrorist) Islamic law.

Against this vision of civilization is the barbaric principle of the U.N. and its proxies, such as IANSA, that self-defense is a privilege that the government can and should take away. If the U.N. can take away anyone's legitimate self-defense rights, it can take away everyone's. And, indeed, it is trying to do precisely that—to prohibit you from owning any firearm for personal and national protection.

As a moral issue, it doesn't matter whether an innocent victim is attacked by a lone criminal, by disorganized gangs of predators (as in New Orleans after Hurricane Katrina), by organized criminals kidnapping girls for sex slavery (as in Cambodia or Albania), by U.N.-funded terrorists, or by a terroristic, genocidal government. The innocent have a right to own firearms to defend themselves anywhere and everywhere.

It is this right that the U.N. and its terrorist allies are working aggressively to destroy, and the National Rifle Association vows to fight them every step of the way.

Chapter 15

The U.N., the Internet, and a Free Press

Just as there is a powerful movement to "control" private ownership of firearms out of existence, using the tendrils of the United Nations, there is an equally dangerous effort to "control" the most effective means that free people have ever possessed to express the political ideals needed to preserve or gain their liberty—the Internet.

The Internet is solely an American creation, born as an integral part of our national defense. We share it with the world as the most open avenue for free expression and the exchange of ideas ever created. It reflects the principles contained in America's unique First Amendment. It also serves to protect what is becoming recognized as a most basic human right for all peaceable peoples—the individual right to own and use firearms.

But the Internet, as Americans know it and use it, is in danger, especially if it falls under the influence of the U.N. and its allies. When you think of global Internet control, think global gun control. They are the same thing—the taking of individual freedom by international despots.

A few headlines tell a powerful story about what is beginning to happen to American's First Amendment rights.

"U.N. to Control Use of Internet?"[1] "E.U. Wants Shared Control of Internet."[2] "China Again Tightens Control of Online News and Information."[3] "China charges U.S. monopolizes the Internet, seeks global control."[4]

The article that goes with that last headline, published by the *World Herald Tribune*, reported that China's U.N. ambassador demands international Internet control:

Sha Zukang told a U.N. conference that controls should be multilateral, transparent and democratic, with the full involvement of governments, the private sector, civil society and international organizations.

"It should ensure an equitable distribution of resources, facilitate access for all and ensure a stable and secure functioning," he said at the conference on Internet governance.

Sha said China opposes the "monopolization" of the Internet by one state, a reference to the United States, which ultimately controls the digital medium.

China? Democratic? Transparent? Let's inject a little reality here. For a feel of what life would be like for Americans were the Internet in the hands of a U.N. body controlled by the likes of China, look no farther than the laws and regulations that nation uses to repress the Chinese people's speech on the Internet.

A remarkable white paper, "Freedom of Expression and the Internet in China: A Human Rights Watch Backgrounder," says, "As of January 2001, sending 'secret' or 'reactionary' materials over the Internet became a capital crime."[5]

Human Rights Watch (HRW) reports that the People's Republic of China (PRC), through its Ministry of Public Security, issued a series of decrees including "Regulations for the Safety Protection of Computer Information Systems," requiring that "all Internet users register with a police bureau in their neighborhood within thirty days of signing up with an ISP. Police stations in provinces and cities followed up on this almost immediately. They also set up computer investigation units."[6]

As Tom Malinowski, HRW's Washington Advocacy Director, points out:

The stakes here are much greater than the future of freedom in China. China is already exporting technology for monitoring the Internet to other repressive governments—Zimbabwe, for example. And such governments in every part of the world are now watching to see if China can bend Internet providers to its will. If China succeeds, other countries will insist on the same degree of compliance, and the companies will have no standing to refuse them. We will have two Internets, one for open societies, and one for closed societies. The whole vision of a world wide web, which breaks down barriers and empowers people to shape their destiny, will be gone. Instead, in the 21st Century, we will have a virtual Iron Curtain dividing the democratic and undemocratic worlds.[7]

Of all the amazing technological developments I have seen in my lifetime, I would have to say that the creation and growth of the Internet has had the most profound effect on the dissemination of knowledge and the sharing of ideas. With a relatively small investment of money and training, someone in a cabin a hundred miles from the nearest town can search the world's most prestigious libraries or communicate instantly with individuals on the other side of the world. As the U.S. Supreme Court has noted, "Through the use of chat rooms, any person with a phone line can become a town crier with a voice that resonates farther than it could from any soapbox."[8]

In the same instant, we can express our views and convince others to share our ideas and ideals. And just as the ability to print and disseminate the written word changed the political face of the medieval world, so has the Internet opened a whole new means of political discussion in our time. As Americans accustomed to our freedom of speech, we see this development as positive—an opportunity to consider any political notion—or to promote any idea.

And as Americans, we should be grateful for the speech Secretary of State Clinton gave on Internet freedom at the Newseum in Washington, D.C., on January 21, 2010. It would by a colossal understatement to say that I—and other gun owners—have had great disagreements (see chapter 18) with Hillary Clinton, but I applaud her Internet speech. She said:

There are many other networks in the world [but] the Internet is a network that magnifies the power and potential of all others. And that's why we believe it's critical that its users are assured certain basic freedoms . . .

As I speak to you today, government censors are working furiously to erase my words from the records of history. But history itself has already condemned these tactics. Two months ago, I was in Germany to celebrate the 20th anniversary of the fall of the Berlin Wall. The leaders gathered at that ceremony paid tribute to the courageous men and women on the far side of that barrier who made the case against oppression by circulating small pamphlets called samizdat. These leaflets questioned the claims and intentions of dictatorships in the Eastern Bloc, and many people paid dearly for distributing them. But their words helped pierce the concrete and concertina wire of the Iron Curtain . . .

Some countries have erected electronic barriers that prevent their people from accessing portions of the world's networks. They have expunged words, names and phrases from search engine results. They have violated the privacy of citizens who engage in non-violent political speech. These actions contravene the Universal Declaration on Human Rights, which tells us that all people have the right "to seek, receive and impart information and ideas through any media and regardless of frontiers." With the spread of these restrictive practices, a new information curtain is descending across much of the world. Beyond this partition, viral videos and blog posts are becoming the samizdat of our day.[9]

To a tyrant or a demagogue, nothing could be more threatening than the free exchange of ideas. Nothing could be more dangerous than the notion that governments exist at the sufferance of their citizens. That an individual can better choose how to live and take care of family and community than a bureaucratic behemoth such as the U.N., for example, simply does not compute. The deep-seated urge to control how people live or what they think is basic—from the pettiest dictator to the most bloated bureaucracy.

We have seen how the desire to manipulate information and ideas works, even in the United States. Can we count on the national media for a factual accounting of issues relating to our Second Amendment rights? Hardly ever. When did you read or hear anything fair or factual about firearms rights or about the Second Amendment or NRA in the national mainstream media? The Internet has changed the old media's monopoly of information.

Anyone who wants to examine all aspects of an issue can do so freely, without what NBC's Tom Brokaw called a "gatekeeper"—a network filter to politically cleanse what you learn. But that information is available on the Internet. How threatening this freedom must be to those accustomed to presenting their own opinion as fact, and manipulating fact to support their own opinion. To be challenged by a well-informed audience—dangerous!

Most of the people in the world cannot begin to imagine the freedom we have here. And we have a hard time imagining what it would be like *not* to have that freedom. Envision this. You are sitting at your computer, ready to take action against a gun ban pending before Congress, a ban the media says will likely become law. First, you do what you always do, seek the most up-to-date and accurate facts and information. Your local newspaper says the gun ban will be a great benefit to society. The national media is touting it. You want access to the truth so you can convince your friends and neighbors to contact their senators and representatives.

You type in the URL for the National Rifle Association—www.nra.org—and you get an error message: "Host not found." Then you type the Web address of a civil liberties think tank—a known, proven source for accurate information and analysis—and you find yourself looking at a screen saying, "Content blocked."

You can access the Violence Policy Center and the Brady Campaign. No problem. But every pro-gun site is blocked or filtered. Nothing is coming into your in-box from any of the pro–Second Amendment online newsletters you always get. Nothing from your state association. Their sites are blocked as well.

So you send an e-mail to your state representative and U.S. senators telling them about the Internet blackout and urging them to vote against the gun-ban legislation, and you copy the e-mail to friends and family and coworkers who care about First Amendment rights as a shield for the Second Amendment. Your e-mails are blocked. Your urgent political speech falls into a cyber trash can, while the voices of those hyping the bans on speech and gun ownership sail through. Your in-box fills with returned mail, with cover messages listing the "Postmaster" at the address of your Internet Service Provider (ISP) saying, "Action: failed" or "Status: Permanent failure—no additional status information available."

As a hedge, you consider sending your congressional letters through the U.S. Postal Service—but the bill is up for floor action in three days, and you know your message of opposition won't arrive in time because federal mail screening to counter active terrorism threats causes weeks or months of delays in delivery to Congress.

You try again to reach the site of your activist state association, and you get a new error message: "ACCESS FORBIDDEN BY THE UNITED NATIONS INTERNET GOVERNANCE AUTHORITY. Your attempted access has been recorded."

You go to another pro-gun site, and it is there, but wait a minute—the headline on the main page says they *support* the gun ban. The site has been hacked, the original content dumped, and fraudulent material added.

The International Telecommunication Union (ITU) is a U.N. agency based in Geneva. Its purpose is to create standards for international telecommunication—for example, so that the phone systems in different nations can interoperate. But now, it is engaged in a much more ominous project.

At the behest of the Chinese government, the ITU is creating Internet standards to eliminate anonymity, so that the government would always be able to trace the source of any communication. An ITU document that was leaked to the technology news site CNET described the problem that the new ITU standards are meant to overcome: "A political opponent to a government publishes articles putting the government in an unfavorable light. The government, having a law against any opposition, tries to identify the source of the negative articles but the articles having been published via a proxy server, is unable to do so protecting the anonymity of the author."

The ITU is working in secret, and U.S. government officials are also participating. The final proposal has not yet been released, and there is evidence that some members of the ITU committee oppose the elimination of anonymity. The ITU does not have the power to impose a new standard, but governments usually adopt whatever the ITU says. Arguably, the proposal would be unconstitutional in the United States. The Supreme Court's 1995 decision in *McIntyre v. Ohio Elections Commission* affirmed, "Under our Constitution, anonymous pamphleteering is not a pernicious, fraudulent practice, but an honorable tradition of advocacy and of dissent. Anonymity is a shield from the tyranny of the majority."[10] However, State Department legal adviser Harold Koh has already written that the First Amendment should be narrowed to be harmonious with international standards, as I discuss in chapter 20.

The ITU's effort to take over the web should have been easy to resist, since the ITU only has jurisdiction over "telecommunications." For decades, it was generally agreed that government authority to regulate telephone calls did not include the authority to control computer communications. But in the United States, the Obama-controlled Federal Communications Commission (FCC) is moving to claim that the Internet is part of "telecommunications services."

Robert McDowall, a dissenting FCC Commissioner, warns that the FCC's decision could "trigger ITU and, ultimately, U.N. jurisdictions over parts of the Internet." He warns that the United States has no veto at the ITU, "and may not be able to stop it."[11]

China Censors the Internet

All of these things—all of this censorship, including replacing site content—are already worldwide realities for millions of people today. A chilling account of Internet repression—including some of the error messages I cited—was recently published in the London *Independent*. Author Daniel Howden wrote: "China remains the benchmark in censorship. Beijing has cajoled major U.S. players such as Google, Microsoft and Yahoo into adapting their sites and services to suit the censors. A Chinese web surfer typing the word [*sic*] 'democracy' or 'freedom' or 'human rights' into their server will probably receive an error message announcing: 'This item contains forbidden speech.'"[12]

Howden quoted Brad Adams, Asia director of Human Rights Watch, saying, "When companies like Yahoo!, Microsoft, and Google decide to put profits from their Chinese operations over the free exchange of information, they are helping to kill that dream."

China's rapidly growing technological skill, in league with greedy big business, gives the government the means to track and control Internet use. China has been particularly outspoken in its goal of controlling the flow of "dangerous" ideas. Its U.N. ambassador, Sha Zukang, in March 2005 told a U.N. Conference: "It is of crucial importance to conduct research on establishing a multilateral governance mechanism that is more rational and just and more conducive to the Internet development in a direction of stable, secure and responsible functioning and more conducive to the continuous technological innovation."[13]

At this same moment, China closed forty-seven thousand Internet cafés. "The cafes closed in the crackdown had been 'admitting minors and engaged in dissemination of harmful cultural information,' the Communist Party newspaper *People's Daily* said on its Web site."[14]

Equally disturbing was a report that aired on *Radio Free Europe*:

[R]epresentatives of a group of social investment funds meeting in San Francisco drew attention to another issue that Beijing would prefer not to see in the media, namely the role of Western Internet companies in allegedly helping the Chinese Communist Party suppress free speech and political activism at home.

The investor group and Reporters Without Borders charged that firms including Yahoo, Cisco, Microsoft, and Google face risks in "collaborating to suppress freedom of opinion and expression." The critics called attention to a case in which Yahoo reportedly provided information about one Chinese journalist's e-mails that enabled the authorities to send him to jail.[15]

The following was filed earlier in 2005 by the same Radio Free Europe reporter:

On 16 June, state media reported that the Beijing Security Service Corporation, which is run by the police, is setting up a new Beijing Internet Security Service and is looking for 4,000 recruits to staff it. About 800 of them will go to Internet cafes throughout the city and most of the rest to various other Internet-related businesses. Among their duties will be to "delete all kinds of harmful information" as a part of a drive that is reportedly being extended to other cities as well.[16]

And in a January 17, 2006, editorial, the *New York Times* said:

Microsoft has silenced a well-known blogger in China for committing journalism. At the Chinese government's request, the company closed the blog of Zhao Jing on Dec. 30 after he criticized the government's firing of the editors at a progressive newspaper. Microsoft, which also acknowledges that its MSN Internet portal in China censors searches and blogs, is far from alone. Recently Yahoo admitted that it had helped China sentence a dissident to 10 years in prison by identifying him as the sender of a banned e-mail message.

Even as Internet use explodes in China, Beijing is cracking down on free expression, and Western technology firms are leaping to help. The companies block access to political Web sites, censor content, provide filtering equipment to the government and snitch on users. Companies argue that they must follow local laws, but they are also eager to ingratiate themselves with a government that controls access to the Chinese market.[17]

The *Times* more recently noted, "Starting in late 2008, the Chinese government shut down thousands of Web sites under the pretext of an antipornography campaign."[18]

Indeed, bloggers do not escape Chinese government censorship, either. "Web sites and portals must now 'give priority' to news and opinion material that have already appeared in the state-run print media. This seemingly puts a stop not only to freewheeling, opinion-driven blogging but also to the use of the Internet to break and develop news stories that the official media have not reported . . . the new rules could be interpreted broadly enough to enable the authorities to punish anyone who sends friends an e-mail describing a local riot."[19]

Expanding Internet censorship from an internal function to an international reality is a short step. Obviously, our free exchange of ideas is anathema to countries such as China. The notion of using a U.N. bureaucracy to gain greater control over the free dissemination of thought among their citizens is very attractive.

"In my opinion, freedom of speech seems to be a politically sensitive issue. A lot of policy matters are behind it," observed Houlin Zhao, the man who wants to control the greatest forum for free expression in history. As a director of the U.N.'s International Telecommunication Union (ITU) and a former senior Chinese government official, Zhao is a leader in the world body's effort to supplant the U.S. government in the supervision of the Internet.[20]

China, of course, is not the only U.N. member determined to control the free flow of information on the Internet. Take Syria, for example:

> Today the Syrian government relies on a host of repressive laws and extralegal measures to suppress Syrians' right to access and disseminate information freely online. It censors the Internet—as it does all media—with a free hand. It monitors and censors written and electronic correspondence. The government has detained people for expressing their opinions or reporting information online, and even for forwarding political jokes by e-mail. Syrian bloggers and human rights activists told Human Rights Watch that plainclothes security officers maintain a close watch over Internet cafes.[21]

How about Cuba? The group Reporters without Borders (in French, Reporters sans Frontières) reports that under dictator Fidel Castro's iron fist, "Internet use is very restricted and under tight surveillance. Access is only possible with government permission and equipment is rationed. [A] Cuban who wants to log on to it or use public access points must have official permission and give a "valid reason" for wanting to and sign a contract listing restrictions."[22]

Castro, by the way, was named "World Hero of Solidarity" by the U.N. General Assembly in 2009.[23]

And then there is Iran. On February 11, 2010, Reporters without Borders condemned that government's "latest offensive against the Internet coinciding with celebrations marking the Islamic Revolution's thirty-first anniversary. Online access has again been disrupted, as it is whenever opposition protests are expected."

The press freedom group noted further:

> Unable to control the new media, the [Iranian] government has responded by resorting to cyber-attacks, filtering and blocking undesirable websites, including conservative sites at times. It has also developed its online surveillance capabilities, it has put government propaganda online and it has made many arrests. But it still has not been able to stop unwanted information circulating online. At least 18 bloggers and netizens are currently detained.[24]

Conspiracy against the Free Flow of Information

The U.N. World Summit of Information Society (WSIS) was held in mid-November 2005 in Tunis, Tunisia. It was a follow-up of a meeting held in Geneva, Switzerland, under the aegis of the U.N.'s ITU. The Tunis meeting was one of a series of U.N. events in which participants discussed a variety of difficulties affecting worldwide use of the Internet—from practical problems such as spam, cybercrime, and securing the Internet against terrorism, to Internet access in third-world countries. At the same time, the WSIS provided a platform for attacks on U.S. stewardship over the Internet.

And, in what seems like some kind of a U.N. in-joke, not only is the ITU headed by a representative from Communist China; the U.N. WSIS was held in an especially repressive country, Tunisia. None of this was lost on New Zealand journalist Gwynne Dyer, who noted:

> The scenes in Tunis itself reinforce the notion that this conference is really a conspiracy against the free flow of information.
> Tunisian police rough journalists up outside the conference centre, and an alternative "Citizens' Symposium on the Information Society" finds its reservations for hotel meeting rooms mysteriously canceled.

Seven leading Tunisian figures including the head of the Union of Tunisian Journalists are on hunger strike to demand greater freedom of speech in their own country while the world's attention is temporarily turned their way.[25]

Another concerned journalist, Rohan Jayasekera, who is a Toronto-based Internet expert, noted with justifiable alarm: "In the run up to the 16–18 November conference, Christophe Boltanski, a journalist with the Paris daily *Liberation*, was tear-gassed, beaten and stabbed in Tunis under the eyes of police who later refused to log his assault. The attack occurred less than 24 hours after *Liberation* ran Boltanski's story on how plain-clothes police had beaten human rights activists in the weeks before WSIS."[26]

Much closer to home, former Delaware governor Pete du Pont wrote in the *Wall Street Journal*'s online *Opinion Journal*:

When the U.S. attends those IGF [Internet Governance Forum] meetings, our representative will surely be reminded of the repeated advice Tony Mauro, the Supreme Court correspondent for *The American Lawyer*, recalls receiving from Europeans at a run-up meeting of the U.N. Internet group in Budapest three years ago. *Do not invoke the First Amendment in Internet discussions, he was told, for it is viewed as a sign of U.S. arrogance.*

If the U.N. establishment believes free speech is arrogance, we can be confident that U.N. control of the Internet would be calamitous.[27]

Perhaps the most outrageous critic of U.S. maintenance of the Internet is Robert Mugabe, the dictator of Zimbabwe. Bitter, jealous, and oozing paranoid suspicion, he illustrates the fear in the heart of every tyrant. The U.N. actually seems to give credence to this racist lunatic. Judge for yourself—here is Mugabe in his own words:

Yes, we seek equal access to information and the control of communication technologies whose genesis in fact lies in the quest for global hegemony and dominance on the part of rich and powerful nations of the north. The ICTs [Information and Communications Technologies] that we seek to control and manage collectively are spin-offs from the same industries that gave us the awesome weapons that are now being used for the conquest, destruction and occupation of our nations. The ICTs by which we hope to build information societies are the same platforms for high-tech espionage, the same platforms and technologies through which virulent propaganda and misinformation are peddled to de-legitimise our just struggles against vestigial colonialism, indeed to weaken national cohesion and efforts at forging a broad Third World front against what patently is a dangerous imperial world order led by warrior states and kingdoms.[28]

Mugabe then offers his two cents' worth on the war against terrorism in Iraq:

My country Zimbabwe continues to be a victim of such aggression, with both the United Kingdom and United States using ICT superiority to challenge our sovereignty through hostile and malicious broadcasts calculated to foment instability and destroy the state through divisions. Our voice has been strangled and our quest to redeem a just and natural right has been criminalized. Today we are very clear. Beneath the rhetoric of free press and transparency is the iniquity of hegemony. The quest for an information society should not be at the expense of our efforts towards building sovereign national societies."[29]

U.N Moves to Curtail Free Speech

In a 2007 joint declaration, U.N. secretary-general Kofi Annan, the European Union foreign policy coordinator, and the secretary-general of the Organisation of the Islamic Conference announced that the United Nations Human Rights Charter would be rewritten to "protect the sanctity of religions and the prophets." In other words, freedom of speech would be curtailed to prevent criticism of Islam.

In 2007, the U.N. General Assembly passed, by a vote of 108 to 51, a resolution against the "defamation" of religions. Islam was the only religion specifically mentioned in the resolution.[30] "Defamation" as used in the resolution is not what free countries call "defamation"—which is knowingly telling damaging lies about someone. Rather, in the Islamic countries that successfully pushed the General Assembly resolution, people are criminally punished for "defamation" for any criticism of Islam, even if the criticism is factually correct, and even if (*especially if*), the critic is a Muslim who is pointing out problems with the government-controlled version of Islam.[31] The resolution was passed again in 2009.[32] The vote provides a pretext for domestic laws against criticizing the government's version of Islam or whatever other religion the government favors, and provides the starting point for the fabrication of an international law "norm" against speech that offends a religious or ethnic group.

The Obama administration made things worse by cosponsoring, with Egypt, a similar resolution that passed the Human Rights Council. Even the normally timid Europeans found the resolution's tolerance for repression so worrisome that they objected.[33]

The U.N. has also moved to suppress media that shed light on how the U.N. itself really works. The *Inner City Press* is a small online newspaper in New York City with in-depth coverage of the United Nations. In February 2008, Google eliminated the *Inner City Press* from its search results, so that a person searching for information about the U.N. (or, for that matter,

411

entering "Inner City Press" as a search term) would never find the *Inner City Press* website.

Google said that it had taken the actions because of a single complaint against the *Inner City Press*, and Google refused to disclose who had made the complaint. However, circumstantial evidence indicated that the complainant was probably the United Nations Development Programme (UNDP) which was irked about a recent *Inner City Press* story exposing problems at the UNDP. As I explain in chapter 10, on U.N. Corruption, the UNDP is at the forefront of the U.N.'s global gun confiscation program; from 1999 to 2005, George Soros's man at the U.N., Mark Malloch Brown, ran the UNDP.

When other media began reporting on the Google/U.N. censorship, Google relented and restored *Inner City Press* to its search results.[34] U.N. assistant secretary-general Michael Adlerstein asked a representative of the *Inner City Press*, "How should you be punished?"[35]

Adlerstein has apparently found the answer, as part of the renovation of U.N. headquarters he is overseeing. In May 2009, U.N. officials, in a closed-door meeting, brought forth a plan to start charging the press rent for using space at the U.N. The annual fee would be twenty-three thousand dollars for print, and seventy thousand dollars for broadcast media. The pretext for the fee is that some U.N. offices are going to have to pay rent in other buildings while the renovation takes place, but the plan is that the media rent charges will continue even after the renovation is completed and everyone moves back to the headquarters building.

The U.N. is also planning to move journalists into an open area with un-walled offices. The absence of walls obviously makes private communication impossible, turning the journalist workspace into a "whistleblower-free" zone.[36]

Charging rental to the media is certainly not the norm in the United States. The White House does not do so, nor does the U.S. Department of State, nor does New York City Hall. After all, the taxpayers have already paid for the buildings used by government organizations (including the U.N.), so those organizations have a duty to make themselves accessible to media who can tell the taxpayers what is going on at those organizations. At the U.N., General Assembly resolutions affirm that the U.N. should make itself easy for the media to cover.[37]

At a time when print media are already under severe economic pressure, the U.N. is in effect making the press pay a tax equal to half or a third of the salary of a full-time reporter, just to have a reporter at the U.N. For small media, such as the *Inner City Press*, the cost may perhaps be enough to force a drastic reduction in coverage. Which might be just what the U.N. wants.

The U.N. has many thousands of employees, and plenty of them work hard and try to make the world better. The U.N. has been shutting down their freedom of speech too. For example, the U.N.'s own computer system blocks employees from viewing websites that criticize anti-CNN.com (a Chinese website) or Islam.[38] The problem has grown so severe that the U.N. Staff Council passed a resolution calling on the U.N. administration to stop "censorship, harassment, intimidation or punishment, or the threat or implication thereof." One of the worst offenders has been the United Nations Development Programme.[39]

The U.N. is also quite cooperative with dictatorships that want to control and spy on U.N. employees. For example, the U.N. has allowed the Sudanese dictatorship to censor and block e-mail by the staff of the U.N. Mission in Sudan.[40] Likewise, as I discussed in the chapter on U.N. corruption, the U.N. allowed the North Korean government to monitor communications by U.N. employees in Pyongyang.

A small glimpse of a media future under U.N. control was seen at a U.N. Internet Governance Forum, held at Sharm El-Sheik, Egypt, in November 2009. Some activists from the OpenNet Initiative put up a poster criticizing the Great Firewall of China (China's censorship regime, which prevents Chinese web users from seeing sites that criticize the Chinese government, or discuss human rights in Tibet, or acknowledge Taiwan's independence). The head of the U.N. forum said that the poster was removed not because of content, but because the U.N. has a "no poster policy."[41]

That's a pretty dubious claim if you've ever been to one of the U.N.'s antigun conferences, which are replete with posters from gun ban lobbies.

U.N. Plans to Tax the Internet and Firearms

U.S. Supreme Court chief justice John Marshall observed that "the power to tax involves the power to destroy."[42] The United Nations has long been striving to create its own power to tax. A U.N. taxing power would make its bureaucracy freer to act against the interests and rights of the nations that pay most of the annual dues, starting with the United States. In addition, because the power to tax does create a power to destroy, or to control, the U.N. is aiming to assert taxing power over the Internet, and lots more.

At a little-reported conference in early 2006, secretary-general Kofi Annan called for taxing power for the United Nations. He wanted a tax on aviation fuel—supposedly to help the environment (by making air travel so expensive that fewer people would fly). He also wanted a U.N. tax on airplane tickets, and on air flight corridors (as if the U.N. owned the air route between Los Angeles and Melbourne). He also wanted to tax international currency transactions and carbon emissions—including a 4.8 cent per gallon tax on gasoline. The new taxes would total $200 billion per year.[43] In September 2010, sixty U.N. member governments announced that they were banding together to push a U.N. tax on international currency transactions.[44]

The World Health Organization is working on proposals for U.N. taxes on the Internet, on financial transactions, and on alcohol, tobacco, and arms. Regarding arms, the WHO wants a 10 percent tax on international arms sales.[45] So when you buy an imported gun, you'll pay a significantly higher price, for the benefit of the corrupt U.N. bureaucracy.

By the way, federal law prohibits government agencies from using taxpayer money to lobby for higher taxes. But United Nations officials use U.S. taxpayer money to lobby for more taxes on American taxpayers. Of course, any tax paid to the United Nations would destroy our American principle of "No taxation without representation."

Miguel d'Escoto, the Nicaraguan Communist who was president of the General Assembly, proposed that the U.N. create a Taxation Authority to regulate, or perhaps tax, the Internet.[46] In fact, the U.N. has begun setting up an Internet tax, without the consent of national governments, or of taxpayers. It's called the "Digital Solidarity Fund." At the 2005 World Summit, the U.N. called for the creation of a voluntary Digital Solidarity Fund. In the U.N.'s usual doublespeak, by "voluntary" they mean "mandatory."

Here's the way it would work: a local government—such as San Francisco, California, or Geneva, Switzerland—signs up for the plan. Anytime a high-tech company wants to do business with the local government, the price gets raised by an extra 1 percent. Of course the company will end up passing the cost along to consumers.

The money thus extracted from consumers gets passed on to the United Nations, which promises that it will use the money to pay for computers and other technology in poor countries. In 2005, at the World Summit of Cities and Local Authorities on Information Society (held in the vacation town of Bilbao, Spain), the delegates agreed to begin creating a World Agreement for Digital Solidarity; participating in the conference were the governments of Denver, Los Angeles, Houston, Nashville, Oakland, and San Francisco. Initially, the Fund is supposed to be voluntary (in the sense that local governments can choose whether or not to extort the 1 percent from the public), but the long-term objective is for the U.N.'s high-tech tax to be mandatory.[47]

ICANN and the Internet

A great deal of spleen from anti-American U.N. members has been directed at supposed U.S. control of the Internet. This ire is directed at a nonprofit organization in Marina Del Rey, California, called ICANN—the Internet Corporation for Assigned Names and Numbers. ICANN regulates top-level domain names such as ".com" and ".org." It determines what companies run the thirteen "root servers," the computers that hold the master list of all Web addresses worldwide.

Historically, ICANN worked under a memorandum of understanding (MOU) with the U.S. Commerce Department, which "plays no role in the internal governance or day-to-day operations of the organization."[48] As the Internet has grown into a worldwide entity, eight of its thirteen root servers are located outside the U.S. It is, in practice, an international organization.

However, the fact that a U.S. nonprofit corporation controls the domain names and addresses for the Internet is threatening to some of the more repressive or anti-American countries in the world. This issue was debated—but not resolved—at the U.N.'s Tunis summit.

Meetings and jawboning are the obvious products of the U.N.— but, as in meetings on the control of small arms, bureaucratic hot air can eventually result in concrete results. Envision the U.N.'s official gun control NGO, the International Action Network on Small Arms—IANSA—vetting your computer for "dangerous" speech.

In the face of international pressure to relinquish U.S. control of the Internet, the Bush administration firmly stated at the end of June 2005 that the management of root directories and domain names by ICANN would remain a U.S function. Michael D. Gallagher, assistant secretary at the National Telecommunications and Information Administration, said:

> The United States Government intends to preserve the security and stability of the Internet's Domain Name and Addressing System (DNS). Given the Internet's importance to the world's economy, it is essential that the underlying DNS of the Internet remain stable and secure. As such, the United States is committed to taking no action that would have the potential to adversely impact the effective and efficient operation of the DNS and will therefore maintain its historic role in authorizing changes or modifications to the authoritative root zone file.[49]

Speaking at a press conference at the Tunis Summit, ambassador David Gross, of the U.S. Department of State, expressed Bush administration support for the agreement that would, for the time being, leave the management of domain names to ICANN: "It [the agreement] reaffirms the importance of technology and particularly the Internet to the world . . . It focuses and refocuses and reaffirms the importance of the free flow of information . . . It reaffirms the importance of technology and particularly the Internet to the world. It preserves the unique role of the United States government in assuring the reliability and stability of the Internet."[50]

And in the same press conference, Michael Gallagher pointed out that "the Internet itself is not controlled by any single government; it is not controlled by any single person. It is a manifestation of the creativity and the genius of the world spirit."[51]

Ambassador Gross also made an important point, saying that the Internet has prospered "largely because governments have not played a dominant role; but rather, private enterprise and very importantly, individuals have done that. It has allowed for innovation, it has allowed for changes, both in terms of the network itself, and the applications, the sorts of software that run over the Internet. And that freedom to innovate is very, very important."[52]

In a pointed rebuke to regimes that stifle free speech on the Internet, John Marburger, White House Office of Science and Technology Policy director, told the Tunis Summit:

Phase I of this Summit produced a Declaration of Principles that was our shared focus on the ability of all peoples to access information through the reaffirmation of their right of freedom of opinion and expression.

It is vital that the Internet remain a neutral medium open to all in order to realize that access for our citizens. It is the role of governments to ensure that this freedom of expression is available to its citizens and not to stand in the way of people seeking to send and receive information across the Internet . . . The legacy of WSIS should be an environment that nourishes the growth of the Internet not only as a vehicle of commerce, but also as an extraordinary vehicle for freedom and personal expression.[53]

The possibility of the Internet being controlled by the U.N., or any other international entity, evoked a strong response by Congressional leaders. A sense of the Senate resolution introduced by Norm Coleman (R-MN) unanimously passed the Senate on November 18, 2005, and upheld the United States' role in overseeing the governance of the Internet. Senator Coleman said:

The Internet has flourished under the supervision and market-based policies of the United States.

This resolution makes clear the determination of the Senate to oppose any attempt by the United Nations or any other international group to control or politicize the Internet now or in the future. The potential risks to our economy, security, and freedom of expression are too profound to allow the World Wide Web to be governed by the U.N. or any other international entity.

The senator (who as I mentioned earlier unfortunately has been replaced in the Senate by the pro-U.N. and antigun Al Franken) went on to say:

The resolution supports the four governance principles articulated by the Bush administration on June 30, 2005. These are:

Preservation of the security and stability of the Internet domain name and addressing system (DNS).

Recognition of the legitimate interest of governments in managing their own country code top-level domains.

Support for the Internet Corporation for Assigned Names

and Numbers (ICANN) as the appropriate technical manager of the Internet DNS.

Participation in continuing dialogue on Internet governance in multiple existing fora, with continued support for marked-based approaches toward, and private sector leadership of, its further evolution."[54]

Senator Coleman also said the dispute is not over. "It has been put on hold, but it is not dead."[55]

On the House side, Rep. John Doolittle, (R-CA) introduced H. Con. Res. 268. The resolution, which also expressed the sense of the House that the U.S. should not relinquish control of the Internet to the U.N., passed 423 to 0. A press release from Representative Doolittle noted:

The United States invented the Internet and it has been our gift to the world, paid for by our taxpayers. The U.N.'s desire to take that gift as a means of increasing its power must be stopped.

If the U.N. were to be successful in its efforts to control the Internet, countries where human rights records range from questionable to criminal could be put in charge of determining what is and is not allowed to appear online. For example, we need only look back to 2003 when the U.N. decided that Libya, a country frequently condemned by human rights groups, was the U.N.'s choice to head its Human Rights Commission.[56]

However, in 2009, the Obama administration retreated from the firm line President Bush had drawn in the Tunisian sand. ICANN became an entirely independent body. It is now purely an international private corporation. It is supposed to take advice from a Governmental Advisory Committee, of which the United States is just one member.[57]

For the time being, ICANN has continued operating as it did before. But over the long term, ICANN will be increasingly under the influence of other governments, not one of which has the centuries-long commitment to the freedom of speech and of the press that we enjoy in America.

Not too long ago, I heard a pundit referring to "First Amendment Rights worldwide." I realized that we are so accustomed to free speech and a free press that we often forget that our precious American constitutional freedoms truly do not exist worldwide. Our Bill of Rights is a uniquely American document and is a threat to dictators and bureaucratic busybodies alike.

Were the U.N.—or the kinds of governments that dominate the U.N.—to gain influence over the most important means of communications in history since the invention of moveable type, you can bet globalist billionaire George Soros and his minions would be suppressing Internet access by those who oppose their world vision of a global gun ban. This fight, like the global efforts to disarm Americans, will never go away.

And neither will our duty to protect the sanctity of the First Amendment with the vigor equal to our defense of the Second Amendment. We had better not underestimate the monumental patience of international organizations like the United Nations. All of the seemingly useless summits and committees, the endless busywork of meetings and "programmes," can eventually bear fruit—and result in the loss of our God-given rights.

Chapter 16

Don't Trust Direct Democracy

F irst lesson is, don't trust direct democracy," said Rubem Fernandes.[1] At a United Nations forum, Lessons from the Brazilian Referendum, that country's self-appointed gun-ban czar showed an arrogant contempt for a free people.

That disdain for democracy by the likes of Fernandes's group, Viva Rio, is the core reason Brazilian citizens made world history by rejecting a total ban on civilian sales of firearms and ammunition in October 2005. In voting down the firearms prohibition by a 63 percent margin, 100 million voters chose for themselves a right that is universally rejected by the U.N. disarmament cadres. To the simple question, "Should the sale of firearms and ammunition be banned in Brazil?" they answered with a resounding "NO."

Fernandes later told assembled U.N. officials, World Council of Churches delegates, and representatives of a host of gun-control NGOs in New York, "The notion of rights came up . . . The debate on rights was new to Brazil . . . The notion of rights was new, it grew."

"'I have a right to a gun;' this was an argument that started weak and grew . . . The debate on rights rose as a very profound matter."[2] Fernandes said that putting the question to the very people he would disarm was a mistake: "First lesson is, don't trust direct democracy." This was a sentiment echoed in private conversations with other gun-ban advocates who were in an ugly, I-told-you-so mood.

Days before Brazilians went to the polls on October 23, 2005, the global gun-ban movement was electrified with a certainty that the world's first nationwide "civil disarmament" plebiscite would provide a huge payoff for their years of massive investments of time and money in propaganda campaigns and grassroots organizing.

The international and domestic forces arrayed to bring about the firearms and ammunition ban included a complex web of global gun-confiscation groups, official U.N. entities, private billionaires, foreign governments, leftist international church groups, the Brazilian government and much of the country's entertainment industry. All of this was stage-managed by a radical social engine called Viva Rio, and by the International Action Network on Small Arms (IANSA), which describes itself as "the organization officially designated by the U.N Department of Disarmament Affairs (DDA) to coordinate civil society involvement to the U.N. small arms process."[3]

IANSA head Rebecca Peters told the *Washington Post*, "If the ban is passed, then I definitely expect other countries to try the same thing."[4] Before the historic vote, IANSA was ecstatic in its prediction: "Brazilians will be able to vote in a radical referendum that is without precedent in the world . . . *for IANSA members in Brazil, the referendum is a huge opportunity and the culmination of years of campaigning* . . . Opinion polls show that 60 to 80% of Brazilians favour a prohibition on gun sales to civilians . . . a message that the majority of people do not believe that having guns in their communities makes them safer."[5]

In virtually all of the world press, there was a premature sense of celebration over the impending ban.

In an October 13, 2005, opinion piece titled "Follow Brazilian lead and close the arms industry," Terry Crawford-Browne, head of a South African gun-control group called Economists Allied for Arms Reduction, predicted the ban would pass in a 4-to-1 landslide. "The yes vote is being supported by a broad civil society coalition," Crawford-Browne wrote. "Churches, schools and universities are rallying around in solidarity that disarmament provides people with the greatest security."[6]

"Significantly," he wrote, "it is in the poor areas—the *favalas*—where this sentiment is strongest. Gangsters have in the past terrorized the residents with guns, and the people have responded that they intend to take control of their own lives." As for middle-class gun owners, he predicted a yes vote "with the realization that guns are often taken from their owners and used against them."

On the day of the voting in Brazil, the *Sunday Herald* in Scotland told its readers, "More than 122 million Brazilians will make history today by voting in the world's first national referendum on the sale of guns."[7]

Brazil made history, all right. And the vote was stunning in its breadth and depth. But it was a vote for freedom, not repression. The overwhelming pro-ban victory IANSA's Peters was predicting for the future of her whole civil disarmament movement was, in fact, a defeat on a cosmic level.

In a lengthy December 2005 interview in NRA's magazine, *America's 1st Freedom*,[8] Luciano Rossi, who was among the prime movers in the winning "No ban" campaign, provided an analysis of the vote—perhaps the only such breakdown published in the U.S. Rossi is the managing director of the firearms firm that has borne his family name for well over a century. The ban did not win anywhere, he said, not in any city, state, or with any segment of the population. The poor—the slum dwellers whose vote had been seen as a given and who were the object of millions in targeted expenditures—voted to defeat the ban.

"Maybe 40% of the 100 million people who went for voting that Sunday, maybe 40% know only how to write their own names. And we won with them. It was amazing."

The vote against the ban won in all twenty-six Brazilian states. As for urban areas where the poor were expected to obey the government propagandists, Rossi said the victory was "the stuff of history . . . In Rio, where all the criminals, the gangs, the banditos supported the ban . . . 64% said 'no!'"

"Some cities were 99%," Rossi said. "And the state in the north where the 'no' won by the smallest percentage, we won by 55%. I think if the campaign had lasted for one more week, it would be an even bigger victory all over the country—like 85%."

This was a true example of the most basic democratic process at work where the will of the people was expressed. It was the people versus the iron will of a cabal of self-appointed international civil disarmament groups not elected by anyone anywhere.

Indeed, this was history in the making, but it was history that was briefly rationalized, quickly forgotten, and even erased in many quarters. The reaction from U.S. antigun groups was virtual silence. They had not a word to say. But they—and particularly IANSA—were directly a party to the defeat.[9] Among the North American groups listed as IANSA members are the Brady Campaign, the Million Mom March, the Coalition to Stop Gun Violence, Join Together, and the HELP Network.

The same silence marked the response of the government of Brazil. It had invested massive effort and treasure in pressing for the ban. Politicians wanted the referendum to disappear, much like Soviet Union leaders who were airbrushed out of historic photographs. For the politicians in Brazil who supported the ban, there is good reason for silence: fear.

"There is no doubt that those people lost a lot of credibility, people who joined the ban, and number one was the president [Luiz Inácio] Lula," Rossi said.

"We have to thank him that he was the propaganda boy of the other side. For sure, he lost a lot of credibility with this try of taking rights away. And below him, just about every senator, congressman who got engaged on the pro-ban has been burned. I don't know how many will lose elections next year, but probably a lot of them."

While the global firearms-confiscation crowd would rather forget its crushing defeat, gun owners everywhere must study what happened in Brazil. That victory, that resonance with ordinary citizens of the world who understood that they possess a basic human right to own firearms, must be studied, amplified, and replicated.

Had the vote gone the other way, the media would have endlessly analyzed the issue, and proponents of the ban would be trumpeting it with every breath. It would be major news well into the future. The defeat, however, left the world press stunned and angry. The international media was desperate for excuses.

"Many in Brazil and abroad had hoped that a yes-vote on the referendum would make the world's fifth-largest nation an example to the many other countries where gun use is out of control, especially the U.S.," whined the indie-media website www.corpwatch.com.[10]

The *Khaleej Times* in Dubai, United Arab Emirates, was typical, saying, "Yet it is hard to justify the overwhelming opposition to gun sales ban. *It only goes to show that majority is not necessarily always right.*"[11]

That editorial rant continued, "It is believed that it is not so much that Brazilian voters' belief in the so-called right to own guns but their opposition to the extremely unpopular government of President Luiz Inácio Lula da Silva and its policies could have undermined the proposed ban . . . The proposed ban had wide support from human rights groups and the clergy before campaigning on the referendum began."

That was the same excuse offered in many U.S. publications. The big lie repeated and repeated was that the huge majority against the ban was nothing more than a vote against the Lula government.

The *Japan Times* tried a different spin:

Last Sunday in Brazil, a country with the second-highest rate of gun deaths on the planet, almost two-thirds of Brazilians voted against a total ban on the sale of firearms. Explain that.

Part of the answer was a ruthless media campaign by the local gun lobby that exploited the free television time both sides are granted in Brazilian referendums . . . They translated reams of propaganda from the National Rifle Association in the U.S. and pumped it out over the air unaltered, with the result that millions of Brazilians now believe they have a constitutional right to bear arms. (They don't.)[12]

This theme was echoed in many media outlets as well—the failure of the gun-ban referendum in Brazil was, they opined, the National Rifle Association's fault. While NRA has been aggressive in fighting the global metastasizing of gun control, and has a presence at the U.N., the assertion that the victory in Brazil hinged on NRA was overblown and diversionary to say the least.

In terms of protecting freedom in nations under attack from the likes of George Soros, Rebecca Peters, and their army of radical political carpetbaggers, something far more significant and far more remarkable happened in Brazil. The threat of the ban was the catalyst for an indigenous grassroots movement to protect what liberty the people had left. The truth is, the campaign against the ban was totally homegrown. It was purely the hard work of Brazilians telling other Brazilians the truth about what the ban would mean for their future.

Brazil was a remarkable turning point, and Brazilians who told the world what they stood for and what the gun-ban crowd stood for are due all of the credit. Above all, ordinary Brazilians saw the same flame that was lit in 1776. Rights. Liberty. Freedom. Self-protection. Protection of family.

What the organizers of the brilliant "No" campaign did take from NRA is what we hope all other such movements take—something all American gun owners would be more than willing to give: our love of freedom. And that love of freedom is what the gun-ban crowd fears the most worldwide.

In "Gunning for the World," *Foreign Affairs* observed: "The number of civilians in Brazil who legally own a gun is estimated to be only about 2 million. In other words, some 59 million Brazilians voted to preserve a prerogative the vast majority of them will never enjoy."[13]

That thought was a critical key to what really happened in Brazil. In all of the brief media lip-biting and blame-laying, almost no one went to the source of the winning campaign. No one except the editors at *America's 1st Freedom* asked Luciano Rossi how the victory came about. He explained in the December 2005 issue:

> At the beginning, when the subject of the referendum started to get hot, 40 days before the voting day, everybody was very much believing that with the strong lobby of network television, together with the government, would be strong enough to bring the victory to their side. Their target vote was mainly among the poor population which in Brazil, is by far the largest block.
>
> Every side of the "yes" and the "no" had 10 minutes every day on television to explain its ideas—time that is given each side by the government. (Allotted for 20 days leading up to two days before the actual voting.)
>
> So for our side, we developed a campaign that was designed to clarify what was really being decided. We made it very clear to the most simple people in Brazil, that what was in consideration was that voting "yes" to the ban means everybody will lose forever the right to buy a legal firearm.
>
> We said that we know that most of you don't have a firearm, don't now want to have a firearm, but by voting no, you are at least having the possibility of someday, if you want to buy a firearm, you can.
>
> In 20 days, it changed the whole debate. The people started really understanding what game was being played against them. It was fantastic, it was historical stuff that happened in Brazil.
>
> The mainstream media in Brazil was worked hard by Viva Rio and its axis. And also the U.N. directly in the form of UNESCO.

A year before the official campaigns for and against the referendum were allowed to begin, UNESCO, through the U.N. International Programme for the Development of Communication, provided significant funding to influence the outcome of the vote through a grant that "aims at increasing the quality and quantity of coverage . . . in the lead-up to the 2005 gun-ban referendum." Among the specifics was a zealous core of organized and trained "women from affected communities to build capacity for media advocacy and develop skills for working with journalists from all media."[14]

The recipient of this largesse was Viva Rio, which the UNESCO funding documents said "coordinates national and regional campaigns, including a women's disarmament campaign called 'Choose Gun Free! It's Your Weapon or Me,' and other projects and research programmes on disarmament in Brazil . . . News and information websites developed and hosted by Viva Rio will facilitate networking and communications."

As for the Viva Rio's arguments, its English website reveals a single-minded goal: "to reform permissive and inefficient legislation on arms control, seeking to end civilian use of firearms."[15] Among its disarmament efforts were "Public awareness campaigns on the need for civil disarmament [in order that] 'honest citizens' and their families do not become victims of their own guns in accidents or do not fall victim to armed assailants if they try to defend themselves with a gun."

For the beleaguered Brazilian population—the victims of real criminal violence—what Rossi and his allies offered made far better sense: the right to choose to exercise the basic human right to own a gun for self-defense. "Our argument was very well-focused. What will be the next right the government will take from you? It was like giving an electrical discharge on the people, to really wake up."[16]

In addition to recognizing the issue of gun ownership as a basic and universal human right, Rossi said that honest, law-abiding people began to realize that they were being punished for the acts of violent criminals.

"We started putting out our arguments, and saying, 'Look, the government is saying that the crime rate in Brazil is your fault—the fault of the law-abiding population!"

Remarkably, the truth of just who was committing violence was often spelled out in the media, but with a total disconnect between criminals and the honest citizens who would pay the price of disarmament.

In its hand-wringing about the defeat, corpwatch.com inadvertently made that point, saying, "Most of the gun-related violence has its roots in the cocaine trafficking."[17] Quoting a Dutch social worker in Rio, the article said, "And today gangsters have even more sophisticated weapons, such as laser-guided weapons they use to shoot police helicopters out of the sky . . . When quantities of these inexpensive and readily available weapons enter Brazil and get into the wrong hands at the wrong time, they transform criminal activities and gang rivalries into major wars; they turn minor, often domestic, incidents into massacres; change tranquil societies into battlegrounds; and undercut efforts for peace and reconciliation."

Another argument that Brazilian voters apparently found specious was that legal guns are a danger because they may be stolen and used by criminals. A Viva Rio propaganda piece titled "Brazil: Most crime guns start out legally" is typical:

> In Brazil, most of the crime guns seized by police were once legally owned, according to a report from the government of Rio de Janeiro state (Brazil), released on 3 October 2005.
>
> The findings disprove claims by the Brazilian gun lobby that the illegal gun trade is responsible for most gun crime in Rio de Janeiro, which suffers higher rates of gun violence than many war-torn regions.[18]

From the get-go in Brazil that was a theme of the civil disarmament crowd: if only we take guns from honest people, criminals will no longer be criminals. Like all gun control, at a local level, national level, or on a global scale, there is a universal failure of the gun-ban crowd to recognize any difference between good and evil—between honest citizen and criminal predator. But ordinary people—including the vast majority of Brazilians—understand the difference between good and evil, and they are the victims of evil every day.

Blaming law-abiding gun owners for the acts of real criminals was, Rossi explained, "like a punch on the face of the population, because the government was insisting that the high rate of murders in Brazil was being caused by people who had legal firearms. The pro-ban propaganda hid the truth about the murder rate which is one of the highest in the world—most of the killing is between gangs and drug dealers."

In addition to the radio and television campaign waged by the antiban forces, Rossi said a key news story helped change the political dynamic. It was something never revealed in the U.S. media.

"The outlaws from the slums in Rio de Janeiro, the drug dealers that control the slums 100%, it came up in the news that they were financing the pro-ban campaign. The banditos were financing it in the slums! Everybody got very angry, and said look, 'If the banditos are supporting the ban, something is wrong, you know?'"

Gun Bans and Soap Operas

Where the antiban side was limited to government allotted time, gun-ban forces had massive additional help from Brazil's Globo television network and its soap operas, which net huge audiences, especially among Brazil's poor. Rossi explained:

> The government was 100% sure that they could present distortion statistics, they could use artists of the soap operas. Because in Brazil, the population loves soap operas. There are three every day, different time between 6 o'clock at night and 9 o'clock at night, three different soap operas that have 65% of the televisions tuned on the Globo network television. This year, Globo Television

created fictional situations on their soap operas to start establishing on the brains of the people that firearms in the hands of legal guys were dangerous.

In fact, the use of soap opera stars and other entertainment and sports figures had been critical to enacting the 2003 law that brought the referendum into being. A story in the *Guardian* (London)—covering a protest march in Rio demanding passage of the "The Statute of Disarmament"—admired the effectiveness of daily dramatized propaganda:

> The protest had been heavily promoted in the soap opera "Women in Love." For weeks, the show's characters have talked about the march and their presence guaranteed a large turnout despite the weather.
>
> The popular soap opera, which threads together the stories of several women, has hit hard on the issue of gun violence in recent weeks. A scene where a character was killed by a stray bullet was front-page news last month, eclipsing many real killings.

But according to Rossi, that constant media propaganda and the enlistment of big television and movie stars in the ban campaign backfired: "The ban propaganda started very heavily with celebrities like 80% of the programs of television and then, like on day 10, when 50% of the days were done, they started collecting their polls; they were losing like crazy. And they just banned the celebrities. They just put those people away," he said.

Of all of the facts that came out in NRA's interviews with Rossi, a stunner was the cost: the equivalent of $200 million U.S. for the first-ever national referendum. Brazil is a relatively poor nation. But the real shock was something never mentioned anywhere in the U.S. media—the actual number of firearms that would have been subject to a ban on sales. Rossi said:

The whole country will spend about $80 million this year to buy all the apparel and the equipment for the police. And they spend $200 million on the referendum to ban the sale of under 2000 units a year! That's the number of guns allowed as legal sales. Two thousand. For 180 million people. It's unbelievable . . . That's the total legal civilian sales in Brazil. Everything. Shotguns. Rifles. Revolvers. It's almost a zero market already because, the new law that came into effect two years ago is so restrictive.

The Statute of Disarmament

So what was this new law that so discouraged legal commerce in firearms for Brazilian citizens? The Statute of Disarmament was adopted at the end of 2003 after a long and shrill campaign by a host of global pressure groups.[19] These players included U.N. entities such as UNESCO, a collection of U.N.-favored gun-ban NGOs such as IANSA, and, directly and indirectly, the governments of Canada and the United Kingdom, among others. (As host nation, the UK provides abundant financial support for IANSA.)[20]

Bear in mind that for years, law-abiding Brazilian gun owners have lived under very strict laws. They were limited as to the caliber of handguns: nothing larger than .38 caliber. They were limited to no more than fifty rounds of ammo a year. And they were limited in the number of firearms and types they could own.

There is never an end to the demands of the world gun-ban crowd. Rebecca Peters is fond of saying that the law merely "regulates" firearms, but in truth, for many poorer Brazilians the new law disarmed them or caused them to secretly fade into the ranks of good people that the likes of Peters can now call "gun criminals."

The Statute of Disarmament created a draconian system of universal firearms registration and gun owner licensing, all compounded with exorbitant fees beyond the reach of a majority of Brazilians.

To get a license to continue owning a firearm under the law, an ordinary citizen has to prove psychological fitness; undergo a background check in which even having been sued once in civil court is a disqualifier; must prove legal employment; and must provide "proof of technical capacity" to handle firearms. And he or she must present an approved reason to own a gun. All of this involves a complex bureaucracy of government and court officials at the federal, state, and military levels. Getting a license takes months. Additionally, it is unlawful for a citizen to openly carry a firearm for any reason.

Under the Statute of Disarmament, registration fees and reregistration fees alone made compliance impossible for millions of law-abiding Brazilian gun owners. Those fees amount to one-third of average family incomes in Brazil's rural states. And there was no grandfather clause to allow continued legal possession of firearms owned prior to the law's enactment.

The law further requires that guns seized by police be destroyed within forty-eight hours. Millions of legally owned guns, mostly common sporting arms, became "illicit small arms"—the U.N. term for contraband.

At the heart of the Brazilian gun ban were Lula's far-Left federal government, and Brazil's gun-ban lobby, Viva Rio. Campaigning on fear of violent crime—which indeed was rampant in urban Brazil—gun banners imposed harsh strictures on law-abiding Brazilians, making the continued ownership of firearms impossible for most of them.

A self-serving study created by Viva Rio claimed there are 15.5 million firearms in the hands of Brazilian citizens, and that 8.7 million of them are not registered and are therefore illegal.[21] For Brazilians fearful that continued gun ownership would make them criminals, the government created an amnesty period during which they could give up their guns and receive between $50 and $150 compensation, regardless of actual value. After that, firearms possession without registration and licensing became a no-bail criminal offense.

Unlike other firearm confiscation schemes in Canada, Australia, or England, this one was not aimed at any particular type of demonized firearm. No "assault weapons" or "Saturday Night Specials." This was directed at all guns—any guns in private hands.

The amnesty period in Brazil was accompanied by a political orgy of gun burnings and crushings, with confiscation advocates joyously participating. According to the Canadian group Project Ploughshares:

> The State Government of Rio, Brazil, in partnership with the NGO Viva Rio, organised the public destruction of 4,158 firearms . . . crushed with a steam roller. Three hundred rifles and shotguns were also destroyed in a pyre. This "Flame of Peace" was the first arms destruction by this method to take place in South America, and is a method favoured by the United Nations due to its strong anti-violence symbolism.[22]

For peaceable Brazilian gun owners, seeing their seized personal firearms go up in smoke had become a reality. For gun-ban groups pressing their war against individual freedom worldwide, Brazil had become paradise.

For its part, IANSA took a share of the credit, saying it "coordinated the third Week of Action Against Small Arms . . . with International Gun Destruction Day," and featured an event in Brazil where "6,500 illegal firearms confiscated by police were destroyed by Viva Rio, the Brazilian Army, and the Rio state government."[23]

This frontal attack on freedom was achievable only with generous financial assistance from the global disarmament community and propaganda from those who control the airwaves in Brazil. The massive gun collection and destruction program would receive a UNESCO prize in the Human Rights and Peace Culture category.[24]

In terms of the rats' nest of connections between activist gun-ban funders and participants in the Brazil gun-control free-for-all leading up to and including the referendum, look no farther than IANSA, Viva Rio, and the World Council of Churches (WCC).

The "Summary Report on the WCC's Microdisarmament Efforts 2000–2001" provides a glimpse at the complexity of the political and funding network.[25] I won't attempt to map these entangled relationships; let the WCC paint the picture:

> The WCC is a founding member of the International Action Network on Small Arms (IANSA), which it described as working to co-ordinate activities and campaigning by bringing together human rights organisations, foreign policy think tanks, gun control groups, development and humanitarian relief agencies, victim support groups, and local community and public health groups. IANSA has a range of objectives to reduce the demand for small arms by civilians.

The WCC is an active IANSA partner and is making its particular contribution through facilitating the formation of the Ecumenical Network on Small Arms (ENSA). It is also a member of the Geneva Action Network on Small Arms (GANSA), a working group of the NGO Committee for Disarmament, of which WCC is a board member.

Under "Capacity-building," the report says, "In the development of the Ecumenical Network on Small Arms, seed funding was provided," by what it calls "the Microdisarmament Fund," to Viva Rio, Brazil, for "the nationwide campaign, 'Enough, I Want Peace' (*Basta! Eu Quera Paz*) . . . particularly networking in community centres, as well as *training of partners in a large scale gun collection and destruction initiative*." (Emphasis added.)

Viva Rio

So there is a circle. This is global political and funding inbreeding on a colossal scale. Viva Rio, which rose from humble socialist activist beginnings in the early 1990s, has become a combination crypto-political party and quasi-government body, bloated by international foundation largesse and funding from foreign governments.

By its own description the NGO says, "Viva Rio is funded by the public sector (Federal, State and Municipal governments), the private sector (national private companies and multinational corporate organisations), foreign government development agencies (e.g., DFID of the U.K. government and DFAIT of the Canadian government), donor foundations (e.g., Ford Foundation), NGOs (e.g., Save the Children Sweden) and international agencies (e.g., UNESCO and UNICEF)."[26]

Viva Rio is also largely self-sufficient, funded by its own banking and venture-capital operations, which amount to profit centers based on an amalgam of socialism and capitalism. The only comparison to this party-state-business marriage is Communist China.

An article published by another NGO called South North Network Cultures and Development touted Viva Rio as "fully autonomous . . . It gets state and municipality subsidies and is increasingly self-sufficient thanks to its own profit-generating activities, e.g., the insurance brokers company, the microcredit bank, etc. Business is sponsoring its activities . . . 'Viva Rio' is a brilliant example of a lively social and cultural movement engendered by civil society . . . In this sense, it is a deeply democratic movement. Yet it is not reduced to US-inspired democracy, based on individualism."[27]

So what are Viva Rio's origins and how did it become so powerful in the global civil disarmament movement? A 2004 analysis of how Viva Rio came into being may also go a long way toward explaining why Brazilians overwhelmingly voted no on the gun-ban referendum.

Adèle Kirsten, former director of Gun Free South Africa (another IASNA partner), has attempted to explain the inception and growth of various national gun-ban movements including Viva Rio. Kirsten is a close associate of Rebecca Peters and a self-proclaimed "non-violent, social justice activist." She describes the origins of civil disarmament movements in Brazil and Australia as being similar, having been born out of what she called "defining moments": mass killings.

"Gun massacres in Australia and Brazil . . . acted as internal stimuli for social mobilisation in the fight against gun violence," she says.[28] But her attempt to connect the dots between the Port Arthur massacre in Australia and Brazil is truly bizarre. On one hand, the Australian government's 1997 confiscation and destruction of seven hundred thousand long guns that had been the lawful property of law-abiding Aussies came a year after a sociopath murdered thirty-five vacationers at Port Arthur, Tasmania.

On the other hand, the creation of Viva Rio and its ultimate rise as the center of the civil disarmament movement in Brazil, according to Kirsten, involved a 1993 massacre in which "eight street children were gunned down by police on the steps of the Candeleria church in central Rio de Janeiro."

Innocent vacationers senselessly murdered by a lone sociopath, children murdered on church steps by agents of the state—only a gun prohibitionist would see a parallel. And only a gun prohibitionist would think that you can prevent such atrocities by stripping away the means of self-defense from potential victims.

As seen by the repressive confiscation of firearms from law-abiding citizens—be they in Australia, Brazil, or England—the only way to enforce the "end to civilian use of firearms" is through the threat of government force or with the actual brutal application of police power.

Kirsten explains that in its newfound role of being an agent for civil disarmament in Brazil, Viva Rio discovered its initial forays into gun control *were critical in building the relationship with the state.* (Emphasis added.)

This is the same state that Kirsten said had such recent history of brutality and fear. And that relationship between Viva Rio and the state—formerly the instrument of repression and "gun massacres"—provides massive funding for Viva Rio for a diversity of activities. And it provides a connection with corporate funding, and funding from foreign governments and U.N. entities. Kirsten says that with the advent of IANSA, Vivo Rio took on a global aspect with respect to disarming the civilian populations of the world.

As it gathered power—as a campaigner for government disarmament of law-abiding Brazilians—Viva Rio, now with full assistance and support from IANSA and its other partners, embarked on a massive organizing, networking, and propaganda campaign to impose draconian gun controls on Brazilians.

Again, in her telling of history, Kirsten says:

In 1999, Viva Rio organized the "*Rio, Abaixe essa Arma*" (Rio, Put that Gun Down) campaign to mobilise support for a change in firearms legislation. Over a million signatures were collected in support of a law banning the commerce of small arms in Brazil. This focus on firearms and the strengthening of legislation and arms control management systems has remained central in subsequent campaigns.

Not coincidentally, this was a time when a conference of global gun-ban groups met in Rio. The U.N. Non-Governmental Liaison Service (NGLS) November 1999 newsletter noted, "Among other activities, Viva Rio has mobilized a network of 1,815 public schools, or nearly one and a half million school children and teachers, in its campaign to control small arms in the country."[29] As for direct U.N. support, the newsletter announced that:

the campaign has received the support of the United Nations Educational, Scientific and Cultural Organization (UNESCO),

438

which is sponsoring the initiative within the framework of actions taken to mark the year 2000 as International Year for Culture and Peace.

In addition to calling for government legislation to ban small arms, Viva Rio is also encouraging citizens in Rio de Janeiro to hand in their weapons. A network of church organizations has been set up in the city where citizens can turn in their guns, which are immediately destroyed by trained personnel.

Again returning to Kirsten's history of the growth of Viva Rio, she fast-forwards to September 2003, "when 50,000 people, including Brazil's Minister of Justice, the Secretary of Public Security, the Governor of Rio, and other representatives of government joined community associations, civil society organisations, actors and singers, religious leaders and students on the famous Copacabana beach to march for a gun free Brazil. This public display of support was timed to coincide with a decision in Congress regarding sweeping reforms to the country's gun legislation."

Kirsten's analysis ignores a whole other dynamic to the complex of "actors" revolving around Viva Rio and confiscatory gun control. There is a moral disconnect—a kind of resonant dissonance—in all of this, which is also reflected by Amnesty International's involvement in the Brazil gun ban. Amnesty International's online newsletter, *The Wire*, declared: "On Mother's Day, 13 May 2001, the Brazilian non-governmental organization (NGO) Viva Rio launched a campaign under the slogan '*Arma Nao! Ela Ou Eu*' ('Choose gun-free! It's your weapon or me'). Their aim was to bring together women from all sections of Brazilian society to force the men of Brazil to give up their guns."[30]

But the rest of the story had little to do with an argument that the women of Brazil didn't buy into after all. What it did have to do with was the sociopathic split personality that marks what I call "humanitarian tyranny."

Amnesty said, "Urban violence in Brazil is endemic, and there is no doubt that Brazilian society lives in fear. Those living in poor urban communities are trapped in a no-man's land between the violence of criminal gangs, who commit serious crimes including torture and killings, and that of the state response to them. The police forces . . . resort to brutal, ad hoc solutions and human rights violations in the absence of a coherent approach to public security issues."

Juxtapose that thought with what Amnesty says next: "Viva Rio is working with the poorest communities of Rio de Janeiro to find practical local solutions to the problems of gun crime. Initiatives include working with the local police to set up a system for storing and recording guns that are seized, with the aim of tracing the source of the guns and ensuring that they are not reintroduced into the community."

This is schizophrenic. On one hand the state—the police—are brutal human rights violators. On the other hand, all that is forgiven when it comes to disarming ordinary civilians. The organs of the state—what Kirsten calls the "agents of political repression [that] were known for their use of torture and human rights abuses"—morph into partners when it comes to "microdisarmament" or civil disarmament, creating a "civil society" by taking firearms from law-abiding people.

Neither Amnesty nor anyone in the phony international human rights community ever made the connection. When it comes to gun control, they far too often ally with the oppressors. They celebrate the loss of the most important human right of all: armed self-protection by decent men and women.

Although unintended by Kirsten or by Amnesty, the emphasis on what they describe as a long history of repression by police—especially recent history still fresh in the minds of many Brazilians—could not have been lost on voters, especially the poor, who most likely are victims of brutal repression.

The failed referendum was supposed to have been the crown jewel for world "microdisarmament." It was no coincidence that Rio was the host for a meeting where the gun-ban crowd made real their intentions with respect to world citizens anywhere who had the temerity to freely possess and use firearms.

As part of the lead up to the concerted U.N. effort in 2006 to press an international treaty to disarm civilians worldwide, a meeting of gun-ban NGOs was held in Rio de Janeiro in March 2005, just seven months before the Brazilian plebiscite. With the theme being how to end or suppress private possession of firearms, any group or individual in support of civilian ownership of arms was specifically excluded. This is U.N. democracy at work.

A key paper presented at that March 2005 meeting was a manifesto against gun ownership in the United States.[31]

Titled "The regulation of civilian ownership and use of small arms," the document declared that the "U.S. public holds one-third of the global gun arsenal: an estimated 234 million guns" and claimed that "the permissive and massive legal market for small arms in the U.S. is a major source of illicit firearms throughout the western hemisphere."

Chief among its recommendations was that global "awareness raising campaigns could help all societies move from a culture of 'rights' for weapons owners to one of 'responsibility' for ensuring that society is not harmed with their weapons."

"A culture of rights." That is precisely what the Brazilian people realized that they had in their grasp. After decades of oppressive government, they saw the light of real freedom.

But there is another point made in this manifesto against basic human rights, as part of its conclusion: "Along with weapons collection, however, it is critically important that appropriate regulatory regimes be implemented to *establish norms of non-possession.*"

"Norms of non-possession." In U.N.-speak, that means making possession "abnormal." It means making peaceable private ownership and use of firearms an aberration. It means propagandizing a generation or two of children to associate nothing good with firearms. It is a kind of brainwashing for citizens who seek only to exercise a basic human right.

It is everything that was rejected by Brazilians who stood up to Viva Rio and its U.N. fellow travelers and loudly proclaimed, "We trust direct democracy."

Chapter 17

Barack Obama: The Most Antigun President in American History

Extremism, lies, and threats. These are the consistent themes of Barack Obama's policy on gun control. Extremism in his advocacy for banning guns. Lies when his record is exposed. And threats against whoever tells the truth about him. During the 2008 election, the NRA warned that "Obama would be the most antigun president in American history." Unfortunately, that warning is already coming true, most ominously in his Supreme Court appointments.

The enduring theme of Obama's gun policy—from the early days when he was a political newcomer trying to join the state legislature, and all the way through his 2008 presidential campaign—has been support for handgun prohibition.

Barack Obama's elective career began with his 1996 campaign for an Illinois State Senate seat from the South Side of Chicago. In a questionnaire from the organization Independent Voters of Illinois, candidate Obama was asked: "Do you support state legislation to: (a) ban the manufacture, sale and possession of handguns? (b) ban assault weapons? (c) mandatory waiting periods and background checks?"

His answers were yes, yes, and yes.

When the brochure came to light during the 2008 presidential campaign, Obama—stealing a page from Bill Clinton's playbook—asserted that the questionnaire had been mistakenly answered by an aide. Obama claimed that he personally "never saw or approved the questionnaire." He insisted, "No, my writing wasn't on that particular questionnaire. As I said, I have never favored an all-out ban on handguns."

But the Washington newspaper and website *Politico* obtained the questionnaire itself, and found Obama's own handwriting on it.[1]

When Obama in 2003–04 was running for the United States Senate, he was asked again about handgun bans. This time, he answered, "While a complete ban on handguns is not politically practicable, I believe reasonable restrictions on the sale and possession of handguns are necessary to protect the public safety."[2]

That's not the answer of someone who opposes banning handguns. That's the answer of someone who, accurately, recognized that a handgun ban would not be enacted by Congress during the time that Obama would be in Congress.

If you asked me, "Do you favor banning handguns?" I wouldn't mumble about a complete ban being "politically impracticable." I would just say, "Heck no!"

On the other hand, if you asked me, "Do you favor repealing California's gun registration scheme?" I would tell you that a repeal is not "politically practicable" right now, and then I would tell you about some of things that NRA is working on right now to help gun owners in California. If you took my words to mean that I hope that California registration is repealed, and that as soon as it becomes politically practicable, I will work very hard to make it happen, you would be absolutely right.

Obama endorsed handgun prohibition yet again when the Supreme Court agreed to hear *District of Columbia v. Heller*. Asked about the case, the Obama campaign told the *Chicago Tribune*: "Obama believes the D.C. handgun law is constitutional" and that "local communities" should have the ability "to enact common sense laws."[3]

Obama himself said the same thing during a February 11 interview on WJLA television in D.C., shortly before the "Potomac primaries" in D.C., Maryland, and Virginia.[4] This was consistent with his statement in one of his books that "I believe in keeping guns out of our inner cities, and that our leaders must say so in the face of the gun manufacturer's lobby."[5] As if people in inner cities have no right to self-defense.

A bipartisan majority of Republican and Democratic senators (along with a similar majority from the House of Representatives) filed an amicus curiae (friend of the court) brief in the *Heller* case, urging that the Supreme Court enforce the Second Amendment and overturn the D.C. laws that banned handguns and that outlawed the use of any firearm for self-defense in the home.[6]

Of course Obama refused to join that brief. During a debate before the Pennsylvania primary, Obama was asked his opinion on the *Heller* case. He refused to answer.[7]

When the Supreme Court delivered the *Heller* decision, the Obama campaign had the audacity to claim that Obama supported the decision because it affirmed the Second Amendment as an individual right. The campaign apparently hoped that the media would forget that Obama had repeatedly declared his support of handgun prohibition, including the D.C. ban. Most of the media went along with Obama's strategy, but ABC, shortly before the *Heller* decision was announced, did ask about the campaign's November 2007 endorsement of the D.C. ban. The network was told that the November statement had been "inartful," which is apparently the Obama term for telling the truth.[8]

As for Obama's claim that he has always been a supporter of the Second Amendment individual right, that assertion is refuted by the fact that Obama had actually served on the board of directors of the antigun Joyce Foundation. In that capacity, he steered huge grants to the Violence Policy Center (the most extreme of the national gun-ban organizations, and an advocate of imposing a national handgun ban by bureaucratic decree), and to Ohio State University history professor Saul Cornell. The Cornell grants were for the express purpose of countering the individual rights Standard Model understanding of the Second Amendment.[9]

Just before Pennsylvania's April 2008 primary, Obama had told the voters: "I have never favored an all-out ban on handguns."[10] Whether or not the statement was "artful," it was not the truth.

Barack Obama has put his gun-banning beliefs into practice by voting to ban guns at every opportunity—and not just handguns.

During the presidential campaign, Obama said that he wanted to ban so-called assault weapons because such guns should only be found on "foreign battlefields." Yet the so-called assault weapons Obama has tried to ban are not guns used by the military, but guns used by ordinary Americans.

Demonstrating his hostility to defensive gun ownership, and his ignorance about firearms, Obama claimed that so-called "assault weapons . . . have only one purpose, to kill people."[11] In truth, such guns are commonly used for sporting purposes, including for the premiere target competition in the United States, the annual matches at Camp Perry, Ohio.

In the Illinois State Senate, Obama voted for an "assault weapon" ban even more sweeping than the Clinton ban of 1994. The ban Obama supported would have banned many more guns than the Clinton ban did, would not have sunset after ten years (as the Clinton ban did), and would have made a felon of anyone who retained a pre-ban gun.[12]

In 1998, Obama said that he wanted to "ban the sale or transfer of all forms of semi-automatic weapons."[13] That would include a Colt 1911 pistol, a Ruger 10/22 rifle, a Winchester Model 1907 shotgun, and thousands of others traditional American firearms, including well over half of all handguns.

Ammunition bans are also part of the Obama agenda. In 2005, he voted for an amendment by Senator Edward Kennedy that would have given the attorney general the unilateral authority to outlaw any centerfire rifle ammunition.[14] One can only cringe at what Obama's attorney general, Eric Holder, might do with such unchecked power.

In 2000, given that banning handguns was "not politically practicable," Obama co-sponsored a bill for gun rights rationing, to limit handgun purchases to one per month.[15] As the gun prohibition lobbies are well aware, once the principle of rationing is established, the rationing can be constricted, down to two handguns per year, or to just a few (or one) handgun per lifetime.

Obama also has been hostile to defensive gun ownership. His presidential campaign website claimed that Obama supported gun ownership "for the purposes of hunting and target shooting." Not for self-defense.

Thus, when running for the U.S. Senate in 2004, Obama told the *Chicago Tribune* that he wanted a national law to outlaw concealed handgun carry licenses.[16] Although he had voted for a 2004 Illinois bill to allow concealed carry by retired police officers, he emphasized, "I am consistently on record and will continue to be on record as opposing concealed carry."[17] Of course he also said that he supported the "common sense" D.C. gun laws that not only banned handguns, but also prohibited the use of any firearm for self-defense in the home.

In 2001, the Illinois legislature was considering a genuinely common-sense reform to the state's gun laws. Along with Wisconsin, Illinois is one of only two states that has no procedure for citizens to be issued permits to carry concealed handguns. Of the forty-eight other states, eight of them issue licenses arbitrarily, rather than according to the fair and reasonable standards that most states use. California is one of the arbitrary states, but it does have a sensible provision: if a court has issued a protective order because a person is the victim of a stalker, or of domestic violence, the victim is entitled to a concealed carry permit.

When the Illinois legislature considered a similar law, to authorize concealed carry by persons whom a court had determined to be victims of domestic violence or stalking, state senator Obama repeatedly spoke against the bill on the Senate floor, and helped defeat it.[18]

He was less successful in fighting another self-defense measure. In Wilmette, one of the Chicago suburbs with a handgun ban, fifty-two-year-old Hale DeMar was the victim of two home invasion burglaries by the same criminal. During the second burglary, DeMar used his handgun to shoot and wound the attacker.[19]

As a result, DeMar was arrested, and charges were filed against him for violation of the Wilmette handgun ban. After a public outcry, the Cook County prosecutor's office dropped the case.

In March 2004, Illinois Senate Bill 2165 came to the floor. The bill stated that if a person actually used a handgun for lawful self-defense in his or her own home, then the person could not be criminally prosecuted under a local handgun ban. Barack Obama complained that the bill would erode the effectiveness of the Chicago handgun ban. Defending Chicago's handgun ban as a legitimate exercise of local discretion, he said, "What works in Chicago may not work in Mattoon." In other words, people in Mattoon might not like handgun bans, but they should not interfere with the Chicago ban—not even to protect the victims of violent home invaders in Chicago or the suburbs. Obama voted against the bill in March, and again in May.[20]

During the presidential campaign, Barack Obama and Joe Biden told audiences all over America that they would not "take away" people's guns. It was an artful word choice. If you make it nearly impossible for people to buy guns or ammunition, then you can keep your promise not to "take away" guns.

Obama did vote against confiscation in 2006, when he joined eighty-three other U.S. senators in barring the use of federal funds for the illegal confiscation of guns, as took place after Hurricane Katrina.

One way to get rid of guns without gun confiscation is to bankrupt the firearms manufacturers. In 1998–2000, some big-city mayors launched a series of abusive lawsuits against firearms manufacturers. At the vanguard of the suits was the man who would be a key Obama supporter in 2008, Chicago mayor Richard Daley.

The lawsuits by Daley and the rest threatened to cripple the firearms industry—not because the lawsuits were meritorious, but because they had been carefully structured to exhaust the financial resources of the gun companies, driving their legal defense costs so high that the companies would be forced to capitulate to the agenda of the antigun lobby, or be driven into bankruptcy.

Obama helped defeat legislative efforts in Illinois to stop these abusive suits. In the U.S. Senate, he was less successful. The 2005 Protection of Lawful Commerce in Arms Act passed despite his negative vote, and stopped most of the abusive suits.[21]

But there's more than one way to get rid of guns. In 1999, Obama ran for the U.S. House of Representatives, challenging incumbent Democrat Bobby Rush, who represented the South Side of Chicago. Rush, by the way, is a former member of the Black Panthers, a domestic terrorist organization active in the 1960s and 1970s. Rush himself is a convicted gun felon.

It was not surprising that Obama did not try to use the Black Panther issue against Rush; instead, he tried to outdo Rush as an antigun advocate. This was not easy.

Rush is one of the most active antigunners in Congress, who pushed legislation that would create a national licensing and registration scheme for handguns and for semiauto long guns.

Yet Obama did find a way to outdo Bobby Rush in opposition to civil rights. Barack Obama promised that, if elected, he would push for a national ban on all gun stores located within five miles of a school or park. That is, essentially, everywhere. You can't go to an inhabited portion of the United States without coming within five miles of some kind of school or park. The only gun stores left might be a few home businesses in very rural farm areas.[22]

State Senator Obama took a soft line regarding gun criminals. He voted "present" on a bill that required that persons aged fifteen years or greater who illegally fire guns near a school be tried as an adult.[23]

Candidate Obama also pressed for a 500 percent increase in the federal tax on firearms and ammunition.[24] Currently, the federal excise tax is 11 percent, paid by the manufacturer and passed on to the consumer. The Obama gun tax plan would raise the tax rate to 66 percent. In other words, a $264 tax on a $400 gun, or a $13.33 tax on a $20 box of ammunition.

Significantly, Obama has never backed away from his plan to eliminate gun stores and make guns and ammunition difficult to afford. When the media asked the Obama campaign about these proposals during the presidential election, the campaign refused to answer. "We asked the Obama campaign about his position on an ammunition tax but have received no response."[25]

The campaign against Bobby Rush was the only one Barack Obama ever lost. In 2008, Rush was a strong supporter of Obama's presidential bid. And why not? In 2001 and again during the 2007–08 presidential campaign, Obama (like Rush) promised to work for national gun owner licensing and registration.[26]

However, on January 15, 2008, the late Tim Russert, of NBC television, asked in a debate, "Senator Obama, when you were in the state senate, you talked about licensing and registering gun owners. Would you do that as president?"

Obama answered, "I don't think that we can get that done."[27]

Another way to say, "I don't think we can get that done" is that it is "not politically practicable." It's a good idea, but not one that can be passed right now. If a candidate actually opposed national licensing and registration, then he would say something different, such as, "Tim, I oppose national gun licensing and registration."[28]

Why is Obama so antigun? To start with, we may have never had a president with less personal knowledge of firearms.[29]

This is perhaps one explanation for Obama's infamous remarks to an invitation-only gathering of the mega-rich in San Francisco in March 2008, when he asserted that the people of small towns in Pennsylvania and the Midwest "cling" to guns, religion, and xenophobia because they are "bitter" about their economic circumstances.[30]

His remark was obviously the product of extreme ignorance and bigotry, but such attitudes are not uncommon in the isolated, far-left milieu of the Chicago elite.

Moreover, Obama seems to have a knack for choosing mentors who are themselves bitter, and who are no friend to lawful gun ownership.

As a youth in Hawaii, Barack Obama picked a mentor named Frank Marshall Davis. Davis had been a member of the Communist Party, and admired the Soviet Union.[31] Certainly the Soviet Union, like all Communist dictatorships, was a gun control paradise.

Obama's father, Barack Hussein Obama Sr., was mostly an absentee father, but he was nevertheless the object of his abandoned son's lifelong fascination and admiration, as detailed in Obama Jr.'s autobiography, *Dreams from My Father.* Obama Sr. was an ally of Kenyan politician Oginga Odinga, an anti-Western communist. He was also an academic, and his article "Problems Facing Our Socialism" (*East Africa Journal,* July 1965) urged that the government confiscate private land, and also confiscate small stores belonging to families who had immigrated to Kenya from Asia or Europe.[32] In other words, Obama Sr. favored the kind of oppressive, discriminatory government that almost necessarily requires a disarmed populace.

In Chicago, Obama did not confine himself to the spiritual mentorship of the infamous Rev. Jeremiah Wright. An admiring article about Obama in the *Chicago Sun-Times* reported: "Friends and advisers, such as the Rev. Michael Pfleger, pastor of St. Sabina Roman Catholic Church in the Auburn–Gresham community on the South Side, who has known Obama for the better part of 20 years, help him keep that compass set, he [Obama] says."[33]

So who is Rev. Michael Pfleger, the man whom Obama credits with helping to keep his compass set?

Well, first of all, he has long been a key Obama ally in the church network that is so important to South Side Chicago politics. Not only did Pfleger endorse Obama early for the 2004 U.S. Senate race; he was one of the few prominent backers of Obama during his 1999–2000 primary challenge to incumbent U.S. representative Bobby Rush.

The Obama presidential campaign relied on Pfleger's support. Early in the race, the Obama campaign advertised Pfleger as one of a dozen leading ministers who endorsed Obama.[34] The Obama campaign sent Pfleger to an Obama-organized forum in Iowa on religion and politics.[35]

Obama, in turn, has supported Pfleger. While in the Illinois legislature, Obama steered $225,000 in taxpayer grants to Pfleger's St. Sabina Church.[36]

Like Obama's Rev. Jeremiah Wright, Pfleger is a fervent admirer of the racist hatemonger Louis Farrakhan, whom Pfleger calls "a great man."[37]

Pfleger is also a fanatic enemy of gun ownership. The closest gun store to Chicago is Chuck's Gun Shop, in Riverdale, a town on Chicago's southern border. Pfleger has waged an incessant, hateful campaign to destroy the store and its owner, John Riggio.

Like all law-abiding gun stores in Illinois, Chuck's Gun Shop sells firearms only to customers who have a Firearms Owner's Identification Card (FOID); the Illinois State Police issue the card only after conducting a background check, which takes several weeks.

Chuck's Gun Shop has gone beyond the letter of the law, and had its employees take training from the "Don't lie for the other guy" program, that shows gun store staff how to detect straw purchasers. The program is jointly sponsored by the National Shooting Sports Foundation and the Bureau of Alcohol, Tobacco, Firearms and Explosives.

No one has ever pointed to any instance of Chuck's Gun Shop violating any gun control law. Yet Pfleger has targeted the store and its owner for destruction. Month after month, Pfleger and Jesse Jackson brought in crowds to picket the store.

Pfleger—the man whom Obama credits with keeping Obama's moral compass pointed in the right direction—simply objects to the lawful sale of firearms, period. He demands that the Riverdale city council "vote Riverdale gun-free." Making an explicit analogy to the former prohibition of alcohol, the Pfleger crowd chants, "Vote Riverdale gun dry."[38]

In a scene reminiscent of George Wallace blocking the schoolhouse door, obstructing civil rights, and defying the law, Pfleger and Jackson criminally obstructed the entrance to the store, and were arrested.[39]

Another time, Pfleger told the mob outside the store to murder owner John Riggio: "We're going to find you and snuff you out . . . Like a rat you're going to hide. But like a rat, we're going to catch you and pull you out . . . We're going to snuff out John Riggio." Pfleger continued: "We're going to snuff out legislators that are voting against our gun laws. We're coming for you because we're not going to sit idly."

In response to the death threats, Chicago's Cardinal Francis George remonstrated: "Publicly delivering a threat against anyone's life betrays the civil order and is morally outrageous, especially if this threat came from a priest."[40]

According to Pfleger, he had no idea that "snuff out" means "kill." He said that he was merely delivering a colorful metaphor about discovering the home address of John Riggio, an address that was not in public records. The claim is implausible, since Pfleger also vowed to "snuff out" Illinois legislators, and their home addresses were in the public record.

Besides, Riggio was not exactly hiding in secret. He was right inside the store when Pfleger spoke. So what lawful purpose could Pfleger have in mind for taking his mob to Riggio's home?

And Michael Pfleger is the guy who has been, according to Obama himself, guiding Obama's moral compass. Pfleger is also a close ally of Arne Duncan, Obama's antigun secretary of education.[41]

Pfleger's criminal trespass against the civil rights of the gun store owner and customers, and his threat to "snuff out" the store's owner, came in the summer of 2007. Although the crimes were reported in the Chicago newspapers, they apparently provided no impediment to Obama sending Pfleger on the road that fall as a "spiritual" spokesman for the Obama campaign.

So how did Barack Obama respond when the NRA and some journalists exposed his record of gun ban extremism during the presidential campaign? I've already told you about how he lied about his record of supporting handgun bans, and refused to answer questions about his proposal to ban gun stores, and to impose huge taxes on firearms and ammunition.

Like a typical Chicago machine politician, like a man who takes his moral guidance from an extremist who issues death threats and criminally blocks the entrance to a store, Obama resorted to bullying.

The NRA Political Victory Fund purchased television and radio advertisements in key states, informing voters about the truth of the Barack Obama and Joe Biden records on guns. In response, the Obama campaign sent threat letters to television and radio stations, warning that if they aired the ads, they might lose their broadcast licenses from the Federal Communications Commission. This is serious intimidation from a man who was seeking, and won, the power to appoint the FCC commissioners.

Supposedly, the ads were "false and misleading," yet the Obama campaign was unable to document a single factual error in any of our advertising. Instead, the campaign just pointed to sources such as a *Washington Post* editorial that naively (or cynically) asserted that because Obama claimed to respect the Second Amendment, the NRA must be wrong in warning that he is antigun.

During the campaign, Obama insisted, "I have always believed that the Second Amendment protects the right of individuals to bear arms." Not exactly true.

During the presidential campaign, Obama told *Field & Stream* magazine that "if you talk to sportsmen in my home state of Illinois, they will tell you that I've always been a forceful advocate on behalf of the rights of sportsmen, on behalf of access for sportsmen and hunters."[42]

In fact, no one can point to a single time in Illinois that Obama ever acted as a "forceful advocate . . . on behalf of sportsmen and hunters." As executive director of the Illinois State Rifle Association, Richard Pearson has been lobbying for sportsmen in the Illinois state legislature during the entirety of Obama's political career. Pearson reported that Obama had *never* advocated in the legislature for sportsmen and hunters, or, for that matter, even on behalf of fishing.[43]

Candidate Obama promised, "As President, I will uphold the constitutional rights of law-abiding gun-owners, hunters, and sportsmen. I know that what works in Chicago may not work in Cheyenne."

Yet in fact, if we lived in nation with the laws that Barack Obama has endorsed, you could not own a handgun. You could not own any self-loading firearm.

To own any of the guns that were left, you would need a government-issued license and registration. Your state permit to carry a firearm for lawful protection would be null and void.

Buying a new gun, or ammunition, would be nearly impossible, since gun stores would have been banned from the inhabited portion of the United States. If you did manage to find a store somehow, the price would reflect a 66 percent federal excise tax on the arms or ammunition.

Already, the Obama administration has begun its campaign to shrink the Second Amendment so small you won't be able to tell it exists. The Obama administration tried a regulatory maneuver with the Customs Bureau that would have outlawed 80 percent of folding knives by labeling them "switchblades." Fortunately, we were able to defeat them.[44]

Within a few weeks of taking the oath of office, President Obama and the rest of his administration began blaming America for Mexico's violent crime problem, and saying that so-called assault weapons should be banned. He used the Mexican gun hoax to start pushing for Senate ratification of the CIFTA international gun control treaty that would outlaw reloading, and require most gun owners to get a federal firearms "manufacturing" license.

His Department of Homeland Security issued an "Intelligence Assessment," to law enforcement all over the country, warning that advocates of Second Amendment might be right-wing extremist terrorists.[45]

Worst of all, he is stacking the Supreme Court with foes of the Second Amendment, as I'll detail in chapter 20.

We know that there will be much more to come from the most antigun president in American history.

Chapter 18

Hillary Clinton

During the 2008 election, I warned that the Barack Obama administration would be the most antigun in history. Certainly the closest competitor in that regard is the Clinton administration, and Hillary Clinton was at the heart of the antigun campaigns of the 1990s. As secretary of state, Hillary Clinton has the means, motive, and opportunity to wage war on our Second Amendment.

Indeed, she has already begun to do so. An easy way to see the difference that the secretary of state can make is to contrast Clinton with former secretary of state Condoleezza Rice, who called herself a "Second Amendment absolutist." As secretary of state, she was in charge of the United States delegation to the United Nations. It was that delegation, led by the heroic John Bolton, who stopped the creation of a binding international antigun treaty in 2006.

When foreign governments tried to enlist the U.S. State Department in promoting gun control, Secretary of State Rice quickly rejected them. For example, in December 2008, she met with Mexican foreign secretary Patricia Espinosa. At a joint press conference, Espinosa said that Mexico's problem of gun crime perpetrated by drug cartels was the fault of the United States. Espinosa announced that the Mexican government wanted the U.S. to reimpose the federal ban (which had expired in 2004) on so-called assault weapons.

Secretary of State Rice retorted, "I follow arms trafficking across the world, and I've never known illegal arms traffickers who cared very much about the law. And so I simply don't accept the notion that the lifting of the ban somehow has led arms traffickers to increase their activity."

The Mexican secretary of state's demands got only a little attention in the American media.

Contrast that with what Secretary of State Clinton has done. She did exactly what the NRA told you she would. She arranged very public events with Mexican government officials, and announced that the Mexicans were right to blame America. She agreed that the "assault weapon" ban should be reinstituted. She used her power to influence the media to place the Mexican gun issue, and the alleged urgency of American gun control, on network television and on the front pages and editorial pages of all the major newspapers all over America.

I explained the real facts about the Mexican government campaign against American gun rights in chapter 8. But for now, the key point is that Secretary of State Clinton is ready, willing, and able to use her tremendous power to advance the antigun agenda.

These days, if you ask Hillary Clinton a question about her antigun advocacy, she will be sure to begin by affirming how she thinks the Second Amendment is very important. As I detail in the chapter on George Soros, that's exactly what antigun political consultants have been telling gun-hating Democrats to do: to go right on promoting their antigun agenda, but to first insist that they care about Second Amendment rights. For several weeks in the 2008 primaries, she effectively hammered Obama on his comment that people "cling" to guns because they are "bitter."[1] Her campaign postcards to voters highlighted Obama's antigun record, but cleverly remained silent about Clinton's own record on guns. Her attacks on the Obama gun record helped her win the Pennsylvania primary in a landslide, and to beat Obama in Indiana.[2] Whatever sporting privilege Hillary Clinton might be willing to tolerate, she has established a decades-long record as a staunch enemy of Second Amendment rights. It was during the Clinton administration that Janet Reno's Department of Justice insisted that *no* American (not even a National Guardsman) has any Second Amendment rights. Rather, in the Clinton-Reno view, the Second Amendment right belongs exclusively to the government.

We may never know how much Hillary Clinton did behind the scenes to promote the antigun agenda when she was First Lady. We do know that she often used the Office of the First Lady to organize the vanguard of antigun extremism.

In the spring of 1999, Missouri voters were deciding on a "Proposition B," about whether to adopt licensed carry. The Clinton/Reno U.S. Attorneys for Missouri-Edward Dowd and Stephen Hill—sent a letter on U.S. Department of Justice letterhead, asking sheriffs and police to campaign against Proposition B. Dowd even set up a toll-free telephone number in his office for voters to request anti-B campaign materials. Their actions were a flagrant violation of the federal law against using federal funds and resources to influence an election, but, of course, the Clinton/Reno Department of Justice let them get away with it.

Mrs. Clinton also reportedly helped with fund-raising for the anti-carry campaign, led by Robin Carnahan, who went on to become Missouri secretary of state.

Then, the weekend before the April election, Mrs. Clinton taped a telephone message that was delivered to seventy-five thousand homes, targeted to women. She urged people to vote against licensed carry, claiming, "It's just too dangerous for Missouri families."[3]

At other times, when Mrs. Clinton has been campaigning in rural areas on her own behalf, she will say things like, "I don't have anything against guns if guns are used by responsible people."[4] Yet based on what she did in Missouri, even if you pass a safety class and a fingerprint-based background check, she still doesn't think you are "responsible" enough to carry a handgun for lawful protection.

Two weeks after the Missouri vote, a pair of young felons (who had skated through a diversion program) murdered thirteen people at Columbine High School, in Colorado. Before the victims had even been buried, Mrs. Clinton came out swinging: "We need to stand up and say what needs to be said about guns and firearms," she declared. "Why on earth would we permit any young person access to the firearms those two young men brought into that school?"[5]

Well, those two "young men" should have had felony records for the felony burglary to which they pled guilty, which would have resulted in a permanent ban on their possession of any firearm. But again, the laws we have were not enforced.

The criminals used four guns. One of them was a Tec-9 pistol, a so-called assault weapon, so it was not surprising for Mrs. Clinton to express outrage that anyone had access to that gun. Yet the other three guns—a double-barreled shotgun, a pump shotgun, and a carbine—were what the gun control lobbies like to call "legitimate" hunting arms.[6] This just provides another example of how phony the "assault weapon" issue is.

Mrs. Clinton seemed to be saying that she didn't think that "young men" (including, apparently eighteen-year-olds, since that was the age of one perpetrator) should have any "access" to firearms, including old-fashioned rifles or shotguns.

As she said in her 2000 Senate campaign, "We have to enact laws that will keep guns out of the hands of children and criminals and mentally unbalanced persons."[7]

It is outrageous for her to equate children with criminals and the insane. Of course the NRA wants to keep criminals and the insane from ever holding a gun in their hands, and we have pushed for laws to help do so. Yet Mrs. Clinton refuses to acknowledge the difference between a man with an armed robbery conviction, and a fourteen-year-old going hunting with her father. The former has forfeited his right to arms; the latter has every right to participate in America's tradition of responsible gun ownership.

Speaking to middle school students in Nassau County, New York, in 1999, Mrs. Clinton told them: "It is really important for each of you to make sure you stay away from guns. If you have guns in your home, tell your parents to keep them away from you and your friends and your little brothers and sisters."[8]

She was not telling the twelve- to fifteen-year-olds to stay away from guns without adult supervision. She was telling them to stay away from guns unequivocally. "Guns and children are two words that should never be put together in the same sentence," she said on another occasion.[9]

One of Clinton's books is *It Takes a Village to Raise a Child*. It's a nice idea to think about people in a local community helping each other with their children. But the title is misleading in two senses. First, what it really takes to raise a child are good parents. For four centuries, many good parents in America have taught their children about responsibility, safety, and conservation by teaching them about hunting and shooting. Often, friends and neighbors have participated in these wholesome activities.

Yet the "village" that Mrs. Clinton extols seems to be Washington, D.C.—a "village" whose bureaucracy will intrude into every small town, city, farm, and ranch in America, to make sure that children never use guns.[10] As she said in 1996, "As adults we have to start thinking and believing that there isn't really any such thing as someone else's child."[11] Put another way, your children are also Mrs. Clinton's children.

First Lady Marches with Rosie O'Donnell

Hillary Clinton's longtime best friend and political adviser is Susan Thomases. Ms. Thomases' sister-in-law is Donna Dees-Thomases. Ms. Dees-Thomases had been a Democratic Senate staffer, and in 1999 was working as a publicist for *The Late Show with David Letterman*. After Columbine, this experienced political and media operator announced the formation of the "Million Mom March."

Although most of the media unquestioningly accepted Mrs. Dees-Thomases's claim that she was just a housewife from New Jersey who wanted to protect kids from the gun lobby, the Million Mom March (MMM) appeared to be carefully calculated to get suburban married women to vote Democratic in the next election.

The Office of the First Lady provided extensive planning support to the MMM. When the march was held in Washington, D.C., in May 2000, Mrs. Clinton herself was the opening speaker. She shared the stage with extremists such as Rosie O'Donnell, the angry paranoid who had announced that all guns should be banned, and that everyone who did not obey the ban should be sent to prison.

By 2001, the "Million Mom March" had been exposed as an AstroTurf sham. Although the organizers claimed that 750,000 people had attended their 2000 rally in Washington,[12] photographs showed that the crowd was much smaller.

The much-touted (by the media) network of grassroots antigun activists failed to materialize for the 2000 election. Eventually, the "Million" Mom March was merged into the Brady Campaign, amounting to little more than a different letterhead on the same old antigun propaganda from a D.C. lobby. Their 2001 rally in Washington drew only a hundred people.

Yet Mrs. Clinton still gamely showed up in May 2001 to address a MMM rally in White Plains, New York, sharing the stage with Senator Charles Schumer, Governor George Pataki, and New York attorney general Eliot Spitzer.

"We have a right as mothers and fathers to do everything we can to keep our children safe, and that, at bottom, is what this whole fight over gun safety is about," she told the crowd.

I agree that parents have the right to protect their children, and this is the right that Mrs. Clinton and her crowd have been taking away. They have tried to take away the right of parents to carry licensed firearms to protect their families, and they have even tried to take away the constitutional right of parents to own defensive guns at all.

Mrs. Clinton continued: "We have an epidemic of gun violence in this country."[13] This is the textbook language of the gun prohibition groups. It avoids saying anything about the criminals who cause "gun violence." Instead, it equates "violence" with a disease. It is designed to make people think that guns are like germs, and gun owners are like disease carriers.

Mrs. Clinton's involvement in the gun prohibition movement long predates her time as First Lady. From 1986 to 1992, she served as chair of the board of directors of the Children's Defense Fund, and is still an emeritus member of the board.[14] Although the group has a nice name, its long-standing priority was opposing welfare reform.[15] The group has also campaigned for decades against Second Amendment rights, and has endorsed even the most extreme antigun proposals, such as Senator John Chafee's 1992 bill for a national handgun ban.

When Hillary Clinton began her own political career with her campaign for the United States Senate in New York, she was questioned about whether her Senate seat would merely be used as a stepping-stone to higher office. (As, in fact, it was.) She insisted that she was really interested in the Senate, and that one of her main reasons for wanting to run was to fight for gun control.

She did keep her antigun promise.

Clinton Votes to Use Your Money to Confiscate Your Guns

Perhaps the height of Senator Clinton's antigun extremism came in her 2006 vote to allow federal taxpayer money to be used to *illegally* confiscate guns from law-abiding citizens.

After Hurricane Katrina, good citizens formed neighborhood patrols to protect their families, neighbors, and communities from the gangs of murderers, rapists, and looters who were running wild. Instead of sending the police out to stop the criminals, New Orleans Police superintendent Eddie Compass sent his minions to confiscate guns from the people of New Orleans. They broke into houses, threw old ladies to the ground, and made off with lawfully owned firearms.[16]

In doing so, they violated not only the Second Amendment and the Louisiana Constitution; they also broke the statutory law of Louisiana, which made it very clear that gun confiscation is *not* among police powers during an emergency. Unfortunately, some of the gun confiscation was assisted by police from other jurisdictions, and by some federal officers. Similar abuses took place in St. Tammany's Parish, adjacent to New Orleans.

An emergency lawsuit by the National Rifle Association halted the gun confiscations.[17] Yet for years the New Orleans police have dithered and delayed in refusing to return the illegally confiscated arms.

I'm proud to say that at the urging of the National Rifle Association, many state legislatures have enacted or strengthened laws against gun confiscation during disasters or emergencies.

In the U.S. Congress, Louisiana senator David Vitter sponsored an amendment to the Department of Homeland Security appropriations bill.[18] The amendment says that federal funds cannot be used to *illegally* confiscate guns during a natural disaster. The bill also applies to state and local agencies that receive federal grants.[19] Rather notably, the bill does not even block gun confiscation if the confiscation is authorized by a state or local law, or a court order.

To vote against spending federal taxpayer money on something that's illegal is not exactly a difficult vote. If ever there was an easy way to vote pro–Second Amendment, this was it. Eighty-four senators voted for the Vitter Amendment, including Barack Obama, casting the only significant pro-gun vote of his career.

Only a minority, sixteen of the most extremist anti-rights senators, voted against the Vitter Amendment. One of them was Hillary Clinton.

So the next time Mrs. Clinton tells you she thinks the Second Amendment is "very important," remember that she doesn't think that it's important enough to stop lawless police from breaking into your home, assaulting you, and confiscating your guns *with no legal justification at all.* She may say that she is opposed to "people on the other extreme who want to take everybody's guns away,"[20] but she voted to give them your tax money to do so.

Except on the Vitter Amendment, the Clinton and Obama antigun records have been remarkably similar.

Senators Clinton and Obama both voted against the Protection of Lawful Commerce in Arms Act, the federal law that blocks junk lawsuits against gun manufacturers and gun stores.[21] Despite the disinformation put out by the gun ban lobbies behind the lawsuits, the Act only forbids lawsuits if the store or manufacturer obeyed all of the many laws about the making and sale of guns.

Clinton also has endorsed the licensing of all gun owners, federal registration of all new guns and all gun transfers, and registration of all existing handguns.[22] She is an enthusiastic advocate of banning so-called assault weapons, a ban Bill Clinton treated as the signature accomplishment of his first term. She has even endorsed random metal detector searches of people walking down the street, to detect people carrying guns.[23]

Clinton also has worked to change the political system to the disadvantage of Second Amendment advocates. The first bill she introduced as a U.S. senator was a bill to abolish the Electoral College. The Founders wisely set up the Electoral College to give the less-populated states some protection from the whims of the giant states. The Electoral College encourages presidential candidates to campaign in a diverse collection of states, rather than just concentrating on the huge urban population centers.

If the Clinton plan had been in effect in 2000, then Al Gore would have become the president of the United States. And you can be certain that President Gore would have used the September 11 attacks as the pretext for imposing California-style gun controls on the entire country.

Mrs. Clinton has also been a leading advocate of the campaign finance censorship laws, which are designed to reduce the ability of the National Rifle Association and its members to influence elections by informing the public about candidates' records. She even cochaired a fund-raising dinner that raised eight hundred thousand dollars for an organization that was created to promote such laws.[24]

Hillary Clinton Picks the U.S. Delegation

As I explained in chapter 3, Secretary of State Clinton picked the U.S. delegation to the U.N.'s 2010 Biennial Meeting of the States on gun control. There, her delegation endorsed far-reaching antigun laws.

In September 2010, it was announced that the U.S. delegation to the U.N. will have a representative who specializes in antigun extremism. Former Seattle mayor Greg Nickels was named "alternate representative of the United States of America to the Sixty-fifth Session of the General Assembly of the United Nations." Before being defeated for reelection as mayor in 2009, Nickels had been the most prominent gun control advocate in the state of Washington. He had promoted a wide variety of antigun laws, and had even banned the lawful carrying of firearms in city parks—a flagrant defiance of Washington state law, which forbids local gun controls. At the U.N. Nickels may have the opportunity to make real progress on his gun ban agenda.

With the endorsement of President Obama and Secretary Clinton, the United Nations is busy negotiating an Arms Trade Treaty (ATT). That treaty is designed to prevent arms transfers to human rights violators. While the final content of the treaty is yet to be decided, treaty advocates such as IANSA and Control arms want the treaty to be used against the United States and Israel. The U.N. thinks that Israel is by far the worst country in the world, and the U.N. has already declared that it is a human rights violation for the United States to allow crime victims to use guns against violent attacks, and it is also a human rights violation for the U.S. not to have severely repressive gun laws.

Along with President Obama, Secretary of State Clinton is pushing the Senate to ratify the CIFTA treaty, which would require that most American gun owners be licensed the same as gun manufacturers.

In chapter 3, I explained CIFTA and other international agreements in depth. Yet even if we put aside these particular threats, the secretary of state (and the president) already have tremendous unilateral power to impose their will via international law.

For example, treaties require Senate ratification, but a *multilateral agreement* does not, nor do some other international agreements. A multilateral agreement can go into effect simply by being signed by the president or the secretary of state.

What's the difference between a treaty and a multilateral agreement? Well, in general, a multilateral agreement is supposed to be less significant. But the dividing line is really a judgment call, and courts are very, very reluctant to second-guess an executive branch decision that something is a multilateral agreement rather than a treaty.

Significantly, arms control has frequently been the subject of multilateral agreements. In the past, this has meant national military arms (e.g., how many and what types of naval vessels are allowed in a particular body of water). Yet the international gun-ban groups have been quite successful in turning traditional arms control mechanisms into vehicles for citizen firearms control. The international gun ban movement was created by activists who seek to replicate the achievement of the international ban on land mines. At the United Nations, the U.N. Office for Disarmament Affairs, created for national military disarmament, has enthusiastically taken up the cause of disarming civilians.

Could Secretary of State Clinton advance the gun prohibition agenda with a multilateral agreement, designed to avoid Senate ratification? It would be dangerous to presume that she will not.

The secretary of state and the president can also "reinterpret" already-ratified treaties, or other international legal documents that already bind the United States.

For instance, back in the George H. W. Bush administration, the U.S. Senate ratified the International Covenant on Civil and Political Rights (ICCPR). The Covenant requires that governments not violate the right to life. That's a good principle.

Yet as interpreted by the United Nations, the right-to-life section of the ICCPR requires governments to prohibit firearms use by civilians or police, unless there is an immediate threat to life. So if you shoot a rapist, a robber, a carjacker, or an arsonist, you are violating his right to life. If the government does not punish you, the government is also violating the criminal's right to life—at least that's what the U.N. now says.

Again, an Obama-Clinton administration would not be the first to try to use dubious interpretation of an old treaty as a basis to claim massive new powers for the executive branch. For example, the Mexican government has long been upset about United States capital punishment of Mexican illegal aliens who have murdered Americans.

The George W. Bush administration argued that it had the power to order state governments not to execute certain murderers who were illegal aliens.[25] The Bush administration asserted that various sources of international law, including the United Nations Charter (the document that created the U.N., and sets forth its basic rules) gave the president the authority to issue binding orders to state governments.

That view was rejected by a 6-3 vote of the U.S. Supreme Court in the 2008 case *Medellin v. Texas*. Yet there were three justices who agreed that the United Nations Charter (and other international treaties) gives the president domestic law powers *beyond* what he is granted by Article II of the U.S. Constitution. With more Supreme Court appointments, such as Sonia Sotomayor and Elena Kagan, the majority of the Court might soon agree.

Hillary Clinton, Bill Clinton, George W. Bush, and Barack Obama have all had various disputes with one another over the years. But all four have been staunch advocates of unchecked, unilateral executive power. It has long been established that a president's unilateral power is at its height in foreign affairs.

Because of this unilateral power, nearly a million collectible rifles have been kept out of the hands of American consumers.

In 2009, the U.S. State Department gave its approval to the routine import into the United States of 87,310 M1 Garands and 770,160 M1 Carbines, currently in the hands of the South Korean government.

But in March 2010, Mrs. Clinton's State Department withdrew the approval. A State Department spokesperson explained that "the transfer of such a large number of weapon[s] . . . could potentially be exploited by individuals seeking firearms for illicit purposes."

The purported fear was ridiculous. Anyone who bought one of these excellent, historic rifles would have to pass through the same National Instant Check System that is used for all gun store sales in the United States.

Needless to say, the Brady Campaign was thrilled that the Obama/Clinton administration had kept nearly a million guns out of the hands of American citizens.[26]

One thing that links the Clintons and Obama is how much they owe to George Soros. As I detail in chapter 19, Soros has been their long-standing political patron, spending millions and millions of dollars to help them acquire and retain power. Pragmatically speaking, they have every reason to use their power for his benefit, including on his pet cause of gun control.

We cannot know for sure all the ways that Mrs. Clinton and Mr. Obama will turn executive branch power against American gun owners, or how they may try to turn international law into domestic gun control. But we do know that they have already begun, and there may be much worse to come.

Chapter 19

George Soros

The marching axis of adversaries of First and Second Amendment rights has a central banker, and his name is George Soros. The billionaire bankroller is trying to revoke the Bill of Rights through his checkbook.

There are some folks who say that George Soros is fundamentally a bad guy. He has been criminally convicted in France of "financial misdeeds," which is their term for insider trading.[1] His company, Soros Fund Management, was fined by Hungary's State Financial Supervisory Authority for illegal short selling, which destroyed much of the value of the largest Hungarian bank.[2]

Other people say he is a good guy because he supplied resources to activists in eastern Europe who were seeking to change the Communist regimes in their countries, or to open up their societies after Communism fell.[3]

Still others would argue that Soros is the very model of the modern major megalomaniac.[4] He wrote: "If the truth be known, I carried some rather potent messianic fantasies with me from childhood, which I felt I had to control, otherwise they might get me in trouble."[5] And, "I admit I have always harbored an exaggerated sense of my self-importance—to put it bluntly, I fancied myself as some kind of god or an economic reformer like Keynes, or, better, a scientist like Einstein."[6]

Interviewed by a British newspaper, Soros was asked about his messianic self-image. He explained: "It is a sort of disease when you consider yourself some kind of god, the creator of everything, but I feel comfortable about it now since I began to live it out."[7]

In his own mind, says he, "I am sort of a deus ex machina" (Latin for "God from the machine"[8]). "Next to my fantasies about being God, I also have very strong fantasies of being mad," he once said. "In fact, my grandfather was actually paranoid. I have a lot of madness in my family. So far I have escaped it."[9]

Whatever he is, he is not what the public thinks: "I am something unnatural. I'm very comfortable with my public persona because it is one I have created for myself. It represents what I like to be as distinct from what I really am. You know, in my personal capacity I'm not actually a selfless philanthropic person. I've [sic] very much self-centered."[10]

Neither gods nor madmen think they have to obey human rules, and neither does George Soros: "I do not accept the rules imposed by others. If I did, I would not be alive today. I am a law-abiding citizen, but I recognize that there are regimes that need to be opposed rather than accepted. And in periods of regime change, the normal rules don't apply."[11] "Regime change," as we shall see, is the term he uses to characterize an American election.

Personally, I'm not interested in looking into George Soros's eyes and trying to see his soul. I'm interested in what he actually does. And what he is actually doing—and has been doing for over a decade—is bankrolling the destruction of American constitutional rights and the freedom of other people around the world.

Soros Bankrolls "Junk" Lawsuits against U.S. Gun Industry

Soros first drew public notice on the gun issue in late 1998 when he funded a junk lawsuit against firearm manufacturers. The suit had been brought by Elisa Barnes, an antigun attorney in New York City, and it helped set up the tidal wave of junk lawsuits that were later filed by big-city mayors.[12] Rebecca Peters, Soros's top antigun employee, was sent into the courtroom, claiming that she was merely an observer in the case.[13] The case resulted in a $4 million verdict against three handgun manufacturers, and attorney Barnes said that Soros's money "made all the difference in the world."[14] (The verdict was later overturned in a unanimous 7–0 decision of the New York Court of Appeals, New York's highest state court.[15])

By spring 1999, Soros's Center on Crime, Communities and Culture (part of his Open Society Institute) was running a meeting of thirty private foundations, convincing them to put money into antigun work.[16] He anted up $5 million for the Funders' Collaborative for Gun Violence Prevention, and placed Rebecca Peters in charge.[17]

Next came a grant to the NAACP (National Association for the Advancement of Colored People) for another junk lawsuit against gun companies, a sad betrayal of the NAACP's historic advocacy of civil rights.[18]

Soros also provided a major grant to fund the planning of the so-called "Million" Mom March (MMM)—a series of nationwide rallies featuring shrill gun-haters such as Rosie O'Donnell.[19] The MMM organizers were so grateful that they called Rebecca Peters "our fairy godmother."[20] The MMM was one of many Clinton-Soros collaborations during the Clinton presidency, and the Office of the First Lady was closely involved in MMM organizing.

Promoting antigun research is another Soros specialty. His Funders' Collaborative for Gun Violence Prevention has made grants to pay for research from the antigun Harvard Injury Control Center.[21] One reason that Soros got into the research business was that Congress had ordered the federally funded Centers for Disease Control to stop producing junk science gun control propaganda masquerading as public health research.[22] Another Soros grant went to the Educational Fund to Stop Gun Violence, the research/legal affiliate of a handgun prohibition lobby.

Rebecca Peters directed Soros's Center on Crime, Communities and Culture in producing a report titled "Gun Control in the United States."[23] According to the report, "42 states fall below minimum standards for public safety, since they lack basic gun laws such as licensing and registration." The rating scale was 0 to 100, with only seven states scoring above 30 percent, and 20 states getting negative numbers. The average score was a mere 9 percent.

Notably, the report refused to examine the strength of state laws to punish criminals who use guns.

The claims about "minimum standards for public safety" probably surprised many people in the states that the Soros group praised, since, as of the time of the report, they suffered a 21 percent higher crime rate than the "below minimum standard" states.[24]

The Soros report called for prohibiting *possession* of long guns by anyone under eighteen, and handguns by anyone under twenty-one. In other words, Soros and his team want to make it illegal for you to take your seventeen-year-old son hunting, or to take your twenty-year-old daughter to the pistol range when she comes home on leave from the U.S. Army. The obvious agenda was to destroy the American gun culture by sending you to prison if you try to pass it on to the next generation.

The 2000 election was supposed to be the year of victory for the gun prohibition movement. Soros was generous in state antigun initiatives. For example, in Oregon, few people were interested in gathering petitions to put an antigun show initiative on the ballot. So George Soros gave money to Handgun Control, Inc., with the purpose of passing the money through to the Oregon antigunners. The Oregonians then hired paid petition gatherers, earning $1.45 per signature, and were able to make the ballot.[25]

Soros also donated to an antigun show initiative in Colorado.[26] Both campaigns were built around the lie of the "gun show loophole," a phrase designed to trick voters into believing that laws about the sales of guns at gun shows are different, and weaker, than laws about the sales of guns anywhere else.

The Oregon and Colorado initiatives both passed. In California, antigun advocates credited the money from Soros and his foundation allies for the legislative enactment of gun rationing laws and a ban on small handguns.[27]

Taking Away Your Gun Rights

The international gun prohibition lobby is essentially George Soros's creation. IANSA's funding is secret, but the Soros connection is not. From the creating of IANSA until July 2010, the group was run by Rebecca Peters. IANSA has networked hundreds of other organizations around the world into its prohibition web, and IANSA has also spun off affiliates, such as Control Arms. If there were no IANSA, there would be no international gun ban movement.

IANSA is "the organization officially designated by the U.N. Department of Disarmament Affairs (DDA) to coordinate civil society involvement to the U.N. small arms process."[28]

IANSA's dangerous and deadly machinations are not confined to the corridors of the United Nations. Soros's organization works around the world for the destruction of the human right of self-defense.

Chapter 7 tells the tragic story of how countries that have been trapped by the Soros axis have fallen prey to increased violence and decreased freedom. Soros's network is vast.

Soros got his way in South Africa; and so in a country where more than half of all women will be raped in the course of their lives (and, very possibly, infected with AIDS as a result), the police told women that they could not have handgun permits for protection. They should just stay home, the police said, or only go out when accompanied by their husbands.

Soros compared the Bush administration to Hitler's dictatorship, and called the United States "a danger to the world."[29] Yet it is Soros himself who promotes the kind of gun laws favored by Hitler's National Socialists, and it is Soros himself who is endangering the people of the world by exterminating their right of self-defense against *genocidaires*, tyrants, and criminals.

The South African law was the model that Soros's proxies brought to Panama, and then to Costa Rica.[30] In Costa Rica, the bill was pushed by President Oscar Arias. Who funds the Arias Foundation? George Soros.[31]

Who is the world's leading "humanitarian" spokesman for the United Nations Arms Trade Treaty, a Soros project to impose an embargo on arms sales to the United States and Israel? Oscar Arias.

Make no mistake that IANSA and Soros have any long-run agenda that is nothing short of total prohibition. IANSA even wants the police to be disarmed, because, as Rebecca Peters says, "When police begin to carry guns, that motivates criminals to carry guns."

IANSA is so extreme that it complains that the gun laws of England are too lax, and that gun ownership rates in England are too high. IANSA gloats when guns are taken from sportsmen; the group's website celebrated when the government of Uruguay destroyed thousands of firearms, the majority of which had been "gathered" from the Ministry of Livestock, Agriculture and Fishing. IANSA was pleased with "the country's first destruction of weapons previously used for hunting and sports."[32] So it is no surprise that Soros and his minions went all out to try to pass the gun confiscation referendum in Brazil.[33]

But the people of Brazil stood together, and repudiated Soros's anti-freedom agenda. So did the people of the United States in the 2004 election, when they rejected Soros's candidate, John Kerry, who would have let Soros and IANSA have their way at the 2006 U.N. antigun conference, creating a worldwide binding global antigun treaty, with the United States under its thumb.

John Kerry would have picked a U.S. ambassador to the U.N. who would have done the bidding of Soros and Peters. But President Bush nominated under secretary of state John Bolton, and the Soros machine went to war.

The website of Soros's Open Society Institute hosted a well-funded campaign titled "Stop Bolton!" Laughably, the Soros website used the heading "United Nations Reform" for its attempt to destroy one of the most pro-reform diplomats in U.N. history. One of the many organizations serving in Soros's anti-Bolton campaign was the Center for American Progress—run by John Podesta, who had been President Bill Clinton's White House chief of staff, and who would later run transition planning for president-to-be Barack

Obama.[34] As usual, much of the American media picked up the talking points generated by Soros and his proxies.

The NRA and other groups fought back. In the end, there were plenty of senators ready to vote to confirm John Bolton, but they could not vote because for the first time in history, a nominee for United Nations Ambassador was filibustered. President Bush hung tough, and used the constitutional provision allowing him to make a "recess appointment." Thus, Bolton was able to serve from August 2005 until December 2006, which, at least, was long enough to thwart Soros at the U.N.'s antigun conference in June-July 2006.

Soros and Censoring Free Speech

The McCain-Feingold campaign speech restriction law was written to impair the ability of National Rifle Association members to collectively participate in elections. It is a law that was bought and paid for George Soros and his ultra-rich buddies, carefully written to suppress your speech while empowering theirs. And that law was just the beginning of their plans to take away your First Amendment rights.

The McCain-Feingold law set up a sixty-day period of censorship before general elections, and thirty days before primaries. During that period, corporations (which include public interest groups like the NRA) and unions are forbidden from buying "issue advocacy" advertising that mentions a federal candidate, or which refers to the candidate by title (e.g., "our senator").

Here's an example of an illegal act under McCain-Feingold: In mid-September, the Senate is considering a bill to register all guns. The NRA buys ads on national television networks, saying: "Gun registration doesn't solve crimes. It invades your privacy rights, and makes gun confiscation easy. Please call your senator and ask him to vote against the gun registration bill."

The advertisement is inside the sixty-day pre-election censorship period. The ad does not mention any names, but it does say "your senators." So viewers in Pennsylvania would know that the ad is referring, in part, to the two senators from Pennsylvania. One of the senators from Pennsylvania is running for reelection, and so are two dozen other senators around the country.[35]

Thus, the advertisement was forbidden under McCain-Feingold, with criminal penalties attached. It was the worst federal censorship law in American history—worse even than the Sedition Act of 1798. (At least for the Sedition Act, speech could not be punished if it was truthful.)

Congress passed and, unfortunately, President Bush signed the McCain-Feingold censorship law because they thought that the American people were demanding it, to "get the money out of politics." As it turned out, Congress was tricked. The "grassroots" support was a fabrication, the creation of a coterie of the ultra-rich and their foundations. Soros put in $18 million.[36] Eighty-eight percent of the $140 million that was spent to push McCain-Feingold came from Soros's Open Society Institute and seven of its foundation allies.[37]

One of the groups in the Soros axis was the Pew Charitable Trusts. After McCain-Feingold had been signed into law, a former program officer at Pew, named Sean Treglia, spilled the beans. Journalist Ryan Sager obtained a videotape of Treglia speaking at the University of Southern California, Annenberg School for Communication, in March 2004.

"I'm going to tell you a story that I've never told any reporter," said Treglia. "Now that I'm several months away from Pew and we have campaign-finance reform, I can tell this story."

The billionaires would spread their money around "to create an impression that a mass movement was afoot—that everywhere they looked, in academic institutions, in the business community, in religious groups, in ethnic groups, everywhere, people were talking about reform."[38]

Some asked, "What would have happened had a major news organization gotten ahold of this at the wrong time?"

"We had a scare," Treglia answered. "As the debate was progressing and getting pretty close, George Will stumbled across a report that we had done and attacked it in his column. And a lot of his partisans were becoming aware of Pew's role and were feeding him information. And he started to reference the fact that Pew had played a large role in this—that this was a liberal attempt to hoodwink Congress."

Treglia continued: "But you know what the good news is from my perspective?" He answered his own question: "Journalists didn't care . . . So no one followed up on the story. And so there was a panic there for a couple of weeks because we thought the story was going to begin to gather steam, and no one picked it up."

What Pew, and Soros, and the rest of the axis did to the First Amendment is little different from what they have been trying with the Second Amendment: create groups such as the Million Mom March or IANSA that purport to speak for the views of vast numbers of ordinary citizens—but that really represent little more than the views of the Soros axis itself. Count on a compliant media to amplify these voices and present them as if they were true citizen organizations. And then have your most powerful political friends— such as Hillary Clinton and Kofi Annan—use their power to further bolster the groups and their Soros message.

The NRA has fought Soros every step of the way, defending the First and Second Amendments. We helped beat him in 2006 at the U.N., and saved the Second Amendment. But he won in Congress with McCain-Feingold in 2002, and dealt a devastating blow to the First Amendment. The NRA took the case to the U.S. Supreme Court, while the Soros axis paid lawyers to defend the censorship law. Soros won 5–4 in the case of *McConnell v. Federal Election Commission*.

Dissenting in *McConnell v. FEC*, Justice Clarence Thomas warned that the Court had paved the way for censorship of other media. The Obama Department of Justice agreed. In the spring 2009 case of *Citizens United v. Federal Election Commission*, the Obama administration told the Supreme Court that it would be constitutional for the censorship law to be extended even to block the publication of books.

Fortunately, the Court's January 2010 decision in *Citizens United v. Federal Election Commission* removed unconstitutional restrictions on NRA's ability to speak freely at election time. The ruling is a victory for anyone who believes that the First Amendment applies to each and every one of us. It is a defeat for arrogant elitists such as George Soros who wanted to carve out free speech as a privilege for themselves; and for those who believed that speech had a dollar value and should be treated and regulated like currency, and not a freedom. The Court's decision reaffirms that the Bill of Rights was written for every American, and it will amplify the voice of average citizens who want their voices heard.

The NRA has been in the forefront of defending the First Amendment so we can protect the Second Amendment. This ruling is clearly a victory for our continuing efforts to educate voters on where politicians stand on our fundamental, individual right to keep and bear arms.

Soros Axis and Obama Target the Airwaves

It is radio, however, where the Soros axis and Obama have set their sights next. They want to control the content of radio programs.

There has been a lot of discussion about Obama using the Federal Communications Commission (FCC) to restore the so-called Fairness Doctrine. This doctrine was applied to television and radio from 1949 until 1987, when the Reagan administration lifted it. In theory, it was supposed to mean that radio and TV stations had to present balanced viewpoints. In practice, it was rarely applied to news programs, no matter how egregiously biased, or how unfairly they slanted a program against gun owners. The Fairness Doctrine was very effective in deterring radio stations from airing talk programs where the host forthrightly declared his or her own position or ideology. In fact, talk radio programs as we now know them came into existence only because the Fairness Doctrine was repealed.

GEORGE SOROS

Certainly there are some in Congress and other advocates—almost all
of whom happen to be antigun—who have called for reinstating the Fairness
Doctrine, and even for extending it to other media, such as the Internet.

Although the First Amendment forbids government infringement of
the freedom of the press, there used to be a common view that radio and
television were not entitled to the same protections as newspapers or other
print media. The theory was that the broadcast spectrum was very finite;
since a given city might have only three or five television stations, and since
the government "owned" the airwaves (supposedly), the government should
ensure that programming was balanced.

That rationale is no longer plausible. Thanks to cable TV, satellite
TV and radio, and the Internet, there is near-infinite availability of different
television and radio channels—delivered by traditional radio and TV airwaves,
or by cable TV lines, or by satellite transmission, or by any of the many ways
that the Internet is accessed.

While the threat of a reimposed Fairness Doctrine remains, I think
that Obama will more likely try another approach—taken from the Soros-
Clinton mastermind John Podesta.[39] (More on Podesta in a little bit.)

Here's how it would work. Every radio and television station needs
a broadcast license from the Federal Communications Commission. The
five FCC Commissioners are appointed to staggered terms by the president.
Already, four of the five commissioners are Obama picks.

The radio and television licenses must be renewed every few years.
Now, it would be a little crude (and too obviously unconstitutional) for
Obama-appointed commissioners to create a rule saying, "In order to renew
a broadcast license, a radio station must drop conservative talk programs such
as those hosted by Glenn Beck, Rush Limbaugh, or Sean Hannity. The station
must replace these popular hosts with other programs that will not criticize
President Obama, and that will support his agenda, including gun control."

But there's a way to impose this same rule without saying so directly.
Podesta's think tank, the Center for American Progress (CAP), has outlined

481

the plan. Obama's campaign adopted it. CAP's 2007 research paper, *The Structural Imbalance of Political Talk Radio*, reports how many hours of right-wing and left-wing talk radio are broadcast in different U.S. markets. The paper shows that the number of hours of right-leaning programs greatly exceeds the number for left-leaning programs.

The explanation is easy, although Podesta's group ignored it: radio stations are in business to make money. They make money by attracting large audiences, since the bigger the audience, the higher the advertising rate a station can charge. Radio stations often pick conservative hosts because they attract the largest audiences. Perhaps one reason audiences like to listen to conservative talk radio hosts is that the opposite perspective dominates most network and local television news programs, and most newspapers. The difference is that the leftist writers and television reporters pretend to be neutral, whereas the radio hosts are honest about their perspectives.

Podesta and CAP were not interested in encouraging more balance in newspapers or television. Rather, they figured that if they could change the ownership of the radio stations, then the radio stations might stop buying the conservative talk programs:

> We believe that minority and female owners, who tend to be more local, are more responsive to the needs of their local communities and are therefore less likely to air the conservative hosts because this type of programming is so far out of step with their local audiences. Additionally, minority-owned stations are more likely to be found in areas with high minority populations—areas that also report high percentages of progressives and liberals.[40]

So under the CAP theory, radio stations are forcing conservative talk radio hosts onto reluctant listeners, and the solution is to use FCC ownership rules so that more stations are locally owned, especially by nonwhite owners.

The analysis is dubious. The residents of Washington, D.C., are overwhelmingly Democratic and nonwhite. Yet the *Rush Limbaugh Show* gets great ratings there. Meanwhile, the all-Left-all-the-time Air America had such a tiny D.C. audience that the ratings agencies could not even rate it. Even in Madison, Wisconsin, where Leftist ideas are very popular, Air America ratings have been dismal.[41]

So dismal, in fact, that on January 21, 2010, Air America Radio ceased live programming and announced that it would file for Chapter 7 bankruptcy protection. The problem with Air America was that, in terms of pure radio skill, none of its hosts were as talented as Limbaugh, Hannity, or Beck. Besides, if you lived in D.C. or Madison and you wanted left-leaning radio, you could just tune into a National Public Radio station, with its high production values and program quality.

The CAP report concludes: "Ultimately, these results suggest that increasing ownership diversity, both in terms of the race/ethnicity and gender of owners, as well as the number of independent local owners, will lead to more diverse programming, more choices for listeners and more owners who are responsive to their local communities and serve the public interest."[42]

Barack Obama's campaign plan to change radio adopts the CAP strategy: "Barack Obama believes that the nation's rules ensuring diversity of media ownership are critical to the public interest. Unfortunately, over the past several years, the Federal Communications Commission (FCC) has promoted the concept of consolidation over diversity."[43]

So, "as president, he will encourage diversity in the ownership of broadcast media, promote the development of new media outlets for expression of diverse viewpoints and clarify the public interest obligations of broadcasters who occupy the nation's spectrum. An Obama presidency will promote greater coverage of local issues and better responsiveness by broadcasters to the communities they serve."[44]

In other words: Adopt new FCC rules or guidelines against one company owning several radio stations. When license renewal time comes, force the company to sell some or most of its stations to local owners, with female or minority owners being favored. The radio corporations, knowing that they need to curry favor with the FCC on a wide range of regulatory issues, will obediently sell to local insiders who are favored by the Obama machine.

Now, once the new, Obama-favored owners have their own local stations, some of them might decide they just want to make the most profits possible, and so they would keep the conservative hosts, in order to attract the largest audiences.

Most owners, however, would probably be savvy enough to know that their new broadcast license will itself be coming up for renewal in a few years. And when it does, the owners had better be in the good graces of the Federal Communications Commission. So the owners will dump the conservative talk show hosts, and replace them with something "local" that will not annoy the Obama machine. Like a sports talk program. Or a program by a "community activist" who spouts the Obama line.

Obama has taken the first step, appointing as chief diversity officer at the Federal Communications Commission a far-left radical named Mark Lloyd. Lloyd favors extensive new federal controls over the political content of radio and television programs, and dismisses "exaggerated" concern for the First Amendment.[45]

From Maine to Hawaii, radio programs that criticize the Obama administration may be taken off the air—thanks to technical regulatory changes that can be passed off to the American public as promoting local business and giving minorities a break. You can hardly deny that George Soros made a good investment in John Podesta and the Center for American Progress.

More Paid Speech for Soros

McCain-Feingold became law thanks in part to $18 million from the George Soros axis. According to *USA Today*, "Soros says he always suspected that any campaign-finance changes would have 'loopholes' because money and power are elemental forces."[46]

"Suspected" is probably an understatement. "Knew in advance and planned for it" might be more accurate, since Soros could hire the finest lawyers in the world to tell him about the loopholes in the McCain-Feingold draft bill. And perhaps to make sure that they stayed in the bill.

Senator Mitch McConnell of Kentucky could also see some of the loopholes. He warned the Senate: "We haven't taken a penny of money out of politics, we have only taken the parties out of politics. This is a massive transfer of speech away from the two great political parties to the press, to academia, to Hollywood, to billionaires . . . This is a stunningly stupid thing to do."[47]

Or it's a stunningly clever thing to do, for a billionaire with a long-term strategy. In the 2004 presidential election, George Soros would spend $27 million,[48] and the circle of ultra-rich allies he recruited would spend much more, exploiting the McCain-Feingold loopholes. The *Wall Street Journal* observed that by drastically reducing donations to political parties, Soros had "cleared a path to make himself the biggest bankroller in Democratic politics."[49]

The spending of the Soros axis was all the more powerful because their McCain-Feingold law had restricted not only donations to parties, but had also infringed the freedom of speech of citizen groups such as the National Rifle Association. As the *Wall Street Journal* had observed, "Joining with other small donors in one larger cause (the Sierra Club or NRA) is sometimes the only way, other than voting, that the non-rich can influence politics," but (thanks to Soros), "small donors have had their speech restricted by the limits on advertising imposed on traditional lobbying groups 60 days before an election."[50]

Speaking on behalf of McCain-Feingold, antigun senator Chris Dodd of Connecticut had inveighed against "money that threatens to drown out the voice of the average voter of average means." Yet McCain-Feingold cracked down on "the average voter of average means" who supported groups such as the NRA, leaving those voters silenced while the plutocrats tried to buy the election.

Soros's Open Society Institute had promoted McCain-Feingold by warning about "the corrupting influence of very large donors." Yet Soros asserted that it was all right for him to spend vastly more than what might have been spent by one of the "large donors" who had been shut down by McCain-Feingold: "Campaign reform was designed to get special interests out of politics. And I have no special interests; I'm not interested in any favorable treatment of any kind. I'm really concerned with the public interest."[51]

In an article titled "Super Rich Step into Political Vacuum: McCain-Feingold Paved Way for 527s," the *Washington Post* explained how Soros organized the plutocracy to exploit the McCain-Feingold loopholes.[52]

Harold Ickes, a hatchet man from the Clinton administration, wrote a memo in 2001, well before McCain-Feingold had been enacted, warning that because McCain-Feingold would drastically reduce donations to political parties, the Democrats should start using 527 organizations for fund-raising.

A "527" gets its name from the section of the Internal Revenue Code that defines what it is. A 527 is not allowed to urge the election of a candidate, but it can engage in activities such as voter registration, get-out-the-vote, or issue advocacy.

One of the perversities of McCain-Feingold was that it left 527s completely free to advocate on issues, whereas the NRA was restricted from issue advocacy during the sixty-day preelection censorship period.

Ickes and some other Democratic powerhouses decided to create a 527, and to call it America Coming Together (ACT). Ickes also planned another 527, dubbed "the Media Fund," to buy campaign ads. (The Media Fund ads would be the kind of "sham ads" that McCain-Feingold had aimed to shut down; although they did not explicitly urge a vote for or against a candidate, they promoted Kerry and attacked Bush.)

George Soros was angry at George W. Bush, and had hired political consultants to figure out how he could use the 527 loophole. Soros and his consultants studied ACT, to decide if it were structurally sound, and decided that it was.[53]

Soros set up a small meeting in July 2003 at his estate in Southampton, Long Island. Exactly who was at the meeting remains a secret, but the result was that Soros pledged $10 million to get ACT started, and his wealthy friends also joined in.

Clinton to Soros: "This Is the Ball Game."

Soros hosted a dinner that November in Manhattan, featuring former president Bill Clinton, to raise millions more for ACT and the Media Fund. Clinton told the donors: "If we'd had these two groups in 2000, we wouldn't be sitting here tonight. This is the ball game."

The Clintons have long been part of the Soros network. Strobe Talbott—who had been Clinton's Oxford roommate, and who served as his deputy secretary of state—worked closely with Soros and considered him "a sort of shadow arm of the State Department."[54] When the Clintons were in the White House, Soros never had trouble when he wanted to meet with the president or First Lady.[55]

Soon, the National Rifle Association was spreading the word about Soros's scheme. Soros fired back with an op-ed.[56] He wrote that there had been "a lot of name-calling about my donations," by the National Rifle Association.

He insisted: "I have scrupulously abided by both the letter and the spirit of the law . . . I have contributed to independent organizations that by law are forbidden to coordinate their activities with the political parties or candidates."

Back when McCain-Feingold was being pushed through Congress, Soros had given money to a group called Democracy 21 to help support the bill. The group's president, Fred Wertheimer, now said that "George Soros started out as part of the solution, and he's ended up as part of the problem." He accused Soros of helping to start "a soft-money arms race."[57]

Brigham Young University political science professor David Magleby explained that "Soros breathed life and funds into what has become a well-developed array of new groups tailor-made to operate under the new rules . . .

He was a beacon for the old Democratic soft money . . . Soros put the new groups in business. He set up the storefront."[58]

As Soros had written, his 527s were legally forbidden to coordinate with political parties or candidates. But they did coordinate.

The *Washington Post* observed that "ACT often seems remarkably in sync with Democratic Party activities."[59]

Harold Ickes, the chief of staff of ACT (and formerly, director of the Media Fund) was also a member of the executive committee of the Democratic National Committee. According to the *Post*, "Official minutes and meeting transcripts show the executive committee got campaign briefings from Kerry's campaign manager, Mary Beth Cahill, and top DNC officials."[60]

Ickes told the *Post* that his dual role did not violate the anti-coordination law, because the DNC Executive Committee meetings did not discuss DNC communication strategies. Besides that, the DNC supposedly kept its own executive committee in the dark about almost everything: "The executive committee of the DNC knows less about what the DNC is doing than the average newspaper reader."[61] Sure.

ACT's purpose was voter registration and turn-out in swing states. The Democratic National Committee, by some odd but uncoordinated coincidence, mostly abandoned the traditional party roles of voter registration and turn-out in some key swing states, and ACT filled the gap.[62] Not that ACT and the DNC were illegally coordinating, of course.

ACT had nearly six thousand paid employees, and seventy-eight field offices.[63] Ninety-one percent of ACT's money came from people who gave $100,000 or more.[64] Soros put six million dollars into the Media Fund, for its sham ads on TV and radio.[65]

MoveOn.org had been set up during the latter part of the Clinton administration, to defend Clinton against impeachment and conviction. The group stayed in business, and by the 2004 election, had set up its own 527. Soros gave them $15 million during the 2003–04 election cycle.[66]

The laws against coordination with political parties did not stop MoveOn. org from working with the Democratic National Committee. For example, the DNC website announced, "The Democratic Party is partnering with MoveOn. org" for "a massive public mobilization" against the Bush tax cuts.[67]

Likewise, the party's website enthused:

> The DNC is also conducting a major petition drive in partnership with MoveOn.org. More than 310,000 Americans have signed the petition to protect our courts—with more than 172,000 of those signatures coming in the past 36 hours. The petition calls on Bush and the Republicans to stop nominating judges that are out of step with mainstream Americans and praising the Democrats for standing up for their rights.

Other Soros expenditures were to more mysterious groups. Soros Fund Management gave $500,000 to the Campaign for a Progressive Future (CPF). So did the Irene Diamond Fund, Soros's old partner in financing antigun junk lawsuits. Soros also made a separate personal donation. CPF did nothing to draw attention to itself, but another group described the CPF as an "organization that supports candidates opposed by the National Rifle Association."[68]

There was also America Votes, a get-out-the-vote organization consisting of some respectable organizations, as well as ACORN (a far left entity infamous for fraudulent voter registration), plus the Brady Campaign and its subsidiary the Million Mom March. George's son Jonathan Soros gave them $250,000, and George himself contributed $500,000 in 2005[69]

One of the ironies of the 2004 election was that some ordinary citizens who were sincerely opposed to George Bush put "Billionaires for Bush" bumper stickers on their cars. The bumper stickers were supposed to be an ironic comment about Bush. Probably very few of the folks driving the cars with the bumper stickers realized that Kerry himself was married to a billionaire, and that the pro-Kerry campaign was dependent on a small coterie of the ultrarich led by George Soros. Perhaps never in American history has a major party presidential candidate been so indebted to a few plutocrats as was John Kerry to the Soros cabal in 2004.

The web of Soros is immense. A report by Discover the Networks revealed that Soros and his Open Society Institute have funded 143 different organizations in recent years.[70] Among the beneficiaries of his largesse are the Alliance for Justice and People for the American Way—a pair of misnamed lobbies dedicated to opposing the confirmation of judges who support First and Second Amendment rights. Also on the list are a host of organizations that promote gun control, including the American Constitution Society, American Friends Service Committee, The American Prospect, Amnesty International, ACORN, Brookings Institution, the Nation Institute, Physicians for Social Responsibility, Sojourners, and the infamous Southern Poverty Law Center, which has a specialty in bogus reports claiming that gun rights activists are incipient terrorists. There's also the Coalition for an International Criminal Court, anti-hunting groups such as Defenders of Wildlife, and numerous anti-Israel, anti-U.S., pro-illegal immigration, and extreme Left organizations.

The Soros Philosophy: No Sovereignty for You!

One of the groups that agreed with Soros about the importance of stopping the nomination of John Bolton was Citizens for Global Solutions, formerly known as the World Federalist Association. It is the leading U.S. organization promoting the eradication of U.S. sovereignty and its replacement with global government by the United Nations.[71]

George Soros thinks that America is a deeply flawed nation. He has written that he has always "felt that modern society in general and America in particular suffer from a deficiency of values."[72]

Speaking at Columbia University's commencement, he told the students and their parents: "If President Bush is reelected, we must ask the question, 'What is wrong with us?'"[73]

In the upside-down world of George Soros, America is what's wrong with the world. Soros opposed not only the invasion of Iraq, but also the invasion of Afghanistan that destroyed al-Qaeda's training camps there.[74]

Soros scolded: "When President Bush says, as he does frequently, that freedom will prevail, in fact he means that America will prevail."[75] Well, that's how things usually work out. When America wins, freedom wins (as in the American Revolution and World War II). When America loses (as in Vietnam), there's never a democracy on the winning side.

Soros considers him an acolyte of the great philosopher Karl Popper. Soros took Popper's classes at the London School of Economics.[76] Popper's great work is the two-volume *The Open Society and Its Enemies*.[77] Popper, having experienced Nazi and Communist totalitarianism in Europe, argued that successful societies must be "open" rather than "closed," must embrace change, must have transparent and responsive governments, must be tolerant of all opinions, must recognize that all "truths" are contingent rather than absolute, and must never assume that their own beliefs or morals are infallible or are superior to those of others.

Soros adored Popper's work, and Soros's Open Society Institute is named after Popper's books. Many of Soros's good works in Eastern Europe, helping to build civil society, have been precisely the kind of projects that Popper might have applauded.

Popper was also extremely distrustful of strong nationalism, which he viewed as leading to closed, retrograde, intolerant societies, and to tribalism. According to Soros, what really got him upset about George W. Bush was Bush's strong sense of American nationalism.[78]

However, Soros's war on the First and Second Amendments indicates that Soros, who has always fancied himself a great philosopher,[79] has drastically misunderstood Popper. At the least, the anti–Bill of Rights projects of Soros's "Open Society Institute" promote the opposite of what Popper meant by an open society.

The Open Society and Its Enemies is built around Popper's critique of three philosophers: Plato, Georg Wilhelm Friedrich Hegel (a nineteenth-century German who elaborated on Plato's political ideas and created the intellectual basis for fascism), and Karl Marx. All three were advocates of government censorship. Soros's efforts to suppress political speech in the United States have much more in common with Plato, Hegel, and Marx than with the openness advocated by Popper.

Second, Plato and Hegel strongly believed that the government should have a monopoly of force. Every government that has ever called itself "Marxist" has adopted the same principle.

Popper believed the opposite. He devoted considerable energy to arguing that Plato was an ally of the Thirty Tyrants, who took over Athens in 404 BC. The Tyrants murdered approximately 8 percent of the Athenian population. Popper lauded the Athenian resistance: "The democrats fought on. At first only seventy strong, they prepared under the leadership of Thrasybulus and Antyus the liberation of Athens, where Critias [leader of the Thirty Tyrants] was meanwhile killing scores of citizens." After months of warfare, the democrats destabilized the Tyrants, who then lost their support from Sparta, and democracy was restored to Athens.[80]

Yet IANSA and Soros are doing everything possible to ensure that a democratic rebellion against a dictatorship becomes impossible. Soros proxies, such as IANSA, are absolutely insistent that the world's citizens not have arms with which to resist tyranny and mass murder by government. At the U.N. gun control conferences, and in the Arms Trade Treaty, they are attempting to outlaw the supplying of arms to democratic groups that are fighting to liberate their nations from tyrants. Soros here is working against what Karl Popper advocated:

> I am not in all cases and all circumstances against a violent revolution. I believe with some medieval and Renaissance Christian thinkers who taught the admissibility of tyrannicide that

there may indeed, under a tyranny, be no other possibility, and a violent revolution may be justified.[81] . . . In other words, the use of violence is justified only under a tyranny which makes reforms without violence impossible, and it should have only one aim, that is, to bring about a state of affairs which makes reforms without violence possible . . .

There is only one further use of violence in political quarrels which I should consider justified. I mean the resistance, once democracy has been attained, to any attack (whether from within or without the state) against the democratic constitution and the use of democratic methods. Any such attack, especially if it comes from the government in power, or if it is tolerated by it, should be resisted by all loyal citizens, even to the use of violence. In fact, the working of democracy rests largely on the understanding that a government which attempts to misuse its powers and to establish itself as a tyranny (or which tolerates the establishment of a tyranny by anybody else) outlaws itself, and that citizens have not only a right but also a duty to consider the action of such a government as a crime, and its members as a dangerous gang of criminals.[82]

Although Popper's writing style is different from that of James Madison or Thomas Jefferson, his viewpoint on the issue of resistance to tyranny is the same. The above paragraphs are an excellent summary of the philosophy of the Second Amendment. The Soros war on the Second Amendment is a war on the Open Society itself.

It says a lot that Soros's closest ally at the United Nations, Mark Malloch Brown, was not only a fervent gun ban advocate, but also ran something that was nicknamed the United Nations Dictators Program. Despite Soros's past good works in Eastern Europe, he has become one of the chief modern enemies of the Open Society.

Soros is a critic of what he calls "excessive individualism."[83] There's no doubt that to both friends and enemies of the Second Amendment, the firearm is a very powerful symbol of individualism, and that the possession of firearms promotes attitudes of individualism and self-reliance.

Yet there's one more twist in trying to figure out what motivates Soros. Consider what Soros did to political speech: in the name of "reform," he successfully pushed for a law that partly suppressed the speech of the political parties and of citizen organizations. With traditional speech (including the spending of money to communicate that speech to large audiences) diminished, Soros became the grand moneybags of the Democratic, and his fund-raising network was essential to the party's 2004 presidential campaign.

Now, Soros and his agents are working hard to drastically reduce gun possession around the world by ordinary people. Yet even while promoting gun bans, Soros was funding armed revolutionaries. In Serbia in the final years of the twentieth century, he spent lavishly to fund sympathetic organizations, including an organization all-Left-all-the-time of seventy thousand militant youths, called Otpor. On Serbian election night, September 26, 2000, the vote was disputed, because both sides had cheated. A few days later, Soros's forces took to the streets. Although they worked hard to gain the support (or at least not the opposition) of the police and military, they did use guns and Molotov cocktails. And Otpor blockaded the capital of Belgrade, leading forces armed with AK-47 rifles, mortars, and antitank weapons. The government collapsed, and Soros's side took over.[84]

I'd say that this counts as a good deed by Soros, since the Serbian president whom he ousted was the mass murderer Slobodan Miloševic. But it does make me wonder. Some campaign finance activists were sincere in wanting to "get the money out of politics," and never realized until it was too late that they might have been a pawn in a broader Soros strategy of getting *other people's* money out of politics, thereby making his own political money much more important. I wonder if Soros-funded groups such as the Brady Campaign (who are unquestionably sincere and earnest in wanting to get rid of guns) may also be pawns. Perhaps the bumper sticker for the twenty-first century might read, "When guns are outlawed, only George Soros's friends will have guns."

There were plenty of people, including perhaps Senators McCain and Feingold, who did not realize what a gigantic loophole that campaign finance "reform" would create for George Soros. Who knows what the Soros loophole might be in some future gun ban?

We do know that George Soros does not feel obliged to play by other people's rules during times of "regime change"—a time he defines to include American elections. He asserts that his efforts to oust George W. Bush were essentially the same as his (successful) efforts to overthrow dictatorships in Yugoslavia, Croatia, and Slovakia.[85]

George Soros and Barack Obama

George Soros came very close to successfully buying the election for John Kerry. Had he prevailed, the U.N. would have created a global gun control treaty in 2006. President Kerry would have appointed two Supreme Court justices (Sonia Sotomayor was already being mentioned as a nominee), and *District of Columbia v. Heller* would have been a 6–3 loss instead of 5–4 win. The Second Amendment would have been judicially nullified, and the Soros/IANSA axis of global gun banners would be marching toward final victory.

If not for the National Rifle Association, Soros would have been triumphant. About six million votes were cast in Ohio, a state where about a third of households own firearms. So there were about two million votes cast by gun-owning families. If John Kerry had gotten just sixty thousand of George Bush's votes, Kerry would have become president of the United States. Did NRA convince at least sixty thousand Ohio voters not to believe John Kerry's bogus claim that he was a staunch friend of the Second Amendment? I'm sure of it.

One of the Soros 527 groups, America Coming Together, had hoped to keep going after 2004, but had to shut down because once Bush was reelected, many donors lost interest.[86] Soros, however, knows how to work in the long term. He soon went to work with his fellow far-left billionaires to build a political infrastructure that would put a suitable agent in the White House in 2009.

Billionaires for Big Government is the title of the report from the Capital Research Center (CRC) that describes what happened next: "In April 2005, Soros and the other major players assembled a large group for a secret planning session. Seventy millionaires and billionaires met in Phoenix, Arizona, to discuss how to develop a long-term strategy."[87]

At first they called it the "Phoenix Project." Then the name was changed to the "Democracy Alliance"—a rather inaccurate moniker for a plutocratic cabal dedicated to a secret political takeover of the United States.

Reporting on Soros's machinations in the *Washington Post*, the *Post* explained that the "Democracy Alliance" was "made up of billionaires and millionaires." As one California trial lawyer put it: "Like a lot of elite groups, we fly beneath the radar."[88]

According to the *Post*, "The goal was to invest in groups that could be influential in building what activists call 'political infrastructure'—institutions that can support Democratic causes not simply in the next election, but for years to come." The *Post* said that more than two dozen organizations had already been funded by the DA.[89]

One of the DA's beneficiaries has been People for the American Way (an antigun organization that vehemently fought the confirmation of Supreme Court Justices John Roberts and Samuel Alito). Another has been the Association of Community Organizations for Reform Now (ACORN), a deeply corrupt organization known for fraudulent voter registration. Barack Obama had worked closely with ACORN since his early days on the South Side of Chicago, and in 2008, ACORN put a massive effort into electing him.[90]

The DA has also been funding John Podesta and his Center for American Progress (CAP), the organization that forms the key link between the gun banning of the Clinton and the Obama administrations. I've already told you how CAP created Barack Obama's blueprint to get rid of pro-gun talk radio hosts.

Soros had given CAP $3 million in 2003.[91] In the first round of DA funding, CAP got $5 million more.[92] As White House chief of staff under Bill Clinton from 1998 to 2001, John Podesta had been at the top of the chain of command for Clinton's final gun control programs: the lawsuits against the firearms industry, the exploitation of the Columbine murders for political gain, the fabrication of the Soros-funded and Clinton-directed "Million" Mom March as a supposedly grassroots organization of housewives, and the rest of the dirty work carried out by Rahm Emanuel, Eric Holder, and the Clinton crew.

Back in July 2008, Barack Obama began planning his presidential transition. The *Atlantic* reported that "Podesta's Center for American Progress is working with the Third Way think tank on a Homeland Security Presidential Transition Initiative."[93]

The *Atlantic* called CAP a "Third Way think tank" because it is related to an organization called the Third Way. ("Third Way" is a political term of art for the policies of politicians such as Bill Clinton and Tony Blair, who see themselves as charting a "third way" between capitalism and socialism.) The Third Way group was founded in 2004. Jonathan Cowan is its president, and Jim Kessler is vice president for policy.

Kessler had once been Sen. Charles Schumer's main staffer on gun control.[94] Cowan had been chief of staff to Clinton's Housing and Urban Development secretary, Andrew Cuomo—at the time when Cuomo was cooking up a plan for public housing authorities all over the United States to file junk lawsuits against gun companies. (The NRA found out, and convinced Congress to shut down the plan.)

Between the Clinton years and the 2004 creation of Third Way, Cowan and Kessler ran a gun control organization called Americans for Gun Safety (AGS). That group (now defunct) had its own billionaire funder, Andrew McKelvey, owner of the job search website Monster.com. AGS, Cowan, and Kessler strove to portray themselves as sensible moderates on the gun issue, but they could not even bring themselves to acknowledge that the Second Amendment is an individual right, or to criticize the D.C. handgun ban.

They did, however, make an important contribution to the rhetoric of antigun politicians. They conducted polling that showed that "gun safety" was a more popular term than "gun control." (As it should be, since the NRA is the nation's oldest gun safety organization. But referring to gun control as "gun safety" is a deception.)

Kessler and Cowan also wrote the gun control script that Barack Obama, Hillary Clinton, and John Kerry would later follow: don't retreat an inch on any of your positions on gun control; but begin every answer to a question about gun control by declaring how much you respect the Second Amendment.[95]

Like George Soros's manipulative trading of foreign currencies, much of what his Axis of Plutocracy does is hidden from public view. For example, although we know that the Soros-funded Center for American Progress took the early lead in guiding Obama's staffing of the Department of Homeland Security, we cannot know for sure whether CAP helped set the stage for the Department's report—released just a few weeks after Obama took office—that was sent to every law enforcement agency in the United States, and that warned that people who were worried about Obama's gun control policy might be domestic terrorists.

We do know that since the late twentieth century, two donors have stood far above all the rest as consistent, extremely generous funders of the gun prohibition movement. One of those donors was George Soros. The other was the Joyce Foundation. Barack Obama served on the Joyce Foundation board for years, and, after being defeated in a 2000 race for the U.S. House of Representatives, considered becoming its president. As a member of the board of directors of the Joyce Foundation, Obama voted over and over for large grants for anti–Second Amendment research and for gun prohibition advocacy.[96]

George Soros worked for years and invested shrewdly in everything that was necessary for "regime change" in America—for a president who shared his views on guns, and who would embrace rather than resist Soros's domestic and international antigun agenda. Soros has succeeded.

Chapter 20

Obama Appointments

Barack Obama and Hillary Clinton have plenty of helpers for their anti-rights schemes. First of all, there's the legal quadumvirate: State Department legal adviser Harold Koh, for inventing new antigun legal theories loosely based on international law; attorney general Eric Holder, to take those theories to the Supreme Court; and justices Sonia Sotomayor and Elena Kagan, to turn those theories into the law of the land.

At the head of the antigun army was White House chief of staff Rahm Emanuel, formerly the director of President Bill Clinton's antigun campaign. The Obama team stands ready for the day when gun owners will become the target of Emanuel's rule: "You don't ever want a crisis to go to waste; it's an opportunity to do important things that you would otherwise avoid."[1]

Rahm Emanuel: Top General in Bill Clinton's Antigun Army

Every army needs a general, and in the Obama army, that man was White House chief of staff Rahm Emanuel. And make no mistake—Emanuel is a ruthless and fierce enemy of the Second Amendment.

After raising millions of dollars for Bill Clinton's presidential campaign, Emanuel served as assistant to the president for political affairs, and then as senior adviser to the president for policy and strategy. In practice, he was in charge of the Clinton antigun campaign.

To pass the 1994 ban on so-called assault weapons, Clinton had told reluctant Democrats that once the ban was passed, the Clinton administration would be finished with gun control. Add this to the list of Clinton lies.

Clinton never relented on making life harder and harder for licensed firearms dealers. He got back into the gun ban business in 1998, using administrative power to outlaw the importation of fifty-eight types of firearms, as well as accessories for those guns. "We're bending the law as far as we can to ban an entirely new class of guns," boasted Rahm Emanuel.

Using the same type of rhetoric that Obama would employ during the presidential campaign, Emanuel asserted that the outlawed guns were "military weapons, not sporting weapons." And "those weapons were designed for one purpose—military—and they don't belong on our streets." According to Emanuel, the new import ban applied to "the AK-47."[2]

None of this was true. Not one of the banned guns was manufactured primarily for military use. The AK-47, a fully automatic rifle that is common in the Third World, but very rare in the United States, was not affected by the ban. None of the banned guns were fully automatics.

The Firearms Owners' Protection Act of 1986 requires that import of a gun must be allowed if the gun is "particularly suitable for or readily adaptable to sporting purposes."[3] Many of the banned guns were, as attested by their trade names, such as "Hunter" or "Sporter."

Emanuel and Clinton, however, argued that the guns could be banned because a survey had shown that hunting guides rarely recommended those guns. So according to Clinton and Emanuel, the only true "sporting" use of a gun is to take it on a guided hunting trip.

Another reason to ban the guns, Emanuel argued, was that they "accept rounds in the 20, 30, 40, in some cases 100 rounds at a case [sic]."[4] But that's true for any gun that has a detachable magazine. If the gun uses a detachable magazine, it can use a detachable magazine of any size.

Emanuel was providing a rationale for outlawing any gun that takes a detachable magazine. Some countries have done so. Since the late 1980s, the American gun ban lobbies have been pushing to give federal regulators the same power.

Another Emanuel success was his campaign to mandate that trigger locks be sold with handguns. Never mind whether the buyer wanted or needed one, or if the buyer already had a gun safe.

One Emanuel effort that did not work was trying to impose a permanent waiting period on handgun purchases. As noted earlier, then deputy attorney General Eric Holder was a lead spokesman on Emanuel's effort.

Thanks to an NRA amendment that had been added to the Brady Bill in 1993, the "waiting period" of the Brady Act expired in February 1998. Congress had wanted to end the waiting period as soon as a National Instant Check System was operational. Congress also, wisely, worried that attorney general Janet Reno would never voluntarily certify that NICS was working well enough to let the waiting period end. So Congress ordered that if Reno had not ended the waiting period by February 1998, the waiting period would end automatically, and NICS would go into effect.

In 1998, Bill Clinton and Rahm Emanuel fought hard to keep the waiting period. Clinton declared it to be among his "top priorities." The waiting period "is very, very important," said Emanuel.

Why was it so important? Testifying before Congress on September 30, 1993, Clinton's assistant attorney general, Eleanor Acheson, had affirmed that there was no statistical evidence showing that handguns were often used in crimes just a few days after being bought.

In 1998, however, Emanuel told the American people: "Based on police research, 20 percent of the guns purchased that are used in murder are purchased within the week of the murder."

Absolutely false. When the NRA telephoned Emanuel's office, his staff admitted that the "factoid" was not based on police research—it was copied from "briefing materials provided by Handgun Control, Inc." (Handgun Control was one of the two prior names for the group that now calls itself the Brady Campaign.)

So the NRA called Handgun Control to ask them the source of their claim about "police research" and the 20 percent figure. We called them repeatedly, but they refused to answer. As is so often the case, their "research" was fiction, to put it politely.

Although Emanuel's high intelligence is beyond dispute, he apparently did not recognize when Handgun Control was misleading him. Emanuel showed a similar lack of perception after he left the White House in October 1998. Clinton appointed him to the board of directors for the Federal Home Loan Mortgage Corporation ("Freddie Mac"), where he drew a salary of $231,655.

During Emanuel's time as director, Freddie Mac was building the house of cards for the mortgage disaster that would send the U.S. into the worst financial crisis since the Great Depression. Freddie Mac used accounting tricks to hide the problems it was creating. The Securities and Exchange Commission later determined that Freddie Mac had defrauded investors by creating fake reports of multibillion-dollar profits. These fake reports were produced in 2000–2002, when Emanuel was on the board of directors, and when he was supposed to be protecting the public. But the board "failed in its duty to follow up on matters brought to its attention," according to the Office of Federal Housing Enterprise Oversight (OFHEO).[5]

Ironically, as White House chief of staff, Emanuel played a key role in the government programs that are supposed to fix the mess caused by the disaster Emanuel and Freddie Mac did so much to cause.

Emanuel was elected to the U.S. House of Representatives in 2002, taking a Chicago seat that had previously been held by such exemplars of honest public service as Rod Blagojevich and Dan Rostenkowski.

As a U.S. representative, Emanuel cosponsored H.R. 1312 to create a permanent ban on so-called assault weapons, even more sweeping than the 1994 Clinton ban, which expired in 2004. The bill would also have allowed the executive branch to do to domestic gun manufacture what Emanuel had done to imports in 1998: impose a ban with a stroke of the pen, without needing permission from Congress.

Emanuel also voted repeatedly against the Protection of Lawful Commerce in Firearms Act, which finally passed in 2005, and stopped most of the predatory lawsuits.

These days, Chicago and its suburb of Oak Park are the only U.S. cities with handgun bans. Emanuel proposed a plan to make a handgun ban national: outlaw the sale of normal handguns and allow only so-called smart guns to be sold. Never mind that "smart gun" technology is still far too primitive to be reliable for self-defense, which is why the police refuse to adopt it.

By the 2006 elections, the hardworking and highly partisan Emanuel became head of the Democratic Congressional Campaign Committee (DCCC). He accurately recognized that while gun control might be popular on the Gold Coast of Chicago, it was very unpopular in most of America. So in many districts, he recruited pro-gun Democratic candidates. Many of them became the Blue Dogs who would hold the balance of power in the 2009–10 House.

That, of course, doesn't mean that Emanuel has become a friend of the Second Amendment. It does mean that he has learned from the Clinton experience that keeping the antigun agenda permanently on the front burner is a political mistake.

My guess is that Obama and Emanuel have an antigun program that they are ready to unleash the moment there is a terrorist attack or some other atrocious crime. As Emanuel said, "You don't ever want a crisis to go to waste; it's an opportunity to do important things that you would otherwise avoid."[6]

As I've warned before, we know the attack is coming. Unless we are ready with all the necessary resources to fight back, the final disarmament of law-abiding Americans could very well occur beneath the shroud of antiterrorism legislation.

Harold Koh: Hillary Clinton's Legal Right Arm

Formerly the dean of the Yale Law School, Harold Hongju Koh is now legal adviser to the U.S. Department of State. He provides the legal support for what Secretary of State Hillary Clinton wants to do.

In April 2009, a coalition of pro-freedom scholars and activists sent a letter to the Senate Foreign Relations Committee, warning about Koh's long-standing efforts to undermine American sovereignty.[7] Among the signers was NRA First Vice-president David Keene, in his capacity as chairman of the American Conservative Union.

The letter explained that:

> due to the international nature of the position, the Legal Adviser must be relied upon to protect and defend the rights of American citizens and the interests of American institutions from the increasing (and to us, unwelcome) influence of international organizations, and must promote policies that preserve U.S. national security prerogatives, self-governance, and constitutional principles while defending American values from encroachment by transnational actors.

Koh's record has been the opposite. He is the mastermind of "transnationalism"—of working with foreigners to restrict American freedom of action, and the freedom of the American people.[8]

The legal adviser to the State Department represents the United States in every aspect of international law: drafting treaties and U.N. resolutions, and deciding their meanings; presenting the official legal views of the United States in international courts and other international organizations. And also deciding (based on the wishes of the secretary of state and the president) American government positions and policies on international law.

Koh has written that the "skill and maneuvering of particular well-positioned individuals" who are "serving as key institutional chokepoints" have a huge effect on American and international law.[9] Koh is now in that choke point position, and it is Second Amendment rights that are going to be choked.

Before becoming dean at Yale, Koh had been the Clinton administration's assistant secretary of state for democracy, human rights and labor, leaving office when Clinton did, in 2001. In a speech published in the *Fordham Law Review* in 2003, Koh explained that he felt that during his time under Clinton, there was "too much work left undone." So, said he, "after a few sleepless nights, I wrote for myself a list of issues on which I needed to do more in the years ahead. One of those issues was global regulation of small arms."[10]

Now, a Clinton is back in power, and so is Koh.

The title of Koh's speech at Fordham was "A World Drowning in Guns." According to that speech, Americans do not have any right to own guns. Instead, preventing people from having guns is a "human right." (That's also the official position of the misnamed "Human Rights Council" at the U.N., which I discussed in chapter 13).

According to Koh, "If we really care about human rights, we have to do something about the guns."[11]

He praised American scholars who were producing articles that argued against the view that the Second Amendment is a normal individual right. He sternly denounced John Bolton, who, as one of President Bush's delegates to the 2001 U.N. antigun conference, had warned that the United States would not sign any agreement that "contains measures abrogating the constitutional right to bear arms."[12]

Apparently looking forward to a total ban on guns, while acknowledging that such a ban could not be imposed immediately, Koh wrote, "We are a long way from persuading governments to accept a flat ban on the trade of *legal* arms."[13] It was Koh who, in the published version of his speech, put the emphasis on "legal," thus making it clear that a ban on legal arms is the ultimate goal.

What to do until "we" (Koh and his allies) can persuade governments to ban the trade of legal arms? Well, a good step on the way to banning guns is to first get them registered. That's the strategy laid out in 1976 by Pete Shields, who was running the group that now calls itself the Brady Campaign.[14]

That was the strategy used by gun banners in New York City, in the United Kingdom, in Australia, and in dictatorships such as Nazi Germany.[15] Before you ban guns, get them registered first. It's much easier to confiscate them if you already know where they are.

Speaking at Fordham, Koh said that international arms registries should be created. Kofi Annan, as secretary-general of the United Nations, had urged the same thing.

Remember back in the Bill Clinton administration, when the Brady Center was organizing mayors to bring junk lawsuits against firearms manufacturers? One of the explicit goals of the lawsuits was to put the manufacturers under the thumb of a special regulatory committee, with the regulatory committee under the control of the antigun lobbies.

Koh has a similar idea. He wants to give nongovernmental organizations official power to monitor how governments comply with international gun laws.[16] I don't think that Koh was trying to find a role for genuine civil rights organizations, such as the National Rifle Association, or similar organizations in other countries. Rather, Koh's official international monitors would likely be groups such as George Soros's International Action Network on Small Arms (IANSA), the international gun ban network that the U.N. has declared to be the "official" representative of civil society on gun issues.[17]

The U.N. gun-ban bureaucracy sometimes claims that it is only interested in controlling the transfer of arms from one country to another. Koh, at least, forthrightly stated that the goal is "stronger *domestic* regulation."[18] (Koh's emphasis.)

One reason that more restrictive *domestic* gun laws (and, ultimately, "a flat ban on the trade of *legal* arms") are needed is that "more guns have been associated with more, rather than less, crime." He told that audience that the idea "that more guns have been associated with less crime in American society" was wrong.[19]

In short, the world needs "a global system of effective controls on small arms."[20] According to Koh, "harmonizing our own national approach with those of other countries" is realistic and is politically possible.[21]

Of course "harmonizing our own national approach with those of other countries," is exactly the opposite of why the United States has fought for its independence and sovereignty again and again. The freedom-loving immigrants from every corner of the world who made their way to the United States came precisely because it was different from other countries. Precisely because our nation cherished the civil liberties that other countries did not.

Koh is not anti-American in the sense of disliking the United States. But he is hostile to the idea that our Constitution guarantees stronger rights than what might be found in the European Union.

For example, in an article in the *Stanford Law Review*, he derided John Bolton for saying that United States would not sign a global gun treaty that infringed the Second Amendment. Koh characterized Bolton's position as "claiming a Second Amendment exclusion from a proposed global ban on the illicit transfer of small arms and light weapons."[22] In Koh's view, the invocation of the Second Amendment was "the most problematic face of American exceptionalism."[23] To rely on the Second Amendment is not to "obey global norms." Such disobedience, in Koh's view, is the worst—in "order of ascending opprobrium"—form of American exceptionalism.[24]

Now, you may wonder how, legally speaking, Koh gets around the problem of the Second Amendment. At the time that Koh published his *Fordham* and *Stanford* articles, the lower federal courts were split on the meaning of the Second Amendment. Groups such as the Joyce Foundation (with Barack Obama on the board of directors) were giving money to gun ban groups such as the Violence Policy Center, and to disingenuous professors such as Saul Cornell, in order to produce "research" asserting that ordinary Americans do not have Second Amendment rights. Koh's *Fordham* article cheered on the anti-rights advocates.[25]

But those advocates were defeated in the *Heller* case in 2008. At Koh's 2009 confirmation hearing before the Senate Foreign Relations Committee, he insisted that he respected the Second Amendment. He assured senators that he did not believe foreign law could override the Second Amendment.

Yet there is less to these answers than meets the eye. Koh is an extremely intelligent and very talented wordsmith. What Koh said amounted to: "I agree that if there is a conflict between an international law and the Second Amendment, the Second Amendment would win."

But what does the Second Amendment mean? Koh's approach would be to use foreign law to guide the interpretation of the Second Amendment. Then, with the Second Amendment interpreted as narrowly as possible, there would be no conflict between the Second Amendment and the foreign laws.

We can see the outlines of the assault on the Second Amendment in his writings against the First Amendment. In the same *Stanford* article that complained about "American exceptionalism" for refusing to accept an international agreement that infringed Second Amendment rights, Koh also complained about the First Amendment: "Our exceptional free speech tradition can cause problems abroad, as, for example, may occur when hate speech is disseminated over the Internet. In my view, however, our Supreme Court can moderate these conflicts by applying more consistently the transnationalist approach to judicial interpretation."[26]

The same tactic can be used against the Second Amendment. That Amendment tells us that the right "shall not be infringed." The Supreme Court's decision in *District of Columbia v. Heller* says that a ban on handguns is an infringement, but that regulations on the commercial sale of arms are not an infringement, and neither is a ban on machine guns.

Regardless of whether one agrees with the particular examples that the Court picked, the Court made it clear that at least some kinds of gun control are not infringements.

Now, suppose a Supreme Court justice takes the "transnationalist" approach favored by Koh. The justice does not feel bound to follow the original understanding of the Constitution. Instead, he or she follows Koh's rule that the Supreme Court "must play a key role in coordinating U.S. domestic constitutional rules with rules of foreign and international law."[27]

So the justice looks at gun laws in other countries, finds that they are much more repressive than American laws, and decides to "coordinate" America's Constitution with the foreign and international laws. Then the court announces that it's fine to have an onerous licensing and registration system like that found in England, which was designed to drive people out of the shooting sports, and has reduced household gun ownership to only 4 percent.[28]

Or the court decides that it's all right to outlaw all gun stores (as Obama proposed), as long as there is one single government-run store where people can buy guns. And at that government-run store, the only gun that most people can buy is a .22 pistol, and nobody can own more than one gun. That's how they do things in Mexico, even though the Mexican Constitution guarantees a right to arms. (See chapter 8 for more on Mexico.)

If the Supreme Court did "harmonize" the Second Amendment with the gun laws of Mexico and similar nations, Koh could claim that the Second Amendment was not being trumped by foreign law. Rather, the Court was simply taking foreign law into account when interpreting an ambiguous portion of the Second Amendment.

Who decides what arguments the U.S. government will present to the U.S. Supreme Court about international law? Well, that's usually the role of the legal adviser, and that's Mr. Koh. Would the Supreme Court go along with Koh's ploys? If Obama gets to nominate some more justices such as Sonia Sotomayor and Elena Kagan (more on them to come), the answer is yes.

Charming Betsy Meets Harold Koh

Koh has some other tricks up his sleeve. According to Hofstra University law professor Julian Ku's report of a Koh speech, Koh "argued for a 'Constitutional *Charming Betsy* Canon' that would guide courts in the interpretation of the U.S. Constitution."[29]

You may wonder, what's a "*Charming Betsy* canon"? A canon is a rule of legal interpretation. For example, if two statutes conflict, there is a canon that states that the most recent statute should prevail.

Supreme Court chief justice John Marshall invented the *Charming Betsy* canon in an 1804 case over who owned the *Charming Betsy*, a schooner that had been captured during the Napoleonic wars, in which the United States was neutral. Part of the case turned on the interpretation of law that Congress had enacted regarding neutral trade. Chief Justice Marshall announced the principle that "an act of Congress ought never to be construed to violate the law of nations, if any other possible construction remains."[30] In other words, if the statute is ambiguous, adopt the interpretation that would not create a conflict with international law.

Koh, however, wants to make *Charming Betsy* into what it has never been: a rule for interpreting the Constitution. Thus, whenever something in the Constitution is ambiguous, the Supreme Court would be *required* to adopt the interpretation that matches international law.

The rub here is that almost every constitutional case that the Supreme Court takes involves some kind of ambiguity. What is an "unreasonable" search and seizure? What kinds of punishments are "cruel and unusual"? What types of "arms" does the Second Amendment protect, and what kinds of controls "infringe" the right to arms?

Koh's *Charming Betsy* rule would dumb down the U.S. Constitution to the standards of Koh's fellow left-wing transnationalists.

There's another twist to Koh's scheme to "harmonize" the Constitution to international norms. Back when Chief Justice Marshall wrote the *Charming Betsy* decision, international law covered only a few topics—mainly laws of war and trade, and some rules for how to treat diplomats. International laws regarding the rights and restrictions of neutral trade with wartime belligerents were long established and clear.

These days, however, international law—or at least something that pretends to be international law—exists on almost every subject imaginable.

510

You see, there are two key sources of international law. One is treaties, or similar international agreements. Treaties may have ambiguities, but at least you can recognize a treaty when you see one.

The other source of international law is the customary practices of nations. For example, long before the Geneva Conventions were written, civilized nations believed that it was a violation of international law to execute a prisoner of war. Nations (usually) obeyed this law, believing that they were legally required to do so.

Koh and his fellow transnationalists, however, are in the business of fabricating customary international law. They collect various things that in themselves have no legal force—such as resolutions of the United Nations General Assembly, or pronouncements made at some meeting of leftist nongovernment organizations. They blend the concoction and announce that they have discovered new "customary international law." Then they set off to impose their creation on various nations, with the assistance of compliant judges.

It's all part of the process of "transnationalism" advocated by Koh as a strategy for his admirers and their international compatriots. The transnationalists work in alliance, some on the inside, some on the outside. Or in Koh's words, "These governmental norm sponsors work inside bureaucracies and governmental structures to promote the same changes inside organized government that non-governmental norm entrepreneurs are urging from the outside."[31]

For example, even without a legally binding international gun control treaty, one article in a U.N. publication takes the position that U.N. gun control documents and statements constitute new international law "norms."[32]

Koh advises activists to "trigger transnational interactions, that generate legal interpretations, that can in turn be internalized into the domestic law of even resistant nation states."[33] What's a "resistant nation state"? Let's take a look.

As I discussed in chapter 13, the United Nations Human Rights Council, Subcommittee on Human Rights, has already declared that international law requires all nations to adopt extremely severe gun controls. Supposedly, the controls are required because various treaties and customs protect the right to life. The U.N. also says that gun owners may not be allowed to use deadly force against non-deadly attacks (e.g., against a rapist, an arsonist, or a carjacker).

So the legal adviser to the State Department can urge that the Second Amendment be "harmonized" with international law: First, interpret "infringed" so that nothing short of a ban on all handguns constitutes an infringement. Second, "clarify" the self-defense right recognized in *Heller* so the right does not include armed defense against rapists, arsonists, or carjackers.

And by the way, Koh has ways to make this happen even without a constitutional *Charming Betsy* canon. Federal courts have always applied customary international law. For example, by the early 1800s, it was well established that foreign ambassadors could be deported, but they were immune from criminal prosecution. So say that the Spanish ambassador committed a crime in Virginia, and the county government in Virginia initiated a prosecution. A federal district court in Virginia would have the duty to issue a writ of habeas corpus freeing the Spanish ambassador from the Virginia jail.

Koh takes the simple rule and expands it into a principle of staggering proportions. Since federal courts have to apply international law (which includes customary international law) the courts must therefore apply whatever Koh and his transnationalists claim to be customary international law.

These arguments may be especially persuasive to lower-court federal judges. Such judges may not care much one way or the other about gun rights, but they may be very deferential when the U.S. Department of State tells them that if they rule in favor of gun rights, they will be putting the United States in violation of international law.

Because of the Supremacy Clause of the U.S. Constitution, federal law overrides any conflicting state law, including the right to arms and right to self-defense provisions of state constitutions.

Harold Koh's longtime goal has been to "bring international law home."[34] Regarding gun rights, this is a program for choking off the Second Amendment, as an essential step toward his announced goal of banning the legal trade in firearms.

Attorney General Eric Holder's Antigun Pedigree

If Harold Koh is the mastermind of legal theory for using international law to crush the Second Amendment, Attorney General Eric Holder is the man running the crusher.

As attorney general, he is the boss of all the United States attorneys' offices; these are the offices that prosecute federal criminal cases, defend federal gun laws that are being challenged, and conduct almost all the litigation of the United States government. Holder also directs the office of the solicitor general, who is in charge of presenting arguments to the U.S. Supreme Court, and of deciding what the government position will be.

Finally, as attorney general, Holder is in charge of the FBI, and of the Bureau of Alcohol, Tobacco, Firearms and Explosives, both of which are part of the U.S. Department of Justice.

Eric Holder has the perfect pedigree for an administration of low ethics and anti-rights extremism. During the terrible reign of Janet Reno, he was her second-in-command, the deputy attorney general.

He argued that that no one should be allowed to own a handgun without a federal license, and that there should be national gun registration. He also contended that the best way to close the so-called gun-show loophole was with a bill whose fine print would have made it possible for gun shows to be eliminated entirely.

He insisted that more gun laws were a national necessity, because "every day that goes by, about 12, 13 or more children in this country die from gun violence." But if you look at the underlying data, the deaths for actual children is much, much smaller. Holder's assertion was valid only if you say that eighteen-year-old gangbangers who murder each other in a turf battle are "children."[35]

Holder was especially tough on gun bans for "children." He wanted to ban anyone under age twenty-one (even a soldier who was home on leave) from possessing a handgun or the ordinary guns he called "assault weapons." This would be backed up by mandatory prison sentences.[36] Thus, if your son's birthday was on December 28, and you gave him an old family heirloom gun on Christmas Day—when he was 20 years and 362 days old—a federal judge would be *required* to send you to prison.

Thanks to the NRA's work in Congress, the five-government-working-day waiting period for handguns ended in 1998, and was replaced by the National Instant Check System. Holder, however, argued that there should still be a three-day wait for handgun purchases—an unnecessary delay that could prove fatal to someone who needs a gun right away for protection from a stalker or other predator.[37] And he wanted to ration handgun sales, so that no one could buy more than one per month. Once the rationing principle is established, it sets the foundation for tightening the ration—down to two per year, or (as is the practice in Mexico) one per lifetime.

Washington insiders expected that if Al Gore won the presidential election in 2000, Holder would become the new attorney general. But as President Clinton himself later stated, the gun issue and the NRA cost Gore the election.[38]

However, considering that Florida was one of the swing states that Gore lost, it appears that Holder himself played a crucial role in Gore's defeat.

Elián González was a six-year-old boy who with his mother had fled the Castro tyranny in Cuba. The mother died during the boat trip, but Elián survived and was taken in by relatives in Florida.

Fidel Castro demanded the boy's return, and used Elián's divorced father as his proxy advocate. The Clinton-Gore and Reno-Holder teams were eager to comply.

Under Holder's command, the home of Elián and his relatives was surrounded by paramilitary agents. Holder promised the American people that there would no invasion of the home at night.

He broke the promise and launched an invasion an hour before dawn. He later claimed that he had kept his promise, since supposedly an hour before the sun has risen is not part of the night.

The federal agents broke into the home with a battering ram and, waving machine guns, screamed, "Get down, get down! We'll shoot." One agent found Elián in the arms of Donato Dalrymple, one of the fishermen who had first rescued Elián. With his finger *on* the trigger of his machine gun, the agent pointed the gun at the terrified boy a few inches away, and screamed obscenely at Dalrymple.

Eric Holder, though, falsely told the American people that Elián "was not taken at the point of a gun." Holder praised the agents for acting "very sensitively."[39]

Holder's attack squad had worked diligently to prevent the media from seeing the abduction of Elián Gonzalez. But a daring news photographer, Alan Diaz, had snuck into the home. He snapped the photograph that won the Pulitzer Prize that year: the "sensitive" federal agent with his finger on the machine gun trigger, screaming, pointing the gun at the little boy.

Elián Gonzalez was returned to Fidel Castro's island-sized concentration camp. The Cuban-American population of Florida, which had been trending toward the Democrats, overwhelming voted against the administration in the next election. Al Gore narrowly lost the state. Eric Holder did not become the new attorney general.

Out of office, Holder stayed active on the antigun front. After the September 11 terrorist attacks, he demonstrated the kind of "Patriot Act" that would have come from the administration of a President Gore and an

Attorney General Holder. In an op-ed for the *Washington Post*, he said that there should be a national gun registration law, giving "the Bureau of Alcohol, Tobacco and Firearms a record of every firearm sale."[40]

In addition, wrote Holder, a person should lose his right to arms if he is on one of the secret "watch lists" that various government agencies have created. That is, somebody on a watch list would become a prohibited person for federal gun laws—making it a federal felony for the person even to hold a gun in her hands. Since the watch lists are secret, a person would not know that she was on the list, and thus might inadvertently commit a serious federal felony just by continuing to own guns that she bought years before.

Of course, a big difference between a felony conviction and being on a "watch list" is that for the felony conviction, the government has to prove a case against you, and a judge or jury decides if the evidence is sufficient. There's no due process when a government employee just adds somebody's name to a secret list.

Now that Eric Holder is attorney general, you can bet that when the administration uses a terrorist attack or other infamous crime as the moment for its offensive on gun control, use of the secret lists to take away Second Amendment rights will be a top priority. So will as much gun registration as they think they can get away with.

Holder's Radical View on the *Heller* Case

Holder's role in the *Heller* case showed his complete hostility to gun ownership and gun rights. The District of Columbia Circuit Court of Appeals announced its decision in *Parker v. District of Columbia* in March 2007. The Court said that D.C. could not ban the possession of handguns in the home, and could not prohibit the use of firearms in the home for lawful self-defense.

Holder did not like the result. He warned that the *Parker* case "opens the door to more people having more access to guns and putting guns on the streets."[41] To Holder, "access to guns" was in itself something that should not be allowed.

D.C.'s Mayor Adrian Fenty agreed, and appealed the case to the United States Supreme Court, where its name became *District of Columbia v. Heller*. In January 2008, the America's antigun advocates filed their amicus briefs in support of the bans on handguns and self-defense.

Eric Holder and Janet Reno teamed up again, joining with some other former Department of Justice employees (mostly from the Reno era) to file the most radical anti-rights brief of all. Most of the briefs in support of the D.C. bans had agreed that the Second Amendment does protect an individual right, but that the right is so small as to be almost nonexistent. In other words, a National Guardsman on active duty might have some type of individual right under the Second Amendment, although the briefs were vague about what this right meant.

Holder and Reno, however, went even further. Their brief argued that *no one* has a Second Amendment right.[42] Instead, said they, the Second Amendment is a "collective" right. In other words, it is like "collective property" in a Communist country. The "right" belongs only to the government, which exercises the right on the supposed behalf of the people in general.

Not a single justice agreed with Holder and Reno's radical claim about a "collective" right.

Holder may be more successful in future Supreme Court cases, when his view will be the official view of the United States government. When international law can somehow be brought into the case, Holder will be able to use the legal theories invented by Harold Koh. Koh is certainly clever enough to offer the Supreme Court a better antigun theory than something as self-contradictory and inherently absurd as a "collective right" to possess a gun.

However, there are many things that Holder can do to change the nation's gun laws, without needing to convince a majority of the Supreme Court. As attorney general, Eric Holder is in charge of the Bureau of Alcohol, Tobacco, Firearms and Explosives (BATFE).

The Bureau has some fine, dedicated agents, but it has long suffered from serious management problems, and unwillingness to rein in agents who bully law-abiding citizens and abuse constitutional rights.

The NRA is promoting the "Bureau of Alcohol, Tobacco, Firearms and Explosives Reform and Firearms Modernization Act." This bill would rewrite the system of administrative penalties for licensed dealers, manufacturers, and importers of firearms. It would allow fines or license suspensions for some violations, while still allowing license revocations for intentional violations that could block an investigation or put guns in the hands of criminals. This will help prevent the all-too-common situations where BATFE has revoked licenses for insignificant technical violations—such as improper use of abbreviations, or filing records in the wrong order.

As things stand now, BATFE can write regulations that are related to the federal gun statutes, and can get away with almost anything it wants—because courts usually allow federal regulators almost unlimited discretion in writing regulations.

Holder and his BATFE could make life much more difficult for law-abiding licensed firearms dealers. They can bring more guns under the scope of the National Firearms Act (NFA)—meaning that even continuing to own such a gun would require one to go through the same onerous process needed to buy a fully-automatic gun.

Already Holder's BATFE has taken a major step to make life difficult for firearms publications. Ever since the enactment of the Gun Control Act of 1968, BATFE allowed firearms writers to temporarily use firearms for testing, without having to go through the paperwork and permissions needed for firearms purchases. For example, if a writer for *Guns & Ammo* wanted to write a review of a new Remington rifle, Remington could ship the rifle directly to the writer, and then the writer would ship it back to Remington after a few weeks of testing.

Likewise, if a firearms manufacturer needs to have some prototypes tested, the manufacturer can ship the firearms directly to the testing center, and then the center will ship them back after the testing is completed.

According to BATFE, in the forty-two years since 1968, there has never been a single instance of firearms misuse related to these temporary loaner guns. Nevertheless, BATFE has declared that henceforth, the loaner guns must be treated just like firearms sales. In other words, the guns must now be shipped to a licensed firearms dealer, who can only transfer the guns to the writer for the testing after going through the same process as if he were selling a gun. In states with highly restrictive gun laws, this creates a nightmare. For example, in a state like New Jersey, the writer or the testing center may have to wait months for local police to approve the gun transfer. "One handgun a month" laws may prevent the writer or testing center from conducting comparative research on several handguns at once. Licensing and registration fees may cost the writer more than he would earn from writing the article.

Because there had never been *any* problem under the loaner system, it is difficult to characterize the actions of Holder's BATFE as anything other than a malicious attempt to harm firearms manufacturers and firearms publications.

The Supreme Court

When the Holder Department of Justice brings Harold Koh's transnationalist ideas to the U.S. Supreme Court, will the justices be receptive?

Koh has written that the Supreme Court has four members in what he calls its "transnationalist faction."[43] The four transnationalists happened to be the very same justices who voted to uphold the handgun and self-defense bans in *Heller*: Justices Stevens, Ginsburg, Breyer, and Souter.

This is not at all a coincidence. The point of transnationalism, as one can see by reading Koh's speeches exhorting his transnationalist allies, is that the transnationalists constitute an international alliance to advance a leftist, "progressive," big-government vision everywhere. If a transnationalist is wondering about whether something would be a good idea in his own country, his sensibility is that his country should probably do things the same way they are done in Belgium or Sweden and the rest of the world that is "enlightened" (by the standards of America's leftist elite).

It's the same reason that the gun prohibition groups never tire of complaining that American gun laws are very different from those in most other highly developed countries. Never mind that we have much less violent crime than places that strongly discourge self-defense, such as England or Scotland. To the transnationalist, being different from the rest of the world is considered shameful.

Transnationalism is the opposite of a mode of thought that cherishes the unique, distinctive, historical, traditional, and "exceptional" features of one's own culture, especially of one's legal culture. Thus, Koh says that the justices who do not follow his line of thinking are "the nationalist faction."

Justice Sonia Sotomayor

The change from Justice David Souter to Justice Sonia Sotomayor is the replacement of one transnationalist by another. Speaking to a meeting of the American Civil Liberties Union in Puerto Rico in April 2009, she said that "to suggest to anyone that you can outlaw the use of foreign or international law is a sentiment that's based on a fundamental misunderstanding. What you would be asking American judges to do is to close their minds to some good ideas."

At her confirmation hearings before the Senate Judiciary Committee, she ducked and weaved in her description of the role of foreign law in American constitutional decision making. Her follow-up written answers, however, made it clear that she had retreated not one inch from what she had spoken in April.

She did say that foreign law (except to the extent that it is reflected in a ratified treaty) could not be used as a precedent to compel a particular result.

But that is no real concession. If there is a clearly controlling precedent, then the case will not even get to the U.S. Supreme Court. The very nature of most Supreme Court cases is that they involve important issues where the precedents are unclear, or where constitutional or statutory language is ambiguous.

When Supreme Court opinions cite anyone or anything, whatever gets cited becomes much more prestigious and influential in American legal culture. Other than papal encyclicals, there are probably no modern writings that receive such intensive, line-by-line study as do Supreme Court opinions.

So when Justices Ginsburg, Souter, and Breyer wrote an opinion citing the CEDAW treaty that the U.S. Senate for three decades has refused to ratify, they were in essence end-running the legislative branch of our government, and bringing that foreign law into American legal culture.[44]

Foreign law is on Justice Sotomayor's list of "good ideas" but something else is missing: the right of the people to keep and bear arms.

Before moving up to the Supreme Court, Sotomayor was a judge on the federal Second Circuit Court of Appeals, which covers New York, Vermont, and Connecticut. In the January 2009 case of *Maloney v. Cuomo*, she was part of a three-judge panel that ruled that people in those three states have no Second Amendment rights that state or local governments are bound to respect.[45] Under Sotomayor's decision, if the New York State government outlawed and confiscated every handgun, long gun, and knife in the state, the confiscation would be completely constitutional.

The *Heller* decision had involved the District of Columbia, which is part of the federal government; the only powers that the D.C. city council has are those that have been delegated by Congress. So *Heller* did not decide the question of whether the Second Amendment also applies to state and local governments, or only to the federal government.

Various Supreme Court decisions have made most, but not all, of the Bill of Rights enforceable against the states; these decisions say that particular parts of the Bill of Rights are "incorporated" in the due process clause of the Fourteenth Amendment, which says: "nor shall any State deprive any person of life, liberty, or property, without due process of law."

Until the *McDonald* case in 2010, the Supreme Court had never definitively ruled whether or not the Second Amendment is made applicable to the states by the due process clause of the Fourteenth Amendment.

In *Maloney*, Judge Sotomayor and the other two judges on her appellate panel ruled that New York, Vermont, and Connecticut (as well as local governments there, since local governments derive their powers from the state) have no obligation to obey the Second Amendment.

Incredibly, Judge Sotomayor did not even *acknowledge* the issue of due process incorporation. Instead, she based her decision on some nineteenth-century Supreme Court cases that did not involve the due process clause. Those older cases were about a separate part of the Fourteenth Amendment, namely the "Privileges or Immunities" clause. Judge Sotomayor was acting disingenuously when she pretended that Supreme Court cases about one clause in the Constitution had created a binding precedent about an entirely different clause.

Judge Sotomayor's supporters said that the *Maloney* decision was very narrow; it just involved New York's complete prohibition on the possession of nunchakus. (New York is the only state in the Union with a total ban.) But *Maloney* was not a narrow decision about nunchakus; it was a broad decision that wiped out Second Amendment protection for the people of New York, Vermont, and Connecticut from abusive state or local laws.

Testifying before the Senate Judiciary Committee, Sotomayor said that the ban on nunchakus was legally appropriate because nunchakus could injure someone. Which is true. It's also true about firearms, airguns, knives, swords, bows, arrows, baseball bats, chemical defense sprays, tasers, and lots of other things. That is what "arms" are.

In addition, Judge Sotomayor was a member of the panel in the case of *United States v. Sanchez-Villar*, where (in a summary opinion) the Second Circuit dismissed a Second Amendment challenge to New York State's pistol licensing law. That panel, in a terse footnote, cited dicta from a previous Second Circuit case to claim, "The right to possess a gun is clearly not a fundamental right."[46]

It is only by ignoring history that any judge can say that the Second Amendment is not a fundamental right and does not apply to the states.

The one part of the Bill of Rights that Congress clearly intended to apply to all Americans in passing the Fourteenth Amendment was the Second Amendment. History and congressional debate are clear on this point.

During Senate confirmation hearings, Sotomayor readily offered platitudes such as "I understand the individual right fully that the Supreme Court recognized in Heller" and, "I understand how important the right to bear arms is to many, many Americans." Senator Mark Udall (D-CO) told the Associated Press that "Sotomayor told him during a private meeting that she considers the 2008 ruling that struck down a Washington, D.C., handgun ban as settled law that would guide her decisions in future cases."[47] She repeated the "settled law" phrase several times during her Judiciary Committee testimony.

Yet what did Sotomayor do once she was on the Supreme Court? In *McDonald v. Chicago*, she joined Justice Breyer's dissent urging that *Heller* be overruled. According to Sotomayor and Breyer, the Second Amendment should be held to protect *no* individual right to possess a firearm for self-defense.

When Sotomayor told the Senators and the American people that she considered *Heller* to be "settled law," she was creating the impression that she had no wish to unsettle it. But it is now clear that Sotomayor was parsing her words Clinton-style. "Settled law" merely meant that the case had been decided and everyone had a "settled" understanding of the basic legal meaning of the case.

Based on Sotomayor's antigun record as a federal appeal court judge, and on her testimony to the Senate, the NRA figured out what she was up to, and we strongly opposed her confirmation to the Supreme Court.

Justice Elena Kagan

The day that the Supreme Court released the *McDonald* decision, including Justice Sotomayor's vote to destroy Second Amendment rights, confirmation hearings began on the nomination of Elena Kagan.

Once again, President Obama had chosen a nominee with a strongly antigun record. Kagan had served in the Clinton White House, and had invented the legal theory for Clinton to unilaterally ban the import of dozens of models of semiauto rifles and shotguns. Anticipating the Supreme Court ruling in *Printz v. United States*, in which the Court would rule that Congress could not force state and local law enforcement officials to carry out federal background checks on handgun buyers, Kagan requested research on whether the president might have executive power to prohibit handgun sales.

She compared the National Rifle Association to the Ku Klux Klan as "bad guy" organizations. As a clerk to Supreme Court Justice Thurgood Marshall, she had sniffed, "I'm not sympathetic" to the plight of a law-abiding D.C. citizen who was being persecuted because of the District's handgun ban.[48]

Finally, as a law professor, she had spoken out in favor of greatly constricting First Amendment rights.

When Senators asked her about the Second Amendment rights, she would offer nothing more than the repeated platitude about "settled law," even though Sotomayor's actions that very week had proven that assurances about "settled law" meant absolutely nothing.

The NRA fought hard against the Kagan confirmation, but President Obama achieved another victory in ensuring that the Supreme Court will have anti–Second Amendment Justices for decades to come.

So your Second Amendment rights hang by literally a single vote on the Supreme Court. Pro–Second Amendment Justices Antonin Scalia and Anthony Kennedy were born in 1936 and cannot be expected to serve forever. If an Obama nominee cut from the same judicial cloth as Sonia Sotomayor or Elena Kagan replaces any of the five justices from the *Heller* majority, the Second Amendment is going to be in very deep trouble.

Even if a court with Justices Sotomayor and Kagan in an anti–Second Amendment majority did not formally overrule *Heller*, it could make the Second Amendment so weak that almost any antigun law short of total prohibition would be allowed.

Barack Obama has made his personal feelings clear about four of the five justices who rendered the Supreme Court's decision upholding the Second Amendment as protecting an individual right and recognizing the right to self-defense in the home.

While a U.S. senator, he voted to defeat the nominations of both Chief Justice John Roberts and Justice Samuel Alito. And during a 2008 presidential debate with John McCain, Obama volunteered: "I would not have nominated Clarence Thomas . . . I profoundly disagree with his interpretations of a lot of the Constitution. I would not nominate Justice Scalia . . . because he and I just disagree."[49]

Justice Scalia—a longtime firearms owner and hunter—wrote the majority opinion in *Heller*, an opinion that includes the following words that stand for what Barack Obama has opposed since he first entered politics: "The Second Amendment protects an individual right to possess a firearm unconnected with service in a militia, and to use that arm for traditionally lawful purposes, such as self-defense within the home."[50]

Questioning the Right to Self-Defense and U.S. Sovereignty

Secretary of State Clinton's warm embrace of a "binding" U.N. treaty on global control of the trade in firearms and ammunition brands the Obama administration as an aggressive participant in what international gun-ban groups have hailed as a "first step" in their march to negate U.S. sovereignty and ultimately outlaw the private ownership of firearms worldwide.

In announcing the radical shift in U.S. policy, Clinton proclaimed, "The United States is committed to actively pursuing a strong and robust treaty that contains the highest possible, legally binding standards for the international transfer of conventional weapons."[51]

She failed to mention either the Second Amendment or U.S. sovereignty. Her silence stands in stark contrast to the vigorous defense of American freedom by President George W. Bush and his U.N. ambassador, John Bolton.

Former ambassador Bolton wasted no time responding to the Obama administration's dangerous shift in U.S. policy, stating, "This has little or nothing to do with the international trade in conventional arms. This will strengthen the hand of a government that wants to regulate private ownership of firearms."[52]

Ambassador Bolton is keenly aware of the key July 2007 report to the U.N.'s Human Rights Council, titled, "Specific Human Rights Issues—Prevention of human rights violations committed with small arms and light weapons." According to this official U.N. report:

> Self-defence is sometimes designated as a "right." There is inadequate legal support for such an interpretation . . . No international human right of self-defence is expressly set forth in the primary sources of international law: treaties, customary law or general principles . . . International law does not support an international legal obligation requiring States to permit access to a gun for self-defence.

So there you have it. This is the heart, the essence, of the United Nations attack on our Second Amendment and our sovereignty. No matter what the gun-ban crowd claims, there is only one true endgame for U.N. arms control officials: crushing the individual rights of the American people under the unrestricted power of the international superstate.

Each of us must work to stop this bowing and scraping by the Obama administration to those evil principles. And none of us, whether we own guns or not, can forget Obama's criticism of U.S. sovereignty in his book *The Audacity of Hope.* He wrote, "When the world's sole superpower willingly restrains its power and abides by internationally agreed-upon standards of conduct, it sends a message that these rules are worth following."

Recognizing the "standards of conduct" and freedom-hating tyrants the U.N. embraces around the world, these words should harden resolve in every American who believes in the supremacy of our Constitution and who believes that the way of life our Founders bequeathed is worth defending at all times, at all costs and against all adversaries.

Notes

In these endnotes, I have provided many URLs to help readers find articles on the World Wide Web. However, URLs sometimes change, so a URL that works now may not work two years from now. If you are looking for an article that no longer appears on the Internet, try going to www.archive.org. That site takes frequent snapshots of the Web so you can read websites that have changed or gone out of business. Enter the old URL into the www.archive.org search box, and there is a good chance that you will find what you're looking for.

Introduction

1. William Jefferson Clinton, *My Life* (New York: Random House, 2004), 928.
2. Statement by John R. Bolton, United States Undersecretary of State for Arms Control and International Security Affairs, U.S. Plenary Session, UN Conference on Illicit Trade in Small Arms and Light Weapons in All Its Aspects, July 9, 2001, http://www.fas.org/asmp/campaigns/smallarms/SAconf-USstmt.htm.
3. Lawrence Auster, "Global Gun Controllers Surrender to U.S.," NewsMax, July 24, 2001, http://www.newsmax.com/archives/articles/2001/7/24/111205.shtml.
4. Dave Kopel, "U.N. Out of North America: The Small Arms Conference and the Second Amendment," *National Review* Online, August 9, 2001, http://old.nationalreview.com/kopel/kopel080901.shtml.
5. Auster, "Global Gun Controllers Surrender to U.S."
6. Ibid.
7. "Programme of Action to Prevent, Combat and Eradicate the Illicit Trade in Small Arms and Light Weapons in All Its Aspects," United Nations Conference on the Illicit Trade in Small Arms and Light Weapons in All Its Aspects, July 20, 2001, http://www.nti.org/e_research/official_docs/inventory/pdfs/sarms.pdf.
8. *The Great U.N. Gun Debate*, King's College, London, DVD, Starcast Productions, Ltd., 2004.
9. Brooks Tigner, "EU Builds Strategy against Small Arms," *Defense News.com*, October 24, 2005, originally at http://www.defensenews.com/story.php?F=1155112&C=landwar.
10. Ibid.
11. Eric Green, "Meeting Aims to Combat Illicit Arms Trafficking in the Americas," State Department News Release, Oct. 7, 2005, usinfo.state.gov/xarchives/display.html?p=washfile-english&y=2005&m=October&x=20051007122742AEneerG0.3076898&t=livefeeds/wf-latest.html.

12. Kelly Hearn, "As Brazil Votes to Ban Guns, NRA Joins the Fight," *Nation,* October 21, 2005, http://www.thenation.com/article/brazil-votes-ban-guns-nra-joins-fight.
13. Monte Reel, "Brazilians Reject Measure to Ban Sale of Firearms," *Washington Post,* October 24, 2005, http://www.washingtonpost.com/wp-dyn/content/article/2005/10/23/AR2005102300394_pf.html.
14. Winston Churchill speech, "The Sinews of Peace," Westminster College, Fulton, MO, March 5, 1946, www.hpol.org/churchill/.

Chapter 1

1. *The Great U.N. Gun Debate*, King's College, London, DVD, Starcast Productions, Ltd., 2004.
2. Ibid.
3. Ibid.
4. Ibid.
5. Ibid.
6. Ibid.
7. Ibid.
8. Ibid.
9. David B. Kopel, "Bypassing U.S. Voters," *National Review Online*, August 3, 2001, http://www.nationalreview.com/kopel/kopel080301.shtml. No longer accessible.
10. Ibid.
11. Julie Lewis, "Gun-ho Diplomacy," *Bulletin*, March 28, 2000, 42.
12. Rebecca Peters, "Turn in the Guns," *Sydney Herald*, April 26, 1997.
13. Ibid.
14. David Gonzalez, "Gun Makers, and a Culture, on Trial," *New York Times*, February 3, 1991.
15. Samantha Lee and Rebecca Peters, "Handguns, Deadly Loophole in Control," *Newcastle Herald*, April 30, 2001.
16. "Compensation for the Surrender of Prohibited Firearms," *Australian Shooters Journal*, September 1996.
17. *The Great U.N. Gun Debate.*
18. Ibid.
19. Ibid.
20. C. Sutton, H. Gilmore, and Simon Kent, "He Could Have Been Stopped: Bungling Let the World's Worst Killer Go Free," *Sydney Sun-Herald*, May 5, 1996.
21. Adèle Kirsten, "The Role of Social Movements in Gun Control: An international comparison between South Africa, Brazil and Australia," Centre for Civil Society Research Report No. 21, September 2004, http://www.armsnetafrica.org/content/centre-civil-society-research-report-no-21-role-social-movements-gun-control-international-c.
22. Ibid.
23. Lewis, "Gun-ho Diplomacy."
24. Rebecca Peters and Roland Browne, "Australia's New Gun Control Philosophy: Public Health Is Paramount," The Drawing Board: An Australian Review of Public Affairs 1, no. 2 (November 2000): 63–73, University of Sydney School of Economics and Political Science, http://www.australianreview.net/journal/v1/n2/peters_browne.pdf.

25. Ibid, 64–65.
26. Ibid, 67–68.
27. Ibid, 69.
28. Ibid, 66.
29. "Common Elements in Firearms and Ammunition Control Legislation: A Framework for the Strengthening of Regulations," in *Small Arms and Light Weapons: Legal Aspects of National and International Regulations*, vol. 4, *Arms Control and Disarmament Law*, eds. Erwin Dahinden, Julie Dahlitz, and Nadia Fischer (Geneva: United Nations), 139–41.
30. E.g., "Arms Control: Critics of the law to curb gun-related crimes say that it attempts to disarm law-abiding citizens while leaving criminals armed," *Guardian* (Johannesburg, South Africa), January 7, 2005, 6.
31. Joseph A. Klein, *Global Deception: The UN's Stealth Assault on America's Freedom* (Los Angeles: World Ahead Pub., 2005), 131.
32. Ibid.
33. The Samuel Rubin Foundation's donees include International Association of Lawyers against Nuclear Arms, the Women's International Link for Peace, the Hague Appeal for Peace, the Institute for Pacific Studies, and Americans for Peace Now (John Gizzi, "The Anti-War Movement Arsenal: Center for National Security Studies, Center for Defense Information, Center for International Policy," *Organization Trend* [Capital Research Center: June 2004]). Other donors include the Public Media Center, Tides Foundation and Tides Center (a major antigun donor), Trauma Foundation (also involved in antigun work), Preamble Center, Winrock International Institute for Agricultural Development, the Institute for Agriculture and Trade Policy, Essential Information.
34. "Institute for Policy Studies," DiscovertheNetworks.org: A Guide to the Political Left, http://www.discoverthenetworks.org/groupProfile.asp?grpid=6991.
35. "Small Arms Survey," http://www.smallarmssurvey.org/home.html.
36. "Welcome to the HD Centre," http://www.hdcentre.org/?aid=2.
37. Funding of the HD Centre, http://www.hdcentre.org/funding.
38. "Putting People First: Rio Meeting," http://web.archive.org/web/20050319111142/www.hdcentre.org/?aid=125.
39. "Chair's Summary of the 'International Meeting on the Regulation of Civilian Ownership and Use of Small Arms'—Rio de Janeiro, March 16–18, 2005: Convened by the Centre for Humanitarian Dialogue in Collaboration with the Government of Brazil, Viva Rio and Sou da Paz," web.archive.org/web/20061007153306/www.hdcentre.org/datastore/Small+arms/Rio_Chair_summary.pdf.
40. *Small arms and light weapons: The response of the European Union* (Luxembourg: Office for Official Publications of the European Communities, 2001), http://eeas.europa.eu/cfsp/salw/docs/small_arms_en.pdf.
41. *Handbook of Best Practices on Small Arms and Light Weapons* (2003), http://www.osce.org/item/13550.html.
42. ECOWAS Moratorium on the Importation, Exportation and Manufacture of Light Weapons, October 31, 1998, http://www.fas.org/nuke/control/pcased/text/ecowas.htm.
43. The Nairobi Protocol for the Prevention, Control and Reduction of Small Arms and Light Weapons in the Great Lakes Region and the Horn of Africa, http://www.recsasec.org/pdf/Nairobi%20Protocol.pdf.

44. Protocol on the Control of Firearms, Ammunition and Other Related Materials in the Southern African Development Community (SADC) Region, www.grip.org/bdg/g2010.html. No longer accessible.
45. Inter-American Convention against the Illicit Manufacturing of and Trafficking in Firearms, Ammunition, Explosives, and Other Related Materials, http://www.oas.org/dsp/documentos/armas_de_fuego/Documentos%20Claves/Texto%20de%20la%20Convencion/text%20of%20CIFTA%20english.doc.
46. Katharine Q. Steele, "National Rifle Association Is Turning to World Stage to Fight Gun Control," *New York Times*, April 2, 1999.
47. "Principles of the WFSA," http://www.wfsa.net.
48. Stefan Halper, "51. The United Nations," *Cato Handbook for Congress: 105th Congress* (Washington, D.C.: Cato Institute, 1999).
49. William Godnick, *Tackling the Illicit Trade in Small Arms and Light Weapons* (London: British American Security Information Council, 2002), 13.
50. Derek Miller, et al., *Regulation of Civilian Possession of Small Arms and Light Weapons*, International Alert Briefing No. 16 (London, United Kingdom: International Alert, 2002), 5.

Chapter 2

1. Edward J. Laurence, "Addressing the Negative Consequences of Light Weapons Trafficking: Opportunities for Transparency and Restraint," in *Lethal Commerce: The Global Trade in Small Arms and Light Weapons,* eds. Jeffrey Boutwell, Michael T. Klare, and Laura Reed (Cambridge, MA.: American Academy of Arts and Sciences, 1995), 149.
2. Many of the books address genuine problems, such as warlords in Africa, but nearly all of them make the mistake of proposing crackdowns on legitimate gun owners as part of the solution. Among the books are:

Afghanistan, Arms and Conflict: Armed Groups, Disarmament and Security in a Post-War Society. Small Arms Survey, 2008.
Ammunition Tracing Kit: Protocols and Procedures for Recording Small-Calibre Ammunition. Small Arms Survey, 2008.
Armed and Aimless: Armed Groups, Guns, and Human Security in the ECOWAS Region. Small Arms Survey, 2005).
Beasley, Ryan, Cate Buchanan, and Robert Muggah. *In the Line of Fire.* Centre for Humanitarian Dialogue, 2003.
Boutwell, Jeff, et al., eds. *Lethal Commerce: The Global Trade in Small Arms and Light Weapons.* Academy of Arts and Sciences, 1995.
Brandt, Don. *A Deadly Pandemic: Small Arms and Light Weapons.* World Vision, 2003.
Buchanan, Cate, and Mereille Widmer. *Putting Guns in Their Place—a resource pack for two years of action by humanitarian agencies.* Centre for Humanitarian Dialogue, 2004.
Buchanan, Cate, and Robert Muggah. *No Relief: Surveying the effects of gun violence on humanitarian and development personnel.* Centre for Humanitarian Dialogue, 2005.

Capie, David. *Small arms production and transfers in Southeast Asia.* Australian National University, 2002.

Capie, David. *Under the Gun—The Small Arms Challenge in the Pacific.* Victoria University Pr., 2004.

The Central African Republic and Small Arms: A Regional Tinderbox. Small Arms Survey, 2008.

Combating the Proliferation of Small Arms and Light Weapons in West Africa: Handbook for the Training of Armed and Security Forces. United Nations, 2005.

Conventional Ammunition in Surplus: A Reference Guide. Small Arms Survey, 2008.

Cukier, Wendy, and Victor W. Sidel. *The Global Gun Epidemic: From Saturday Night Specials to AK47s.* Praeger, 2005.

Curbing the demand for small arms. Centre for Humanitarian Dialogue, 2003.

Dahinden, Erwin, Julie Dahlitz, and Nadia Fischer, eds. *Small Arms and Light Weapons: Legal Aspects of National and International Regulations A Contribution to the United Nations Conference on the Illicit Trade in Small Arms and Light Weapons in All Its Aspects and Its Follow-Up Process.* United Nations, 2002.

Disposal of Surplus Small Arms: A survey of policies and practices in OSCE countries. Co-published by the South Eastern Europe Clearinghouse for the Control of Small Arms and Light Weapons, Saferworld, and the British American Security Information Council, 2004.

Fernanda, Maria, and Tourinho Peres. *Firearm Related Violence in Brazil.* Universidade de São Paulo, 2004.

Florquin, Nicolas, and Shelly O'Neill Stoneman. "A House Isn't a Home without a Gun": SALW Survey of Montenegro. Small Arms Survey and South Eastern Europe Clearinghouse for the Control of Small Arms and Light Weapons, 2004.

Gamba, Virginia, ed., *Governing Arms. The Southern African Experience.* Institute for Security Studies, 2000.

Gamba, Virginia. *Society under Siege: Vol. 1, Crime, Violence and Illegal Weapons.* Institute for Security Studies, 1997.

Gamba, Virginia, and Sarah Meek, eds. *Society Under Siege, Vol. 2, Licit Responses to Illicit Arms.* Institute for Security Studies, 1998.

Gould, Chandré and Guy Lamb. *Hide and Seek. Taking Account of Small Arms in Southern Africa.* Institute for Security Studies , 2004.

Grillot, Suzette R Shelly, O. Stoneman, Hans Risser, and Wolf-Christian Paes. *A Fragile Peace—Guns and Security in Post-Conflict Macedonia.* Commissioned by UN Development Programme and co-published by the Bonn International Center for Conversion and the South Eastern Europe Clearinghouse for the Control of Small Arms and Light Weapons, 2004.

The Handbook of Best Practices on Small Arms and Light Weapons. Organization for Security and Co-operation in Europe (OSCE), 2003.

Hiller, Debbie, and Brian Wood. *Shattered Lives—the case for tough international arms control.* Amnesty International and Oxfam, 2004.

"Insecurity Is Also a War": An Assessment of Armed Violence in Burundi. Small Arms Survey, 2009.

Lumpe, Lora. *The Arms Trade Revealed: A Guide for Investigators and Activists* (Federation of American Scientists, Arms Sales Monitoring Project, 1998).

Lumpe, Lora, ed., *Running Guns: The Global Black Market in Small Arms.* Zed Books, 2000.

Meek, Sarah and Noel Stott. *Destroying Surplus Weapons: An Assessment of Experience in South Africa and Lesotho.* United Nations, 2003.

Meek, Sarah, and Noel Stott. *Guide to the Destruction of Small Arms and Light Weapons: The Approach of the South African National Defence Force.* United Nations, 2004.

Missing Pieces: A guide to reduce gun violence through parliamentary action. Centre for Humanitarian Dialogue and the Interparliamentary Union, 2007.

Mogire, Edward. *A Preliminary Examination of the Linkages between Refugees and Small Arms.* Bonn International Center for Conversion, Germany, 2004.

Nepram, Binalakshmi. *South Asia's Fractured Frontier: Armed conflict, narcotics and small arms proliferation in India's North East.* Mittal Pubs, New Delhi, India, 2002.

The No-Nonsense Guide to the Arms Trade. Gideon Burrows. Verso, 2002.

No Refuge: The Crisis of Refugee Militarization in Africa. Small Arms Survey, 2008.

Oosthuysen, Glenn. *Small Arms Proliferation and Control in Southern Africa.* (SAIIA Southern Africa Press, 1996.

"*The Politics of Destroying Surplus Small Arms*": *Inconspicuous Disarmament.* Small Arms Survey, 2009.

"*Primed and Purposeful*": *Armed Groups and Human Security Efforts in the Philippines.* Small Arms Survey, 2010.

Putting People First. Centre for Humanitarian Dialogue, 2003.

Renner, Michael. *Small Arms, Big Impact: The Next Challenge in Disarmament.* Worldwatch, 1997.

Reviewing Action on Small Arms 2006: Assessing the First Five Years of the Programme of Action. IANSA, 2006.

Schroeder, Emily, and Lauren Newhouse. *Gender and Small Arms—Moving into the Mainstream.* Institute for Security Studies, 2004.

Schroeder, Matthew, Rachel Stohl, and Dan Smith. *The Small Arms Trade: A Beginner's Guide.* Oneworld, 2007.

Security and Post-Conflict Reconstruction: Dealing with Fighters in the Aftermath of War. Small Arms Survey, 2009.

Small Arms Survey 2001: Profiling the Problem. Small Arms Survey. Oxford University Press, 2001.

Small Arms Survey 2002: Counting the Cost. Small Arms Survey. Oxford University Press, 2002.

Small Arms Survey 2003: Development Denied. Small Arms Survey. Oxford University Press, 2003.

Small Arms Survey 2004: Rights at Risk. Small Arms Survey. Oxford University Press, 2004.

Small Arms Survey 2005: Weapons at War. Small Arms Survey. Oxford University Press, 2005.

Small Arms Survey 2006: Unfinished Business. Small Arms Survey. Oxford University Press, 2006.

Small Arms Survey 2007: Guns and the City. Small Arms Survey. Oxford University Press, 2007.

Small Arms Survey 2008: Risk and Resilience. Small Arms Survey. Oxford University Press, 2008.

Small Arms Survey 2009: Shadows of War. Small Arms Survey. Oxford University Press, 2009.

Small Arms Survey 2010: Gangs, Groups, and Guns. Small Arms Survey. Oxford University Press, 2010.

Targeting Ammunition: A Primer. Small Arms Survey, 2006.

United Nations Institute for Disarmament Research:

> *Curbing Illicit Trafficking in Small Arms and Sensitive Technologies: An Action Oriented Agenda.*
> *Disarmament and Conflict Resolution Project: Small Arms Management and Peacekeeping in Southern Africa*
> *Disarmament Study Series: Small Arms*
> *The Scope and Implications of a Tracing Mechanism for SALW.* 2003.
> *Small Arms Control: Old Weapons, New Issues*
> *Small Arms Problem in Central Asia, The: Features and Implications*

United Nations International Study on Firearm Regulation

Yihdego, Zeray. *The Arms Trade and International Law.* Hart, 2007.

Besides the above listing of books, there are literally hundreds of monographs and shorter studies produced by the same organizations.

3. United Nations Information Service, Press Release, UNIS/CP/346, May 12, 1997.
4. The data can be found on the website of the United Nations Register of Conventional Arms, http://disarmament.un.org/un_register.nsf.
5. United Nations, Secretary-General, *Supplement to an Agenda for Peace: Position Paper on the Secretary-General on the Occasion of the Fiftieth Anniversary of the United Nations,* S/1995/1, 1995, Section D, ¶ ¶ 60–65.
6. Swadesh Rana, *Small Arms and Intra-State Conflict* (New York: United Nations Publications, 1995).
7. Most Americans have no idea how extensive the U.N. structure is. The U.N. has three headquarters; in addition to the New York headquarters, there is a huge facility in Vienna and a similarly sized headquarters in Geneva. The Geneva HQ is located in the old Palais des Nations, which itself was the building that housed the League of Nations. There are also regional offices all over the world.
8. "Parents of Japanese boy killed in U.S. appeal for gun control," Kyodo News Service (Tokyo, Japan, 2002).
9. Walter Mondale, "National Press Club Speech," Video Monitoring Services of America, transcript, September 6, 1996, 6.
10. A/RES/50/70 B, http://www.securitycouncilreport.org/atf/cf/%7B65BFCF9B -6D27-4E9C-8CD3-CF6E4FF96FF9%7D/Arms%20A%20RES%2050%20 70.pdf. By the end of 2005, there were almost thirty UN General Assembly resolutions on gun control.
11. At the time, he was Japan's special assistant to the minister of foreign affairs.
12. Boutwell, Klare, and Reed, *Lethal Commerce.*
13. Raymond Bonner, "U.N. Panel May Approve Limit on Guns Despite N.R.A. Pleas," *New York Times,* April 30, 1998.
14. General Assembly, "Report of the Panel of Governmental Experts on Small Arms," August 27, 1997, A/52/298, www.un.org/Depts/ddar/Firstcom/SGreport52/ a52298.html.

15. Definition #1 is from the 1997 "Report of the Panel of Government Experts on Small Arms" paragraph 24: "Small arms and light weapons range from clubs . . . The small arms and light weapons which are of the main concern for the purposes of the present report are those which are manufactured to military specifications for use as lethal instruments of war."

Definition #2 is from the 1997 "Report of the Panel of Government Experts on Small Arms," paragraphs 25 and 26:

> Broadly speaking, small arms are those weapons designed for personal use, and light weapons are those designed for use by several persons serving as a crew. (¶ 25)
>
> Based on this broad definition and on an assessment of weapons actually used in conflicts being dealt with by the United Nations, the weapons addressed in the present report are categorized as follows:
>
> (i) Revolvers and self loading pistols;
> (ii) Rifles and carbines;
> (iii) Sub-machine guns;
> (iv) Assault rifles;
> (v) Light machine-guns

The description continues with heavy machine guns, grenade launchers, etc.) (¶ 26)

Definition #3 is from the 1997 "Report of the Panel of Government Experts on Small Arms," paragraph 28:

> In conflicts dealt with by the United Nations, non-military weapons not manufactured to military specifications, such as hunting firearms and homemade weapons, have been used in violent conflicts, terrorism, and the intentional harming of civilian populations. In such cases, and where such weapons are used and accumulated in numbers that endanger the security and political stability of a State, the Panel considered them relevant for the purposes of this report.[8] [Endnote 8 describes home-made weapons that can be constructed out of readily available material with little skill.]

Definition #4 is from the "Report of the Group of Government Experts on Small Arms," paragraphs 129 and 130:

> The scope of the International Conference will be the illicit trade in small arms and light weapons in all its aspects. (¶ 129)
>
> In this context, the primary focus of attention should be on small arms and light weapons that are manufactured to military specifications (see endnote 5). Other types of firearms used in conflicts may, however, also have to be considered in dealing with the problems in the most effected regions of the world. (¶ 130)

Definition #5 is from the "Report of the Group of Government Experts on Small Arms," endnote 5.

The Group followed the practice of the previous Panel of Governmental Experts on Small Arms in its definitions of small arms and light weapons. Broadly speaking, small arms are those weapons designed for personal use and light weapons are those designed for use by several persons serving as a crew. The category of small arms includes revolvers and self-loading pistols, rifles and carbines, sub-machine guns, assault rifles and light machine guns.

These definitions are overly broad on two counts. First they refer to and include, somewhat convolutedly, civilian firearms, such as hunting rifles (definition #3). More important, they rely on the broad, undefined term "manufactured to military specifications." This is generally thought to mean military design. But if the term "small arms" were interpreted as merely being manufactured to certain standards of increased durability or tolerances, it would be unworkably narrow. For example, an M16 manufactured by a regular producer under a government contract would be within the definition, but a copy of the same firearm made in an illegal workshop would not be within the definition.

16. United Nations General Assembly, resolution 52/38 J, Dec. 9, 1997 (endorsing recommendations of the "Small Arms" report by the Panel of Governmental Experts).
17. "Report of the Group of Governmental Experts on Small Arms," United Nations General Assembly, A/54/258, 122, http://www.iansa.org/un/documents/GGE_small_arms99.pdf.
18. General Assembly, Resolution 53/77 E (introduced by Japan), http://disarmament.un.org/vote.nsf/91a5e1195dc97a630525656f005b8adf/198682e60b83f62e052566b90062b0ba?OpenDocument&ExpandSection=4.
19. "Report of the Group of Governmental Experts on Small Arms," A/54/258, ¶ 123.
20. New York state senator George Washington Plunkitt, known as "the sage of Tammany."
21. United Nations, Preparatory Committee for the United Nations Conference on the Illicit Trade in Small Arms and Light Weapons in All Its Aspects, Draft Programme of Action . . . Third Session, March 19–20 2001, A/CONF.192/PC/L.4/ Rev 1 (Feb. 2, 2001).
22. This is a deadly, yet subtle, combination of legalese and diplomatic terminology.
23. Association Nationale de defense des Tireurs, Amateurs et Collectionners d'armes (ANTAC), France.

Associazione Nazionale Produttori Armi e Munizioni (ANPAM), Italy
British Shooting Sports Council (BSSC), United Kingdom.
Canadian Institute for Legislative Action (CILA), Canada
Fair Trade Group (FAIR), United States
Federation of European Societies of Arms Collectors (FESAC), the Netherlands
Forum Waffenrecht (FW), Germany
International Ammunition Association, Inc. (IAA), United States

National Rifle Association of America—Institute on Legislative Action (NRA-ILA), United States

Safari Club International (SCI), United States

Single Action Shooting Society (SASS), United States

South Africa Gun Owners' Association (SAGA), South Africa

Sporting Clays of America (SCA), United States

Sporting Shooters' Association of Australia (SSAA), Australia

World Forum on the Future of Sports Shooting Activities (WFSA), Belgium

24. The full text of the presentations is at: http://web.archive.org/web/20021217014127/disarmament.un.org/cab/smallarms/ngospeakers.htm.

25. Emphasis added.

26. Aaron Karp, "Small Arms: Back to the Future," *Brown Journal of World Affairs*. 9, no. 1 (Spring 2002), http://www.watsoninstitute.org/bjwa/archive/9.1/SmallArms/Karp.pdf.

27. "Report of the Ninth United Nations Congress on the Prevention of Crime and the Treatment of Offenders," United Nations Congress on the Prevention of Crime and the Treatment of Offenders, Cairo, Egypt, 29 Apr.–8 May 1995, A/CONF.169/16, May 12, 1995, http://www.uncjin.org/Documents/9rep2e.pdf.

28. *Yomiuri Shimben*, reprinted in *Daily News*, Ketchikan, AK, quoted in *Gun Week*, October 20, 1995.

29. United Nations, Economic and Social Council, Resolution 1995/27.

30. United Nations, Economic and Social Council, E/CN.15/1998/L.6/Rev. 1.

31. United Nations, Economic and Social Council, E/CN.15/1998/4, 4–7.

32. "Report of the Ad Hoc Committee on the Elaboration of a Convention against Transnational Organized Crime on the work of its first to eleventh sessions, Addendum Report of the Ad Hoc Committee on the Elaboration of a Convention against Transnational Organized Crime on the work of its twelfth session," United Nations, General Assembly, A/55/383/Add.2 (March 20, 2001), ¶ 11.

33. Ibid., ¶ 10.

34. Under Article 51 of the U.N. Charter, States do have the right of self-defense. Unfortunately, this is not usually interpreted as the right of self-defense for individuals themselves.

35. The Chinese broach no criticism of their policies from the U.N., especially on human rights issues (Joseph Kahn, "China Disputes U.N. Envoy on Widespread Use of Torture," *New York Times*, December 7, 2005, A5).

36. "Report of the Ad Hoc Committee on the Elaboration of a Convention against Transnational Organized Crime," A/55/383/Add.2, ¶ 11.

37. Ibid., ¶ ¶ 5–6.

Chapter 3

1. The treaty is available online: http://www.oas.org/juridico/English/treaties/a-63.html. CIFTA is sometimes called the Inter-American Convention on Illicit Arms Trafficking, although this name obscures how wide-ranging CIFTA really is.

2. In modern international law usage, when an agreement is created by a multinational organization, such as OAS or the U.N., the agreement is called "Convention" instead of "Treaty." In an American constitutional sense, the CIFTA convention is still a "treaty" in that it requires ratification by the U.S. Senate.

3. He made the announcement at the April 2009 OAS meeting of heads of government.

4. CIFTA article VII, § 2: "States Parties shall adopt the necessary measures to ensure that all firearms, ammunition, explosives, and other related materials seized, confiscated, or forfeited as the result of illicit manufacturing or trafficking do not fall into the hands of private individuals or businesses through auction, sale, or other disposal."

5. Some states conduct the checks themselves, rather than handing the check over to the FBI, which runs NICS. A few states do not require NICS checks if the buyer already has a state-issued license to own or carry handguns.

6. CIFTA article I, § 1.

7. CIFTA article IV, § 1.

8. An unlimited number of additional unannounced inspections are allowed if they are part of a criminal investigation.

9. 18 U.S. Code § 923(a).

10. CIFTA article I.

11. Ibid. Emphasis added.

12. Most states are similar, although a few state laws do cover antique guns.

13. The registration requirement would be bolstered by CIFTA's Article XI, Recordkeeping: "States Parties shall assure the maintenance for a reasonable time of the information necessary to trace and identify illicitly manufactured and illicitly trafficked firearms to enable them to comply with their obligations under Articles XIII and XVII." One way to identify "illicitly manufactured" (that is, assembled without a federal license) ammunition or firearms would be to require registration of everything that is assembled pursuant to a license.

14. CIFTA article IV.

15. Indeed, the fact that the preamble lists some things that do not need to be licensed makes it all the more clear that manufacturing must be licensed, since manufacturing is not on the preamble's list of non-requirements. The well-established legal principle is that the inclusion of some things implies the exclusion of other things ("*inclusio unius est exclusio alterius*").

16. At least in modern times. The treaties with Indian nations were frequently violated.

17. Harold Hongju Koh, "Transnational Public Law Litigation," 100 *Yale Law Journal* 2347, 2360–61, 2383–4 (1991); Harold Hongju Koh, "Paying 'Decent Respect' to World Opinion on the Death Penalty," 35 *University of California, Davis Law Review* 1085, 1111 n. 114 (2002); Harold Hongju Koh, "The 1998 Frankel Lecture: Bringing International Law Home," 35 *Houston Law Review* 623, 666 (1998).

18. Harold Kongju Koh, "Lecture: A World Drowning in Guns," 71 *Fordham Law Review* 2333, 2358–59 (2003), http://law2.fordham.edu/publications/articles/500flspub11111.pdf.

19. Harold Kongju Koh, "Is International Law Really State Law?" 111 *Harvard Law Review* 1824, 1828–29 n. 24 (1998).

20. Koh, "Transnational Public Law Litigation," 2383–84.

21. Harold Kongju Koh, "On American Exceptionalism," 55 *Stanford Law Review* 1479, 1509–10 (2003), web.pdx.edu/~kinsella/ps448/koh.html. URL no longer accessible.

22. The Inter-American Court was established by the OAS in 1979. Located in San José, Costa Rica, its duty is to interpret and hear cases on the American Convention on Human Rights.

    An OAS member state would be able to bring a case directly in the court. Strongly antigun governments such as those in Mexico or Brazil might be logical plaintiffs, especially if Secretary of State Clinton told them off the record that she would not be upset if they sued in order to push gun control in the United States.

    A nongovernment plaintiff would have to first bring a complaint to the OAS Inter-American Commission on Human Rights, which could choose to send the matter to the OAS court. The OAS Commission is strongly supportive of the gun confiscation agenda. For example, its 2009 report on Haiti has an extensive discussion of a program to round up guns in Haiti, and does not even mention the Haitian Constitution, which guarantees a right to arms for home defense (*Annual Report of the IACHR 2006: Haiti*, ¶ 113, http://www.cidh.org/annualrep/2006eng/chap.4c.htm). The Haitian Constitution, article 268-1, provides: "Every citizen has the right to armed self defense, within the bounds of his domicile, but has no right to bear arms without express well-founded authorization from the Chief of Police." (In the original: *Tout citoyen a droit à l'auto-défense armée, dans les limites de son domicile mais n'a pas droit au port d'armes sans l'autorisation expresse et motivée du Chef de la Police.*)

    For the OAS court to have jurisdiction over the United States, the U.S. would first have to ratify the American Convention on Human Rights. That treaty was signed by Jimmy Carter in 1977, but the Senate has not ratified it.
23. Fran Spielman, "Daley wants to take suit vs. gunmakers to World Court," *Chicago Sun-Times*, April 28, 2010.
24. No lawsuits could be brought based on state constitutional right to arms clauses, since the Supremacy Clause of the U.S. Constitution means that federal law (including laws enacted pursuant to treaties) trumps any state law.
25. *Reid v. Covert*, 354 U.S. 1 (1957).
26. Harold Hongju Koh, "Why Do Nations Obey International Law?" 106 *Yale Law Journal* 2599, 2658 n. 297 (1997).
27. The CIFTA guidelines include: Model Legislation on the Marking and Tracing of Firearms (Apr.19, 2007); Draft Model Legislation and Commentaries on Legislative Measures to Establish Criminal Offenses (May 9, 2008); Broker Regulations (Nov. 17–20, 2003). Available at www.oas.org.
28. David J. Scheffer, "America's Stake in Peace, Security, and Justice," U.S. Department of State, August 31, 1998, http://www.state.gov/www/policy_remarks/1998/980831_scheffer_icc.html.
29. Bill Clinton, "Statement on the Rome Treaty on the International Criminal Court," Dec. 31, 2000, http://findarticles.com/p/articles/mi_m2889/is_1_37/ai_71360100.
30. Kim R. Holmes, "Smart Multilateralism," in *ConUNdrum: The Limits of the United Nations and the Search for Alternatives*, ed., Brett D. Schaefer (Lanham, MD: Rowman & Littlefield, 2009), 14n9.
31. Ewen MacAskill, "Clinton: It is a 'great regret' the US is not in International Criminal Court," *Guardian* (London), August 6, 2009, http://www.guardian.co.uk/world/2009/aug/06/us-international-criminal-court.

32. Joe Lauria, "Court Orders Probe of Afghanistan Attacks," *Wall Street Journal*, September 10, 2009. The court has also begun collecting similar information regarding Israeli forces in Gaza.

   U.S. forces in Afghanistan, like U.S. forces in most other countries, are protected by an "Article 98" agreement; under that agreement, the host country promises not to turn U.S. soldiers over to the ICC for prosecution. However, the enforceability of Article 98 agreements under international law is contested.

33. The following is from page 21 of the Arms Trade Treaty Steering Committee's *Compilation of Global Principles for Arms Transfers* (revised and updated 2007):

   > Under international human rights law, States are responsible for their own actions and the actions of their agents. They also have a duty to prevent patterns of abuse committed by private persons, whether or not they are acting under the control of the State. Failure to exercise "due diligence" by omitting to take the necessary steps to protect individuals from organised crime such as kidnapping and killing for ransom can amount to a violation of human rights law. In some cases, the obligation to protect individuals from violations perpetrated by private actors is part and parcel of the State's obligation not to commit the violation itself. For example, failing to adopt the necessary measures to prevent acts of torture from being carried out on one's territory may amount to more than a violation of the "due diligence" standard and be treated as a breach of the international norm prohibiting torture.
   >
   > The Rome Statute of the International Criminal Court (ICC), in Article 25 (3)(c), establishes criminal responsibility if a person aids, abets or otherwise assists in the commission or the attempted commission of a crime, including by providing the means for its commission. Providing the weapons used to commit or attempt to commit one of the crimes for which the ICC has jurisdiction is sufficient to give rise to responsibility as an accomplice.

34. Rome Statute of the International Criminal Court, July 17, 1998, article 5(1), www.un.org/children/conflict/keydocuments/english/. No longer accessible.

35. Brett D. Schaefer and Steven Groves, "The U.S. Should Not Join the International Criminal Court," Heritage Foundation, Backgrounder no. 2307, August 18, 2009, http://www.heritage.org/Research/InternationalOrganizations/bg2307.cfm.

36. Ted R. Bromund and Steven Groves, "The U.N.'s Arms Trade Treaty: A Dangerous Multilateral Mistake in the Making," Heritage Foundation, Backgrounder no. 2309, Aug. 21, 2009, http://www.heritage.org/Research/InternationalOrganizations/bg2309.cfm.

37. Rome Statute, article 12(3.)

38. Rome Statute, article 12(1).

39. Rome Statute, article 12(2)(b).

40. Koh, "On American Exceptionalism," 55 *Stanford Law Review* 1479, 1506–9.

41. The official name was "The U.N. Conference to Review Progress Made in the Implementation of the Program of Action to Prevent, Combat and Eradicate the Illicit Trade in Small Arms and Light Weapons."

42. "Douglas was appointed a 'messenger of peace' by Secretary-General Kofi Annan in 1998. His focus has been primarily on disarmament—from nuclear on down to

small arms" ("Michael Douglas backs U.N. gun ban: TV commercial 'spotlights the illicit trade in small arms and light weapons,'" Worldnetdaily.com, May 28, 2006, http://www.wnd.com/news/article.asp?ARTICLE_ID=50407).

43. "Biography for Michael Douglas," *Internet Movie Database*, www.imdb.com/name/nm0000140/bio.

44. At the time, the Brady Campaign called itself Handgun Control, Inc., and its legal/educational affiliate was the Center to Prevent Handgun Violence.

45. "Will U.N. Take Away Americans' Guns?" *Hannity & Colmes* (Fox News); guest: Wayne LaPierre, June 29, 2006.

46. "Annan receives arms petition by one-millionth signer, vows to transmit call onward," UN News Centre, June 26, 2006, http://www.un.org/apps/news/story.asp?NewsID=18997&Cr=small&Cr1=arms.

47. U.N. Department of Public Information, "Global Scourge from Illicit Trade in Small Arms Continues to 'Wreak Havoc', Says UN Disarmament Head, as Meeting on 2001 Action Programme Opens," June 14, 2010, DC/3247, http://www.un.org/News/Press/docs/2010/dc3247.doc.htm.

48. U.N. General Assembly, "Towards an Arms Trade Treaty: Establishing Common International Standards for the Import, Export and Transfer of Conventional Arms," U.N. Document A/C.1/63/L.39*.

49. His full name is Óscar Rafael de Jesús Arias Sánchez.

50. When the Security Council is using its powers under Chapter VII of the U.N. Charter, to address "any threat to the peace, breach of the peace, or act of aggression." The Security Council can also act under Chapter VI of the Charter, to engage in dispute resolution which is not legally binding.

51. The Security Council is separately authorized, by Chapter VI, to make nonbinding recommendations for dispute resolution.

52. "UN Arms Embargoes: An Overview of the Last Ten Years," Control Arms Campaign, March 17, 2006, http://www.oxfamamerica.org/publications/un-arms-embargoes-an-overview-of-the-last-ten-years.

53. David B. Kopel, Paul Gallant, and Joanne D. Eisen, "The Arms Trade Treaty: Zimbabwe, the Democratic Republic of the Congo, and the Prospects for Arms Embargoes on Human Rights Violators," 114 *Penn State Law Review* 891 (2010), ssrn.com/abstract=1437204. Much of this section of the chapter is based on this paper.

54. "Chinese Gunrunners Persist," *Strategy Page*, April 28, 2008, http://www.strategypage.com/htmw/htmurph/articles/20080428.aspx?comments=Y; "Disarming Zimbabwe," *Strategy Page*, April 21, 2008, http://www.strategypage.com/htmw/htproc/articles/20080421.aspx?comments=Y.

55. David Beresford, "Chinese Ship Carries Arms Cargo to Mugabe Regime," *Guardian* (UK), April 18, 2008. (Themba Maseko, South African head of government information: "We are not in a position to act unilaterally and interfere in a trade deal between two countries.")

56. *Phillip & Kearney v. National Conventional Arms Control Comm., et al.*, no. 4975/08 (High Court of South Africa, Durban & Coast Local Div., April 18, 2008); "Zim arms ship reaches Angola," *Independent Online* (South Africa), April 27, 2008, http://www.iol.co.za/index.php?set_id=1&click_id=84&art_id=vn20080427110147534C924469.

57. "Arms from China's 'ship of shame' reach Mugabe," *Sunday Herald* (Scotland), May 17, 2008, http://www.sundayherald.com/international/shinternational/display. var.2278991.0.0.php.

58. "Zim arms ship reaches Angola"; Christof Maletsky, "'Ship of Shame' Cargo Delivered to Country," *Namibian*, May 20, 2008.

Congo-Brazzaville, also called "Congo," or formally, "Republic of the Congo," is a distinct nation from the much larger Democratic Republic of the Congo. Congo borders the western DRC.

59. Maletsky, "'Ship of Shame' Cargo Delivered to Country."

60. General Assembly, "Towards an Arms Trade Treaty," p. 2.

61. David B. Kopel, Paul Gallant and Joanne D. Eisen, *The Human Right of Self-Defense*, 22 *BYU Journal of Public Law* 43 (2008): 137–47; http://davekopel .org/2A/LawRev/The-Human-Right-of-Self-Defense.pdf:

Right of self-defense: Antigua & Barbuda, the Bahamas, Barbados, Belize, Cyprus, Grenada, Guyana, Honduras, Jamaica, Malta, Nigeria, Peru, Samoa, St. Kitts & Nevis, Saint Lucia, Saint Vincent and the Grenadines, Slovakia, and Zimbabwe.

Right to resist tyranny: Andorra, Argentina, Congo, Greece, Guatemala, Honduras, Hungary, Lithuania, Mauritania, Peru, Portugal, Romania, and Slovakia.

Right of security in the home: Afghanistan, Andorra, Angola, Antigua and Barbuda, Armenia, Azerbaijan, Bahamas, Belarus, Belgium, Belize, Benin, Bolivia, Brazil, Bulgaria, Burkina Faso, Burundi, Cambodia, China, Congo, Cuba, Dominican Republic, Egypt, El Salvador, Eritrea, Estonia, Ethiopia, Germany, Grenada, Guatemala, Guyana, Honduras, Hong Kong, Iran, Ireland, Italy, Jamaica, Jordan, Kuwait, Latvia, Lebanon, Liberia, Libya, Luxembourg, Macedonia, Madagascar, Mongolia, Nepal, Nicaragua, Niger, Oman, Panama, Paraguay, Peru, Portugal, Qatar, Romania, Russia, Rwanda, Saint Christopher and Nevis, Saint Lucia, Saint Vincent, Slovakia, Saudi Arabia, South Korea, Spain, Suriname, Switzerland, Syria, Thailand, Trinidad and Tobago, Tunisia, Turkey, Uruguay, Venezuela, Vietnam, Zambia, and Zimbabwe.

Obviously many of the governments of the above countries do not obey the requirements of their own constitutions—a fact which casts further doubt on their willingness to adhere to international arms control treaties.

62. Bromund and Groves, *The U.N.'s Arms Trade Treaty*, 13.

63. Ibid.

64. International Action Network on Small Arms, "Gaza: An ATT Would Reduce Civilian Casualties," June 17, 2009, http://www.iansa.org/regions/nafrica/gaza_ att09.htm. No longer accessible.

65. Control Arms, *Arms without Borders: Why a Globalised Trade Needs Global Controls*, October 2006, http://www.amnesty.org/en/library/asset/POL34/006/2006/ en/30873344-d403-11dd-8743-d305bea2b2c7/pol340062006en.html.

66. Bernd Debusmann, "Soros adds voice to debate over Israel lobby," Reuters News, April 15, 2007.

67. *Op. cit.*, Slater, *Soros* (1996), 120.

68. Eye on the UN, http://eyeontheun.org/browse-un.asp?ya=1&ua=1&sa=1&tpa=1.

69. The Burmese dictatorship has renamed the country "Myanmar," but I use the traditional name—hoping one day that the dictatorship will be gone, and the real name will return, just as Cambodia went back to being "Cambodia," and not "Kampuchea" after the Khmer Rouge lost power.

70. Ben Case, "Disarmament: Inching toward a Global Arms Treaty," Inter Press Service News Agency, July 16, 2009, http://ipsnews.net/news.asp?idnews=47691.

71. Kenneth Anderson, "International Gun Control Efforts?" OpinioJuris.org, July 19, 2008, http://opiniojuris.org/2008/07/19/international-gun-control-efforts/.

72. Micheal E. Bussard and Stanton L. Wormley Jr., *NRA Firearms Sourcebook* (Fairfax, VA: NRA, 2006), 208.

73. National Research Council of the National Academies, Committee on Critical Mineral Impacts on the U.S. Economy, *Minerals, Critical Minerals, and the U.S. Economy* (Washington: National Academies Press, 2008).

74. United States Geological Survey, *Minerals Commodity* Summaries, http://minerals.usgs.gov/minerals/pubs/mcs/.

75. National Academies of Science, *Ballistic Imaging* (Washington: National Academies Press, 2008), http://books.nap.edu/catalog.php?record_id=12162; David Howitt, Frederic A. Tulleners, and Michael T. Beddow, *What Laser Machining Technology Adds to Firearm Forensics: How Viable Are Micro-Marked Firing Pins as Evidence?* (U. Cal. Davis, 2007), http://www.nssf.org/share/legal/docs/0507UCDavisStudy.pdf; G. G. Krivosta, "NanoTag™ markings from another perspective," *AFTE Journal* (Association of Firearms and Toolmarks Examiners) 38, no. 1 (Winter 2006): 41–47.

76. John Bolton, "Obama's U.N. Record," *National Review Online*, September 20, 2010, http://www.nationalreview.com/articles/247029/obama-s-u-n-record-john-bolton?page=1.

Chapter 4

1. "Press Briefing on Small Arms Conference," United Nations, July 5, 2001, http://www.un.org/News/briefings/docs/2001/SmallArmsConfBrf.doc.htm; Edith M. Lederer, "U.N. Investigating Whether E-Mails From U.S. Gun Enthusiasts a Security Threat," Associated Press, July 5, 2001; Dave Kopel, "Score One for Bush: A U.N. conference concludes without too much permanent damage," *National Review Online*, July 30, 2001, http://old.nationalreview.com/kopel/kopel073001.shtml.

2. United Nations Department of Public Information in cooperation with the Department for Disarmament Affairs, "Setting the Record Straight: UN Conference on the Illicit Trade in Small Arms and Light Weapons in All Its Aspects, New York, 9–20 July 2001," http://www.calguns.net/calgunforum/showthread.php?t=233266&page=5.

3. Dave Kopel, Paul Gallant, and Joanne D. Eisen, "Jamaican War Zone: An island of intoxicative beauty? Try again, mon," *National Review Online*, October 30, 2000, http://www.nationalreview.com/kopel/kopel103000.shtml.

4. Preparatory Committee for the United Nations Conference on the Illicit Trade in Small Arms and Light Weapons in All Its Aspects, Second session—January 8–19,

2000, "Working paper by the Chairman of the Preparatory Committee. Draft Programme of Action, January 9, 2001," § 6(f).

5. Canadian War Museum, "Temporary Exhibitions: The Art of Peacemaking," April 26, 2001, http://web.archive.org/web/20041113095142/http://www.civilization.ca/cwm/ihuman/cwmhumeng.html.

6. Ad Hoc Committee on the Elaboration of a Convention against Transnational Organized Crime, "Revised draft Protocol against the Illicit Manufacturing of and Trafficking in Firearms, Their Parts and Components and Ammunition, supplementing the United Nations Convention against Transnational Organized Crime, Twelfth session, Vienna, 26 Feb.–2 Mar. 2001," Dec. 18, 2000, A/AC.254/4/Add.2/Rev.6.

7. Peter Lock, "Pervasive Illicit Small Arms Availability: A Global Threat," European Institute for Crime Prevention and Control, affiliated with the United Nations; HEUNI Paper no. 14 (Helsinki, 1999), 27. (The "affiliated with the United Nations" phrase appears as part of the group's name, on the title page of this document.)

8. Kopel, "Score One for Bush."

9. "Report of the Panel of Government Experts on Small Arms," A/52/298, Aug. 27 1997, ¶ 26, http://www.fas.org/asmp/campaigns/smallarms/UN_A_52_298.pdf.

10. *Small Arms Survey 2001* (New York: Oxford Univ. Pr., 2001), http://www.smallarmssurvey.org/nc/de/publications/by-type/yearbook/small-arms-survey-2001.html?sword_list%5B0%5D=small&sword_list%5B1%5D=arms&sword_list%5B2%5D=survey&sword_list%5B3%5D=2001.

11. David B. Kopel, Paul Gallant, and Joanne D. Eisen, "How Many Global Deaths from Arms? Reasons to Question the 740,000 Factoid Being Used to Promote the Arms Trade Treaty," *NYU Journal of Law & Liberty* 5 (2010), 672; http://papers.ssrn.com/sol3/papers.cfm?abstract_id=1580225.

12. John Hughes-Wilson and Adrian Wilkinson, "Safe and Efficient Small Arms Collection and Destruction Programmes: A Proposal for Practical Technical Measures," United Nations Disarmament Programme (May 2001), 16, ¶ 4.1.2, http://www.smallarmssurvey.org/fileadmin/docs/L-External-publications/2001/2001-Hughes-Wilkinson-Small-Arms-Collection-Destruction.pdf:

> It may be possible to start a programme of weapon registration as a first step towards the physical collection phase . . . The advantage to the local community is that they can retain their weapons until they feel that the security environment is sufficiently safe to allow for weapons surrender . . . Assurances must be provided, and met, that the process of registration will not lead to *immediate* weapons seizures by security forces. [Emphasis added.]

13. "Conference on Small Arms Set to Convene at Headquarters, 9–20 July," Press Release, DC/2782, July 5, 2001, http://www.un.org/News/Press/docs/2001/dc2782.doc.htm.

14. Of course, smokeless powder never explodes; it deflagrates.

15. Kopel, "Score One for Bush."

16. Ibid.

17. The Laogai Research Foundation provides extensive information on human rights abuses in China, including on China's system of de facto slave labor, at http://www.laogai.org/.
18. Lock, "Pervasive Illicit Small Arms Availability," 27.
19. Kofi A. Annan, "Small arms, big problems," *International Herald Tribune*, July 10, 2001, http://www.un.org/News/ossg/sg/stories/articleFull.asp?TID=24&Type=Article.
20. The ICBL's website is http://www.icbl.org/intro.php /.
21. Annan, "Small arms, big problems."
22. Kopel, "Score One for Bush."
23. David B. Kopel, Paul Gallant, and Joanne D. Eisen, "Does the Right to Bear Arms Impede or Promote Economic Development?" *Engage* 6, no. 1 (2005): 85, http://www.davekopel.com/2A/Foreign/Development.pdf.
24. Adèle Kirsten, *A Nation without Guns: The Story of Gun Free South Africa* (Scottsville, S.A.: University of KwaZulu-Natal Press, 2008), 176 (describing the 2006 WHO conference in Durban, South Africa).
25. David Kopel, Paul Gallant, and Joanne D. Eisen, "The Guns of Sudan. Gun confiscation in South Sudan makes a bad situation for human rights even worse," *New Ledger*, July 7, 2009, http://newledger.com/2009/07/the-guns-of-sudan/.
26. Amir Attaran, et al., "WHO, the Global Fund, and medical malpractice in malaria treatment," 363 *Lancet* 237 (2004).
27. In a letter to the *New York Times*, answering a *Times* editorial criticizing the U.S. for not allowing the conference to be used as a tool to disarm civilians, Whittlesey elaborated:

> The highest priority of freedom-loving people is liberty, even more than peace. The small arms you demonize often protect men, women and children from tyranny, brutality and even the genocide too frequently perpetrated by governments and police forces. The world's numerous dictators would be delighted to stem the flow of small arms to indigenous freedom fighters and civilians alike to minimize any resistance . . .
>
> The right of individual self-defense in the face of criminal intimidation and government aggression is a deeply held belief of the American people dating back to 1776, when small arms in the hands of private individuals were the means used to secure liberty and independence.

(Faith Whittlesey, "Small Arms in a Big, Brutal World," *New York Times*, July 13, 2001, p. A20.)
28. Remarks by U.S. Undersecretary of State John R. Bolton at the UN Conference on Illicit Trade in Small Arms and Light Weapons in All Its Aspects Plenary, New York, July 9, 2001, usinfo.state.gov/topical/pol/arms/stories/01070902.htm. No longer accessible.
29. David B. Kopel, Paul Gallant, and Joanne D. Eisen, "Firearms Possession by 'Non-State Actors': the Question of Sovereignty," 8 *Texas Review of Law and Politics* 373 (2004), http://www.davekopel.com/2a/LawRev/Non-state-actors.pdf.
30. Ibid.
31. The Declaration of Independence (1776), ¶ 2.
32. *Mandel v. Mitchell*, 325 F. Supp. 620, 629 (E.D.N.Y., 1971).

Chapter 5

1. Patrick F. Fagan, "How U.N. Conventions on Women's and Children's Rights Undermine Family, Religion, and Sovereignty: Supplemental Material: Quotations from CRC and CEDAW Committees of the United Nations" Heritage Foundation, Backgrounder no. 1409, February 5, 2001, http://www.heritage.org/Research/Reports/2001/02/How-UN-Conventions-On-Womens.

2. Austin Ruse, "Diplomat Charges UN Committee with Misuse of UN Documents," *C-Fam* (a publication of the Catholic Family and Human Rights Institute) 4, no. 32, July 27, 2001, http://www.c-fam.org/publications/id.199/pub_detail.asp.

3. *Reid v. Covert*, 354 U.S. 1, 16 (1957) ("No agreement with a foreign nation can confer power on Congress, or on any other branch of Government, which is free from the restraints of the Constitution").

4. Phyllis Schlafly, "Can Globalism Amend Our Constitution?" *Eagle Forum*, August 11, 2003, http://www.eagleforum.org/column/2003/aug03/03-08-13.shtml.

5. *Knight v. Florida*, 528 U.S. 990, 993–99 (1999) (Breyer, J., dissenting from denial of certiorari).

6. *Gratz v. Bollinger*, 539 U.S. 244, 302 (2003) (Ginsburg, J., dissenting, joined by Justices Souter and Breyer); *Grutter v. Bollinger*, 539 U.S. Ct. 306, 344 (2003) (Ginsburg, J., concurring, joined by Justice Breyer).

7. Ruth Bader Ginsburg, "Looking beyond Our Borders: The Value of a Comparative Perspective in Constitutional Adjudication," *Idaho Law Review* 40 (2003): 1, 8.

8. 536 U.S. 304, 316 n. 21 (2002).

9. Joseph Bruce Alonso, "The Second Amendment and Global Gun Control," *Journal on Firearms & Public Policy* 15 (2003), http://www.saf.org/journal/15/TheSecondAmendmentandGlobalGunControl.pdf. The article is based on a paper that won first place in the NRA Civil Rights Legal Defense Fund student lawyer essay contest in 2002.

10. Barbara Frey, "Progress report on the prevention of human rights violations committed with small arms and light weapons," E/CN.4/Sub.2/2004/37 (2004), ¶ 58, http://www1.umn.edu/humanrts/demo/smallarms2004-2.html; Barbara Frey, "Specific Human Rights Issues," United Nations Economic and Social Council, Human Rights Commission, Sub-Commission on the Promotion of Human Rights, E/CN.4/Sub.2/2003/29 (June 25, 2003), ¶¶ 36, 47. The theory is that the state is culpable for criminal violence due to failure to exercise "due diligence" in preventing crime.

11. Frey, "Progress report on the prevention of human rights violations."

Chapter 6

1. Act of July 16, 1866, 14 Stat. 173, 176.

2. The significance of the Freedmen's Bureau Act to the Fourteenth Amendment is recognized in the following: Akhil Amar, "The Bill of Rights and the Fourteenth Amendment," 101 *Yale Law Journal* (1992): 1193, 1245n228; Michael Kent Curtis, *No State Shall Abridge: The Fourteenth Amendment and the Bill of Rights* (1986); H. Flack, *The Adoption of the Fourteenth Amendment* 17 (1908).

The definitive book on the subject is Stephen P. Halbrook, *Securing Civil Rights: Freedmen, the 14th Amendment, and the Right to Bear Arms* (Oakland: Independent Institute, 2010). See also Nelson Lund, "Outsider Voices on Guns and the Constitution," 17 *Constitutional Commentary* 701 (2000).

3. Cong. Globe, 39th Cong., 1st Sess. 129 (1866). All debates and proceedings from the 39th Congress can be accessed at http://memory.loc.gov/ammem/amlaw/lwcglink.html#anchor39.

4. P. Foner and G. Walker, eds., *Proceedings of the Black State Conventions, 1840–1865* (1980), 302.

5. Cong. Globe, 39th Cong., 1st Sess. 337 (1866).

6. Ibid. 512.

7. Ibid., 517.

8. Ibid., 585

9. Ibid., 654.

10. Ibid.

11. Ibid., 657.

12. Executive Document No. 70, 39th Cong., 1st Session (1866), 233, 236 (emphasis in original).

13. Cong. Globe, 39th Cong., 1st Sess. 1292 (1866).

14. Ibid., 688.

15. Ibid., 742.

16. Ibid., 743.

17. Ibid., 748.

18. Ibid., 775.

19. Ibid., 1292.

20. Ibid., 908–9.

21. *Loyal Georgian* (Augusta), February 3, 1866, 1.

22. Ibid., 2.

23. Ibid., 3.

24. Cong. Globe, 39th Cong., 1st Sess. 916 (1866).

25. Ibid., 936.

26. Ibid., 941.

27. Ibid., 943.

28. Ibid., 1238.

29. Ibid., 3412.

30. Ibid., 1291.

31. Ibid., 1292.

32. Ibid.

33. Ibid., 606 (Senate); 1367 (House).

34. Ibid., 1679.

35. Ibid., 1757.

36. Ibid., quoting James Kent, *Commentaries on American Law.*

37. Ibid., 1809.

38. "The Civil Rights Bill in the Senate," *New York Evening Post*, April 7, 1866, 2.

39. Ibid.

40. 14 Stat. 27 (1866) (emphasis added).

41. See 42 U.S.C. § 1981.

42. Cong. Globe, 39th Cong., 1st Sess. 2743 (1866).
43. Ibid., 3412.
44. Ibid., 2545.
45. Ibid., 2765.
46. Ibid.
47. Ibid., 2766.
48. Ibid., 2773.
49. Ibid.
50. Ibid., 2774.
51. Ibid., 2775.
52. Ibid., 2878.
53. Ibid.
54. Ibid., 3042.
55. Ibid., 3149.
56. Ibid., 3210.
57. Ibid., 3412.
58. Ibid.
59. Ibid.
60. Ibid.
61. Ibid., 3524.
62. Ibid., 3562.
63. Ibid., 3849.
64. Ibid., 3850.
65. Ibid., 3842.
66. 14 Stat. 173 (1866).
67. Ibid., 176–77, emphasis added.
68. P.L. 274, 77th Cong., 1st Sess., Ch. 445, 55 Stat., pt. 1, 742 (October 16, 1941).
69. *New York Times*, November 11, 1938, 1.
70. Ibid., 4.
71. Ibid., November 4, 1939, 5.
72. Ibid., July 1, 1940, 3.
73. Ibid., July 2, 1940, 4.
74. Ibid., September 5, 1940, 17.
75. Ibid., January 4, 1941, 7.
76. Brief for the United States, *United States v. Miller*, 15.
77. *United States v. Miller*, 307 U.S. 174, 178 (1939).
78. Letter reprinted in Cong. Rec., 77th Cong., 1st Sess., at A2072 (May 2, 1941).
79. Hearings before the Committee on Military Affairs, House of Representatives, 77th Cong., 1st Sess., on S. 1579 to Authorize the President of the United States, July 31, 1941, at 18 (1941).
80. Rep. No. 1120 [to accompany S. 1579], House Committee on Military Affairs, 77th Cong., 1st Sess. 1 (Aug. 4, 1941).
81. Ibid. at 2. The Report should have said, "Amendment 2" instead of "section 2."
82. 87 Cong. Rec., 77th Cong., 1st Sess. 6778 (August 5, 1941).
83. Ibid.
84. Ibid, 6811 (August 6, 1941).

85. Ibid. Chandler later served as commissioner of Major League Baseball, and—against stiff opposition from fifteen of the sixteen club owners—supported Branch Rickey's decision to bring Jackie Robinson to the Brooklyn Dodgers. Still later, as governor of Kentucky, Chandler used National Guard troops to protect black children from violence during school desegregation.

86. Ibid.

87. Ibid., 7097 (August 13, 1941).

88. Ibid., 7098.

89. Ibid.

90. Ibid., 7100.

91. Ibid., 7100–1.

92. Ibid., 7101.

93. Ibid., 7101.

94. Ibid.

95. Ibid.

96. Ibid., 7102.

97. Ibid.

98. Ibid., 7103.

99. 87 Cong. Rec., 77th Cong., 1st Sess. 7164 (August 13, 1941).

100. Rep. No. 1214, Conference Report [to accompany S. 1579], 77th Cong., 1st Sess. 2 (September 25, 1941).

101. P.L. 274, 77th Cong., 1st Sess., Ch. 445, 55 Stat., pt. 1, 742 (October 16, 1941).

102. Federal Firearms Legislation: Hearings before the Subcommittee to Investigate Juvenile Delinquency, Judiciary Committee, U.S. Senate, 90th Cong., 2nd Sess. 56 (1968).

103. Ibid., 479, 481.

104. § 1(b), P.L. 99-308, 100 Stat. 449 (May 19, 1986).

105. *The Right to Keep and Bear Arms: Report of the Subcommittee on the Constitution,* Senate Judiciary Committee, 97th Cong., 2d Sess. 12 (1982), http://www.guncite.com/journals/senrpt/senrpt.html. In addition, two other scholarly studies were inserted into the legislative record in support of Congress' finding during Senate debate: David I. Caplan, "Restoring the Balance: The Second Amendment Revisited," *Fordham Urban Law Journal* 5 (1976): 31, reprinted in 131 Cong. Rec. S8692 (June 24, 1985); Stephen P. Halbrook, "To Keep and Bear Their Private Arms: The Adoption of the Second Amendment, 1787–1791," *Northern Kentucky Law Review* 10 (1982): 13, reprinted in 131 Cong. Rec. S9105 (July 9, 1985).

106. 18 U.S.C. § 926(a).

107. 18 U.S.C. § 926A.

108. 131 Cong. Rec. S9114 (July 9, 1985).

109. 132 Cong. Rec. H1695 (April 9, 1986).

110. P.L. 109-92, 119 Stat. 2095 (October 26, 2005).

111. Ibid., § 2.

112. Ibid., § 2(a)(3).

113. Ibid., § 2(a)(4).

114. Ibid., § 2(a)(5).

115. Ibid., § 2(a)(6).

116. Ibid., § 2(a)(7).

117. Ibid., § 2(a)(8).
118. Ibid., § 2(b)(1).
119. Ibid., § 2(b)(2), (3).
120. Ibid., § 2(b)(4).
121. Ibid., § 2(b)(5).
122. Ibid., § 3.
123. 151 Cong. Rec. S9374, S9378 (July 29, 2005).
124. Ibid., S9394.
125. Ibid., S9385.
126. Ibid., S9396.
127. 151 Cong. Rec. H8996 (October 20, 2005).
128. Ibid., H906-07.
129. Ibid., H9009.
130. Ibid., H9010.

Chapter 7

1.   David B. Kopel, Carl Moody, and Howard Nemerov, "Is There a Relationship between Guns and Freedom? Comparative Results from 59 Nations," *Texas Review of Law and Politics* 13 (2008): 1, http://papers.ssrn.com/sol3/papers.cfm?abstract_id=1090441.
2.   Ibid., 30:

> Almost every legitimate purpose for which a person might own a gun can strengthen the person's feelings of competence and self-control. The hunter thinks, "I am a capable outdoorsman. I can put food on my family's table, and don't have to rely entirely on the supermarket." The defensive gun owner thinks, "I am ready to protect my family, because I know that the police may not come in time." The target shooter thinks, "I am skilled at a precise, challenging sport." Many gun owners may think, "If, God forbid, my country ever succumbed to tyranny, I could help my community resist." Almost all gun owners have made the decision, "Even though some people claim that guns are too dangerous, I am capable of handling a powerful tool safely."
>
> For the countries in the top quintile for gun ownership (at least one gun per three persons), it is reasonable to assume that many people in those countries have personal experience with a benign, individual-affirming gun culture. Participation in a benign gun culture is hardly the only way in which a person can have personal experiences which affirm and strengthen the individual's beliefs in his or her own competence. But when a country has a benign, thriving gun culture, it is certain that there are great many persons who do have such experiences, and who do so in a context (successful, safe handling of potentially deadly tools) which is especially likely to induce and strengthen feelings of personal competence. The effect of a gun culture in promoting greater levels of individual competence and personal responsibility may be one reason for the statistically significant association between higher rates of gun ownership and higher rates of freedom from corruption, of economic freedom, of and economic success.

3. Don B. Kates and Gary Mauser, "Would Banning Firearms Reduce Murder and Suicide? A Review of International and Some Domestic Evidence," *Harvard Journal of Law and Public Policy* 30 (2007): 649, www.law.harvard.edu/students/orgs/jlpp/Vol30_No2_KatesMauseronline.pdf.
   As the authors have explained elsewhere, the Luxembourg data that they cite is incorrect, because the official statistical source from which they obtained the data has a typographical error.

4. Much of the material in this section is based on David B. Kopel, Paul Gallant, and Joanne D. Eisen "Human Rights and Gun Confiscation," *Quinnipiac Law Review* 26 (2008): 383, http://davekopel.org/2A/Foreign/Human-Rights-and-Gun-Confiscation.pdf.

5. Ben Knighton, "Historical ethnography and the collapse of Karamojong culture: Premature reports of trends," http://www.eldis.org/fulltext/knighton_karamoja.pdf.

6. "Uganda: Focus on Karamoja Disarmament," *U.N. Integrated Regional Information Networks*, January 10, 2002, www.irinnews.org/report.aspx?reportid=29684.

7. His title was director of the external security organisation.

8. Matthew Russell Lee, "Disarmament Abuse in Uganda Leads UN Agency to Suspend Its Work and Spending," *Inner City Press*, June 27, 2006, http://www.innercitypress.com/unhq062706.html.

9. Joanne D. Eisen, Paul Gallant, and David B. Kopel, "Guns Don't Kill People, Gun Control Kills People: Uganda terrorizes its own citizens under the auspices of UN gun control mandate," *ReasonOnline*, February 23, 2007, http://reason.com/archives/2007/02/23/guns-dont-kill-people-gun-cont.

10. Kiflemariam Gebre-Wold, Bonn International Centre for Conversion (BICC), "Exploring the Relationship between Human Security, Demand for Arms, and Disarmament in the Horn of Africa," paper presented at International Physicians for the Preservation of Nuclear War Conference, Helsinki, Finland, September 28, 2001, 4, http://www.ncbi.nlm.nih.gov/pubmed/12498403.

11. Taya Weiss, *Guns in the Borderlands* (Pretoria: Institute for Security Studies, 2004), 15, http://www.iss.co.za/pubs/Monographs/No95/Intro.htm ("While not every organization identifies small arms as a specific area of work, all acknowledge that the presence of illegal weapons is crucial to a cycle of violence that sustains meso-level conflict in both urban and rural borderlands."); E. Hogendoorn et al., *Playing with Fire: Weapons Proliferation, Political Violence, and Human Rights in Kenya*, Human Rights Watch (May 2002), 8, http://www.hrw.org/reports/2002/kenya/Kenya0502.pdf ("In Kenya and other countries not at war, the ready availability of these weapons undermines security [including with relation to crime], erodes prospects for development, contributes to social disintegration, and makes the resort to violence more likely—and more deadly").

12. Halakhe D. Waqo, Oxfam Great Britain, Kenya Programme, "Peacebuilding and Small Arms: Experiences from Northern Kenya," presented to a workshop on field experiences, at the U.N. Biennial Conference of States on Small Arms Programme of Action, New York, July 7–11, 2003, available at http://www.docstoc.com/docs/17691476/PEACEBUILDING-AND-SMALL-ARMS-EXPERIENCE-FROM-NORTHERN-KENYA.

13. Samuel Mburu, "Repeal Laws Barring Kenyans from Keeping Arrows, Urges Kaguthi," *Standard* (Nairobi), December 8, 2004; Peter Mwaura, "Owning a Gun Sign of Power and Success," *Daily Nation* (Nairobi), February 25, 2006.

14. Margie Buchanan-Smith and Jeremy Lind, *Armed Violence and Poverty in Northern Kenya*, Center for International Cooperation & Security at Bradford University (March 2005), 11, http://www.brad.ac.uk/acad/cics/publications/AVPI/poverty/AVPI_Northern_Kenya.pdf.

15. John Oroni and Beatrice Obwocha, "Residents Unwilling to Surrender Guns," *Standard* (Nairobi), July 2, 2005; "Operation to Disarm North Rift Residents Starts Today," *Standard* (Nairobi), May 30, 2005 ("Yesterday, Internal Security minister Mirugi Kariuki said the Government would stop at nothing to recover the arms"); Fred Mukinda and Mwaura Kimani, "Protests at 'Shoot to Kill' Order," *Nation* (Nairobi), March 23, 2005 ("The Kenya National Commission on Human Rights cautioned Kenyans to brace themselves for a killing field if police officers were to effect the order"); "Law Society Condemns Shoot-to-Kill Order," *Standard* (Nairobi), March 22, 2005 ("The Law Society of Kenya (LSK), doctors, human rights groups and churches yesterday criticized National Security minister John Michuki's shoot-to-kill order on those found with illegal firearm . . . . Speaking in Nakuru, Ojienda [newly elected LSK chairman, Tom Ojienda] urged Michuki to revoke the order, which, he said, would give the police the leeway to kill innocent Kenyans in the guise of fighting crime"); Okech Kendo, "Genesis of the Pokot's Love for the Gun and the Bullet," *Standard* (Nairobi), April 27, 2006 (fifty disarmament attempts during the last 100 years, almost constantly in the Borderlands); Gakuu Mathenge, "War-Like Activities and the Question of Disarmament," *Daily Nation* (Nairobi), May 7, 2006 (quoting Krop Muroto: "In his 24-year rule, President Moi ordered 20 military disarmament operations on the Pokot. President Kibaki's government is on the third, and biggest operation so far").

16. C. Bryson Hull, "Kenya's Pokot Haunted by Past as Soldiers Hunt Guns," Reuters, May 11, 2006.

17. Mathenge, "War-Like Activities and the Question of Disarmament."

18. Hull, "Kenya's Pokot Haunted by Past as Soldiers Hunt Guns."

19. Karen Allen, "Kenya Firearms Hunt Stokes Mistrust," BBC News, May 4, 2006, http://news.bbc.co.uk/2/hi/africa/4974802.stm; Small Arms Survey, *Responses to Pastoral Wars*, Sudan Issue Brief no. 8 (Sept. 2007), 5.

20. Allen, "Kenya Firearms Hunt Stokes Mistrust" ("We are only intimidating villagers by our presence . . . we're telling them 'please hand over your weapons . . . you don't need them,'" said Hassan Noor, the government official in charge); Anderson Ojwang and Stephen Makabila, "18 Firearms Recovered in Gun Hunt," *Standard* (Nairobi), May 10, 2006; Vincent Bartoo and Stephen Makabila, "Hunger, Despair Set in as Disarmament Operation Continues," *Standard* (Nairobi), May 18, 2006 ("Starvation and anguish are now stalking West Pokot residents, since the Government launched a forcible disarmament exercise a month ago . . . The residents now say they have resigned themselves to fate and have become refugees in their own country . . . A recent visit by *The Standard* revealed the sense of hopelessness and vulnerability that the disarmament has brought, forcing majority residents to relocate to Uganda. Schools have also become ghost institutions, with very few pupils . . . Although the Government says the operation has not disrupted the villagers' normal life, a spot-check reveals otherwise").

21. Peter Mutai, "70 Guns Recovered in Disarmament Exercise," *Standard* (Nairobi), May 25, 2006.

22. Ochieng' Oreyo, "Call for Unity in Arms War," *Standard* (Nairobi), July 15, 2006; Kenya National Focal Point on Small Arms and Light Weapons, *Kenya National Action Plan for Arms Control and Management* (2006), viii, http://www.iansa.org/regions/cafrica/documents/Kenya-National-Action-Plan-2006.pdf. No longer accessible.

23. Osinde Obare, "Turkana Herders Flee Kenya-Uganda Border," *Standard* (Nairobi), August 18, 2007; Osinde Obare, "UPDF Releases Hostages," *Standard* (Nairobi), August 6, 2007.

24. Adèle Kirsten, *A Nation without Guns: The Story of Gun Free South Africa* (Scottsville, S.A.: University of KwaZulu-Natal Press, 2008).

25. Ibid., xvi, 179–80.

26. Ibid.,140–41.

27. Ibid., 4, 219n21, citing interview with Martin Hood (SAGA), October 11, 2002, and P. Van der Walt, "The History of Private Firearm Ownership in South Africa" (Johannesburg: unpublished paper, 1998).

28. South African Constitution, ch. 1, § 6(1) ("The official languages of the Republic are Sepedi, Sesotho, Setswana, siSwati, Tshivenda, Xitsonga, Afrikaans, English, isiNdebele, isiXhosa and isiZulu"); e-mail from Richard Wesson, Gun Owners of South Africa, to Paul Gallant, May 11, 2007, cited in Kopel, Gallant, and Eisen "Human Rights and Gun Confiscation."

29. E-mail from Alex Holmes, spokesman, South Africa Arms and Ammunition Dealers Association, to Paul Gallant, May 7, 2007, quoted in Kopel, Gallant, and Eisen, "Human Rights and Gun Confiscation."

30. Firearms Control Act of 2000, ¶¶ 13–20.

31. E-mail from Alex Holmes.

32. Michael Wines, "In South Africa, Licensing Law Poses Hurdles for Gun Buyers," *New York Times*, January 3, 2005, 7.

33. "Gun Crime Continues to Devastate Lives," *U.N. Integrated Regional Information Networks*, May 26, 2006, http://www.irinnews.org/PrintReport.aspx?ReportId=59075.

34. People Opposing Women Abuse (POWA), "Statistics," http://www.powa.co.za/stats.html.

35. Human Rights Watch, *Scared at School: Sexual Violence against Girls in South African Schools* (2001), www.hrw.org/reports/2001/safrica/ ("The age category of zero to eleven years of age reflected a ratio of 130.1 rapes per 100,000 of the female population"); Carolyn Dempster, "Rape—Silent War on SA Women," BBC News, April 9, 2002, http://news.bbc.co.uk/2/hi/africa/1909220.stm ("A woman born in South Africa has a greater chance of being raped, than learning how to read. One in four girls faces the prospect of being raped before the age of 16"); Gavin du Venage, "Rape of Children Surges in South Africa: Minors Account for About 40% of Attack Victims," *San Francisco Chronicle*, February 12, 2002 ("More than 52,000 rape cases were reported in 2000, and about 40 percent of the victims were under 18").

36. E-mail from Alex Holmes.

37. Telephone interview by Joanne D. Eisen with Abios Khoele, chairman of the Black Gun Owners' Association, April 24, 2007, cited in Kopel, Gallant, and Eisen, "Human Rights and Gun Confiscation."

38. Firearms Control Act §§ 120(1)(b) (Schedule 4) ("A person is guilty of an offence if he or she contravenes or fails to comply with any . . . condition of a license, permit or authorisation issued or granted by or under this Act"); Edwin Tshivhidzo, "Hand It Over, or Face 25 Years in Jail," *BuaNews* (Tshwane, S.A.), June 24, 2005, http://www.buanews.gov.za/view.php?ID=05062411451002&coll =buanew05.

39. Wyndham Hartley, "Gun Dealers 'Driven out of Business,'" *Business Day*, August 17, 2006, 4, available at http://allafrica.com/stories/200608170202.html by subscription ("Ninety percent of SA's gun dealers have been driven out of business and lost their livelihoods . . . It was common cause that the South African Police Service [SAPS] was not coping with the relicensing process as prescribed by the law").

40. Kirsten, *A Nation without Guns*, 183–84.

41. Ernest Mabuza, "Figures Confirm Violent Crime Is on the Rise," *Business Day* (Johannesburg), July 4, 2007, 1.

42. Warren Hoge, "U.S. Says South Africa Impedes U.N. Motion to Condemn Rape as a Tactic," *New York Times*, November 8, 2007, http://www.nytimes. com/2007/11/09/world/africa/09nations.html?_r=1&oref=slogin.

43. Benny Avni, "Pretoria's Cynicism at the U.N.," *New York Sun*, February 20, 2007, http://www.nysun.com/foreign/pretorias-cynicism-at-the-un/48919/; Colum Lynch, "South Africa's U.N. Votes Disappoint Some," *Washington Post*, April 16, 2007, http://www.washingtonpost.com/wp-dyn/content/article/2007/04/15/ AR2007041500996.html.

44. Measures included the Royal Ordinance of 27 January 1920, Royal Ordinance of 8 July 1927, Royal Ordinance of 26 April 1929, and Royal Ordinance of 1 July 1935. The most comprehensive was Royal Ordinance No. 55 of 28 March 1938, which provided for a licensing system. Royal Ordinance No. 55 was expanded on May 29, 1953 (Jay Simkin, Aaron Zelman, and Alan M. Rice, *Lethal Laws* [Milwaukee: Jews for the Preservation of Firearms Ownership, 1994], 305).

45. These were the Cambodian People's Armed Forces ("CPAF"), the National Army of Democratic Kampuchea ("NADK," the armed forces of the PDK or Khmer Rouge), the Armée Nationale pour un Kampuchea Indépendent ("ANKI"), and the Khmer People's National Liberation Armed Forces ("KPNLAF").

46. Formally, the "Agreements on a Comprehensive Political Settlement of the Cambodian Conflict."

47. U.N. Security Council Resolution 745 (1992) established UNTAC, which became operational on March 15 of that year. Security Council Resolution 745, U.N. SCOR (1992), http://www.un.org/documents/sc/res/1992/scres92.htm. UNTAC consisted of four distinct components: the Military Component, the Electoral Component, the Civil Administration Component, and the Repatriation Component.

48. Jianwei Wang, *Managing Arms in Peace Processes: Cambodia* (UN Institute for Disarmament Research 1996), 35, table 1.

49. Ibid., 34

50. *Decaying consent* is defined by the U.N. as "a pulling back from willingness to abide by an agreement because circumstances are not working out as hoped or envisioned." Donald C. F. Daniel, "Is There a Middle Option in Peace Support Operations? Implications for Crisis Containment and Disarmament," in *Managing Arms in Peace Processes: The Issues* (UN Institute for Disarmament Research 1996), 60.

51. David R. Meddings and Stephanie M. O'Connor, "Circumstances around Weapon Injury in Cambodia after Departure of a Peacekeeping Force: Prospective Cohort Study," *British Medical Journal* 319 (1999), 412–13. Meddings and O'Connor used data from the International Committee of the Red Cross–supported Mongkol Borei hospital in northwestern Cambodia. Land mine and other weapon injuries, in addition to firearm injuries, were included in the study. Approximately one-third of the victims were injured in noncombat situations, and of that category, civilian intentional firearm-related injuries comprised the largest category.

52. Ibid., 412. The authors found that:

> 30% of weapon injuries occurred in contexts other than interfactional combat. Most commonly these were firearm injuries inflicted intentionally on civilians. Civilians accounted for 71% of those with non-combat injuries, 42% of those with combat related injuries, and 51% of those with weapon injuries of either type . . . The incidence of weapon injuries remained high when the disarmament component of a peacekeeping operation achieved only limited success. Furthermore, injuries occurring outside the context of interfactional combat accounted for a substantial proportion of all weapon injuries, were experienced disproportionately by civilians, and were most likely to entail the intentional use of a firearm against a civilian.

53. Ibid., 75–76:

> There would be a three-week grace period to allow people either to surrender their weapons or to get their papers in order. Gun holders were supposed to surrender their arms at the local UNTAC, CIVPOL, or military contingent where they would be given a receipt for their weapon and would face no legal action. Those who wished to retain their weapons could apply to the police force of the relevant authorities for a firearm licence.

54. Sivaraman, "Violent Crime Thrives in Wounded Society," Inter Press Service, August 25, 1998 (quoting Mouen Chhean Nariddh: "While the world focuses on the human rights and political situation in Cambodia, silent but steady violent crime is emerging as one of the country's biggest killers").

55. "UN Ban Starts in Cambodia," BBC News, April 7, 1999.

56. Ibid.

57. Press Release, "United Nations Conference on the Illicit Trade in Small Arms, Small Arms Conference Hears Call for Stepped-Up Control of Illicit Trade: But Several States Insist on Right to Acquire Arms for Security Purposes" U.N. Doc. DC/2787, July 10, 2001, (3d meeting), http://www.un.org/News/Press/docs/2001/dc2787.doc.htm.

58. Ibid.

59. Bertil Lintner, "Drugs and Politics," *Far East Economic Review*, February 7, 2002; Craig Skehan, "Thais Run Huge Arms Trade," *Sydney Morning Herald*, August 14, 1999 ("Smuggling is largely controlled by corrupt military officers").

60. For example, there is the *Protocol to Prevent, Suppress and Punish Trafficking in Persons, Especially Women and Children, Supplementing the United Nations Convention against Transnational Organized Crime*, G.A. Res. 25, Annex II, U.N. GAOR, 55th Sess., Supp. No. 49, p. 60, U.N. Doc. A/45/49 (2001).

61. Bonn International Center for Conversion, *Help Desk for Practical Disarmament: Cambodia*,; BBC, "UN Ban Starts in Cambodia," ("Many Cambodians remain skeptical, saying they keep weapons precisely because they have little faith in the public institutions that are meant to maintain law and order").

62. *Small Arms Survey 2002*, 296. The Small Arms Survey may have been naive in concluding that most Cambodians support the weapons collection program in theory; when speaking to foreigners or in public, Cambodians may be reluctant to go on record contradicting the government. It would not be unreasonable to fear that voicing disagreement with the weapons confiscation program would be a quick way to have one's home put at the top of the list for searching by the government.

63. John Locke, *Two Treatises of Government* (1690).

64. For a detailed account of how the Khmer Rouge thoroughly disarmed the Cambodian people before beginning the genocide, and how such disarmament almost always is completed before genocide begins, see Aaron Zelman and Richard W. Stevens, *Death by "Gun Control": The Human Cost of Victim Disarmament* (2001). See also David B. Kopel, "Book Review: Lethal Laws," *New York Law School Journal of International and Comparative Law* 15 (1995): 355, http://www .davekopel.com/2A/LawRev/lethal.htm.

65. "Japan Provides Aid to Help Cambodia's Small Arms Management," *WorldSources, Inc.*, Jan. 13, 2003. This program evolved into Japan Assistance Team for Small Arms Management in Cambodia ("JSAC") in April 2003. For more, see the JSAC website, http://www.jics.or.jp/jsac/jsacEN.html.

66. Press Release, Embassy of Japan, Japanese ODA News, "Signing of Grant Contracts for the Japanese Grant Assistance for Grass-roots Projects (HUSANONE)," March 16, 2001.

67. "Japan Provides Aid to Help Cambodia's Small Arms Management."

68. "Berisha and Nano: Albania's Rivals," BBC News, September 13, 1998, http:// news.bbc.co.uk/1/hi/world/europe/170543.stm ("An estimated 90% of Albania's population invested around $2bn in the get-rich-quick schemes, and lost the best part of their money—often their life savings—when the crisis came").

69. Georgios A. Antonopoulos, "Albanian Organized Crime: A View from Greece," *Crime & Just. Int'l*, Nov./Dec. 2003, 7.

70. Support to Security Sector Reform (SSSR)—The United Nations Development Programme (UNDP), *Albania, Background*, § 1; Afrim Krasniqi, "Demilitarizing Communities in Albania," *Choices*, December 2002, 14; Chris Smith, "Illegal Arms in Albania and European Security" (speech, Seminar on Contemporary Arms Control and Disarmament, Geneva, Switzerland), September 16, 1998. (Between January 1997 and March 1997, "an estimated 750,000–1 million light weapons were stolen from government armories [the OSCE (Organization for Security

and Co-Operation in Europe) estimates a figure of 1.5 million]. The state lost approximately 80 per cent of its weaponry stock, in addition to 1.5 billion pieces of ammunition.")

The weapons stolen during the Albanian upheaval were stored in government armories, not in civilian homes and closets; thus, the stolen weapons had been secured under what the antigun activists call "safe-storage" conditions.

The claim is often made by firearm-prohibitionists that civilian gun stocks serve as "piggy-banks" for criminals, and therefore restrictive legislation concerning civilian ownership and use of firearms is necessary to prevent criminal acquisition from civilian sources. For example, Canadian prohibitionist Wendy Cukier has stated, "Diversion of civilian held small arms also fuels the illicit supply" (Wendy Cukier, "Small Arms and Light Weapons: A Public Health Approach," *Brown Journal of World Affairs* 9, no. 1 [2002]: 272).

71. Jan Wahlberg, *Weapons for Development: The Economic, Social and Political Context*, http://web.archive.org/web/20020728141315/http://katu-network.fi/Artikkelit/kirja03/Wahlberg.htm.

72. United Nations Development Programme, Gramsh Pilot Programme, Weapons in Exchange for Development, Progress Report, February 23, 1999.

73. "U.N. Arms Control of a Different Type Gets Promising Results in Albania," Associated Press, August 31, 2002, http://209.157.64.200/focus/f-news/742498/posts.

74. Eric Roman Filipink, "SALW Issues and OSCE Field Missions: The Experience of the Presence in Albania" (Joint Azerbaijani-Swiss Workshop, 21–22 June 2001).

75. United Nations Development Programme: Albania, *SALWC 2002–2003, Results and Current Situation, Situation after 4 Aug 2002*.

76. UNDP Albania, *Small Arms and Light Weapons Control Project, Background*, 6.

77. Ibid.

78. Jolyon Naegele, "Albania: Weapons-Collection Program Meets with Mixed Results," Radio Free Europe/Radio Liberty (2001).

79. Ibid. Also, according to the *Socio-Economic Analysis and Impact Assessment* (SALWC Project, Centre for Rural Studies, page 26), whose site I visited in September 23, 2003, "the main reason for having a weapon is self/family protection for more than 73.7% of the respondent[s]." The researchers explained that although many Albanians said they would be willing to disarm, "many of them would like to keep one weapon (with the reason to protect himself and his family and business) as the others still have weapons." Site no longer available.

80. Human Rights Watch, *Albania, Human Rights Watch World Report 2003*, http://www.hrw.org/wr2k3/europe1.html.

81. Antonopoulos, "Albanian Organized Crime: A View from Greece," 6.

82. The case of the Cambodian genocide illustrates how encouraging governments to limit small arms ownership can have terrible consequences. As the killing began, Cambodian soldiers undertook an extraordinary house-to-house search to confiscate weapons people could have used to defend themselves. A witness recounted that the soldiers would "knock on the doors and ask the people who answered if they had any weapons. 'We are here now to protect you,' the soldiers said, 'and no one has a need for a weapon any more.' People who said that they kept no weapons were [nevertheless] forced to stand aside and allow the soldiers to

look for themselves" (Don B. Kates, "Democide and Disarmament," *SAIS Review* 23 (2003): 305 [quoting Alec Wilkinson, "A Changed Vision of God," *New Yorker*, January 24, 1994, 54–55]).

83. Moses and Rikha Havini, "Bougainville—The Long Struggle for Freedom," http://www.eco-action.org/dt/bvstory.html.

84. *Bougainville: The Peace Process and Beyond*, Parliament of Australia, Joint Standing Committee on Foreign Affairs, Defence and Trade, chap. 2: "History of the Bougainville Conflict," http://www.aph.gov.au/house/committee/jfadt/bougainville/bv_chap2.htm.

85. Ibid.

86. Yauka Aluambo Liria, *Bougainville Campaign Diary* (Melbourne: Indra Press, 1993), 61.

87. David B. Kopel, Paul Gallant, and Joanne D. Eisen, "Firearms Possession by 'Non-State Actors': The Question of Sovereignty," *Texas Review of Law and Politics* 8 (2004): 373, 396, http://www.davekopel.com/2A/LawRev/Non-state-actors.pdf.

88. Plaintiffs' Complaint in class action lawsuit by Hagens Berman LLP. The case is still going on, with the most recent decision being *Sarei v. Rio Tinto PLC*, 650 F. Supp. 2d 1004 (C.D. Cal., 2009).

89. Aziz Choudry, "Bougainville—Small Nation, Big Message," *Scoop* (November 21, 2001), http://www.scoop.co.nz/stories/HL0111/S00127.htm.

90. *Bougainville: The Peace Process and Beyond*, chap. 2.

91. Liria, *Bougainville Campaign Diary*, 191.

92. *Bougainville: The Forgotten Human Rights Tragedy*, Amnesty International, ASA 34/001/1997, February 26, 1997.

93. Secretary-General Kofi Annan's address to the Parliament of Rwanda, in Kigali, May 7, 1998. U.N. Press Release SG/SM/6552, AFR/56, May 6, 1998, http://www.un.org/News/Press/docs/1998/19980506.SGSM6552.html>.

94. Liria, *Bougainville Campaign Diary*, 118–19.

95. Choudry, "Bougainville—Small Nation Big Message."

96. Dorothy Hunt, *Conflict in Bougainville—Part 3: Interview with Sam Kauona Sirivi*, June 30, 2000; Choudry, "Bougainville—Small Nation Big Message."

97. "PNG and Bougainville Seal Peace after Decade of War," *Sydney Morning Herald*, Aug. 31, 2001, 1.

98. The Rotakas Record: Joint Bougainville Ex-Combatants Agreement on Weapons Disposal, May 3, 2001, http://www.c-r.org/our-work/accord/png-bougainville/key-texts34.php.

99. "Kiwi's Supply Gun Lockers," *P.N.G. Post-Courier*, November 21, 2001.

100. Ibid.

101. Damien Murphy, "Ona Refuses to Lay Down Arms," *Sydney Morning Herald*, June 11, 1999.

102. Thomas Kilala, "Bougainville Bill Clears First Hurdle," *National*, Jan. 24, 2002.

103. *Report of the Secretary-General on the United Nations Political Office in Bougainville*, UN Security Council, U.N. SCOR S/2003/345, ¶ 16 (2003) ("The predecessor of the Bougainville Peace Agreement, the Lincoln Agreement, did call for rehabilitation and reintegration, but this aspect has not kept pace with weapons disposal"); "PMG Out," *P.N.G. Post-Courier*, July 1, 2003 (promised funds for Bougainville development were not provided); "Tanis: Gov't Is Not Serious,"

P.N.G. Post-Courier, February 24, 2004 ("the autonomous Bougainville government establishment grant had been used for purposes other than the one it was meant for").

103. Alpers and Twyford, *Small Arms in the Pacific*, Small Arms Survey Occasional Paper No. 8 (March 2003), 87.

104. "B'ville Restoration Not Moving Ahead," *P.N.G. Post-Courier*, May 29, 2003; "Services Collapse in Bougainville," *P.N.G. Post-Courier*, May 30, 2003.

105. Art. 21, ¶ 3.

106. Art. 25.

Chapter 8

1. "Scotland Worst for Violence—UN," BBC News, September 18, 2005 ("Scotland has been named the most violent country in the developed world by a United Nations Report").

2. Pat Mayhew, *Residential Burglary: A Comparison of the United States, Canada and England and Wales* (Washington: National Institute of Justice, 1987).

3. David B. Kopel, "Lawyers, Guns, and Burglars," 43 *Arizona Law Review* 345 (2001), davekopel.org/2A/LawRev/LawyersGunsBurglars.htm.

4. The official Spanish text is:

    Artículo 10. Los habitantes de los Estados Unidos Mexicanos tienen derecho a poseer armas en su domicilio, para su seguridad y legítima defensa, con excepción de las prohibidas por la Ley Federal y de las reservadas para el uso exclusivo del Ejército, Armada, Fuerza Aérea y Guardia Nacional. La ley federal determinará los casos, condiciones, requisitos y lugares en que se podrá autorizar a los habitantes la portación de armas.
    (http://pdba.georgetown.edu/Constitutions/Mexico/textovigente2008.pdf)

5. The 1857 version stated: "Article 10: Every man has the right to have and to carry arms for his security and legitimate defense. The law will indicate which arms are prohibited and the penalty for those that will carry prohibited arms." (In Spanish, *"Artículo 10: Todo hombre tiene derecho de poseer y portar armas para su seguridad y legítima defensa. La ley señalará cuáles son las prohibidas y la pena en que incurren los que las portaren."*)
    (http://www.juridicas.unam.mx/infjur/leg/conshist/pdf/1857.pdf)

6. The store's name is UCAM (*Unidad de Comercialización de Armamento y Municiones*).

7. Fred Burton and Scott Stewart, "Mexico: The third war. While drug cartels battle each other and the Mexican government, a third criminal front much more dangerous to civilians has opened," *World*, February 19, 2009).

8. "Bush Says America Should Work to Stop Guns from Entering Mexico from U.S.," *Cybercast News Service*, January 14, 2009, http://cnsnews.com/public/content/article.aspx?RsrcID=41937; Kristin Bricker, "Mexico's Drug War Death Toll: 8,463 and Counting" *Narcosphere*, December 31, 2008, http://narcosphere.narconews.com/notebook/kristin-bricker/2008/12/mexicos-drug-war-death-toll-8463-and-counting.

9. Congressional Research Service, *The Bureau of Alcohol, Tobacco, Firearms and Explosives (ATF): Budget and operations* (May 30, 2008), http://www.fas.org/sgp/crs/row/RL32724.pdf.

10. Dudley Althaus, "Obama to help Mexico cut drug violence," *Express News* (San Antonio), January 13, 2009, http://www.mysanantonio.com/news/Obama_to_help_Mexico_cut_drug_violence.html.

11. E.g., *The United States and Mexico: Towards a Strategic Partnership* (Wilson Center, Mexico Institute, January 2009), http://www.wilsoncenter.org/events/docs/The%20U.S.%20and%20Mexico.%20Towards%20a%20Strategic%20Partnership.pdf; Todd Bensman, "Lax rules aid flow of ammo to Mexico," *Express-News* (San Antonio), December 21, 2008, http://www2.mysanantonio.com/gun_run/part3/part3.html.

12. William La Jeunesse and Maxim Lott, "The Myth of 90 Percent: Only a Small Fraction of Guns in Mexico Come from U.S.," *FOXNews.com*, Apr. 2, 2009, http://www.foxnews.com/politics/elections/2009/04/02/myth-percent-guns-mexico-fraction-number-claimed/.

13. Jo Tuckman, "Mexico considers banning toy guns to cut child aggression," *Guardian* (London), January 12, 2009, http://www.guardian.co.uk/world/2009/jan/12/mexico-toy-guns.

14. Todd Bensman, "Gunrunners' land of plenty," *Express-News* (San Antonio), November 30, 2008, http://www.mysanantonio.com/Gun_Running_Series_part_1.html. The *Guardian* article in the previous note mentions the Reynosa seizure, and is more precise in describing what was seized than in the *Express News* article, so I have used it for the item inventory.

15. Ibid.

16. Stewart M. Powell, Dudley Althaus, Gary Martin, "Obama vows action of flow of guns into Mexico: He pledges to help stem violence related to drug gangs," *Houston Chronicle*, January 13, 2009; Jonathan Roeder and Jorge Alejandro Medellín, "U.S. arms fuel drug violence on border," *El Universal* (Mexico City), August 3, 2005, http://www2.eluniversal.com.mx/pls/impreso/noticia.html?id_nota=11425&tabla=miami.

17. La Jeunesse and Lott, "The Myth of 90 Percent."

18. *Firearms Trafficking: U.S. Efforts to Combat Arms Trafficking to Mexico Face Planning and Coordination Challenges*, GAO-09-709 (Washington: Government Accountability Office, June 2009), http://www.gao.gov/new.items/d09709.pdf.

19. "U.S. and Mexican government and law enforcement officials also stated this scenario seemed most likely, given the ease of acquiring firearms in the United States; specifically, they told us they saw no reason why the drug cartels would go through the difficulty of acquiring a gun somewhere else in the world and transporting it to Mexico when it is so easy for them to do so from the United States" (ibid., 16).

20. *Washington Diplomat*, June 2009, 14.

21. Clare Ribando Seelke, *Mérida Initiative for Mexico and Central America: Funding and Policy Issues*, Congressional Research Service, April 19, 2010, http://wilsoncenter.org/news/docs/Merida%20Initiative%20for%20Mexico%20and%20Central%20America.pdf.

Suppose we consider only gun homicides. Here are the figures for each year, according to Mexico's *Secretaria de Seguridad Publica* (Ministry of Public Security):

year 2000: 3,605 gun homicides; 2001: 3,512; 2002: 2,606; 2003: 3,006; 2004: 2,858; 2005: 3,209; 2006: 3,610; 2007: 3,930; 2008: final data not available, but more than 5,000.

Was there a rise in gun homicides from 2004 to 2005? Yes. Yet even after rising in 2005–07, the number of gun homicides had simply returned to the level of 2000. The high numbers in 2000–01, followed by a dip, followed by a rise to the earlier level, do not support Calderón's theory that American availability of semi-automatics has been the key factor in Mexican homicides. After all, the number of homicides in 2005 (after the Clinton ban had expired) was lower than in 2000–01, when the Clinton ban was in effect.

22. *Economist Intelligence Unit*, March 2, 2010.
23. Susana Hayward, "A Report from Juarez, the Bleeding Front Line of the War on Drugs," *Dallas Observer*, April 28, 2010, http://www.dallasobserver.com/2010-04-29/news/a-report-from-juarez-the-bleeding-front-line-of-the-war-on-drugs/ ("Calderón maintains that most of the murders are related to cartel violence, that about 5 percent are innocent or bystanders").
24. Hector Tobar, "A cartel army's war within: Hit men known as the Zetas are aiming at their own as a power struggle spreads in Mexico," *Los Angeles Times*, May 20, 2007.
25. Ana Lucía Blas, "Desaparacen más de 2.000 Arms de la PNC," *Prensa Libre* (Guatemala City), December 10, 2008.
26. Lizbeth Diaz, ""Narco Juniors' Paid to Do the Dirty Work," *National Post* (Canada) (Reuters), January 15, 2009:

> Mexican teenagers as young as 15 are killing rivals for a few hundred dollars in a brutal drug war on the U. S. border . . . Feuding gangs in the violent cities of Tijuana and Ciudad Juarez prize teenage drug cartel members, known as "narco juniors," because they give the attacks an added element of surprise and because they can't be given long prison sentences, police and social workers say.
>
> "There are lots of us, and we get $300 for each kill," said Eduardo, 17, a middle-class student who was arrested in December after an army raid on a drug safe house in Tijuana.

27. *The United States and Mexico: Towards a Strategic Partnership* (Wilson Center, Mexico Institute, Jan. 2009), http://www.wilsoncenter.org/events/docs/The%20 U.S.%20and%20Mexico.%20Towards%20a%20Strategic%20Partnership.pdf.
28. Althaus, "Obama to help Mexico cut drug violence."
29. Stratfor, *Mexico: Dynamics of the Gun Trade*, October 24, 2007.
30. Ibid.
31. David Hardy, "Thoughts on tracing of guns in Mexico," *Of Arms and the Law*, September 18, 2010, http://armsandthelaw.com/archives/2010/09/thoughts_on_tra_1.php.
32. National Shooting Sports Foundation, "Firearms Industry Responds to Mexico's Threats of Litigation," April 22, 2011, http://www.nssfblog.com/firearms-industry-responds-to-mexico%e2%80%99s-threats-of-litigation/.

33. Cable 09MEXICO880, "SCENESETTER FOR THE FIREARMS-TRAFFICKING," American Embassy in Mexico City to U.S. State Dept., Washington, March 25, 2009 http://www.wikileaks.ch/cable/2009/03/09MEXICO880.html (repeating assertions that most Mexican firearms come from the U.S., but noting that "at least 90 percent of military origin weapons) such as grenades and light anti-tank weapons) are traced to Central American military stocks") (parentheses in quote are in original); Cable 09GUATEMALA106, "UNDER NARCO THREAT, RULE OF LAW COLLAPSING IN COBAN," American Embassy in Guatemala to U.S. State Dept., Washington, February 9, 2009, http://www.wikileaks.ch/cable/2009/02/09GUATEMALA106.html (rule of law is collapsing in Coban, Guatemala, as it has in other parts of Guatemala, allowing the Zetas cartel to smuggle weapons with impunity); cable 10MEXICO77, "MEXICO: TAPACHULA ARMS CONFERENCE FOCUSES ON SOUTHERN BORDER," U.S. Embassy in Mexico to U.S. State Dept., Washington, January 10, 2010, http://groups.google.com/group/frontera-list/browse_thread/thread/81e5075921266a9b ("our visit to three border crossings between Guatemala and Mexico in Chiapas revealed neither country presently works seriously to enforce these laws . . . Limited resources also undermine the effort: while there are 30,000 U.S. CBP officers on the 1,926 mile Mexican/U.S. border, only 125 Mexican immigration officials monitor the 577 mile border with Guatemala. Mexican immigration officials repeatedly confirmed that they do not have the manpower or resources to direct efforts effectively along the southern border . . . One of the most memorable images of the day was the steady flow of rafts transporting people and goods across the river illegally within sight of the legal border crossing").

34. Cable 09GUATEMALA538, "ROUGE ELEMENTS IN GUATEMALAN MILITARY SELLING WEAPONS TO NARCOS," U.S. Embassy in Guatemala to U.S. State Dept., Washington, June 8, 2009, http://www.mcclatchydc.com/2011/04/21/112594/cable-guatemalan-military-selling.html.

35. Cable 08STATE105491, "LAX HONDURAN CONTROLS ON U.S.-SUPPIED WEAPONS," U.S. State Dept. to U.S. Embassy in Honduras, October 2, 2008, http://www.mcclatchydc.com/2011/04/21/112595/cable-lax-honduran-controls-on.html.

36. Bill Conroy, "The Mexican Drug War Has Become a Hot Market for U.S. Weapons Sales: U.S.-Backed Programs Supplying the Firepower for Mexico's Soaring Murder Rate," GlobalResearch.ca, April 16, 2011, http://www.globalresearch.ca/index.php?context=viewArticle&code=CON20110416&articleId=24353 (reporting data from U.S. State Dept).

37. William La Jeunesse, "America's Third War: Is the U.S. Arming Mexican Cartels?" *Foxnews.com*, April 28, 2011, http://www.foxnews.com/us/2011/04/28/americas-war-arming-mexican-cartels/.

38. Cable of Nov. 9, 2009, http://www.wikileaks.ch/cable/2009/11/09MEXICO3376.html. A follow-up report, including information from a confidential informant in Mexico, is available in a May 31, 2011 *Fox News* report by La Jeunesse, http://video.foxnews.com/v/968667204001/us-arming-mexican-cartels.

39. Stratfor, "Mexico Security Memo: March 29, 2011," http://www.stratfor.com.

Stratfor reports are for subscribers only, but nonsubscribers can obtain free access to one article.

40. Stratfor, "Mexico Security Memo: Dec. 6, 2011," http://www.stratfor.com.

41. Scott Stewart, *Mexico's Gun Supply and the 90 Percent Myth*, Stratfor.com, February 10, 2011, http://www.stratfor.com/weekly/20110209-mexicos-gun-supply-and-90-percent-myth.

42. U.S. Department of Justice, Office of the Inspector General, Evaluation and Inspections Division, *Review of ATF's Project Gunrunner*, Evaluation and Inspections Report I-2011-001, November 2010, http://www.justice.gov/oig/reports/ATF/e1101.pdf.

43. Colby Goodman, *Update on U.S. Firearms Trafficking to Mexico Report*, Woodrow Wilson Center for International Scholars, Mexico Institute, April 2011, 4, http://wilsoncenter.org/news/docs/Goodman%20Update%20on%20US%20Firearms%20to%20Mexico.pdf.

44. Ibid., 7.

45. Gary Kleck, "The Myth of Big-Time Gun Trafficking," *Wall Street Journal*, May 21, 2011, C2, http://online.wsj.com/article/SB10001424052748704904604576333443343499926.html; Gary Kleck and Shun-Yung Kevin Wang, "The Myth of Big-Time Gun Trafficking and the Overinterpretation of Gun Tracing Data, *UCLA Law Review* 56 (2009): 1233; http://uclalawreview.org/pdf/56-5-6.pdf.

46. Sharyl Attkisson, "Congressional investigators back in Arizona for 'Gunwalker,'" *CBSNews.com*, May 16, 2011, http://www.cbsnews.com/8301-31727_162-20063373-10391695.html#ixzz1NWKCzYqg ("Insiders allege ATF allowed more than 2,500 assault rifles and other weapons to hit the streets or 'walk'"); Sharyl Attkisson, "Gunrunning scandal uncovered at the ATF," *CBSNews.com*, February 23, 2011, http://www.cbsnews.com/stories/2011/02/23/eveningnews/main20035609.shtml?tag=contentMain;contentBody ("On the phone, one Project Gunrunner source (who didn't want to be identified) told us just how many guns flooded the black market under ATF's watchful eye. 'The numbers are over 2,500 on that case by the way. That's how many guns were sold—including some 50-calibers they let walk'") (parenthetical in original).

47. Sharyl Attkisson, "NRA reacts to CBS News investigation on ATF 'gunwalking'," March 21, 2011, http://www.cbsnews.com/8301-31727_162-20045576-10391695.html?tag=cbsnewsMainColumnArea. BATFE sources say that Wide Receiver began in 2008, and that there were other similar operations (Sharyl Attkisson, "Documents point to ATF 'gun running' since 2008," *CBSNew.com*, March 8, 2011, http://www.cbsnews.com/stories/2011/03/08/eveningnews/main20040803.shtml?tag=cbsnewsMainColumnArea).

48. Sharyl Attkisson, "ATF gunwalking scandal: Second agent speaks out," *CBSNews.com*, March 21, 2011, http://www.cbsnews.com/8301-31727_162-20045650-10391695.html?tag=cbsnewsMainColumnArea.

49. Nacha Cattan, "Mexico lawmakers livid over US 'Operation Fast and Furious,'" *Christian Science Monitor*, March 9, 2011, http://www.csmonitor.com/World/Americas/2011/0309/Mexico-lawmakers-livid-over-US-Operation-Fast-and-Furious.

50. John Solomon, "Gun shy: Firearms dealer worried ATF would let weapons slip to bad guy," *Center for Public Integrity*, April 14, 2011, http://www.iwatchnews.

org/2011/04/14/4150/gun-shy-firearms-dealer-worried-atf-would-let-weapons-slip-bad-guy.

51. Jerry Seper, "ATF criticized for failing to respond to committee subpoena," *Washington Times*, April 21, 2011, http://www.washingtontimes.com/news/2011/apr/20/atf-criticized-failing-respond-committee-subpoena/. The e-mails, along with a letter from Senator Grassley summarizing the e-mails, are available at http://www.cbsnews.com/htdocs/pdf/gunwalking_emails_041411.pdf?tag=contentMain; contentBody.

52. Jerry Seper, "ATF criticized for failing to respond to committee subpoena," *Washington Times*, April 21, 2011, http://www.washingtontimes.com/news/2011/apr/20/atf-criticized-failing-respond-committee-subpoena/.

53. John Solomon, David Heath, and Gordon Witkin, "ATF let hundreds of U.S. weapons fall into hands of suspected Mexican gunrunners," Center for Public Integrity, March 4, 2011, http://www.iwatchnews.org/2011/03/03/2095/atf-let-hundreds-us-weapons-fall-hands-suspected-mexican-gunrunners.

54. Letter of March 16, 2011, http://grassley.senate.gov/about/upload/Judiciary-ATF-03-16-11-Letter-to-CBP-Fast-and-Furious.pdf.

55. William La Jeunesse, "More Than 1,300 Guns Were Bought Illegally by Suspect Buyers Under ATF's 'Gunrunner' Program," *Fox News*, May 4, 2011, http://www.foxnews.com/politics/2011/05/04/1300-guns-bought-illegally-suspect-buyers-atfs-gunrunner-program/.

56. Sharyl Attkisson, "Mexican attorney general says 'full force of law' to be used in ATF gunwalking scandal investigation," *CBSNews.com*, March 28, 2011, http://www.cbsnews.com/8301-31727_162-20048028-10391695.html?tag=cbsnewsMainColumnArea; Sharyl Attkisson, "ATF gunwalking: Who knew, and how high up?" *CBSNews.com*, March 25, 2011, http://www.cbsnews.com/8301-31727_162-20047027-10391695.html?tag=cbsnewsMainColumnArea.

57. Ibid.

58. Ibid.

59. Attkisson, "ATF gunwalking: Who knew, and how high up?"

60. The memo is available at http://www.foxnews.com/projects/pdf/ATF_document_guns.pdf.

61. Katie Lopez, "Valley law enforcement taking measures to stop gun trafficking," *KGBT* (Harlingen, TX), May 24, 2011, http://www.valleycentral.com/news/story.aspx?id=621893.

62. Tim Johnson, "WikiLeaks dispute claims U.S. ambassador to Mexico," *Miami Herald* (McClatchy Newspapers), March 19, 2011, http://www.miamiherald.com/2011/03/19/2124329/wikileaks-dispute-claims-us-ambassador.html (President Calderón demanded Pascual's removal).

63. Sharyl Attkisson, "'Gunwalking' scandal final straw leading to resignation of U.S. ambassador to Mexico," *CBSNews.com*, March 20, 2011, http://www.cbsnews.com/8301-31727_162-20045147-10391695.html?tag=cbsnewsMainColumnArea.

64. Alejandra Xanic von Bertrab, "ATF allegations, anger spread through Mexico," Center for Public Integrity, March 16, 2011, http://www.iwatchnews.org/2011/03/16/3576/atf-allegations-anger-spread-through-mexico.

65. Solomon, Heath, and Witkin, "ATF let hundreds of U.S. weapons fall into hands of suspected Mexican gunrunners."

66. The transcript of my speech to the NRA Annual Meeting about the Fast and

Furious scandal is available at http://home.nra.org/pdf/Wayne_LaPierre_MM_Speech.pdf. A video of the speech is available at http://home.nra.org/#/home.

67. Ms. Attkisson's reporting is available at http://cbsnews.com/sharylattkisson.

68. Sharyl Attkisson, "ATF memo after CBS report: We need positive press," *CBSNews. com*, March 4, 2011, http://www.cbsnews.com/8301-31727_162-20039251-10391695.html?tag=contentMain;contentBody.

69. Sen. Charles Grassley, letter of April 8, 2011, to Kenneth Melson, acting director, BATFE, http://grassley.senate.gov/about/upload/Judiciary-ATF-04-08-11-letter-to-Melson-Whistleblowers-Gillett.pdf (discussing BATFE orders to staff on February 3, 2011, and noting that it was unclear how widely the orders were disseminated).

70. David Heath, "E-mails allege strife within ATF over Grassley probe," Center for Public Integrity, April 8, 2011, http://www.iwatchnews.org/2011/04/08/3971/e-mails-allege-strife-within-atf-over-grassley-probe.

71. Rep. Daryl Issa, letter of March 29, 2011, to Secretary of State Hillary Clinton, http://www.cbsnews.com/htdocs/pdf/Issa-Letter-2011-03-29.pdf.

72. Sharyl Attkisson, "ATF chief won't appear at Senate hearing in wake of 'gunwalking' scandal," *CBSNews.com*, March 29, 2011, http://www.cbsnews.com/8301-31727_162-20048331-10391695.html?tag=cbsnewsMainColumnArea.

73. Chairman Daryl Issa, letter of April 20, 2011, to BATFE acting director Kenneth Melson, http://oversight.house.gov/images/stories/Other_Documents/4-20-11_Melson_Follow_up_letter.pdf; Anna Palmer, "Issa Threatens to Begin Contempt Proceedings against ATF Official," *Roll Call*, April 20, 2011, http://www.rollcall.com/news/issa_threatens_to_begin_contempt_proceedings_against_atf_official-205054-1.html; Nedra Pickler, "Chairman threatens ATF with contempt in gun probe," Associated Press, April 20, 2011, http://www.centredaily.com/2011/04/20/2661123/chairman-threatens-atf-with-contempt.html; Louise Radnofsky, "Issa Steps Up Fight over ATF Documents," *Wall Street Journal*, April 20, 2011, http://blogs.wsj.com/washwire/2011/04/20/issa-steps-up-fight-over-atf-documents/;

74. Jerry Seper, "ATF criticized for failing to respond to committee subpoena," *Washington Times*, April 21, 2011, http://www.washingtontimes.com/news/2011/apr/20/atf-criticized-failing-respond-committee-subpoena/.

75. Sharyl Attkisson, "Justice Memo to Self: No Gunwalking Allowed," *CBSNews. com*, March 15, 2011, http://www.cbsnews.com/8301-31727_162-20043411-10391695.html?tag=cbsnewsMainColumnArea.

76. Sharyl Attkisson, "Senator Grassley tells Attorney General Holder: 'You may be ill-served'," *CBSNews.com*, May 3, 2011, http://www.cbsnews.com/8301-31727_162-20059453-10391695.html?tag=cbsnewsMainColumnArea.

77. BATFE, Phoenix Field Division, Phoenix Group VII (Gunrunner/Strike Force), Briefing Paper, January 8, 2010, http://oversight.house.gov/images/stories/Other_Documents/4-7.pdf.

78. Lanny A. Breuer, assistant attorney general, memorandum to Paul M. O'Brien, Director of Enforcement Operations, Criminal Division, March 10, 2010, http://oversight.house.gov/images/stories/Other_Documents/2-3.pdf.

79. Sharyl Attkisson, "DOJ's Breuer authorized wiretap in ATF Fast and Furious case," *CBS News.com*, May 4, 2011, http://www.cbsnews.com/8301-31727_162-20059640-10391695.html.

80. Transcript at House Committee on Government Oversight and Reform, "What Attorney General Holder Won't Tell on Controversial Gun Operation, Documents Do," http://oversight.house.gov/index.php?option=com_content&view=article& id=1272:what-attorney-general-holder-wont-tell-on-controversial-gun-operation-documents-do&catid=22:releasesstatements. A three-minute excerpt of Holder's testimony is available at http://www.cbsnews.com/8301-31727_162-20059360-10391695.html?tag=cbsnewsMainColumnArea.

81. The Grassley letters are available at: http://grassley.senate.gov/about/upload/ Judiciary-03-03-11-letter-to-Holder-Melson-ATF-SW-Border.pdf (March 3); http://judiciary.senate.gov/resources/documents/upload/021611GrassleyToHolder. pdf (February 16); http://grassley.senate.gov/about/upload/Judiciary-02-09-11-Letter-to-Holder-notifying-of-ATF-issues.pdf (February 9) (The letter begins: "During our meeting on January 31, I provided you with copies of my recent letters to Acting ATF Director Kenneth E. Melson. I had received serious allegations from ATF whistleblowers. ATF agents told my staff that the agency allowed the sale of assault rifles to known and suspected straw purchasers for an illegal trafficking ring near the southwest border"); http://grassley.senate.gov/about/ upload/Judiciary-01-31-11-Whistleblower-retaliation-letter-to-ATF.pdf (January 31); http://grassley.senate.gov/about/upload/Judiciary-01-27-11-letter-to-ATF-SW-Border-strategy.pdf (January 27).

82. "Is Obama a Gunrunner?" *Investor's Business Daily*, May 9, 2011, A16, http://www. investors.com/NewsAndAnalysis/Article/571468/201105061854/Is-Obama-a-Gunrunner-.htm.

83. Solomon, Heath, and Witkin, "ATF let hundreds of U.S. weapons fall into hands of suspected Mexican gunrunners."

84. Matthew Boyle, "What we know about Project Gunrunner," *Daily Caller*, April 21, 2011, http://dailycaller.com/2011/04/21/what-we-know-about-project-gunrunner/.

85. Solomon, Heath, and Witkin, "ATF let hundreds of U.S. weapons fall into hands of suspected Mexican gunrunners."

86. The question and answer are available at http://www.youtube.com/ watch?v=AROf30JpY-8.

87. Jason Horowitz, "Over a barrel? Meet White House gun policy adviser Steve Croley," *Washington Post*, April 11, 2011.

88. Sam Stein,"Obama Looking for Ways around Congress on Gun Policy," *Huffington Post*, Mar. 23, 2011, http://www.huffingtonpost.com/2011/03/15/obama-gun-laws-congress_n_836138.html.

89. Matthew Huisman, "Gun sales alert gets key support," *Dallas Morning News*, May 18, 2011, A9, http://www.dallasnews.com/news/politics/headlines/20110517-rule-would-require-texas-dealers-to-track-mass-sales-of-high-powered-guns.ece (quoting Brady president Paul Helmke).

90. Brady Center to Prevent Gun Violence, *Officers Gunned Down: How Weak Gun Laws Put Police at Risk* (May 2011), http://bradycenter.net/xshare/pdf/reports/ Officers-Gunned-Down.pdf.

91. For an example of the continuing denials, see Assistant Attorney General Ronald Weich, Assistant Attorney General, letter of May 2, 2011, to Sen. Charles Grassley, http://grassley.senate.gov/about/upload/Judiciary-ATF-05-02-11-letter-from-DOJ-denial-2-to-allegations.pdf.

92. Arturo Sarukhan, Ambassador of Mexico to the U.S., Washington, "Choose labels carefully," Letters to the Editor, *Dallas Morning News*, April 11, 2011, http://letterstotheeditorblog.dallasnews.com/archives/2011/04/on-mexico-and-v.html:

> Re: "Let's call México's Cartels what they are: terrorists," Friday Editorials. The editorial should be better headed "Let's Call Mexico's cartels what they are: very violent, well-financed transnational criminal organizations." . . .
>
> Misunderstanding the challenge we face leads to wrong policies and bad policy making. If you label these organizations as terrorist, you will have to start calling drug consumers in the U.S. "financiers of terrorist organizations" and gun dealers "providers of material support to terrorists." Otherwise, you really sound as if you want to have your cake and eat it too. That's why I would underscore that the editorial page should be careful what it advocates for.

Chapter 9

1. As of late 2008, there were 112,000 personnel (Edwin J. Feulner, introduction to Brett D. Schaefer, ed., *ConUNdrum: The Limits of the United Nations and the Search for Alternatives* [Lanham, MD: Rowman & Littlefield, 2009], 4, citing U.N. Department of Public Information, "United Nations Peacekeeping Operations: Background Note," December 31, 2008, http://www.un.org/Depts/dpko/dpko/bnote.htm); "Call the Blue Helmets," *Economist*, January 4, 2007, 22, 24, http://www.economist.com/world/displaystory.cfm?story_id=8490163.
2. "U.N. Dispute Reignited over Corruption," *New York Times* (Associated Press), Feb. 22, 2006, http://www.nytimes.com/aponline/national/AP-UN-Power-Struggle.html.
3. Feulner, in Schaefer, *ConUNdrum*, 4.
4. Greg Mills and Terence McNamese, "Mission Improbable," ibid., 62, citing U.N. Security Council, "Peacekeeping Procurement Audit Found Mismanagement, Risk of Financial Loss, Security Council Told in Briefing by Chief of Staff," SC/8645, February 12, 2006.
5. Mills and McNamee, citing Colum Lynch, "Audit of U.N.'s Sudan Mission Finds Tens of Millions in Waste," *Washington Post*, February 10, 2008, 16.
6. The corrupt U.N. officials were the Russians Alexander Yakovlev and Vladimir Kuznetsov, who were caught by the Procurement Task Force, which the Russians later eliminated. (Details in chapter 10.)

   For more on the suits, see Compass Group, "Announcement in relation to ESS/ES-KO and Supreme (UN) litigation," October 16, 2006 (announcing the settlement, stating that "the terms of the settlement are confidential but the total legal, professional and related costs associated with investigation, litigation and settlement are below £40,000,000"; and noting that the settlement avoided a trial in which there likely "would have been various attacks on the privileges and immunities of the United Nations"); Liza Porteus, "British Food Company Slapped with U.N. Bid-Rigging Scheme Suit," *Fox News*, March 30, 2006, http://www.foxnews.com/story/0,2933,189676,00.html; "Compass Has 2nd Complaint on U.N. Contract," *New York Times* (Associated Press), March 30, 2006, http://www.nytimes.com/aponline/business/AP-Britain-Compass-Group.html;

Salamander Davoudi and Stephen Fidler, "Compass faced with new UN lawsuit," *Financial Times*, March 29, 2006, news.ft.com/cms/s/6831ecb8-bf57-11da-9de7-0000779e2340.html; Liza Porteus, "Food Services Company Files Lawsuit over U.N. Procurement Contracts," *Fox News*, March 10, 2006, www.foxnews.com/story/0,2933,187454,00.html.

7. Brett D. Schaefer, *Time for a New United Nations Peacekeeping Organization*, Heritage Foundation Backgrounder no. 2006, February 13, 2007, http://www.heritage.org/research/reports/2007/02/time-for-a-new-united-nations-peacekeeping-organization.

8. Mills and McNamee, in Lynch, "Audit of U.N.'s Sudan Mission," 78 (citing "a senior regional official in Bukavu interviewed by the authors).

9. Matthew Russell Lee, "UN in Africa Needs Further Oversight, Should Protect Trucks to Darfur, of Double-Standards," *Inner City Press*, June 11, 2008, http://www.innercitypress.com/unsc1postafrica061108.html.

   CNDC is the French acronym for National Congress for the Defense of the People. Like the rest of the warlord armies, its name sounds much better than the actions that the group actually takes—which are mainly massacring, raping, and looting.

10. Matthew Russell Lee, "Eastern Congo Violence Allowed by UN, Fancy Uvira Camp as Council Visits Goma, Gold and Guns Denied," *Inner City Press*, June 9, 2008, http://www.innercitypress.com/unsc1goma060808.html.

11. Matthew Russell Lee, "UN Accused of Inaction As LRA Kills in Congo, Denies but without Specifics, No Bosco," *Inner City Press*, February 4, 2009, http://www.innercitypress.com/drc1msf020409.html.

12. David B. Kopel, Paul Gallant, and Joanne D. Eisen, "The Arms Trade Treaty: Zimbabwe, the Democratic Republic of the Congo, and the Prospects for Arms Embargoes on Human Rights Violators," *Penn State Law Review* 114 (2010): 891, http://ssrn.com/abstract=1437204. Much of this section of the chapter is based on this paper.

13. Martin Plaut, "UN Troops 'traded gold for guns'," BBC News, May 23, 2007.

14. Martin Plaut, "UN troops 'helped smuggle gold'," BBC News, August 11, 2007.

15. Matthew Russell Lee, "On UN's Congo Scandal, Ban Defers to OIOS, Which Itself Stands Accused," *Inner City Press*, May 5, 2008, http://www.innercitypress.com/un4oiosmonuc050508.html.

16. Martin Plaut, "UN Troops 'armed DR Congo rebels'," BBC One *Panorama*, BBC News, April 28, 2008, http://news.bbc.co.uk/2/hi/programmes/panorama/7331077.stm.

17. Colum Lynch, "Pakistani Forces in Congo Aided Gold Smugglers, the U.N. Finds: Rights Group Alleges Direct Involvement by the Peacekeepers," *Washington Post*, July 23, 2007, http://www.washingtonpost.com/wp-dyn/content/article/2007/07/22/AR2007072201242_pf.html; "Peacekeeper 'smuggled Congo gold': A United Nations inquiry has confirmed that a Pakistani peacekeeper in the Democratic Republic of Congo was involved in smuggling gold," BBC News, July 13, 2007, http://news.bbc.co.uk/2/hi/south_asia/6896881.stm.

18. Plaut, "UN Troops 'armed DR Congo rebels'" (Doss speaks in the online video).

19. "DRC: Interview with MONUC chief William Swing," *IRIN News*, January 14, 2009, http://www.irinnews.org/Report.aspx?ReportId=45492.

20. Plaut, "UN Troops 'traded gold for guns.'"
21. Plaut, "UN Troops 'armed DR Congo rebels.'"
22. Peter Wallensteen, Paul Holtom, Alex Vines (discussant) and Claire Spencer, *United Nations Arms Embargoes: Their Impact,* February 28, 2008, 1119, Chatham House, http://www.chathamhouse.org.uk/files/11170_280208unarmsembargoes.pdf.
23. "Uganda accuses UN peacekeepers of arming DR Congo rebels," MONUC, April 30, 2008, http://www.monuc.org/news.aspx?newsID=17212; "Clarification Regarding the MONUC (the United Nations Mission in the Democratic Republic of Congo) Scandal Involving Gold and Armstrafficking in Mongbwalu, Ituri District, Oriental Province, DRC, at #1," BBC, http://news.bbc.co.uk/nol/shared/bsp/hi/pdfs/24_04_08_rebel_letter.pdf (Confession of the captured gun-runners, dated May 23, 2007, stating: "The MONUC Pakistani Blue Helmets were engaged in the sale of various items (computers, freezers, mobile phones, food stuffs, . . .) for which we were used as intermediaries between them and buyers and, at times, we were buyers ourselves").
24. Lee, "On UN's Congo Scandal, Ban Defers."
25. "UN: Hold Peacekeepers Accountable for Congo Smuggling, Letter to Chief of UN Peacekeeping Urges Follow-Through," Human Rights Watch, July 23, 2007, http://www.hrw.org/legacy/english/docs/2007/07/23/congo16448_txt.htm. Human Rights Watch is a vicious and dishonest organization with regard to Israel, but still sometimes does accurate work on other countries. For the story of HRW's grotesque participation in the international campaign to destroy Israel, see Robert L. Bernstein, "Rights Watchdog, Lost in the Mideast," *New York Times,* October 19, 2009 (op-ed by the founder of Human Rights Watch).
26. "UN: Hold Peacekeepers Accountable for Congo Smuggling."
27. Ibid.
28. Ibid.
29. Matthias Basanisi, "Who Will Watch the Peacekeepers?" *New York Times,* May 23, 2008, http://www.nytimes.com/2008/05/23/opinion/23basanisi.html.
30. Matthew Russell Lee, "UN's Congo Scandal Was Covered-Up, Former OIOS Investigator Says, Accountability Delayed," *Inner City Press,* May 23, 2008, http://www.innercitypress.com/un7oiosmonuc052308.html.
31. Lynch, "Pakistani Forces in Congo Aided Gold Smugglers."
32. David B. Kopel, Paul Gallant, and Joanne D. Eisen, "Microdisarmament," *UMKC Law Review* 73 (2005): 969
33. Amnesty International, *Democratic Republic of the Congo: arming the east,* AI Index: AFR 62/006/2005 (July 2005), 36–37.
34. "Annan vows to end sex abuse committed by UN mission staff in DR of Congo," *UN News Centre,* November 19, 2004, http://www.un.org/apps/news/story.asp?NewsID=12k590&Cr=democratic&Cr1=congo; Human resources management, "Report of the Secretary-General on the activities of the Office of Internal Oversight Services, Financing of the United Nations Organization Mission in the Democratic Republic of the Congo," UN document A/59/661, January 5, 2005, ¶ 35, http://www.monuc.org/downloads/0520055E.pdf ("Although MONUC has prepared directives on the prevention of sexual exploitation and abuse, at present, little has been done to implement an effective prevention programme in Bunia"), and ¶ 38 ("On several occasions, the commanders of these contingents [in

Bunia] either failed to provide the requested information or assistance or actively interfered with the investigation").

35. The U.N., to its credit, now has a website on Sexual Exploitation and Abuse and Peacekeeping: http://www.un.org/Depts/dpko/dpko/ctte/SEA.htm.

36. "French court convicts UN worker of rape in Africa," Reuters, September 12, 2008, http://africa.reuters.com/top/news/usnBAN227489.html; "UN to probe sex abuse allegations against DR Congo staff," *Agence France Press*, December 24, 2008, http://www.google.com/hostednews/afp/article/ALeqM5j-b-SyMAasnGGTazBj2QAAm_xyrQ.

37. Bradley S. Klapper, "UN finds 217 sex abuse claims against blue helmets," Associated Press, Jan. 14, 2009, http://www.google.com/hostednews/ap/article/ALeqM5hgvsctOxCKOZVwadLLMtgZwci6JAD95N1PBG0. The report was leaked and placed on the Wikileaks.org website ("United Nations Organization Mission in the Democratic Republic of the Congo: Allegations of sexual exploitation and abuse in the Ituri region, Bunia (ID Case No. 0618-05," January 30, 2007, http://wikileaks.org/wiki/United_Nations_Organization_Mission_in_the_Democratic_Republic_of_the_Congo:_Allegations_of_sexual_exploitation_and_abuse_in_the_Ituri_region%2C_Bunia_%28ID_Case_No._0618-05%29%2C_30_Jan_2007.

38. "India probes UN sex charges in DR Congo," Agence France Press, August 12, 2008, http://afp.google.com/article/ALeqM5h31znoknlmnZnUuVFyumyU3lv-hQ.

39. Jeffrey Gettlemen, "Latest Tragic Symbol of an Unhealed Congo: Male Rape Victims," *New York Times*, August 5, 2009, A1.

40. Gettlemen, "Latest Tragic Symbol of an Unhealed Congo," A7.

41. Thalif Deen, "U.N. Lacks Muscle to Fight Sex Abuse in Peacekeeping," *IPS News*, July 2, 2008, http://www.ipsnews.net/news.asp?idnews=43041.

42. Eve Ensler, "A Broken U.N. Promise in Congo," *Washington Post*, June 30, 2009, http://www.washingtonpost.com/wp-dyn/content/article/2009/06/29/AR2009062903456_pf.html.

43. Matthew Russell Lee, "Congolese Doctor Says UN Witnessed, Contributes to Rape, Lumo Shows Pol Blaming Women," *Inner City Press*, May 31, 2009, http://www.innercitypress.com/drc1lumo060109.html.

44. Grace Kwinjeh, "When Will MONUC Stop Blundering?" *New Times* (Rwanda), November 10, 2009.

45. "UN Peacekeepers Failed DR Congo Rape Victims: Official," *Agence France Press*, September 7, 2010; Louis Charbonneau, "Number of Victims in Congo Mass Rape Increases: U.N.," Reuters, September 1, 2010; Josh Kron and Jeffrey Gettleman, "U.N. E-mail Shows Early Warning on Congo Rapes," *New York Times*, August 31, 2010; Matthew Russell Lee, "On Congo Rapes, UN Inaction & Dissembling Stretches to Special Representative on Sexual Violence and Conflict," *Inner City Press*, August 31, 2010; Matthew Russell Lee, "On Congo Rapes, Email about Rebels Exposes UN Lies, Security Council's Buzzword 'Elements' Must Extend to Probe of UN," *Inner City Press*, August 26, 2010; Matthew Russell Lee, "As UN's Inaction on Congo Rapes Triggers Belated Trips, Why No Flares or Sat Phones?" *Inner City Press*, August 24, 2010.

46. Kron and Gettleman, "U.N. E-mail Shows Early Warning on Congo Rapes."

47. David Smith, "UN Peace Mission Fueling Violence in Congo, Report Says," *Guardian* (London), November 25, 2009; Michelle Faul, "Report: UN-backed Congo Troops Killing Civilians," *Associated Press*, December 15, 2009.
48. Kenneth Cain, Heidi Postlewait, and Andrew Thomson, *Emergency Sex and Other Desperate Measures: A True Story from Hell on Earth* (New York: Miramax Books, 2004), 255.
49. Ibid., 265–66.
50. U.S. House of Representatives, Committee on International Relations, Subcommittee on Oversight and Investigations. Investigative Report, The Oil-for-Food Program: The Systemic Failure of the United Nations, 109th Cong., 1st sess. (2005), 31; Editorial, "Sex and the UN: when peacemakers become predators," *New York Sun*, January 11, 2005.
51. "Note for Implementing and Operational Partners by UNHCR and Save the Children-UK on Sexual Violence & Exploitation: The Experience of Refugee Children in Guinea, Liberia and Sierra Leone based on Initial Findings and Recommendations from Assessment Mission 22 October–30 November 2001," U.N. High Commissioner for Refugees, February 2002, http://www.unhcr.ch/cgi-bin/texis/vtx/partners/opendoc.pdf. See also "UN DR Congo sex abuses 'on film,'" BBC News, November 23, 2004; Kate Holt, "How the UN Was Forced to Tackle Stain on Its Integrity," *Independent*, February 11, 2005.
52. "UNHCR remedial actions and preventive measures against sexual exploitation and abuse of refugees," U.N. High Commissioner for Refugees, October 22, 2002, http://www.unhcr.ch/cgi-bin/texis/vtx/news/opendoc.htm?tbl=NEWS&page=home&id=3db54e985.
53. Colum Lynch, "U.N. Faces More Accusations of Sexual Misconduct: Officials Acknowledge 'Swamp' of Problems and Pledge Fixes amid New Allegations in Africa, Haiti," *Washington Post*, March 13, 2005, A22.
54. Save the Children U.K, *From Camp to Community: Liberia study on exploitation of children*, May 8, 2006, http://www.eyeontheun.org/assets/attachments/articles/3264_Save_the_Children--Sex_Exploitation_Study.pdf.
55. Sarah Lyall, "Aid Workers Are Said to Abuse Girls," *New York Times*, May 9, 2006, http:// www.nytimes.com/2006/05/09/world/africa/09liberia.html?_r=1&oref=slogin.
56. Matthew Russell Lee, "UN in Africa Needs Further Oversight, Should Protect Trucks to Darfur, of Double-Standards," *Inner City Press*, June 11, 2008, http://www.innercitypress.com/unsc1postafrica061108.html.
57. Matthew Russell Lee, "On Sudan, UN Ban Admits Limit on Peacekeepers, Gambari Summoned, Change Pledged," *Inner City Press*, September 9, 2010.
58. Kate Holt and Sara Hughes, "UN staff accused of raping children in Sudan," *Telegraph* (London), January 3, 2007, http://www.telegraph.co.uk/news/main.jhtml;jsessionid=I2SFT5PVNXEYVQFIQMFCFFWAVCBQYIV0?xml=/news/2007/01/03/wsudan03.xml.
59. Peter Murphy, "Survival Sex?" Reuters, July 24, 2007, http://www.theglobeandmail.com/servlet/story/RTGAM.20070724.wivorycoast0724/BNStory/International/; Parfait Kouassi, "U.N. Warns Moroccans on Sex Abuse," *Washington Post* (Associated Press), July 22, 2007.
60. Evelyn Leopold, "UN teams go to Ivory Coast to probe sex abuse," Reuters, July 26, 2007, http://uk.reuters.com/article/worldNews/idUKN2633420120070726.

61. Lee, "UN in Africa Needs Further Oversight."
62. "Peacekeepers 'abusing children': Children as young as six are being sexually abused by peacekeepers and aid workers, says a leading UK charity," BBC, May 27, 2008, http://news.bbc.co.uk/1/hi/7420798.stm.
63. Joseph Guyler Delva, "Haitian policemen said beaten by U.N. peacekeepers," Reuters, August 7, 2008, http://www.reuters.com/article/homepageCrisis/idUSN07366700._CH_.2400.
64. "AP Interview: UN envoy in Haiti works to prevent peacekeeper sex abuse," Associated Press, December 26, 2007, http://www.iht.com/bin/printfriendly.php?id=8913015.
65. "Peacekeeping and sex abuse," *Economist*, May 29, 2008.
66. Reed Lindsay, "U.N. peacekeepers accused of rape," *Washington Times*, December 17, 2006, http://www.washtimes.com/world/20061217-122119-4767r.htm.
67. Carol J. Williams, "U.N. confronts another sex scandal," *Los Angeles Times*, December 15, 2007, http://www.latimes.com/news/nationworld/world/la-fg-haitisex15dec15,1,1408756.story?track=crosspromo&coll=la-headlines-world&ctrack=1&cset=true. The U.N. said that the Pakistanis had been sent back to Pakistan, where the Pakistani government sentenced them to a year in prison (Lindsay, "U.N. peacekeepers accused of rape").
68. "UN troops face child abuse claims: Children have been subjected to rape and prostitution by United Nations peacekeepers in Haiti and Liberia, a BBC investigation has found," BBC, November 30, 2006, http://news.bbc.co.uk/2/hi/americas/6195830.stm.
69. "UN and aid workers accused of abusing children," *Final Call*, June 24, 2008, http://www.finalcall.com/artman/publish/article_4892.shtml.
70. Matthew Russell Lee, "At UN, Happy Talk of Haiti Means Stonewall of Shootings and Sexual Abuse, Kidnapping," *Inner City Press*, September 12, 2009, http://www.innercitypress.com/ungo6haiti090909.html.
71. Steve Stecklow and Joe Lauria, "U.N. Mum on Probes of Sex-Abuse Allegations," *Wall Street Journal*, March 21, 2010, http://online.wsj.com/article/SB10001424052748704188104575083334130312808.html.
72. "UN and aid workers accused of abusing children."
73. Ibid.
74. "Comprehensive review of the whole question of peacekeeping operations in all their aspects. Letter dated 24 March 2005 from the Secretary-General to the President of the General Assembly," A/59/710, Fifty-ninth session, Agenda item 77
75. Warren Hoge, "Report Finds U.N. Isn't Moving to End Sex Abuse by Peacekeepers," *New York Times*, October 19, 2005; Abby Wisse Schachter, "The Rapes Continue," *New York Post*, October 24, 2005. See also Editorial, "The Worse U.N. Scandal," *New York Times*, October 24, 2005.
76. Hoge, "Report Finds U.N. Isn't Moving to End Sex Abuse"; Schachter, "The Rapes Continue"; "The Worse U.N. Scandal."
77. Schachter, "The Rapes Continue."
78. Patrick Goodenough, "U.N. 'Whistleblower' Loses Job," CNSNews.com, Dec. 15, 2004, www.cnsnews.com/ForeignBureaus/Archive/200412/FOR20041215b.html.
79. Schachter, "The Rapes Continue."

80. Liza Porteus, "U.N. Lacks Authority to Punish Misbehaving Peacekeepers," *Fox News*, January 5, 2007, http://www.foxnews.com/story/0,2933,241699,00. html?sPage=fnc.world/unitednations.

81. Claudia Parsons, "UN investigates sex abuse charges in Ivory Coast," Reuters, July 20, 2007, http://africa.reuters.com/wire/news/usnN20284599.html.

82. "UN investigator: Troops from armies that abuse, torture should not be peacekeepers," *PR Insider*, July 28, 2007.

83. Thalif Deen, "U.N. Lacks Muscle to Fight Sex Abuse in Peacekeeping," IPS News, July 2, 2008, http://www.ipsnews.net/news.asp?idnews=43041.

84. Stewart Stogel, "Red Tape Hampering U.N. Peacekeeping Reform," NewsMax, March 2, 2006, http://www.newsmax.com/archives/articles/2006/3/2/94735. shtml.

85. Bea Edwards and Shelley Walden, "U.N. not so clean anymore," *Citizen Times*, July 12, 2008, http://www.citizen-times.com/apps/pbcs.dll/ article?AID=200880707042.

86. Mills and McNamee, 67 (noting that the U.N. pays troop-contributing countries $1,110 per month per soldier, which is far more than what most developing countries actually pay those soldiers).

87. "Peacekeeping and sex abuse," *Economist*, May 29, 2008; Mills and McNamee, 67, citing U.N. Department of Peacekeeping Operations, "Contributions to United Nations Peacekeeping Operations," May 31, 2008, http://www.un.org/Depts/ dpko/dpko/contributors/2008/may08_1.pdf.

88. James Reinl, "UN peacekeeping marred by abuse," *National*, June 1, 2008, http://www.thenational.ae/article/20080531/FOREIGN/881915422/1103/ SPORT&Profile=1103.

Chapter 10

1. Claudia Rosett, "How Corrupt Is the United Nations?" *Commentary* magazine, April 2006, http://www.commentarymagazine.com/article.asp?aid=12104031_1 ("On UN websites devoted to procurement, where the idea is not to minimize the official amount of UN spending but on the contrary to attract suppliers to a large and thriving operation, the estimate of money spent yearly on goods and services by the entire UN system comes to $30 billion").

2. For a good overview of U.N. budget problems, see Brett D. Schaefer, *Time to Rein in the U.N.'s Budget*, Heritage Foundation, Backgrounder no. 2368, February 3, 2010, http://www.heritage.org/Research/Reports/2010/02/Time-to-Rein-in-the-UNs-Budget.

3. Holmes, "Smart Multilateralism," in Schaefer, *ConUNdrum*, 21.

4. Irwin Arieff, "Need a Job? UN Payroll Is a Bright Spot in Bleak Times," *UNA-USA World Bulletin*, March 3, 2010, http://www.unausa.org/worldbulletin/030310/ arieff.

5. Ibid.

6. U.N. Security Council Resolution 687, April 3, 1991.

7. Much of the information in this section comes from the U.S. House of Representatives, Committee on International Relations, Subcommittee on Oversight and Investigations. Investigative Report, *The Oil-for-Food Program: The*

Systemic Failure of the United Nations, 109th Cong., 1st sess. (2005) [hereinafter cited as *Systemic Failure*].

8. Ibid., 10.

9. Ibid., 11, citing a confidential interview with a diplomat at the U.N.

10. Ibid., 2. See also pages. 12–17.

11. Michael Soussen, "The Cash-for-Saddam Program," *Wall Street Journal*, March 8, 2004; Jed Babbin, *Inside the Asylum: Why the United Nations and Old Europe Are Worse Than You Think* (Washington, D.C.: Regnery, 2004), 24–25. See also *Systemic Failure*, 21–22, citing Rehan Mullick, Testimony before the Committee on International Relations Subcommittee on Oversight and Investigations, March 17, 2005.

12. *Systemic Failure*, 21–22.

13. Judith Miller, "Panel Pegs Illicit Iraq Earnings at $21.3 Billion," *New York Times*, November 16, 2004.

14. Claudia Rosset, "Oil-for-Terror?" *National Review*, April 18, 2004.

15. Dore Gold, *Tower of Babble: How the United Nations Has Fueled Global Chaos* (New York: Three Rivers Pr., 2005), 122, citing U.S. General Accounting Office, statement of Joseph A. Christoff, director, International Affairs and Trade, Testimony before the Committee on Foreign Relations, U.S. Senate, "United Nations: Observations on the Oil-for-Food Program," April 7, 2004.

16. *Systemic Failure*, 9–10, citing "Comprehensive Report of the Special Adviser to the DCI on Iraq's WMD, Section on Regime Intent, 2004," 1 ("the Duelfer Report").

17. Ibid., 19.

18. Barbara Slavin, "Scope of oil-for-food fraud 'overwhelming'," *USA Today*, November 18, 2005.

19. Ibid., 121–22.

20. Ibid., 124–25.

21. Ibid.

22. Editorial, "Kofi Annan's 'leadership'," *Washington Times*, April 24, 2005.

23. Ibid.

24. "2,000 firms 'paid oil-for-food kickbacks,'" *Daily Telegraph* (London), October 27, 2005.

25. Slavin, "Scope of oil-for-food fraud 'overwhelming.'"

26. Editorial, "Kofi Annan's 'leadership.'"

27. Claudia Rosett, "Scandal Central," *New York Post*, July 18, 2008, http://www.nypost.com/seven/07182008/postopinion/opedcolumnists/scandal_central_120413.htm.

28. Francis Harris, "UN investigator claims Annan lied about son's role," *Daily Telegraph* (London), December 9, 2005.

29. Joseph A. Klein, *Global Deception: The UN's Stealth Assault on America's Freedom* (L.A.: World Ahead Pub., 2005), 25.

30. Harris, "UN investigator."

31. "Annan Says Exoneration by Iraq Oil-for-Food Report 'Great Relief,'" UN News Centre, March 29, 2005.

32. Harris, "UN investigator."

33. Ibid.

34. *Systemic Failure*, 2–3.

35. Meghan Clyne, "Trump Tells Congress U.N. Should Abandon Turtle Bay," *New York Sun*, July 22, 2005, http://www.nysun.com/foreign/trump-tells-congress-un-should-abandon-turtle-bay/17391/.

36. Judi McLeod, "UN's $1.9 Billion Taj Mahal on the East River," Canada Free Press, July 31, 2007.

37. Paul D. Colford, "Show me the money to fix up the UN, Annan tells members" (New York) *Daily News,* November 30, 2006.

38. David M. Walker, Comptroller General of the United States, *United Nations: Internal Oversight Controls and Processes Need Strengthening*, GAO-06-701T, April 27, 2006, http://www.gao.gov/new.items/d06701t.pdf.

39. Thomas Melito, GAO Director of International Affairs and Trade, *United Nations: Weaknesses in Internal Oversight and Procurement Could Affect the Effective Implementation of the Planned Renovation*, GAO-06-877T, June 20, 2006, http://www.gao.gov/new.items/d06877t.pdf.

40. Erling Grimstad, *Review of the OIOS Investigations Division, United Nations Submitted to the Under-Secretary-General of Office of Internal Oversight Services*, Review of Investigations Division/OIOS/UN, June 26, 2007, 7, http://www.innercitypress.com/oiosrev1.pdf.

41. Matthew Russell Lee, "UN's Congo Scandal Was Covered-Up, Former OIOS Investigator Says, Accountability Delayed," *Inner City Press*, May 23, 2008, http://www.innercitypress.com/un7oiosmonuc052308.html.

42. Melito, *United Nations.*

43. Ibid.

44. Irwin Arieff, "US lawmaker presses UN on renovations," Reuters, June 12, 2006; Alec Russell, "US failing to aid the UN, says Annan's deputy," *Telegraph* (London), June 8, 2006, http://www.telegraph.co.uk/news/main.jhtml?xml=/news/2006/06/08/wun08.xml; James Bone and Richard Beeston "Apologise or we'll cut your funding, US envoy tells UN," *Times* (London), June 9, 2006, http://www.timesonline.co.uk/article/0,,11069-2217839,00.html.

45. John Podesta and Richard C. Leone, "Time for U.S. Leadership, Not Bullying at the United Nations," The Century Foundation, June 16, 2006, http://www.tcf.org/list.asp?type=TN&pubid=1335.
When Bolton resigned at the end of his term, in December 2006, Brown was asked for a reaction. He responded, "No comment—and you can say he said it with a smile." Edith M. Lederer, "Bush Agenda Came 1st for Bolton at U.N.," *Washington Post* (Associated Press), December 5, 2006, http://www.washingtonpost.com/wp-dyn/content/article/2006/12/05/AR2006120500209.html.

46. The Palais is the former headquarters of the League of Nations, the failed predecessor of the United Nations.

47. Laura MacInnis, "U.N. seeks facelift for aging offices in Geneva," *Forbes,* February 6, 2009.

48. Joseph Abrams, "Cost of Rebuilding U.N.'s Palace? A Billion Dollars," Fox News, November 24, 2008, http://www.eyeontheun.org/articles-item.asp?a=5651&id=6989.

49. Kevin J. Kelley, "Report faults UN complex expansion job," Nation (Kenya), October 9, 2008, http://www.eyeontheun.org/articles-item.asp?a=5587&id=6893 (reporting on findings by the UN Advisory Committee on Administrative and Budgetary Questions).

50. David Lee Miller and Jonathan Wachtel, "Valuable Works of Art 'Unaccounted For' at the U.N.," Fox News, March 5, 2009, http://www.eyeontheun.org/articles-item.asp?a=5871&id=7393.

51. Harvey Morris, "UN scours corridors for lost art ahead of $2bn refit," *Financial Times*, March 2, 2009, http://www.ft.com/cms/s/0/4025c9f2-06ca-11de-ab0f-000077b07658.html?nclick_check=1.

52. January 26, 2009, *Chicago Tribune*, http://www.chicagotribune.com/news/opinion/chi-0126edit2jan26,0,454107.story.

53. Thalif Deen, "Cheques, chocolates and wrist watches: Vote buying at UN elections," (London) *Sunday Times*, May 31, 2009, http://sundaytimes.lk/090531/Columns/inside.html.

54. Rosett, "How Corrupt Is the United Nations?"

55. George Russell, "Floating Your Boat? U.N.'s 'Flotel' in Haiti Is Vastly Overpriced, Says Expert," *Fox News*, June 10, 2010, http://www.foxnews.com/world/2010/06/10/floating-boat-uns-flotel-haiti-vastly-overpriced-says-expert/.

56. Dvir Abramovich, "Is It Time for the UN to Be Scrapped?" *Sydney Morning Herald* (Australia), January 25, 2010, http://www.smh.com.au/opinion/blogs/chutzpah/is-is-time-for-the-un-to-be-scrapped/20100125-mtxy.html.

57. U.N. Division for Public Administration and Development Management (DPADM).

58. Betsy Pisik, "Report: U.N. official diverted funds," *Washington Times*, June 12, 2008, http://www.washingtontimes.com/news/2008/jun/12/report-top-official-diverted-funds/?page=1; Rosett, "Scandal Central." The Greek government had donated funds for the Thessaloniki Centre for Public Service Professionalism, in order to help former Soviet states set up transparent and accountable governments. Bertucci mismanaged the trust fund for the center, obstructed its work, and wasted money on consultants who did little or nothing. During the course of the OIOS investigation, he stopped cooperating, and refused to let OIOS see important documents (Betsy Pisik, "U.N. 'good governance' chief spared disciplinary actions," *Washington Times*, August 1, 2008, http://www.washingtontimes.com/news/2008/aug/01/un-good-governance-chief-spared-disciplinary-actio/.)

59. Pisik, "U.N. 'good governance' chief spared disciplinary actions."

60. George Russell, "Disgraced Former U.N. Official Welcomed at High-Level U.N. Conference," *Fox* News, May 12, 2009, http;//www.foxnews.com/story/0,2933,519929,00k.html.

61. Joseph Abrams, "U.N. 'Good Governance' Official May Escape Penalties for Alleged 'Gross Negligence,'" *Fox News*, July 15, 2008, http://www.foxnews.com/story/0,2933,382861,00.html.

62. Rosett, "Scandal Central."

63. Matthew Russell Lee, "At UN, Questions of Ban's Son in Law's Hirings and Promotion Unanswered, In Denmark," Inner City Press, July 23, 2009.

64. Matthew Russell Lee, "As UN's 'Faux' Financial Summit Begins, Host D'Escoto Calls Nepotism 'Entertaining'," Inner City Press, June 23, 2009, http://www.innercitypress.com/unpga1entertain062309.html.

65. The seventy thousand figure does not include the more than eighty thousand United Nations "peacekeepers" who, although they serve as the U.N.'s army, are technically employed by other nations (Greg Mills and Terence McNamee,

"Mission Improbable," in *ConUNdrum*, 65). That number does include twenty thousand Palestinians who work for UNRWA, which elsewhere in this book I call "the Mother of Terrorism." I suspect that the percentage of UNRWA employees who see their U.N. employment as an opportunity to help build a peaceful, tolerant world is considerably lower than at most other U.N. agencies.

66. Joseph A. Christoff, "Observations on the Oil-for-Food Program," testimony before the Committee on Foreign Relations, U.S. Senate, April 7, 2004, http://www.gao.gov/new.items/d04651t.pdf.

67. Brett D. Schaefer, "The Demise of the U.N. Procurement Task Force Threatens Oversight at the U.N." (web memo), Heritage Foundation, February 5, 2009, http://www.heritage.org/Research/InternationalOrganizations/wm2272.cfm; Editorial, "Corruption? The U.N. buries its head," *Chicago Tribune*, January 26, 2009, http://www.realclearpolitics.com/news/tms/politics/2009/Jan/27/corruption__the_u_n__buries_its_head.html.

68. Colum Lynch, "U.N. Seeks U.S. Probe of Alleged Misuse of Afghan Aid, *Washington Post*, June 11, 2009. Helseth was the director of the U.N. Office for Project Services (UNOPS) in Afghanistan from 2002 to 2006.

69. Neil MacFarquhar, "Report Details Corruption Cases Involving U.N. Purchasing," *New York Times*, October 21, 2008, http://www.nytimes.com/2008/10/22/world/22nations.html?_r=1&ref=world&oref=slogin.

70. Patrick Worsnip, "U.N. seen slow to address corruption," Yahoo News, October 23, 2008, http://uk.news.yahoo.com/22/20081023/tpl-uk-un-corruption-43a8d4f.html.

71. Schaefer, "The Demise of the U.N. Procurement Task Force Threatens Oversight at the U.N."

72. Lynch, "Russia Seeks to Thwart U.N. Task Force."

73. Editorial, "Corruption?" *Chicago Tribune*.

74. Schaefer, "The Demise of the U.N. Procurement Task Force." The convicted Russian U.N. official was Vladimir Kuznetsov, who had been chief of the U.N. budget committee (Lynch, "Russia Seeks to Thwart U.N. Task Force."

75. Lynch, "Russia Seeks to Thwart U.N. Task Force."

76. "Corruption?" *Chicago Tribune*; Lynch, "Russia Seeks to Thwart U.N. Task Force"; Steve Stecklow, "U.N. Allows Its Antifraud Task Force to Dissolve," *Wall Street Journal*, January 8, 2009, http://online.wsj.com/article/SB123138018217563187.html?mod=googlenews_wsj.

77. John Heilprin, "UN Scales Back Efforts to Deal with Internal Corruption," Associated Press, January 12, 2010, http://www.eyeontheun.org/articles-item.asp?a=6256&id=8007.

78. John Heilprin, "UN's Internal Watchdog Faces Leadership Vacuum," *Boston Globe* (Associated Press), July 14, 2010, www.boston.com/news/nation/articles/2010/07/14/uns_internal_watchdog_faces_leadership_vacuum/?page=full.

79. Stecklow, "U.N. Allows Its Antifraud Task Force to Dissolve"; Schaefer, "The Demise of the U.N. Procurement Task Force." Appleton has filed a grievance charging that he was discriminated against on the basis of gender (John Heilprin, "Ex-US Prosecutor Accuses UN Chief of Hiring Bias," *San Francisco Examiner* [Associated Press], August 4, 2010, http://www.sfexaminer.com/world/99947934.html).

80. George Russell, "Ban Ki-Moon's New Weapons in Battles over U.N. Oversight," *Fox News*, July 26, 2010, http://www.foxnews.com/world/2010/07/26/analysis-

ban-ki-moons-new-weapon-battles-oversight/?utm_source=feedburner&utm_
medium=feed&utm_campaign=Feed%3A+foxnews%2Fworld+%28Internal+-
+World+Latest+-+Text%29.

81. Colum Lynch, "Departing U.N. Official Calls Ban's Leadership 'Deplorable' in
50-page Memo," *Washington Post*, July 20, 2010; Inga-Britt Ahlenius, "Note to the
Secretary General. End of Assignment Report," July 14, 2010, http://www
.washingtonpost.com/wp-srv/hp/ssi/wpc/nations2.pdf?sid=ST2010071904739.

82. Claudia Rossett, "Keep an Eye on the U.N.," *Forbes.com*, January 28, 2010.

83. John Bolton, "Obama's U.N. Record," *National Review Online*, September 20,
2010, http://www.nationalreview.com/articles/247029/obama-s-u-n-record-john-
bolton?page=1.

84. George Russell, "'Reform' Is Just a Word at the U.N., Its Own Investigation
Shows," *Fox News*, October 8, 2009, http://www.foxnews.com/world/2009/10/22/
reform-just-word-investigation-shows/.

85. Oklahoma Senator Tom Coburn explained:

> Ironically, on the same day in April when the U.N. budget committee
> authorized more spending on the renovation project, the committee also
> voted down Secretary General Kofi Annan's modest management reform
> package. I note that the countries who voted down these reforms contribute
> 12% of the UN budget. The 50 nations that voted for the reforms contribute
> 87%. Those of us paying most of the bills were outvoted by those who
> contribute much less to UN operations. And yet some of these developing
> countries are the very same ones dependent on UN programs, and who in
> theory should most want efficient, transparent, effective and honest United
> Nations operations

86. Stephen M. Lilienthal, "Reform—Not More Revenue—Is Needed By the United
Nations," *American Daily*, July 6, 2006, http://americandaily.com/article/14426)

87. Joseph Abrams, "U.N. Secretary-General Tears into Top Officials over
Bureaucratic Bog," *Fox News*, September 9, 2008, http://www.foxnews.com/
story/0,2933,419481,00.html.

88. Benny Avni, "Report: U.N. Commits Human Rights Abuses Against Its Staff,"
New York Sun, June 13, 2006, http://www.nysun.com/article/34352.

89. Matthew Russell Lee, "UN Whistleblower in Tokyo Raises Questions of Fraud,
Cover-Up and Retaliation from Below," *Inner City Press*, August 26, 2008, http://
www.innercitypress.com/undpi1koda082708.html.

90. Andrew Higgins and Steve Stecklow, "U.N. Push to Stem Misconduct Flounders,"
Wall Street Journal, December 26, 2008, http://online.wsj.com/article/
SB123025080391234345.html.

91. Ibid.

92. Matthew Russell Lee, "UN Tells Press to Pay $23,000 for Space to Cover It,
Sources Say, Scant UN Media Coverage to Further Decrease?" Inner City Press,
June 1, 2009, http://www.eyeontheun.org/articles-item.asp?a=5987&id=7623.

93. Colum Lynch, "Is Ban Ki-moon in Contempt of Court?" *Foreign Policy*, May
12, 2010, turtlebay.foreignpolicy.com/posts/2010/05/12/is_ban_ki_moon_in_
contempt_of_court; Neil MacFarquhar, "Review Panel Judges See a Culture of
Secrecy," *New York Times*, June 17, 2010.

94. Claudia Rosett, "Iran Wields the Gavel at the UNDP," *Forbes*, January 15, 2009, http://www.forbes.com/2009/01/14/iran-undp-board-oped-cx_cr_0115rosett. html.

95. Melanie Kirkpatrick, "The U.N.'s North Korea Chutzpah," *Wall Street Journal*, June 12, 2008, http://online.wsj.com/article/SB121323111102166531.html.

96. Lynch, "U.N. Seeks U.S. Probe of Alleged Misuse of Afghan Aid." He was the director of the U.N. Office for Project Services (UNOPS) in Afghanistan from 2002 to 2006.

97. Lee, "UN Tells Press to Pay $23,000 for Space to Cover It."

98. George Russell, "How Much Discretion? U.N.'s Anti-Poverty Program Wants Unlimited Spending Power," *Fox News*, August 20, 2008, http://www. myfoxlubbock.com/myfox/pages/News/Detail?contentId=7246677&version=1&lo cale=EN-US&layoutCode=TSTY&pageId=3.4.1.

99. UNDP/UNFPA Executive Board, "Compendium of decisions adopted by the Executive Board at its second regular session 2008," (September 8–12 and September 19, 2008, New York), http://www.unfpa.org/exbrd/2008/secondsession/ compendium_decisions.doc

100. Rosett, "Iran Wields the Gavel."

101. Matthew Russell Lee, "UNDP Whitewashing Whistleblower's Claims in Somalia, Resists Backpay and Ethics Office," *Inner City Press*, July 1, 2008, http://www. innercitypress.com/undp2wbsomalia070108.html.

102. Ibid.

103. Bea Edwards and Shelley Walden, "U.N. not so clean anymore," *Citizen Times*, July 12, 2008, http://www.citizen-times.com/apps/pbcs.dll/ article?AID=200880707042. Edwards and Walden work for the Government Accountability Project, which says that it is a "30-year-old nonprofit public interest group that promotes government and corporate accountability by advancing occupational free speech, defending whistleblowers, and empowering citizen activists." www.whistleblower.org.

104. Rosett, "Iran Wields the Gavel."

105. External Investigative Review Panel, *Confidential Report on United Nations Development Programme Activities in the Democratic People's Republic of Korea 1999–2007*, May 31, 2008, http://www.undp.org/dprk/docs/EIIRP_Final_ Report_31%20May.pdf.

106. Ibid.

107. Ibid. The rules are in the UNDP document "Internal Control Framework for UNDP Offices." George Russell, "International Fight at U.N.'s $5 Billion Anti-Poverty Agency over Secrecy," *Fox News*, September 19, 2008, http://www.foxnews. com/story/0,2933,425325,00.html.

108. 108. External Investigative Review Panel, *Confidential Report.*

109. Ibid.

110. Ibid.; Kirkpatrick, "The U.N.'s North Korea Chutzpah."

111. External Investigative Review Panel, *Confidential Report.*

112. Ibid.

113. Russell, "International Fight at U.N.'s $5 Billion Anti-Poverty Agency Over Secrecy."

114. Kirkpatrick, "The U.N.'s North Korea Chutzpah." The subcommittee was the United States Senate Permanent Subcommittee on Investigations of the U.S. Senate Committee on Homeland Security and Governmental Affairs.

115. Rosett, "Iran Wields the Gavel."
116. External Investigative Review Panel, *Confidential Report.*
117. Ibid.
118. Ibid.
119. Ibid.; George Russell, "Report Shows U.N. Development Program Violated U.N. Law, Routinely Passed on Millions to North Korean Regime," *Fox News*, June 12, 2008, http://www.foxnews.com/story/0,2933,365676,00.html.
120. George Russell, "Does the United Nations Accept the Rule of Law?" *Fox News*, July 3, 2008, http://www.foxnews.com/story/0,2933,375668,00.html; Russell, "International Fight at U.N.'s $5 Billion Anti-Poverty Agency over Secrecy"; Rosett, "Iran Wields the Gavel."
121. External Investigative Review Panel, *Confidential Report.*
122. Security Council Resolution 1695 (April 15, 2006) (equipment usable in ballistic missile development), Resolution 1718 (October 14, 2006) (any equipment usable for weapons of mass destruction).
123. Kirkpatrick, "The U.N.'s North Korea Chutzpah."
124. Matthew Russell Lee, "Senate Report Confirms North Korea Errors of UNDP While Letting Wider UN, Kemal Dervis and U.S. Allies Off the Hook," *Inner City Press*, January 23, 2008, http://www.innercitypress.com/sen1usundp012308.html.
125. External Investigative Review Panel, *Confidential Report*; Russell, "Report Shows U.N. Development Program Violated U.N. Law."
126. Rosett, "Iran Wields the Gavel."
127. External Investigative Review Panel, *Confidential Report*; Russell, "Report Shows U.N. Development Program Violated U.N. Law."
128. Russell, "Does the United Nations Accept the Rule of Law?"
129. Benny Avni, "Compensation Urged for U.N. Whistleblower," *New York Sun*, July 2, 2008, http://www.nysun.com/foreign/compensation-urged-for-un-whistle-blower/81082/?print=1174994121; Russell, "Does the United Nations Accept the Rule of Law?"
130. Brett D. Schaefer, "Suspend UNDP Activities in North Korea, Again," Heritage Foundation, WebMemo no. 2387, April 8, 2009, http://www.heritage.org/Research/InternationalOrganizations/wm2387.cfm.
131. George Russell, "Questions Are Raised about Who Profits from UN Aid to North Korea," *FoxNews.com*, July 27, 2009.
132. Russell, "Report Shows U.N. Development Program Violated U.N. Law."
133. Rosett, "Iran Wields the Gavel."
134. Matthew Russell Lee, "UNDP Admits Herfkens Broke Rules, Dodges on Currency Exchange Losses," *Inner City Press*, September 4, 2008, http://www.innercitypress.com/undp1forex090408.html.
135. Matthew Russell Lee, "As UN Admits 25% Loss in Myanmar, Demand for Return of Cash Grows, No UNDP Answers," *Inner City Press*, July 25, 2008, http://www.innercitypress.com/un14myanmar072508.html; George Russell, "US Asked UN about Exchange Rate Issues in Burma Year before Latest Scandal," *Fox News*, August 1, 2008, http://www.foxnews.com/story/0,2933,396143,00.html. For example, as of 2007, one U.S. dollar was worth 1,100 kyat on the open market, but a dollar used to buy a Foreign Exchange Certificate would yield only 880 kyat. The difference very likely went into the pockets of the military dictators and

their business cronies (Thomas Bell, "UN aid disappearing in Burma cash scam," *Telegraph* [London], July 29, 2008, http://www.telegraph.co.uk/news/worldnews/asia/burmamyanmar/2469426/UN-aid-disappearing-in-Burma-cash-scam.html).

136. Russell, "US Asked UN about Exchange Rate Issues."

137. Ibid.; Bell, "UN aid disappearing in Burma cash scam."

138. Russell, "US Asked UN About Exchange Rate Issues."

139. Bell, "UN aid disappearing in Burma cash scam."

140. Matthew Russell Lee, "Leaked Minutes Show UN Knew of 20% Loss in Myanmar 2 Weeks Prior to $300 Million Request," *Inner City Press*, July 28, 2008, http://www.innercitypress.com/fec1myanmar072808.html.

141. Russell, "US Asked UN about Exchange Rate Issues."

142. Ibid.

143. Benny Avni, "Ex-Deputy U.N. Chief Joins with Soros," *New York Sun*, May 7, 2007, http://www.nysun.com/article/53955; "Mark Malloch Brown appointed Vice-Chairman of Soros Fund Management, Open Society Institute," Global Public Policy Institute, May 21, 2007, http://www.gppi.net/news/detail/article/mark-malloch-brown-appointed-vice-chairman-of-soros-fund-management-open-society-institute/. Brown resigned the Quantum Fund position after being appointed to the Foreign and Commonwealth Office ("A new rich friend for Mr Brown," *Observer* [London], September 16, 2007).

144. Rosett, "How Corrupt Is the United Nations?" http://www.commentarymagazine.com/article.asp?aid=12104031_1.

145. "Axis of Soros," *Wall Street Journal*, May 9, 2007, A16.

146. Ibid.

147. Ibid.

148. United Nations Office of Internal Oversight, *Findings Resulting from Oversight Activities of the Oil-for-Food Programme*, OIOS audit report AF03/120/1 (2004). The report was kept in "draft" status, and not officially finalized.

149. Rosett, "How Corrupt Is the United Nations?"

150. Rosett, "Iran Wields the Gavel."

151. United Nations Development Programme, Bureau for Crisis Prevention and Recovery, *How to Guide: Small Arms and Light Weapons Legislation* (Geneva, July 2008). The book's opening page indicates that it is part of an "Advocacy Series" of publications.

152. Ibid, 23.

153. Ibid, 28.

154. Ibid, 35. The guide does caution that its use of "should" must be "understood as suggesting an advised course of action which experience has shown to be effective, rather than indicating any requirement" (Ibid, 3). In other words, the UNDP is not yet claiming that it can legally order governments to adopt repressive gun laws.

155. Ibid, 39.

156. A few examples: United Nations: Ma. Ceres P. Doyo, "Small Arms, Wrong Hands," *Philippine Daily Inquirer*, October 23, 2003 (Annan: "In short, the excessive accumulation and illicit trade of small arms is threatening international peace and security, dashing hopes for social and economic development, and jeopardizing prospects of democracy and human rights"); "Secretary-General Calls for Redoubled Efforts to Curb 'Global Scourge' That Kills 60 People an Hour,

as Biennial Meeting Opens on Small Arms," M2 *Presswire*, July 8, 2003 (Kofi Annan: "Less quantifiable, but no less palpable, were the wider consequences of small arms proliferation, in terms of conflicts fueled, peacekeepers threatened, aid denied, respect for law undermined and development stunted"); *Unless Adequately Addressed, Proliferation of Small Arms, Mercenaries Will Continue to Pose Severe Threat to West Africa, SG Says*, SG/SM/8641 SC/7695 AFR/587, March 18, 2003 (Secretary-General's office: "The uncontrolled proliferation of small arms and light weapons . . . impedes political, economic and social development"); Center for Defense Information, *Weekly Defense Monitor*, February 11, 1999 (quoting Annan: "These weapons [small arms] of personal destruction impair economic and social progress and impede our best development efforts."); United Nations Development Programme, *Development Can Help Curb Small Arms Trade, UNDP Tells UN Conference*, March 19, 2001 (Larry de Boice, Deputy Director of the UNDP Emergency Response Division: "The proliferation of arms . . . will prevent our development objectives from being reached"); IANSA, *Implementing the Programme of Action 2003: Action by States and Civil Society*, 14: ("small arms and light weapons (SALW) . . . escalate and exacerbate conflicts, obstruct achievement of peace and good governance and undermine efforts to promote development"); "Made-in-USA Guns Widely Available in Mexico," *Join Together Online*, October 29, 2003 (Jessica Galeria, Latin American coordinator for IANSA: "Made-in-U.S.A. guns continue to fuel conflicts, exacerbate poverty, and impede development").

157. David B. Kopel, Paul Gallant, and Joanne D. Eisen, "Does the Right to Bear Arms Impede or Promote Economic Development?" *Engage* (journal of the Federalist Society) 6, no. 1 (2005): 85, http://davekopel.org/2A/Foreign/Development.pdf.

158. Matthew Russell Lee, "Myanmar Opposition's Letter to UN Gets Lost in UNDP's Mail, as China Is Missing from Stakeout," *Inner City Press*, March 18, 2008, http://www.innercitypress.com/un2myanmar031808.html.

159. Ibid.

160. Stephen Hull, *Development by Decree: The politics of poverty and control in Karen State*, Karen Human Rights Group, April 2007, http://www.khrg.org/khrg2007/khrg0701.html.

Chapter 11

1. The Convention on the Prevention and Punishment of the Crime of Genocide, 78 U.N.T.S. 277, 102 Stat. 3045, Oct. 9, 1948 (adopted by U.N. General Assembly 1948, entered into force 1951.

2. R. J. Rummel, "Democide Since World War II," http://www.hawaii.edu/powerkills/GENOCIDE.ENCY.HTM; Tables 1–5, http://www.hawaii.edu/powerkills/POSTWWII.TAB.GIF; http://www.hawaii.edu/powerkills/WF.CHAP6.HTM; http://www.hawaii.edu/powerkills/POSTWWII.HTM.

3. Ibid.

4. Ibid.

5. Ibid.

6. Most of the information about Rwanda is from Dore Gold, *Tower of Babble: How the United Nations Has Fueled Global Chaos* (New York: Three Rivers Pr., 2005), 137–54.

7. Jean Hatzfeld, *Machete Season: The Killers in Rwanda Speak*, transl. Linda Coverdale (France, 2003; repr., New York: Farrar, Straus & Giroux, 2005), 177.

8. Ibid., 179.

9. "Report of the Independent Inquiry into the Actions of the United Nations During the 1994 Genocide in Rwanda," December 15, 1999, 6–7, http://www.un.org/Docs/journal/asp/ws.asp?m=S/1999/1257. [Hereinafter cited as "Inquiry into Genocide in Rwanda."]

10. For details see Hatzfeld, *Machete Season.*

11. Ibid., 91.

12. "Inquiry into Genocide in Rwanda."

13. Ibid., 57.

14. Matthew Russell Lee, "At UN's Rwanda Genocide Commemoration, Questions of FDLR, Darfur and UNDP's Mbarushimana," *Inner City Press*, April 7, 2008, http://www.innercitypress.com/un1rwanda040708.html.

15. Joseph A. Klein, *Global Deception: The UN's Stealth Assault on America's Freedom* (L.A.: World Ahead Pub., 2005), 30, citing Associated Press, "Kofi Annan Was Aware of Tutsis' Peril," *Pioneer Press*, May 4, 1998, http://geocities.com/CapitolHill/Lobby/4621/rwanda1.html.

16. Thalif Deen, "UN Declares War on Small Arms," *Asia Times*, October 1, 2002.

17. U.N. Resolution 713, September 25, 1991, http://www.cco.caltech.edu/~bosnia/natoun/unres713.html.

18. U.N. Charter, art. 51 ("Nothing in the present Charter shall impair the inherent right of individual or collective self-defence if an armed attack occurs against a Member of the United Nation").

19. "The promise made by UN general Morillon in 1993 to the people of Srebrenica that they were under the protection of the UN and would not be abandoned . . . The proclamation of the zone as a safe area created an illusion of security for the population" (*Summary for the Press*, an authorized summary of the conclusions from the epilogue of the main report *Srebrenica, a 'Safe' Area—Reconstruction, Background, Consequences and Analyses of the Fall of a Safe Area*, http://www.srebrenica.nl/en/content_perssamenvatting.htm.

20. Report of the Secretary-General Pursuant to General Assembly Resolution 53/35 (1998): Srebrenica Report, November 30, 1998, http://www.haverford.edu/relg/sells/reports/Unsrebrenicareport.htm.

21. U.N. Resolution 819, S/RES/819 (Apr. 16, 1993), http://gopher.undp.org/00/undocs/scd/scouncil/s93/20.

22. *Srebrenica: A Cry from the Grave*, WNET Television (New York City), www.pbs.org/wnet/cryfromthegrave.

23. For a history of the case, which has been before the ICJ in various settings ever since 1993, see http://www.icj-cij.org/icjwww/ipresscom/ipress2004/ipresscom2004-37_bhy_20041208.htm.

24. *Application of the Convention on the Prevention and Punishment of the Crime of Genocide (Bosnia & Herzegovina v. Yugoslavia (Serbia and Montenegro)*, 1993 I.C.J. 3 (Request for the Indication of Provisional Measures Order of April 8) (hereinafter *Bosnia v. Yugoslavia*).

25. Ibid., at 438.

26. Ibid. at 439–44.

27. Ibid. at 501. Craig Scott, "A Memorial for Bosnia: Framework of Legal Arguments Concerning the Lawfulness of the Maintenance of the United Nations Security Council's Arms Embargo on Bosnia and Hercegovina," 16 *Michigan Journal of International Law* 1 (1994).

28. Geraldine Coughlan, "Dutch Felt Srebrenica 'not worth sacrifice,'" BBC News, December 6, 2002.

29. Gold, *Tower of Babble*, 169.

30. "The 10,000 to 15,000 men gathered in Šušnjari's moonlit fields knew the stakes couldn't be any higher. Only one-third of them were armed. The first groups to leave would have the best chance of survival. The last ones would face Serb troops who could pick and choose when to ambush the Muslims they'd seen coming for days . . . At midnight, the lead scouts in the column slipped out of the enclave. What would become known as the 'Marathon of Death' had begun" (David Rohde, *Endgame: The Betrayal and Fall of Srebrenica* [1997], 179–80. See also Mike O'Connor, "Bosnian Men Tell of Survival Deep in Serb Territory," *New York Times*, April 9, 1996).

31. Laura Silber and Allan Little, *Yugoslavia: Death of a Nation* (New York: Penguin, repr. ed. 1997), 345, 349–50.

32. William Drozdiak, "Milosevic to Stand Trial for Genocide," *Washington Post*, November 24, 2001.

33. "Security Council Decides on Phased Lifting of Arms Embargo against Former Yugoslavia by Vote of 14 to None, with Russian Federation Abstaining," UN Press Release SC/6127, November 27, 1995, http://www.un.org//News/Press/docs/1995/19951122.sc6127.html.

34. Drozdiak, "Milosevic to Stand Trial for Genocide."

35. UN Press Release, August 2, 2001, http://www.un.org/icty/pressreal/p609-e.htm.

36. *Srebrenica: Reconstruction, Background, Consequences and Analyses of the Fall of a Safe Area, Netherlands Institute for War Documentation*, April 10, 2002, http://194.134.65.22/srebrenica. No longer accessible.

37. Convention on the Prevention and Punishment of the Crime of Genocide, adopted by Resolution 260 (III)A of the U.N. General Assembly (December 9, 1948).

38. *American College Dictionary* (Random House, 1967 ed.).

39. Case Study: The Srebrenica Massacre, July 1995, Gendercide Watch, http://www.gendercide.org/case_srebrenica.html.

40. Report of the Secretary-General Pursuant to General Assembly Resolution 53/35 (1998) Srebrenica Report, ¶¶ 503–4, http://www.haverford.edu/relg/sells/reports/UNsrebrenicareport.htm.

41. "Dutch court agrees UN has immunity in Srebrenica massacre claim," Agence-France Press, July 10, 2008, http://afp.google.com/article/ALeqM5glExJfzoYz5GAffRrDpoE8jnKRRw; "Survivors of Srebrenica massacre seek damages from UN, Netherlands," Canadian Press, June 18, 2008, http://canadianpress.google.com/article/ALeqM5hEiK59W0LsQWZDaGiYE_XnQsStrw; "Dutch Court to Hear Case on Srebrenica Massacre," Deutsche Welle, June 16, 2008, http://www.dw-world.de/dw/article/0,2144,3415139,00.html; Alexandra Hudson and Daria Sito-Sucic, "Dutch court rules Srebrenica families can sue U.N.," Reuters, November 27, 2007, http://www.reuters.com/

article/worldNews/idUSL2712448720071127?sp=true; Matthew Russell Lee, "On Genocide, UN Cites Immunity to Srebrenica Claims, Lack of Jurisdiction Over Peacekeepers," *Inner City Press*, June 26, 2008, http://www.innercitypress.com/un1srebrenica062608.html.

42. Aida Cerkez-Robinson, "Srebrenica Massacre Memorial to Point Finger at UN," Yahoo News, July 10, 2010.

43. John G. Taylor, *East Timor: The Price of Freedom* (London: Zed Books, 1999), 154.

44. Ibid., 158–60.

45. Charles Scheiner, speech at "Guns Know No Borders" rally, July 17, 2001, Dag Hammarskjold Plaza, New York, http://www.pcug.org.au/~wildwood/01julguns.htm.

46. Andrew Latham, "Light Weapons and Human Security—A Conceptual Overview," *Small Arms Control: Old Weapons, New Issues*, eds. Jayantha Dhanapala, et al) (UK: United Nations Institute for Disarmament Research, 1999), 13–14; http://www.unog.ch/unidir/.

47. Letter by James F. Dunnigan to Paul Gallant and Joanne D. Eisen, February 23, 2002, quoted in David B. Kopel, Paul Gallant, and Joanne D. Eisen, "Firearms Possession by 'Non-State Actors': The Question of Sovereignty," *Texas Review of Law and Politics* 8 (2004): 373, 389, http://davekopel.org/2A/LawRev/Non-state-actors.pdf.

48. Michael Wagner, "Army in the Way of Freedom," *Sydney Morning Herald*, April 29, 1999.

49. Jonathan Head, "Militia Terror in Timor," BBC News, July 10, 1999.

50. Ibid.

51. UN Press Release SG/SM/6966, April 23, 1999, http:..srch1.un.org/plweb-cgi/fastweb?state_id=1014054694&view=unsearch&numhitsfound=1&query=SG/SM/6966&&docid=581&docdb=pr1999&dbname=web&sorting=BYRELEVANCE&operator=adj&TemplateName=predoc.tmpl&setCookie=1.

52. UN Press Release SG/SM/6980, May 6, 1999, http://srch1.un.org/plweb-cgi/fastweb?state_id=1014054353&view=unsearch&numhitsfound=1&query=SG/SM/6980&&docid=671&docdb=pr1999&dbname=web&sorting=BYRELEVANCE&operator=adj&TemplateName=predoc.tmpl&setCookie=1.

53. Kopel, et al., "Non-State Actors," 391.

54. UN Report of the Secretary General: Question of East Timor, S/1999/862, August 9, 1999, http://srch1.un.org/plweb-cgi/fastweb?state_id=1014054432&view=unsearch&docrank=1&numhitsfound=5&query=S/1999/862&&docid=97&docdb=screports&dbname=web&sorting=BYRELEVANCE&operator=adj&TemplateName=predoc.tmpl&setCookie=1

55. UN Resolution 1246, S/Res/1246 (1999), June 11, 1999, http;//srch1.un.org/plweb-cgi/fastweb?state_id=1014054536&view=unsearch&numhitsfound=1&query=S/RES/1246(1999)&&docid=371&docdb=scres&dbname=web&sorting=BYRELEVANCE&operator=adj&TemplateName=predoc.tmpl&setCookie=1

56. Mark Dodd, "Fears of Bloodbath Grow as Militias Stockpile Arms," *Sydney Morning Herald*, July 16, 1999, 9.

57. According to UNAMET, 98.6 percent of registered voters did so (Taylor, *East Timor*, 228).

58. Janine de Giovanni, "East Timor's Aftermath," *New York Times*, October 24, 1999.

59. Kopel, et al., "Non-State Actors," 392.

60. Seth Mydans, "East Timorese, First Wary, Then Jubilant, Greet U.N. Troops in Village Near Capital" *New York Times*, September 22, 1999.

61. Barbara Frey, "Progress report on the prevention of human rights violations committed with small arms and light weapons," E/CN.4/Sub.2/2004/37 (2004), ¶ 50, http://www1.umn.edu/humanrts/demo/smallarms2004-2.html.

62. Paul Daley, "Falintil Resists Move to Give Up Weapons," *The Age* (Melbourne, Australia), October 6, 1999, 13.

63. Mark Dodd, "Cosgrove Sees Falintil as a Legal Police Force," *Sydney Morning Herald*, December 2, 1999, 10.

64. Mark Dodd, "Viva the Defence Force: Guerilla Veterans Join the Army," *Sydney Morning Herald*, February 2, 2001, 8.

65. http://www.un.org/peace/etimor/untaetR/reg00105E.pdf.

66. "UN forces labeled 'cowards' by Ramos-Horta's brother," *ABC News*, February 14, 2008, http://www.abc.net.au/news/stories/2008/02/14/2163293.htm?section=world.

67. Eric Reeves, "Darfur: Genocide Before Our Eyes," in *Darfur: Genocide Before Our Eyes*, ed., Joyce Apsel (New York: Institute for the Study of Genocide, 2005), 29.

68. Alex de Wall, "Counter-Insurgency on the Cheap," *London Review of Books*, August 5, 2004, http://www.lrb.co.uk/v26/n15/waal01_.html.

69. Jay Nordlinger, "About Sudan," *National Review*, May 23, 2005, 39.

70. Scott Straus, "What's in a Name?" *Foreign Affairs* 84 (January–February 2005): 123; *Darfur Rising: Sudan's New Crisis*, International Crisis Group, Africa Report no. 76, March 25, 2004, http://www.crisisweb.org/home/getfile.cfm?id=1132&tid=2550, 18–19:

> The SLA drew its first recruits from Fur self-defence militias that had arisen during the 1987–1989 conflict. The emergence in 2001 of a group of largely Fur and Massaleit fighters in southern and western Darfur coincided with the decision of Zaghawa young men to rebel against the government. The Zaghawa insurgents were unhappy about the government's failure to enforce the terms of a tribal peace agreement requiring nomads of Arab background to pay blood money for killing dozens of Zaghawas, including prominent tribal chiefs. The SLA grew out of this increased cooperation between the Fur, Massaleit and Zaghawa groups. "Massaleit" is spelled in a variety of ways depending on the author.

71. *Targeting the Fur: Mass Killings in Darfur*, Human Rights Watch Paper, Jan. 21, 2005, hrw.org/backgrounder/africa/darfur0105/darfur0105.pdf, at 6.

72. Stuart Taylor, "Genocide in Darfur: Crime without Punishment?" *National Journal*, February 21, 2005; U.S. State Department Pub. 11182, September 2004, http://www.state.gov/g/drl/rls/36028.htm ("The UN estimates the violence has affected 2.2 million of Darfur's 6 million residents"); Jonathan Karl, "The Darfur Disaster," *Weekly Standard*, May 2, 2005; Eric Reeves, "Who Is Dying?" *New Republic Online*, July 20, 2005, http://www.tnr.com/etc.mhtml?pid=2732.

73. Roger Sandall, "Can Sudan be Saved?" *Commentary*, December 2004, 38. Although "Janjaweed" is the more common term, "Jajaweed" is also used.

74. "Sudan 'bombing Darfur villages,'" BBC News, January 27, 2005 ("The Sudanese air force has bombed villages in Darfur despite agreeing to stop using planes in the war-torn region, aid agencies say").

75. *Sudan: Arming the Perpetrators of Grave Abuses in Darfur*, Amnesty International, November 16, 2004, ¶ 8, http://web.amnesty.org/library/index/engafr541392004. The president of the JEM, Khalil Ibrahim stated: "About 90% of our armament comes from what we have captured from Sudanese army barracks." However, arms are readily available to them from other opposition groups. (Ibid.)

76. Ibid., ¶ 4.1. See also "Sudan—Darfur in Flames: Atrocities in Western Sudan," *Human Rights Watch* 16, no. 5 (April 2004): 19 ("Clearly there was SLA presence in certain villages, which provides military justification for the use of force, however the use of force must be proportional . . . to the expected military gain"); *Darfur Rising: Sudan's New Crisis*, International Crisis Group, Africa Report no. 76, March 25, 2004, http://www.crisisweb.org/home/getfile.cfm?id=1132&tid=2550.

77. Straus. "What's in a Name?"

78. "New Clashes Break out in Darfur," BBC News, July 25, 2005 ("Last week, the commander of the African Union peacekeeping force in Darfur, Festus Okonkwo, told the BBC that there had been no major attacks in the region since January and that there had also been a reduction in attacks on villages. But US aid official Andrew Natsios said this was chiefly because there were no villages left to burn down").

79. *Sudan: Arming the Perpetrators of Grave Abuses in Darfur*, ¶ 4.1.

80. *Sudan—Darfur in Flames*. The Human Rights Watch report also noted:

> In yet another telling example of the government's refusal to provide security for civilians, a number of tribal leaders of the Fur, Zaghawa and Masaalit communities reportedly made repeated attempts to inform government authorities of the grave abuses taking place. They appealed to the highest levels of government in Khartoum. They presented documented cases of violations, with no response. In at least one case, the Sudanese government warned the Darfurian representative to stop his appeals.
>
> Jan Pronk, the UN secretary-general's special representative for Sudan stated: "Those responsible for atrocious crimes on a massive scale go unpunished . . . The government has not stopped them." See generally, *Targeting the Fur: Mass Killings in Darfur*, A Human Rights Watch Paper, January 21, 2005, http://hrw.org/backgrounder/africa/darfur0105/darfur0105.pdf. (Summary: "To date, the Sudanese government has neither improved security for civilians nor ended the impunity enjoyed by its own officials and allied militia leaders.")

81. Judy Aita, *Brutal Attacks Still Occurring in Darfur, United Nations Reports*, States news Service (Wash., May 12, 2005).

82. Eric Reeves, "Darfur Mortality Update: April 30, 2005," *Sudan Tribune*, May 1, 2005.

83. "Sudan: Arms Trade Fuelling Human Rights Abuse in Darfur," Amnesty International Press Release, November 16, 2004, http://web.amnesty.org/library/index/engafr541422004. Egeland made the statement on July 1, 2004.

84. Ibid.

85. S/Res./1556, U.N. SCOR, July 30, 2004, ¶7, http://www.un.org/News/Press/docs/2004/sc8160.doc.htm.

86. *Sudan: Arming the Perpetrators of Grave Abuses in Darfur*. The Amnesty report additionally notes that "oil now accounts for more than 11% of Sudan's Gross Domestic Product (GDP)" (ibid., ¶ 9.1). Furthermore, the report noted: "Sudan's oil wealth has played a major part in enabling an otherwise poor country to fund the expensive bombers, helicopters and arms supplies which have allowed the Sudanese government to launch aerial attacks on towns and villages and fund militias to fight its proxy war" (ibid., ¶ 9.2).

87. Ibid., ¶ 6.

88. Catherine Flew and Angus Urquhart, *Strengthening Small Arms Controls: An Audit of Small Arms Control in the Great Lakes Region and the Horn of Africa,* Safer Africa and Saferworld, February 2004, http://www.saferworld.co.uk/publications/Horn%20narrative%20report.pdf.

89. U.S. State Dept. Pub. 11182, September 2004, http://www.state.gov/g/drl/rls/36028.htm.

Peter Verney, editor of London-based *Sudan Update*, describes "the government policy of selectively arming tribesmen while removing the weapons of the farmers, the Fur, Masalit and Zaghawa." Moreover, "Since 2001, Darfur has been governed under central government decree, with special courts to try people suspected of illegal possession or smuggling of weapons, murder and armed robbery. The security forces have misused these powers for arbitrary and indefinite detention" (Peter Verney, "Darfur's Manmade Disaster," *Middle East Report Online*, July 22, 2004, http://www.merip.org/mero/mero072204.html). See also *Sudan: Arming the Perpetrators of Grave Abuses in Darfur*, ¶ 2 ("Special Courts set up under a state of emergency declared in Darfur in 2001 . . . have been handing down summary justice after flagrantly unfair trials").

90. See generally *Sudan: Arming the Perpetrators*. See also *Armed Conflicts Report 2004*, Project Ploughshares, Sudan-Darfur, January 2004, http://www.ploughshares.ca/content/ACR/ACR00/ACR00-SudanDarfur.html ("The Jajaweed and other Arab militias are alleged to have been armed by the Sudanese government, previously in order to fight against the Sudan People's Liberation Army (SPLA), and recently to engage non-Arab populations in Darfur"); Verney, "Darfur's Manmade Disaster," ("One directive from February 2004, evoking the authority of President Omar Bashir, calls upon Darfur security heads to step up 'the process of mobilizing loyalist tribes and providing them with sufficient armory to secure the areas'").

91. *Targeting the Fur: Mass Killings in Darfur*, A Human Rights Watch Paper, January 21, 2005, http://hrw.org/backgrounder/africa/darfur0105/darfur0105.pdf, at 22. (Among the recommendations of Human Rights Watch was that the government of Sudan "clearly and unequivocally state that no one is entitled to retain or use any land illegally acquired during the conflict. A temporary measure interdicting any permanent land transfers should also be put in place.") See generally, *Sudan: Darfur: Rape as a Weapon of War: Sexual Violence and Its Consequences*, Amnesty International, AI Index: AFR 54/076/2004, July 19, 2004, http://web.amnesty.org/library/index/engafr540762004.

92. *Sudan: Arming the Perpetrators*, ¶ 6.2.

93. Ibid.

94. *Targeting the Fur*, 8.

95. Dimitri Vassilaros, "Gun Control's Best Friend," *Pittsburgh Tribune-Review*, April 1, 2005. The official was Bill Garvelink, acting assistant administrator of the Bureau for Democracy, Conflict, and Humanitarian Development, which is part of the U.S. Agency for International Development.

96. The official was Trish Katyoka, director of Africa Advocacy for Amnesty International. Unlike many other human rights groups, Amnesty International has never officially used the word "genocide" to describe the Darfur situation.

97. Reeves, "Darfur: Genocide Before Our Eyes."

98. Ibid., 37.

99. Ibid., 46.

100. Ibid., 45.

101. Eric Reeves, "Khartoum Triumphant: Managing the Costs of Genocide in Darfur," December 17, 2005, http://www.sudanreeves.org/index.php?name=News&file=article&sid=81.

102. "A Working Formula for Arms Management and Reduction," in *Small Arms and Lights Weapons: Legal Aspects of National and International Regulations*; vol. 4 *Arms Control and Disarmament Law*, eds., Erwin Dahinden, Julie Dahlitz and Nadia Fischer (Geneva: United Nations, 2002) (sales no. G.V.E.02.0.4), 145; emphasis added.

103. Louis Charbonneau, "Darfur is now a 'low-intensity conflict': U.N," Reuters, April 27, 2009, http://www.reuters.com/article/worldNews/idUSTRE53Q4LR20090427.

104. Lydia Polgreen, "Peacekeeping in Darfur Hits More Obstacles," *New York Times*, March 24, 2008.

105. "The score at half-time: Ban Ki-moon has turned in a mixed performance so far. He needs to improve," *Economist*, June 11, 2009, http://www.economist.com/world/international/displaystory.cfm?story_id=13825201.

106. Matthew Russell Lee, "As Sudan Expels UN Officials from Darfur for Rape Detection, UN Silent, Menkorios One Year & Out, Gration's Khartoum Jaunt," *Inner City Press*, August 18, 2010, http://www.innercitypress.com/ossg2sudan081810.html.

107. Dave Kopel, Paul Gallant, and Joanne Eisen, "Ripe for Genocide," *National Review Online*, February 13, 2001, http://davekopel.org/NRO/2001/Ripe-for-Genocide.htm.

108. Brian Kagoro, "The Prisoners of Hope: Civil Society and the Opposition in Zimbabwe," *African Security Review* 14, no. 3 (2005): 19, 22.

109. David Blair, "Pressure Mounts for Mugabe to Quit," *Telegraph* (London), February 18, 2000.

110. David Blair, "Court Rules Mugabe's Land Grab Is Illegal," *Telegraph* (London), November 11, 2000; David Blair, "Farm Grab Is Noble Effort, Says Mugabe," *Telegraph* (London), August 12, 2000.

111. Abel Mutsakani, "Govt Arms War Vets," *Financial Gazette*, January 1, 2001.

112. Anton LaGuardia, "There's No Room for Whites Here, Says 'Hitler' Hunzvi," *Telegraph* (London), April 8, 2000.

113. "Zimbabwe youth militias accused of holding women as sex slaves," *Los Angeles Times*, July 7, 2008.

114. Roger Bate, American Enterprise Institute, "Life Is Too Short Here to Worry about HIV," *Tech Central Station*, March 11, 2005, http://www.aei.org/article/22116.

115. R.W. Johnson, "Millions missing, but UN ignores Zimbabwe's quiet genocide," *The Australian*, January 8, 2007 (reprinting article from the Sunday Times, London), http://www.theaustralian.news.com.au/story/0,20867,21025366-2703,00.html.

116. Donna Dees-Thomases and Alison Hendrie, *Looking for a Few Good Moms: How One Mother Rallied a Million Others against the Gun Lobby* (Emmaus, PA: Rodale, 2004), 75.

117. "Harare compels public to surrender their guns," ZimOnline (South Africa), June 30, 2005, http://www.zwnews.com/issuefull.cfm?ArticleID=12207 ("At the peak of its chaotic and often violent farm seizure programme in 2000, the government issued a decree compelling civilians to surrender their guns. The move was targeted at white commercial farmers who at that time held a number of assault guns for self-protection").

118. David Blair, "Police Search Beseiged Farms for Guns," *Telegraph* (London), April 18, 2000.

119. Mutsakani, "Govt Arms War Vets."

120. Kopel, et al., "Firearms Possession by 'Non-State Actors,'" http://davekopel. org/2A/LawRev/Non-state-actors.pdf (e-mail from the farmer to one of the authors).

121. *Strategy Page* (November 19, 2003)(no title), http://www.strategypage.com/qnd/ pothot/articles/20031119.aspx.

122. Brett D. Schaefer and Marian L. Tupy, "Africa's Zimbabwe Problem: Why do African nations line up in support of such a disreputable nation?" *National Review*, May 24, 2007, http://article.nationalreview.com/print/?q=MzYyOGFjZTkwODJh ZGY4NjMxZWI5YTkwNjgzYThkOGU. Gratwicke's website is zimconservation. com/.

123. Radio VOP, "Ministers and Senior Government Officers Involved in Rhino Poaching," *The Zimbabwean* (UK), September 3, 2009, http://www. thezimbabwean.co.uk/2009090324153/weekday-top-stories/ministers-and-senior-government-officers-involved-in-rhino-poaching.html.

124. "Harare compels public to surrender their guns."

125. Schaefer and Tupy, "Africa's Zimbabwe Problem."

126. Colum Lynch, "Another One Bites the Dust," *Foreign Policy*, August 20, 2010, http://turtlebay.foreignpolicy.com/posts/2010/08/20/another_one_bites_the_dust.

127. "Millions missing, but UN ignores Zimbabwe's quiet genocide."

128. Ibid.

129. Schaefer and Tupy, "Africa's Zimbabwe Problem."

130. "Zimbabwe vows to block Western efforts at UN Security Council," Agence France Presse, December 15, 2008, http://www.google.com/hostednews/afp/article/ ALeqM5iPIr7GbrfGwCugGme-JYul4on1XA.

131. Anne Applebaum, "Robert Mugabe's Roman holiday highlights the United Nations' ineffectiveness," *Slate*, June 3, 2008, http://www.slate.com/id/2192718/; Joseph Klein, "Moral Poverty at the UN," *FrontPage Magazine*, June 9, 2008, http://frontpagemagazine.com/Articles/Read.aspx?GUID=681BDC29-ACBB-49D7-80DA-A65E6EB5478E.

132. Matthew Russell Lee, "At UN, Re-Sale of AIDS Drugs and Zimbabwe Diversions Downplayed, as Ban Met Mugabe," *Inner City Press*, December 1, 2008, http://www.innercitypress.com/un2aids120108.html.

133. Schaefer and Tupy, "Africa's Zimbabwe Problem."

134. Ibid.

135. Claudia Rosett, "Call It the U.N. Commission on Sustainable Dictatorships: Business as usual as Zimbabwe takes a seat," *National Review*, May 13, 2007, http://article.nationalreview.com/?q=YjRiNzRjOTVhZjZiNTkzMDhkYzAwNTVmZGJkZmNlMWQ=.

136. Tracy McVeigh, "Fury at Zimbabwe UN role: West outraged as African nations help elect key minister to head environmental body," *Guardian* (London), May 13, 2007, http://observer.guardian.co.uk/world/story/0,,2078488,00.html.

137. Ibid.

138. Schaefer and Tupy, "Africa's Zimbabwe Problem."

139. Ibid.

140. Ibid.

141. "Mugabe's presence at UN food summit 'obscene': Australia," *Agence France Presse*, June 1, 2008, afp.google.com/article/ALeqM5jV0AtOAzpcD1-066wrGXd03oRX5w.

142. Klein, "Moral Poverty at the UN."

143. Colum Lynch, "South Africa's U.N. Votes Disappoint Some," *Washington Post*, April 16, 2007, http:www.washingtonpost.com/wp-dyn/content/article/2007/04/15/AR2007041500996.html.

144. Ibid.

145. "The score at half-time," *Economist*.

146. Colonel T.J. Dube, the chief delegate of Zimbabwe on Arms Control. For Dube's career as an arms smuggler, see "Duped by Zimbabwe," *Sunday Times* (Sri Lanka), September 6, 1998, http://www.sundaytimes.lk/980906/spec.html; Raymond Bonner, "Rebels in Sri Lanka Fight with Aid of Global Market in Light Arms," *New York Times*, March 7, 1998 (Dube's role taking money for arms smuggling to Sri Lanka, but never delivering the arms); Brian Wood, "The Prevention of Illicit Brokering of Small Arms and Light Weapons: Framing the Issue," in *Developing a Mechanism to Prevent Illicit Brokering in Small Arms and Light Weapons—Scope and Implications* (New York: United Nations Institute for Disarmament Research (UNIDIR), 2007), 4–5, http://www.unidir.org/pdf/articles/pdf-art2590.pdf; David Pallister, "Murky tale of a mercenary adventure: Speculation grows as Equatorial Guinea claims plot to kill president was foiled," *Guardian* (London), March 13, 2004; Erika Gibson, "Op pad na 'n staatsgreep: SA huursoldate se bestemming was glo land in Wes-Afrika," *Beeld* (South Africa), March 10, 2004, at 1, http://152.111.1.88/argief/berigte/beeld/2004/03/10/B1/01/02.html (Dube's role in arms smuggling to Equatorial Guinea for a coup); Mduduzi Mathuthu, "South Africa, Zimbabwe trained 'mercenaries'," *New Zimbabwe*, March 9, 2004, http://www.zimbabwesituation.com/mar10_2004.html#link2.

147. Speech of Zimbabwe at the Conference to Review Progress Made in the Implementation of the Programme of Action to Prevent, Combat and Eradicate the Illicit Trade in Small Arms and Light Weapons in All Its Aspects, presented by the chief delegate of Zimbabwe on Arms Control, Col. T. J. Dube, June 26–July 7, 2006, New York.

Chapter 12

1. Nairobi Secretariat on Small Arms, The Nairobi Protocol for the Prevention, Control and Reduction of Small Arms and Light Weapons in the Great Lakes Region and the Horn of Africa (Nairobi, Kenya). See also Ramazani Baya, Minister of Foreign Affairs and International Cooperation Democratic Republic of the Congo, "Editorial," *Progress* (June 2005), 1 (newsletter of the Nairobi Secretariat, Saferworld, and the Security Research and Information Centre).
2. Nairobi Protocol, art. 23.
3. Ibid., art. 3(c)
4. Ibid., arts. 5(b)(i), 9, 12, 13
5. Protocol on the Control of Firearms, Ammunition and Other Related Materials in the Southern African Development Community (SADC) Region.
6. The nations are Angola, Botswana, Congo, Lesotho, Malawi, Mauritius, Mozambique, Namibia, Seychelles, South Africa, Swaziland, Tanzania, Zambia, and Zimbabwe. One measure of corruption is the Corruption Perception Index compiled every year by Transparency International. Using objective criteria, nations are rated on a scale from 1 to 10, with 10 being the least corrupt. In the 2009 CPI, New Zealand scored at the top, with a 9.4 rating; the United States was 19th [[stet numerals]], with a 7.5. In sub-Saharan Africa (the target of the U.N. antigun regional treaties), the highest scores were Botswana (5.6), Mauritius (5.4), Seychelles (4.8), South Africa (4.7), and Namibia (4.0). Every other country in sub-Saharan Africa was below 4.0, indicating extreme and pervasive corruption. The 2009 survey is available at http://www.transparency.org/.
7. David B. Kopel, Paul Gallant and Joanne D. Eisen Microdisarmament: The Consequences for Public Safety and Human Rights," *UMKC Law Review* 73 (2005): 969, 1003–9 (Mali), http://www.davekopel.com/2A/Foreign/MicroDisarmament.pdf; David B. Kopel, "U.N. Gives Tyranny a Hand," *National Review Online*, August 6, 2001 (Niger), http://www.nationalreview.com/kopel/kopel080601.shtml.
8. Mark Huband, "Liberia," Crimes of War website, http://www.crimesofwar.org/thebook/liberia.html.
9. Haruna Bahago, "Don't Turn Other Cheek, Says Nigerian Archbishop," *Independent* (London), November 29, 2002 (Associated Press).
10. Dennis C. Jett, *Why Peacekeeping Fails* (Palgrave Macmillan, 2001), xii.
11. Kenneth Roth, *International Injustice: The Tragedy of Sierra Leone*, Human Rights Watch, http://www.hrw.org/editorials/2000/ken-sl-aug.htm.
12. The report is available at http://www.freedomhouse.org/uploads/fiw09/FIW09_Tables&GraphsForWeb.pdf. Free: Benin, Botswana, Cape Verde, Ghana, Mali, Mauritius, Namibia, South Africa. Partly free: Burkina Faso, Burundi, Central African Republic, Djibouti, Ethiopia, Gabon, the Gambia, Guinea-Bissau, Kenya, Lesotho, Liberia, Madagascar, Malawi, Mozambique, Niger, Nigeria, Seychelles, Sierre Leone, Senegal, Tanzania, Togo, Uganda, Zambia. Not Free: Angola, Brunei, Cameroon, Chad, Congo (Brazzaville), Cote d'Ivoire, Democratic Republic of the Congo (Kinshasa), Equatorial Guinea, Eritrea, Guinea, Mauritania, Rwanda, Somalia, Sudan, Swaziland, Zimbabwe.

13. The Convention on the Prevention and Punishment of the Crime of Genocide, 78 U.N.T.S. 277, 102 Stat. 3045, October 9, 1948 (adopted by U.N. General Assembly 1948, entered into force 1951, ratified by United States 1981).

14. Genocide Convention, art. I (emphasis added). The affirmative duty is consistent with the long-established duty in Jewish law and in Napoleonic Codes for an individual to act to rescue another person in danger. E.g., Code Pénal, art. 434-1 (France); David B. Kopel. "The Torah and Self-Defense," *Penn State Law Review* 17 (2004): 109, http:// www.davekopel.com/2A/LawRev/The-Torah-and-Self-defense.pdf.

15. *Application of the Convention on the Prevention and Punishment of the Crime of Genocide (Bosnia and Hercegovina v. Yugoslavia [Serbia and Montenegro], Further Requests for the Indication of Provisional Measures,* I.C.J. Reports 325, 443–44 (September 13, 1993) (Lauterpacht, J.).

16. *Prosecutor v. Akayesu* (Case No. ICTR-96-4-T), Judgment 2, September 1998, ¶ 731.

17. William A. Schabas, *Genocide in International Law* (Cambridge University Press: 2000), 170–71, citing *United States of America v. von Weizaecker et al.* ("Ministeries Case"), 14 T.W.C. 314, 557–58 (United States Military Tribunal, 1948) (government cuts in special food rations applied only to Jews, and not to general German population, but cuts were not a form of genocide, because they were not so severe as to cause sickness or death).

18. Notably, the Genocide Convention abrogates the head of state immunity, which applies in most other applications of international law (Genocide Convention, art. IV; *A-G Israel v. Eichmann,* 36 I.L.R. 18, ¶ 28 [Dist. Ct., Jerusalem, 1968]; *A-G Israel v. Eichmann,* 36 I.L.R. 277, ¶ 14 [S. Ct. 1968]; *Prosecutor v. Blaskic* [Case No. IT-95-14-AR108*bis*], *Judgment on the Request of the Republic of Croatia for Review of the Decision of Trial Chamber II of July 18, 1997,* ¶ 41 [October 29, 1997]; Schabas, 316). Given that the Genocide Convention explicitly abrogates one of the most well-established principles of general international law, it would hardly be surprising that the Convention also abrogates, by implication, some forms of ordinary internal state authority, such as the power to set standards for food rations, medical rations, or arms possession.

19. Universal Declaration of Human Rights, G.A. Res. 217 A (III), U.N. Doc A/810, art. 3.

20. Ibid.; International Covenant on Civil and Political Rights, 999 U.N.T.S. 171, 1976, art. 6; Convention for the Protection of Human Rights and Fundamental Freedoms, 213 U.N.T.S. 221, E.T.S. 5, 1955, art. 2; American Convention on Human Rights, 1144 U.N.T.S. 123; O.A.S.T.S. 36, 1979, art. 4.

21. Universal Declaration, art. 3.

22. Convention for the Protection of Human Rights and Fundamental Freedoms, 213 U.N.T.S. 221, E.T.S. 5, 1955), art. 2 (2); Gilbert Guillaume, "Article 2," in Louis-Edmond Pettiti, Emmanuel Decaux, and Pierre-Henri Imbert, *La Convention Européenne des Droits de l'Homme: Commentaire Article par Article 152* (Paris: Economica, 2d ed. 1999). See also M. Cherif Bassiouni, *A Draft International Criminal Code and Draft Statute for an International Criminal Tribunal* (Boston: Martinus Nijhoff, 1987), 109–10 (right to self-defense recognized in model code written by leading scholar of international criminal and human rights law, who serves as president of the International Human Rights Law Institute, as president of the International Institute of Higher Studies in Criminal Sciences, and as president of the International Association of Penal Law).

23. Rome Statute of the International Criminal Court, U.N. Doc. A/CONF.183/9, art. 31.

24. Universal Declaration of Human Rights.

25. Johannes Morsink, *The Universal Declaration of Human Rights: Origins, Drafting & Intent* (University of Pennsylvania Press: 1999), 307–12.

26. Ibid.

27. Compare *Bivens v. Six Unknown Named Agents of the Federal Bureau of Narcotics*, 403 U.S. 388 (1971) ("where federally protected rights have been invaded, it has been the rule from the beginning that courts would be alert to adjust their remedies so as to grant the necessary relief").

28. The rights in the Universal Declaration's Articles 1–3, including the right to armed self-defense as a last-resort defense of other rights, clearly belong to individuals:

    Article 1. All human beings are born free and equal in dignity and rights. They are endowed with reason and conscience and should act towards one another in a spirit of brotherhood.

    Article 2. Everyone is entitled to all the rights and freedoms set forth in this Declaration, without distinction of any kind, such as race, colour, sex, language, religion, political or other opinion, national or social origin, property, birth or other status. Furthermore, no distinction shall be made on the basis of the political, jurisdictional or international status of the country or territory to which a person belongs, whether it be independent, trust, non-self-governing or under any other limitation of sovereignty.

    Article 3. Everyone has the right to life, liberty and security of person.

29. United States v. Cruikshank, 92 U.S. 542, 551–53 (1875) (quoting *Gibbons v. Ogden*, 22 U.S. 1, 211 (1824)). The "civilized man" quote comes from the Court's discussion of the right to assemble; the right to arms discussion follows immediately, and adopts the same reasoning as the right to assembly analysis. For a more detailed analysis of *Cruikshank*, see David B. Kopel, "The Supreme Court's Thirty-Five Other Second Amendment Cases." St. Louis Univ. Public Law Review 18 (1999): 99, 177, http://www.davekopel.com/2A/LawRev/35FinalPartOne.htm.

30. William Blackstone, *Commentaries*, vol. 1 (1765), 143–44.

31. Abram L. Sachar, *The Redemption of the Unwanted* (New York: St. Martin's/Marek, 1983), 60.

32. V.V. Stanciu, "Reflections on the Congress for the Prevention of Genocide," in ed., Livia Rothkirchen, *Yad Vashem Studies on the European Jewish Catastrophe and Resistance*, vol. 7 (Jerusalem, Israel: Yad Vashem, 1968), 187.

33. Samuel C. Wheeler III, "Arms as Insurance," *Public Affairs Quarterly* 13, no. 1 (April 1999): 121.

34. E-mail from anonymous U.S. Soldier to Dave Kopel (January 2003) (on file with author).

Chapter 13

1. Editorial, "The U.N.'s Latest," *New York Sun*, August 26, 2005.

2. Anne Bayefsky, "U.N. vs. Israel," *National Review Online*, April 20, 2004, http://www.nationalreview.com/bayefsky/bayefsky200404200848.asp.

3. Ibid.

4. Ibid.
5. "UK freezes assets of 5 Hamas leaders," *Rediff India Abroad*, March 25, 2004, http://us.rediff.com/news/2004/mar/25hamas.htm.
6. "Secretary-General Strongly Condemns Israel's Assassination of Hamas Leader, Which Resulted in Deaths of Eight Others," United Nations Information Service, SG/SM/9210, March 23, 2004, http://www.unis.unvienna.org/unis/pressrels/2004/sgsm9210.html?print.
7. Bayefsky, "U.N. vs. Israel."
8. Hamas Charter, The Covenant of the Islamic Resistance Movement, August 18, 1988, MidEast Web Historical Documents, http://www.mideastweb.org/hamas.htm.
9. Bayefsky, "U.N. vs. Israel."
10. Ibid.; Office of the High Commissioner for Human Rights, "Grave situation in the Occupied Palestinian Territory," Commission on Human Rights Resolution 2004/1, March 24, 2004, http://ap.ohchr.org/documents/E/CHR/resolutions/E-CN_4-RES-2004-1.doc.
11. Bayefsky, "U.N. vs. Israel."
12. "The UN's Blinkers," (Toronto) *Globe and Mail*, July 22, 2004.
13. International Court of Justice, "Legal Consequences of the Construction of a Wall in the Occupied Palestinian Territory," Advisory Opinion, July 9, 2004, http://www.icj-cij.org/icjwww/idocket/imwp/imwpframe.htm.
14. "The UN's Blinkers."
15. United Nations International Meeting on the Question of Palestine. *Theme: Implementing the ICJ Advisory Opinion on the Legal Consequence of the Construction of a Wall in the Occupied Palestinian Territory—The role of Governments, intergovernmental organizations and civil society*, United Nations Office at Geneva, 8 and 9 March 2005, http://domino.un.org/unispal.nsf/9a798adbf322aff38525617b006d88d7/bcb37133df60c4e085256fc400757804!OpenDocument.
16. Ruth Wisse, "The U.N.'s Jewish Problem: Anti-Semitism has found a comfortable home on the East River," *Weekly Standard*, April 8, 2002, http://weeklystandard.com/content/protected/articles/000/000/001/076zcpic.asp.
17. Anne Bayefsky, "How the U.N.'s Human Rights Investigations Do Yasser Arafat's Dirty Work," *New York Sun*, April 29, 2002; Gold, *Tower of Babble*, 41–42; Nile Gardiner and Baker Spring, *Reform the United Nations*, Heritage Foundation, Backgrounder no. 1700, October 27, 2003, http://www.heritage.org/Research/InternationalOrganizations/BG-1700.cfm; Brett D. Schaefer, "No funding for U.N.'s farcical rights council," *Baltimore Sun*, October 10, 2007, http://www.baltimoresun.com/news/opinion/oped/bal-op.un10oct10,0,1259104.story; Joseph Klein, "They Deserve Each Other," *FrontPageMagazine.com*, April 10, 2006, http://www.frontpagemag.com/Articles/Read.aspx?GUID={F4D00D8E-263D-4AE6-98DB-101F4EDAF2B0}.
18. Najat Al-Hajjaji, the Libyan ambassador to the United Nations.
19. "Human Rights Council," General Assembly Resolution 60/251, April 3, 2006.
20. 20. John Bolton, "The Key to Changing the United Nations System," in Schaefer, *ConUNdrum*, xxiii.
21. Brett D. Schaefer and Steven Groves, "Human Wrongs," in ibid., 132.
22. Hillel Neuer, "The UN's elite apologists," *Canadian Jewish News*, February 15, 2007, http://www.cjnews.com/viewarticle.asp?id=11228.

23. Anne Bayefsky, "U.S. on Human Rights Council," *Washington Times*, May 14, 2009, http://washingtontimes.com/news/2009/may/14/us-on-human-rights-council/.

24. Ibid.

25. Ibid.

26. Ben Evansky, "Libya Wins Seat on UN Human Rights Council," *Fox News*, May 13, 2010, http://liveshots.blogs.foxnews.com/2010/05/13/libya-wins-seat-on-un-human-rights-council/.

27. Anne Bayefsky, "Since When Is Iran a Champion for Women's Rights?" *FoxNews. com*, April 29, 2010, http://www.foxnews.com/opinion/2010/04/29/anne-bayefsky-iran-united-nations-commission-status-women-congress/; Nir Boms and Shayan Arya, "Iran's War on Women," *Wall Street Journal, Opinion Journal*, June 15, 2010, http://online.wsj.com/article/SB10001424052748703561604575282363858858700.html.

28. "Andres Oppenheimer, "Little hope for U.N. rights council," *Miami Herald*, August 7, 2008, http://www.miamiherald.com/news/columnists/andres-oppenheimer/story/631994.html.

29. David J. Rusin, "UN to Britain: Stop Being Islamophobic," Israel Hasbara Committee, August 13, 2008, http://www.infoisrael.net/cgi-local/text. pl?source=5/a/130820081.

30. Ibid.

31. Jeffrey Imm, "Jihad against Freedom of Speech at the United Nations," Counterterrorism blog, June 19, 2008, counterterrorismblog.org/2008/06/jihad_against_un.php.

32. Haviv Rettig, "Analysis: How Reform Jews almost got kicked out of UN," *Jerusalem Post*, June 10, 2008, http://www.jpost.com/servlet/Satellite?apage=1&cid=1212659690981&pagename=JPost%2FJPArticle%2FShowFull; Anne Bayefsky, "UN-speakable hypocrisy," *Daily News* (New York), June 2, 2008, http://www.nydailynews.com/opinions/2008/06/02/2008-06-02_unspeakable_hypocrisy.html.

33. Patrick Goodenough, "U.S. Returns to Human Rights Council as an Observer, for Now," CNS News, March 2, 2009, http://www.cnsnews.com/public/content/article.aspx?RsrcID=44298.

34. Steven Groves, "Why the U.S. Should Oppose 'Defamation of Religions' Resolutions at the United Nations," Heritage Foundation, Backgrounder no. 2206, November 10, 2008, http://www.heritage.org/research/legalissues/bg2206.cfm.

35. Stephen Brook, "WAN conference: newspapers attack UN Human Rights Council," *Guardian* (London), June 3, 2008, http://www.guardian.co.uk/media/2008/jun/03/pressandpublishing.unitednations.

36. Bayefsky, "U.S. on Human Rights Council." Iran and Uzbekistan had been part of the "1503" procedure (a response to a request by NGOs for an investigation based on credible evidence presented by the NGOs). Belarus and Cuba had been the subject of special rapporteur investigations (Brett D. Schaefer, *U.N. Human Rights Council Whitewash Argues against U.S. Participation*, Heritage Foundation, Backgrounder no. 2255, April 2, 2009, http://www.heritage.org/Research/Reports/2009/04/UN-Human-Rights-Council-Whitewash-Argues-Against-US-Participation.

37. Jonah Goldberg, "Obama's bailout for the despots: By investing political capital in the U.N. Human Rights Council, the president gives validation to a tainted organization," *Los Angeles Times*, April 7, 2009, http://www.latimes.com/news/opinion/commentary/la-oe-goldberg7-2009apr07,1,4243939.column.

38. Vincent Gioia, "The Mislabeled 'United Nations Human Rights Council'," *Post Chronicle*, August 20, 2008.

39. Bayefsky, "U.S. on Human Rights Council"; Goldberg, "Obama's bailout for the despots."

40. Schaefer, *U.N. Human Rights Council Whitewash.*

41. Editorial, "Selective on Rights," *Globe and Mail* (Toronto), January 13, 2009.

42. Patrick Goodenough, "Human Rights Council Rejects 'Interference' in Sri Lanka—But Not in Israel," CNS News, May 28, 2009, httwww.cnsnews.com/public/content/article.aspx?

43. Colum Lynch, "Is the U.N. Complicit in Sri Lankan War Crimes" *Foreign Policy*, May 24, 2010, http://turtlebay.foreignpolicy.com/posts/2010/05/24/is_the_un_complicit_in_sri_lankan_war_crimes.

44. Joseph Klein, "The U.N.'s Hypocrisy in Tibet," *FrontPageMagazine.com*, March 28, 2008, http://www.frontpagemag.com/Articles/Read.aspx?GUID=C0058CAB-F932-4EB8-B2C1-2C8CABB01F53.

45. Claudia Rosett, "U.S. Seeks to Join a Despots' Club," *Forbes*, May 7, 2009, http://www.forbes.com/2009/05/06/united-states-united-nations-opinions-columnists-human-rights-council.html.

46. "TV crew expelled from UN meeting on freedom of expression: The journalists were working on a documentary on how the issue of human rights is debated at the United Nations," *Expatica.com*, Jan. 23, 2009, http://www.expatica.com/es/news/local_news/TV-crew-expelled-from-UN-meeting-on-freedom-of-expression-b-U_48911.html.

47. Thor Halvorssen, "Durban II—A Conference about Nothing," *Fox News*, May 14, 2009, http://foxforum.blogs.foxnews.com/2009/05/14/halvorssen_thor_durban_un/; Anne Bayefsky, "How Durban II Undermined Human Rights," *Forbes*, April 27, 2009, http://www.forbes.com/2009/04/27/durban-conference-racism-geneva-opinions-contributors-geneva.html.

48. Henry Gombya, "Durban II did not help the war against racism," *Daily Monitor* (Uganda), April 29, 2009, http://www.monitor.co.ug/artman/publish/features/Durban_II_did_not_help_the_war_against_racism_83979.shtml

49. Bayefsky, "How Durban II Undermined Human Rights."

50. Ibid.

51. Ibid.

52. Ibid.; "Outcome document of the Durban Review Conference," http://blog.unwatch.org/wp-content/uploads/2009/04/durban_review_outcome_document_en.pdf.

53. Halvorssen, "Durban II—A Conference about Nothing."

54. Gombya, "Durban II did not help the war against racism"; "Outcome document," ¶ 62.

55. "Human rights & wrongs," *Jerusalem Post*, December 10, 2008, http://www.jpost.com/servlet/Satellite?cid=1228728146806&pagename=JPost%2FJPArticle%2FShowFull.

56. Ruth Lapidoth, *The Legal Basis of Israel's Naval Blockade of Gaza*, Jerusalem Center for Public Affairs, July 18, 2010, http://www.jcpa.org/JCPA/Templates/ShowPage. asp?DRIT=1&DBID=1&LNGID=1&TMID=111&FID=442&PID=0&IID=440 2&TTL=The_Legal_Basis_of_Israel%E2%80%99s_Naval_Blockade_of_Gaza.

57. "Israel rejects claims of 'crime against humanity,'" Yahoo News, December 10, 2008, http://news.yahoo.com/s/afp/20081210/wl_mideast_afp/ unrightsisraelpalestinian_081210152356.

58. The Turkish name is *Insani Yardim Vakfi*, commonly translated a "Humanitarian Relief Foundation."

59. Joel Mowbray, "Flotilla Focus Turning to Terror Ties," *Washington Times*, August 12, 2010.

60. Gerald M. Steinberg, "The War against Israel," *Wall Street Journal, Opinion Journal*, June 7, 2010, http://online.wsj.com/article/SB100014240527487040253045752 83832128809598.html; Ben Evansky, "Gaza Flotilla Group Part of U.N. NGO Branch," *Fox News*, June 4, 2010, http://liveshots.blogs.foxnews.com/2010/06/04/ gaza-flotilla-group-part-of-u-n-ngo-branch/?test=latestnews.

61. Ibid.

62. "Arab Media Reports on Flotilla Participants," Middle East Media Research Institute (MEMRI), Special Dispatch no. 2990, June 1, 2010, http://www.memri. org/report/en/print4265.htm; Israel Defense Forces, "Pistols Found on Flotilla Activists," May 31, 2010, http://idfspokesperson.com/2010/05/31/pistols-found-on-flotilla-activists-31-may-2010/.

63. Joel Leyden, "UN Remains Silent as Terrorists Strike Israel from Lebanon, Egypt," Israel News Agency, August 3, 2010, http://www.israelnewsagency.com/

64. "Fenton Communications," DiscoverTheNetworks.org, http://www. discoverthenetworks.org/groupProfile.asp?grpid=6958.

65. Fenton Communications, This Just In: 10 Lessons from 25 Years of Public Interest Communications (2009), 3, http://www.fenton.com/FENTON_IndustryGuide_ ThisJustIn.pdf.

66. "The Grave Violations of Human Rights in the Occupied Palestinian Territory Including the Recent Aggression in the Occupied Gaza Strip," Human Rights Council, Resolution S-9/1, January 12, 2009, 9th Special Session, http://www. eyeontheun.org/assets/attachments/documents/7683_HRC_Resolution_Gaza_1-12-09.doc: The "Human Rights Council . . . . Decides to dispatch an urgent, independent international fact-finding mission, to be appointed by the President of the Council, to investigate all violations of international human rights law and international humanitarian law by the occupying Power, Israel, against the Palestinian people throughout the Occupied Palestinian Territory, particularly in the occupied Gaza Strip, due to the current aggression, and calls upon Israel not to obstruct the process of investigation and to fully cooperate with the mission."

67. "The Judges: Israel Is Already Guilty," Eye on the UN, http://www.eyeontheun.org/ view.asp?l=47&p=984; Alan Dershowitz, "An Anti-Israel Extremist Seeks Revenge Through Goldstone Report," *Huffington Post*, February 12, 2010, http://www. huffingtonpost.com/alan-dershowitz/an-anti-israel-extremist_b_460187.html.

68. European Centre for Law and Justice, "Legal Memorandum in Opposition to Erroneous Allegations and Flawed Legal Conclusions Contained in the UN Human Rights Council's Goldstone Report," January 26, 2010, http://www

.eclj.org/pdf/ECLJ_MemoonGoldstoneReport_20100126.pdf; Jonathan D. Halevi, "Blocking the Truth of the Gaza War: How the Goldstone Commission Understated the Hamas Threat to Palestinian Civilians," *Jerusalem Issue Brief* 9, no. 10, Jerusalem Center for Public Affairs, September 18, 2009, http://www.jcpa.org/JCPA/Templates/ShowPage.asp?DRIT=1&DBID=1&LNGID=1&TMID=111&FID=442&PID=0&IID=3086&TTL=Blocking_the_Truth_of_the_Gaza_War; Trevor Norwitz, "Open Letter from Trevor Norwitz," October 19, 2009, http://www.goldstonereport.org/pro-and-con/critics/316-trevor-norvitz-open-letter-to-judge-goldstone-191009; Israeli Ministry of Foreign Affairs, "Israel's analysis and comments on the Gaza Fact-Finding Mission Report," September 15, 2009, http://www.mfa.gov.il/MFA/About+the+Ministry/MFA+Spokesman/2009/Press+releases/Israel_analysis_comments_Goldstone_Mission_15-Sep-2009.htm; Joseph Klein, "A Response to Israel's Haters," *Canada Free Press*, April 12, 2010, htto://canadafreepress.com/index.php/article/21883; Dore Gold, "The Dangerous Bias of the United Nations Goldstone Report," *U.S. News & World Report*, March 24, 2010, http://politics.usnews.com/opinion/articles/2010/03/24/the-dangerous-bias-of-the-united-nations-goldstone-report.html; Alan Dershowitz, "How Goldstone Is Making Peace More Difficult," *Huffington Post*, September 1, 2010, http://www.huffingtonpost.com/alan-dershowitz/how-goldstone-is-making-p_b_701950.html.
     Goldstone was presented to the world as a courageous human rights activist. The truth is rather different. See R. W. Johnson, "Who Is Richard Goldstone?" Radio Free Europe, October 20, 2009, http://www.rferl.org/content/Who_Is_Richard_Goldstone/1856255.html; Ashley Rindsberg, "UN's Goldstone Sent 13-Year-Old Boy to Prison for Protesting Apartheid," *Huffington Post*, November 19, 2009, http://www.huffingtonpost.com/ashley-rindsberg/uns-goldstone-sent-13-yea_b_359696.html; Nissan Ratzlav-Katz, "When Goldstone Indicted a Fictional Character (and a Dead Man)," *Arutz Shevna*, September 29, 2009, http://www.israelnationalnews.com/News/News.aspx/133631; Tehiya Bank, "Judge Goldstone's Dark Past," Ynetnews, May 6, 2010, http://www.ynetnews.com/articles/0,7340,L-3885999,00.html; Alan Dershowitz, "Legitimating Bigotry: The Legacy of Richard Goldstone," *Hudson New York*, May 7, 2010, http://www.hudson-ny.org/1189/legitimating-bigotry-the-legacy-of-richard-goldstone.

69. Benjamin Weinthal, "Goldstone Committee Denies Bias," *Jerusalem Post*, July 25, 2010, http://www.jpost.com/International/Article.aspx?id=182483.

70. Bradley Burston, "The Plot: Use the UN to rid the world of Israel," Haaretz, March 12, 2007, http://www.haaretz.com/hasen/spages/836274.html.

71. John Bolton, "Israel, the U.S. and the Goldstone Report," *Wall Street Journal*, October 19, 2009, online.wsj.com/article/SB10001424052748704500604574480932924540724.html.

72. *Jean Ziegler's Campaign against America: A Study of the Anti-American Bias of the U.N. Special Rapporteur on the Right to Food*, United Nations Watch (Geneva, Switzerland: October 2005), http://www.unwatch.org/atf/cf/%7B6DEB65DA-BE5B-4CAE-8056-8BF0BEDF4D17%7D/Jean_Zieglers_Campaign_Against_America.pdf .

73. With respect to Sudan, by contrast, Darfur is merely a cause for grave concern; the Khartoum regime has only "allegedly" perpetrated atrocities. "Eight UN Human Rights Experts Gravely Concerned about Reported Widespread Abuses in Darfur, Sudan," UN press release, AFR/873, HR/CN/1065, March 29, 2004.

74. "Jean Ziegler s'attaque aux Etats-Unis, au FMI et a l'OMC," *SDA*, January 27, 2003, cited in *Jean Ziegler's Campaign against America.*
75. "U.N. Swiss envoy warns of apocalyptic consequences of U.S. strikes on Afghanistan," Swiss Radio International's Swissinfo website, September 22, 2001, cited in *Jean Ziegler's Campaign against America.*
76. In February 2003, Ziegler publicly stated that war in Iraq should be avoided at all costs, and even proposed that Switzerland offer exile to Saddam Hussein. See "Swiss rights campaigner urges Swiss exile for Saddam," Agence France Presse—English, February 5, 2003. By April 2003, he was accusing Coalition forces of violating the rights to food and water in Iraq. See "UN expert de l'ONU denonce les violations du droit a l'alimentation en Irak," Agence France Presse, April 3, 2003; "UN rights expert demands aid agencies get access to feed Iraqis," Agence France Presse—English, April 3, 2003, cited in *Jean Ziegler's Campaign against America.* Also, "Nearly twice as many Iraqi children going hungry since Saddam's ouster, U.N. expert says," Associated Press, March 30, 2005, cited in *Jean Ziegler's Campaign against America* (condemning coalition forces, but not terrorists, for causing malnutrition in Iraq, while only expressing "concern" about hunger in other countries, including Sudan and North Korea).
77. Nat Hentoff, "U.N. Hypocrisy on human rights," *Washington Times,* February 13, 2006.
78. *Jean Ziegler's Campaign against America.* (Note: The dictator's first name is variously spelled *Muammar, Mu'ammar,* and *Moammar*; his last name is variously spelled *al-Gaddafi, Gadaffi, Gadhafi, Qadaffi, Kadafi, el-Qaddafi,* and various other ways, depending on the newspaper or news service.)
79. Ibid.
80. Ibid. The magazine's website was http://www.empire-americain.com.
81. U.N. Commission on Human Rights, Sub-Commission on Human Rights, *The Prevention of Human Rights Violations Caused by the Availability and Misuse of Small Arms and Light Weapons,* Resolution 2002/25, August 14, 2002, http://www.unhchr.ch/huridocda/huridoca.nsf/6d123295325517b2c12569910034dc4c/10a32527edc27cd4c1256c1d0038ee46?OpenDocument.
82. Burston, "The Plot: Use the UN to rid the world of Israel."
83. U.N. Human Rights Council, Sub-Commission on the Promotion and Protection of Human Rights, 58th Sess., *Prevention of Human Rights Violations Committed with Small Arms and Light Weapons,* U.N Doc. A/HRC/Sub.1/58/27 (July 27, 2006) (prepared by Barbara Frey), http://www.geneva-forum.org/Reports/20060823.pdf. [hereinafter Frey Report].
84. *Prevention of Human Rights Violations Committed with Small Arms and Light Weapons,* endorsed Sub-Com. res. 2006/22, U.N. Doc A/HRC/Sub.1/58/L.11/Add.1 (2006) (Small Arms Principles), http://www1.umn.edu/humanrts/instree/smallarmsprinciples.html.
85. Frey Report, ¶ 16:

> Minimum effective measures that States should adopt to prevent small arms violence, then, must go beyond mere criminalization of acts of armed violence. Under the principle of due diligence, it is reasonable for international human rights bodies to require States to enforce a minimum

licensing requirement designed to keep small arms and light weapons out
of the hands of persons who are likely to misuse them . . . The criteria
for licensing may vary from State to State, but most licensing procedures
consider the following: (a) minimum age of applicant; (b) past criminal
record including any history of interfamilial violence; (c) proof of a legitimate
purpose for obtaining a weapon; and (d) mental fitness. Other proposed
criteria include knowledge of laws related to small arms, proof of training on
the proper use of a firearm and proof of proper storage. Licences should be
renewed regularly to prevent transfer to unauthorized persons. These licensing
criteria are not insurmountable barriers to legitimate civilian possession.
There is broad international consensus around the principle that the laws
and procedures governing the possession of small arms by civilians should
remain the fundamental prerogative of individual States. While regulation of
civilian possession of firearms remains a contested issue in public debate—due
in large part to the efforts of firearms manufacturers and the United States
of America-based pro-gun organizations—there is in fact almost universal
consensus on the need for reasonable minimum standards for national
legislation to license civilian possession in order to promote public safety and
protect human rights. This consensus is a factor to be considered by human
rights mechanisms in weighing the affirmative responsibilities of States to
prevent core human rights violations in cases involving private sector gun
violence.

86. Ibid., ¶ 21.
87. Ibid., note 14, discussing David B. Kopel, Paul Gallant, and Joanne D. Eisen, "Is
    Resisting Genocide a Human Right?" *Notre Dame Law Review* 81 (2006): 1275.
88. Emile LeBrun, Lora Lumpe, and Cate Buchanan, "Reducing gun violence,
    improving security: National arms control efforts," *Small Arms and Human Security
    Bulletin* (Centre for Humanitarian Dialogue), April 2005, 3, http://www.hdcentre.
    org/files/Bul2English.pdfHumantarian Dialogue.
89. According to Frey, a government violates the human right to life to the extent that
    a state allows the defensive use of a firearm "unless the action was necessary to save
    a life or lives." Frey Report, ¶ 26:

> International bodies and States universally define self-defence in terms
> of necessity and proportionality. Whether a particular claim to self-defence
> is successful is a fact-sensitive determination. When small arms and light
> weapons are used for self-defence, for instance, unless the action was necessary
> to save a life or lives and the use of force with small arms is proportionate to
> the threat of force, self-defence will not alleviate responsibility for violating
> another's right to life.

90. Ibid., ¶27:

> The use of small arms and light weapons by either State or non-State
> actors automatically raises the threshold for severity of the threat which must
> be shown in order to justify the use of small arms or light weapons in defence,

as required by the principle of proportionality. Because of the lethal nature of these weapons and the *jus cogens* human rights obligations imposed upon all States and individuals to respect the right to life, small arms and light weapons may be used defensively only in the most extreme circumstances, expressly, where the right to life is already threatened or unjustifiably impinged.

91. International Covenant on Civil and Political Rights, article 6, part 1, http://www2.ohchr.org/english/law/ccpr.htm.

92. Frey Report, ¶¶ 28–29.

93. For example, the Vienna Convention on the Law of Treaties says that the *jus cogens* rule means that a treaty is void if it violates "a norm accepted and recognized by the international community of States as a whole as a norm from which no derogation is permitted and which can be modified only by a subsequent norm of general international law having the same character" (Vienna Convention on the Law of Treaties, 1969 U.N. Juridicial Year Book 140, art. 53). A legitimate example (not one invented by the Axis of Soros) would be that if two countries signed a treaty to jointly commit genocide, the treaty would be void under international law.

94. Frey Report, ¶ 27: "Because of the lethal nature of these weapons and the '*jus cogens*' human rights obligations imposed upon all States and individuals to respect the right to life, small arms and light weapons may be used defensively only in the most extreme circumstances, expressly, where the right to life is already threatened or unjustifiably impinged."

95. "Fragmentation of International Law: Difficulties Arising from the Diversification and Expansion of International Law," Report of the Study Group of the International Law Commission, UN Doc. A/CN.4/L.682, April 13, 2006, 189, ¶ 374.

96. Article I, section 8, grants Congress the power "to define and punish Piracies and Felonies committed on the high Seas, and Offenses against the Law of Nations."

97. James Brown Scott, *The Spanish Origin of International Law: Francisco de Vitoria and His Law of Nations* (1934; repr., Union, NJ: Lawbook Exchange, 2000), 75.

98. Francisci de Vitoria, *De Indis et De Iure Belli Relectiones*, ed., Ernest Nys ed., transl. John Pawley Bates (1532; repr., Buffalo: William S. Hein, 1995), 2:167.

99. Ibid.

100. Brian Tierney, *The Idea of Natural Rights* (Grand Rapids: Wm. B. Eerdmans, 1997), 301.

101. Ibid., 314.

102. "Neither could the aforesaid remedy [of jurisdiction] with respect to a subject, reasonably have been applied to those things through which it would have been possible to do away with the right of self-defence—springing from the law of nature—against a criminal charge, especially a charge that was so grave; for it would not be permissible that the Emperor should abolish those things which proceed from the natural law" (Francisco Suárez, "A Treatise on Laws and Gods the Lawgiver," in Francisco Suárez, *Selections from Three Works*, ed., Gwladys L. Williams [Buffalo: William S. Hein, 1995] [collecting three books originally published in the early seventeenth century], 2:273.

103. Francisco Suárez, *A Defense of the Catholic and Apostalic Faith*, in *Selections from Three Works*, vol. 2; Francisco Suárez, "A Work on the Three Theological Virtues of Faith, Hope, and Charity: Divided into Three Treatises to Correspond with the Number of the Virtues Themselves," in Francisco Suárez, *Selections from Three Works* 2:854–55 (the state is the superior of the ruler; the state retains its natural right of self-defense against a tyrant; the state can enforce its implicity contract with the ruler that the ruler act for the public good).

104. Alan, Watson, transl., *The Digest of Justinian* (Philadelphia: Univ. of Penn. Pr., 1985) (first published in AD 530–533), book 43, section 16, ¶ 1, item 27 ("Cassius writes that it is permissible to repel force by force, and this right is conferred by nature. From this it appears, he says, that arms may be repelled by arms"). The *Digest* was one portion of a massive compilation of Roman law, ordered by the Byzantine Emperor Justinian. Many of the items, such as the words just quoted, were the opinions of Roman legal scholars; the *Digest* considered them to be correct and authoritative statements of the law.

105. J. H. M. Salmon, "Catholic Resistance Theory, Ultramontism, and the Royalist Response, 1580–1620," in J. H. Burns, ed., *The Cambridge History of Political Thought 1450–1700* (1996), 238, citing Francisco Suárez, *De Legibus Ac Deo Legislatore* (1612), 4:123.

106. John Dalberg Acton, *The History of Freedom and Other Essays*, eds., John Neville Figgis and Reginald Vere Laurence (London: Macmillan, 1907), 82, http://oll.libertyfund.org/index.php?option=com_staticxt&staticfile=show. php%3Ftitle=75&Itemid=99999999.

107. James Scott Brown, "Introduction," in Suárez, *Selections from Three Works*, 18a–19a.

108. Hugo Grotius, *The Rights of War and Peace* (Indianapolis: Liberty Fund 2005) (reprint of 1737 English translation by John Morrice of the 1724 annotated French translation by Jean Barbeyrac; first published 1625), vol. 2, inside jacket.

109. George B. Davis, *The Elements of International Law* (1901; repr., Boston: Adamant Media, 2005), 15.

110. Ibid.

111. Grotius, *The Rights of War and Peace*, vol. 1, inside jacket.

112. Ibid., 183–84.

113. Ibid., 184–85.

114. Ibid., 2:397, 401–2, 408.

115. Samuel Pufendorf, *Of the Law of Nature and Nations* (Union, NJ: The Lawbook Exchange, 2005) (reprint of 1726 London edition of the 1706–07 Barbeyrac French translation and annotation, with English translation by Mr. Carew, first published 1672), 184.

116. Ibid.

117. Ibid. Likewise: "But what Possibility is there of my living at Peace with him who hurts and injures me, since Nature has implanted in every Man's Breast so tender a concern for himself, and for what he possesses, that he cannot but apply all Means to resist and repel him, who either respect attempts to wrong him" (214).

118. Ibid., 191. "As if the Aggressors were so generous, as constantly to give notice to the other Party of their Design, and of the Arms they purpos'd to make use of; that they might have the Leisure to furnish themselves in like manner for the Combat.

Or if these Rencounters we were to act on our Defence by the strict Rules of the
common Sword Plays and Tryals of Skill, where the Champions and their Weapons
are nicely match'd and measur'd for our better Diversion."
119. Ibid., 192:

> For what an age of Torments should I undergo, if another Man were
> allow'd perpetually to lay upon me only with moderate Blows, whose Malice
> I could not otherwise stop or repel, than by compassing his Death. Or if
> a Neighbour were continually to infest me with Incursions and Ravages
> upon my Lands and Possessions, whilst I could not lawfully kill him, in my
> Attempts to beat him off? For since the chief Aim of every human *Socialness*
> is the Safety of every Person, we ought not to fansy in it such Laws, as would
> make every good and honest Man of necessity miserable, as often as any
> wicked Varlet should please to violate the Law of Nature against him. And it
> would be highly absurd to establish Society amongst Men on so destructive a
> Bottom as the Necessity of enduring Wrongs.

Also, 186, 190, 192–94, 198.
120. Ibid., 190, 192–94.
121. Ibid., 723.
122. Ibid. 719n2.
123. Emmerich de Vattel, *The Law of Nations; or, Principles of the Law of Nature, applied
to the Conduct and Affairs of Nations and Sovereigns* (Union, NJ: The Lawbook
Exchange, 2005) (reprint of 1854 translation, first published 1758), http://www.
constitution.org/vattel/vattel.htm; Robert Ward, *An Enquiry into the Foundation of
the Law of Nations in Europe from the Time of the Greeks and Romans to the Age of
Grotius* (1795; repr., Clark, NJ, The Lawbook Exchange, 2005), 2:375.
124. Vattel, *The Law of Nations*, 22.
125. "On all these occasions where the public authority cannot lend us its assistance, we
resume our original and natural right of self-defence. Thus a traveler may, without
hesitation, kill the robber who attacks him on the highway; because it would,
at that moment, be in vain for him to implore the protection of the laws and of
the magistrate. Thus a chaste virgin would be praised for taking away the life of
a brutal ravisher who attempted to force her to his desires" (ibid., 84). Also: "A
subject may repel the violence of a fellow-citizen when the magistrate's assistance
is not at hand; and with much greater reason may he defend himself against the
unexpected attacks of foreigners" (ibid., 399).
126. Ibid., 18. Also, 22 (if the prince murders innocents, he "is no longer to be
considered in any other light than that of an unjust and outrageous enemy, against
whom his people are allowed to defend themselves"), 82, note * (lauding "past
generations" who had "made effectual use of arms" against abusive sovereign,
including John II, who had been King of Aragon and Navarre), 155.

Henry Clay, who has long been regarded as one of the greatest United States
Senators of all time, used Vattel to justify the wars of independence of Spain's
South American colonies:

I maintain that an oppressed people are authorized, whenever they can, to rise and break their fetters. This was the great principle of the English Revolution. It was the great principle of our own. Vattel, if authority were wanting, expressly supports this right. We must pass sentence of condemnation upon the founders of our liberty, say that you were rebels, traitors, and that we are at this moment legislating without competent powers, before we can condemn the cause of Spanish America

. . . Spanish America for centuries has been doomed to the practical effects of an odious tyranny. If we were justified, she is more than justified. (Henry Clay, "The Emancipation of South America," speech delivered to the United States House of Representatives, March 24, 1818, http://www.bartleby.com/268/9/5.html.)

127. *Quando lex aliquid alicui concedit, omnia incidentia tacite conceduntur.*
128. *Quando lex aliquid alicui concedit, conceditur et id sine quo res ipsa esse non protest.*
129. Joseph Loconte, "Human Rights at 60: They aren't what they used to be," *Weekly Standard*, December 10, 2008, http://www.weeklystandard.com/Content/Public/Articles/000/000/015/899uarzx.asp.
130. Vaclav Havel, "A Table for Tyrants," *New York Times*, May 11, 2009, http://www.nytimes.com/2009/05/11/opinion/11havel.html.
131. In the 2009–10 Congress, the bill is H.R. 557. The H.R.C. is covered in sections 401–2 (http://www.govtrack.us/congress/billtext.xpd?bill=h111-557).
132. H.R. 2376, http://www.govtrack.us/congress/bill.xpd?bill=h111-2376.

Chapter 14

1. The dates on which government was designated a state sponsor of terrorism are: Cuba, March 1, 1982; Iran, January19, 1984; North Korea, January 20, 1988; Sudan, August 12, 1993; Syria, December 29, 1979 (U.S. State Dept., "State Sponsors of Terrorism," http://www.state.gov/s/ct/c14151.htm). Libya was on the list from 1979 until 2006, when it was removed after having renounced terrorism and agreed to the supervised destruction of its WMDs.

   For an in-depth report on Syria's sponsorship of terrorism, see Reuven Ehrlich, *Terrorism as a Preferred Instrument of Syrian Policy*, Institute for Counter-Terrorism, http://www.ict.org.il/inter_ter/st_terror/syrian_terror.htm.
2. Terrorist states on the Security Council include: Cuba (1990–91), Libya (1976–77) (although not yet so designated by the U.S. State Department), and Syria (2002–03).
3. "Bin Laden 'received UN cash'," BBC, October20, 2001, http://news.bbc.co.uk/1/hi/world/middle_east/1610214.stm.
4. "Muwafaq" is Arabic for "blessed relief" (ibid.). The BBC reported that the U.N. had delivered $1.4 million to a consortium of Sudanese "charities." The article did not specify how much was delivered to Muwafaq.
5. Ibid.
6. Rachel Ehrenfeld, "The Saudi Buck Stops Here," *FrontPageMagazine.com*, March 3, 2005, http://www.frontpagemag.com/Articles/authors.asp?ID=579.

7. "Bin Laden 'received UN cash.'"

8. Ibid.

9. Eric Shawn, "Did Terrorists Benefit from Oil-for-Food?" *Fox News*, September 23, 2004, http://www.foxnews.com/story/0,2933,133212,00.html.

10. Stephen Hayes, "Saddam's Terror Training Camps," *Weekly Standard*, January 6, 2006, http://weeklystandard.com/Content/Public/ Articles/000/000/006/550kmbzd.asp.

11. Claudia Rossett, "The Buck Still Hasn't Stopped," *Weekly Standard*, October 3, 2005, http://www.weeklystandard.com/Content/Public/ Articles/000/000/006/118nzmcw.asp?pg=1.

12. "Excerpts: Annan Interview," *BBC News*, September 16, 2004.

13. E.g, Allan H. Meltzer, "New Mandates for the IMF and World Bank," *Cato Journal* 25, no. 1 (Winter 2005): 13–16, http://www.cato.org/pubs/journal/ cj25n1/cj25n1-2.pdf; Ana I. Eiras, *Time for the International Monetary Fund and World Bank to Reconsider the Strategy for Millennium Development Goals*, Heritage Foundation, Backgrounder no. 1880 (September 16, 2005), http:// www.heritage.org/Research/TradeandForeignAid/bg1880.cfm; Ana Isabel Eiras and Brett D. Schaefer, *A Blueprint for Paul Wolfowitz at the World Bank*, Heritage Foundation, Backgrounder no. 1856 (June 2, 2005), http://www. heritage.org/Research/TradeandForeignAid/bg1856.cfm; Ana I. Eiras, *IMF and World Bank Intervention: A Problem, Not a Solution*, Heritage Foundation, Backgrounder no. 1689 (September 17, 2003), http://www.heritage.org/Research/ InternationalOrganizations/bg1689.cfm. President George W. Bush nominated Paul Wolfowitz, a strong opponent of terrorism, to be president of the World Bank, and he was unanimously approved by that body's board of executive directors on March 31, 2005. I hope that Mr. Wolfowitz manages to turn the World Bank around, but he faces enormous powers of inertia and bureaucracy.

14. Brett D. Schaefer, *Stop Subsidizing Terrorism,* Heritage Foundation, Backgrounder no. 1485 (October 4, 2001), http://www.heritage.org/Research/NationalSecurity/ BG1485.cfm.

15. Ibid.

16. Itamar Marcus, "World Bank Indirect Funding of Suicide Terror," *Palestinian Media Watch Bulletin*, April 2, 2004, http://www.pmw.org.il/Latest%20bulletin .html#worldbank. Among the terrorists who came straight from a Palestinian college or university are:

Bir Zeit University:
Mahmud Shuraytakh: chairman of the campus chapter of Hamas of the Student Council. Organized the September 19, 2002, terror attack on a Tel Aviv bus, which killed 6 and injured 71 victims.

Ihab Abdul-Qadir Mahmud Abu Salim: member of the Hamas student chapter. Murdered people and injured 20 in a terrorist attack in Zerifin on September 9, 2003.

Daya Muhammad Hussein Al-Tawil, member of the Hamas student chapter. Injured 29 people in a terrorist attack in Jerusalem on March 27, 2001 Ramiz Ubaid: member of the Islamic Jihad student chapter. Perpetrated a terrorist attack killing 13 and injuring 118 in Tel Aviv on Mar. 3, 1996.

Al-Najah University:
Hamid Abu Hajlah: Member of the Hamas student chapter. Injured 3 victims in a terrorist attack in Netanya on January 1, 2001.

   Muhammad Al-Rul: Hamas activist. Murdered 19 and injured 42 in a Jerusalem terrorist attack on June 18, 2002.

Al-Quds Open University:
Ramiz Abu Salim: Hamas student activist. Murdered 7 Israelis and injured about 20 in a terrorist attack on Jerusalem on September 9, 2003.

17. Ibid.
18. Ibid.
19. Ibid.
20. A/RES/61/259, March 28, 2007.
21. Muhammad Saman, "Almost all intifada funds by Arab donors has arrived," *Arab News*, August 26, 2001, http://www.arabnews.com/?page=4&section=0&article =4976&d=26&m=8&y=2001; Anne Bayefsky, "Bank of the Intifada to Join the U.N.," *National Review Online*, March 26, 2007, http://article.nationalreview.com /?q=Nzc2YjJlMWFiMzllODE4NjY2YzVkNTc0YjcxMjc5MjM=.
22. Steven Stalinsky, "Saudi Royal Family's Financial Support to the Palestinians 1998–2003: More than 15 Billion Riyals ($4 Billion U.S.) Given to 'Mujahideen Fighters' and 'Families of Martyrs,'" Middle East Media Research Institute, Special Report no. 17, July 3, 2003, http://www.memri.org/report/en/0/0/0/0/0/0/902. htm; Bayefsky, "Bank of the Intifada."
23. Bayefsky, "Bank of the Intifada."
24. Claudia Rossett, "UNICEF's Proliferation-Prone Banker," *Forbes*, September 3, 2009.
25. Kate Clark, "UN quake aid went to extremists," BBC, October 3, 2006, http:// news.bbc.co.uk/2/hi/south_asia/5402756.stm; Matthew Russell Lee, "Questions about Jamaat ud Dawa and UN's Pakistan Aid in Mumbai's Wake," *Inner City Press*, December 8, 2008, http://www.innercitypress.com/un1jamaat120808.html.
26. Clark, "UN quake aid went to extremists."
27. David B. Kopel, "Tragedy in Africa gets scant notice," *Rocky Mountain News/ Denver Post*, June 18, 2005; David B. Kopel, "Dailies ignoring Zimbabwe crisis," *Rocky Mountain News/Denver Post*, September 1, 2002; David B. Kopel, Paul Gallant, and Joanne D. Eisen, "Ripe for Genocide: Disarmament endangers Zimbabwe," *National Review Online*, February 13, 2001, http://www.davekopel. com/NRO/2001/Ripe-for-Genocide.htm.
28. Ariel David and Frances D'Emilio, "Critics Say UN Food Summit Wasteful, Ineffective," Associated Press, November 19, 2009.
29. George Russell, "U.N. Ignores Its Own Freeze on Deals with Alleged Somali Food Distribution 'Cartel,'" *FoxNews.com*, July 23, 2010; Jeffery Gettleman, "Somali Food Aid Bypasses Needy, U.N. Study Finds," *New York Times*, March 8, 2010.
30. Aaron Goldstein, "Kofi Annan's Double Talk on Terrorism," *American Daily*, March 14, 2005, http://www.americandaily.com/article/7101.
31. United Nations Security Council, Resolution 1559, S/RES/1559, September 2, 2004, http://www.eyeontheun.org/documents-item.asp?d=269&id=418.

32. Goldstein, "Kofi Annan's Double Talk on Terrorism."
33. "U.N. Delays Disarming of Hizbullah," Media Line, April 7, 2005, http://www. themedialine.org/news/news_detail.asp?NewsID=9649.
34. Goldstein, "Kofi Annan's Double Talk on Terrorism"; Kofi Annan, "A Global Strategy for Fighting Terrorism," Keynote Address to the Closing Plenary of the International Summit on Democracy, Terrorism and Security, Madrid, Spain, March 10, 2005, http://www.eyeontheun.org/assets/attachments/documents/a_ global_strategy_for_fighting_terrorism--annan--madrid.doc.
35. Benny Avni, "Annan Envoy Visits Hezbollah Leader," *New York Sun*, February 18, 2005.
36. Aluf Benn, "Israel accuses UN of collaborating with Hezbollah," Haaretz, September 11, 2005.
37. Ibid.
38. Ibid.
39. Ibid.
40. Reuven Koret, "UN soldiers reportedly helped Hizbullah kidnap Israelis," *Israelinsider*, July 15, 2001, http://www.israelinsider.com/channels/diplomacy/ articles/dip_0061.htm.
41. Ibid.
42. Ibid.
43. Ibid.
44. "Investigation onto UN Handling of Video Launched," *ICEJ News*, July 23, 2001 (International Christian Embassy Jerusalem).
45. Ibid.
46. Ibid.
47. House Resolution 191, Cong. Rec. H4814.
48. "U.N to release Mideast kidnap tape," *CNN*, July 7, 2001, http://archives.cnn. com/2001/WORLD/meast/07/07/mideast.unvid/.
49. Julia Weller, "The U.N.'s Complicity in Hezbollah Kidnappings," *FrontPageMagazine.com*, August 2, 2006, http://www.frontpagemag.com/Articles/ ReadArticle.asp?ID=23634; Jack Kelly, "No peace from the U.N.: Israel must take its own steps to defang the terrorists," *Jewish World Review*, July 24, 2006, http:// jewishworldreview.com/0706/jkelly072406.php3.
50. Lori Lowenthal Marcus, "What did you do in the war, UNIFIL? You broadcast Israeli troop movements," *Weekly Standard*, September 4, 2006, http://www. weeklystandard.com/Content/Public/Articles/000/000/012/622bqwjn.asp.
51. Joseph Klein, "The UN Shield for Terror," *FrontPageMagazine.com*, August 11, 2006, http://www.frontpagemag.com/Articles/ReadArticle.asp?ID=23766.
52. Ibid.
53. Benny Avni, "Annan's Claims on Casualties May Unravel," *New York Sun*, July 27, 2006; Ricki Hollander, "New York Times Story on UN Position Hit by Israel Omits Crucial Context," Committee for Accuracy in Middle East Reporting in America, July 27, 2006, http://www.camera.org/index.asp?x_context=2&x_ outlet=35&x_article=1160.
54. "UNfit for purpose," *Telegraph* (UK), August 13, 2006, http://www.telegraph. co.uk/news/main.jhtml?xml=/news/2006/08/13/wmid313.xml; Joseph Klein, "Kofi Annan's Latest Big Lie," *FrontPageMagazine.com*, July 31, 2006, http://www.

frontpagemag.com/Articles/ReadArticle.asp?ID=23603; Joel Kom and Steven
Edwards, "Hezbollah was using UN post as 'shield': Canadian wrote of militia's
presence, 'necessity' of bombing," *Ottawa Citizen*, July 27, 2006.

55. Megan K. Stack, "Unarmed in the Crossfire," *Los Angeles Times*, July 28, 2006,
http://www.latimes.com/news/printedition/la-fg-border28jul28,1,5243162.story.

56. Jeff McKay, "Annan Mum on Hizballah's Wounding of UN Workers," CNS
News, August 7, 2006 (UNIFIL report of July 25, 2006: "This morning,
Hizballah opened small arms fire at a UNIFIL convoy consisting of two armored
personnel carriers (APC) on the road between Kunin and Bint Jubayl. There
was some damage to the APCs, but no casualties, and the convoy was obliged
to return to Kunin"), http://www.cnsnews.com/ViewForeignBureaus.asp?Page=/
ForeignBureaus/archive/200608/INT20060807e.html.

57. A FTO is designated by the State Department's Coordinator for Counterterrorism,
pursuant to section 219 of the Immigration and Naturalization Act. A designated
FTO must meet three conditions: It must be a foreign organization; it must engage
in terrorism or terrorist activity; and it must threaten U.S. citizens or U.S. national
defense, foreign policy, or economic interests (U.S. Dept. of State, Office of
Counterterrorism, *Foreign Terrorist Organizations* [*FTOs*], Fact Sheet [Washington,
D.C., October 11, 2005], http://www.state.gov/s/ct/rls/fs/37191.htm).

According to United States law (8 U.S. Code sect 1182(a)(3)(B)(iii)) the
definition of "terrorist activity" is:

> any activity which is unlawful under the laws of the place where it is committed
> (or which, if committed in the United States, would be unlawful under the laws
> of the United States or any State) and which involves any of the following:
> (I) The highjacking or sabotage of any conveyance (including an aircraft,
> vessel, or vehicle).
> (II) The seizing or detaining, and threatening to kill, injure, or continue to
> detain, another individual in order to compel a third person (including a
> governmental organization) to do or abstain from doing any act as an explicit
> or implicit condition for the release of the individual seized or detained.
> (III) A violent attack upon an internationally protected person (as defined
> in section 1116(b)(4) of title 18, United States Code) or upon the liberty of
> such a person.
> (IV) An assassination.
> (V) The use of any . . .
>
> > (b) explosive, firearm, or other weapon or dangerous device (other than
> > for mere personal monetary gain), with intent to endanger, directly or
> > indirectly, the safety of one or more individuals or to cause substantial
> > damage to property.
>
> (VI) A threat, attempt, or conspiracy to do any of the foregoing.

To "engage in terrorist activity" includes not just to perform the terrorist act itself,
but also assisting in the planning and fund-raising for the terrorist act (8 U.S.
Code § 1182(a)(3)(B)(iv):

"Engage in Terrorist Activity" Defined

As used in this chapter, the term "engage in terrorist activity" means in an individual capacity or as a member of an organization—

(I) to commit or to incite to commit, under circumstances indicating an intention to cause death or serious bodily injury, a terrorist activity;
(II) to prepare or plan a terrorist activity;
(III) to gather information on potential targets for terrorist activity;
(IV) to solicit funds or other things of value for–

(aa) a terrorist activity;
(bb) a terrorist organization described in clause (vi)(I) or (vi)(II); or
(cc) a terrorist organization described in clause (vi)(III), unless the solicitor can demonstrate that he did not know, and should not reasonably have known, that the solicitation would further the organization's terrorist activity;

(V) to solicit any individual—

(aa) to engage in conduct otherwise described in this clause;
(bb) for membership in terrorist organization described in clause (vi)(I) or (vi)(II); or
(cc) for membership in a terrorist organization described in clause (vi)(III), unless the solicitor can demonstrate that he did not know, and should not reasonably have known, that the solicitation would further the organization's terrorist activity; or

(VI) *to commit an act that the actor knows, or reasonably should know, affords material support, including a safe house, transportation, communications, funds, transfer of funds or other material financial benefit,* false documentation or identification, weapons (including chemical, biological, or radiological weapons), explosives, or training —

(aa) for the commission of a terrorist activity;
(bb) to any individual who the actor knows, or reasonably should know, has committed or plans to commit a terrorist activity;
(cc) to a terrorist organization described in clause (vi)(I) or (vi)(II); or
(dd) to a terrorist organization described in clause (vi)(III), unless the actor can demonstrate that he did not know, and should not reasonably have known, that the act would further the organization's terrorist activity. [Emphasis added.]

An alternative or a supplement to the Foreign Terrorist Organization designation is naming an organization or an individual as a Specially Designated Global Terrorist. The U.S. Department of the Treasury is in charge of naming a SDGT.

58. U.S. Dept. of State, Office of Counterterrorism, *Foreign Terrorist Organizations.*

59. Jamie Glazov, "Blocking UNRWA's Terror Ties," *FrontPageMagazine.com*, October 16, 2009, http://frontpagemag.com/2009/10/16/blocking-unrwa%e2%80%99s-terror-ties-by-jamie-glazov-2/; Claudia Rosett, "Gaza Bedfellows UNRWA and Hamas," *Forbes*, January 8, 2009, http://www.forbes.com/opinions/2009/01/07/gaza-hamas-unrwa-oped-cx_cr_0108rosett.html; Ron Kampeas, "Battle gets nasty at critical juncture for U.N. agency aiding Palestinians," Jewish Telegraphic Agency, February 9, 2009, http://jta.org/news/article/2009/02/09/1002854/unrwa-under-fire-in-gaza-and-in-washington.

60. James Lindsay, *Fixing UNRWA: Repairing the UN's Troubled System of Aid to Palestinian Refugees*, Washington Institute for Near East Policy, Policy Focus no. 91, January 2009, https://www.washingtoninstitute.org/templateC04.php?CID=306.

61. Ibid.

62. Joseph Klein, "UNRWA Cries Wolf," *Canada Free Press*, May 10, 2006, http://www.canadafreepress.com/2006/klein051006.htm.

63. Stan Goodenough, "UN official equates Arab terror and Israel's self-defense," Jerusalem Newswire, February 19, 2008, http://www.jnewswire.com/article/2341.

64. Herb Keinon and Tovah Lazaroff, "UNRWA offers political cover to Hamas," *Jerusalem Post*, February 25, 2009, http://www.jpost.com/servlet/Satellite?cid=1235410706632&pagename=JPost%2FJPArticle%2FShowFull. Commendably, UNRWA did once condemn Hamas, on February 3, 2009, for a recent theft of UNRWA supplies, without at the same time criticizing Israel more sternly for something else (Joseph Klein, "The Robbing of Gaza," *FrontPageMagazine*, February 9, 2009, http://frontpagemagazine.com/Articles/Read.aspx?GUID=D3AC314B-782C-4E96-95E2-1D8C146E9E1A); "UNRWA accuses Hamas of stealing Gaza aid packages," Agence France Press, February 4, 2009, http://www.google.com/hostednews/afp/article/ALeqM5jl-efmp-pcq0wQv5O8OLJgMkWECw.

65. Question: Does the Secretary-General consider Hamas to be a terrorist organization?

Spokesman: The Secretary-General has denounced in clear terms every time any organization has done a terrorist act, including when those acts were claimed by Hamas.

Question: But that doesn't answer my question.

Spokesman: There is no United Nations label that I know of, of a terrorist organization

(Joseph Klein, "The UN Shield for Terror," *FrontPageMagazine.com*, August 11, 2006, http://www.frontpagemag.com/Articles/ReadArticle.asp?ID=23766, quoting a briefing from January 2006)

66. Joseph Klein, "The 'Blessed' Terrorist Martyrs," *FrontPageMagazine.com*, September 15, 2008, http://frontpagemagazine.com/Articles/Read.aspx?GUID=61BB1920-1530-477C-B1A2-6C9272F0E6B1.

67. Rosett, "Gaza Bedfellows UNRWA and Hamas." As noted in chapter 9, United Nations peacekeeping operations have more than a hundred thousand personnel, but most of them are soldiers who remain in the employ of their national armies, even while they are under U.N. command.

68. "Perpetuating Refugees," *Jerusalem Post*, February 11, 2007, http://www.jpost.com/servlet/Satellite?cid=1170359835454&pagename=JPost%2FJPArticle%2FShowFull.

69. Rosett, "Gaza Bedfellows UNRWA and Hamas."

70. Arlene Kushner, *UNRWA: Its Role in Gaza*, Center for Near East Policy Research, August 2009, http://israelbehindthenews.com/library/pdfs/MY_UNRWA_Report_2009_US_.pdf.

71. Asaf Romirowsky, "How UNRWA Supports Hamas," Jewish Policy Center, Fall 2007, http://www.jewishpolicycenter.org/article/53.

72. "Perpetuating Refugees."

73. Peter Berkowitz, "Plans for Mideast peace," *Washington Times*, August 5, 2008, http://www.washingtontimes.com/news/2008/aug/05/plans-for-mideast-peace/.

74. Lindsay, *Fixing UNRWA*, xi.

75. James Tisch, "UNRWA's Hamas problem," *Jerusalem Post*, December 18, 2004. The money comes from the United States Agency for International Development and from the U.S. State Department.

76. Malkin, "Ambulances."

77. Dov B. Fischer, "The Overseers of Jenin: What exactly is the U.N. doing in its refugee camps (with our money)?" *Weekly Standard*, May 13, 2002, http://www.weeklystandard.com/content/public/articles/000/000/001/213cgjov.asp; David Meir-Levi, "Terrorism: The Root Causes," *FrontPageMagazine.com*, November 9, 2005, http://www.frontpagemag.com/Articles/ReadArticle.asp?ID=20117.

78. Yaakov Lappin, "UNRWA's shady donors," *Jerusalem Post*, Nov. 23, 2004.

79. Ibid.

80. Ibid.

81. Ibid.

82. United Nations General Assembly, Resolution "302 (IV). Assistance to Palestine Refugees," A/RES/302(IV), December 8, 1949, http://www.eyeontheun.org/assets/attachments/documents/un_resolution_establishing_unrwa.doc.

83. Arlene Kushner, *The United Nations Relief and Works Agency for Palestine Refugees in the Near East: A Hard Look at an Agency in Trouble* (Center for Near East Policy Research: Brookline, MA, March 2005), http://israelbehindthenews.com/pdf/UNRWAReport-Consolidation.pdf.

84. Danny Ayalon, "The Flotilla Farce," *Wall Street Journal, Opinion Europe*, July 29, 2010, http://online.wsj.com/article/SB10001424052748703940904575395022140188274.html.

85. Anne Bayefsky, "U.N. vs. Israel," *National Review Online*, April 20, 2004.

86. Foreign Assistance Act of 1961 (as amended), Public Law 87-195, § 301(c): "No contributions by the United States shall be made to [UNRWA] except on the condition that [UNRWA] take all possible measures to assure that no part of the United States contribution shall be used to furnish assistance to any refugee who is receiving military training as a member of the so-called Palestine Liberation Army or any other guerilla type organization or who has engaged in any act of terrorism."

87. U.S. Government Accountability Office, *Department of State and United Nations Relief and Works Agency Actions to Implement Section 301(c) of the Foreign Assistance Act of 1961*, GAO-04-276R-UNRWA (November 17, 2003), http://www.gao.gov/new.items/d04276r.pdf; James Tisch, "UNRWA's Hamas problem," *Jerusalem Post*, December 18, 2004.

    For UNRWA offices in Lebanon, Syria, and Jordan, UNRWA does ask the host governments about whether job applicants have terrorist connections. Government Accountability Office, (Although it is hard to believe that Syria—or the Syrian-influenced regime in Lebanon are very interested in helping keeping terrorists off the U.N. payroll.) In the West Bank and Gaza, UNRWA does not even attempt to screen out terrorist employees. Ibid. UNRWA refuses to ask Israel for information about whether a potential employee is a terrorist. Arlene Kushner, "UN Dollars for Terror," *FrontPage Magazine.com*, Aug. 18, 2004, www.frontpagemag.com/Articles/ReadArticle.asp?ID=14703.

    GAO reports UNRWA's excuse was that its staff would be endangered (e.g., killed by terrorists) if they attempted to screen out terrorists. Even if one believes that UNRWA would genuinely prefer to screen out terrorists, and is failing to do so solely because of the danger, the excuse does not give a reason for the U.S. government to keep funding UNRWA. As long as UNRWA money goes to Hamas, *existing* U.S. law forbids the transfer of foreign aid to UNRWA, if UNRWA is incapable of taking *any* steps to ensure that it does employ terrorists. It is long past time for the State Department and the U.S. Agency for International Development to fully abide by the law, and to stop giving money to UNRWA.

    The State Department does have fourteen monitors at UNRWA offices, but these monitors have obviously not been successful in preventing UNRWA from hiring Hamas employees.

    Three members of Congress have called on the State Department to cut off U.S. taxpayer UNRWA funding until UNRWA stops employing Hamas members (Office of Rep. Jerrold Nadler, "Nadler Calls on Powell to Suspend Funding for UNRWA Until Terrorists are Removed from its Staff," press release, October 12, 2004, http://www.house.gov/apps/list/press/ny08_nadler/PowellUNRWA101204.html).

88. Jonathan S. Tobin, "At UN, no division between aid and terror," *israelinsider*, Oct. 12, 2004. Hansen spoke to the CBC on October 4, 2004. Hansen claimed that the Hamas employees were not necessarily terrorists (even though Canadian and American laws state that *any* member of Hamas is a member of a terrorist organization).

89. Government Accountability Office; Tisch, "UNRWA's Hamas problem."

90. Kushner, "UN Dollars for Terror" (quoting Yoni Fighel, who formerly served as military governor in disputed territories).

91. Ibid.; Rachel Ehrenfeld and Alyssa A. Lappen, "The UN Gives Hamas a Raise," *FrontPage Magazine*, January 6, 2006, http://www.frontpagemag.com/Articles/ReadArticle.asp?ID=20788.

92. David Bedein, "How Can the UN Address the Subject of Palestinian Refugees and Not Allow Israel to Attend the Meeting?" *Israel Behind the News*, June 12, 2004, http://israelbehindthenews.com/#unrwa.

93. Ehrenfeld and Lappen, "The UN Gives Hamas a Raise."

94. Greg Myre, "Israel Feuds with Agency Set Up to Aid Palestinians," *New York Times*, October 18, 2004.

95. Government Accountability Office.

96. Ronen Bergman, *Authority Given* (Tel Aviv: Yedi'ot Aharonot, 2002) (Hebrew), 266, quoted in Yagil Henkin, "Urban Warfare and the Lessons of Jenin," *Azure Online,* no. 15 (2003), http://www.azure.org.il/article.php?id=240.

97. Isabel Kershner, "The Refugees' Choice?" *Jerusalem Report,* August 12, 2002 (quoting Peter Hansen's attachment to a letter which Kofi Annan sent to U.S. Rep. Tom Lantos).

98. Interview conducted by Jeff Arner and Sylvia Martin, October 1991, in the UNRWA West Bank Field Office in East Jerusalem, quoted in Kushner, *The United Nations Relief and Works Agency for Palestinian Refugees in the Near East: Links to Terrorism.*

99. Kushner, "UN Dollars for Terror" (confession of Ala'a Muhammad Ali Hassan, a terrorist sniper who was a member of the terrorist organization Tanzim, which is one of Yassir Arafat's groups); Herb Keinon, "Shin Bet documents terrorists' misuse of UNRWA facilities," *Jerusalem Post,* December 11, 2002.

100. Kushner, "UN Dollars for Terror." Kushner attended the conference, and observed Hansen's finger quotes.

101. Ibid. Hansen backtracked and said, "Well, there was one case." In fact, there have been many cases.

102. Kushner, *The United Nations Relief and Works Agency for Palestinian Refugees in the Near East: Links to Terrorism.*

103. Khaled Abu Toameh, "Hamas wins teachers union elections for UN schools in Gaza," *Jerusalem Post,* March 29, 2009, http://www.jpost.com/servlet/Satellite?cid=1237727563424&pagename=JPost%2FJPArticle%2FShowFull.

104. Harris O. Schoenberg, "The UN reaction to Gaza," February 4, 2009, http://www.eyeontheun.org/articles-item.asp?a=5784&id=7214.

105. Joel Mowbray, "U.N. Agency That Runs School Hit in Gaza Employed Hamas and Islamic Jihad Members," *Fox News,* January 14, 2009, http://www.foxnews.com/story/0,2933,479940,00.html.

106. Itamar Marcus and Nan Jacques Zilberdik, "UNRWA Football Tournament Named after Terrorist Abu Jihad," *Palestinian Media Watch,* February 18, 2010, http://palwatch.org/main.aspx?fi=157&doc_id=1660. UNRWA denied the story, which had been published in the Palestinian paper *Al-Hayat Al-Jadida* on February 17, 2010. The paper retracted the story—which was probably a sensible decision given the propensity of Palestinian terrorists to murder journalists who provide unwanted publicity.

107. Ibid. (reporting estimate of Jonathan Halevi, a former IDF intelligence officer who has built a terrorist attack database for the Jerusalem Center for Public Affairs of terrorist attacks).

108. Lindsay, *Fixing UNRWA,* 21.

109. Adam Entous, "Gaza headmaster was Islamic Jihad 'rocket-maker,'" Reuters, May 5, 2008, http://www.reuters.com/article/middleeastCrisis/idUSL05686115; "UNRWA teacher also built bombs," Jewish Telegraph Agency, May 7, 2008, http://www.jta.org/cgi-bin/iowa/breaking/108447.html; Asaf Romirowsky, "Defund UNRWA," *Washington Times,* May 19, 2008, http://www.washingtontimes.com/article/20080519/EDITORIAL/629937213/1013/editorial.

110. Melanie Phillips, "Who could know?" *Spectator,* May 6, 2008, http://www.spectator.co.uk/melaniephillips/657011/who-could-know.thtml.

111. Barry Rubin, Asaf Romirowsky and Jonathan Spyer, *UNRWA: Refuge of Rejectionism*, Global Research in International Affairs, May 8, 2008, http://www.gloriacenter.org/index.asp?pname=submenus/articles/2008/rubin/5_8.asp.

112. Maayana Miskin, "Slain Senior Hamas Terrorist Was Employed by UN," *Arutz Shevna*, August 2, 2010, http://www.israelnationalnews.com/News/News.aspx/138884.

113. Kushner, "UNRWA 2009."

114. Lindsay, *Fixing UNRWA*, xi.

115. Dan Robinson, "US Lawmakers Renew Effort for More Accountability on UN Aid to Palestinians," Voice of America, March 5, 2009, http://www.voanews.com/english/2009-03-05-voa65.cfm.

116. Heather Robinson, "Will $40 Million US Tax Dollars Subsidize UN Agency That Tolerates Teaching Martyrdom to Palestinian Kids?" *Huffington Post*, February 7, 2010, http://www.huffingtonpost.com/heather-robinson/will-40-million-us-tax-do_b_452681.html.

117. Naomi Lakritz, "UN Denies Holocaust to Appease Terrorists," *Calgary Herald*, September 4, 2009 (UNRWA's pretext for Holocaust denial was that teaching about the Holocaust is not age appropriate for eighth graders; this is absurd, since the Holocaust is routinely taught in middle school world history courses in civilized nations, and since *The Diary of Anne Frank* is a very common text in middle school English classes).

118. Nicole Brackman and Asaf Romirowsky, "Dubious refugee relief," *Washington Times*, June 21, 2007, http://washingtontimes.com/apps/pbcs.dll/article?AID=/20070621/EDITORIAL/106210010/1013/EDITORIAL&template=printart; Arlene Kushner, "Inside the Palestinian Refugee War in the UNRWA camps in Lebanon," *IsraelBehindTheNews.com*, May 26, 2007, http://israelvisit.co.il/cgi-bin/friendly.pl?url=May-26-07!Advisory3; Betsy Pisik, "U.N. Agency Knew of Armed Fighters In Lebanon Camp," *Washington Times*, May 24, 2007, http://washingtontimes.com/world/20070524-121319-1575r_page2.htm.

119. S/RES/1208, November 19, 1998, http://www.reliefweb.int/unpm/documents/SeccoRes1208.pdf.

120. Michael J. Jordan, "Resolution on militancy shows clear double standard, critics say," Jewish Telegraphic Agency, March 15, 2006, http://www.jta.org/page_view_story.asp?intarticleid=16408&intcategoryid=1.

121. Item 5 of Resolution 1208 "recognizes the primary responsibility of the UNHCR, with the assistance of other relevant international bodies and organizations, to support African States in their actions directed towards the full respect and implementation of the provisions of international law relating to the status and treatment of refugees." As AbuZayd admits, even though the Resolution speaks about African camps run by the U.N. High Commissioner for Refugees, it also applies to the Asian camps operated by UNRWA. Therefore, it is "the primary responsibility" of UNRWA to support states in fully respecting and implementing international law against camps being taken over by armed terrorists. Because the Lebanese government's sovereignty over south Lebanon is tenuous at best, UNRWA could and must exercise its "primary responsibility" to help Lebanon by making genuine efforts to keep terrorists out of camps.

122. Jordan, "Resolution on militancy shows clear double standard."
123. Jacob Shrybman, "The Gaza Siege Myth," *YnetNews.com*, March 18, 2010, http://www.ynetnews.com/articles/0,7340,L-3864592,00.html.
124. James Kirchick, "A Real Refugee Problem," *New York Sun*, February 26, 2007, http://www.nysun.com/article/49278.
125. "Help, Not Hate," *National Post* (Canada), January 25, 2010.
126. United Nations Security Council, Resolution 11267, S/Res/1267, Oct. 15, 1999.
127. Anne Bayefsky, "U.N.derwhelming Response: The U.N.'s approach to terrorism," *National Review Online*, September 24, 2004, http://www.nationalreview.com/comment/bayefsky200409240915.asp.
128. Ibid.
129. Thalif Deen, "The Most Elusive Word," Inter Press Service News Agency, December 1, 2005, http://www.ipsnews.org/news.asp?idnews=31267.
130. "UN gives up on completing anti-terrorism treaty by year-end," Haaretz (Reuters), December 1, 2005, http://www.haaretzdaily.com/hasen/spages/652457.html.
131. Ibid.
132. Joshua Muravchik, "The U.N.'s terrorism gap," *Los Angeles Times*, September 18, 2005, http://articles.latimes.com/2005/sep/18/opinion/oe-muravchik18.
133. Deen, "The Most Elusive Word."
134. Ibid.
135. Ibid. (noting use of "state terrorism" language against U.S. and Israel).
136. Mark Steyn, "Let's give Iran some of its own medicine," (London) *Daily Telegraph*, January 17, 2006, http://www.telegraph.co.uk/opinion/main.jhtml?xml=/opinion/2006/01/17/do1702.xml (quoting advisor Hassan Abbassi).
137. IAEA Statute, arts. III.B.4, XII.C, www.iaea.org/About/statute_text.html.
138. Anne Bayefsky, "Doing Business with Iran: Top U.N. officials responsible for nuclear nonproliferation are facilitating Iran's acquisition of nuclear weapons," *National Review Online*, January 16, 2006, http://nationalreview.com/bayefsky/bayefsky200601161051.asp.
139. Benny Avni, "Terror Sponsors as Decision Makers," *New York Sun*, October 3, 2005.
140. Evelyn Gordon, "How the IAEA Encourages Proliferation," *Commentary Magazine*, November 17, 2009.
141. Joseph Klein, "The UN Shield for Terror," *FrontPageMagazine.com*, August 11, 2006, http://www.frontpagemag.com/Articles/ReadArticle.asp?ID=23766.
142. Claudia Rosett, "Where's the U.N. on Iran?" *Forbes*, June 25, 2009, http://www.forbes.com/2009/06/24/wheres-united-nations-iran-opinions-columnists-ban-ki-moon.html.
143. Joseph Klein, "Moral Poverty at the UN," *FrontPage Magazine*, June 9, 2008, http://frontpagemagazine.com/Articles/Read.aspx?GUID=681BDC29-ACBB-49D7-80DA-A65E6EB5478E.
144. Brett D. Schaefer and Steven Groves, *Preventing Repressive Regimes from Using the U.N. to Advance Their Interests*, Heritage Foundation, Webmemo no. 1445, May 4, 2007, http://www.heritage.org/Research/Reports/2007/05/Preventing-Repressive-Regimes-from-Using-the-UN-to-Advance-Their-Interests.
145. Charter of the United Nations, Preamble and arts. 1–2.
146. Faye Bowers, "Iran Holds Al Qaeda's Top Leaders," *Christian Science Monitor*, July

28, 2003, http://www.csmonitor.com/2003/0728/p01s02-wome.html.

147. Michael R. Gordon, "The Struggle for Iraq: Deadliest Bomb in Iraq Is Made by Iran, U.S. Says," *New York Times*, February 10, 2007, A1.

148. United Nations Security Council, Resolution 1373, United Nations Document S/RES/1373, September 28, 2001, http://www.un.org/Docs/scres/2001/sc2001.htm.

149. Schaefer and Groves, *Preventing Repressive Regimes from Using the U.N. to Advance Their Interests.*

150. "A Member of the United Nations which has persistently violated the Principles contained in the present Charter may be expelled from the Organization by the General Assembly upon the recommendation of the Security Council" (Charter of the United Nations, art. 6).

151. Richard Saccone, "United Nations fail to protect civilians," *South Florida Sun-Sentinel*, March 13, 2008, http://www.sun-sentinel.com/news/opinion/sfl-forum13terrorsbmar13,0,2259695.story.

152. Roee Nahmias, "Israel complains to UN over Iranian general's remarks," *Ynetnews*, Feb. 18, 2008, http://www.ynetnews.com/articles/0,7340,L-3508442,00.html.

153. Benny Avni, "Disarming Hezbollah Should Be U.N.'s Top Priority," *New York Sun*, August 20, 2007, www.nysun.com/article/60878.

Chapter 15

1.   "U.N. to control use of Internet?" *World Net Daily*, February 22, 2006, http://www.worldnetdaily.com/news/article.asp?ARTICLE_ID=42982.

2.   Aoife White, "EU Wants Shared Control of Internet," Associated Press, September 30, 2005.

3.   Daniel Schearf, "China Again Tightens Control of Online News and Information," *Voice of America*, September 26, 2005, http://www.clearharmony.net/articles/200509/29033.html.

4.   "China charges U.S. monopolizes the Internet, seeks global control," *WorldTribune.com*, March 2, 2005, http://www.worldtribune.com/worldtribune/05/breaking2453432.0569444443.html.

5.   "Freedom of Expression and the Internet in China: A Human Rights Watch Backgrounder," *Human Rights Watch*, 2004, http://www.hrw.org/backgrounder/asia/china-bck-0701.htm.

6.   Ibid.

7.   Testimony of Tom Malinowski, Washington Advocacy Director, Human Rights Watch, to the Congressional Human Rights Caucus Members' Briefing: Human Rights and the Internet—The People's Republic of China, http://hrw.org/english/docs/2006/02/02/china12595.htm.

8.   *Reno v. American Civil Liberties Union* 521 US 844 (1997).

9.   Lynn Sweet, "Hillary Clinton on Internet Freedom. Speech Text and Q&A at Newseum," *Chicago Sun-Times*, January 22, 2010, http://blogs.suntimes.com/sweet/2010/01/hillary_clinton_on_internet_fr.html.

10. Declan McCullagh, "U.N. agency eyes curbs on Internet anonymity," *Cnet news*, September 12, 2008, http://news.cnet.com/8301-13578_3-10040152-38.html.

11. Robert M. McDowell, "The U.N. Threat to Internet Freedom," *Wall Street Journal*, July 22, 2010.

12. Daniel Howden; "On the Line, the Internet's Future," *The Independent* (London), November 16, 2005.

13. "China charges U.S. monopolizes the Internet, seeks global control."

14. "China shuts down 47 'harmful' internet cafes," *The Scotsman*, March 3, 2005.

15. Patrick Moore; "China: Beijing's Own Goals," Radio Free Europe/Radio Liberty, November 8, 2005.

16. Patrick Moore, "China: Acting to Keep Out 'Harmful Information,'" Radio Free Europe/Radio Liberty, August 14, 2005.

17. Editorial; "Beijing's New Enforcer: Microsoft," *New York Times*, November 17, 2006, http://query.nytimes.com/gst/fullpage.html?res=9F06EED8143FF934A257 52C0A9609C8B63.

18. Edward Wong, "China Rebuffs Clinton on Internet Warning," *New York Times*, January 22, 2010.

19. Patrick Moore, "China: Bullying the Bloggers," Radio Free Europe/Radio Liberty, September 29, 2005.

20. Carlos Ramos-Mrosovsky and Joseph Barilli, "World Wide (Web) Takeover: The United Nations Wants the Internet," *National Review*, September 28, 2005.

21. "False Freedom: Online Censorship in the Middle East and North Africa: Syria," *Human Rights Watch*, http://hrw.org/reports/2005/mena 1105/6 htm.

22. "The Internet under Surveillance," Reporters sans Frontières, http://www.rsf.org.

23. "La Asamblea General de la ONU considera a Castro y Morales 'Héroes Mundiales,'" *ElDiarioExterior.com*, September 1, 2009, http://www.eldiarioexterior .com/articulo.asp?idarticulo=33819.

24. "Connections severed or slowed and Google Mail blocked in latest anti-Internet offensive, Reporters sans Frontières, http://www.rsf.org/spip.php?page=article&id_ article=36434.

25. Gwynne Dyer, "The spoilers and the web," *Evening Standard* (Palmerston North, New Zealand), November 18, 2005.

26. Ibid.

27. Pete du Pont; "Cease-Fire in Tunisia," *Wall Street Journal, Opinion Journal* (emphasis added).

28. Robert Mugabe, Speech, World Summit on the Information Society, Geneva, Switzerland, December 10, 2003, http://www.itu.int/wsis/geneva/coverage/ statements/zimbabwe/zw.html.

29. Ibid.

30. Patrick Goodenough, "Islamic Bloc Scores 'Defamation of Religions' Resolution at UN, *Cybercast News Service, December* 20, 2007, http://*www.eyeontheun.org/ articles-item.asp?a=4733&id=5570.*

31. Joseph Klein, "UN Gag Order," *FrontPage Magazine*, January 11, 2008, http:// www.frontpagemag.com/Articles/Read.aspx?GUID=517977FB-9A49-499D-9AFF-38140DB3F70A.

32. Patrick Worsnip, "Support Lower for U.N. Text on Religion Defamation," Reuters, December 18, 2009, http://ca.reuters.com/article/topNews/ idCATRE5BH4H120091218 (80 votes in favor, 61 against, 42 abstentions).

33. Anne Bayefsky, "You Can't Say That," *Weekly Standard*, October 5, 2009, http:// sroblog.com/2009/10/05/you-cant-say-that-by-anne-bayefsky-weekly-standard/; Anne Bayefsky, "Why Is U.S. Supporting Sham U.N. Human Rights Council? *Fox News*, June 22, 2010, http://www.foxnews.com/opinion/2010/06/22/anne-bayefsky-human-rights-council-obama-israel-kyrgyzstan-syria-durban-cuba/.

34. Matthew Russell Lee, "A Week's Exclusion from Google Raises UN-answered Questions," *Inner City Press*, February 19, 2008, http://www.innercitypress.com/un2google021908.html; Matthew Russell Lee, "Google, Asked at UN About Censorship, Moved to Censor the Questioner, Sources Say, Blaming UNDP," *Inner City Press,* February 14, 2008, http://www.eyeontheun.org/articles-item.asp?a=4953&id=5848.

35. Matthew Russell Lee, "UN's Censorship and Press Punishment Slammed by Staff Union, From Google to Photos of the Dead," *Inner City Press*, March 13, 2008.

36. Matthew Russell Lee, "UN Says and Shows It Won't Cover Stories Countries Don't Like, Critics Targeted," *Inner City Press*, July 1, 2009, http://www.innercitypress.com/unrules1media070109.html.

37. Matthew Russell Lee, "UN Tells Press to Pay $23,000 for Space to Cover It, Sources Say, Scant UN Media Coverage to Further Decrease?" *Inner City Press,* June 1, 2009, http://www.eyeontheun.org/articles-item.asp?a=5987&id=7623.

38. Matthew Russell Lee, "UN Censors Internet in Its NY Headquarters, Blocking Media Critique and Non-Google Video Sites," *Inner City Press*, April 10, 2008, http://www.innercitypress.com/un1censorweb041008.html. Websites that were blocked included anti-CNN.com (a Chinese website that criticizes alleged media bias against China), and dailymotion.com (because it hosted the film *Fitna*, which criticizes Islam).

39. Lee, "UN's Censorship and Press Punishment."

40. Matthew Russell Lee, "Sudan Blocks UN Peacekeeping Mission's E-mail Access, UN Remains Silent," *Inner City Press*, February 8, 2008, http://www.innercitypress.com/un1unmis020808.html.

41. Tarek El-Tablaway, "UN Defends Removal of China Poster at Net Event," Associated Press, November 16, 2009.

42. *McCulloch v. Maryland*, 17 U.S. 316, 431 (1819).

43. Paul M. Weyrich, "United Nations Proposal: World Taxation Without Representation," *Accuracy in Media,* March 14, 2006, http://www.eyeontheun.org/articles-item.asp?a=2907&id=3211; Richard W. Rahn, "Halting global tax tyranny," *Washington Times*, July 19, 2006, http://www.washingtontimes.com/commentary/20060718-083429-4191r.htm. See also Stephen M. Lilienthal, "Reform—Not More Revenue—Is Needed by the United Nations," *American Daily,* July 6, 2006, http://www.eyeontheun.org/articles-item.asp?a=3573&id=4060. Lilienthal traces some of the tax push to the UN Financing for Development Coordinating Secretariat.

44. The member nations are pushing the tax through the Leading Group on Innovative Financing for Development. The Group's website is www.leadinggroup.org/rubrique20.html.

45. George Russell, "U.N.'s World Health Organization Eyeing Global Tax on Banking, Internet Activity," *FoxNews.com*, January 15, 2010, http://www.foxnews.com/world/2010/01/15/uns-world-health-organization-eyeing-global-tax-banking-internet-activity/.

46. Matthew Russell Lee, "EU Attacks UN Tax and Cyberspace Authority Proposal, D'Escoto Advisers Muse," *Inner City Press*, May 15, 2009, http://www.innercitypress.com/unpga1taxnet051509.html.

47. Joseph Klein, "The Digital Solidarity Fund: An Internet tax in disguise," *Canada Free Press*, January 30, 2006, http://www.canadafreepress.com/2006/klein013006.htm.

48. John M. R. Kneuer, Deputy Assistant Secretary for Communications and Information, U.S. Department of Commerce, testimony before the U.S. Senate Subcommittee on Communications, Committee on Commerce, Science and Transportation, September 30, 2004.

49. Administration (NTIA), "U.S. Principles on the Internet's Domain Name and Addressing System," http://www.ntia.doc.gov.

50. "World summit Agrees on Status Quo for Internet Governance," http://usinfo. state.gov/gi/Archive/2005/Nov/16-609244.html.

51. Ibid.

52. Tim Receveur; "Ambassador David Gross participates in video webcast December 13," available at http://www.usinfo.state.gov.

53. "U.S. Official Calls for Stable, Free, Accessible Internet," http://usinfo.state.gov/gi/ Archive/2005/Nov/19-134756.html.

54. Press Release; "Senate Unanimously Passes Coleman Resolution to Maintain U.S. Oversight Role for Internet," Office of U.S. Sen. Norm Coleman (R-Minn.), http://coleman.senate.gov/index.cfm.

55. Kevin Diaz, "Norm Coleman, Annan now tangle over Web name control, The senator sees an attack on Internet openness, the U.N. chief wants to close the digital divide," *Star Tribune* (Minneapolis), November 21, 2005.

56. Press Release, "Doolittle: Don't Hand the Internet Over to U.N.," Office of U.S. Rep. John T. Doolittle (R-CA), http://www.house.gov/doolittle/press/press05/ pr11-16-05.html.

57. David Meyer, "Icann gains independence from the US," ZDNet UK, September 30, 2009, http://www.zdnet.co.uk/news/networking/2009/09/30/icann-gains-independence-from-the-us-39780163/.

Chapter 16

1. Remarks by Rubem Fernandes, director of NGO, Viva Rio, to a forum hosted by the World Council of Churches, "Lessons from the Brazilian Referendum," New York, January 17, 2006.

2. Ibid.

3. *IANSA's 2004 Review—the Year in Small Arms*, http://www.iansa.org/ documents/2004/iansa_2004_wrap_up_revised.doc.

4. Monte Reel, "Brazil Weighs a National Gun Ban—Country Is First to Vote on Issue," *Washington Post*, October 1, 2005, A1.

5. "Brazilian gun referendum approaches: a historic opportunity to make people safer from gun violence," IANSA website, http://www.iansa.org/regions/samerica/brazil-referendum.htm (emphasis added).

6. Terry Crawford-Browne, "Follow Brazilian lead and close the arms industry," *Cape Times & Independent*, October 13, 2005.

7. Karin Goodwin, "Brazil Makes History in Vote to Ban Sale of Guns," *Sunday Morning Herald* (Scotland), October 23, 2005, http://www.sundayherald. com/52406.

8. James O.E. Norell (interviewer), "Victory in Brazil: A Talk with Luciano Rossi," *America's 1st Freedom*, January 2006.

9. List of IANSA members in North America, available at http://www.iansa.org/ about/members/namerica.htm.

10. Anton Foek, "Shot Down: Lobby Kills Brazil Gun Ban," CorpWatch.org, October 25, 2005.
11. Editorial; "Of arms and men," *Khaleej Times Online*, October 26, 2005 (emphasis added).
12. Gwenne Dyer; "Gun control loses yet again," *Japan Times*, October 30, 2005.
13. David Morton; "Gunning for the World," *Foreign Affairs*, January/February 2006.
14. *Brazil . . . Strengthening of Communication Networks and International Partnerships*, International Programme for the Development of Communication, UNESCO, March 2005, http://portal.unesco.org/ci/en/file_download.php/53d7121e58bd59 5db8571998a273f592Latin+America+and+Caribbean+2005++new+projects+appr oved+.pdf.
15. *Projects . . . Disarmament campaigns*; Viva Rio website, vivario.org.br.
16. Norrell, "Victory in Brazil."
17. Foek, "Shot Down."
18. *Brazil: Most crime guns start out legally says report*, IANSA.
19. The Statute of Disarmament; Law no. 10,826/03 (December 2003), http://www. iansa.org/regions/samerica/ documents/statute-of-disarmament.pdf.
20. E.g., *Implementing the Programme of Action 2003*, IANSA, 3, http://www.iansa.org/ documents/report/bandw/mono.pdf ("The Biting the Bullet project partners wish to acknowledge the generous support received from the governments of Canada, Finland, the Netherlands, Switzerland and the United Kingdom and from the International Development Research Center [IDRC]").
21. Juan Michel, WCC media relations officer, "To disarm, body and soul: Brazilian churches participate in national disarmament campaign," World Council of Churches, May 2, 2005; http://www2.wcc-coe.org/pressreleasesen.nsf/index/Feat-05-13.html.
22. "Rio's 'Flame of Peace," *Ploughshares Monitor*, Autumn 2003.
23. *IANSA's 2004 Review—the Year in Small Arms*, IANSA, available at the United Nations Non-Governmental Liason Service website, http://www.un-ngls.org/cso/ cso6/cso6.htm.
24. "Antigun Caravan Crisscrosses Brazil," *Brazil Magazine Online*, October 26, 2004, http://www.brazzilmag.com/content/view/513/41/.
25. "Summary Report on the WCC's Microdisarmament Efforts 2000–2001," World Council of Churches International Affairs, Peace & Human Security Peacebuilding and Disarmament Programme, September 2001, http://www.wcc-coe.org/wcc/ what/international/summary.html.
26. *Fight for Peace Sports Centre—Alternatives for youth to crime, drug faction employment and armed violence*, Viva Rio, 2004.
27. Thierry Verhelst; "A New Type of NGO in Brazil," *Journal of Cultures and Development*, May 2000, http://www.networkcultures.net.
28. Adèle Kirsten, *The Role of Social Movements in Gun Control: An international comparison between South Africa, Brazil and Australia*, Center for Civil Society, Research Report no. 21 (Durban South Africa), September 2004.
29. "Momentum Grows to Address Problem of Small Arms," *NGLS Roundup* no. 45, November 1999, United Nations Non-Governmental Liaison Service.
30. "Women in Brazil take a stand against guns," *The Wire,* http://web.amnesty.org/ wire/February2003/brazil.

31. Lora Lumpe, *Briefing paper on the regulation of civilian ownership and use of small arms in advance of the international meeting in Rio de Janeiro, 16–18 March 2005,* Center for Humanitarian Dialogue, February 2005.

Chapter 17

1. Kenneth P. Vogel, "Obama had greater role on liberal survey," *Poltico.com,* March 31, 2008, http://www.politico.com/news/stories/0308/9269.html; "2008 Democratic primary debate in Philadelphia, Apr. 16, 2008: on Gun Control," http://www.ontheissues.org/2008_Dems_Philly.htm. The Obama campaign claimed: "Sen. Obama didn't fill out these state Senate questionnaires—a staffer did—and there are several answers that didn't reflect his views then or now. He may have jotted some notes on the front page of the questionnaire, but some answers didn't reflect his views" (Vogel, "Obama had greater role on liberal survey").
2. Lynn Sweeton, "Obama's 2003 IVI-IPO questionnaire may be getting closer scrutiny," *Chicago Sun-Times* weblog, December 11, 2007 (including full text of the questionnaire), http://blogs.suntimes.com/sweet/2007/12/sweet_column_obamas_2003_iviip.html.
3. James Oliphant and Michael J. Higgins, "Court To Hear Gun Case," *Chicago Tribune,* November 20, 2007.
4. **Q:** You said in Idaho recently, quoting here, "I have no intention of taking away folks' guns." But you support the D.C. handgun ban, and you've said that it's constitutional. How do you reconcile those two positions?

    A: Because I think we have two conflicting traditions in this country. I think it is important for us to recognize that we've got a tradition of handgun ownership and gun ownership generally. And a lot of people, law-abiding citizens use it for hunting, for sportsmanship, and for protecting their families. We also have a violence on the streets that is a result of illegal handgun use. And so there is nothing wrong I think with a community saying we are going to take those illegal handguns off the streets, we are going to trace more effectively how these guns are ending up on the streets to unscrupulous gun dealers who oftentimes are selling to straw purchases. And cracking down on the various loopholes that exist in terms of background checks for children, the mentally ill. Those are all approaches that I think the average gun owner would actually support. The problem is is that we've got a position oftentimes by the NRA that says that any regulation whatsoever is the camel's nose under the tent, and that I think is not where the American people are at. I think we can have reasonable, thoughtful gun control measures that still respect the Second Amendment and people's traditions. (www.politico.com/candidateinterviews/obama/indexpart2.html)

5. Barack Obama, *The Audacity of Hope* (New York: Crown, 2006), 215.
6. Brief for Amici Curiae 55 Members of United States Senate, The President of the United States Senate, and 250 Members of United States House of Representatives in Support of Respondent, *District of Columbia v. Heller,* http://www.nraila.org/heller/proamicusbriefs/07-290_amicus_congress.pdf.

7. MR. GIBSON: Senator Obama, the District of Columbia has a law, it's had a law since 1976, it's now before the United States Supreme Court, that prohibits ownership of handguns, a sawed-off shotgun, a machine gun or a short-barreled rifle. Is that law consistent with an individual's right to bear arms?

SENATOR OBAMA: Well, Charlie, I confess I obviously haven't listened to the briefs and looked at all the evidence.

As a general principle, I believe that the Constitution confers an individual right to bear arms. But just because you have an individual right does not mean that the state or local government can't constrain the exercise of that right, and, you know, in the same way that we have a right to private property but local governments can establish zoning ordinances that determine how you can use it.

And I think that it is going to be important for us to reconcile what are two realities in this country.

There's the reality of gun ownership and the tradition of gun ownership that's passed on from generation to generation. You know, when you listen to people who have hunted, and they talk about the fact that they went hunting with their fathers or their mothers, then that is something that is deeply important to them and, culturally, they care about deeply.

But you also have the reality of what's happening here in Philadelphia and what's happening in Chicago.

("Democratic Debate in Philadelphia," *New York Times*, April 16, 2008, http://www.nytimes.com/2008/04/16/us/politics/16text-debate.html?_ r=1&pagewanted=all, transcript from Federal News Service)

8. "Obama Camp Disavows Last Year's 'Inartful' Statement on D.C. Gun Law," *ABC News*, June 26, 2008, http://blogs.abcnews.com/politicalradar/2008/06/obama-camp-disa.html; Ben Smith, "Getting ready for a gun ruling," *Politico*, June 26, 2008, http://www.politico.com/blogs/bensmith/0608/Inartful.html.

9. David Hardy, "Obama and the Attempt to Destroy the Second Amendment," Pajamas Media, October 6, 2008, pajamasmedia.com/blog/obama-and-the-attempt-to-destroy-the-second-amendment/.

10. "Democratic Debate in Philadelphia."

11. "Let's be honest. Mr. Keyes does not believe in common gun control measures like the assault weapons bill. Mr. Keyes does not believe in any limits from what I can tell with respect to the possession of guns, including assault weapons that have only one purpose, to kill people. I think it is a scandal that this president did not authorize a renewal of the assault weapons ban" (Illinois Senate Debate #3: Barack Obama vs. Alan Keyes, October 21, 2004, http://www.ontheissues.org/IL_2004_ Senate_3rd.htm).

12. Senate Bill 1195 (2003 legislative session), http://www.ilga.gov/legislation/ BillStatus.asp?DocNum=1195&GAID=3&DocTypeID=SB&LegId=4124&Sessio nID=3&GA=93.

13. "Illinois State Legislative Election 1998 National Political Awareness Test," Project Vote Smart, http://www.votesmart.org/npat.php?can_id=9490 (Obama checked a box indicating that he supported this position).

14. Senate Amendment. 1615 to S. 397, http://www.senate.gov/legislative/LIS/
roll_call_lists/roll_call_vote_cfm.cfm?congress=109&session=1&vote=00217. The
amendment would have given the attorney general the power to ban any and all
handgun ammunition that can penetrate a typical bullet-resistant vest. Because
there are handguns that can fire the vast majority of common rifle rounds, the
Kennedy amendment would also have applied to rifle ammunition. Most vests are
designed to stop standard handgun rounds (e.g., .38 Special) but not rifle rounds
used in a handgun (e.g., a .30-'06) (David B. Kopel, "The Return of a Legislative
Legend: Debating 'cop-killers,'" *National Review Online*, March 1, 2004, http://
davekopel.org/NRO/Return-of-a-Legislative-Legend.htm, discussing the same
proposal in 2004). As a result, almost all centerfire rifle ammunition could have
been banned.

  The Kennedy amendment purported to contain a limit of only applying
to ammunition "designed or marketed as having armor piercing capability." No
ammunition would be covered by the "marketed" part of the definition, because no
manufacturer of rifle ammunition advertises armor-piercing capability.

  On the other hand, the "or designed" could cover all rifle ammunition, at
least as applied by an attorney general like Eric Holder. As David Kopel wrote:

> Almost every automobile in the United States is "designed" to drive over
> 100 miles per hour. The speedometers show this capability, and even if they
> did not, every automobile manufacturer is fully aware that its autos can be
> driven at very fast, unsafe speeds. The auto engines are "designed" to have a
> certain amount of power, and this "design" is based on the full knowledge that
> that auto can be driven over 100 mph. Among the definitions of "design"
> in *Black's Law Dictionary* is "The pattern or configuration of elements in
> something, such as a work of art."
>
> Just as the deliberate configuration of the elements of every automobile
> can be accurately said to be "designed" to drive over 100 mph, so every deer-
> hunting round can be said to be "designed" to penetrate body armor. Notably,
> the ammunition ban language did not say "designed and intended."
>
> . . . Senator Kennedy, the sponsor of the bill, [did say] that he did
> not want to ban hunting ammunition. Nevertheless, the plain language of
> the bill, and not Senator Kennedy's floor statements, were what would be
> enacted into law. If there were ever a judicial challenge to ban on particular
> rifle ammunition ban, a court might well find that the language of the
> statute, along with judicial deference to agency interpretation of the statute,
> meant that there was no need to look to legislative history. (David Kopel,
> "FactCheck flubs Obama gun fact check," *The Volokh Conspiracy*, September
> 23, 2008, http://volokh.com/archives/archive_2008_09_21-2008_09_27.
> shtml#1222201928)

15. John K. Wilson, *The Improbable Quest* (Boulder: Paradigm, 2007), 148.
16. John Chase, "Keyes, Obama are far apart on guns; Views on assault weapons
at odds," *Chicago Tribune*, September 15, 2004; David Mendell, "Democratic
hopefuls vary a bit on death penalty," *Chicago Tribune*, February 20, 2004:

Obama . . . backed federal legislation that would ban citizens from carrying weapons, except for law enforcement. He cited Texas as an example of a place where a law allowing people to carry weapons has 'malfunctioned' because hundreds of people granted licenses had prior convictions.

"National legislation will prevent other states' flawed concealed-weapons laws from threatening the safety of Illinois residents,' Obama said."

Mike Wereschagin and David M. Brown, "Candidates' gun control positions may figure in Pa. vote," *Pittsburgh Tribune-Review*, April 2, 2008, http://www.pittsburghlive.com/x/pittsburghtrib/news/s_560181.html ("I am not in favor of concealed weapons . . . I think that creates a potential atmosphere where more innocent people could [get shot during] altercations").

17. "I didn't find that [vote for carry by retired police] surprising. I am consistently on record and will continue to be on record as opposing concealed carry. This was a narrow exception in an exceptional circumstance where a retired police officer might find himself vulnerable as a consequence of the work he has previously done—and had been trained extensively in the proper use of firearms" (David Mendell, *From Promise to Power* (New York: Amistad, 2007), 250–51).

18. Illinois Senate bill 604 (2001), http://www.ilga.gov/legislation/legisnet92/status/920SB0604.html.

19. Lisa Black and M. Daniel Gibbard. "Wilmette man shoots intruder in his home," *Chicago Tribune*, December 31, 2003.

20. Illinois 93rd General Assembly. Senate Bill no. 2165, March 25 2004 (3d reading in Senate); May 25, 2004 (to concur with House amendments), http://www.ilga.gov/legislation/votehistory.asp?DocNum=2165&DocTypeID=SB&LegID=7961&GAID=3&SessionID=3&GA=93&SpecSess=.

21. U.S. Senate, 109th Cong., 1st Sess., Protection of Lawful Commerce in Arms Act, S. 397, http://thomas.loc.gov/cgi-bin/bdquery/z?d109:SN397.

22. Chinta Strausberg, "Obama Unveils Federal Gun Bill," *Chicago Defender*, December 13, 1999.

23. Dave McKinney, "Hillary slams Obama 'present' votes on abortion, gun laws," *Chicago Sun-Times*, December 4, 2007, 8, http://www.suntimes.com/news/politics/obama/679446,CST-NWS-obama04.article.

24. Strausberg, "Obama Unveils Federal Gun Bill."

25. "NRA Targets Obama," FactCheck.org, Sept. 22, 2008, www.factcheck.org/elections-2008/nra_targets_obama.html.

26. The Obama presidential campaign website quoted Obama's views as expressed in a 2001 article in the *Chicago Defender*: "I know that the NRA believes people should be unimpeded and unregulated on gun ownership. I disagree. I do not object to the lawful use and ownership of firearms, but I do think it is entirely appropriate for the state to monitor it . . . Too many of these guns end up in the hands of criminals even though they were originally purchased by people who did not have a felony. I'll continue to be in favor of handgun law registration requirements and licensing requirements for training" ("Fact Check: No News In Obama's Consistent Record," *Organizing for America*, December 11, 2007, http://factcheck.barackobama.com/factcheck/2007/12/11/fact_check_no_news_in_obamas_c.php).

27. **Q:** When you were in the state senate, you talked about licensing and registering gun owners. Would you do that as president?

     A: I don't think that we can get that done. But what we can do is to provide just some common-sense enforcement. The efforts by law enforcement to obtain the information required to trace back guns that have been used in crimes to unscrupulous gun dealers. As president, I intend to make it happen. We essentially have two realities, when it comes to guns, in this country. You've got the tradition of lawful gun ownership. It is very important for many Americans to be able to hunt, fish, take their kids out, teach them how to shoot. Then you've got the reality of 34 Chicago public school students who get shot down on the streets of Chicago. We can reconcile those two realities by making sure the Second Amendment is respected and that people are able to lawfully own guns, but that we also start cracking down on the kinds of abuses of firearms that we see on the streets.

     The transcript is available at http://www.lasvegassun.com/news/2008/jan/15/debate-transcript/.

28. Shortly before the April 2008 Pennsylvania primary, Obama refused to repudiate his previous support for licensing and registration:

     Q: But do you still favor the registration and licensing of guns?

     A: I think we can provide common-sense approaches to the issue of illegal guns that are ending up on the streets. We can make sure that criminals don't have guns in their hands. We can make certain that those who are mentally deranged are not getting a hold of handguns. We can trace guns that have been used in crimes to unscrupulous gun dealers that may be selling to straw purchasers and dumping them on the streets. ("Democratic Debate in Philadelphia")

     Perhaps Obama thought that Pennsylvania voters would be too stupid to notice that he had refused to answer the question. He was wrong, and Obama lost the primary in a landslide.

29. His campaign claims that he fired a gun in college, when he went target shooting in the woods (Matt Gouras, "Pro-gun Montanans a tough audience for Obama, Clinton," Associated Press [Mont.], April 17, 2008, http://www.missoulian.com/articles/2008/04/17/bnews/br37.txt). Obama attended Occidental College in Los Angeles, and Columbia University, in Harlem. Neither college is very close to woods where target shooting could take place.

30. "It's not surprising they get bitter," because of economic problems, Obama said. So "they cling to guns or religion or antipathy to people who aren't like them or anti-immigrant sentiment or anti-trade sentiment as a way to explain their frustrations" (Mayhill Fowler, "Obama: No Surprise That Hard-Pressed Pennsylvanians Turn Bitter," *Huffington Post*, April 11, 2008, http://www.huffingtonpost.com/mayhill-fowler/obama-no-surprise-that-ha_b_96188.html).

     Obama tried to defend his remarks with the absurd spin that he meant that people "cling" to good things like guns or religion in tough times. But his list of things that people "cling" to also included things he obviously considered to be bad: "antipathy" to different people; "anti-immigrant" sentiment, and "anti-trade" sentiment.

31. David von Drehle, "The Five Faces of Barack Obama," *Time*, August 21, 2008.

32. The article is available at http://www.politico.com/static/PPM41_eastafrica.html. Obama Sr. spelled his first name "Barak."

33. Cathleen Falsani, "'I Have a Deep Faith' Series: The God Factor," *Chicago Sun-Times*, April 5, 2004, http://www.suntimes.com/news/falsani/726619,obamafalsa ni040504.article.

34. Eric Krol, "Clinton 'conceding nothing' in her home state," *Daily Herald* (Arlington Heights, IL), May 8, 2007.

35. Carol Marin, "No honeymoon for Democrats in Iowa caucuses," *Chicago Sun Times*, September 12, 2007.

36. Ray Long, Ray Gibson and David Jackson, "State pork to Obama's district included allies, donors," *Chicago Tribune*, May 3, 2007.

37. "Sticking Up for Rev. Jeremiah Wright and Louis Farrakhan," *The O'Reilly Factor* (Fox News), April 4, 2008, http://www.foxnews.com/story/0,2933,346391,00. html. (Pfleger: "He has—first of all, he has not called Judaism a gutter religion of bloodsuckers. That is not what he has said because I have heard that talk. I stick up for Louis Farrakhan because he is another person that the media has chosen to define how they want to do it. And they demonize how they want to demonize somebody. I know the man, Louis Farrakhan. He is a great man. I have great respect for him. He has done an awful lot for people and this country, black, white and brown. He's a friend of mine.")

  Pfleger often had the Black Muslim Farrakhan to speak at St. Sabina's (Susan Hogan/Albach, "'I'm also a Christian': Warm welcome from Pfleger's flock for Muslim minister," *Chicago Sun Times*, May 26, 2007; Stella Foster, "PUSH pols," *Chicago Sun Times*, May 10, 2007).

38. *Chicago Defender*, October 29, 2007.

39. The crime took place on June 23, 2007. Later, the charges were dropped—just as racist Alabama governor George Wallace also was not prosecuted for his own criminal obstruction. Wallace's June 1963 obstruction of a door at the University of Alabama was a pure publicity stunt; after making the show in the doorway, he stood aside and let the black students enter the building. In contrast, Pfleger and Jackson stayed in the doorway to prevent the exercise of constitutional rights until the police physically removed them.

40. Susan Hogan/Albach, "Cardinal rebukes Pfleger for 'threat': Priest says words against gun shop owner misconstrued, *Chicago Sun Times*, June 8, 2007.

41. Dave Kopel, "Education at the Extremez," *America's 1st Freedom*, April 2009, http://www.nraila.org/Issues/Articles/Read.aspx?ID=349.

42. "An Exclusive Interview with Senator Barack Obama," *Field & Stream* Online, September 16, 2008, http://www.fieldandstream.com/articles/hunting/2008/09/ exclusive-interview-senator-barack-obama.

43. David Kopel interview with Richard Pearson, iVoices.org podcast, October 14, 2008, http://audio.ivoices.org/mp3/iipodcast228.mp3.

44. Details are on the website of Knife Rights, www.kniferights.org/. As the website details, the NRA was deeply involved in lobbying to block the Customs knife ban.

45. Department of Homeland Security, Office of Intelligence and Analysis Assessment, "Rightwing Extremism: Current Economic and Political Climate Fueling Resurgence in Radicalization and Recruitment," April 7, 2009, http://wikileaks.org/wiki/US_DHS:_Rightwing_Extremism:_Current_Economic_and_Political_Climate_Fueling_Resurgence_in_Radicalization_and_Recruitment,_7_Apr_2009.

Chapter 18

1. For example, in a speech in Valparaiso, Indiana, she recalled that when she was a child in Illinois, her family sometimes vacationed in Scranton, Pennsylvania, where her father taught her how to shoot. "People enjoy hunting and shooting because it's an important part of who they are," she accurately acknowledged. "Not because they are bitter."

2. Her 2 percent win in Indiana saved her from being pushed out of the race. That slim victory was the product of her winning by 22 percent among gun-owning households, who comprised over half of the total voters. Her biggest win of the 2008 race was her 10 percent drubbing of Obama in Pennsylvania, a margin made possible by her 25 percent margin of victory among gun-owning households (who were about a third of the voters in the Democratic primary).

3. Andrew Bluth, "Missouri Rejects Bid to Allow Concealed Guns," *New York Times*, April 8, 1999, A24.

4. "Hillary: Guns Not All Bad," *Newsday*, April 4, 2000, A33. At the same Senate campaign appearance (in Coxsackie, near Albany) where she made the cited quote, she also said "I've gone hunting."

5. Michael Grunwald, "First Lady Denounces 'Culture of Violence,'" *Washington Post*, April 23, 1999, A23 (speech to New York State United Teachers).

6. 12 gauge Savage-Springfield 67H pump-action shotgun; Hi-Point 995 Carbine 9 mm semi-automatic rifle; 12 gauge Stevens 311D double barrel.

7. "Hillary Clinton on Gun Control," *Issues 2000*, http://www.ontheissues.org/Senate/Hillary_Clinton_Gun_Control.htm, citing "Gun Safety," http://www.hillary2000.org, September 9, 2000.

8. "Hillary Clinton on Gun Control," citing Forum at South Side Middle School in Nassau County, July 15, 1999. Similarly:

   > We have to do everything possible to keep guns out of the hands of children, and we need to stand firm on behalf of the sensible gun control legislation that passed the Senate and then was watered down in the House. It does not make sense for us at this point in our history to turn our backs on the reality that there are too many guns and too many children have access to those guns—and we have to act to prevent that. (Hillary Clinton, remarks to National Education Association, Orlando, Florida, July 5, 1999, quoted in "Hillary Clinton on Gun Control")

9. Bennett Roth, "Clinton makes new push for gun-control measures," *Houston Chronicle*, Apr. 28, 1999, p. A1.

10. During the second half of the 2008 Democratic primary season, Sen. Clinton did begin saying that she thought that most gun laws should be left to the states. E.g., Matt Gouras, "Pro-gun Montanans a tough audience for Obama, Clinton," Associated Press (Mont.), April 17, 2008, http://www.missoulian.com/articles/2008/04/17/bnews/br37.txt. The respect for local preferences is certainly inconsistent with the policies she helped push during the Clinton presidency, and with the positions she took as United States senator.

11. Message to the meeting of the United Methodist General Conference, Denver, Colorado, April 24, 1996, quoted in Terry Mattingly, "Different Messages, Shared Concern," *Fresno Bee*, May 11, 1996, B8.

12. Donna Dees-Thomases, "NRA and Its Allies Are in the Line of Fire," *Boston Globe*, July 31, 2000, A13.

13. Karen Matthews, "Pataki Joined by Democrats Clinton, Schumer, Spitzer at Million Mom March Rally," Associated Press, May 13, 2001.

14. Other emeritus members are Susan P. Thomases, and Donna E. Shalala (chair 1992–1993), who served as secretary of health and human services in the Clinton administration (CDF Board of Directors Emeritus, http://www.childrensdefense.org/who-is-cdf/cdf-board-of-directors/emeritus.html).

15. President Clinton's signing of the welfare reform law in 1996 led to rupture in Hillary's long-standing, highly publicized friendship with Marion Wright Edelman, the head of the CDF (Michael Crowley, "Skin Deep," *New Republic*, February 13, 2008, http://www.tnr.com/politics/story.html?id=2165a62c-1a13-43af-8808-50c884193e4c&p=2). ("In July 1996, Bill signed a tough welfare-reform bill crafted by the Gingrich Congress. Behind the scenes, Hillary supported his decision—a stance that ruptured her friendship with her one-time mentor, Children's Defense Fund chairwoman Marion Wright Edelman.")

16. Gordon Hutchinson and Todd Masson, *The Great New Orleans Gun Grab* (Boutte, LA, Louisiana Publishing, 2007).

17. The day after the lawsuit was filed, New Orleans and St. Tammany's entered into a Consent Decree in which they acknowledged that they had no legal authority to confiscate guns, but claimed (absurdly) that they had never had a policy of confiscating guns from Katrina victims. The Consent Decree is available at www.stephenhalbrook.com/lawsuits/nagin-order.pdf.

18. Homeland Security appropriations bill, H.R. 5441, http://www.rules.house.gov/109_2nd/text/hr5441/1092nd_homeland_5441cr.pdf.

19. The amendment reads:

> SEC. 557. Title VII of the Robert T. Stafford Disaster Relief and Emergency Assistance Act (42 U.S.C. 5201) is amended by adding at the end the following: "SEC. 706. FIREARMS POLICIES. "(a) PROHIBITION ON CONFISCATION OF FIREARMS.—No officer or employee of the United States (including any member of the uniformed services), or person operating pursuant to or under color of Federal law, or receiving Federal funds, or under control of any Federal official, or providing services to such an officer, employee, or other person, while acting in support of relief from a major disaster or emergency, may—"(1) temporarily or permanently seize, or authorize seizure of, any firearm the possession of which is not prohibited

under Federal, State, or local law, other than for forfeiture in compliance with Federal law or as evidence in a criminal investigation; "(2) require registration of any firearm for which registration is not required by Federal, State, or local law; "(3) prohibit possession of any firearm, or promulgate any rule, regulation, or order prohibiting possession of any firearm, in any place or by any person where such possession is not otherwise prohibited by Federal, State, or local law; or "(4) prohibit the carrying of firearms by any person otherwise authorized to carry firearms under Federal, State, or local law, solely because such person is operating under the direction, control, or supervision of a Federal agency in support of relief from the major disaster or emergency."(b) LIMITATION.—Nothing in this section shall be construed to prohibit any person in subsection (a) from requiring the temporary surrender of a firearm as a condition for entry into any mode of transportation used for rescue or evacuation during a major disaster or emergency, provided that such temporarily surrendered firearm is returned at the completion of such rescue or evacuation. "(c) PRIVATE RIGHTS OF ACTION.— "(1) IN GENERAL.—Any individual aggrieved by a violation of this section may seek relief in an action at law, suit in equity, or other proper proceeding for redress against any person who subjects such individual, or causes such individual to be subjected, to the deprivation of any of the rights, privileges, or immunities secured by this section. "(2) REMEDIES.—In addition to any existing remedy in law or equity, under any law, an individual aggrieved by the seizure or confiscation of a firearm in violation of this section may bring an action for return of such firearm in the United States district court in the district in which that individual resides or in which such firearm may be found. "(3) ATTORNEY FEES.—In any action or proceeding to enforce this section, the court shall award the prevailing party, other than the United States, a reasonable attorney's fee as part of the costs."

20. "Hillary: Guns Not All Bad." At the same Senate campaign appearance (in Coxsackie, near Albany) where she made the cited quote, she also said "I've gone hunting."
21. Protection of Lawful Commerce in Arms Act, Bill S 397, vote number 2005-219, July 29, 2005.
22. Adam Nagourney, "Mrs. Clinton Backs Gun Control Initiatives," *New York Times*, May 10, 2000, B8. "'The moms who are marching in Washington this Sunday have it right: we have to license and register all handguns,' said Mrs. Clinton, who plans to participate in the march." The article continued: "Under the other proposals supported by Mrs. Clinton, prospective gun buyers would have to obtain a photo license, which would be issued only after they had undergone a criminal record check and passed a gun safety examination. Also, all sales of new guns, or transfers of guns, would be recorded in a national registry."

As CNN reported:

U.S. Senate hopeful Hillary Rodham Clinton appeared at a Manhattan press conference on Friday to offer her support for a legislative proposal to license handguns, just as her Republican rival, Rep. Rick Lazio, was winding up his three-day bus tour. The legislation, sponsored by Sen. Charles Schumer (D-New York), would require anyone who wants to purchase a gun to obtain a state-issued photo gun license.

"I stand in support of this common sense legislation to license everyone who wishes to purchase a gun," Clinton said. "I also believe that every new handgun sale or transfer should be registered in a national registry, such as Chuck is proposing." ("Hillary Clinton offers support for gun licensing bill; Lazio wraps up three-day bus tour," June 2, 2000, http://archives.cnn.com/2000/ALLPOLITICS/stories/06/02/lazio.bustour/index.html)

At the Las Vegas, Nevada, presidential debate on January 15, 2008, Senator Clinton said that she was a "political realist" who realized that registration and licensing would be very difficult politically. Asked "But you've backed off a national licensing registration plan?" she answered "Yes." The transcript is available at http://www.lasvegassun.com/news/2008/jan/15/debate-transcript/.

23. Tony Snow, interview with George Pataki, *Fox News: Special Report with Brit Hume*, March 17, 2000 (transcript from Federal Document Clearing House): "SNOW: What do you make of a proposal that was briefly floated by Hillary Rodham Clinton that also authorities be allowed to do basically metal checks of people walking up and down the streets?"

24. Bradley A. Smith, "Enron Didn't Corrupt Washington," *Wall Street Journal*, February 12, 2002, A22. The group is the Brennan Center, in New York City.

25. When these illegal aliens had been arrested, the arresting police had not immediately notified the local Mexican consulate, although an existing treaty required such notification. However, not every procedural mistake by the police means that a murderer is entitled to an automatic exemption from capital punishment. In the cases of the illegal aliens, their guilt of horrific murderers had been firmly proven.

26. Maxim Lott, "Obama Administration Reverses Course, Forbids Sale of 850,000 Antique Rifles," *FoxNews.com*, September 1, 2010, http://www.foxnews.com/politics/2010/09/01/obama-administration-reverses-course-forbids-sale-antique-m-rifles/.

Chapter 19

1. Floyd Norris, "Insider-Trading Conviction of Soros Is Upheld in France," *New York Times*, March 25, 2005; John Tagliabue, "Soros Is Found Guilty in France on Charges of Insider Trading," *New York Times*, December 21, 2002, C1. Soros's lawyers have appealed the case to the European Court of Human Rights, on the grounds that there was too long of an interval between his 1988 offense and his 2001 prosecution; prosecutors say that the investigation took so long because documents had to be obtained from Switzerland. Soros's defenders say that the French prosecutors used the case to greatly expand the scope of the French law, and that reasonable people at the time could not have foreseen the expansive interpretation of the law (Robert Slater, *Soros: The World's Most Influential Investor* [New York: McGraw-Hill, 2009], 264–68). In September 2010, the European

Court agreed to consider the question of whether Soros was being punished for an act that was legal at the time he did it (Matthew Saltmarsh, "Soros to Get Day in Court over Insider Trading Case," *New York Times*, September 16, 2010).

2. "Soros fund to turn to court over fine," *Budapest Times*, May 4, 2009, http://www.budapesttimes.hu/content/view/11853/219/. The fine was upheld on appeal (MTI-Econews, "Budapest court upholds fine against Soros Fund for market manipulation," *realdeal.hu*, April 26, 2010, http://www.realdeal.hu/20100426/budapest-court-upholds-fine-against-soros-fund-for-market-manipulation). George Soros claims that he is not responsible, because he no longer manages Soros Fund Management ("Soros Fund to turn to court"). According to the financial information service Hoover's, the chairman of Soros Fund Management is George Soros. The president and deputy chairman is his son Jonathan ("Soros Fund Management LLC," http://www.hoovers.com/free/co/people.xhtml?ID=47147).

3. For example, he bought photocopy machines for Hungarian dissidents, and paid for Internet connections for Russian college professors (Jeanne Cummings, "Soros Has a Hunch Bush Can Be Beat: Billionaire Puts His Weight, Money behind Democratic Effort to Oust President in '04," *Wall Street Journal*, February 5, 2004, A4; see also Rick Hampson, "George Soros putting his fortune behind a new cause: Ousting Bush," *USA Today*, June 1, 2004, 1A; this article lists numerous good works to promote democracy in Eastern Europe).

4.

I am the very model of a modern Major-General,
I've information vegetable, animal, and mineral . . .

I'm very well acquainted, too, with matters mathematical,
I understand equations, both the simple and quadratical,
About binomial theorem I'm teeming with a lot o' news,
With many cheerful facts about the square of the hypotenuse.
I'm very good at integral and differential calculus;
I know the scientific names of beings animalculous . . .

In fact, when I know what is meant by "mamelon" and "ravelin",
When I can tell at sight a Mauser rifle from a javelin . . .

When I have learnt what progress has been made in modern gunnery,
When I know more of tactics than a novice in a nunnery—
In short, when I've a smattering of elemental strategy—
You'll say a better Major-General has never sat a-gee.
For my military knowledge, though I'm plucky and adventury,
Has only been brought down to the beginning of the century;
But still, in matters vegetable, animal, and mineral,
I am the very model of a modern Major-General.

("Major-General's Song" from Gilbert and Sullivan's 1879 operetta *The Pirates of Penzance*)

"Mamelon" and "ravelin" are terms used in construction of fortifications.

5. George Soros, *Underwriting Democracy* (New York: Free Press, 1991), 3.
6. George Soros, *The Alchemy of Finance* (1987; repr., New York: Wiley, 1994), 362–63.
7. Gail Counsell, "The billionaire who built on chaos: Gail Counsell charts the rise of a speculator who considers himself 'some kind of god,'" *The Independent*, June 3, 1993, http://www.independent.co.uk/news/business/the-billionaire-who-built-on-chaos-gail-counsell-charts-the-rise-of-a-speculator-who-considers-himself-some-kind-of-god-1489380.html.
8. Lyle Crowley, "George Soros," *New York Times*, April 3, 1994. The phrase refers to a common device in ancient Greek plays, when a hero's problems might be solved by a god, who suddenly appeared onstage, being lowered from a crane, or elevated through a trapdoor by a riser.
9. Rachel Ehrenfeld and Shawn Macomber "George Soros: The 'God' Who Carries around Some Dangerous Demons," *Los Angeles Times*, October 4, 2004, B11 (opinion piece attributing the quote to an interview on British television).
10. Crowley, "George Soros."
11. George Soros, *Soros on Soros: Staying Ahead of the Curve* (New York John Wiley & Sons, 1995).
12. The grant for the case of *Hamilton v. Accu-Tek* was for $300,000, from the Center on Crime, Communities and Culture at Soros's Open Society Institute. "Soros's Foundation Awards $300,000 Grant to Aid Hand-Gun Suit," *Wall Street Journal*, October 23, 1998.
13. David Gonzalez, "About New York: Gun Makers, and a Culture, on Trial," *New York Times*, February 3, 1999, B1.
14. David B. Ottaway, "Legal Assault on Firms Is Armed by Foundations," *Washington Post*, May 19, 1999, A01.
15. Frank J. Murray, "N.Y. court rules gun manufacturers not liable," *Washington Times*, April 27, 2001.
16. Ottaway, "Legal Assault on Firms."
17. James Dao, "Gun Control Groups Use N.R.A. Tactics for Fall Elections," *New York Times*, July 24, 2000, A1.
18. The NAACP grant was made jointly by Soros's Center on Crime, Communities and Culture and the Irene Diamond Fund, which, like Soros's group, is also based in New York City (Paul M. Barrett, "Guns: NAACP Suit Puts Race on Table in Gun Debate," *Wall Street Journal*, August 13, 1999). The Educational Fund to End Handgun Violence (a handgun prohibition organization) said that it helped get Soros to fund the suit (Frank J. Murray, "N.Y. court rules gun manufacturers not liable," *Washington Times*, April 27, 2001).
19. Megan Rosenfeld, "A Force of Nurture Readies for Battle; Born on Labor Day, Gun Control Rally Is Set for Mother's Day," *Washington Post*, March 23, 2000, C1 ("Some $300,000 has come from a collaborative to prevent gun violence funded by philanthropists Irene Diamond and George Soros"); Amy Westfeldt, "Gun control campaign 'looking for a few good moms,'" Associated Press (NJ), April 12, 2000 ("The group also has received a $300,000 grant from the Funders' Collective for Gun Violence Prevention, part of the nonprofit Open Society Institute established by billionaire George Soros")

    Soros has also given millions of dollars to the Tides Foundation, which itself is a major funder of gun ban organizations.

20. Donna Dees-Thomases and Alison Hendrie, *Looking for a Few Good Moms: How One Mother Rallied a Million Others against the Gun Lobby* (Emmaus, PA: Rodale, 2004), 74.

21. Dao, "Gun Control Groups."

22. "When Congress forbade the CDC from using money to 'advocate or promote gun control,' a handful of private granting organizations stepped in to help. Among them: The Joyce Foundation, the California Wellness Foundation, the John D. and Catherine T. MacArthur Foundation and the Soros Foundation" (Sarah A. Webster, "Few study solutions for guns Lack of money, political pressure and threats block hard look at violence with firearms," *Detroit News*, November 28, 2000, 9).

23. *Gun Control in the United States: A Comparative Study of Firearm Laws* (Open Society Institute, Center on Crime, Communities and Culture and the Funders' Collaborative for Gun Violence Prevention), http://www.soros.org/ initiatives/usprograms/focus/justice/articles_publications/publications/gun_ report_20000401/GunReport.pdf. The report was immediately put to its intended use of promoting antigun laws. For example, antigun legislators in Maine cited it, even though Maine (the worst state in the country, according to Soros) had violent crime only one-fifth of neighboring Massachusetts, which Soros declared to the best state (Emmet Meara, "Senate rejects panel on gun laws: Study ranks state least restrictive," *Bangor Daily News*, April 11, 2000; NRA Institute for Legislative Action, "George Soros: The Antigunner who would Remake America," November 13, 2003, http://www.nraila.org/Issues/factsheets/read.aspx?ID=151).

24. Ibid.

25. Oregon State Senator Ginny Burdick "said Monday that about 47,000 signatures—more than half of those she turned in—came from paid petitioners. Her campaign, despite its earlier pledge to run a voluntary effort, ended up paying $1.45 per signature, thanks to $60,000 in contributions from the Washington, D.C., lobbying group Handgun Control Inc. and $7,500 from its education awareness arm, the Center to Prevent Handgun Violence. Burdick said an unspecified amount of money originated with billionaire-philanthropist George Soros before being passed through the gun-control group to her campaign" (David Steves, "Volunteers Help Gain Signatures for Gun Initiative Petition," *Register Guard* [Eugene, OR], July 12, 2000).

26. Carla Crowder, "NRA gives $75,000 to fight Amendment 22," *Rocky Mountain News*, September 16, 2000, 4A.

27. Domenica Marchetti, "Grant Makers, Once Cautious on the Issue, Begin to Seek Ways Stop Shootings," *Chronicle of Philanthropy*, October 5, 2000.

28. IANSA's *2004 Review—The Year in Small Arms*, http://www.iansa.org/ documents/2004/iansa_2004_wrap_up_revised.doc.

29. Soros believes a "supremacist ideology" guides this White House. He hears echoes in its rhetoric of his childhood in occupied Hungary. "When I hear Bush say, 'You're either with us or against us,' it reminds me of the Germans." It conjures up memories, he said, of Nazi slogans on the walls, Der Feind Hort mit ("The enemy is listening"): "My experiences under Nazi and Soviet rule have sensitized me," he said in a soft Hungarian accent (Laura Blumenfeld, "Billionaire Soros takes on Bush," *Washington Post*, November 11, 2003, A3).

30. "Earlier this year when I addressed a conference of the Panamanian Association of Gun Owners (APPA), I heard a Panamanian speaker detail the bill that APPA is fighting in the Panamanian National Assembly. Not surprisingly, it has the same provisions as the South African law. Then a Costa Rican member of that country's National Assembly described the gun control bill in their legislature. Care to guess what is in the Costa Rican bill? The same provisions" (Larry Pratt, "The International Noose Is Tightening," *NewsWithViews.com*, May 6, 2008, http://www.newswithviews.com/Pratt/larry87.htm).

31. Ibid.

32. Chris W. Cox, "Barack Obama and the Global Gun Banners," September 11, 2008, http://www.nrapvf.org/News/Article.aspx?ID=321.

33. Mario Osava, "Gun ban referendum appears headed for approval," Inter Press Service (Brazil), September 21, 2005: "For his part, Wagner Vasconcelos, director of the Movement for the Promotion of the Culture, Language and Wealth of Brazil and an opponent of the gun sales ban, said that disarmament is promoted by non-governmental organizations funded by foreign capital from sources like the Ford Foundation and international financier George Soros. His group has put up posters throughout Rio de Janeiro reading, 'Turn in Your Gun and Turn into a Slave.'"

34. James O.E. Norell, "WE'RE BARAAACK! The Billionaire Gun-Banners Who Back Obama's 'Change'," http://www.nraila.org/Issues/Articles/Read.aspx?ID=322.

35. McCain-Feingold did not change the law about advertising that advocated or opposed the election of federal candidates. That kind of advertising is not purchased by the National Rifle Association, but instead by the National Rifle Association Political Victory Fund. The NRA-PVF is a political action committee (PAC), which is legally a separate entity from NRA, and which raises its own money from donations. Donation amounted are capped by federal election law.

36. James O. E. Norell, "George Soros Bought Campaign Finance Reform. Now he's selling the entire liberal agenda," *FrontPage Magazine*, May 31, 2004, http://www.frontpagemag.com/Printable.aspx?ArtId=12828.

    For much more on the forces behind the censorship law, see the American Conservative Union Foundation, Election Law Enforcement Project, *Who's Buying Campaign Finance 'Reform'?* (March 2001), http://www.foley.com/files/tbl_s31Publications/FileUpload137/2285/campaignfinancereform.pdf.

37. Ryan Sager, "Buying 'reform': Media missed millionaires' scam," *New York Post*, March 17, 2005, 33 (op-ed).

38. Sager, "Buying 'reform.'"

39. As a candidate, Obama said he did not want to bring back the Fairness Doctrine, but his campaign promises have a way of expiring whenever he wants them to.

40. Norell, "WE'RE BARAAACK."

41. Ibid.

42. Ibid.

43. Ibid.

44. Ibid.

45. Mark Lloyd, *Prologue to a Farce: Communication and Democracy in America* (Champaign, IL: Univ. of Illinois Pr., 2006).

46. Rick Hampson, "George Soros putting his fortune behind a new cause: Ousting Bush," *USA Today*, June 1, 2004, 1A.

47. "Excerpts from Senate Debate on Donations: Skirmishing and Predictions," *New York Times*, March 30, 2001, http://www.nytimes.com/2001/03/30/us/excerpts-from-senate-debate-on-donations-skirmishing-and-predictions.html.

48. Sharon Theimer, "Campaign watchdogs look to courts, Congress to rein in 'soft money' groups," Associated Press, November 9, 2004; "Money, politics and more money—After the election," *Economist*, November 20, 2004.

49. Editorial, "Who Is George Soros?" *Wall Street Journal*, November 10, 2008, A16.

50. Editorial, "The Billionaire's Boon," *Wall Street Journal*, November 3, 2004, A14.

51. Melissa Block, "Soros Makes Waves with Contributions," *National Public Radio*, November 12, 2003, http://www.npr.org/templates/story/story.php?storyId=1503707.

52. James V. Grimaldi and Thomas B. Edsall, "Super Rich Step into Political Vacuum: McCain-Feingold Paved Way for 527s," *Washington Post*, October 17, 2004, A1.

53. Jeanne Cummings, "Soros Has a Hunch Bush Can Be Beat: Billionaire Puts His Weight, Money behind Democratic Effort to Oust President in '04," *Wall Street Journal*, February 5, 2004, A4.

54. Connie Bruck, "The World According to Soros," *New Yorker*, January 23, 1995, 57.

55. Robert Slater, *Soros: The World's Most Influential Investor* (New York: McGraw Hill, 2009), 258.

56. George Soros, "Why I Gave," *Washington Post*, December 5, 2003.

57. Hampson, "George Soros putting his fortune behind a new cause."

58. Ibid.

59. Grimaldi and Edsall, "Super Rich Step into Political Vacuum," A1.

60. Ibid.

61. Ibid.

62. Ibid.

63. Glen Justice, "Democratic Fund-Raiser Unit Is Curtailing Most Operations," *New York Times*, August 4, 2005, 14.

64. Grimaldi and Edsall, "Super Rich Step into Political Vacuum."

65. Thomas B. Edsall, "Panel Backs Bill to Rein In '527' Advocacy Groups," *Washington Post*, April 28, 2005, p. A21; Jeffrey H. Birnbaum, "The New Soft Money: Campaign-finance reform didn't kill big political donations, it just changed the rules of the game," *Fortune*, November 10, 2003, 155.

66. Benjamin Ginsberg, "How McCain-Feingold Downsized American Politics," *American Enterprise*, Oct.–Nov. 2004, http://www.taemag.com/issues/articleID.18243/article_detail.asp; Chris Cillizza, "GOP Group Joins Soft-Money Fray," *Roll Call*, November 24, 2003.

Not all of the MoveOn donations were directly counted toward presidential election spending.

67. Norell, "George Soros Bought Campaign Finance Reform."

68. Ibid. The other group was the Center for Public Integrity, which monitors campaign spending.

69. David Horowitz and Richard Poe, *The Shadow Party: How George Soros, Hillary Clinton, and Sixties Radicals Seized Control of the Democratic Party* (Nashville: Thomas Nelson, 2006), 192–95, 212. The group is still around. Their website is www.americavotes.org/site/; the MMM is no longer listed as a member organization.

70. "Organizations Funded Directly by George Soros and His Open Society Institute," Discover the Networks, September 17, 2010, http://www.discoverthenetworks.org/groupProfile.asp?grpid=7476.

71. Frank J. Gaffney Jr., "What the world (body) needs now," *Washington Times*, April 12, 2005, A17, http://www.washtimes.com/commentary/20050411-091454-3375r.htm.

72. Ehrenfeld and Macomber "George Soros: The 'God' Who Carries around Some Dangerous Demons."

73. George Soros, "Victims Turning Perpetrators," speech delivered to the Columbia School of International and Public Affairs, at the Cathedral of St. John the Divine, New York City, May 17, 2004. Transcript at: www.arabworldbooks.com/arab/soros.htm.

74. Horowitz and Poe, *The Shadow Party*.

75. George Soros, *The Bubble of American Supremacy* (New York: PublicAffairs, 2003), 11.

76. Robert Slater, *Soros: The Unauthorized Biography* (New York: McGraw Hill, 1996), 33–35.

77. Karl Popper, *The Open Society and Its Enemies* (2 vols.)(1945; repr., Princeton, NJ: Princeton Univ. Pr., 1971)

78. Robert Slater, *Soros: The World's Most Influential Investor* (New York: McGraw Hill, 2009), 262–63.

    Antinationalism is a family tradition. George Soros's birth name was György Schwartz. His father was devoted to Esperanto, a synthetic language that Esperantists hoped would become a universal language, and thereby increase international understanding. He changed the family name to "Soros," which is Esperanto for "Will soar" (Horowitz and Poe, *The Shadow Party*, 78–79).

79. Slater, *Soros: The World's Most Influential Investor*, vii, 308.

80. Popper, *The Open Society*, 1:192. Thrasybulus was an Athenian general, and Antyus was a politician.

    Aristotle explained that the dictatorial clique disarmed the Athenians in order to impose tyranny: "Thereupon the Thirty decided to disarm the bulk of the population and to get rid of Theramenes . . . Theramenes having been thus removed, they disarmed all the people except the Three Thousand, and in every respect showed a great advance in cruelty and crime" (Aristotle, *The Athenian Constitution*, transl. Frederic G. Kenyon [350 BC], chap. 37, http://www.constitution.org/ari/athen_05.htm).

81. Some of the Christian thinkers to whom Popper was probably referring are discussed in David B. Kopel, "The Catholic Second Amendment," *Hamline Law Review* 29 (2006): 519, http:// www.davekopel.com/Religion/Catholic-Second-Amendment.pdf.

82. Popper, *The Open Society*, 2:151–52.

83. Slater, *Unauthorized Biography*, p. 257.

84. David Holley, "The Seed Money for Democracy," *Los Angeles Times*, January 26, 2001. ("The multibillionaire philanthropist quietly played a key role in the dramatic overthrow last year of President Slobodan Milosevic. His Soros Foundations Network helped finance several pro-democracy groups, including the student organization Otpor, which spearheaded grass-roots resistance to the

authoritarian Yugoslav leader. We were here to support the civil sector—the people who were fighting against the regime of Slobodan Milosevic the past 10 years," said Velimir Curgus of the Soros network's Belgrade branch. "Most of our work was undercover."); Steven Erlanger and Roger Cohen, "From a Summons to a Slap: How the Fight in Yugoslavia Was Won," *New York Times*, October 15, 2000; *pp. cit.*, Horowitz and Poe, *The Shadow Party*, 234–36, citing "The Balkans," *Jane's Sentinel Security Assessments*, November 30, 2000 (both sides stuffed ballots; arms used in Belgrade blockade); and Bob Graham and Sue Masterman, "The Storming of Belgrade: Parliament and HQ Burn as Mobs Tell Milosevic to Go," *Evening Standard* (London), October 5, 2000 (use of guns and Molotov cocktails).

85. **Soros:** By putting up $10 million [his initial donation to Americans Coming Together] and getting people engaged, there's enough to get the show going. In other words, to get the organizing going. Half of it still needs funding.

Brancaccio: What is the show? It's a get out the vote effort.

Soros: Get out the vote and get people engaged on issues. This is the same kind of grassroots organizing that we did or we helped in Slovakia when Mechar was defeated, in Croatia when Tudjman was defeated, and in Yugoslavia when Milosevic.

Brancaccio: But gee whiz, Tudjman, Milosevic, George Bush, almost in the same phrase? Those are fighting words?

Soros: But I do think that our leaders . . . If you take John Ashcroft, I don't think he's an Open Society person, Donald Rumsfeld . . . I do think that we have an extremist element in the government. I think that President Bush has been captured by those people as a result of September 11.

"David Brancaccio interviews George Soros," PBS *Now*, September 12, 2003, http://www.pbs.org/now/transcript/transcript_soros.html (ellipses in original).

86. Glen Justice, "Democratic Fund-Raiser Unit Is Curtailing Most Operations," *New York Times*, August 4, 2005, 14.

87. Matthew Vadum and James Dellinger, "Democracy Alliance: Billionaires for Big Government," *Foundation Watch*, Jan. 2008, http://www.capitalresearch.org/news/news.html?id=551. Additional information can be found on David Horowitz's www.discoverthenetworks.org.

88. Jim VandeHei and Chris Cillizza, "A New Alliance of Democrats Spreads Funding," *Washington Post*, July 17, 2006, A1.

89. Norell, "WE'RE BARAAACK."

90. Ibid.

91. Jeanne Cummings, "Soros Has a Hunch Bush Can Be Beat," A4.

92. VandeHei and Cillizza, "A New Alliance of Democrats."

93. Marc Ambinder, "Obama Team Begins Work on Presidential Transition," *Atlantic.com*, July 24, 2008, http://marcambinder.theatlantic.com/archives/2008/07/obama_team_begins_work_on_pres.php

94. Norell, "WE'RE BARAAACK." The Third Way website is www.thirdway.org/.

95. Michael S. Brown and Dave Kopel, "Demon's in the Details: Dems try to put together a new gun strategy, but wind up in the same place—falsely demonizing gun owners," *National Review Online*, July 24, 2001, http://www.davekopel.org/NRO/2001/Demon's-in-the-Details.htm; Jim Kessler, *Taking Back the Second Amendment: Seven Steps Progressives Must Take to Close the Gun Gap. A Third Way Message Memo* (January 2006), http://www.thirdway.org/data/product/file/21/taking_back_2nd_amendment.pdf ("The problem that progressives have on the gun issue has far less to do with policies" than with "the rhetoric they employ"); Jonathan Cowan and Jim Kessler, "Changing the Gun Debate," *Blueprint Magazine* (Democratic Leadership Council), July 12, 2001, http://www.dlc.org/ndol_ci.cfm?kaid=127&subid=170&contentid=3560. Cowan and Kessler were the president and the policy director of Americans for Gun Safety.

96. David Hardy, "Obama and the Attempt to Destroy the Second Amendment," Pajamas Media, October 6, 2008, http://pajamasmedia.com/blog/obama-and-the-attempt-to-destroy-the-second-amendment/.

Chapter 20

1. Jeff Zeleny and Jackie Calmes, "Obama, Assembling Team, Turns to the Economy," *New York Times*, November 6, 2008, http://www.nytimes.com/2008/11/07/us/politics/07obama.html?_r=1.

2. "Taking Aim," *The NewsHour with Jim Lehrer*, transcript, April 6, 1998, http://www.pbs.org/newshour/bb/law/jan-june98/guns_4-6.html.

3. 18 U.S. Code § 925(d)(3).

4. "Taking Aim," *The NewsHour with Jim Lehrer*.

5. Brian Ross and Rhonda Schwartz, "Emanuel Was Director of Freddie Mac during Scandal," *ABC News*, November 7, 2008, http://abcnews.go.com/Blotter/story?id=6201900&page=1; Bob Secter and Andrew Zajac, "Rahm Emanuel's profitable stint at mortgage giant," *Chicago Tribune*, March 26, 2009, http://www.chicagotribune.com/news/politics/obama/chi-rahm-emanuel-profit-26-mar26,0,5682373.story; "Jane Hamsher, Grover Norquist Call for Rahm Emanuel's Resignation," *Naked Capitalism*, December 24, 2009, http://www.nakedcapitalism.com/2009/12/jane-hamsher-grover-norquist-call-for-rahm-emanuel%e2%80%99s-resignation.html.

6. Jeff Zeleny and Jackie Calmes, "Obama, Assembling Team, Turns to the Economy," *New York Times*, November 6, 2008, http://www.nytimes.com/2008/11/07/us/politics/07obama.html?_r=1.

7. The letter is available at http://preservesovereignty.wordpress.com/koh_letter/. Signers were:

> Dr. Herbert I. London, President, The Hudson Institute; Hon. Rick Santorum, Former United States Senator and Senior Fellow, Ethics and Public Policy Center; Andrew C. McCarthy, Senior Fellow, National Review Institute; David Keene, Chairman, American Conservative Union; Matt Brooks, Executive Director, Republican Jewish Coalition; Dr. Michael Ledeen, Senior Fellow and Holder of the Freedom Chair, Foundation for Defense of Democracies; Jeremy A. Rabkin, Professor of Law, George Mason

University; Frank J. Gaffney Jr., Founder and President, Center for Security Policy; Wendy Wright, President, Concerned Women for America; Clifford D. May, President, Foundation for Defense of Democracies; Christopher C. Horner, Senior Fellow, Competitive Enterprise Institute; Mathew Staver, Dean and Professor of Law, Liberty University School of Law; Edward Whalen, President, Ethics and Public Policy Center; Phyllis Schlafly, Founder and President, Eagle Forum; MG Vincent E. Falter, U.S. Army (Ret.) Former Deputy Assistant to the Secretary of Defense (Atomic Energy); Michael Farris, Chancellor, Patrick Henry College; Vice Admiral Robert Monroe, U.S. Navy (Ret.), Former Director, Defense Nuclear Agency; Daniel Pipes, Director, Middle East Forum; John Fonte, Senior Fellow, Hudson Institute; Brigitte Gabriel, President, ACT! for America; Hon. Tidal W. McCoy, Acting Secretary of the Air Force and Assistant Secretary of the Air Force (1981–1988); Doug Bandow, Former Special Assistant to President Ronald Reagan; Susan A. Carleson, Chairman/CEO, American Civil Rights Union; Jim Backlin, Vice President for Legislative Affairs, Christian Coalition of America; Gary Marx, Executive Director, Judicial Confirmation Network; Andrea Lafferty, Executive Director, Traditional Values Coalition; Austin Ruse, President, Catholic Family & Human Rights Institute; Dr. William Van Cleave, Professor Emeritus, Department of Defense & Strategic Studies, Missouri State University; Thomas McClusky, Senior Vice President, Family Research Council Action; Terrence Scanlon, President, Capital Research Center; Thomas P. Kilgannon, President, Freedom Alliance; Colin A. Hanna, President, Let Freedom Ring; Dr. Thomas G. Barnes, Professor Emeritus of History & Law; Co-Director, Canadian Studies Program, University of California, Berkeley; Gary Aldrich, Chairman, CNP Action, Inc.; Michael D. Ostrolenk, President, American Conservative Defense Alliance; Keith Pavlischek, Senior Fellow, Ethics and Public Policy Center; Brian T. Kennedy, President, The Claremont Institute; Kevin L. Kearns, President, U.S. Business and Industry Council; Dr. Jack Wheeler, President, Freedom Research Foundation; Dr. Peter Leitner, President, Washington Center for Peace and Justice; Frances Brigham Johnson, Strategic Planning Initiatives from the Marshall Plan to USAID; Dr. Robert Kaufman, Professor of Political Science, Pepperdine University; Martin "Buzz" Hefti, The Hefti Group; Dane von Breichenruchardt, President, U.S. Bill of Rights Foundation; Curt Levey, Executive Director, The Committee for Justice; Frank S. Besson III, Managing Director, Besson Consulting; Dr. Douglas Macdonald, Professor of Political Science, Colgate University; Amy Ridenour, President, The National Center for Public Policy Research; C. Preston Noell III, President, Tradition, Family, Property, Inc.; Susan Yoshihara, Director, International Organizations Research Group, Catholic Family & Human Rights Institute; Piero A. Tozzi, Director, International Organizations Law Group, Catholic Family & Human Rights Institute; Tom Fitton, President, Judicial Watch; Peter Huessy, President, GeoStrategic Analysis; R. Peter Weaver, Director of Compliance and Safety, International Liquid Terminals Association; David Kopel, Research Director, Independence Institute; Dr. Joseph Morrison Skelly, Professor of Political Science, College of Mt. St. Vincent; Mark Williamson,

Founder and President, Federal Intercessors; Ron Pearson, President, Council for America; Dr. William Greene, President, RightMarch.com; Beth Gilinsky, Co-Director, Jewish Action Alliance; Dr. Jay Bergman, Professor of History, Central Connecticut State University; Jeff Gayner, Americans for Sovereignty; David Yerushalmi, Esq., General Counsel, Center for Security Policy; Tom Trento, Executive Director, Florida Security Council; Fred Gedrich, Former U.S. Department of State and Defense Official; Tom DeWeese, President, American Policy Center; Jeff Bell, Visiting Fellow, Ethics and Public Policy Center; Richard Falknor, Chairman, Maryland Center-Right Coalition; Rev. Dr. Keith Roderick, Secretary-General, Coalition for the Defense of Human Rights; Andrew F. Quinlan, President, Center for Freedom and Prosperity; Dr. James Hutchens, President, The Jerusalem Connection International; Irwin Hochberg, Board Member, Jewish Institute of National Security Affairs; Judy Smith, State Director, Concerned Women for America of Kansas; Sancha Haysbert-Smith, State Director, Concerned Women for America of Louisiana; Carrie L. Walker, Director, Concerned Women for America of Michigan; Bev Ehlen, State Director, Concerned Women for America of Missouri; Ann Hettinger, State Director, Concerned Women for America of Texas; Janet Robey, State Director, Concerned Women for America of Virginia; Tanya Ditty, State Director, Concerned Women for America of Georgia; Cathie Adams, President, Eagle Forum Texas; Bobbie Patray, President, Eagle Forum Tennessee; Alyssa A. Lappen, Investigative Journalist; Carol Greenwald, President, Potomac Investment Co.; Susanne M. Reyto, Author, speaker; Dr. John Karch, Slovak League of America.

8. M. Edward Whelan III, "Harold Koh's Transnationalism," Ethics & Public Policy Center, April 20, 2009, http://www.eppc.org/publications/pubID.3793/pub_detail.asp.

9. Harold Koh, "On American Exceptionalism," *Stanford Law Review* 55 (2003): 1479, 1496.

10. Harold Kongju Koh, "A World Drowning in Guns," *Fordham Law Review* 71 (2003): 2333, 2361, http://law.fordham.edu/publications/articles/500flspub11111.pdf.

11. Ibid., 2341.

12. Ibid., 2348.

13. Ibid., 2351.

14. "The first problem is to slow down the number of handguns being produced and sold in this country. The second problem is to get handguns registered. The final problem is to make possession of all handguns and all handgun ammunition—except for the military, police, licensed security guards, licensed sporting clubs, and licensed gun collectors—totally illegal" (Richard Harris, "A Reporter at Large: Handguns," *New Yorker*, July 26, 1976, 58, quoting Nelson "Pete" Shields, whom the article describes as the "present director" of the National Council to Control Handguns). The Brady Campaign currently claims that it does not want to ban handguns, although the group's legal affiliate (the Brady Center) did file an amicus brief in the case of *NRA v. Chicago*; the brief strongly argued that handgun prohibition in Chicago and Oak Park, Illinois, was an important strategy for governments to protect public safety.

15. For Nazi Germany, see Stephen P. Halbrook, "Arms in the Hands of Jews Are a Danger to Public Safety: Nazism, Firearm Registration, and the Night of the Broken Glass," 21 *St. Thomas Law Review* 109 (2009), www.stephenhalbrook.com/law_review_articles/Halbrook_macro_final_3_29.pdf.

16. Koh, "A World Drowning in Guns," 2342.

17. The IANSA website brags that the group is "the organization officially designated by the UN Department of Disarmament Affairs (DDA) to coordinate civil society involvement to the UN small arms process."

18. Koh, "A World Drowning in Guns," 2354.

19. Ibid. 2359–60.

20. Ibid. 2341.

21. Ibid. 2360.

22. Koh, "On American Exceptionalism," 1486.

23. Ibid., 1485.

24. Ibid., 1483.

25. Koh, "A World Drowning in Guns," 2359.

26. Koh, "On American Exceptionalism," 1483n14.

27. Harold Hongju Koh, "International Law as Part of Our Law," *American Journal of International Law* 98 (2004): 43, 53–54.

28. Joseph Olson and David B. Kopel, "All the Way down the Slippery Slope: Gun Prohibition in England, and Some Lessons for America," *Hamline Law Review* 22 (1999): 399, http://papers.ssrn.com/sol3/papers.cfm?abstract_id=149029.

29. Julian Ku, "Ten Questions for Legal Advisor-Nominee Harold Hongju Koh," *Opinio Juris* weblog, April 9, 2009, http://opiniojuris.org/2009/04/09/ten-questions-for-legal-advisor-nominee-harold-hongju-koh/.

30. *Murray v. Schooner Charming Betsey*, 6 U.S. 64, 118 (1804).

31. Harold Hongju Koh, "The 1998 Frankel Lecture: Bringing International Law Home," *Houston Law Review* 35 (1998): 623, 646.

32. Nadia Fischer, "Outcome of the United Nations Process: The Legal Character of the United Nations Programme of Action," in Erwin Dahinden, Julie Dahlitz, and Nadia Fischer, eds., *Arms Control and Disarmament Law* 4 (2002), 165–66.

33. Koh, "On American Exceptionalism," 1503.

34. Koh, "The 1998 Frankel Lecture: Bringing International Law Home."

35. David B. Kopel, "Guns, Gangs, and Preschools: Moving beyond Conventional Solutions to Confront Juvenile Violence," *Barry Law Review* 1 (2000): 63, http://davekopel.org/2A/LawRev/Guns-Gangs-Preschools.htm.

36. Statement of Eric Holder Jr., Deputy Attorney General, United States Department of Justice and James E. Johnson, Undersecretary for Enforcement, U.S. Department of the Treasury, Before the Subcommittee on Crime, of the Committee on the Judiciary, U.S. House of Representatives, Concerning Firearms Legislation and Enforcement, May 27, 1999, http://judiciary.house.gov/legacy/holder.pdf; Eric Holder, "Weekly Briefing," May 20, 2000.

37. For example: "On March 5, 1991, Bonnie Elmasri called a firearms instructor, worried that her husband—who was subject to a restraining order to stay away from her—had been threatening her and her children. When she asked the instructor about getting a handgun, the instructor explained that Wisconsin has a 48-hour waiting period. Ms. Elmasri and her two children were murdered by the man 24 hours later" (David B. Kopel, "Waiting Periods," in Dave B. Kopel, ed., *Guns: Who Should Have Them?* [Amherst, New York: Prometheus Books, 1995], 61–62).

38. Bill Clinton, *My Life* (New York: Knopf, 2004).
39. Fox News Channel, April 23, 2000 (Holder interviewed by FNC legal analyst Andrew Napolitano).
40. Eric Holder, "Keeping Guns Away from Terrorists," *Washington Post*, October 25, 2001.
41. David Nakamura and Robert Barnes, "D.C.'s Ban on Handguns in Homes Is Thrown Out," *Washington Post*, March 10, 2007, A1.
42. Brief for Former Department of Justice Officials as Amici Curiae Supporting Petitioners. All the case filings are available at www.nraila.org/heller/.
43. Harold Hongju Koh, "Why Transnational Law Matters," *Penn State International Law Review* 24 (2006): 745, 749.
44. The CEDAW treaty and Supreme Court use of it are discussed at pages 54–56 of *The Global War on Your Guns*.
45. 554 F.3d 56 (2d Cir. 2009).
46. 99 Fed. Appx. 256, 2004 WL 962938 (2d. Cir. 2004).
47. "Sotomayor's views on guns prompt questions," Associated Press, June 11, 2009, http://www.msnbc.msn.com/id/31255491/ns/politics-white_house/.
48. David B. Kopel and Stephen P. Halbrook, "Testimony on Second Amendment and Related Issues," Confirmation Hearings for the Appointment of Elena Kagan to the Supreme Court of the United States of America, Hearings before the Judiciary Committee of the United States Senate, July 1, 2010, http://davekopel.org/2A/Speech/Kopel-Kagan.pdf.
49. Transcript, Saddleback Presidential Forum, August 17, 2008, Lake Forest, CA.
50. *District of Columbia v. Heller*, 128 S. Ct. 2783 (2008).
51. Colum Lynch, "U.S. Is Open to Talks on Conventional Weapons," *Washington Post*, October 16, 2009.
52. Ibid.